AF269645

Robert E. Howard

The Life and Times of a Texas Author

Willard M. Oliver

University of North Texas Press
Denton, Texas

©2025 Willard M. Oliver
Foreword ©2025 Rob Roehm

All rights reserved.
Printed in the United States of America.

10 9 8 7 6 5 4 3 2 1

Permissions:
University of North Texas Press
1155 Union Circle #311336
Denton, TX 76203-5017

The paper used in this book meets the minimum requirements of the American National Standard for Permanence of Paper for Printed Library Materials, z39.48.1984. Binding materials have been chosen for durability.

Library of Congress Cataloging-in-Publication Data

Names: Oliver, Willard M, author.
Title: Robert E. Howard : the life and times of a Texas author / Willard M Oliver.
Description: Denton, Texas : University of North Texas Press, [2025] | Includes bibliographical references and index.
Identifiers: LCCN 2025000035 (print) | LCCN 2025000036 (ebook) | ISBN 9781574419634 (cloth) | ISBN 9781574419740 (ebook)
Subjects: LCSH: Howard, Robert E. (Robert Ervin), 1906-1936. | Authors, American--Texas--Biography. | Pulp literature, American--History and criticism.
Classification: LCC PS3515.O842 Z83 2025 (print) | LCC PS3515.O842 (ebook) | DDC 813/.52 [B]--dc23/eng/20250211
LC record available at https://lccn.loc.gov/2025000035
LC ebook record available at https://lccn.loc.gov/2025000036

The electronic edition of this book was made possible by the support of the Vick Family Foundation.

Typeset by vPrompt eServices.

To Brianna Oliver
Welcome to the family!

My desire for personal freedom has been the ruling passion of my whole life.

—Robert E. Howard.

Contents

Foreword

In the late 1990s, in the early days of the internet, I became reacquainted with a writer I'd enjoyed as a teenager: Robert E. Howard, commonly referred to as REH. My main objective at the time was to find something—*anything*—that my tenth-grade language arts students would read without (too much) complaint. While I was somewhat successful in that objective, rediscovering REH had a more profound effect on me than it did on my students. In trying to find out-of-print Howard stories, I stumbled upon Howard fandom and was soon immersed in the various chat groups and web forums that existed at the time. This got me interested in Howard's biography, and here I am.

Between writing articles for the fan press and discovering "lost" Howard writings, I've also edited many of the titles available from the REH Foundation Press (three volumes of *Collected Letters* and various other collections) and published a few things on my own. I have been called many things—including obsessive; of the things I care to mention, the most complimentary is "The hardest working man in Howard fandom," but the most accurate is "Captain Footnote." Just have a look at any recent Howard biography, including the one in your hands, and there I am. I've spent the last twenty years engaged in "internet archaeology" and the exploration of Howard's Texas. Why? Because when I came into fandom, the only biography of Howard available to me was flawed in a variety of ways, the worst of which was the incessant psychoanalyzing of its subject. Another problem was the footnotes. They often referred to something that had no bearing on the text they referred back to. It was frustrating. And then, when I went looking, I started finding courthouse documents that contradicted what I'd read, that added to the story of Howard and his family. What I really wanted was a well-researched, well-written, all-inclusive biography without the psychobabble.

As the years went by, new biographies appeared and my hopes rose with each publication, but after reading each, none had all that I wanted.

One was well-written but lacked citations; another had citations but was bland; another's focus was more on Howard's writing than the details of his life. All of these biographies have their merits, they just weren't what I was looking for. Enter Will Oliver.

I first met Will in the pages of a REHupa mailing in 2018. REHupa is the Robert E. Howard United Press Association, a group that shares its Howard-related writings with each other with comments on each other's work, all on paper, old school. Anyway, it soon became clear that Will is just as obsessive as I am, maybe more. We started exchanging emails, chatting regularly at Howard Days (an annual event held in Cross Plains, Texas), and sharing our findings with each other. More, since Will is located in Texas (I'm in California), he was able to help in my research by going to courthouses I've not yet been able to investigate. "Hey Will, there's this Howard cousin down in Wharton County. How close is that to you?" And away he'd go. It's good to have friends.

And it was clear from the beginning that he intended to write a biography. There were quick mentions of it in his emails and REHupa contributions. Given his obsessive behavior, I had high hopes. But would this biography be the well-researched, all-inclusive (with citations!) biography I was looking for? I got my answer in January 2022 when I received an email with the subject "Big Favor." Will was asking me to review his chapters for errors as he completed them and, from the first, I knew this was the Howard biography I was hoping for. See for yourself . . .

Rob Roehm
Lancaster, California

Prologue

Cross Plains, Texas

March 1932

When I was a fighting-man, the kettle-drums they beat,
The people scattered gold-dust before my horse's feet;
But now I am a great king, the people hound my track
With poison in my wine-cup, and daggers at my back.
—"The Phoenix on the Sword"[1]

"Well, I'll try to give you some idea of the country I live in," Robert E. Howard once wrote to fellow author E. Hoffmann Price in 1932, before describing his hometown in North Central Texas.[2] In so doing he tried explaining just how large the state of Texas truly is with all its varied terrain, but it seems words failed the writer. "All I can say is," Howard concluded, "Texas is just too big for me to grasp."[3] Price, the only author who ever visited Howard agreed when he later wrote, "To say that Texas is a large state is not a crisp observation. However, the words get a pointed meaning for anyone who has driven from out of the state and into Cross Plains."[4]

The small town is situated along the Callahan Divide between, broadly speaking, West and East Texas. The divide and the county were named for James Hughes Callahan, a soldier in the Texas Revolution who survived the

Goliad Massacre.[5] "Cross Plains," Howard wrote, "is in the southeastern corner of the county." He then described the area this way: "To the north, the country slopes down somewhat into the valley of the Brazos and its tributaries, before rising to the Caprock and the Staked Plains of the Panhandle. West the land likewise slopes a little before rising to the Edwards' Plateau and the region of the South Plains. Southward it drops swiftly from plateau to plateau until it reaches the coastal plains. Eastward the divide runs until it breaks west of the Palo Pinto hills, which further east drop swiftly into the Grand Prairie."[6] Fort Worth lay in the last direction some 165 miles distant by the mostly dirt roads of the day. Abilene, to the northwest, was closer by 100 miles, but Fort Worth boasted a population of 163,447 in 1930, while Abilene was home to a mere 23,175 souls. Brownwood to the south, with only a population of 12,789, was 50 miles closer.

"To the northwest are a pair of peaks," Howard continued, writing of a land feature closer to home, "known collectively as the Caddo Peaks and individually as East Peak and West Peak."[7] When approaching the peaks, he described how they rise "abruptly from the level of the surrounding country and appearing to be of great height," and elsewhere he explained "this appearance was mainly an illusion created by the flatness of the surrounding country."[8] This was because the area around Cross Plains sits at an elevation of 1,742 feet above sea level, while East Peak stands at 2,029 feet and West at 2,090.

"In this region post-oaks dominate the landscape," Howard wrote of the local trees, while "elms, willows and pecans grow along the rivers, and Spanish oaks among the hills." He then added how "brambles, prickly pears and chaparral thickets constitute the undergrowth."[9] Cross Plains was "hemmed in by a dense growth of post-oaks on all sides," and he detailed them with greater depth.[10] "This post-oak growth is low, scrubby and thick; in the summer it is not unpleasing to the sight, densely cloaking the hills and valleys as it does, but in the winter it presents the most dreary, drab appearance imaginable."[11] Like the Caddo Peaks, these landscape descriptions often found their way into the fiction he was writing, such as this painting with words in his story "The Marchers of Valhalla": "The sky was lurid, gloomy and repellent, of the blue of tarnished steel, streaked with dully crimson banners. Against the muddled red smear glowered the low hills that are the peaks of that barren upland which is a dreary expanse of sand drifts and post-oak thickets, checkered with sterile fields where tenant farmers toil out their hideously barren lives in fruitless labor and bitter want."[12]

Howard also tried to explain just how "gloomy and repellent" the weather could be in West Texas. "Two or three years of medium-dry weather," he wrote, "then a year or more of scorching, searing burning drouth, followed by a period of storms and terrific floods when the entire country seems to be on the point of washing away."[13] Texas is known for some harsh weather extremes, giving rise to the oft repeated saying in the Lone Star State, "If you don't like the weather in Texas, wait five minutes."

The weather in March of 1932 averaged 51 degrees; it was mostly in the low 60s during the day and dropped into the upper 30s at night. As if to highlight the weather extremes though, on March 11 the temperatures suddenly dropped to 18 degrees, while nine days later the high reached 90 degrees. At that time the region was in drought conditions, for there was no rain the entire month.[14]

The roads into and out of Cross Plains only numbered two: one from the east and another southwest of town. The road from the east came from the nearby town of Pioneer, a narrow packed-dirt road that entered town on Eighth Street. At that time the trees along the road were just beginning to bloom, something reported upon by the local newspaper, *The Cross Plains Review*: "Driving in here in the Springtime, eight street gives Cross Plains an unusually good 'front.' The tall poplar trees along the highway . . . makes an entrance that even the most extensive travelers will compliment."[15] It was easy enough for the news reporters to observe, for they were located on Eighth Street, just a half block from Main. The only paved street in town was Main, which ran north and south; at its intersection with Eighth Street lay the heart of downtown Cross Plains.[16]

On the northwest corner of the intersection stood a two-story brick building with two stately columns that once housed Farmer's National Bank—a victim of the Depression. Just north of that was a long row of one-level business establishments including Smith's Drug Store. On the southwest corner there stood another two-story brick affair that housed

Citizens State Bank. In that building Howard once worked briefly as a stenographer. Two doors down the block sat Robertson's Drug Store, where Howard had also worked briefly as a soda jerk. In fact, Dr. Robertson, the owner of the drugstore, had just recently celebrated his "seventh birthday"—he had been born on February 29—in 1883.[17]

Across the street were still more businesses, including the biggest of them all, Higginbotham's general merchandise. Billed as the "largest store under one roof between Fort Worth and El Paso," according to one lifelong resident, it was the consensus among local folk that "if Higginbotham's didn't have it, you probably didn't need it."[18] Because the store sold infant supplies and operated a funeral home out of the north end of the building, Higginbotham's could honestly boast they had "Everything from the cradle to the grave."[19]

Despite being in the depths of the Great Depression that March, Cross Plains was faring well. While the local paper wrote one week that "a branch of the Federal farm loan bureau has been established in Cross Plains, and is now extending credit cash to tenants and landowners of this section," a week later it reported, "Few farm loans being made here" and that "only $750 has been applied for to date."[20] The reason the town was faring well may be found in one thoughtful saying of the time period: "Nothing will get people together like getting them into a hole. As long as things are going smoothly we are all independent, but let misfortune come and there is at once a community interest that binds us together." Misfortune had certainly come, but Cross Plains had a strong community base. As one example, "The ladies of Cross Plains churches," as was reported on March 18, "will serve a 'swell feed' in the Higginbotham building, to which anyone with 35 cents is cordially invited, tomorrow (Saturday) at noon. This time it is the Methodists and they specialize in chicken. Better plan to take advantage of this workday banquet."[21]

In light of the limited amounts of cash available in this agricultural community that was used to bartering and trade, many had to stretch their cash as far as they could. Cecil A. Lotief, who ran Lotief's Dry Goods Company, advertised for this purpose. "Lotief says," began all his advertisements, "Trade where you get more goods for less money. Special low

Prices for—Saturday and Monday" and he listed "Ladies House Dresses" for $1.00, "Men's Oxford all leather shoes" for $2.75, and "Good Grade Work Pants" for 98 cents.[22]

The grocery stores in town included the A&P, which advertised it was selling milk for 10 cents a quart bottle, as well as "Grandmother's bread—delivered fresh daily" for 6 cents, and sliced bacon 15 cents a pound.[23] The following week the Piggly Wiggly advertised "A delicious baked ham for your Easter Dinner" for only 17 cents a pound.[24] And despite it being the Great Depression, many people still found enough money to afford a picture show at one of the movie theaters in town, which included the Liberty Theater, "where sound sounds best," showing "James Dunn and Sally Eilers in 'Over the Hill,'"[25] and a week later, Tim McCoy in "Shot Gun Pass."[26]

"Cross Plains is a small town of—well, I guess at present the population is about 1800," Howard wrote his friend, and the comings and goings of these 1,800 souls was dutifully reported by the hometown paper.[27] "Miss Enid Gwathmey spent the week end in Brownwood," it was announced, while "Abney McInnis of Brownwood was in Cross Plains Sunday" and poor "Harold Clark has been confined to his bed several days with rheumatism."[28] Other people were celebrating good news for "An eight pound baby boy was born to Mr. and Mrs. Jimmie Franklin here, Sunday night. He has been named 'Billy.'"[29] And Mr. and Mrs. C. B. McGee "celebrated their 50th wedding anniversary." By that day in 1932, they had "eight children, twenty-seven grand-children, and four great, grand-children living."[30]

In the Burkett news column, a small nearby town where Howard had previously lived, all were informed that "Mrs. Wesley Webb is visiting a sister at Burkburnett" and "Miss Vera Pearly Oliver is substituting in the school for Mrs. J. C. Bowden who is ill." In still another former home of Robert E. Howard, the even smaller town of Cross Cut, the *Review* featured several notes on Lindsey Tyson, Howard's closest friend in Cross Plains. "Lindsey Tyson and Margaret Wagner attended community night here last Friday," and he attended a "bridge party given at Mrs. Henry Davis' home Saturday." No comment was made on community night, but regarding the latter it was noted that "a grand time was had by everyone."[31]

Despite the reporting of all the goings-on in town, the biggest topic of conversation was the upcoming election that was to take place on April 5 at the Anderson-Dodson Chevrolet building. This was because the election was practically a clean slate to elect the fifth mayor of Cross Plains and four aldermen.[32] The newspaper called for nominees who would "make the race and render unto your community those services which you justly owe," and it must have worked, for a week later it was reported that "3 seek mayorship, 12 for aldermen."[33]

Traveling south three blocks from the center of town, Main Street crossed over a set of railroad tracks. The tracks continued west to the train depot situated between Sixth and Seventh Streets. On the west side of Main Street, just south of the tracks, sat the local icehouse, a place where Howard had fought in many amateur boxing bouts and drank "ice cold beer" with his friends, notwithstanding the fact the country was supposedly dry because of Prohibition.

Despite the bucolic sounding appearance of the downtown area of Cross Plains, there were many things that marred this image, but the biggest was the result of the many oil booms the town had experienced over the previous decade along with its "sudden slumps."[34] "The town presents an appearance about like the thousand other small West Texas towns," Howard wrote, "one wide main street, unpaved back alleys, oil derricks rising up here and there all over the business and residential sections."[35] "Here and there were littered heaps of rusted metal . . . in the town, but no drilling was going on," he once described in a realism piece that did little to hide the fact he wrote about his hometown. "Here and there rose the gaunt forms of derricks in empty lots but their walking beams were still and no storage tanks were visible. The townsite oil boom which had brought the town of [Cross] Plains into sudden publicity and prosperity had slumped and most of the promoters had gone into other fields. The flotsam which still lingered found a modicum of work in the shallow fields and only a percent of the oil workers were now seen." These oil workers had once "swarmed in the streets" and brought with them "a whole spirit one of turbulent restlessness," but now they were gone, leaving behind a blight upon the town of Cross Plains.[36] Howard's friend and next-door neighbor, Leroy Butler, once told the sad truth when he said, "It just wasn't—well, it just wasn't a very pretty town in those years."[37]

Howard lived with his parents just west of Main Street down an unpaved road that was Fourth Street. It was located near Turkey Creek, the original site of Cross Plains. Just past the creek, the road turned southwest toward the town of Coleman, approximately thirty miles away.[38]

The Howard and Butler homes were separated by a white picket fence and a big live oak tree. Howard and Leroy Butler often played in that tree as kids. The fence extended across the front of the Howards' wood-frame house, and in the middle stood the gate with a walkway leading up to the front porch steps where hung a sign announcing, "Doctor Howard, Residence." There was some semblance of grass in the yard, but it was still mostly brown because spring had only just come to Texas and, as Butler once explained, "Cross Plains didn't have enough water at that time for people to have decent lawns."[39] Ivy vines grew up around the windows, over the front of the porch, and around to the side of the house. Howard's mother, Hester, always tried to keep color in the yard and, as Butler's wife, Floyce, recalled, "She had pretty roses. Crepe myrtle in the yard." More specifically, "I remember that window box," she fondly recalled, "she had flowers; she had pretty roses."[40]

Farther back along the side of the house, there was another window, frequently open because of the heat of the day. "He had a glassed-in back porch on the southeast side of the house there," Leroy Butler recalled, "and it wasn't too far from my mother's bedroom."[41] The home had an L-shaped porch in the back with the long portion running along the southwest side of the house and served as a sleeping porch on hot summer nights, while the short end was Howard's bedroom. It was in that room, on a tiger oak table he used for his desk, that Howard typed out the stories of his most famous characters. It is this image that led another contemporary pulp author, Leigh Brackett, to imagine him there: "Howard had a great love for all that was lost and strange and faraway. One thinks of him sitting at his typewriter in Cross Plains, Texas, a young man dreaming great dreams of gods and heroes far beyond the narrow boundaries of his own space and time, roaming free across the wonderful landscapes he saw in his mind."[42]

What most of his neighbors recalled, however, was Howard working late into the night, banging away on his typewriter.[43] The editor of *The Cross Plains Review*, Jack Scott, recalled how, "Robert Howard wrote into the night. There was no air conditioning and he raised all the windows, to let the air in. Robert would be writing over there and he would keep all his neighbors in houses nearby awake."[44] Of course it was the Butlers he was keeping awake, particularly Mrs. Butler, who bore the same first name as Hester Howard. "A lot of times at night," Leroy explained, "he'd wake her up with that typewriter clacking at, you know, one or two o'clock in the morning."[45]

It was not just the banging of the typewriter keys that kept Hester Butler awake nights; it was Howard's booming voice as well. His one and only girlfriend in his lifetime, Novalyne Price, recalled the first time she had gone to visit Howard during the day. "I went up the steps and across the porch," she wrote in her memoirs. "I could hear the sound of a typewriter and someone talking at the very top of his voice. It sounded as if somebody were reading from a book while someone else typed. I stood still at the door, listening. Bob was writing and talking at the top of his voice as he wrote."[46]

In the late winter of 1932, Hester Butler no doubt heard passages like, "Conan leaped to the wall and tore therefrom an ancient battle-ax which, untouched by time, had hung there for half a century." He was working on the first story featuring a new character, one he called Conan of Cimmeria. No doubt the action intensified in his mind as he transferred his thoughts to paper, and the intensity came through in his voice: "As he sprang from the wall his ax dropped an outlaw with a severed shoulder, and the terrible back-hand return crushed the skull of another. Any other man would have already died there, and Conan himself did not hope to survive, but he did ferociously wish to inflict as much damage as he could before he fell. His barbaric soul was ablaze, and the chants of old heroes were singing in his ears."[47]

Annoyed by the clacking of the typewriter and the shouting of Hester Howard's son, Mrs. Butler would shout out, "Hester, make him be quiet, we're trying to sleep!"[48] Mrs. Howard, quick to protect her son whenever he happened to be writing, would call back from across the yard, "You leave my boy alone! He's working!"[49]

"Conan put his back against the wall and lifted his ax," Howard continued. It is questionable if he heard his mother or neighbor.

> He stood like an image of the unconquerable primordial—legs braced far apart, head thrust forward, one hand clutching the wall for support, the other gripping his ax on high, with the great corded muscles standing out in iron ridges, and his features frozen in a death snarl of fury—his eyes blazing terribly through the mist of blood which veiled them.
>
> "Who dies first?" he mumbled through smashed and bloody lips.[50]

Howard once explained to his girlfriend this unusual method of writing. "I find that if I talk them out—hear the words as I put them down, the yarn goes a little smoother. Sounds better when you read it."[51] Leading scholar Rusty Burke once wrote that Howard "may be said to have a direct connection to the oral tradition," for he notes that he had "been a spellbinding oral yarnspinner among his friends."[52] This is one of the reasons Howard was such a good writer, for he heard his stories as he wrote them. As John W. Clark noted in his book *Early English*, "It is easy to forget, or even not realize, that language is originally and primarily speech, not writing; that it is something heard before it is something seen."[53] It is this knowledge of Howard's writing that led author and critic John Clute, in an introduction to Howard's fiction, to so eloquently write, "Every word he types is being sung to every reader he will ever have. If I had never read a word he had written, this would have been enough for me to start. I would have loved him already, because he was a teller. Having read Robert E. Howard before learning that he sang Conan in the night, I love him all the more."[54]

The talent to write in this manner may have been, in part, a gift from his father. A friend of the family recalled how Dr. Isaac Mordecai Howard "was a master at using strong language to describe violent action," and he believed that there was "no doubt this conversation influenced Robert's writing."[55] Dr. Howard also used dramatic gestures to tell his stories, and his son most likely adopted this from his father as well. "He had to be moving around," Novalyne Price recalled, "gesturing, telling the story, and a whole lot of that same thing went into the writing of his stories. Talking them aloud, and sitting there at the typewriter, and going through . . . many of the movements."[56] Because of this, as a neighbor remembered, "He made a racket, big racket," and added that he often "typed all night long."[57] That was also what his father remembered, for he would often tell friends, "Robert's been writing for two days and two nights, now. . . . He'd get started and he'd just keep going."[58] Even his friend next door remembered that "he just worked all hours."[59]

Howard was young and virile. He stood just shy of six feet in height and weighed a little over two hundred pounds. He had dark hair, a rugged but handsome face, and blue eyes.[60] Most people summed up Howard's stature by saying, as Butler did, "He was exceptionally strong," while newspaper editor Jack Scott described him as "a big robust man."[61] This was wholly due to his earlier workouts with weights, time spent boxing, and long hours chopping wood for the express purpose of exercising.

For his entire life, Robert E. Howard was rarely ever called by his first name, except for his parents or those who did not know him well. To his friends he was always Bob. In fact, being called Robert by his friends evidently got under his skin. As one of his closest friends from high school recalled, "One night we kept calling him Robert. Howard responded petulantly, 'Why do youse bastards keep calling me Robert?'"[62]

The first time Howard sang of Conan was when he was in Mission, Texas, and wrote a poem of Conan's homeland, titled by the same name "Cimmeria." The poem opens powerfully with a single line in italics, "*I remember*," before continuing:

> The dark woods, masking slopes of sombre hills;
> The grey clouds' leaden everlasting arch;
> The dusky streams that flowed without a sound,
> And the lone winds that whispered down the passes.[63]

In a letter to a fan and future writer Emil Petaja, Howard noted the poem was "suggested by the memory of the hill-country above Fredericksburg seen in a mist of winter rain."[64] In those hills sits the aptly named Enchanted Rock, a smooth, exposed pink granite mountain.

Yet it is Howard's imagination that moves the mountain to wild northern climes. "I have lived in the Southwest all my life," he wrote to a friend, "yet most of my dreams are laid in cold, giant lands of icy wastes and gloomy skies, and of wild, wind swept fens and wildernesses over which sweep great sea-winds, and which are inhabited by shock headed savages with light fierce eyes."[65] The land was the land of barbarians, the lands of Cimmeria, the home of Conan.

"Conan simply grew up in my mind," Howard wrote, "when I was stopping in a little border town on the lower Rio Grande. I did not create him by any conscious process. He simply stalked full grown out of oblivion and set me at work recording the saga of his adventures."[66] And in another letter, he gave a much more in-depth explanation when he wrote that although he had been barren of ideas for some time, "Conan seemed suddenly to grow up in my mind without much labor on my part and immediately a stream of stories flowed off my pen—or rather off my typewriter—almost without effort on my part." "I did not seem to be creating, but rather relating events that had occurred," he added, and how "for weeks I did nothing but write of the adventures of Conan. The character took complete possession of my mind and crowded out everything else in the way of story-writing."[67]

Howard continued writing Conan tales over the next three years, completing twenty-one stories, of which seventeen were published in his lifetime. Perhaps the reason his Conan tales are so well loved is because he never lost interest in the character. After writing ten of the stories, Howard told a friend, "I still write of Conan more powerfully and with more understanding than any of my other characters," and, while typing the last Conan yarn he would ever write, he explained, "It may sound fantastic to link the term 'realism' with Conan; but as a matter of fact—his supernatural adventures aside—he is the most realistic character I ever evolved."[68] It may also be because of the way he described the character to his girlfriend, telling her, "That Conan's the damndest bastard I ever saw. He gets himself into all kinds of scrapes."[69] Or perhaps because, as he once wrote, "I enjoy writing about him more than any character I have ever created. He almost seems to write himself."[70]

Although Howard makes it sound like he was merely transcribing Conan's own yarns, another eminent Howard Scholar, Patrice Louinet, explained, "Research has since demonstrated that the Texan had worked much more intensively on the stories than his desultory tone suggests."[71] That was certainly the case, for in the first story, "The Phoenix on the Sword," the world was first introduced to Conan: "Behind an ivory, gold-inlaid writing-table sat a man whose broad shoulders and sun-browned skin seemed out of place among those luxuriant surroundings. He seemed more a part of the sun and winds and high places of the outlands. His slightest movement spoke of steel-spring muscles knit to a keen brain with the co-ordination of a born fighting-man."[72]

The first Conan yarn was a salvaged unpublished story called "By This Axe, I Rule," about an earlier character, King Kull, who lived before Conan's time. Howard kept the physical description of Kull for Conan but changed the eyes from gray to blue and made the more dour Kull into the more ebullient Conan.[73] Thus, phrases like Kull "gloomily eyed the man who stood before him" were altered to read how Conan "fixed his smoldering blue eyes enviously on the man who stood before him."[74] He also dropped the love interest in the Kull story and added a supernatural element into the Conan tale.[75]

When the revisions were finished, he sent the manuscript to Farnsworth Wright, the editor of *Weird Tales* magazine, and the turnaround on the story was quick. Although Wright said the story "has points of real excellence," after providing him with needed changes, the editor wrote, "I hope you will see your way clear to touch it up and resubmit it."[76] The biggest problem was that while the story opened well, it became bogged down in details describing the lands through which Conan roamed.

Howard rewrote the story per Wright's suggestions, removing much of the historical background and writing a stronger opening. The only thing that seemed to be missing now, at least as Howard saw it, was an understanding of Conan's world.[77] In order to provide this historical background, he added the now famous epigraph to the story:

> Know, oh prince, that between the years when the oceans drank Atlantis and the gleaming cities, and the years of the rise of the Sons of Aryas,

> there was an Age undreamed of, when shining kingdoms lay spread across the world like blue mantles beneath the stars—Nemedia, Ophir, Brythunia, Hyperborea, Zamora with its dark-haired women and towers of spider-haunted mystery, Zingara with its chivalry, Koth that bordered on the pastoral lands of Shem, Stygia with its shadow-guarded tombs, Hyrkania whose riders wore steel and silk and gold. But the proudest kingdom of the world was Aquilonia, reigning supreme in the dreaming west. Hither came Conan, the Cimmerian, black-haired, sullen-eyed, sword in hand, a thief, a reaver, a slayer, with gigantic melancholies and gigantic mirth, to tread the jeweled thrones of the Earth under his sandalled feet.[78]

The new version was accepted for publication by Wright, who offered Howard $85.00 for the story ($1,700 in modern dollars). Now the world had to wait until November when the December 1932 issue of *Weird Tales* hit the newsstands. When it did, "The Phoenix on the Sword" was not the cover story. That honor went to Otis Adelbert Kline for his serial adventure that resembled an Edgar Rice Burroughs novel, *Buccaneers of Venus*.[79] (Kline would soon become Howard's literary agent.) Howard's story was the third in the issue, behind two other popular *Weird Tales* authors, Seabury Quinn and Edmond Hamilton. Howard had a strong reputation in the magazine, but when this story appeared in the pages of *Weird Tales*, as Burke noted, "Howard solidified his standing as one of the two or three most popular writers."[80]

Two months later, in the February issue of the magazine, Howard learned his story had placed second in the readers' poll.[81] In "The Eyrie," the reader forum for *Weird Tales,* there were three fan letters printed regarding his story. Frederick John Walsen wrote, "*The Phoenix on the Sword* fairly took my breath away with its fine intrigue and excellent action and description. It was a magnificent story. Mr. Howard never writes but that he produces a masterpiece."[82] Claude Cameron commented, "Howard has that certain something that makes a good weird tale," while John H. Bate of Philadelphia gave this positive endorsement: "Welcome to Conan the Reaver, Mr. Howard's picturesque fighting man."[83] Harold Preece, Howard's friend, perhaps summed it up best for fans of Conan both then and now when he said, "I am glad that Conan found his bard."[84]

Howard's Conan stories, like many of his others, were so well received by the readers that each of his next four published Conan yarns was voted the best story of the issue. "It is hard to describe precisely what made Mr. Howard's stories stand out so sharply," wrote one of the most popular writers of *Weird Tales* magazine, H. P. Lovecraft, in his memoriam after Howard had died, "but the real secret is that he himself is in every one of them." Howard, he said, "always drew something from his own experience and knowledge of life."[85] Perhaps more than anyone, his girlfriend, Novalyne Price, understood this best because Howard had taught it to her. She later reflected upon his words in her diary, "One thing he wanted to stress, was that stories had to be real and important; the characters—real people with real problems, important problems. He was sure, he said (and he was right), that I wondered how Conan could be a real person, but I needed to remember that deep inside every man there was something of the barbarian, something that civilization could not destroy. A man reading his story about Conan, then, would feel again in the depth of his being those barbaric impulses; consequently, Conan acted as they felt they would act in similar circumstances."[86] Howard was not Conan, but there were so many characteristics of Howard in Conan that he brought the character to life. Nor was this in any sense wish fulfillment writing, for as Louinet explains, Conan was "much more a projection of what Howard *was*, than what he *wanted to be*."[87]

Although Howard was in each of his characters, it did not end there, for as Burke has succinctly stated, "The art of Robert E. Howard was storytelling."[88] "Robert Ervin Howard was preternaturally gifted in the art of telling stories," he explains, "From making up the adventures that he and his young playmates would act out as they wandered the woods and fields around their homes, to keeping Novalyne Price enthralled as they drove around Callahan County with tales of the days when he rode with 'Jenghiz Khan.'"[89] She indeed loved his stories. "I've never dated a man who can talk on so many different subjects nor one who uses words so beautifully. Let him describe a scene from history, or a cowboy riding these Texas hills in search of adventure, and I hear English spoken at its best."[90] This is certainly high praise coming from one who taught speech, drama and debate.

Still others praised him for his gift of writing. Fellow writer E. Hoffmann Price wrote that, "Bob . . . was a natural story teller," before emphasizing, "These are exceedingly rare!"[91] And Lovecraft wrote how, "The really lucky guy is the one whose *natural* mode of expression happens—through pure chance—to coincide with some form of writing in popular demand," before stating, "Robert E. Howard is the best example of this I can think of. . . . His stories sell," he continued, "but they have a zest & naturalness."[92]

Yet, because Howard was a storyteller, he often stretched the truth, all for the sake of telling a good yarn. The story was more important than the truth. This is not to say he lied, but, as one of his friends wrote, "Howard undoubtedly told whoppers of his own."[93] As Howard biographer Mark Finn observed, this is what folklorist Mody C. Boatright called, "The Art of Tall Lying," who notes it is "one of the most characteristically American forms of folk humor."[94] It was certainly a common style of storytelling in Texas and is one Howard came to master. But regardless of the style of his storytelling, as Burke states, "It is clear that telling stories was deeply embedded in Howard's nature."[95]

Although Howard was assuredly a good raconteur, he was a writer by trade. "To be a writer," Novalyne Price once said, "you have to do what Bob did—go into a room, sit down at the typewriter, and write for hours at a time."[96] And "When he wasn't typing on that typewriter," his neighbor Butler recalled, "he was thinking up something . . . I think that was his life, just [those] stories."[97] It was his life, but it runs deeper than that, for as he explained in a letter to Lovecraft, "I took up writing simply because it seemed to promise an easier mode of work, more money, and more freedom than any other job I'd tried."[98] It was his life because it gave him the most freedom to do what he enjoyed and to be his own man in the small agrarian town in which he lived.

Cross Plains was not a thriving center of culture that fostered an up-and-coming author. "I became a writer in spite of my environments," Howard once wrote. He was not ridiculing the people but was addressing the reality of his situation. He lived among men who "made their living from cotton, wheat, cattle, oil, with the usual percentage of business men and professional men." He wrote, "The idea of a man making his living by writing seemed in that hardy environment so fantastic that even today I am sometimes myself assailed by a feeling of unreality."[99] Just the year before, he told his editor that "while I haven't been a howling success . . . I've managed for several years now to get by without grinding at some time-clock punching job. There's freedom in this game, that's the main reason I chose it." He also seemed to suggest just how important his freedom was to him, when he added the statement, "Life's not worth living if somebody thinks he's in authority over you."[100] Through his storytelling and writing, Howard's entire life was spent in the pursuit of his own personal idea of freedom, however elusive that may be, and he carried that pursuit to its tragic end all in the timespan of thirty short years.

What follows is the story of those thirty years, yet it is also a story that is complicated. In late 1928 Howard wrote a letter to one of his best friends stating that "the world at large don't know the half of me and if I can help it, they never will."[101] And when E. Hoffmann Price was asked to write a memoriam for Howard after his death, he responded, "I'm baffled. Describing Howard is like trying to tell you, in words written or spoken, the difference between rye whiskey and bourbon whiskey—only infinitely more difficult."[102] Howard was a complicated man, and his story is just as complicated. Nevertheless, this is the story of a Texas author, the life and times of a pulp writer in the 1920s and 1930s, who created a literary subgenre, gave the world fantastic characters such as Conan of Cimmeria, and cherished his freedom more than anything else in both life and death.

Chapter 1

"I Seek a Vicarious Pride in My Ancestry"

My people came from Munster
and rugged Nevis-side;
Their hearts were black with ancient wrongs
and hate and bitter pride.
—"Heritage"[1]

"Like most men who have nothing to be proud of in themselves," Robert E. Howard once wrote to a close friend in March of 1931, "I seek a vicarious pride in my ancestry."[2] While the former sentiment is most certainly self-deprecating, the latter is entirely true, for he did hold a strong personal pride in his family heritage, boasting of it often in his letters and numerous autobiographical sketches and essays. In another letter, written about the same time, he noted that "the study of genealogy is one of my hobbies, or rather, would be, if I had time and opportunity to pursue it."[3] Although Howard grew up hearing of his family ancestry from both of his parents, it was not until the late 1920s that he began researching his family genealogy in earnest.

In coming to know the nature of both sides of his family, Howard described them as "a race of wanderers," for they "seldom stayed long in the locality in which they were born." In order to emphasize this point, he elaborated: "I've had aunts, uncles and cousins born in every southern state there is except Kentucky and Florida, and a few in the mid-west. Most of them I've never seen. I have relatives all over east Texas, northern Louisiana, southern and western Arkansas, southern and northern Missouri, and eastern and middle Oklahoma, and very few of them have I ever seen."[4] Wallace C. Howard, a relative of the family, said it more succinctly when he declared, "The Howards are a moving people."[5] Robert E. Howard's own childhood would bear this truth out, for his father's wanderlust led the family to move no fewer than ten times before Howard was 14 years old.

This restlessness was not uncommon among the immigrants who first came to America, and those who later found the original thirteen colonies becoming too crowded. "My ancestors were among the early settlers of America, and after a hundred years or so spent in Georgia and the Carolinas, began drifting West," he once recounted to a friend, before telling him how "the Civil War caught the Howards in Arkansas and the Ervins in Mississippi, and ruined both families financially. The Ervins landed in Texas in 1866, the Howards in 1885. Both lines were of restless disposition, and I've had kin in nearly every movement of conquest and colonization from the Revolution on—War of 1812, Gold Rush of '49, Civil War, settling and developing of West Texas, Apache uprising in New Mexico, settling of the Indian Territory—etc."[6]

Although that biographical sketch is certainly not a false account of his family record, the true stories may not be as adventurous as he makes them sound. Howard simply wrote it in this manner to tell a good story about his family lineage, rather than to achieve any historical accuracy or specificity. In a letter he wrote of the imposing height of his ancestors he stated, "My grandfathers, both of whom were six feet two inches tall, my great-grandfather Ervin who was six feet four inches, my great-grandfather Henry who was about the same height, and my great-grandfather Howard who was six feet eight inches."[7] Although Howard did not quite achieve these impressive heights himself, reaching only about six feet tall, he could, once again, boast of the good stock of his forebears.

When describing the ethnic lines of his heritage and the lineage he traced, Howard once boasted, "Well, I am largely Gaelic; Irish, and Scotch-Irish, and Norman-Irish, and Anglo-Irish, and straight Norman, with a touch of the Dane—Dano-Irish, from a red-headed great-grandmother. Mainly I am Irish and Norman, with the Irish predominating."[8] Howard wrote and spoke often of his Irish roots to his friends and correspondents. "I have the dark hair and skin of the Gael," he once described himself, though explaining how "my blue eyes are a heritage of the Danes." As if to make amends for this deficiency, Howard quickly adds, "Blue eyes, dark skin and black hair, are an [ac]cepted Irish type but it comes from a Norse strain, which you know, runs strong in Ireland."[9] He told of his many Irish ancestors, such as "My great-great-grandfather—he was of the old Gaelic family of the MacEnry," and recounted how "he married Anna O'Tyrrell, who was born in Connaught."[10] In a letter to another friend he explained how he inherited some of her particularly Irish traits, when he wrote, "When I seem to radiate gall and rattlesnake venom, please put it down to the personal devil I inherited from Anna O'Tyrrell, who my great-grandfather married in an absentminded moment."[11] Howard wrote another correspondent, "Looking back over three hundred years I can find only one member of the family who did not trace his line back to Ireland," and to still another he wrote, "By nationality I am predominately Gaelic, in spite of my English name—some three fourths Irish while the rest is a mixture of English, Highland, Scotch, and Danish."[12]

The reason for the overemphasis on his Irish heritage was because Howard had come under the spell of the Irish mystique in the late 1920s and found a friend who shared that interest.[13] The prominence he placed on his lineage may have been derived, in part, from the American disdain for Irish immigrants throughout the nineteenth century, thus making them underdogs of American society, and Howard always favored the underdog. But it runs deeper than that, for the Irish had the reputation of being a fighting people with a streak of the barbaric in them and embracing frontier life. As historian T. R. Fehrenbach wrote, "The Scotch-Irish were the only major immigrant group in American history that completely avoided all existing civilization and settlement," for they had "passed through no coastal screen, but headed for the western, Indian frontier." They "had not crossed the sea," he concluded, "to become servile tenants."[14] Howard recognized this thirst for freedom in his ancestors, as he would come to recognize it in himself.

Despite his desire to be and boast of his pure Irish stock, Howard's tales of being predominately Irish are not quite accurate. As Howard scholar Burke explained, "There is little evidence for any significant Irish heritage in either the Ervin or the Howard lines."[15] Howard identified with all the traits of the Irishman so much that he desired to become one, and because of that strong desire, Howard scholar Patrice Louinet explains, "Howard had become an Irishman not because he was descended (or not) from mostly Irish ancestors, but simply because he had *willed* himself to be an Irishman."[16] Still, as Burke noted, Howard's belief in his Irish ancestry "certainly led to some great fiction," for Howard was able to draw upon both his real and imagined ancestry to tell a good story and boast of the good stock of people from which he had come—again, part of that vicarious pride.[17]

Robert Ervin Howard's own name is a combination of his two lines of ancestors in which he took so much pride—his father, Dr. Isaac Mordecai Howard, from whom he inherited his Anglo surname, and his mother, who bears the more Celtic-rooted surname, Hester Jane Ervin, from which Howard's middle name is derived. Modern genealogical research traces the direct line of Howard's heritage as far back as the birth of his paternal great-great-grandfather Mordecai Howard, from whom Dr. Howard was given his own middle name. Mordecai was born in Virginia in 1759 and likely came from Anglo-Saxon ancestors.[18]

Hester Ervin's direct line traces back to John Sr. Ervin, Howard's maternal great-great-grandfather, born about 1774, in South Carolina.[19] Although it is likely his ancestors were Celtic in origin, there is no known direct lineage. The few known Irish ancestors all came from the maternal sides of both families or those who married into the Howard and Ervin clans. Howard, who later took a strong interest in all things Irish, spent more time researching his mother's family history than his father's, and wrote of it more frequently. In one lengthy letter explaining his family genealogy, Howard dedicated only one paragraph to the family line that bore his surname, being sure to note several Irish connections before writing for pages about the family from which his middle name came. This led the preeminent scholar of Howard's genealogy, Rob Roehm, to comment, "It seems that [Robert E. Howard] didn't have much to say about his Howard ancestors."[20] Fortunately, Roehm's research presents a fuller picture of that lineage.

The origins of the Howard name are many, which Robert E. Howard evidently knew. In a letter to a friend, he wrote of three historical origins of the name, the first coming from "Hog-ward, or hog-herder," which he immediately dismissed as inaccurate. The next came from "the occupation name of Hayward, meaning a fence-tender—Hayward—Hawyard—Haward—Howard," and the other from Hereward the Wake, from whom was derived "Hereward—Heward—Haward—Howard."[21] Hereward the Wake is believed to have been an Anglo-Saxon nobleman who led kith and kin with sword and axe against the invading forces of William the Conqueror.[22] Howard reasoned that because of an unknown "law suit in my family nearly a hundred years ago," demonstrating his family lineage was not derived from Hayward, he "naturally" assumed, "I am a direct descendant of Hereward the Wake."[23]

Howard believed that the first of his line arrived in America in the early eighteenth century. "My branch of the Howards came to America with Oglethorpe in 1733," he wrote, "and lived in various parts of Georgia for over a hundred years."[24] "Oglethorpe" was James Edward Oglethorpe, the founder of the Georgia Colony. Howard scholar Roehm's genealogy research, however, has found that "Robert E. Howard's belief that his family landed with Oglethorpe in 1733 is a mistake." According to Roehm, "By all indications, the Howard line had deep roots in Virginia, possibly stretching back to the early 1600s," but he found that it was "not until the early 1800s that the family arrived in Georgia."[25]

It was Howard's great-great grandfather, Mordecai Howard, who brought the family from Virginia to Georgia. Born in Brunswick, Virginia, sometime in 1759, he would have been of the proper age for military service in the American Revolution, but according to Roehm there is the strong possibility that he paid for a substitute. He details that in 1832 a William Wilkinson testified in a Brunswick court hearing regarding his pension that he had enlisted "as a substitute and served a term of three months for Mordecai Howard in the year 1779." Not much later, on February 23, 1784, he married Jane Anderton, who had also been born in Brunswick.[26] They had, by all accounts, eight children, with their last child, Henry, being born in 1795.[27] Although Roehm's research shows Mordecai was a farmer, he also found that Mordecai was "fairly active in land deals." For instance, "On December 23, 1793, Mordecai purchased some Brunswick County land from his brother Thomas, who had moved to North Carolina."[28] It seems Mordecai Howard also finally decided to move south, for according to Roehm, "There are indications that the family arrived in Georgia around 1805."[29]

The last of Mordecai's children, Henry (Howard's great-grandfather) was born on June 11, 1795, in Brunswick, Virginia, and moved with the family to Georgia.[30] There, he met Elizabeth "Betsy" Ann Collier, and they were married on January 27, 1820. Over the next twenty years, Betsy would give birth to nine children, beginning with Charles Henry, who was born on June 27, 1821.[31] Howard described his great-grandfather as "a planter and a schoolteacher" who "was living on a farm in Oglethorpe County, in what I would describe as the middle northeastern part of the state, no great distance from the Savannah River."[32]

After his father, Mordecai, died in 1830, Henry inherited a plot of land, but likely because of some financial difficulties sold the parcel of land to his sister, Nancy Hopkins, for three hundred dollars in 1838.[33] Roehm believes it was at this point Henry decided to move the family 120 miles southwest to settle in Upson County, Georgia.[34] His financial circumstances appear not to have improved any with the sale or the move, for by 1845 he was forced to send out notices to "avail myself of the benefit of the Act entitled an Act for the Relief of Honest Debtors," and the county sheriff began selling off his assets to pay down his debts.[35]

Henry died on April 27, 1876, and according to the *Thomaston Herald*, he "died at his home . . . from old age." The paper also noted, "He has been a good and useful citizen and served his country as a faithful officer in a few instances."[36] His wife remained a widow for four years before she passed away on July 19, 1880. "'Aunt Betsey' (as she was best known)," recalled one neighbor fondly, lived "a life of nearly eighty years, blameless and bright in virtue."[37]

Henry and Aunt Betsey's third child, William Benjamin Howard, was Robert E. Howard's grandfather, and according to the Howard family Bible he was born on July 23, 1827.[38] "As far as I know," Howard once wrote in a biographical essay, "my grandfather, William Benjamin Howard, was born on the plantation."[39] However, "Given the state of Henry Howard's finances," writes Roehm, "it is doubtful that he owned a 'plantation.'"[40] While Henry may have been better off when William Benjamin Howard was born, by 1845 his financial distress had resulted in his plea for debtors' assistance. It may very well have been these financial troubles that motivated William and two of his brothers to leave for California in 1849.[41]

"The gold fever has rapidly increased since the last news arrived," reported *The Constitutionalist*, a Georgia newspaper in January of 1849.[42] Gold had been discovered in California at John Sutter's mill and the race was on.[43] "The streets are filled with adventurers preparing for a start," the article read and "most of those who had gone, or made arrangements to go . . . were men who were in moderate circumstances, young commencing the world, or those who had been disappointed in their calculations here."[44] It is likely all of these were motivations for the Henry boys as Robert E. Howard wrote, "In '49 three brothers started for California."[45] While Howard only gives the name of his grandfather, William Benjamin, Roehm believes the other two are Isaac Mordecai Howard (Robert E. Howard's grand-uncle, not his father) and John Hubbard Howard. William was 22 years old, Isaac was 23, and John was 19 when they set out seeking their fortune in the California Territory.[46] Only one of them would make it there.

"If it had not been for a scourge of cholera," Howard wrote, "I'd have been a Californian instead of a Texan."[47] He explained that the outbreak reduced the party's "number from nineteen to seven," and so weakened the leader, "he was forced to turn back."[48] They had only traveled one-third the distance before tragedy struck in Pine Bluff, Arkansas, located along the Arkansas River.[49] It was there that the three brothers were forced by circumstances to go their separate ways. Howard wrote of their fates when he related how, "one went on to California where he lived the rest of his life, one went back to Georgia and one, William Benjamin Howard, went to Mississippi."[50] The one who likely "went on to California," Roehm informs us, was Isaac, for he was established in Sonora, California, by 1866, while the one who "went back to Georgia" was likely "John Hubbard Howard, Henry Howard's fourth oldest son." It was this breakup of the three brothers that led Howard's grandfather to follow the Arkansas River south into Mississippi, stopping in Oktibbeha County, close to the Alabama line. There, he found employment with James Henry, a farmer and family man with seven children.[51] The Henrys soon became an important part of the Howard family.[52]

If Robert E. Howard could boast of any Irish heritage on the Howard side of the family, it most certainly came from the Henrys. "Of all the branches of my line," he wrote, "the pioneer flame burned in none so brightly as in the Henrys."[53] He says this because the earlier generations had moved between Scotland and Ireland and eventually crossed the Atlantic Ocean to settle in America beginning with his ancestor Reverend John Henry. If the family legend Howard tells can be believed ("My great-great-grandfather, James Henry, was born on the Atlantic Ocean on the way over"), then the year would have been 1765, for James W. Henry, whom Howard referred to as Shamus, was born on May 7 that year.[54] Howard states the reverend, his family, and their new son, "landed in New York" and "drifted southwestward."[55] They settled in the town of Somerset, located in the British Colony of Maryland.

The Reverend John Henry remained there until his death, but the wanderlust grew in his son Shamus, who set his sights on the deeper south, making his way to South Carolina. While in his late 20s, Shamus met Anna Terrell Grimes, and according to the Howard family Bible, they were married on January 4, 1796.[56] Shamus and Anna had eight children, including James W. Henry, who was born on January 11, 1811. With the birth of James, James W. "Shamus" Henry became senior and his son junior, so in order to keep them straight, Howard generally referred to them as Shamus Henry (the father) and Squire Henry, the son.[57]

The year after Squire Henry's birth, war broke out with Britain, lasting until early 1815. "The echoes of the War were scarcely done reverberating," Howard wrote, when Shamus "was pushing westward" and "before Alabama was a state, he came there. It was a southern frontier—sparsely settled, thickly timbered, swarming with game; Indians still dwelt there." It was there, Howard describes, "In the Black Warrior River country, in what came to be Tuscaloosa County, my great-grandfather, James Henry, grew up."[58] They had settled beside a "family named Walser from Georgia," and at the age of 23, Squire James Henry married one of the girls, Mary Ann Walser, on September 25, 1834.[59]

The young family continued to farm the land there for another dozen years, but Howard wrote that "Squire Henry was a typical pioneer," so "when the country about him began to settle up and grow tame, he grew restless and moved on."[60] In 1847 the family relocated approximately a hundred miles to the west, in Oktibbeha County, Mississippi.[61] According to the 1850 Census, James Henry was 39 years of age at the time, a farmer who held real estate estimated to be valued at eight hundred dollars, and he and Mary had seven children.[62] Looking for work, William Benjamin Howard found employment on that farm where he met his future wife.

Robert E. Howard briefly described his grandfather in several letters, once noting that he was "the only one of my recent masculine ancestors I can think of who didn't drink" and that he "stood six feet two in his socks, and weighed two hundred pounds."[63] Whether his abstemious ways came before or after meeting the daughter of Squire Henry, there is little doubt that his imposing size attracted Eliza to him. Born Louisa Elizabeth Henry in Alabama on July 25, 1835, Eliza was the oldest child of Squire Henry and his wife, Mary. William B. Howard must have had an eye on her, for according to the family Bible, on December 6 (possibly 16), 1856, William became the son-in-law of the man he worked for.[64] It seems the aborted trip to California had proven fortuitous.[65]

The Howard family Bible, which still exists, is believed to have been purchased around this time, and may possibly have been a wedding gift.[66] Located in the center of the large leather-bound 1857 Bible are the recorded births, marriages, and deaths of the Howard family that would eventually include Robert E. Howard. In addition to their wedding, the births of William and Eliza Howard's first children were also recorded. Mary Elizabeth A. Howard was their first, born in 1857 in Mississippi, after which Squire Henry decided to move to southwestern Arkansas, and William and his young family went with them.[67] The Henrys and Howards settled near each other on the Ouachita–Dallas County line, close to Holly Springs, and while "the Henrys prospered," Roehm explains, "the Howards not so much."[68] Despite their struggles, they brought their second child into the world, James H. "Jim" Howard in 1858.[69] Not long after, however, war broke out between the states, and there would be no more children for some time.

During the war, William served with the 3rd Arkansas Cavalry in the Confederacy and Howard mentions the family legend, that he "rode for four years with Bedford Forrest."[70] Nathan Bedford Forrest was known as the Wizard of the Saddle for his service as the commanding general of a cavalry regiment during the war. Although it is possible William was attached to the 3rd Regiment, there were no known Arkansas cavalry units attached to Forrest during the war.[71] According to the interview notes of Howard's first biographer, L. Sprague de Camp, one member of the family, Ollie Lorene Davis, told him that during the war, William "was wounded and was an invalid through the latter part of his life," which is confirmed by the 1880 census that lists him as "maimed or crippled."[72]

He returned home to Arkansas after the war and, like most residents of the South, faced the trials and tribulations of a wrecked economy and the constraints of Reconstruction. Still, Arkansas fared better than many other states, for it was the first to be readmitted into the Union in 1868. William also appeared to be faring well, for he and Eliza began having more children, David Terrell Howard in 1866 and Alfonzo T. Howard in 1869.[73] Then, on April 1, 1871, according to the family Bible, Eliza gave birth to Isaac Mordecai Howard, Robert E. Howard's father.[74]

Robert Ervin Howard's middle name is derived from his mother's side of the family, and there are multiple sources for her maiden name, including Irish, Scottish, and Old English, although it is possible that all were derived from the name of a Celtic River, meaning "green, fresh, water." Howard once explained his meager knowledge of the Ervins' settlement in America when he wrote, "The Eiarbhins, or Ervins, to give the name its present Anglicized spelling, came to America a very long time ago; just when I am not sure, but it was before 1700." The family history of his great-grandfather prior to that is scant, but it does appear they were present in the Carolinas as Howard mentioned. "The family was originally Scotch," he believed, when he wrote: "It was a wild Highland clan in the days of Robert Bruce and because they followed him and were granted favors by him, it is a tradition in the family that a male child in every generation be named Robert. My great-grandfather was Robert Ervin, and my great-great grandfather the same; my grandfather, by some chance, was named George Washington Ervin, but he named his youngest son Robert, and I have several cousins of that name."[75] Howard refers to his grandfather as having the middle name of Washington; however, there is no documented evidence for this assertion, although it was not uncommon for children in that time period to be named after America's first president.[76] Regardless, Howard did know that the early American Ervins were established on a plantation in North Carolina as early as 1724 because of "a will made by a slave-holder in North Carolina and witnessed by one Robert Ervin; date, 1724," and that the family "lived there until 1840."[77] It was then, Howard believed, that his great-grandfather began moving the Ervin clan west toward Texas.

According to the Ervin family Bible, Robert Ervin was born in North Carolina on June 5, 1800, although Howard claimed the year was 1801 in an essay on his family history.[78] On February 28, 1825, at the age of 24, Robert Ervin married Jane "Jenny" Tennison in Rowan County, North Carolina.[79] Jenny had been born in that same county on May 15, 1806, which was also recorded in the family Bible, and their son George W. Ervin was also born in North Carolina on May 9, 1830.[80]

Howard wrote that in the early 1840s, "wanderlust took hold of Robert Ervin." Because it was "an age of westward drift," Howard described how Ervin "crossed the Blue Ridge Mountains, drifted on through Tennessee, turned south and in 1842 settled near Iuka, in Tishomingo County, Mississippi, . . . in the northeastern corner of the state, bordered by the Tennessee River."[81] Although the year is not certain, Roehm notes that the 1845 state census does list them as living in Tishomingo at the time.[82]

"In that country and along the river, George Washington Ervin grew to manhood," Howard wrote in a genealogical essay.[83]

In 1848, at the age of 18, George met his future wife, Sarah Jane Martin, when her family moved from across the Tennessee River into Tishomingo County. Sarah had been born in Rutherford, Tennessee, on May 9, 1832, making her precisely two years younger than her husband. The year after they met, on July 26, 1849, George and Sarah were married, after which they settled down and began having children over the next ten years.[84] Christina was born in 1852, Christopher in 1855, John P. in 1856, William in 1860, and Georgia in 1862.[85]

Although the Civil War broke out in 1861, George W. Ervin did not enlist immediately. Rather, he waited until December 7, 1862, when he joined Captain Isham J. Warren's Partisan Rangers, Mississippi State Troops, formed in Tupelo, Mississippi.[86] When the unit was absorbed by the 12th Mississippi Cavalry, George evidently left and joined the 4th Alabama Cavalry and later the 10th. Because the 10th Cavalry at times operated under Nathan Bedford Forrest, Howard believed that "both my grandfathers rode for four years with Bedford Forrest."[87] No doubt echoing the stories told by his mother about her father, Howard boasted of his grandfather's prowess when he wrote to one correspondent, "My grandfather George Ervin was accounted the strongest man in his regiment and one of the strongest men in Forrest's command," while to another he wrote, "My grandfather, Colonel G. W. Ervin . . . was a crack shot with a rifle. He could knock a man out of his saddle at every shot, at any distance within rifle-range—and frequently did."[88] How accurate these statements are is unknown, but typical of Howard, they most certainly voiced that "vicarious pride" he held for his ancestry.

When the war was over, George Ervin returned home to the family farm, but while his family was there, clearly his fortunes were not. As for so many others in the postwar Reconstruction era, the economic situation was bleak, and Mississippi endured five long years under the control of the Fourth Military District; Mississippi was not readmitted to the Union until February 23, 1870. By that time Ervin had moved his family, which now included David, born in 1865, to Texas.

According to Howard, "Colonel George Ervin came into Texas when it was wild and raw," and he "settled on the rich black, waxy prairie lands of Hill County," located between the cities of Fort Worth and Waco.[89] Since the frontier life his grandfather encountered there was important to Howard, he wrote just how "wild and raw" it truly was when he described it to one correspondent in this manner: "From the Palo Pintos to the Gulf roamed thousands and thousands of longhorned cattle, unbranded, worthless. . . . Thirty or forty miles west of G. W. Ervin's farm there stretched the long thin strip of settlements which was the ultimate frontier, and beyond which the Indians roamed and raided unhindered. The Comanches were making their last stand against the white men, and whirlwinds of war and foray shook the border . . . northward, in the unknown land known as the Indian Territory, a half-breed named Jesse Chisholm was dragging a plough through the unbroken prairie to mark a trail for government supply wagons."[90] Since there was no market yet for cattle, the family settled on a farm, but in addition to working the land, Ervin also began purchasing it. According to Roehm, the earliest document showing such a land purchase occurred on March 4, 1868, for $1,047.[91] In addition, Howard describes his grandfather as being somewhat of a "money-lender" who provided needed funds to local ranchers in dire straits, and, despite the risks, Howard noted, "He never lost a cent to the old timers."[92]

The Ervins continued to have more children, and Robert T. Ervin became their first Texas-born child on January 30, 1867.[93] Sadly, one of their children, John P. Ervin, who had been born in 1856, died the following year on October 11, 1868. However, George and Sarah soon welcomed to the family their second Texan and eighth child, Hester Jane Ervin, who was born on July 11, 1870. Hester was Robert E. Howard's mother.

Chapter 2

Dr. Isaac and Hester Ervin Howard, 1870–1906

Sing of my ancestors!
Sing of them with pride!
Sing of fair America,
Green praises and blue tide!
—"An American"[1]

"My father, Dr. Howard, was the son of William Benjamin Howard, of Georgia," wrote Robert E. Howard, noting also that he "was born in southern Arkansas."[2] Although it is known that he was born on April 1, some confusion arose regarding the year of his birth. Dr. Howard created the uncertainty when he changed the year from 1872 to 1871.[3] The Howard family Bible recorded, "Isaac M. Howard, Born April 1, 1871," and both his headstone and obituary in the *Texas State Journal of Medicine* reflect that date.[4] However, the genealogical research of Howard scholars Burke and Roehm demonstrate that until 1918, Dr. Howard consistently recorded his birth year as 1872, and because the 1880 US Census listed him as being 8 years old, the 1871 date is believed incorrect.[5] This led Roehm to conclude, "Isaac Mordecai Howard was born April 1, 1872, in Ouachita County Arkansas."[6]

Isaac was the eighth child of William Benjamin and Eliza Howard and their fifth son. The boy grew up on a farm and no doubt had many chores to help the family farm operate, because his father may have been somewhat incapacitated due to the injury he suffered during the Civil War.[7] Although according to Burke "little is known of the family's life in Arkansas," the Howards likely faced the same conditions as author Tom Barton's father, who was born at approximately the same time. According to Barton, "The South was emerging from Reconstruction with its economy deeply depressed under the dual burden of financing its recovery while paying the cost of its occupation."[8]

When Isaac was 12 years old, he became a Texan. "Following the 1884 death of James Henry," Roehm explains, "the Howards relocated to Texas, settling in the nexus of Hill, Limestone, and McLennan Counties."[9] There, in 1885, they began farming, but tragedy soon struck twice. First, Isaac's oldest brother, James, died not long after the move, and second, on August 2, 1888, at the age of 61, Isaac's father, William, died.[10]

With his father's death, Isaac's older brother, David Terrell Howard, was left in charge of the family, although he was only five years older than Isaac. David was described by the family as "a very stern man and hard to work for," so when his plans were for Isaac to live and work on the farm, Isaac demurred. Most likely out of a desire for his own freedom, Isaac is said to have told his brother he "had other plans," though he was not entirely sure what those plans were. One of David's sons, Wallace Howard, recalled that Isaac considered going into the ministry, but after apparently causing some altercation at church, he concluded his temperament was not well suited for that occupation.[11] He eventually made up his mind. Isaac Mordecai Howard decided to sell his interest in the family property to his brother because he was going to practice medicine.[12]

There was already a family precedent for this since Isaac's maternal uncle, James T. Henry, had previously graduated from the Medical University of Nashville in 1873 and had an established practice in Ouachita County, Arkansas. Dr. Henry's biography notes that he was "one of the very foremost of the professional men of the county" and that he was "an especially skillful physician and surgeon."[13] Closer to home, Isaac's brother David had married into a family with two practicing doctors. Roehm speculates that Isaac apprenticed under one of them, either Dr. Mortier LaFayette Wortham, David Howard's father-in-law, or Dr. John C. Clark, who was married to another of Wortham's daughters and lived in the same community as the Howards.[14]

Whoever he apprenticed with, Isaac managed to catch a rising tide, for as medical historian Caldwell explains, "Toward the end of the 1800s the medical profession was growing—so fast and so uncontrollably, in fact, that doctors who paid attention to the situation were becoming frightened for the future of their calling."[15] Edward Livingston Trudeau, the great-grandfather of *Doonesbury* cartoonist Gary Trudeau, became a physician himself in 1871, and explained the problem when he wrote,

> There was no entrance examination. All the student had to do was to matriculate at the college and pay a fee of five dollars, attend two or more courses of lectures at the college, and pass the very brief oral examinations which each professor gave the members of the graduating class on his own subject. In addition the law required that every student enter his name with some reputable practicing physician for three years as a student in his office—a rather hazy and indefinite relation, for which he paid the physician one hundred dollars a year. If these requirements were met the long-hoped-for sheepskin was forthcoming, and the new M.D. was turned loose on the world.[16]

There was assuredly a growth of medical schools in the last half of the nineteenth century, for although only 52 such schools existed in 1850, by the turn-of-the-century, there were 160. While the population of America grew by 138 percent between the years 1870 and 1910, Caldwell states the "number of physicians grew by 153 percent." Such rapid growth created all manner of deficiencies in the medical schools, leaving Caldwell to conclude that "the training they underwent ranged from the rudimentary to the lunatic."[17] By the beginning of the twentieth century, there was a growing awareness of the problem, and one 1910 report by Dr. Abraham Flexner provides an example of the many calls for change when he wrote, "The improvement of medical education cannot . . . be resisted on the grounds that it will destroy schools and restrict output: that is precisely what is needed. . . . The country needs fewer and better doctors."[18]

Isaac Howard's own training met the minimum requirements of the state of Texas, and on April 19, 1899, he received his own "long-hoped-for sheepskin" when he was granted a "Certificate of Qualification to Practice Medicine in all its branches through the State of Texas" by the Medical Board of Examiners of the Fifth Judicial District, Texarkana, Texas.[19] The documentation lists him as living in Limestone County, but he did not stay there long. As Texas historian Burns wrote, "The frontier stirred wanderlust among [both] doctors and patients."[20]

On July 20, 1899, Roehm tells us that the newly minted Dr. Howard "registered to practice in Freestone County, adjoining Limestone to the east."[21] At the time doctors had to file their credentials with each county in order to practice medicine there. In Dr. Howard's case in Freestone County, the filing certified "that the foregoing attached medical certificate of I. M. Howard was filed in my office for record on the twentieth day of July, 1899."[22]

Roehm catalogued all of the existing county filings of Dr. Howard and finds that the doctor did not stay long in Freestone County either. On May 30, 1901, Dr. Howard was "presenting his credentials at the courthouse in Montague County, on the border between Texas and what was then the Indian Territory (now Oklahoma)."[23] He had family nearby since his favorite sister, Willie Price Howard, had married William McClung, and they were living near the small town of Petersburg, population twenty-five, just across the Red River in Indian Territory.[24] Dr. Howard had likely gone there to assist Willie because, as her daughter, Fannie, once said, "Papa was in the Army."[25] Her father was in the army, but not in the way she likely thought. He was at Fort Leavenworth, Kansas, serving a five-year sentence in the disciplinary barracks for stealing mules.[26] Unfortunately, while helping his sister, Dr. Howard took sick, and the illness developed into pneumonia. Fannie, who called Dr. Howard "Uncle Que," remembered how he wanted to travel to Mount Calm, Texas, to convalesce in the home of his mother.[27] Fannie recalled her mother telling the following story:

> Mama with us two kids and Uncle Que took the train . . . they had to lay over two or three hours in Fort Worth, Texas before they could catch a train to Mt. Calm. She was having a pretty bad time trying to take

> care of Uncle Que and keep up with Clarence and me. . . . As Uncle Que had fever so high that he was delirious—Mama had to have help to get him on the train. As she was a Rebecca [a beautiful woman with an outgoing personality]—she made this know[n] and that she needed help. In minutes she had plenty of help and two of the men made the rest of the trip with her. Uncle Que was not married at the time and I'm not sure how long he stayed in Mt. Calm.[28]

He did not stay long, for on January 8, 1902, he was filing to practice medicine in Palo Pinto County, about one hundred miles northwest of Mount Calm, just west of Fort Worth.[29] He practiced throughout the county while living in the small town of Graford, just northwest of the larger town of Mineral Wells. It was in the latter town that he likely met his future wife, Hester Jane Ervin, who was there visiting her relatives.[30]

X Ξ

As only a proud son can do, Howard once boasted of his father, "There is no better physician in the state of Texas," before adding, "He is a rare combination of a scholar and a worker."[31] Others less biased would not dispute the good doctor's son, for, like Jack Scott, the editor of the *Cross Plains Review*, who described him as an "old country doctor" and "well educated for his time," the people who knew him could not help but love and respect him.[32] Scott recalled him physically as "a big strong, virile kind of man" who "wore a suit of clothes, a white shirt, and tie every day."[33] This is likely why Scott said, "He looked like a United States Senator. Gray headed and strong and upstanding who would look you straight in the eye. I don't believe he was afraid of the devil himself."[34] Pulp writer E. Hoffmann Price, who visited the Howards in Cross Plains, described Dr. Howard in a similar manner as "a man of iron: human, kindly, but a fierce and independent old man."[35] The good doctor evidently treasured his independence.

One friend recalled his best-known character trait when he said, "He was a talkative person," but it seems nearly everyone enjoyed hearing what he had to say.[36] "I liked to hear him talk. He would tell a lot of interesting things," recalled Scott, before adding the colorful Texas colloquialism, "He was unusual as a three dollar bill."[37] Another friend, Norris Chambers, stressed that, "He was *likable*. He was a *good* guy," before explaining, "If he talked, he talked about somebody else, he didn't talk about the guy he was talkin' to." Chambers remembered well the conversations Dr. Howard and his father, a fellow country doctor, often had: "Sometimes him and Papa would get talking about somebody, and they would say all kinds of bad things, but it didn't mean anything. He'd talk about all the bad things he could do, about 'hangin' their guts on a fence' and stuff like that. But it was just talk. He was a good guy. I guess everybody liked him. I don't reckon he had any enemies." When asked if he ever got angry, Chambers replied, "Well, he got angry about *anything*, Dr. Howard did," although it seems it was most commonly rooted in Dr. Howard's passions rather than any actual hatred toward a person.[38]

Other than Dr. Howard's penchant for talking, most people recalled his insatiable appetite. Scott remembered, "He had a ravenous appetite," while many of the women, like Marie Baker Andrews, reminisced how "Dr. Howard loved his food, you just couldn't cook enough for him."[39] The doctor made his rounds to the homes of his friends and patients, often one and the same, and always shared meals with them. "Dr. Howard came by our house at all hours of the day or night," Chambers recalled, and "always my mother, and later my wife and mother, asked him if he had eaten, and usually fixed him a good meal. He was a very hearty eater, and nothing seemed to disagree with him."[40] Another friend and patient, Howard O. Newton, who had been delivered by Dr. Howard and was named after him, explained that "anytime Dr. Howard came to our house, he came in the door telling my mother he was hungry, and that he wanted ham or chicken, and always hot biscuits and gravy."[41] The reason for this insatiable appetite may possibly have been undiagnosed diabetes, since that is a common symptom, and he was later diagnosed with the disease.[42] This may also explain why people like J. H. Childs remembered Dr. Howard coming to their house "four or five times a week at least" and eating "anything [that] wasn't nailed down."[43]

Despite all his demands for food, Dr. Howard remained well loved by his friends and those he served. Many had their favorite stories about Dr. Howard, and all described him as a man who enjoyed many interests. For instance, he liked to have fun with people at their expense. Chambers told the story of how he went into a pharmacy one day with his father. "I wanted a drink of water. So Dr. Howard told his pharmacist, 'Get the boy some water.' So the pharmacist filled up a glass and I took a drink. Carbonated water! And they all just laughed and laughed about that. They thought that was the funniest thing. I didn't! Of course, I didn't know what it was."[44] Still others, like Scott, recalled a more reflective side of the doctor. One day he had pulled his car up in front of the newspaper office and started honking his horn and would not stop. Scott finally came out and told him, "Hell, Doc, we don't give curb service here. What do you want?" Dr. Howard told him to get inside the car, which Scott did, and he began talking: "I just came from Cottonwood. You know how the road is. Trees overlapping. As those leaves fell, and would float down across, I just stopped my car and thought about the people . . . they're just like those leaves. They float down to earth and die, and they're dead and forgotten."[45] Probably uncertain if this was one of the doctor's jokes or not, Scott didn't say anything. Finally, Dr. Howard said, "That's all there is to it. Get out: Just wanted to tell you that."[46]

Most people also remembered how intelligent, well-read, and diversified his interests were. One family friend, Annie Newton Davis, recalled, "He was interested in everything that was going [on] in the community and nationally." When she lived near the Howards, she admired his collection of books and was interested in his Zane Grey editions. "Every time he got a new one in and finished it," she said, "then I got it."[47] In addition to what was popular at the time, he also read widely in the fields of medicine and the sciences. "There is scarcely any branch of medical science that he has not studied," wrote his son, "any legitimate branch, I mean. Nor medicine alone, but theology, history and economics."[48] Scott thought him so intelligent he once told an interviewer, "That man—I bet he wouldn't have been afraid to try brain surgery, or anything else."[49] There is no record that Dr. Howard ever tried brain surgery, but the sentiment is an example of the great respect people had for Dr. Howard as a physician.

It seems nearly everyone was in agreement that he was an excellent "old-fashioned family doctor."[50] Truett Vinson, a close friend of Robert E. Howard, told one interviewer, "I consider Dr. Howard as a very good doctor, one who served the community of Cross Plains unselfishly."[51] Chambers agreed when he said, "I guess he was about as good a doctor as there was back in those days," adding that, "Papa thought he was a good doctor."[52] High praise, indeed, for Chambers's father had been a doctor himself.

Despite the increase in the number of men who had become doctors at the turn of the century, the small town and rural areas of Texas still lacked an adequate number of physicians. The other problem, as O. G. Lawson, an oil worker in the Texas oil boom town of Ranger, stated, was that "it was very difficult to get a decent doctor."[53] Dr. Bryson, a contemporary of Dr. Howard, explained part of the problem when he wrote, "The majority of doctors who were practicing medicine in the smaller towns and rural districts in 1910 had less than four years of medical college training."[54] Added to this is Trudeau's description of what that medical training entailed, and because medical quackery was pervasive in that era, a good doctor was simply hard to find.[55]

The life of a country doctor was not an easy one either. Lewis Newton, who knew Dr. Howard, noted that "a country doctor was gone all hours of the day and night."[56] While they may have had an office inside their home or at the local pharmacy, country doctors throughout Dr. Howard's life still made house calls. He would be summoned in person and, later, by telephone. Dr. Howard would then hitch up "the horse and buggy," later his automobile, and drive to the residence.[57] "In his early days much of his practice was in primitive communities," wrote Dr. Howard's son, "far removed from any of the inventions and conveniences of civilization. He went into miserable shacks and huts, and without weapons save his own intelligence and a few simple medicines of the time."[58] Once he reached the patient, Tom Barton explained what happened next. "[He] took temperature, listened to the heart, examined the eyes, looked at the tongue and throat."[59] Then the doctor would open up his black bag and pull out his medicines. As Ora Lewis Bradley (the wife of a country doctor in Georgia in the same era) wrote, the doctor "had to furnish all his medicines, mix his own powders and roll his own pills, for there were no drug stores within reach."[60] She remembered her husband showing her his "most poisonous medicines" that included "morphine, atropine, prussic acid, and tincture of opium."[61]

The doctor also never knew what he would find upon his arrival. Newton, who at one time drove Dr. Howard on his house calls, reminisced how, "The most memorable visit was to a farm house, where a boy of 14 or

15 was tied on the iron bedstead on the front porch of the house." The doctor removed the dirty bandage wrapped around his foot, then "proceeded to pull out screw worms from the boy's toe. Before he finished dressing the toe the poor old boy was asleep." And in another case, one of Newton's cousins had been on the losing side of a knife fight and had "a 6-inch gash in his stomach" and "his intestines were showing. Dr. Howard washed him out with soap and water and sewed him up on our back porch."[62]

Once he was through doing all he could physically for the patient, Dr. Howard would then give them some consoling words, for as Barton noted, "Sympathy and consolation were important qualities of our doctors."[63] Tevis Clyde Smith, another close friend of Howard's, recalled one such case when a Mr. Cox "told Dr. Howard of his inability to defecate," so "Dr. Howard told him to quit worrying—that he would have a movement at 3:30 that afternoon and that his constipation would be cured." As it turned out, Mr. Cox felt the urge precisely at 3:30 p.m. and was so amazed with Dr. Howard, "he began to think he was God."[64]

There were also times, Bradley explained, when there was nothing a doctor could do for a patient, suggesting that "just talking, looking wise and sympathetic always had favorable results psychologically."[65] Chambers remembered one such story Dr. Howard told him when he was sent to care for a woman who was "pretty sick." Dr. Howard "went in there, and he really didn't know what was wrong with her. So he messed around a bit, and came out, and someone asked him 'What's the matter?' And he told me, 'I just used a few of the terms I'd learned and smoothed it over there.' And when he started to leave, he heard one of the women say to the other, 'He don't know what's a matter with 'em!'" Dr. Howard then bluntly told Chambers, "That lady was right!"[66]

The situations Dr. Howard found himself in were not always safe either. Scott recalled one story the good doctor told him about being called to deliver a baby deep in the country. After spending a good portion of the night with the woman in labor, he realized her poor state of health and went to her husband and said, "I don't think I'm going to pull her through." The man retrieved a shotgun and told Dr. Howard, "If you don't pull her through, you ain't going out of here alive."[67] Dr. Howard went back in and did everything he could.

The baby was born in the morning and the mother survived. Afterward, the parents proudly announced to everyone, "We've named it Howard, for that fine Doctor Howard."[68]

There was another difficulty with being a country doctor, and that was payment for services rendered. Scott described Dr. Howard as "a man who never had any money."[69] His son wrote, "The reason he is not a rich man is because he's been more interested in humanity than in dollars." Howard estimated, "The charity work he's done would run up into the hundred thousands, and the bills people have beat him out of would about equal that figure."[70] Newton remembered, "He doctored all who called and needed him whether they had money or could ever pay him or not," and Larry McDonough confirmed this by recounting how "ol' Doc would never turn anybody down."[71]

Dr. Howard was much like Dr. Bryson, who admitted, "One of my worse faults . . . was considered by the layman to be one of my finest qualities . . . that is, I was a notoriously poor charger and a poorer collector."[72] Most patients knew that to be the case for Dr. Howard, so they never hesitated to call upon him. Because most of his patients were farmers who were typically "cash poor," they often paid him with things like produce, milk, or eggs, as well as free meals. Wallace Howard remembered, "You fed 'em and paid 'em off in chickens or something else."[73] One other way, Scott noted, was, "They kind of paid it in respect to the man," sometimes by naming their children after him, or paying him compliments like McDonough did when he said of Dr. Howard, "He was our doctor; he was a great man."[74]

"George Ervin," Howard wrote of his maternal grandfather, "prospered on his broad rich lands. Children were born to him and his wife. There, in 1876, just three years after the last Comanche raid in Central Texas, my mother, Hester Jane Ervin, was born."[75] As with Isaac's birth date, a discrepancy arose regarding Hester's actual birth year. The family Bible declares she was born on July 11, 1870, yet it seems both Dr. Howard and his son adhered to 1876 as her birth year.[76] Hester did not appear in the 1870 census, because although it had been recorded on July 19, it only listed family living in the abode as of June 1 that year. Hester had been born after that date. The 1900 census, however, gives the birth month and year of each person recorded, and it shows that Hester gave the census taker the July 1870 date. It seems her birth year remained 1870 until she met Dr. Howard, at which point it became 1876, making her four years younger than Isaac, rather than two years older. So when Howard gives 1876 as her birth year, as Louinet explains, he did so because it was a "known, but respected secret in the Howard family."[77]

Roehm informs us that "Hester Jane Ervin was born July 11, 1870, on a farm near Hillsborough, in Hill County, Texas."[78] She was the second Ervin to be born in Texas, after her brother Robert T., and was likely "named after her grandmothers (Martha) *Esther* (Mason) and *Jane* (Tennyson)."[79] As the family continued to prosper, Sarah Jane Ervin became pregnant once more, but then tragedy struck. "After a lingering illness," according to her obituary, Sarah Jane died on June 2, 1874.[80] "She had given birth to a tenth child on April 6 or 16, a girl named Lizzie who would survive her mother by only one day," Louinet explains, meaning "Hester Jane Ervin, not even 4, had just lost her mother."[81]

George W., now a widower, moved his family to Dallas, for as Howard wrote, "A boom was on in Texas; cities were growing" and Hester's father "went into the real estate business, and was successful."[82] While there, G. W. met and courted Alice Wynne, a native of Mississippi who had only just arrived in Dallas, and they were married on April 14, 1875.[83] Hester's father and stepmother soon moved the family to Lewisville, northwest of Dallas, and in 1876 Alice gave birth to the first of five of Hester's half-siblings. Officially, George W. Ervin ran the Lewisville Hotel, but he primarily used it as a base for dealing in real estate and mineral rights.[84] After reviewing the historic records of G. W.'s property holdings, Roehm was left to conclude, "The family was quite comfortable."[85]

Although there are few details of Hester's early years, Dr. Howard later learned of her early hopes and dreams. "Robert's mother was a poet," the doctor wrote, "She also loved the stage. It was her ambition when a young girl to prepare herself for the stage, but her father opposed it. She often spoke of it as a great disappointment. I am sure she had the talent."[86] Her exposure to theater likely came from living in and around Dallas, but the family's next move most certainly isolated her from that particular interest.

Howard continued his mother's story when he wrote that the family "moved again, this time southwestward to Lampasas, in the cattle country."[87] G. W.'s first land purchase there came on January 9, 1886, and according to Roehm, "He appears to have purchased these lots outright for the tidy sum of fifteen hundred dollars."[88] Although he was clearly profiting from his real estate deals, his main interest was in minerals, for two years later, Howard wrote, "He wandered over into western New Mexico and worked a silver mine not far from the Arizona line."[89] The Robert E. Lee Mine was located in Stein's Pass, and local newspapers reporting on the mining activities there noted that by the end of 1888, gold had also been discovered.[90] G. W. began splitting his time between Lampasas and the mine, but despite all attempts at becoming the mine's sole owner, he failed.[91]

Hester remained in Lampasas during those years, beginning to step out into local society starting in 1889 when she was 19 years old.[92] Louinet explains that Hester had grown up "in a world of affluence, surrounded by men of power" and that not only was her father wealthy, but also "among her siblings and in-laws, she had newspapermen, rich merchants, [and] a banker."[93] She was certainly enjoying life; however, all of that was placed in jeopardy when, in 1891, as Howard explains, "G. W. Ervin made the greatest mistake of his life; he turned eastward again."[94] Throughout 1890 her father sold off his land holdings and announced the family was moving to Exeter, Missouri.[95] "The older children refused to accompany him," wrote Howard, and this included Hester, to a certain degree. For the next twelve years, Hester would split her time between the home in Exeter and living with other relatives. Despite being single and now at an age to seek employment, according to Louinet, she "never worked a single day in her life."[96]

Although Hester was never employed in an official capacity, she often found occasion to work in the home, particularly when a relative took sick, as her older sister did at the end of 1892. Christina Ervin, who had been living in Indian Territory since as early as 1887, married John Oliver Cobb on June 16, 1892.[97] That Christmas the local newspaper recorded that Christina had "la grippe," and Hester was there to care for her.[98] Christina recovered, but sometime later Hester took ill, for the *Muskogee Phoenix* reported on February 16, 1893, "Miss Hester Ervin is quite sick at the home of her sister,

Mrs. J. O. Cobb."[99] Howard scholar Leo Grin explains that although the exact nature of her illness is unknown, Hester spent the years before her marriage "selflessly taking care of sick relatives," and at some point she contracted "the illness that would kill her."[100] That illness was tuberculosis.

As Barbara Barrett writes in her in-depth article on Hester's illness, Hester Jane Ervin Howard's death certificate states she died of tuberculosis on June 12, 1936.[101] Barrett calls this a "puzzling diagnosis" and one that is "difficult to understand," because tuberculosis "is never referred to in any letters written by either her son, Robert E. Howard, or her husband, Dr. Isaac M. Howard."[102] Yet after reviewing the signs, symptoms, and treatments, Barrett leaves little doubt that this is the disease she suffered from throughout much of her life.

"Pulmonary tuberculosis," writes medical historian Thomas Dormandy, is "known as phthisis, consumption, wasting disease, weakness of lungs, graveyard cough and a host of other more or less descriptive synonyms." Although the disease is an ancient one, traced back as far as Egypt around 3000 BC, it was not until 1882 that German bacteriologist Robert Koch identified the cause of consumption and transformed the world's thinking about tuberculosis.[103] Koch showed that consumption was the result of an infection with a microorganism, and that the most common form of the disease affected the lungs, hence pulmonary tuberculosis. "As this realization took hold," another historian, Helen Bynum, explicates "what had been an unrelated family of disorders was recast as a single infectious disease. It changed the way in which its sufferers were viewed and treated. Tuberculosis, rather than consumption, was now set to become visible in new ways."[104]

Knowledge of Koch's discovery soon spread to America, and by 1900 there was a greater awareness of how the disease spread through an infected person coughing and sneezing, and how babies and young adults were the most susceptible to contracting it.[105] Emily Bissell created the Christmas Seals program to raise money and promote awareness of tuberculosis, as did groups like the Texas Anti-Tuberculosis Association, which published public service announcements asking people to cough into handkerchiefs, sleep in rooms with fresh air, and not spit on floors.[106] In addition, word began to spread of the people who had contracted the disease—including John Keats, Ralph Waldo Emerson, Frédéric Chopin, and the Brontë sisters—demonstrating that no class was able to escape the dreaded disease.[107]

Doctors were unsure how to treat tuberculosis in the late nineteenth and early twentieth centuries, and they often disputed over their own pet cures. Yet "while doctors argued," Dormandy writes, "the illness continued to kill men and women of all ages, but especially the young: it wrecked hopes, it broke courtships and it struck down bread-winners leaving large families destitute." One common treatment was to move patients to warmer and drier climates and the out of doors, motivating many to move to the American Southwest.[108] However, by the turn of the century, the "bedrock of treatment" had become the sanatorium.[109]

The physician most widely known for promoting the use of the sanatorium in the United Sates was Lawrason Brown. According to Caldwell, "Brown had become resident physician at the Adirondack Cottage Sanatorium in 1901 and remained there until 1912, refining and systematizing the treatment patients underwent, formulating rules, and governing the minutest details of their days."[110] He then created the popular institute at Saranac Lake for those who could afford it. Although tuberculosis did not discriminate by class, discrimination was found in the sanatoriums themselves. The poorer classes were given rooms "less luxuriously furnished; the food somewhat plainer and less *recherché*; more than one patient are often put into the same bedroom; and a certain amount of the lighter work is expected to be done by those patients who are fit for it."[111]

Of all the treatments for pulmonary tuberculosis, the most extreme was a method known as "artificial pneumothorax," which collapsed the lung by inserting air or nitrogen into the pleural space. After being given morphine, anesthesia, and novocaine as a local, the doctor inserted a needle into the pleura to draw off excess fluid. One patient described the procedure and explained everything was mostly harmless until the needle penetrated, when "there was a crunch, a stab and a prayer, O God, let me die quickly."[112]

While the procedure, assuredly painful, only caused the desire to die, the disease itself was killing Americans at astounding levels.[113] According to the

United States Center for Disease Control, one of the leading causes of death in the early twentieth century was tuberculosis. It often competed with "pneumonia (all forms) and influenza" for being the mostly deadly disease.[114] Tuberculosis proved the most deadly in 1902, 1903, 1905, and 1906, the year Robert E. Howard was born. Deaths by tuberculosis also placed it as the most deadly in both 1908 and 1909, after which it competed with heart disease. From another perspective, in 1906 there were nearly 60,000 deaths from tuberculosis, while in 1936, the year Hester Howard died, there were 71,527 deaths. Sadly, tuberculosis deaths in that year had reached their peak, for afterward the numbers fell steadily due to improved diagnosis and treatment.

The greatest unknown regarding Hester's tuberculosis is exactly when she contracted the disease. A person can contract it, experience flu-like symptoms, and then feel fine for years before any additional symptoms occur. Because of this, Ora Lewis Bradley, the country doctor's wife, called it a "deceptive" disease because "patients never believed they had it."[115] Hester could easily have contracted it from her sister Christina or from any of the other sick relatives she cared for. This is likely, however, something that will never be known, and possibly something she herself did not know.

Hester left Indian Territory at some point in 1892 but returned two years later, for as Louinet tells us, "Hester may have spent the full year 1894 with her sister, or she could have been alternating her stays in Missouri with visits to her siblings, which seems to sum up what she did from 1892 to 1903."[116] She spent time visiting family in Dallas, Ferris, and Galveston, and the 1900 Census placed her in Abilene, living with her sister Christina, who was now estranged from her husband.[117]

In 1902 Hester spent about eight months living in Mineral Wells, Texas, with her half-brother Wynne Ervin and one of her sisters, either Christina or Georgia Alice.[118] Mineral Wells had become a popular resort city, mostly because of the healing powers of the local "Crazy Water." In 1880 James Lynch had drilled a well on his property, but the family was afraid to drink the water because it had a "funny taste." Eventually they overcame their fears and found the water to be beneficial, for it cured Mr. and Mrs. Lynch's rheumatism. Billy Wiggins then dug his own well the following year, known as the Crazy Well, and by the end of 1881, over 3,000 people had flooded into Mineral Wells to pay ten cents a glass for Crazy Water. By 1900 the town had become a spa resort with over 150,000 people visiting there annually.[119]

By the time Hester was staying in Mineral Wells, she was 32 years old, and the benefits of her upper-class life had certainly formed her personality. Overwhelmingly, there seemed to be an impression of those who knew her that Hester Jane Ervin was a lady. Truett Vinson said in an interview, "Mrs. Howard was a quiet, genteel lady, of the old South. Or at least that is the impression I had."[120] He also enthusiastically noted, "She was a good cook!"[121] Marie Baker, who once lived next door to Hester, described her from a woman's perspective in this manner: "She just was a 'lady.' You know, I have lots of friends, and I don't think of all of them as 'ladies,' but there is one or two that I do, because of their attitude and so forth. And that's what I thought of Mrs. Howard."[122] Another neighbor, Lewis E. Newton, once said, "I don't know of anyone that ever had a disgraceful word to say about her."[123] She appears, by all evidence, to have been highly social and outgoing, at least until the ravages of her disease began to take hold.[124]

Howard wrote that his mother "met Dr. Isaac Mordecai Howard, while living in Mineral Wells, in Palo Pinto County, and they were married in the early part of 1904."[125] Dr. Howard was living in the small community of Christian, just north of Graford in Jack County, which only had a population of fifty, and it was likely on a visit to Mineral Wells that he met Hester. She may have been dating another man at the time, but after meeting the tall, blue-eyed, handsome young doctor, she knew she had found her future husband.[126]

Dr. Isaac Mordecai and Mrs. Hester Jane Ervin Howard settled initially in the doctor's home in Christian, but the exact date of their next move becomes murky. Roehm believes they left either in 1904 or early 1905, for they were in the town of Bryson by April 1905.[127] How long they stayed there is also unknown, but at some point in 1905 or 1906, they moved several miles west of Graford, settling on the banks of Dark Valley Creek, a small tributary that fed into the Brazos River.[128] At first they boarded with the Green family while they waited for their own home to be built—possibly a rental home, for there are no land records showing the Howards purchased a home there.[129]

The Greens' residence was a "one-story peaked-roof house" with a typical Texas dogtrot—a breezeway through the center of the home. "There was a kitchen on the side nearest the creek," explained Mrs. Green, "with a very small bedroom beyond it, entered through the kitchen." And she recalled how Hester called Isaac "Howie," and Isaac called her "Hessie," and that they were "very much in love."[130]

A few months later, their home was ready. Built not too far from the Greens' home, it was situated approximately fifty feet from the creek, and a neighbor described it as a "real pretty" house with "a pretty little stone arched front." There was no indoor plumbing, so the outhouse sat perched above the creek, which flowed "not more than ten feet below." They now had their own place, and one with more privacy. Still, it was an austere place to begin their marriage, and certainly not one that Mrs. Howard had been used to most of her life. Very few people lived by Dark Valley Creek, and Graford only had a population of nineteen. This is probably why Mrs. Green commented, "I can't imagine why Doctor Howard moved to such a sparsely settled place—no practice to speak of."[131]

While Dr. Howard may have been based in Graford, he responded to calls all over Palo Pinto County. There was already one doctor there, Dr. R. H. Smith, who had only been practicing in the county since the beginning of 1903.[132] Mrs. Howard, like Dr. Smith's wife, "often accompanied him to the home of his patients to help the sick. When he delivered a baby she often bathed and dressed it until the mother was able to care for it."[133] With her experience taking care of sick family members, Mrs. Howard easily made the transition to assisting her husband with his patients. Dr. Moore, a contemporary of Dr. Howard's in Texas, knew the importance of a doctor's wife when he wrote, "The public looks on doctors and their wives as public servants, and rightly expects them to have a common public interest."[134] More specifically, he believed that a country doctor's wife "must be intelligent, a person of sound integrity, possess good judgement, perception, deep understanding, sympathy, a quiet sense of humor, never-failing tactfulness, and the ability to keep her mouth shut." A doctor's wife also had to learn to "tolerate early, late, and irregular hours."[135] Moore believed, "It's a rare woman who can be a good wife, a mother, a housekeeper, a secretary, a good cook, handle the telephone, the doorbell, and be the doctor's buffer."[136] It seemed Mrs. Howard was adept at all of these things, for as Grin summarizes, "Until her health failed she helped her husband with his medical practice."[137]

Dr. Howard also took steps toward strengthening his credentials by obtaining a medical degree.[138] He enrolled in a correspondence course from the Gate City College of Medicine and School of Pharmacy in Texarkana. Dr. Decker had originally organized the college in Sulphur Rock, Arkansas, before moving it to Texarkana in 1903, having been granted a charter by the state of Texas.[139] Dr. Howard received his diploma on May 1, 1905, and on May 4 he was certified as having "attended a Course of Special Instruction in the School of Operative Surgery in the Gate City Medical College and has passed satisfactory examination on the subject." This proved fortuitous, for the state of Texas created a new Board of Medical Examiners in 1907 to issue medical licenses. Dr. Howard would have been grandfathered in because he was already practicing medicine under the old licensure system, but the degree bolstered his right to continue his practice.[140] However, it should be noted that several years later, Gate City Medical College was exposed as a fraud, and the college's charter was revoked.[141]

With a solidified medical practice and a new home, the Howards now only needed one more thing to make their life complete: a child. They were apparently trying to conceive but with no success. Because they truly wanted a child, they began talking of adoption and considered the possibility of adopting one of David Howard's children. "David Howard," explains Roehm, "was farming in Limestone County at the time, some 125 miles southeast of Christian, and had quite a large family."[142] They were apparently not well off and already had six children when their youngest son, Wallace C. Howard, was born in 1904. As Wallace himself told the story, "They come to mama and papa and wanted to take me and raise me as their—their foster-son." Though they never did, it left Wallace to wonder, as he candidly told an interviewer, if he "wouldn't have been better off."[143] Whether David Howard gave the proposition any serious consideration is unknown, but the adoption never happened because they learned sometime in late spring of 1905 that Hester was pregnant.

Chapter 3

A Peripatetic Childhood, 1906–1915

The nightwinds tossed the tangled trees,
the stars were cold with scorn;
Midnight lay over Dark Valley
the hour I was born.
—"The Dweller in Dark Valley"[1]

"I was born in Peaster, Texas, a small town not far from Weatherford, in January, 1906," Robert E. Howard wrote for a school assignment at the age of 15 (he received a B).[2] Later, at 27, he lamented his birth date: "I was born about a hundred years too late; that's not my fault, it's my misfortune."[3] Named for an uncle who had died before his birth, Howard entered the world on the cusp of Texas's entry into the industrialized world, as its frontier days slipped away.[4] Industrialization had come late to the state, for as Texas historian Fehrenbach writes, "Texas entered the twentieth century with its basic society a full two generations, or about sixty years, behind the development of the American mainstream."[5] Howard scholar Leo Grin describes just what that mainstream was like at the time of Howard's birth: "The average Civil War veteran was sixty-five years old and still very much alive. Teddy Roosevelt was President. Ten days earlier, the Dow Jones had closed above 100 for the first time ever, while in the newspapers the very first radio set had just been advertised for $7.50."[6] Yet while America was becoming more urbanized, Texans remained close to the land; it was still an agricultural state. Because Howard grew up during this transition period, he sensed a loss of freedom closely associated with the industrialization that drove his desire to have been born earlier on the Texas frontier.

The entry in the Howard family Bible succinctly states, "Robert E. Howard, born January 22, 1906," but as with his parents before him, there proved to be some confusion over his actual birthdate.[7] His official birth record filed with the Parker County Clerk's Office shows the birthday as January 24, not the 22.[8] The mistake is believed to have arisen from the fact the doctor who delivered Howard, Dr. J. A. Williams, did not file the birth record until February 1.[9] It is likely he had simply forgotten on which day Howard had been born.[10]

The other oddity regarding Howard's birth record is the location. The Howards had been living in Dark Valley, approximately ten miles from the town of Graford, yet the Howards chose to travel another twenty miles east to the town of Peaster in Parker County for the birth. Roehm's research shows that Dr. Howard had filed to practice in Parker County on May 12, 1905, about the time they knew Hester was with child.[11] Burke surmises that "perhaps thinking that his wife, whose age was in that day considered rather advanced for a first-time pregnancy (she was in her mid-thirties), needed to be assured of medical care even if he was off on calls," so he took the necessary precautions to ensure Hester would be in Peaster for the delivery of their first child.[12] Because of this, Howard wrote, "I was born in the little ex-cowtown of Peaster, about 45 miles west of Fort Worth, in the winter of 1906."[13]

Peaster is located in Parker County, named for Texas pioneer and State Representative Isaac Parker, while the town derived its own from the first person to settle there, H. H. Peaster, who had purchased 160 acres and built a home there in 1882.[14] Oddly enough, the first post office was established by another Dr. Howard that year, although the first bank was not organized until the year of Robert E. Howard's birth.[15] Howard visited the small town approximately twenty-five years later and remarked, "The tide of progress seems scarcely to have touched Peaster, the tiny village where I was born—as then, the few stores are kept by old ranchmen too old for riding and roping—tall, bent old men with flowing white moustaches and keen blue eyes who sit and dream of old times."[16]

The birth appears to have gone well, for Mrs. Green recalled in her interview, "Hester seemed healthy when the baby came."[17] Dr. Howard, of course, was ecstatic to be a father. As one of the local newspapers commented, "Dr. Howard is boasting of the only boy baby of Peaster in 1906."[18] Sometime between the birth and the end of spring, they moved back to their home along the creek, leaving Howard to later write that he spent his "first summer in lonely Dark Valley among the sparsely settled Palo Pinto hills."[19]

"Man is greatly molded by his surroundings," stated Howard in a letter. "I believe, for instance, that the gloominess in my own nature can be partly traced to the surroundings of a locality in which I spent part of my babyhood." He described the land there as a "long, narrow valley, lonesome and isolated," and how "it was very sparsely settled and its name, Dark Valley, was highly descriptive." He continued: "So high were the ridges, so thick and tall the oak trees that it was shadowy even in the daytime, and at night it was as dark as a pine forest—and nothing is darker in the world. The creatures of the night whispered and called to one another, faint night-winds murmured through the leaves and now and then among the slightly waving branches could be glimpsed the gleam of a distant star." The description was written before his visit to the land of his childhood, but it reflected aspects of Howard's moods as an adult that he transposed upon the land itself. "Surely, the silence, the brooding loneliness, the shadowy mysticism of that lonesome valley entered in some part into my vague-forming nature."[20]

Little is known about those first two formative years, and what there is varies. For instance, Mrs. Green recalled, "She never had no trouble with the baby and seemed to know exactly what to do to care for it."[21] Dr. Howard's nephew, Wallace C. Howard, recalled how Hester and her son were both sickly during their stay in Dark Valley.[22] And Kate Merryman, a neighbor who helped take care of Hester on her deathbed, suggested Hester may have become pregnant again in Dark Valley, but suffered a miscarriage.[23] Either Hester or her sister, Merryman claimed, had told her that "Mrs. Howard was pregnant and let Robert nurse too long which caused his sickness, she lost the baby."[24] Merryman also recalled Hester saying of Howard, "she spoiled him when he was little. She wasn't well. I don't think she'd ever been very well. But she said she'd springed him on the bed as long as she could stand up and spring, and then she'd get down underneath and work the springs from underneath."[25] Like most mothers, she was rocking her baby to sleep.

In addition to practicing medicine out of Graford and making house calls throughout the county when needed, Dr. Howard was also speculating on land. Roehm believes he purchased several lots in Palo Pinto County because of rumors of a possible railroad line expansion.[26] There was already a line from Weatherford to Mineral Wells that had been built in 1891, but rumors circulated of a possible extension north toward Graford after the Texas and Pacific Railway Company purchased the line in 1902. They did eventually open the line, but not until 1908.[27] By then the Howards had moved, and they would keep on moving for the next ten years.

It is not known why Dr. Howard moved his family so often. Wallace C. Howard summed it up simply by stating, "Howards are moving people," suggesting it was a family trait, one that the westward movement of his ancestors certainly supported.[28] It most certainly had become a trait of Dr. Howard's. Lindsey Tyson, a friend of Howard's, explained it best when he said of the doctor: "He was a—a restless kind of fellow."[29] In his biography of Howard, Burke concludes that "Isaac Howard seems to have been possessed of a combination of wanderlust and ambition that led him to move his family frequently in search of better opportunities."[30] And those "better opportunities" came by moving near boom towns.[31] "My family has been prone to follow booms," Howard wrote, "and I have lived in oil boom towns, land boom towns, railroad boom towns, and have seen life in some of its crudest and most elemental forms."[32] It was the oil booms that Howard remembered most, for oil had only recently been discovered in Texas—five years before his birth.

On Friday morning, January 10, 1901, the well at Spindletop came in. It sat atop a mound the locals called Big Hill, explains historian

Bryan Burroughs, for there, "silhouetted against the gray morning sky, stood the skeleton of an oil derrick, a latticework triangle of wood, sixty-four feet high."[33] The men working Big Hill felt the ground rumble and then, "Suddenly, the fountain exploded, an eruption of mud that shot straight up into the sky high above the derrick."[34] The men watched it spew mud and rock, but "what happened next," wrote Burroughs, "would change the course of history."[35] Oil had come to Texas, and the rush was on to find more petroleum hidden beneath the land ranging from the pine forests of East Texas to the West Texas plains. Although more oil fields were discovered in Ranger (1917) and Burkburnett (1918), it was the discovery of the Permian Basin oil reserves in 1920 that led to the state's spectacular growth.[36]

The discovery, however, came with a price. "I'll say one thing about an Oil boom," Howard told his editor. "It will teach a kid that life's a pretty rotten thing, about as quick as anything I can think of."[37] He described why this was the case to one correspondent: "I've seen towns leap into being over-night and become deserted almost as quick. I've seen old farmers, bent with toil, and ignorant of the feel of ten dollars at a time, become millionaires in a week, by the way of oil gushers. And I've seen them blow every cent of it and die paupers. I've seen whole towns debauched by an oil boom and boys and girls go to the devil whole-sale. I've seen promising youths turn from respectable citizens to dope-fiends, drunkards, gamblers and gangsters in a matter of months."[38]

Even those who worked the oil fields and lived in the boom towns understood this, for one such man told of the people who followed each discovery of oil: "This floating population went to every new oil field just like the boomers went to the gold mines. The women and the men that made their living off of the laboring man, why, they just followed the booms, and they were just a few days behind them, too."[39] Another oil roughneck added to this when he told the interviewer there would be so many people in these towns, they would cause "congestion in every direction" and that "there was lots of crime too—murders, kidnapping, hijacking, and this, that and the other."[40] These floating populations brought in what the interviewees described as booze dens, dope peddlers, gambling joints, dance halls, and whore houses, and every other imaginable form of vice. Even the residents of the towns found time to participate in making a fast dollar, and Burke remembered interviewing one nice old lady who recalled "her family driving into town on Saturday night just to watch people, hoping fights would break out. They were rarely disappointed."[41] Howard's disgust with the people the booms brought in was on display when he angrily told his girlfriend, Novalyne Price, "When they discovered oil, you wouldn't believe the kind of scum who moved in, drinking, whoring, carousing all night long. Not a decent man in the whole lot of them. Scavengers! Bastards!"[42]

Although Dr. Howard did not intend to bring his family into the oil boom towns, he sometimes located near them, and at other times the oil boom came to the small towns where they lived. "Except for short periods spent in New Orleans and San Antonio," Howard elucidated to a fellow writer, "I've lived in the country and in small towns all my life."[43] To another he wrote of growing up mostly in West Texas: "Since infancy my memory holds a continuous grinding round of crop failures, sandstorms, drouths, floods, hot winds that withered the corn, hailstorms that ripped the grain to pieces, late blizzards that froze the crops in the bud, plagues of grasshoppers and boll weevils that stripped the cotton. I remember year-long drouths that killed the very mesquite trees, when the streams were dry, and the cattle ate cactus until their mouths and bellies were full of the spines and then lay down and died when even the cactus was gone."[44] And to still another, Howard explained how all of "the communities in which I lived were unsophisticated and primitive, made up largely of people with quick tempers and violent passions."[45] And because his family resided in small towns, despite the violence, he once noted, "I have lived for years in communities in which there wasn't an officer of the law within forty miles."[46] Howard grew up in an environment that was not far removed from the hard brutalities of frontier life and lived in small, rural, impoverished towns. This was certainly not an environment to produce a writer, especially one as gifted as Howard, yet these were the type of surroundings in which he was raised.

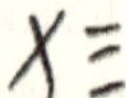

After Christmas of 1907, Dr. Howard packed up the family and headed west. They were moving once again. Mrs. Green recalled their departure, lamenting, "They moved away while Robert was a babe in arms."[47]

Dr. Howard's plan was to move the family to the small town of Seminole, located in Gaines County, not far from the New Mexico border.[48] Along the way the Howards stopped in Big Spring, where Hester's brother William Vinson Ervin Sr. and his family lived.[49] They, too, had only recently welcomed a child into the world, for Robert E. Howard's cousin, Mary "Maxine" Ervin, had been born on October 12, 1906.[50]

Dr. Howard was evidently well received there, for the Big Spring newspaper wrote of the family's visit, calling Dr. Howard "a polished gentleman" and "a fine physician" before noting his plans for possibly settling in Seminole and how "the people of that town will be fortunate if he decides to locate there."[51] Their three-day stay with Hester's brother, however, was extended, for as the newspaper reported, they "were detained here three weeks on account of sickness."[52] Who was sick is unknown, but by the beginning of February, they were on their way.

"As a child," Howard wrote of that journey, "I crossed the South Plains, not in a covered wagon indeed, but in a buggy, in what was about the last big colonization movement in Texas—the settlement of the Great Plains."[53] Seminole is located on the Llano Estacado, which translates as the Staked Plains, and Burke speculates that Dr. Howard may have moved his family there thinking that "Hester would benefit from the drier air and altitude."[54] It was a commonly recommended treatment for tuberculosis at the time.[55]

According to Roehm, Dr. Howard filed his credentials with Gaines County on February 3, 1908, and while Hester tended to their new home, he took to establishing his practice.[56] As for Howard, "I was very young and my memories are scanty," he wrote in a letter, "but I remember illimitable plains stretching on forever in every direction, sandy, drab plains with never a tree, only tufts of colorless bushes, haunted by tarantulas and rattlesnakes, buzzards and prairie dogs; long-horn cattle, driven in to town for shipping, stampeding past the yard where I played; and screeching dust winds that blew for days, filling the air with such a haze of stinging sand that you could see only for a few yards."[57] That was perhaps the one thing he did fully recall, once writing how "I cut my teeth on sandstorms," remembering that "they used to blow three days and nights without a let-up."[58] Due to this, as he wrote in an autobiographical essay for school, "water was scarce there," before adding "too scarce, so we moved."[59]

Dr. Howard set his sights on moving back east toward the Callahan Divide, and according to Roehm, he filed his credentials in Coke County, though still listing his address as Seminole.[60] By late January of 1909, Dr. Howard had delivered a baby in Coke County, for the birth record he filed lists him as living there in the small town of Bronte.[61] The likely reason for the move to Bronte was in hopes of a railroad boom. At the time they moved, the Kansas City, Mexico, and Orient Railroad line between Sweetwater and San Angelo, which passed through Bronte, was under construction. It was also announced that construction of a stone depot "with a tile roof and an elaborately finished interior" would soon begin.[62] It was not completed until 1911, long after the Howards had left.

"Among my earliest recollections as a child, scarce out of infancy," Howard recalled of his time in Bronte, "is that of crouching in dank, dark, or dim-lit, and sometimes reptile-haunted, cellars, while outside the wind shrieked and raved through the night, ripping the branches and leaves from the trees, while rain fell in mad foaming torrents, crashes of thunder shook the very earth, and blinding, insane rips of lightning gleamed through the cracks of the cellar-door."[63] Whether the country was not appealing enough, that there were not enough patients there, or he saw it would be a long time before the rail line was completed, once again, Dr. Howard decided to move.

Although Howard had only crossed the Llano Estacado in a buggy, he once noted, "I did go down the Nueces in a covered wagon."[64] The family had packed all their belongings sometime in late summer or early fall of 1909 and began a journey south.[65] Their destination was Crystal City, located along the Nueces River, so once they reached the river, all they had to do was follow it to their destination. Of this trip Howard remembered "being lulled to sleep in a covered wagon camped on the Nueces River, by the howling of wolves."[66]

They had chosen to travel to Crystal City because Dr. Howard's sister, Willie, lived there with her husband, William Oscar McClung (who had been released from Fort Leavenworth Penitentiary in February 1904) and their daughter, Fannie McClung.[67] Despite the grandeur of the town's name, it was not really a city at the time, nor was it much of a town. "When we lived in Crystal City, it was just a wide place in the road," recalled Fannie. "It was very small. There was just a few stores and the post office. Of course, the railroad run through there. But it was just—I call it a wide place in the road. It had just begun to be a town . . . in 1908." This was actually the only time Fannie ever met her "Uncle Que," as she called him, and she reported that unfortunately, "I was sick." She had the chicken pox. "That's the only time I remember him, or seen him or been around him, was when he visited," she reported; "I guess he come to see Momma."[68] Fortunately for Fannie, Uncle Que was a doctor.

Howard's own memory of the town was that it was one "which had recently sprung up like a mush-room from the wilderness and was still pretty tough."[69] He recounted several stories about just how tough, although none have been corroborated. One memory was that "a little girl in the vicinity fell into a hog-pen and the hogs dismembered her and had her half-devoured before anybody could come to the rescue." Howard then admitted to his correspondent, "I'm naturally leery of pigs."[70] The other was of a playmate of his, when both were about three years old, who "got into the corrals in his play and a killer mule stamped his brains out."[71]

One less violent story he remembered from his time there was when a meteorite fell out of the sky. "I remember waking suddenly and sitting up in bed, seeing everything bathed in a weird blue light, and hearing a terrific detonation." It was only the following day that he learned what it was when he heard people describing it as "being about the size and shape of a barrel" and its impact "making a loud explosion and shedding that strange blue light over everything."[72] Although they looked it was never found.

The visit in Crystal City was short-lived, for by late November 1909 they were living in San Antonio.[73] Roehm speculates that the Howards had continued following the Nueces River "as it meandered east toward Corpus Christi" and "after about 80 miles, in McMullen County, they left the river (or perhaps joined the Atascosa River) and went north another 80 miles to winter in San Antonio."[74] "I well remember when Robert was only four years old," Dr. Howard later wrote, "we spent the winter in San Antonio and the spring months in Atascosa County, some thirty miles south of San Antonio."[75] The stay there was Howard's first chance to live in a big city, and it remained one of his favorite destinations the rest of his life.

As Dr. Howard mentioned, the family moved into Atascosa County, living in the small town of Poteet. Howard had little to say about his short time there, other than "I lived . . . on a ranch in South Texas," and Dr. Howard must not have thought much of the prospects in Poteet, for by the time the 1910 census was enumerated, they had returned to Palo Pinto County.[76] Dr. Howard answered the census questions on May 16 that year in Justice Precinct no. 1, possibly the town of Palo Pinto, and by the end of the year, he was recording his post office address as the small town of Oran.[77] The family remained there for the next several years, but Howard, again, shared few memories from this time period. "When I was five a horse ran away with me," began his most memorable story, recalling how the horse "threw me out of the buggy, giving me a most infernal jolting and bruising." Like the pigs before him, he made note how "I was afraid of horses for a few years afterwards, but soon got over it after moving back to West Texas again."[78] His other memory was of meeting a family whose father had suffered a Comanche attack in which "they shot him full of arrows and scalped him," once again demonstrating Howard was not too far removed from the Texas frontier.[79]

By the end of 1912, Dr. Howard again moved the family. This time they traveled nearly one hundred miles north to what Howard referred to as "the Wichita Falls country up next to Oklahoma."[80] He described it as a "cattle town on the Oklahoma line," the town of Byers located less than five miles from the Red River, which marks the Texas border.[81] Dr. Howard had filed to practice medicine in Clay County on December 19 of that year, and they managed to stay through the winter.[82] Howard apparently did not have the best of memories of Byers for he wrote, "Of all the lousy lands, the Wichita Falls country takes the cake to my mind. There the plains are of white alkali and the glare nearly blinds you. The climate is treacherous. You ride out in the morning in your shirt sleeves, admiring the dreamy slumber of the plains, with the birds singing in the one tree the county boasts, and the heat waves shimmering in the distance; you see a coyote loping along with his tongue hanging out in the heat—and then by noon, maybe, a blue blizzard comes howling over the prairie and freezes your gizzard."[83]Although he talks of the Wichita Falls country, the actual town by that name was located only twenty miles away, and it is possible they made the trip into the larger city. Still, even that town may have been uninspiring to Howard, for as Llerena Friend, who was born there in 1903, recalled, "The only paving was on Tenth Street and was of wooden blocks," and that as a child the biggest adventure was "riding the elevator in the Kemp and Kell Building."[84] Howard's views were evidently shared by his father, for by April of 1913, they had moved again.[85]

This time the family traveled east, their destination over two hundred miles deep into "the piney woods of East Texas."[86] "We moved to Bagwell, Texas," wrote Howard, "which is between Texarkana and Paris." The town seems to have made an impression on Howard, for he later recalled, "It is all piney woods there, and every time I smell the pine scent I get homesick, though I have been away from there for years."[87]

Howard scholar Patrice Louinet provides a different reason for this particular move. Dr. Howard was not chasing a boom this time, but rather there was a need there for a doctor. Dr. Willis Walter Stephens and his father, Dr. Willis Commodore Stephens, had been practicing medicine together in Bagwell. In 1910/1911 the father decided to move to Gunter, Texas, and open up a medical practice there. The son, now needing a new medical partner, thought of Dr. Howard because they had trained together at the Gate City Medical School in Texarkana.[88] So according to Roehm, Dr. Howard filed his credentials in Red River County on April 30, 1913, listing his postal address as Bagwell, Texas.[89] His first delivery of a baby came a week later, for he signed his first known birth record there on May 8.[90]

Bagwell was named for Milas Bagwell, one of its earliest settlers and the local blacksmith. When the Texas and Pacific Railway constructed its lines through the town in 1875/1876, Bagwell became a railroad boom town. According to Burke, because of the railroad Bagwell was "a shipping point for lumber and shingles produced in the town and for cotton and cottonseed from the surrounding area." When the Howards moved to Bagwell, it boasted "a population of 300, several stores, a post office, three hotels, two banks, two cotton gins, a couple of sawmills, and a school."[91] Lee Somerville, a local and contemporary of Howard's, once described the area around the town in a letter: "North of Bagwell was sandy land, swamps and hills and piney woods. Mostly south and west of Bagwell was good rich land, and Becknell's Prairie was good cotton and corn land."[92] The prairie was named for William Becknell, the founder of the Santa Fe Trail, who moved into the area later in life. Although there are as many as three homes in which the Howards possibly lived in Bagwell, one that was then known as "the Old Baker place" was reported to have been in the direction of the prairie, just outside of town.[93]

Bagwell, unlike many of the other places they had lived, actually had a schoolhouse, but as Howard told one correspondent, "I didn't start to school until I was eight"—the year after the family settled there.[94] This was not because of some delay in his education, but rather because a child did not start school in Bagwell until they had reached that age.[95] The Texas legislature did not pass its compulsory school attendance law until 1915, the year after Howard had entered school, but it, too, set the starting age at 8 years.[96]

According to Bagwell historian Sharon Stephens Black, "Robert E. Howard began first grade at Bagwell in a building that was actually a converted home. It was painted white and had lacy Victorian style trim on the porches."[97] Bagwell resident William Archie Kirk, who attended the same school at about the same time, recalled that "the building had three rooms and three teachers. There was usually one man and two lady teachers. The man was necessary to whip the boys when they became unruly."[98] Howard's classroom was likely similar to the schoolroom of fellow Texan William Manire, who fondly remembered "a picture of George Washington centered above the blackboard," above which "was a long black panel of white letters showing the alphabet in both lower and upper case."[99]

Kirk fondly remembered that during recess "the boys and girls played separately. The boys would play ball, marbles, spin the top and leap frog."[100] Somerville did not recall such idyllic games when he wrote to Howard's first biographer that "the day started with wrestling and struggling" and how "teachers didn't try to stop fights among boys, unless there was excess of violence and blood." They believed that this sort of behavior "was a natural way of working off energy."[101] Howard did not record having any such trouble in school, but he did share several memories from his time in Bagwell.

"Once when I was a kid in the edge of the piney woods," began one of those memories, Howard came across two African American boys. They had "caught a big hawk" he remembered, and they "gave it to me." The memory was apparently a vivid one, for Howard continued, "I still remember how fiercely his steely claws bit into the wood of his roost and what an untamable fire blazed in his yellow eyes; and how he seemed to yearn to rend and tear with that scimitar-curved beak of his." Not wanting to deny the bird its freedom, Howard explained, "I took him out into the pines and let him go," and then he watched as the hawk's "wings ripped the air as he shot upward and away." He could not deny the same freedom he so cherished. And unlike the incidents involving pigs and horses, this memory left him to write, "I admire all birds of prey."[102]

Howard also had distinct memories of what he did after war broke out overseas when, on June 28, 1914, Archduke Franz Ferdinand of Austria was assassinated in Sarajevo, triggering the events of World War I. "I well remember that summer," Howard wrote in an autobiographical essay, "and how my playmates and I played at war." America's entry into the war was still three years off, but the war filled the newspapers and conversations of nearly everyone. Howard remembered the first week, "Our sympathies shifted from one side to the other" but that "before the war had been going on a week, I firmly threw in my lot with the Allies and thereafter remained loyal." Howard, being perhaps more introspective than the average student his age at the time, wrote, "I did not reach this decision without much loss of sleep and studying, but I made the announcement firmly, with a determination which would have stood me in good stead since then."[103]

Out of his memories of Bagwell, what appears to have had the most impact on him and his writing career was listening to the stories told by several of the local former slaves. "I well remember the tales I listened to and shivered at, when a child in the 'piney woods' of East Texas, where Red River marks the Arkansaw and Texas boundaries," he wrote, emphasizing, "The one to whom I listened most was the cook, old Aunt Mary Bohannon."[104]

According to Black, "Mary Bohannon cooked for the affluent white folks in Bagwell in the early 1900s," and during their two-year stay there, one of those families included the Howards. Mary Bohannon was born into slavery in Kentucky and, likely because she did not know herself, her birth year is variably listed as sometime between 1825 and 1836.[105] It is said she was owned by Henry Bohannon, from whom she derived her last name, and that the family moved to Red River County, Texas, bringing their slaves with them, sometime in the 1850s. Henry died in 1863, and two years later, with the Juneteenth Emancipation, Mary Bohannon was freed. She remained in the area, and the children of Henry later gave Mary a deed to fifty acres of land and a home for being an "old faithful servant" of the family. She lived there until 1907, when she was forced to sell the land to make ends meet, and by 1910, according to Black, "She was living with a large family working as either a 'servant' or a 'ward,' often cooking for other families, such as the Howards."[106] She would have been between her late 70s and early 90s at the time.

Old Aunt Mary Bohannon excited Howard with the stories and legends she shared with him that the African slaves once told, and he recalled that "she told many tales, one which made my hair rise" and how "Aunt Mary told tales of torture and unmistakable sadism that sickens me to this day when I think of them."[107] She recounted stories of "evil spirits," "a headless giant," and of a "deserted plantation house" that was "huge, brooding and forbidding."[108] And Howard listened, hanging on every word and remembering the stories she told, for one day he would write some of the stories Aunt Mary hard shared.

It seems there was another benefit to Howard's time living in Bagwell, for Burke explains, "It was there that Robert E. Howard had his only real association with African Americans. All of his early homes—Peaster, Dark Valley, Seminole, Bronte, Poteet—had few or no black inhabitants."[109] Indeed, all of the later towns in which he lived also had few African Americans living there, and Cross Plains had none, for they were not allowed to live inside the town. Although Howard's views on race were reflective of the time and place in which he lived, his short stay in Bagwell left him with cherished memories of at least one person he fondly remembered.

"Mary Bohannon never left Bagwell," records Sharon Black. "She died at her home in Bagwell at an advanced age on Feb. 27, 1921." Her death certificate stated she was 100 years old. She was buried in the African American section of the local Becknell Cemetery, and her grave is unmarked.[110]

Howard's only other recorded memories of Bagwell had to do with the rainy, swampy conditions of the area. "If we had too little water at Seminole," he wrote in his autobiographical essay, "we had too much at Bagwell. It rained for weeks at a time; rained until the ground turned green; rained until fish swam around in the roads." He also recalled that he "developed a bad case of nasal catarrh," a buildup of mucus in the sinuses, because "the swampy county was bad for it." So, in true Howard family fashion, they moved—"we went to central west Texas."[111]

Chapter 4

Post Oak Country, 1915–1919

Here where the post-oaks crown the ridge,
and the dreary sand-drifts lie,
I'll sit in the tangle of chaparral
till my enemy passes by —
—"The Sand-Hill's Crest"[1]

When the Howard family moved to "central west Texas," they entered into what was known as the Post Oak country.[2] "In this region," Howard wrote a colleague, "post-oaks dominate the landscape." He added, "Elms, willows and pecans grow along the rivers, and Spanish oaks among the hills," while the undergrowth largely consisted of "brambles, prickly pears and chaparral thickets" and there were "live oaks and mesquites to the west and southwest."[3] The post oak has been described as "a knotty but bold tree, stout and substantial," and "its leaves, when they appeared in the spring, were a 'deep and vital red,' and often clung until pushed off by new growth the next year."[4] Because the post oak is a dense hardwood, it was often used for fence posts and railroad ties. Dr. Howard once noted that his wife "was a lover of the beautiful" and that she passed this on to Robert, who, as he grew, "saw the beautiful around the old country of stunted post-oaks" and how "his imagination wove fantastic pictures of that drab section . . . where he lived."[5]

He now lived in the town of Cross Cut, located in Brown County about eight miles south of Cross Plains, which Howard described as a "small village between Brownwood and Cisco."[6] They had moved there at the beginning of 1915, for Dr. Howard had filed his credentials in the county on January 25, and he was already listing Cross Cut as his home.[7] Although the *Cross Plains Review* announced, "Dr. Howard of Putnam has moved to Cross Cut," the Howards never lived in Putnam.[8] Roehm surmises that the Howards may have been visiting the town for Mrs. Howard's sake because of the medical sanitorium located there.[9] Roehm also notes elsewhere that "the move to Cross Cut signaled an end, of sorts, to wandering," for though "they would move at least two more times, the Howard family had found a permanent home in the post oak country."[10]

The town of Cross Cut was first settled in 1878 by James Bloodworth, who had found the area around the Pecan Bayou and all its tributaries to be suitable for his needs. The bayou was aptly named, for "there were hundreds of large pecan trees on the banks," recalled Norris Chambers, a friend of the Howard family. "Actually," Chambers explained, "it wasn't big enough to be called a river and was too large to be a creek," but it "was a fair sized waterway and had holes that held water during long dry spells."[11]

Bloodworth had decided to open up a general store along one of the tributary creeks, and Richard "Dick" W. Pentecost soon followed.[12] When the two men decided to make it a bona fide town with its own post office, they filled out an application. They had decided to name the new town Cross Out, because "it was cross the country and out of the way."[13] When the post office application was granted, the name had been crossed out and replaced with Cross Cut. Evidently someone thought the original name had been a mistake. So the town became Cross Cut, and the post office opened there in 1879.[14] The town was "duly incorporated and platted," explains Chambers, but it "never had a mayor or council and had no street signs."[15] Despite this, "Cross Cut was a thriving community for many years." At the time the Howards moved there, "the town boasted a blacksmith shop, two general stores, two doctors, [and] a drug store."[16]

By one account they first occupied a house known locally as the Willis home, nearer to the others in the village, but it was small, only being a "one room with a shed."[17] In June of 1915, however, the *Cross Plains Review* reported they had moved "into the house recently vacated by Mr. Pentecost and family."[18] Pentecost, who had helped establish Cross Cut and built his home outside the village by the cemetery, had decided to move his family to Arizona, so the home had come available.[19]

According to Deoma Chambers Morgan, the white house "consisted of four rooms downstairs and two upstairs," a "cellar was attached to the house," and there was a "barn for feed for horses and a milk cow."[20] The home also had a screened-in porch.[21] Since there was no indoor plumbing, the Howards had an outhouse and there was a cistern to catch the rainwater.[22] Another neighbor, Annie Newton Davis, recalled, however, that Dr. Howard "got his drinking water at our cistern. He didn't like it at his house."[23] Because Annie's mother had been sick for some time, Dr. Howard went to visit her every day, and Davis told how Dr. Howard brought over a bucket to carry water back to his house. She remembered that she "always knew when he started from home because of his whistling, he whistled all the way down and all the way back, but very often he came in and sat with us awhile."[24]

Regarding the interior of the Howards' new home, Morgan told the interviewer, "As I remember, they had very ordinary furnishings, only necessary items." She did, however, admire Mrs. Howard's "few pieces of cut glass in her dining room."[25] This style of glassware had become wildly popular in the mid-1800s in America, and many people would recall Mrs. Howard's ornate cut glass fruit bowl.

Dr. Howard quickly found a friend in their new community, for there was another doctor in town, Dr. Solomon Roe Chambers. Born in 1868, Chambers began his medical studies in 1893 and, after becoming a physician, married Martha Jane Williams on December 29, 1896. Their first child, Thomas Spencer, was born in 1897, and a girl, Deoma, soon followed in 1899.[26] Their third child, Winnie, was born in 1908, but did not survive a year. When the Howards moved into the area in 1915, Dr. Chambers had been running the Cross Cut drugstore, preferring the life of a pharmacist over a doctor, and he soon left the doctoring to his newfound friend.[27] The Chamberses would have two more sons, Norris Roe Chambers in 1917 and Thomas R. Chambers in 1918, the former coming to know the Howard family intimately.[28]

As the new town physician, Dr. Howard was well received by the community. As one of his patients, Elsie Byrd, recalled, “He was about average, he wasn’t no handsome thing, but everybody loved him.”[29] When the family came to Cross Cut, they had come by horse and buggy, the same one in which Dr. Howard made his house calls.[30] Morgan, Dr. Chamber’s daughter, remembered those horses, for “they were fiery temperamental, so called Spanish ponies,” and “they would suddenly jump or run if a piece of paper blew across the road or any unusual noise.” Because of this, she said, “It was necessary to keep a stiff rein.”[31] Dr. Howard soon purchased a Ford Model T, which all of the neighbors seemed to recall, for it was the first automobile owned in the area.[32] “It was quite a treat,” Chambers recalled, for he remembered “hearing folks tell about riding in Doctor Howard’s car. He’d come out and take ’em riding.”[33] Despite the new car, Dr. Howard retained his horses and buggy, and Morgan explained he “could only use [the car] in dry weather since roads were so muddy when it rained.” When he first purchased the automobile, he had a local laborer, Ben Gunn, teach him how to drive, but Morgan recalled Dr. Howard once commenting to her father, “You know, Ben didn’t know any more about driving the car than I did.”[34]

Mrs. Howard was actively involved in the Methodist Church in Cross Cut, and the Howards held parties for the children and the ladies of the church in their home.[35] One neighbor, Raymond De Busk, recalled Dr. Howard as being “a little peculiar” and “a little radical.” He shared a story that Dr. Howard and another man in town had organized a religious meeting, but after hearing the other man preach, Dr. Howard told him, “You son of a bitch, if that’s the best you can do, we’ll quit right now.”[36] Apparently Dr. Howard was not much better, for Morgan once told Howard’s first biographer he had preached once, but because “he wasn’t a very good preacher,” he never did it again.[37]

Although the neighbors did not recall Mrs. Howard socializing very often, one person described her as “gracious when you went into her home,” another said that “she was nice, she was a pretty woman,” and still another called her “very refined.”[38] Morgan, who remembered going to the house for dinner, recalled how "she served a nice dinner, and she served it in courses. She was brought up in East Texas, and I think it meant a good deal to her." Of course, Dr. Howard apparently did not like the concept of courses, for every time he finished one, he would yell, "Heck! Have we got anything else to eat?"[39] "Heck" had become Dr. Howard's favorite term of endearment for his wife.[40] Another neighbor recalled that they had a "country phone" and that Mrs. Howard "took the messages for his calls," which may explain another reason why she did not socialize as much as the other women. Someone needed to be home to receive the calls.[41]

As for their son, the neighbors all described him as a quiet, shy boy, but one who was well mannered. For instance, De Busk called him "kind of a loner," and Kate Merryman remembered him as being "shy," though she did add, "he was a real nice lad. I thought a lot of him."[42] Others offered conflicting descriptions of young Howard, such as De Busk, who recalled him as "just a little bitty old boy," while Davis remembered him as "a hefty kid."[43] Either way, Elsie Byrd said, "He was nice looking. I know that."[44] The one thing everyone seemed to agree upon was that Howard was always reading.[45] One neighbor wrote, "When one passed the house south of Cross Cut, he was always on the upstairs porch reading."[46] Another neighbor recalled, "When he had a yen for writing," he would often spend "hours upstairs, alone with his writings."[47] It was there in Cross Cut that Howard first began writing stories. "I remember the first story I ever wrote," he later told a correspondent in a letter, "at the age of about nine or ten." The story "dealt with the adventures of one 'Boealf' a young Dane Viking," although he did note that his "Celtic patriotism prevented him from winning all his battles."[48]

Despite his love for reading and writing, Howard apparently still managed to get outside and play, for Chambers's mother told him, "Mrs. Howard used to get him out in the yard and play ball with him," and others remembered how he went out and played with some of the children in the neighborhood.[49] One of those children was Austin Newton, who later recalled in a letter, "I grew up on a farm ½ mile west of Cross Cut."[50] According to Roehm, he was "born on August 6, 1905," and "had known Howard during elementary and high school."[51] Morgan recalled Newton from those years and described him as "just an all-around average boy."[52]

Austin Newton shared many of his adventures with Howard. "On one occasion," he recounted, "we caught some fish out of Turkey Creek. We broiled them over an open fire and ate them, without any salt, or other seasonings. They tasted horrible, but we thought it was fun." He also remembered how "Robert was greatly interested in boxing" and "he read everything he could find about boxing, and was pretty well informed on the subject." He also told the story that despite not having boxing gloves, "We spent a lot of time sparring out in our back yard." Newton wrote in a letter that one time "I ran into a left jab which hit me on the Adams Apple and knocked me down. That ended the sparring for that day. But sparring continued to be one of our main pastimes."[53]

Like everyone else, Newton also recalled that "Robert read a lot." He noted that "he liked adventure stories" and also acting them out, which often led to them playing "cowboys and Indians, rangers and outlaws." It was this that Newton so fondly remembered, explaining that "Robert was fun to play with because he had such a great imagination. We did a lot of play acting and make believe." Despite the fact that "after elementary school, interests changed, he went one way and I went the other," Newton still said of Howard, "I loved him dearly during those early years of my childhood."[54]

Howard and Newton both attended the Cross Cut School, and Newton recalled Howard as a "pretty fair student."[55] It was the second one-room schoolhouse built on "land specifically designated for that purpose in the original, 1904 town plot by Dick Pentecost."[56] Newton recalled it as a "three teacher school" and that "each teacher taught about three grades. I remember our first grade teacher very well. Her name was Miss Mae Butler. She was an excellent teacher and made quite an impression on me."[57] Howard did not remember her so fondly when he shared this story: "One time when I was a kid, I was out skating—or rather sliding, for I had no skates—on a frozen pond. I must have been a bigger sap then than I am now . . . because the ice buckled and cracked under my weight, and I couldn't swim a stroke and was out there by myself." Fortunately, he managed to make it close to shore before the ice gave way, but he still sank knee-deep into the water. Because he had been told not to play at the pond and did not have a change of socks and shoes, he kept quiet and "splashed off to school in the teeth of a howling blizzard." "When I got to school," he continued, "The teacher, who was enveloped in a fur coat, wouldn't let us go to the stove to warm, because we generally got into a fight if we did. I sat there until noon, at the back of the room where the heat couldn't reach, and I want to say that it was about as lousy a morning as I ever spent. . . . It's a wonder my feet hadn't been frost-bitten."[58] The teacher evidently did make an impression on Howard, just not the same as Newton's, but more importantly, it demonstrates Howard's distaste for being denied his freedom.

Howard also went to school in Cross Cut with one of his cousins, Earl Lee Comer, who was now living in the Howard home.[59] According to Roehm, Earl Lee was the son of Rev. J. Frank Comer and Alice Ervin, Hester's sister. They had been married on March 4, 1896, and had the one child, Earl Lee, born in Saint Louis on July 13, 1898.[60] In the 1900 census, Frank and Alice were no longer living together, and by 1905 Frank had remarried. In 1910 Alice and her son were living near her brother William, the editor of a newspaper in Big Spring, Texas. The following year Earl Comer became part of Boy Scout Troop 1, the first chartered troop in the state of Texas.[61] Sadly, however, Alice died on July 14, 1915, and as Roehm succinctly stated, "Earl's life changed forever."[62]

William temporarily cared for Earl but could not take him under his roof full-time. Earl was not yet an adult and needed to complete his education, so Earl moved to Cross Cut and, despite being much older than Howard, they shared a room together, although this was not uncommon for the time period. They went to school together, and according to Roehm, "Comer joined the basketball squad."[63] It seems Howard's older cousin told him stories, and they did things most teenagers do together. One story Comer apparently shared with Howard was "the details of a camping trip, on which one Boy Scout shot another through the heart with a .22 calibre target rifle."[64] This may have been a retelling of the March 23, 1912, case of Boy Scout Maitland Jarvis, 12, who fatally shot fellow Scout William Luckhardt, 9, with a rifle.[65]

Howard had a penchant for playing on frozen ponds and shared a story of his and Earl's shenanigans together when he wrote, "One of the damndest falls I ever got in my life was on a frozen pool—or tank, as we call them in these parts. I was just a kid, and wrestling with my cousin who was much older and larger. Eventually our feet went from under us, and we both came down on my head. That's the truth. The back of my skull was the first thing that hit the ice, which cracked as though it had been hit with a hammer, although it was several inches thick. I was a tough little devil in those days."[66]

In February of 1918, perhaps to get Howard away from frozen water, the family took a trip to Galveston, Texas, which was Howard's first excursion there. As Chambers later recalled, "My parents had moved to Galveston County from Brown County in 1918," and so the Howards had gone there to visit them. Dr. Chambers had apparently decided to give up the practice of medicine and take up farming near the small town of Hitchcock, about fifteen miles north of Galveston Island. "My dad and my brother had a small farm where they raised many kinds of vegetables," Chambers recalled. "These were hauled in the wagon to Hitchcock" to the train depot there, where "they were loaded in box cars and packed with ice."[67]

Chambers was too young to remember the Howards' visit, but he recalled his mother telling him stories. "Dr. Howard was driving then," he relayed, "and she didn't like his driving." When they went "over that wooden causeway that they had going to Galveston Island at that time . . . she was afraid he was going to run off!" Chambers recalled his mother saying, "He would look this way, and look that way, but he wouldn't be paying any attention to the road!"[68]

While the Howards were there, they had a photo taken that has survived, and on the back it is dated "February 1918."[69] According to Morgan, "The scene is the home of my uncle, which had recently burned."[70] The picture of Drs. Howard and Chambers also has Howard in it, standing off to the side, with one hand playing with a bush, his other hand on his hip; he is looking up into the sky with an inquisitive look on his face. Either he was curious about something he saw or he was lost in thought as his imagination wandered.

The Chambers family remained in Galveston County for the next six years, but in 1924 the company Dr. Chambers was relying on to buy his produce left the area. With no market to support him, he moved his family back to Cross Cut.[71] Although by that time, the Howards were no longer living there, they were close by, and the families often visited one another over the years.

In March of 1918, with the Howards back in Cross Cut and Howard in school, the local newspaper editorialized, "There are only five more weeks of school. There hasn't been much school spirit on account of the war, sickness, and drouth."[72] While that may have been the case for school spirit, the war at least had given Earl Lee some direction in his life. Having turned 18, he decided to enlist in the US Navy. His start date was May 25, and by then he was gone from the Howard home.[73] The Howards also left Cross Cut about the same time.

On April 24, 1919, Dr. Howard filed his first birth record in Coleman County, and later, on June 5, he filed to practice medicine there. In both cases he listed his home as Burkett, which was located eight miles southwest of Cross Cut.[74] The town was named for one of its first settlers, William Burkett, who became the town's first postmaster. Marie Baker described the town and explained, "Burkett didn't have a newspaper, wasn't that big. But we had a post office and . . . we had Baptists and Methodists across the street from each other."[75] Another Texan, Jim Barton, recalled this was a common feature of many small Texas towns. "The Methodists and Baptists had the largest church buildings and the greatest numbers of members," he wrote. "The competition between the two denominations was keen, with a major difference being the manner of baptism. The Baptists had a strong selling point in the 'once saved, always saved' concept."[76] The Baptist Church in Burkett had been erected in 1885, while the Methodist Church was built the following year, as was the first schoolhouse.

Dr. Howard rented a home in Burkett, and although the exact location is not clear, one neighbor referred to their home as the "Cochran House" and recalled "there was a gazebo at this house."[77] Austin Newton visited his good friend in Burkett and recalled that "the house was on the Pecan Bayou, it was painted white, had a big porch with banisters—you could see the bayou from the porch."[78] The Chamberses also visited the Howards there, and Morgan described the homestead. "[The] house consisted of five rooms, a porch across the front of the house and an L porch on the back of the house. A cistern for water was on the back porch—water caught from the house roof when it rained. There was a dirt cellar in the back yard. A barn for the milk cow and horses, a buggy shed, and then there was the out house. No plumbing on inside . . . a fireplace for heat and was of wooden structure."[79]

Howard retained many memories of the years they lived in Burkett. "As my father had his practice and did not attempt to run a farm," he once wrote to a friend, "I had more leisure than the average country kid." He remembered how he "played the rough and savage games popular in those parts then, wrestled, hunted a little, fished a little, trapped a little, stole watermelons, went swimming, and spent more time than all in wandering about over the country-side on foot or on horse-back."[80] Because that country was a common habitat for snakes, Howard recalled many encounters with these reptiles. "I remember one time when I was about twelve years old, a friend and I were trapping in the Coleman county hills, and one warm day in early Spring we went looking to our traps." Howard said when his friend checked one trap, he found he had "set his bare hand within a few inches of a four-foot diamond-back rattler that lay sunning himself."[81] Howard laughed at his friend's predicament, but apparently on another occasion he discovered a snake hiding under "an old discarded stove door," and when he went to grab the door, he saw the snake and jumped. "I've always wished somebody had been there to measure the exact distance that I ascended into the air," he noted in the letter, "for I am positive that I broke several records beyond repair." On another occasion he was climbing up the side of a creek bank and recalled "laying my hand on a live water moccasin." Howard concluded, "I escaped being bitten only because it was as much a surprize to the snake as it was to me, though I doubt if his nervous system suffered as much as mine did."[82]

The Baker family often spent time with the Howards, and the Baker children—Alma, Marie, and Earl—shared many of their memories with Howard's first biographer. Marie remembered how "Dr. Howard *loved* to eat!" She related, "He would swallow mamma's biscuits whole."[83] Because Earl became best friends with Howard, he was over at their house more often and recalled, "Mrs. Howard seemed to have gotten sick around 1918," and "she was in bed a lot, and did a lot of resting because she had to."[84] As for their memories of Howard, Alma recalled him as a "little wild boy"; he and Earl "roamed the pasture with bows and arrows playing Indian." She also said that "Howard learned to ride horseback at the Baker farm."[85] Earl explained that Howard typically rode "Old Charlie, a big gentle dun, kept largely for the children to ride."[86] Howard and a friend also made many trips to the drug store in town where one neighbor recalled they would "get something to drink . . . get candy, and stuff."[87] Still, he did not always have the chance to relax, for at least sometime during the summer, to make some extra money, Howard wrote, "I hoed cockleburs and picked cotton," although he did add that it was "not with pleasure. I detested any kind of work."[88]

In order to spend time with his father, who was often busy with his practice, Howard would sometimes go on house calls with him.[89] One neighbor recalled that when Mrs. Howard was feeling well enough, they both would "accompany him on long drives" and on occasion, they would "stop on their return at some shady spot near a stream and spread lunch." This neighbor also noted that "during the father's absence . . . mother and son keep close contact and were inseparable."[90] In fact, many neighbors recalled how they came to rely on each other because Dr. Howard was not home that often, and she was very protective of her son.[91] Still, what most people seem to remember, such as Lois Garrett, was "how Robert and his mother used to sit in the gazebo, and he spent a lot of time [there]," where he was no doubt reading.[92]

Howard continued his education that fall in the Burkett school that had been built in 1911. "It was a four room frame building," writes Coleman historians Burns and Burkett. "It had two rooms at both the north and south ends, but since there had never been more than two teachers in Burkett, the south side was just one large room with a large stage across the east side."[93] Howard's memories of the school had little to do with his book learning and instead were mostly about the games he played. "When I was a country schoolboy," he once wrote, "there was little systematic and competitive athletics, but all engaged in some playground form of amusement—baseball, snap-the-whip, wolf-over-the-river, wrestling."[94] It was the latter he seemed to like best for, "when I was a kid of ten or eleven, in a country school," he wrote, "I was stockily built and fairly proficient in the brutal and unscientific style of wrestling then prevalent in the country, which depended less on speed and skill, than on strength and endurance." One anecdote stuck with him, and that was when he tried to impress a teacher with those skills by showing off. He had squared off with a small student, but looking around for a "worthier opponent," as he said, "suddenly and stunningly I found myself thrown!" The teacher saw it, laughed, and Howard explained how he "broodingly contemplated my shameful defeat."[95] Still, these skills came in handy, for there were some boys who liked to bully others, but as Howard said, they mostly "fought each other and it was very rare that any of the rest of us ever had any trouble."[96] Howard tried to stay away from these tyrants, but it seems there was "one exception" when he "had a few overgrown bullies make me miserable."[97] Most people, however, did not remember him having much of any problem.[98]

The most significant event that took place that fall was the announcement that on November 11, 1918, there was a cessation of hostilities in Europe. The Great War had ended. The event was significant for Texas because until the war, life there was very different from the rest of the United States. "What started [Texas's] merger with the rest of the country," explains historian John Myers Myers, "was America's entry into World War I."[99] When Texas mobilized for war, according to Texas historian Randolph B. Campbell, "more than 988,000 men registered under national draft laws, and 197,389 either volunteered or were drafted, mostly into the army."[100] As America had stepped out onto the world stage, Texas became more like the rest of the country.

In small-town Burkett, however, the war was still a somewhat abstract concept. Howard wrote a school paper in 1920 based on the question, "What I Did to Help Win the War," and his answer was, "Not much." Despite that opening, he did mention that he "contributed all I could to the Red Cross," even having "a button to prove it," and that he "bought a liberty bond," "joined the Victory boys," and "bought War Saving Stamps, which were for children, who could not buy bonds." They also conserved food, and he stated, "I planted a war garden." He also noted that he had a number of relatives who joined the military, including his cousin Earl.[101] What he remembered the most, however, was that on the evening after the armistice was signed, "I got out on the porch and fired a shotgun into the air," after which, "Everybody took it up, and all the rest of the night you couldn't sleep for the noise."[102]

Two other memorable events for Howard during his time in Burkett was when he acquired some pets. "I used to have a pet coon," he wrote of the first, "and he was a damn sight smarter than I was," after which he humbly added, "That may not be saying much." He recalled how much the raccoon liked to fight, writing that "I carry scars from his talons and teeth to this day."[103] He wrote of Burkett being swarmed by grasshoppers at one point, and "about the only person that really enjoyed that plague was my pet raccoon who ate those big jumbo grasshoppers till he could hardly waddle."[104] One neighbor recalled how Howard could often be seen having "an after dinner romp" with his pet, but he eventually had to let him go.[105] "The wild was always in him," wrote Howard.[106]

His most favored pet, however, was his dog Patch. The dog held such honor in the family, there was even an entry in the Howard family Bible, which read, "Patch, dog of Robert E. Howard born Christmas 1917."[107] "He raised the dog from the time he was a wee thing, before his eyes were barely open," Dr. Howard later wrote in a letter, "through the life of the dog." He recalled, "The dog was an inseparable companion to Robert."[108] Patch must have been a mongrel dog, for not everyone remembered him the same. Dr. Howard called him a "half-collie, half-Walker foxhound," and a neighbor recalled the dog as "half-Walker hound" and was "white and tan spotted."[109] One of Dr. Howard's memories of Patch was that he "was often fed from the table; as Robert ate, sitting down by Robert's chair was Patch. When Robert helped himself, before eating a bite, he helped Patch to food."[110]

Neighbors also held memories of Patch. One neighbor recalled that when it was feeding time for his dog, Howard would call out, "Chuck, Patch! Chuck, Patch, here!"[111] Mrs. Burns, the postmistress of Burkett, remembered one encounter with Howard and his dog. She was sitting on a rock reading and the dog surprised her. Almost immediately she heard Howard call, "Come Patches, come Patches" and she saw "a lad of about ten years crossing the fence." She said he politely came up to her and like a typical impetuous child said, "I'm Robert Howard. I'm sorry if we frightened you; Patches and I are out for our morning stroll. We like to come here where there are big rocks and caves so we can play 'make believe.' Some day I'm going to be an author and write stories about pirates and maybe cannibals. Would you like to read them?"[112] She assured him she would, and he soon ran off after his dog.

She also remembered Howard running through the hills with Patch and placing his brand on everything from trees to sandstone rocks. "His favorite 'brand' as he expressed it, was X≡," the X triple bar, and she claimed that as late as 1936, it could still be seen in places he had once played.[113] Later, Howard would often sign his name using just his personal brand.

X≡

In order to bolster his credentials and enhance his practice, Dr. Howard attended four separate postgraduate courses in New Orleans. The first was in June of 1917, and the last was in January of 1921.[114] On the longest of these trainings, the doctor took his family with him, and they arrived there on March 10, 1919.[115] It seems that their arrival was in keeping with what New Orleans's own sheriff called "a perfect hell on earth."[116] Howard later wrote he was greeted by news of a family who had been violently attacked by a man with an axe.[117]

Remembering his time in New Orleans in an essay, Howard noted, "For months, the fear of the menace known as the axe-man had laid over the city like a fog."[118] An unknown assailant first attacked an Italian immigrant couple who ran a small grocery store in the early hours of May 23, 1918, butchering them with an axe. New Orleans detectives called it "one of the most gruesome in the annals of the New Orleans police."[119] After another such attack, the serial killer became known as "The Axeman of New Orleans."[120] The modus operandi of the killer was to target mostly Italian immigrants after gaining entrance to their home by removing a panel on a rear door. After killing them with an axe while they slept, the perpetrator ransacked the home, taking little, and leaving no fingerprints.

"The morning I arrived in New Orleans," Howard recalled, "the morning papers were full of the latest atrocity, committed across the river among the towns which so crowd the river bank."[121] The Axe Man had attacked the Cortimiglia family (Charles, Rosie, and their 2-year old daughter).[122] As Howard wrote, "The ax-man had butchered an entire family—hacked a young man and his wife almost to death, though they eventually recovered, and killed their baby."[123] Later, Howard remembered "strolling down a narrow street one day when the town was electrified by the shout of the newsboys, 'They've got the ax-man!'"[124] It was later learned that the two men arrested had been falsely accused, and the crimes remain unsolved.

Although it was certainly a horrific welcome to the city of New Orleans, Howard seems to have many cherished memories from his wanderings there. "It was my fortune to be acquainted with some elderly maiden ladies by the name of Durell—gentlewomen of the old school," he wrote of Camille, Delphine, and Marie Durel, who operated their home on Canal Street as a boardinghouse.[125] He commented on the old French Market, noting "It smelled like hell," but he called the gumbo he ate there, "a food for the gods."[126] He also remembered the Sicilians Joe Rizzo and his wife, who sold oysters on Canal Street. "Their sole object in life seemed to be to open oysters," for he recalled "a steady stream of shells and oysters flowed from their hands."[127] And while in the city, Howard evidently found a curio of a bronze-colored bust of Cleopatra that caught his fancy, perhaps because of the snake that creeped across the queen's chest. Yet more than anything, his most memorable experience appears to have been the time he spent in the Canal Street library.

Although Howard assuredly enjoyed exploring all facets of the library, there was one book that caught his attention. He wrote that it was "a book detailing the pageant of British history" that "was written for school-boys and told in an interesting and romantic style."[128] The book was likely G. F. Scott Elliot's *The Romance of Early British Life*.[129] Elliot was a botanist by trade, who was passionate about not only natural history, but antiquarian societies.[130] Howard wrote, "[It was] there I first learned of the small dark people which first settled Britain, and they were referred to as Picts. I had always felt a strange interest in the term and the people, and now I felt a driving absorption regarding them."[131] As depicted in the chapter titled, "The Coming of the Picts," Howard would have read, "This people, or rather this race of mankind, has been called by many different names. The most sonorous is no doubt, 'Homo Mediterraneus,' but they have also been called Basques, Iberians, Silurians, the Firbolg, the Dolmen-builders, the Picts."[132] The Picts—a name that certainly fired the imagination of young Robert E. Howard, especially when he read their powerful description as the "malignant gnome, a dark little dwarf, whose stone arrows are to be dreaded," and how they were "a black-haired tattler, a guileful, tale-telling, noisy, contemptible, wretched, mean, strolling, unsteady, harsh, and inhospitable person."[133] This description and the information about the Picts throughout the book were instrumental in the formation of Howard's writing about this lost race of the Scottish Highlands.

The real Picts were, indeed, a lost race. Scottish historian Neil Oliver tells of how the Romans of 54 BC observed a race of men in Britannia who "painted their bodies with blue woad," whom the legionaries called "Caledonians." When the Emperor Hadrian could not conqueror them, he built an east-west wall to, in his words, "separate Romans from the barbarians."[134] By the fourth century, the Romans began referring to them as Picts, "the painted ones," and although the race "had a rich and complex culture," Oliver also called them a "quintessential warrior society." "For all that," Oliver continues, "they managed somehow to vanish entirely from history; indeed they seem to have perished, in the words of Ecclesiasticus, as though they had never been."[135] It was this lost race of barbarians that captured young Howard's mind and would remain with him for the rest of his life.

The Howards were back in Burkett by May, but already Dr. Howard must have been thinking of another move, for by September 1919, they were living in Cross Plains.

Chapter 5

Cross Plains, Texas, 1919

The days when youth was golden fire
And dreams in dreams were won
And visions came on flaming wings
From night and setting sun
—"Nights to Both of Us Known"[1]

For a school assignment, Robert E. Howard was asked to write his autobiography. It was a short paper, for he was only 15 years old at the time. Howard began with his birth, wrote of the many places he had lived, and concluded that he "later moved to a small town known as Cross Plains," before ending with the line, "I'm still here."[2] Little did he know the move to Cross Plains, located ten miles north of Burkett in Callahan County, would be his last permanent home.[3]

When Howard wrote a correspondent about the town and its surrounding geography, he shared some of the history of Cross Plains. "It first stood near the banks of a small creek known originally as Briar, and later as Turkey Creek."[4] People began settling there in the 1870s, and the small community was called Turkey Creek because of the high prevalence of the birds along the creek's banks.[5] According to local historian Ann Beeler, however, "Because the community sat at the crossroads of the army roads and cattle trails from Coleman to Cisco and Brownwood to Belle Plain, it was given the name of Cross Plains." The town was officially established in 1885, but there was little in the way of civilization because the town only "consisted of a post office in a log cabin, six logs high, a store and a blacksmith shop."[6] While there was plenty of game to support the families living there, which was supplemented by small gardens, as one early settler remarked, "If a feller wanted a biscuit, he went to Fort Worth!" Still, by 1901 the town had its first telephone lines, and in 1909 the town newspaper, the *Cross Plains Review*, began rolling off an old cylinder press.[7]

Howard once wrote that there is "a peculiarity of many Texas towns," for "the first settlers were inclined to build as near the banks of creeks and streams as possible." "Later," he continued, "the towns were moved up on higher grounds, because of various reasons—or sometimes for no apparent reason."[8] In the case of Cross Plains, there were two reasons: the problem of the creek flooding in heavy downpours and the coming of the Texas Central Railroad.

The railroad's 1910 annual report told of the commencement of construction of a branch line from DeLeon, Texas, and how "early in the year we promised the citizens along this line as far as Cross Plains, a distance of about 41 miles, to build that many miles of road this year."[9] The plan was for the line to end in Cross Plains at a train depot to be built on a parcel of land located east of Turkey Creek with the hope of one day extending the line as far as Abilene. Because the end of the line was east of Turkey Creek and railroad depots attract commerce, the people of Cross Plains began making plans to move.

In the fall of 1910, the Cross Plains Townsite Company was created with Charles H. Sharman as its president. Sharman was an Irishman who fought with the 33rd Iowa Infantry during the Civil War before working as a surveyor for the Transcontinental Railroad.[10] Noted frontier author Ernest Haycox wrote: "Sharman swam the broad North Platte River to set the first survey stake for a 2,300-foot-long bridge, watched painted Indians run off his party's horses and mules, and in the final winter, when construction never stopped, saw tracks rushed ahead on temporary embankments raised with blocked ice and snow."[11] He eventually became the chief engineer for the Texas Central Railroad and was in charge of selling off land plots after the line and depot were finished. The day of the land sale was January 12, 1911.

The first train rolled into town that day, and a map of all the lots for sale was posted. An estimated seven hundred people were in attendance, and a Colonel Lackland served as the auctioneer. To begin the sale, he cupped his hand behind his ear and said, "Hark, hark." Once everyone was quiet, in dramatic fashion, he said, "I hear the footsteps of approaching thousands who will someday call Cross Plains their home."[12] He sold $77,000 worth of lots that day, and additional sales were later held in May and during the annual Cross Plains picnic in July.[13]

The presence of the trains allowed the area farmers to reach a larger market. Although the first settlers had mainly raised cattle that fed on the surrounding plains, farmers soon moved into the area and grew both truck crops and cotton. By the time the railroad came to Cross Plains, peanut crops had been introduced and were gaining in popularity. The November 23 issue of the *Review* in 1917 demonstrated how profitable the crop had become when it reported that on the previous Saturday, "thirty-eight cars of peanuts and twenty-six of hay had been shipped from Cross Plains."[14]

The trains also brought various goods into town.[15] No one had to go all the way to Fort Worth for biscuits anymore. It was the establishment of the rail-line into Cross Plains that attracted the Higginbotham family to consider building there. In June of 1914, the three brothers purchased six lots on Main Street at the cost of $1,744.40, then built, as Scott explained, "that enormous building that was advertised as the largest store under one roof between Fort Worth and El Paso."[16] When one of their uncles came to town, he was reported to have asked one of the brothers, "Why didn't you build it bigger?" The brother was said to have replied, "I would have, but the bricks ran out."[17]

The large mercantile store bought from the local farmers, and they in turn bought from the brothers, and Cross Plains came to be the destination for shopping in the surrounding area. Beverly Tatom Ross remembered her grandfather telling her about Saturdays in Cross Plains. "All the farmers and ranchers from the outlying areas would make their one trip to town on Saturdays, joining up with the townspeople for a day of grocery and merchandise shopping, but mostly for a lot of visiting. After a long productive day, everyone would return to their homes—waiting for the next Saturday to come."[18] As automobiles became more prevalent, they would park on both sides of Main Street, and once those spaces were filled, they just began parking in the middle of the exceptionally wide street. "There was a lot of excitement here," recalled Jack Scott.[19]

There was also one day a month that served as another shopping day in Cross Plains, for "it was the custom in West Texas towns to set aside a certain day in the month known as 'trade's-day,'" Howard once wrote a friend. "In this town it was the third Monday of the month and was referred to variously as 'Third Monday' 'Trade Monday' and 'Horse Monday.' On that day the streets and alleys were full of men swapping horses and mules."[20] Scott recalled how it "meant the town would be swarming with people and horse and mule dealers would come far and wide to buy and sell with local farmers."[21] Howard recalled these trade days with some distaste when he wrote, "Farmers would come to town with equally worthless nags and the noise of arguments, assertions and refutations must at times have equalled the clamor in an Oriental bazaar. How anybody ever made anything out of most of the swaps, is more than I can see. It always looked to me as if both parties got gypped."[22] Regardless, it still brought more people and commerce to the growing town of Cross Plains.

If the railroad boom had not brought enough prosperity into Cross Plains, the oil boom was about to. The Great War had made evident the world's desire for oil, and exploration was soon prevalent everywhere. In October 1917, in the town of Ranger north of Cross Plains, an oil field was discovered that brought people and jobs into the area. In February of 1920, the first oil was discovered in Cross Plains and the *Review* excitedly announced, "Vestal Well Comes in a Gusher."[23] The well was located north of town, but as Scott stated, it proved to be a "disappointment" because "it didn't last long."[24] The well brought in twenty thousand barrels of oil and then went to sulfur water.[25] Despite that, as Beeler explains, "It was announced that Cross Plains was in the center of a big oil and gas field," and Cross Plains became a boomtown.[26]

Dr. Howard had evidently begun deciding to move to Cross Plains sometime after the family's return from New Orleans, and on September 20, 1919, he purchased a house located in what was known as the "old section" of town, for the home was closer to Turkey Creek than Main Street. According to Burke, the doctor purchased the home "from Mr. and Mrs. J. M. Coffman for $1500, paying $500 down and promissory notes for the remainder, $250 to be paid each year for four years at 10% annual interest." In addition, the doctor "had the house remodeled, installing electricity, running water, indoor plumbing, and a glassed-in 'sleeping porch' at the rear."[27] Electricity was only recently introduced to Cross Plains, as was gas that came from a limited system that drew upon local gas wells.[28]

Once the remodeling was finished, the Howards left Burkett and made their last move as a family to Cross Plains. In their October 24, 1919 edition, the *Review* reported, "Dr. I. M. Howard and family have moved here from Burkett and are occupying one of the Coffman houses in the old town, which he bought some time ago." In addition, the newspaper told how he had "fixed up a nice office over the Farmers National Bank" and that "he is preparing to practice his profession in earnest here."[29] Although the residence of a country doctor became common knowledge in a community, Dr. Howard was planning to have an office where patients could meet with him, one that was located near several pharmacies.

The house featured a walk from the road to a white picket fence that ran across the front and around the west side of the house. Beyond that side, behind the house, was a detached garage and storage shed. Just to the east of the house stood the Butler home where William; his wife, Hester; and their two children, Leroy and Faustine, lived. Leroy was several years older than Howard, while Faustine was one year younger. It was Leroy Butler who recalled the roses and crape myrtles in the Howards' yard, as well as the ornamental cedar near their front door.[30] In between the two properties stood an old mulberry tree and a large live oak on the Butler property.

Steps led up to a front porch where ivy grew across the support posts, and through the front door was a small foyer and hallway. To the left was Dr. and Mrs. Howard's bedroom, and to the right was the living room. Butler recalled the living room as being furnished with a leather davenport and two leather chairs, and they had a long "library table."[31] Maroon velvet draperies hung as window treatments, and there was a rug on the floor that matched; for additional color Mrs. Howard often set fresh flowers about the room.

The dining room was reached through the living room, which Butler recalled was furnished with a large traditional round oak table and chairs, and there was a buffet with a display of Mrs. Howard's cut glass and vases. In the center of the table sat the cut-glass fruit bowl "which caught the sun's rays in the afternoon."[32] There was also an entryway into the kitchen with another opening into the hallway. Butler's future wife, Floyce, recounted how both her mother and Mrs. Howard "still had their old-fashioned ice boxes . . . you picked up the top and put the fifty pounds of ice in."[33] There was also a gas stove, a counter with a sink, and a small kitchen table in the room.[34]

The kitchen door led into the glassed-in sleeping porch, with the bathroom at the end. A cot remained on the sleeping porch where Dr. Howard often slept. Since he was a country doctor, he was on call any time, day or night, and many people came calling for his services at the house, so he likely slept on the porch to avoid disturbing his wife's sleep. In addition, because Central Texas was unbearably hot in the summer, it is possible the sleeping porch may have been a cooler place to sleep. It may also have been for health reasons, since the medical profession was recommending this type of arrangement. One 1921 medical journal stated, "Absolutely ideal sleeping conditions are hardly possible for the average family, for they would call for a separate room for each individual," but if that was not possible, at least "a separate bed or couch with two or three in the same room."[35] In addition to everyone's health, there was also Mrs. Howard's condition to consider. The same article also recommended, "Every tubercular patient should sleep alone in a well-ventilated room," which reflected the same information Dr. Howard would have been taught in medical school—"A phthisical patient should sleep alone."[36]

Across from the kitchen was Howard's bedroom, a small narrow room that was part of the L-shaped porch; through the glass windows, he could look out into the backyard. On the other side of the room was the window from his parent's bedroom, originally constructed as a porch window.[37] There was also a window that opened to the outside, constructed on the far side of the room, filled with a cot, a dresser, a trunk, and a writing table and chair. Although the room was small, as writer and editor Celia Blue Johnson wrote, "A room is far more than four walls, a ceiling, and a door." She explained that regardless of the room's configuration, it was the place where an author like Howard could embrace their idiosyncrasies, harness their creativity, and develop their "unique work habits."[38] That former sleeping porch certainly proved the point, for it is there in that room where Howard created his many popular characters and wrote his stories for the pulp magazines.

Dr. and Mrs. Howard's bedroom, located between the front porch and Howard's own room, had more ample space, and Butler recalled that it was furnished with an oak chiffonier and an iron bed. There were rag rugs on the floor and white cotton ruffled curtains in the windows. Mrs. Howard kept her sewing machine in the bedroom, and he recalled there were many souvenirs on display in the room, including a conch shell from Galveston and numerous tintypes.[39]

When Howard started school that fall, he walked there because it was located on the west side of the cemetery, about two blocks from home. The first schoolhouse built in Cross Plains, according to Beeler, was "a small boxed school house built about 1883" that was soon replaced "in the fall of 1888 [by] a two-story wooden structure about 24 by 40 feet."[40] When the town moved in 1911, a school bond was issued, and a new two-story brick building was constructed on the same site.[41] Apparently, the construction of the school was somewhat questionable. It was reported that after the building was "partially erected," it "toppled over." Even after it was built, "the building was never too sturdy" and "when a strong wind would blow, the building . . . would sway slightly and the parents would come to take the children home." One girl, it was recalled, became so frightened by the swaying one time, she "jumped out the window, breaking her leg."[42]

According to Beeler, by the time Howard began attending classes, "the school had eleven teachers, electric light and natural gas heat, and 335 students."[43] One of those students was Lindsey Tyson, the son of another physician in Cross Plains, and a person Howard would come to know well. "[Howard] was a fine student," Tyson recalled. "He had one teacher in particular that encouraged Bob and encouraged him about his work. He was writing, you know, and she could see a lot in him."[44] He remembered it was the English teacher, Miss Doris Pyle.

When school was not in session, Howard found work in town to make some spending money. "After moving into town," Howard wrote in a letter, "I worked at various things during vacation, such as a grocery store and a Jewish dry-goods store."[45] One thing he recalled about the former job was that it was during Prohibition and "the amount of lemon extract etc., I've known some of them to buy in one day, would startle one."[46] In regard to the latter job, he remembered having to mark down goods for their sales. "For instance," he wrote, "The regular retail price of a pair of trousers would be $5.00. I would mark in big numbers on the tag—$9.50, then draw a line through that and mark below, $5.50. Thus the duped customer . . . would consider that he was getting a bargain, whereas in reality paying fifty cents more than the regular price of the garment."[47]

When Howard was not working or doing schoolwork, he spent much of his time playing with friends. His best friend, Earl Baker, would often come for weekend visits, but more often than not, Howard spent the weekend with Earl in Burkett.[48] They wandered the countryside, rode horses, fenced some, boxed, and practiced throwing knives.[49] "He was a fanatic about knives and swords," Vera Baker recalled.[50] Sometimes the families would get together, and Vera Baker also remembered how the Howard "home was perfectly kept" and that Mrs. Howard was "a marvelous cook; and such a lovely person. I just loved her."[51] Earl Baker recalled that sometimes dinner conversation could turn volatile and that "when something set him off," Howard "would have explosions of temper at the dinner table." "He would get up abruptly," Baker explained, "go out, and sometimes beat the wall with his fist."[52]

While Howard's best friend in Burkett was Earl Baker, his best friend in Cross Plains quickly became Lindsey Tyson, and by some accounts, Lindsey was his best friend in life.[53] Born in Cross Plains to Dr. John Tyson and his wife, Bamma, Lindsey had five older siblings.[54] "I suppose one thing that drew us together," explained Tyson in an interview, "was that my Father was a Dr. and a good friend of Dr. Howard's" and that "they had none of the jealousies (Professional) that existed among Drs. at that time."[55]

Earl Baker and Lindsey Tyson also got along with each other, for Lindsey once stated, "He was a friend of mine too," and told how, "Bob and I visited with him at Burkett several times."[56] Baker would come to visit Howard in Cross Plains some weekends, and whether with Baker or not, Tyson recalled many good memories of those early years in Cross Plains. Sometimes they would go into town to the soda fountains. "We ganged around those some pretty well," Tyson remembered, while other times they ran around outdoors to which he noted, "We spent quite a bit of time running up and down the creek."[57] They liked to box ("We'd beat each other for an hour or so") and fence, although their fencing equipment only consisted of a pair of foils to which they fastened empty revolver cartridge casings over the points.[58] Tyson also remembered Howard as a "pretty good swimmer" and having a "good sense of humor."[59]

Tyson did note that "Bob was rather moody," and he seemed "happiest when he could get a group of five or six friends to come to his house for a visit."[60] He did have other friends in the area, including Dave Lee, Winfred Brigner, and Tom Ray Wilson. Tyson also remembered that Howard "didn't take to hunting much" since "he didn't like to kill anything."[61] Wilson also remembered this as well, for he once said Howard would join him and his friends on nighttime coon hunts, "but he wouldn't let us kill anything."[62]

One of Tyson's favorite pastimes with his friend was hearing Howard tell stories. "Bob was a remarkable story teller," Tyson recalled, "He had a lot of humor, and would read aloud to his friends parts of some books that he thought was humorous." He also remembered that Howard "liked to take snapshot pictures" and that with him, "There was never a dull moment."[63]

Since both families were Methodists—all save Dr. Howard, who was a Baptist—Tyson recalled how they "went to church and Sunday school together."[64] The Cross Plains Methodist church had been formed in 1886, and at first the members met in the schoolhouse, before a dedicated church was built near Turkey Creek in 1901. When the town moved, the church moved with it, where it was erected on Main Street.[65] "Bob and I never did discuss religion or politics," Tyson once said in an interview, but he added, "I know that he did have some kind of belief as I have seen him pray."[66]

The other friend Howard often played with was his next-door neighbor, Leroy Butler, and sometimes his sister, Faustine. Leroy was two and a half years older than Howard and had been born on a farm outside of Cross Plains before the family moved into town in 1910. After the Howards moved next door in 1919, Leroy became such a fixture around the Howard home that Mrs. Howard took to calling him "Son." Leroy recalled spending many hours with Howard in the big live oak tree between their homes, often playacting pirates or some other characters from a tale Howard had read. He once said that Howard "was very studious in school" and how he was "always coming up with new words, you know, that I had never heard in my life. Where he got 'em I don't know; he might have just made 'em up out of thin air."[67] He did note that Howard "didn't get out and play with the other kids a lot like most kids do," and, like so many others, he did not like to hunt.[68] Yet despite that, Leroy still remembered him as "just another kid. You know, just an average small-town boy."[69]

Howard may have been a small-town boy, but since Cross Plains was the largest town he had ever lived in outside of his visits to San Antonio and New Orleans, he was more used to the freedoms of growing up in the country. One manner in which this created some conflict was Howard's interest in guns.[70] "When I was a kid, with no more sense that a kid usually has," he wrote, "I used to sit on the back porch and shoot at the barn and other outhouses, to the irritation of the neighbors." Although the houses were not built close to one another, some were close enough for the bullets to reach. "I figured to put the bullets into wood alright, and generally did," he continued. "But some of them went on through and buzzed through the backyards of the citizens, most of whom were tolerant enough. But one old gentleman used to wax wroth. He said it was trying on the nerves to get his whiskers combed with hot lead every time he stepped out of his back door—which was an exaggeration, of course; I wasn't always shooting." Howard, at least later, realized the issue was between the freedoms of country life, which he had grown accustomed to, with those of a town. "I'd just moved in from the country where life was free and careless," he wrote, "and it took me a long time to get used to a thickly settled locality."[71] Since Howard cherished his freedoms, there is probably much truth in what he said.

Other neighbors remembered Howard fondly. For instance, Mrs. D. K. Woolridge once said of Howard, "Everybody liked him," although she added that "he didn't mix much." She described him as "a tall, slim boy with blue eyes" who "wore a white shirt all the time" when it was the custom to wear blue denim or plaid shirts. And like so many others, she recalled that he read all the time. "We called him the book fiend," she explained in an interview, "and he was a smart boy."[72]

Other neighbors spoke of the many hours he spent with his dog, Patch. One neighbor who lived south of the Howards recalled how "each afternoon Robert would take his dog, Patches, for a walk or run toward Turkey Creek." It seems they usually passed through her property, and she recalled that the dog often relieved himself along the way. She and her husband would always hear Howard cry out loud, "Patches, Patches, what are you doing?" adding that he never did anything to try to prevent the dog from despoiling their yard.[73] Still, she said, in time they found Howard's delivery of that line humorous. Butler also recalled hearing Howard call to his dog every evening at mealtime when he would shout, "Chuck, Patch. Chuck, Patch."[74]

Although the Howards had only been living in Cross Plains a few months, they were settling into their new life in their new town. Howard's reading and playacting evidently gave him enough confidence to do a public reading at the end of the year. According to the *Cross Plains Review*, on Christmas Eve the Methodist Church put on the "Christmas Tree Program." In addition to an address by Rev. Tyler, there was also a series of songs and readings, and one was "By Robert Howard."[75]

Chapter 6

Influential Authors, 1920–1922

I opened a volume dark and rare,
I lighted a candle of mystic lore—
Bare feet throbbed on the outer stair
And book and candle fell to the floor.
—"Moonlight on a Skull"[1]

Robert E. Howard loved to read. "As a boy and a youth in my 'teens, I read purely for the love of reading," he once wrote in a letter. "I can say with confidence that no man, however mature, ever loved reading for its own sake more than I." He elaborated by saying he did not read to learn, to pass the time, or for escapism; rather, "I read simply because I loved reading for its own sake alone. The printed page was like wine to me."[2]

The only problem with this love came in its acquisition, for as he stated, "Books were scarce in the country." Howard detailed the limitations of living in a rural environment when he wrote, "I could not go into a library or book store and select what I wanted. I had to read whatever came to my hand." There was no library in Cross Plains during Howard's lifetime, or any bookstores, and so he wrote, "My main source of reading material were the hand-made bookcases which served for libraries in the country schools."[3] Yet even these were sorely limited in their holdings, so whenever he could, he acquired his own library, which he described as generally being "the largest in the place I lived, but it was small."[4] He typically received a book for Christmas and one for his birthday, but most of the time he was limited to what he could borrow.

Howard shared one story regarding his acquisition of books from the country schoolhouses during the summers when he "raided those 'libraries.'"[5] "During the long summer vacations which usually lasted six or seven months, schools and bookcases were kept locked and barred," he wrote, noting how on occasion "I could obtain the key and permission to read the books so guarded." But more often than not, he "jimmied the doors or windows of the buildings, and pried the locks off the solidly made book cases" and "if that failed, I removed the hinges." He then loaded up an empty flour-sack with his contraband and with a flourish he claimed, "I departed in a cloud of dust." He moralized he was not stealing the books, for he always returned them when he was finished. Although the story may be apocryphal, it highlights his passion for reading, for when he explained why he so willingly broke the law, he emphasized the point: "I had to read."[6]

The fact that he read whatever he received, borrowed, or stole forced him to read widely, and he noted, "Perhaps that accounts in part for my still rather indiscriminate tastes."[7] For instance, one person recalled Howard "sitting alone reading an ancient history, yogi or hypnotism" noting that it was "nothing that a child his age would usually be interested in reading."[8] Yet this did not mean that he liked all that he read. "In my earlier years I thought it was my duty to read stuff the critics praised," he recalled, but realizing he did not find it all that praiseworthy, he lamented, "I could kick myself when I think of some of the junk I waded through." This early experience, however, led him to his own independent judgment of what he enjoyed reading. Howard stated, "I read what gives me enjoyment, and I avoid what bores me," making the point, "if I don't like it, then I'm not going to bother with it—regardless of the author."[9]

When people recalled Howard, they almost always mentioned his love of reading. One neighbor reported the Howard house was "filled with books and books and books," and another that "Robert always had his nose in a book."[10] The Chamberses remembered that when Howard visited them, "he never was interested in getting out on the farm"; he "would bring his books with him," and "he just sat down and read."[11] His friend Lindsey Tyson once told an interviewer that "most of the time he was either reading or writing," and that "he was an extremely fast reader; he read almost as fast as he could turn the pages."[12] Another friend made a similar comment when he explained, "Bob can go into a library, take down twenty books, scan them" and "in one three or four hour session, absorb the essence of all."[13]

Howard's extensive reading and catholic tastes certainly had a great influence on his life. He even wrote about this in a Cross Plains High School essay titled "Some People Who Had Influence over Me." After first acknowledging his parents, he humorously mentioned the books he read about Captain Kidd. "Reading his biography and fiction based on his eventful life, caused me to determine, at an early age, to lead a life of piracy on the high seas." Still, after reading another book about pirates, he changed his mind. As he wrote, there "was an illustration which shattered my hopes entirely," for it depicted a pirate who was "fastened to the mast of a man-o'-war, by a great spike which was driven through his head into the wood."[14] This caused him to conclude the pirate's life was not for him. Humor aside, it does highlight that other than his parents, the greatest influences upon his life were the books he read.

The first book that had a lasting impact was a volume of the *Arabian Nights*, for Howard recalled "one of my first books was a copy of that great work—I was six, I believe."[15] He read many of the popular folktales, including one of the Icelanders' sagas, "The Saga of Grettir the Outlaw," that he once said "reaches the peak of horror" for its "night-long battle between the outlaw and the vampire."[16] Howard also enjoyed the gothic horror tales of Edgar Allan Poe, once noting, "I have read most of Poe's work."[17]

Howard also read many of the books that were popular while he was growing up, including Mark Twain, whom he listed as a favorite, and the Zane Grey Westerns his father also read. In addition, he liked many of the popular English writers at the time, including Rudyard Kipling, of whom he wrote, "I've got much solid enjoyment out of his prose and verse.

He has guts at least, which so many modern writers utterly lack."[18] Moreover, he read the works of Sir Arthur Conan Doyle, such as his Sherlock Holmes and Lost World novels, and immensely enjoyed the Sax Rohmer stories that were wildly popular at the time about the mysterious and elusive Dr. Fu-Manchu.[19]

Howard read many of the classics, but he held his own individualistic views on these authors. For instance, he clearly read many of Charles Dickens's novels that would have been widely available in his youth, but as Howard wrote, "with the exception of Pickwick Papers which is my favorite of all his books. . . . He gets on my nerves." "Why good gad," Howard elaborated, "his characters submitted to indignities and insults and outrages that made me grind my teeth merely to read about," adding, "and I'm a peaceable man."[20] Or in regard to Shakespeare, whom he also appears to have read, he is said to have commented, "Shakespeare had perspective. That is why he is so great, why he continues to live. It is something so few have. He probably had it more than any man."[21]

Out of all the authors he listed as his favorites, one novelist certainly rose to the top, and that was Jack London; Howard called him one of "the most powerful men . . . in all the world's literature."[22] London was the famous author of *The Call of the Wild*, *White Fang*, and *The Sea-Wolf*, and Howard greatly admired London's tales of adventure about common men who could struggle through feats of physical prowess and overcome the shackles of society and nature. On many occasions Howard told of his love for London's work, such as when he wrote, "As far as I am concerned, he stands head and shoulders above all other American writers," and how reading and appreciating him "makes a man feel life not altogether useless."[23]

Of all of London's books, two stood out for Howard, *Martin Eden* (1909) and *The Star Rover* (1915). The former is a semi-autobiographical novel of London's struggles to become a writer. In the story sailor Martin Eden, who comes from a working-class background, falls in love with Ruth, a girl far above his station in life. Eden decides that his best means for being accepted in her world is to become a writer, but he struggles with not only his writing but also the numerous rejections he receives early in his career. Like so many other authors, such as frontier writer Louis L'Amour, the novel helped prepare Howard for the struggles he would face in becoming a writer.[24] Moreover, it later became the template for his own semi-autobiographical novel.[25]

The other book, *The Star Rover*, was an unusual novel for London to have written because it ventures into science fiction and involves reincarnation.[26] The story is about university professor Darrell Standing, who was wrongfully sentenced to life imprisonment in San Quentin Penitentiary for murder, and because of his continued defiance in prison, he is continually being placed in solitary confinement in a straitjacket. In such a constrained position, Standing learns to project his mind and to experience the past lives he once lived. Howard wrote that "London's *The Star Rover* is a book that I've read and re-read for years, and that generally goes to my head like wine."[27] The novel had such an influence on him, he often incorporated the theme of reincarnation into his stories and developed a character who, like Standing, could project himself to experience past lives lived.[28] Perhaps more than anyone, Frank Belknap Long, a pulp author and a contemporary of Howard's, understood the impact London had on Howard when he wrote, "London was the kind of writer who could instill in his readers a lively awareness of what it means to be very young, eager and strong and confident, and hell-bent for 'red-blooded adventure' . . . Bob Howard was like that too," for he "had all of the tremendous zest, of adventurous delight in fictional encounters on the heroic level that we associate with the novels of Jack London."[29] London's influence was that great.

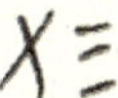

While Howard's penchant for books helped form his writing style, it was the introduction of magazines, particularly the pulp magazines, that made him a writer.[30] In the same letter in which Howard mentioned the scarcity of reading material in the country, he noted, "Magazines were even more scarce than books." "It was after I moved into 'town,'" the town being Cross Plains, that Howard recalled "I began to buy magazines." "I well remember the first I ever bought," he continued: "I was fifteen years old; I bought it one summer night when a wild restlessness in me would not let me keep still, and I had exhausted all the reading material on the place. I'll never forget the thrill it gave me. Somehow it never had occurred to me before that I could buy a magazine. It was an *Adventure.* I still have the copy. After that I bought *Adventure* for many years, though at times it cramped my resources to pay the price. It came out three times a month, then."[31] Howard was actually 13 years old when the family moved to Cross Plains, and 14 the summer after he "moved into 'town,'" so, as Howard scholars Morgan Holmes and George Knight point out, Howard's recollection of his age may have been a "misstatement."[32] They conclude that Howard likely bought his first copy of *Adventure* sometime between September 1919 and July 1920.

Pulp magazines, so called because of the cheap wood pulp paper they were printed on, ushered in the twentieth century; they were first published in 1896. When author Charles Beaumont once asked rhetorically, "What were the pulps?" he answered they were "cheaply printed, luridly illustrated, sensationally written magazines of fiction aimed at the lower and lower-middle classes." Naturally, the next question he asked was, "Were they any good?" and he answered, "No. They were great!"[33] The pulps grew in popularity throughout the first two decades of the new century and reached their heyday from the 1920s into the 1940s.

In the nineteenth century, America had more newspapers than Europe, and they were affordable for most people.[34] Magazines, on the other hand, were far more costly. "Before 1893," pulp historian Tony Goodstone explains, "people with money and education read stately magazines like *Harper's*, *Atlantic*, *The Century*, and *Scribner's*," while "the great masses of low-income workers, immigrants, and youngsters with meager education read Dime Novels and sleazy paperbacks costing five or ten cents."[35] Many of these cheap paper publications featured American frontier heroes such as Daniel Boone, Kit Carson, or Buffalo Bill, and popular detectives like Nick Carter. What led to the demise of the popular dime novels was a change in US postal regulations. The novels no longer qualified for second-class postal rates, and the added shipping costs priced them out of existence.[36] It was this that cleared the way for pulp magazines.

Frank Andrew Munsey is the man responsible for the creation of the pulp magazine when, in 1896, he published *The Argosy* on the cheaper quality paper that measured seven by ten inches.[37] The magazine had existed since 1882 as a boy's weekly paper called *The Golden Argosy*, but Munsey shortened the title and oriented the content more toward adults; it was filled with short stories and serial novels. Howard would purchase *Argosy* throughout the 1920s, once remarking, "I suppose I have every *Argosy* I ever bought, for I have a stack of back numbers about four feet high."[38]

Munsey soon added *Munsey's All-Story Magazine*, and by 1908 he not only had paid off all his publishing debts but also had accumulated a net profit of $9 million.[39] Then, in 1912, what may have been Munsey's greatest publishing success was his serialization of new author Edgar Rice Burroughs's first two novels that year, *Under the Moons of Mars* (a.k.a. *A Princess of Mars*) and *Tarzan of the Apes*.[40] It did not take long before, as Goodstone explains, "Other publishers hurried to cash in on the Munsey rag-paper-to-pulp-riches formula."[41]

One of the first publishers to follow was Street & Smith with *Popular Magazine* beginning in 1903 and *Top-Notch* in 1910.[42] As more and more publishers began releasing new titles, in order to distinguish themselves, pulp magazines began atomizing with specialty topic titles. Munsey, again, was the first when he released *The Railroad Man's Magazine* in 1906, and soon there was *Detective Story*, *Western Story*, *Love Story*, *Sea Stories*, and *Sport Story* appearing on the newsstands.[43] "During their heyday," pulp historian Tim DeForest writes, "any newsstand in the country was overflowing with pulps, with their garish and often bizarre covers competing for the attention of eager readers."[44] And, as fellow Texan Francis Edward Abernathy recalled, growing up in a small town in Texas, they had "the usual drugstores with . . . rows of pulp magazines."[45] It was probably in one of the Cross Plains drugstores that Howard first purchased a copy of *Adventure*.

The Butterick Company, one of the largest magazine publishers in the nation, first released *Adventure* in 1910.[46] Trumbull White, an adventurous explorer himself, served as the magazine's first editor, lending the title some gravitas due to his background, but it was under the skillful editorship of Arthur Sullivant Hoffman that the magazine came to be referred to as "the *Atlantic Monthly* of the pulps."[47] By the time Howard began reading the magazine, according to bibliographer Richard Bleiler, "*Adventure* was without question the most important pulp magazine in the world," and it could not have been more aptly named, for it was the adventure story that Howard cherished most.[48] In those pages he found new authors he came to admire, even going so far as to make a list of his favorite authors and their stories among the issues he had read between September 1, 1919, and July 20, 1922. The list consisted of authors who shared their adventures with Howard, such as Hugh Pendexter's stories of early American history, W. C. Tuttle's humorous Westerns, and Captain Dingle's tales of life at sea.[49] While Arthur O. Friel transported him to the jungles of South America, Gordon Young took him to the islands of the South Pacific, and Talbot Mundy to lands in the far-off Middle East and Afghanistan. Although mostly forgotten today, these authors were well known during the pulp era, especially to those who, like Howard, read *Adventure*.

Another author Howard avidly read was Harold Lamb, of whom he claimed, "I have only respect and a keen admiration."[50] Writing "colorful tales of Cossacks, crusaders, Vikings, and Mongols in the pages of *Adventure,*" Lamb proved to be one of the magazine's most popular authors.[51] His writing style was both compelling and evocative, and it caught the attention of a young Howard. He once went through all of Lamb's stories he owned, listing the foreign words Lamb had used, and on another occasion, according to author and Lamb historian Howard Andrew Jones, regarding Lamb's story "The Wolf Chaser," "Howard wrote a five-hundred-word recap of the story, then wrote nearly a thousand words of his own take on the events, reusing the place names and some of the characters."[52] This was not an uncommon practice for would-be authors learning how to write, for even Jack London, Howard's favorite, "practiced copying page after page of Kipling's work in order to get the hang of it himself."[53]

During the 1920s, because *Adventure* was being released three times a month at the cost of a quarter per issue for "192 pages of eye-straining print," as Howard said, "it cramped my resources to pay the price."[54] As he once told a friend, "There were many stretches of enforced idleness when my pockets were empty. I was never one to make undue calls on my father for spending money. During the idle stretches, I scrimped and saved from one magazine to the next. I'd buy one copy and have it charged, and when the next issue was out, I'd pay for the one which I owed, and have the other one charged and so on."[55]

Yet despite his monetary constraints, *Adventure* motivated Howard to attempt writing the stories he so enjoyed, and it awakened in him the realization that he could make a living writing for the pulp magazines.

"To write! The thought was fire in him."[56] Howard would have read that line in Jack London's novel *Martin Eden*, and he no doubt shared those same sentiments, for those early memories of starting to write for publication remained with him.[57] "I wrote my first story when I was fifteen" (meaning the first for publication) "and sent it—to *Adventure*, I believe," Howard recalled.[58] The story was titled "Bill Smalley and the Power of the Human Eye" and was submitted to both *Adventure* and *Western Story*.[59] The replies he received from both pulp magazines also proved to be another first for Howard—his first rejections.

According to Howard biographer Mark Finn, his first stories were very short and were derived from some of his homework assignments in which he wrote of Steve Bender, an unreliable narrator, and his friends Bill Smalley, Weary McGraw, and the Whale.[60] The stories were handwritten in either his room or at the dining room table, but by the following year, in 1922, Howard acquired a typewriter, and soon all of his stories were composed on this machine.[61] "As Howard's skill as a writer increased, and he became more proficient at the longer forms," Finn explains, "he dialed Steve Bender's age back a bit and tried his hand at what appears to be boy's adventure fiction. Full of sneaking around, snap decisions, and hasty conclusions, these stories, while more finished, lack some of the urgency in Howard's later works."[62] Howard wrote additional stories featuring Steve Bender, including "The Ghost with the Silk Hat" and "Westward, Ho!," but none of them sold.

Other than his homework assignments, which offered him a chance to write, Howard did not enjoy attending school. "I hated school," he once asserted, "simply because the whole system irked me." Howard explained that "sitting still in one place for hours at a time got on my nerves," "having to go and come at certain times irked me," and "I hated for my actions to be controlled by the ringing of a bell." Howard elaborated, writing, "The fact that these things were necessary had nothing to do with it. School, any way it is looked at, was a restriction of my freedom. I accepted it as a necessary evil, and got through with it as quickly as possible."[63] Howard had grown accustomed to the freedom and independence he had in the country; he had not started school until he was 8 years old and then had the long summer breaks that were common for agrarian communities. Yet the school in Cross Plains was larger and more mindful of structure, a structure he could not tolerate. This was not an uncommon trait for a young man who grew up in Texas, for folklorist J. Frank Dobie once noted the strong streak of fierce independence found in Texans and recalled how one nineteenth-century visitor to the state was said to have commented, "These Texians are the most independent people under the whole canopy of heaven."[64] Even Texas historian T. R. Fehrenbach noted this common trait when he wrote, "Texans were independent. No man put his nose in his neighbor's business, unless asked."[65] The fact that the school system dictated Howard's behaviors throughout the day caused him to bristle at his loss of freedom.

This did not mean that Howard was a bad student. As his best friend, Lindsey Tyson, explained to L. Sprague de Camp, "As a high-school student, [Bob] did not appear to be resentful or rebellious, as he depicted himself." Rather, Tyson described him as "quiet, withdrawn, solitary," and despite his not liking the dictates on his time, he "liked his teachers, and breezed through the courses with little effort and excellent marks."[66] Another fellow student, Paula Bond, remembered Howard in a similar manner, stating, "In class, he didn't speak out very much" and described him as "a moody person."[67]

During the 1920–1921 school year, Howard took notes on a number of subjects, including Samuel Taylor Coleridge's famous poem "The Ancient Mariner" (which he memorized in its entirety), Washington's "Farewell Address," and George Eliot's *Silas Marner*. During his last year in the Cross Plains school, 1921–1922, he had notes from his classes in English, physics, geometry, and American history, as well as from reading Shakespeare's *Macbeth* and Robert Louis Stevenson's *The Strange Case of Dr. Jekyll and Mr. Hyde*.[68]

Howard continued writing short stories for his school assignments, including the tales of "Mr. Dowser Buys a Car" and a "Twentieth-Century

Rip Van Winkle," in which he demonstrated a vivid imagination. He also proved to be rather sassy when it came to the more banal essay assignments such as "What I Did in Vacation" and "What My Signature Means to Me."[69] For the former, he told of going to the Rocky Mountains with some friends and one of them climbed a tree and bumped a hornet's nest with disastrous results. Yet he then added that a bear chased another friend, and they had to kill a moose who treed yet another.[70] He received a grade of C on the paper. In regard to the latter essay, he wrote that "Other people's names mean more to me than mine," highlighting how much he admired the signature of J. P. Morgan, before adding (tongue-in-cheek), "I admire it so much that I often practiced writing it." His teacher wrote in the margin, "I meant for you to tell *seriously* what your signature means to you."[71] Still, he earned a B- on that one.

Yet Howard was not always so flippant with his writing assignments. For one essay in English Class III, he wrote a first-person narrative titled "Pictures in the Fire" in which he recalls the dreams he experienced looking into a fireplace.[72] "There were no lights in the room except the firelight, and as the flame rose and fell, the shadows danced on the wall like elves at play. It was a time for reverie and dreams, and with half-closed eyes, I leaned back and watched the marvelous panorama, the mystic pictures in the fire."[73] He then writes of the "fire-breathing dragon" and the "knight in gleaming, crimson armor, carrying a flaming sword" before the scene shifts to "the face of a crimson demon." And then, "The fire died. The coals' glow dimmed. The draft roared down the chimney and scattered the white ashes over the hearth. And the hearth was cold."[74] In the margins of this assignment the teacher presciently wrote, "Robert, I believe that some day you will be one of our major writers. Develop your talents."[75]

The Howard family's move to Cross Plains appears to have been a good one, for they seemed to thrive there. Tyson recalled the Howards as being "a very close-knit family," and they were described as being both active and happy.[76] Dr. Howard added new equipment to his office to better serve his patients in 1921, and he attended a class in Dallas on eye care.[77] That year he also moved his practice into the City Drug Store and worked with other local physicians to establish a hospital in Cross Plains.[78] Still, he was gone both day and night making house calls, while Mrs. Howard tended house. One neighbor recalled some of her activities by noting how her "garden was nice, and Mrs. Howard tried to keep a pretty yard" and that she and her son "would go on trips together."[79]

The Howards also welcomed back Earl Lee Comer, who lived with them for a second time. Toward the end of his enlistment, Comer was in Milwaukee, Wisconsin, and while there he took a mechanical drawing course.[80] Over the holidays in December 1920, he visited his hometown of Big Spring before traveling to Cross Plains, where he moved into the Howards' new home.[81] According to Burke it is believed that Howard and his cousin slept on the sleeping porch, while his mother slept in Howard's room to help with her tuberculosis.[82] Comer stayed approximately one year before moving to Dallas, where he worked as a draftsman, and by 1925 he was living in California.[83]

Howard continued to read, write, and play with his friends, especially Lindsey Tyson and his next-door neighbor, Leroy Butler. One of their pastimes was to dress up like pirates and act out different adventures, possibly some Howard had read in his favorite pulp magazine. Butler recalled how they had ordered several swords from the Francis Bannerman Sons mail-order catalog with a "round hilt on them," and that in the backyard they would "wrap bandana handkerchiefs around our heads like a pirate." He also recalled that his family "had an immense live oak tree in our backyard, and we'd get out in the shade of that ole tree and pretend that we were back maybe in the dark ages or something. In time of the Spanish Main, things like that. He had things like that on his mind all the time."[84]

In light of Howard's distaste for school, he assuredly found the summer months free from the regiment of the "system" and more to his liking.[85] He did, however, recall one incident from the summer of 1920 that he did not particularly enjoy. It occurred at the traveling carnival that was part of the annual Cross Plains picnic in July. Although one disgruntled citizen commented, "The Carnival people came to fill their pockets with the coin of our people," some of the locals, like Howard, managed to get small paying jobs there.[86]

"I was working at a carnival, at one of those blasted cat-stands," Howard wrote in a letter, describing one of the carnival games of knocking down pins, possibly shaped like cats, with a ball. "I was behind the rack bending over to pick up a cat," he wrote, "when some bully let go with everything he had." He then described what happened next: "It dazed me—almost knocked me down. . . . I remember faintly hearing the woman I was working for . . . came up and put her arm around me and asked how bad I was hurt, and I pushed her away roughly like a kid will—embarrassed because everyone was laughing at me . . . it was an hour or more before I could think straight."[87]

The next summer proved to be more to his liking, for when the carnival returned the next year, he was smitten with one of the carnie girls.[88] Howard apparently only mentioned the girl to a friend once later in life, saying "that he'd lost interest in romance because of a let-down from a carnival girl when he was age fifteen."[89] "Carnies—a wild breed—interested him because they lived free of the rules that govern solid home folk," his friend explained, but after standing "there spellbound when he saw her moving around the midway," she "disappeared behind a tent with a man—likely another carnie—for whom she had probably been waiting."[90] The encounter was doubtless as fleeting as his friend states, but one can only wonder what it was about her that attracted him so.

When May of 1922 finally came, Howard graduated from the Cross Plains High School. Although rain caused the ceremony to be postponed twice, finally, on Friday night May 12, commencement exercises were held.[91] The graduating class, family, and teachers were in attendance, and after Professor S. E. Settle delivered a short address, the nine graduates received their diplomas.[92] Although Howard was relieved to have this phase of his education completed, he was not finished with school. He still had one more year to go. The graduating class had only completed ten years of education, but at the time, as Roehm explains, "Texas colleges required 11 years for admittance, so college-bound students had to pick up the 11th years elsewhere."[93] So in the fall of 1922, Howard temporarily moved to Brownwood, Texas, to complete his education.

Chapter 7

Brownwood, Texas, 1922–1923

The sea, the sea, the rolling sea!
High flung, wide swinging, so wild and free,
The leaping waves with their white-capped crest
The plunge and lunge on the ocean's breast.
—"The Sea"[1]

In the fall of 1922, Howard and his mother made their way to Brownwood, Texas, for the start of Robert E. Howard's last year of schooling. Although Brownwood was located only thirty miles south of Cross Plains, there was no direct route at the time. A traveler either went to Rising Star, located east of Cross Plains, and then south to Brownwood, or they had to journey southwest to Coleman and then east to town. The former was the preferred route, for as the *Brownwood Bulletin* commented at the time, "The road from Coleman to Brownwood is in a very deplorable condition."[2]

Brownwood, Texas, is located in Brown County, and both are named for an early pioneer of Texas, Henry Stevenson Brown.[3] The town was first organized in 1857, east of the Pecan Bayou, but in the late 1860s, it was moved west of the river. In the 1880s/1890s, after several railroads were built through Brownwood, the town witnessed significant growth, and by the end of the century it had established two colleges: Daniel Baker and Howard Payne. When Mrs. Howard and her son temporarily moved there, Brownwood had a population of 10,900 and was "the second largest pecan shipping point in the world," had "compressed seventy-three thousand bales of cotton" that year and, because oil had been discovered in 1917, the town produced "775 barrels of crude oil per day." The town could also boast that it had "14 churches," "50 miles of water mains," "29½ miles of sewer main," "six paid and 40 volunteer firemen" and "three fully and modernly equipped hospitals."[4] In addition, the town also prided itself on its Carnegie Library that had been established by a grant from industrialist Andrew Carnegie in 1904.[5] Compared to Cross Plains, Brownwood was a thriving city.

Arrangements had been made for Howard and his mother to rent separate rooms at a boardinghouse located near the school at 316 Wilson Street, run by Mr. John F. Day and his wife, Alice.[6] The practice of a mother staying near her child while attending high school was not, according to Roehm, an uncommon one.[7] Mrs. Howard did not stay the entire time in Brownwood; she returned to Cross Plains for at least one week in November, and Dr. Howard visited his family at least three times that fall.[8]

Despite being in a new town, Howard already had several friends he knew there. C. S. Boyles Jr., a fellow graduate from Cross Plains, had also come to Brownwood for his final year of high school.[9] Just the month before, the two had worked with a group of boys under the direction of Dr. John Rumph to erect a radio relay tower on top of the Higginbotham Brothers' Store.[10] In addition, Howard was reunited with his best friend from Cross Cut, Austin Newton, since he, too, was in town for the same reason.[11]

On Monday morning, September 11, 1922, Howard walked to the high school for the first day of classes. "It was a short walk to school," explains Roehm, for it was "one block to Austin [Avenue] and six blocks to Avenue B" where the school sat "on the corner." He also describes how "Howard would have passed the Brownwood Ice & Fuel Company and gone through the 'Santa Fe Subway,'" an underpass constructed beneath the Santa Fe Railroad tracks in 1913.[12]

Howard found the school "overcrowded—fairly flowing over with students."[13] Even Superintendent George W. Page had to agree, for he commented to the newspaper that it was "crowded to a point at which effective work is well nigh impossible," since there had been growth in both Brownwood and the surrounding feeder schools.[14] Howard wrote about his experience later, explaining, "It was like a sardine can. We had to gang up, two or three to a seat in the main study hall. The Senior class was given separate study halls, but they were eventually abolished, because the students didn't keep order any too well. Some of them were mean as the devil, but most were just exuberant kids, overflowing with a superabundance of vigor and animal spirits."[15]

Howard was certainly one of them. He and Newton initially palled around together, and they both tried out for the basketball team. "I came out for basketball and made the team," recalled Newton, but Howard did not.[16] In a letter Howard explained why: "I remember once I tried out for basket-ball, and quit in disgust during the first practice because I was repeatedly reproved for roughness. I kept instinctively tackling the ball-carrier."[17] Because "Robert didn't care for sports," Newton explained, "I didn't see him much in high school."[18] They had gone their separate ways.

Howard was also visited several times by at least one of his friends from Cross Plains, Tom Ray Wilson.[19] A particular memory of Wilson's was how "Howard suffered from frequent nightmares," and that he would often wake up thrashing and fighting. Because of this, Wilson recalled, "I'd tie him to the bed to keep from hurting himself."[20] Another friend from Cross Plains remembered the same thing, explaining how "Robert would tie his right hand to the bed because he had violent dreams and would wake up swinging."[21] In addition, Howard was prone to sleepwalking, and so he often tied his foot to the bedpost, thus not allowing himself to wander around at night as he had been known to do. The behavior, however, is apparently not uncommon.

Author Charles Duhigg has explained that "sleepwalking is an odd outgrowth of a normal aspect of how our brains work while we slumber." The body goes through phases in sleep, and part of this is a movement into sleep paralysis. Most people can make the switch; "some people's brains, though, experience switching errors. They go into incomplete paralysis as they sleep, and their bodies are active while they dream or pass between sleep phases."[22] When this happens, for some people like Howard, the result is sleepwalking. For most this is a benign experience, but for some, often children, they experience sleep terrors.[23] According to Duhigg, this happens because, "The activity inside people's brains is markedly different from when they are awake, semi-conscious, or even sleepwalking. People in the midst of sleep terrors seem to be in the grip of terrible anxieties, but are not dreaming in the normal sense of the word."[24] Neurologist Mark Mahowald of the University of Minnesota explains, "People with sleep terrors aren't dreaming in the normal sense. There's no complex plots like you and I remember from a nightmare. If they remember anything afterward, it's just an image or emotions—impending doom, horrible fear, the need to defend themselves or someone else."[25] People are acting on their base instincts in these cases, not rational habits as in sleepwalking, so they have been known to jump off roofs or to physically attack someone because they are acting on the basic of instincts, "fight or flight."[26]

Howard's other friend from Cross Plains, Boyles, became somewhat closer to Howard in Brownwood due to his writing; he had obtained the associate editor position for *The Tattler*, the school's student-run newspaper.[27] Boyles announced in late November, "Begin saving your stray pennies now, students, for that big Christmas number of *The Tattler* which will surpass anything you have ever seen in the way of a High School Christmas edition." He was looking for stories and articles that were due to his office by December 15 in time to make the December 22 issue, and there was a contest with prize money for the best stories.[28] Howard made two contributions. The first was "'Golden Hope' Christmas," which opened with, "Red Ghallinan was a gunman. Not a trade to be proud of, perhaps, but Red was proud of it. Proud of his skill with a gun, proud of the notches on the long blue barrel of his heavy .45s." The story focuses on a man who "was born a gun-fighter" and for whom "the killer instinct burned strongly in him—the heritage of Cane."[29] The story, despite its opening, proves to be a sentimental piece, and one that has a redemptive quality to it. The second story was "West Is West," a shorter, humorous Western tale.

The publication of the two stories proved to be a number of firsts for Howard. As Roehm writes of Boyles and *Tattler's* editor-in-chief, Claude Curtis, "They were the first to publish the work of Robert E. Howard."[30]

The two stories were also the first for which Howard received praise other than from his parents and teachers, when the *Brownwood Bulletin* wrote, "Among the several interesting contributions to the Christmas number of *The Tattler*, Brownwood High School student publication, are two stories by Robert E. Howard, a member of the Senior class. 'Golden Hope Christmas' is the title of the better of the two stories, telling briefly of the career of an old-time desperado. The little story is well written and the theme is well chosen. . . . His literary work in Brownwood High School is being done with a view to undertaking journalism as his life profession."[31] And, if publication and praise were not enough, assuming Smith's memory was correct, these also proved to be the first stories for which Howard was paid; "Golden Hope" was awarded a ten-dollar prize, and "West Is West" five dollars.[32]

On December 22, the last day of classes before the Christmas break, Howard possibly participated in the "junior-senior walkout." According to *The Tattler*, which apparently lived up to its name, the students "met at the Carnegie Library at eight-thirty and left for a picnic at the Matlock place. About six cars went, all of which were packed to the utmost with students and good things to eat. A very delightful time was had by everyone, the crowd returning about four-thirty that afternoon."[33] After the New Year, when the students returned, both classes received a reprimand from the superintendent who called the affair "untimely" and "the result of wrong leadership."[34]

After returning to Brownwood, Howard continued to submit stories to the school newspaper, including several about Hawkshaw the Detective, publishing "AHA! Or the Mystery of the Queen's Necklace" in February and "Unhand Me, Villain!" in March.[35] These stories were based on a widely popular comic strip in the newspapers at the time called "Hawkshaw the Detective." As Roehm explains, the word "hawkshaw was fairly prevalent in the 1920s and was synonymous with 'detective.'"[36] The editors of *The Tattler* were certainly well pleased with Howard's stories, for they wrote, "We are fortunate in having such a good writer here in our school and we hope he will keep up his contributions," noting that "HIS stories have plenty of action and are spicy with near-cuss words and slang."[37] Altogether, they would publish five of his short stories and poems.[38]

Howard also began making new friends his senior year, including Truett Vinson.[39] Born Wade Truett Vinson on September 26, 1905, in Erath County, Texas, near Fort Worth, his father was a Baptist minister but a furniture refinisher by trade.[40] The family moved to McCulloch County when Vinson was 5 years old, and by 1920 they were living in Brown County. It is unknown when Howard and Vinson met their senior year, but they became fast friends, despite their differences. "Vinson is six feet two," Howard once described his friend, who, with his dark features, was a handsome young man.[41] Vinson once said of his friendship with Howard, "He took me as I was. I took him as he was—even if I did not understand him. Our friendship had nothing at all to do with his writings," he pointedly stated, before adding, "He understood that I never really liked his stories, and we actually hardly ever discussed them."[42]

The friend who did appreciate Howard's stories, Tevis Clyde Smith, was introduced to him by Truett Vinson. Smith and Vinson already knew each other from their participation in the Lone Scout program.[43] W. D. Boyce, who had started the Boy Scouts of America in 1910, left that organization five years later and started the Lone Scouts of America, to serve rural boys in areas that did not have a scout troop.[44] While no longer active in the program, both Smith and Vinson had remained close friends.[45] "It was a day much like today—cloudless, pleasantly warm—probably in early April, if not late March, 1923 that I asked Truett Vinson if he knew Robert E. Howard," recalled Smith. "We were on the school grounds at Brownwood High, and Truett said, 'Yes, there he is now.' I told Truett that I'd like to meet Bob, and he called Bob over, introducing us to one another . . . and we became good friends before the school term ended."[46]

Smith, who went by his middle name, Clyde, was an only child born in Brownwood on February 17, 1908. He lived with his parents, Tevis Sr. and Maury Elizabeth, in a one-story frame house located at 1917 Avenue D in Brownwood.[47] His father worked for the Walker-Smith Company, a wholesale grocery firm, and his mother taught piano lessons for many years.[48] Howard once described Smith as "a fine upstanding young man, three years younger than myself, six feet one inch in height, a perfect blond type; athletic in appearance."[49] Due to his age, Smith was a sophomore when he met Howard.[50] One friend of Smith's described him as someone who "liked to run," "ran every opportunity he had," and believed he was "full of hard to hold energy." He could be "withdrawn" and was often "impatient with people," and "if you spoke to him in any way with which he might find the slightest fault, he glared at you through those thick glasses, and you quickly decided to let him alone."[51] In addition to being athletic, Smith was also interested in literature and debate, and he and Vinson had organized a boy's club, after they felt they had become too old for the Lone Scouts, which they called "The All-Around Club."[52]

Smith was already familiar with Howard's interest in writing, having read his prize-winning stories in *The Tattler*, but he quickly learned of his interest in literature, as well as his interest in boxing.[53] "By the time I met him," Smith later recalled, "he was reading just about any good book that he could lay his hands on." They often went to the Carnegie Library together, and he remembered Howard "moving along the shelves." He would "race through the books, for he was a fast reader. He scanned through some of them, and read others more thoroughly, eager to get their contents, keeping with, at the same time, trends in the pulp fiction field, as well as reading everything connected to boxing, from *The Police Gazette* to *The Ring*, for he was well balanced in his interests, and enjoyed some sports as much as literature."[54] Smith enjoyed talking with Howard for he recalled that near the Howards' boardinghouse, there were two churches under construction, and "When the men were off from work we would sit in the sand in front of first one and then the other of the churches, and carry on long conversations while the traffic went by, for Bob was an enchanting talker, and also enjoyed what I had to say."[55] It seems they also loved to debate one another. A mutual acquaintance described that when they would argue and debate things, "They sometimes talked to the very tops of their voices, and they used a lot of gestures and they argued and they argued and they discussed things vehemently."[56]

The two friends also went on long walks together, talking and debating while seeking out adventure. "Bob and I went swimming in a small stream on the edge of town in late March, or early April," Smith said, recalling one of their adventures together. Unfortunately, after their swim, Howard missed some school, for, according to Smith, Howard "took the intestinal flu from the swim, and had spent three days in misery."[57]

Howard, Smith, and Vinson, explains Burke, "became the closest of friends, a relationship that continued until almost the end of Howard's life, and these friendships were most important to him."[58] Of the three friends, Howard and Smith were most alike. A friend of all three explained it in this manner: "One of Clyde's characteristics that later reminded me of Bob's was that he raised his voice as loudly as he could when he was arguing and disagreeing with someone, especially if the disagreement was on one of his pet subjects. He shouted and raised his voice and waved his arms frantically."[59] Vinson, however, was not like that. "Truett would stop, sit quietly, and listen," their mutual friend explained. "A lot of times, I imagine, he was amused at Clyde and Bob, at how excited they could get about simple subjects." The friend summarized, "All three of them were different—but Bob and Clyde were more alike. They were more argumentative."[60] As another mutual friend once said of Howard, "I doubt if he ever trusted any chums beside those two."[61]

While Howard still maintained his friends in Cross Plains, his relationship with those in Brownwood was different. Howard scholar Patrice Louinet once remarked of his friends in Cross Plains, such as Lindsey Tyson, that "these were the friends he would have a drink or a walk with, watch a football match or box with." His friends in Brownwood, because they "harbored literary and/or journalistic aspirations," Louinet continues, "soon became his 'intellectual' friends."[62]

Despite having made two new friends, however, Howard still despised school. As he once wrote, "I hated school as I hate the memory of school."[63] "I got through high school by the skin of my teeth," he wrote, although elaborating that the real reason was the lack of freedom it imposed upon him: "Outside of mathematics—at which I was a terrible mug—I didn't particularly mind the studies, but I hated being confined indoors—having to keep regular hours—having to think up stupid answers for equally irritating questions asked me by people who considered themselves in authority over me."[64] Outside of math, he does note that he was not a particularly bad student when it came to grades, for as he honestly stated, "I had no trouble learning the tripe they dished out in the way of lessons—except arithmetic, and I might have learned that if I'd gone to the trouble of studying it.

I wasn't head of my classes—except in history—but I wasn't at the foot either. I generally did just enough work to keep from flunking the courses, and I don't regret the loafing I did."[65] The two classes he affirms to have enjoyed the most were history and his biology class, although in regard to the latter he does note, "The teacher was a poor misfit who didn't know his stuff; that is, he was a good biologist, but he couldn't handle students."[66] Still, he claimed to have had a "knack for biology" and that his teacher had suggested he become a biologist, but as Howard wrote, "I wanted to be a writer; I didn't give a damn about being a scientist."[67]

Although he appears to have been sympathetic to his biology teacher regarding the unruly class, for the most part he did not like many of his teachers. "I always hated teachers who had favorites," he once stated, and by way of explanation he added, "I guess it was because I was never the favorite."[68] He also felt, "All the teachers I had didn't give a damn in hell whether the kids in their classes lived or died or whether they learned or not."[69] Yet, again, it was not so much the uncaring teachers as what he perceived as their authoritarian rule. It was about his loss of freedom: "What I hated was the confinement—the clock-like regularity of everything; the regulation of my speech and actions; most of all the idea that someone considered himself or herself in authority over me, with the right to question my actions and interfere with my thoughts."[70] So in the end he harbored resentment for his time in school. This showed when he facetiously wrote to Smith over a year after his graduation, "Ah, yes, I wish I were back in good old B[rownwood] High—with a couple of bombs."[71]

As graduation day drew near, Howard took advantage of several contests in which he could display his writings. The first was sponsored by Brownwood's Winnie Davis Chapter of the United Daughters of the Confederacy for the best paper on the subject "What the Nation Owes the South."[72] Howard submitted his own essay by that title. The second was a high school poetry contest sponsored by the University of Mary Hardin-Baylor. Each high school was only allowed to submit two poems, and the competition was among all of the submitting high schools in Texas. In the past the contest had only been open to girls, but this was the first year in which it had been opened to boys, so Howard submitted his poem titled "The Sea."[73]

Howard was once again thankful when graduation day arrived. The ceremony took place on the evening of Friday, May 18, 1923, on the campus of Howard Payne College. The list of graduates numbered 140 and included C. S. Boyles, Truett Vinson, and Robert E. Howard.[74] There were so many graduates and family members present, the *Brownwood Bulletin* reported, that the audience "taxed every inch of space at the Howard Payne auditorium, School of Fine Arts building to the limit Friday night."[75] Howard later noted that "the class in which I graduated was the biggest that had ever graduated from a Texas high school, up to that time."[76]

The ceremony included two local reverends leading prayers and a speech from the president of the school board, along with choral songs and piano solos. Finally, the graduates walked across the stage and received their diplomas, leaving Howard to later write, "I graduated from high school at the age of seventeen."[77] Afterward, when everyone was seated, the Winnie Davis Chapter of the United Daughters of the Confederacy announced the winners of their contest for the best essay on "What the Nation Owes the South." The winner of the senior medal was Robert E. Howard. The essay was reprinted in the *Brownwood Bulletin* at the end of May.[78] Howard opened the essay with a statement of heritage: "In order to appreciate to what extent the American union is indebted to the south, one must go back to the first settlements in America. Virginia, the Carolinas and the other Southern colonies were settled by the Cavaliers of England, Scotland and Ireland, the best blood of Europe." He then made note that "From these Cavaliers came Thomas Jefferson, George Washington and General Robert E. Lee," before detailing the prominent characteristics among them, those that became identified as the Southern traits of "loyalty, bravery, chivalry."[79] He continued tracing the development of the South across time and discussed its economic impact through its agricultural and natural resources. Then, with grand eloquence, he ended with this flourish: "But I have scarcely dipped into the great store house, the South's history. To record her greatness in full would be to write a great book. Her glorious annals would fill many volumes. I have but tried to show the great extent to which not only the American nation, but the whole world is indebted to the South."[80] Howard was so excited that his essay had been reprinted in the paper that after he received a copy, he wrote to Smith asking him,

"Did you see my 'What the Nation Owes the South' in the Bulletin? That's what I won the U.D.C. medal on, you know."[81]

The award for the poetry contest was not announced at the graduation ceremony, for the information had stated that "announcement of the awards, together with the publication of the poem winning first place, will be made through the press of the state; and all poems winning prizes or honorable mention will be published in the May issue of the Baylorian."[82] That announcement came after graduation, and although Howard did not win, it did list his name among the honorable mentions.[83] Howard's poem did, however, catch the attention of several people. "I got a letter from the assistant editor of *The Campus*, S[outhern] M[ethodist] U[niversity]," Howard wrote to Smith. "He said he saw my poem 'The Sea' in *The Baylor United Statement* and he asked me to contribute to *The Campus*. I sent him a poem."[84] In addition, everyone who read the *Cross Plains Review* could read the poem in its June 29 issue.[85]

As for receiving his high school diploma, Howard was elated. "I'll never forget the wild and passionate feeling of relief that surged through me as I bounded out of the building where the graduation exercizes had been held," he recalled, "with my diploma in my hand, and halting on the lawn, expressed my pleasure at being through with school, and my opinion of the whole works in language more picturesque than choice."[86] And with that, Smith sadly recalled, Howard "gathered his belongings, and went home."[87]

Chapter 8

Struggling Author, 1923–1924

My rejections slips will all be there
of all the forms and genders—
Of them will I build a gibbet fair,
and hang thereon the sender.
—"Another Hymn of Hate"[1]

"Robert Howard, who has been in Brownwood High School, is back home after graduating," the *Cross Plains Review* announced in their June 1, 1923, issue.[2] Howard settled back into his parents' home and set his sights on becoming a writer.[3] Yet when he went to write, as Smith recalled, "He complained that his words ran through his head, but didn't come out on paper like he had planned them. They dried up when he sat down at the typewriter. He felt that he was in chains."[4] He kept at it though and wrote more stories for submission to the pulp magazines. He sent "The Mystery of Summerton Castle" and "The Phantom of Old Egypt" to *Weird Tales* magazine, "Lal Singh—Adventurer" appropriately to *Adventure*, "The Feminine of the Species" to *Argosy-Allstory*, and "The Iron Terror" to *Cosmopolitan*.[5] They all came back rejected. Like his idol, Jack London, he was "baffled by the incessant stream of rejection slips," so he read the pulp magazines in which he was hoping to publish, "trying to find the magical formula for success."[6]

Although he struggled with the rejections, Howard was determined to become a writer. "I'll make the pulps," he told Smith, "and I'll make them from here in Texas. I'm going to prove that a man doesn't have to live in New York to sell his stories."[7] "He said this more than once," Smith recalled, while the "rejected manuscripts piled up beside his table."[8] Howard later explained his motivations, writing, "I've always had a honing to make my living by writing, ever since I can remember," and so he continued to write and submit for publication.[9]

Despite his determination, however, Cross Plains was not the most conducive environment for such a profession. His best friend in town, Lindsey Tyson, understood this when he explained, "Most of our population was made up of Farmers, Ranchers, Oil field workers, and small storekeepers that did not understand him. They knew about nothing of the things that Bob knew most about, and in turn he knew very little about their things."[10] There were no established writers in town to consult for advice, and there were no other aspiring authors with whom he could discuss his new trade.[11] He was largely on his own. In time the people in town came to look upon him as someone odd or strange. Howard recognized it, for he once told a friend, "I know how people in this part of the country feel about writers. Everybody thinks I'm a lazy, no-good rat, sponging off my family, and they wonder why I don't get out and get a man's job."[12] His friend came to understand, for she later said of Howard, "Writing stories was the only thing he had ever wanted to do in his life. That was the most important thing in the world to him . . . so he was going to write. Come hell or high water he was going to write."[13] And so he wrote.

Of course, life sometimes got in the way of his writing. Almost as soon as he was settled back at home, the family left for Marlin, Texas, located 150 miles southeast of Cross Plains. They stayed there for the next several weeks in a small bungalow located at 508 Coleman Street. The home, Roehm explains, served as "a convenient rental for families wanting to spend time in the healing waters."[14] Across the street from the bungalow stood the Torbett Sanatorium. The Howards had gone there for therapy to treat Mrs. Howard's tuberculosis.

The Sanatorium was owned and run by Dr. John Walter Torbett Sr. "I was born on the 12th day of July, 1871, by Gum Creek, near Jacksonville, Texas," the good doctor wrote in his memoirs before detailing his childhood and how he "completed a four-year course in two years, and graduated April 28, 1891."[15] He then "read medicine" with his brother-in-law, Dr. J. W. Cook, before attending the Medical College of Georgia in Atlanta.[16] After graduation he served as a country doctor in Leon Junction, Texas, but after contracting malaria he convalesced in the home of his brother-in-law.[17] "After I had recovered from my spell of fever," Torbett continued the story, "he asked me to go into partnership with him to help organize an institution for the treatment of chronic diseases."[18] What they envisioned was a health resort, so they purchased a building, and on March 11, 1898, they opened the Bethesda Bath House, in which patients could take advantage of "the hot mineral water."[19] Dr. Torbett soon married and had a son, John Walter Jr., and his brother Bert joined their practice. He then had a new building constructed in 1907, and when it opened the following year, as he wrote, "The institution was called 'Sanatorium' because it used climate and the forces of nature, like heat, light and mineral water."[20] His brother Oscar soon joined the staff, and later his brother Frank. Howard became friends with Frank's son, Frank Thurston Torbett, who was slightly older than he, having been born on November 30, 1901.

While his mother received her treatments, Howard either explored the new town or stayed in the bungalow writing. There, he also sent his first extant letter to Tevis Clyde Smith on June 8, 1923. It is a good example of juvenilia, since he would have been 17 years of age at the time. Opening the letter, he jokingly writes, "May the blessings of Allah rest upon you and your feet never become tangled in your whiskers."[21] He told his friend how the day before, he had secured a hall and advertised for Reverend B. G. Richbourg's lecture on *Ben Hur*, before sarcastically writing, "Who is the enterprizing young gentleman who is going to rake in one-half the proceeds? Me! Ha! Ha! Ha!"[22] He then rambles some more, misquotes the poet Omar Khayyam, writes some free verse, draws a few pictures, and pontificates on the hypocrisy of society discriminating against flappers, progressive women of the 1920s. Much of Howard's early letters are representative of his sense of humor when he writes poetry, short plays, or shares some anecdote.

By the time the Howards returned home on June 22, Howard was ill. As he wrote to Smith, "I have got whooping-cough, curse it."[23]

In addition to exchanging letters, Howard and his friends had another way to keep in contact through the publication of a paper they called the *All-Around Magazine*. By the time Smith met Howard, the All-Around Club had fallen to the wayside, but at that time Smith purchased a small printing press and "before long," he explains, "*The All-Around Magazine*, a small, amateur paper, made its appearance. I was the editor, type-setter, makeup man, and press man, as well as chief contributor and circulation head."[24] His friends also contributed some of the paper's content, and the first issue was dated March 1923.[25] A second issue appeared in April and a third in May/June, in which Howard and Smith published the beginning of their adventure serial titled "Under the Great Tiger."[26] Smith described their serial as "a rather gory, and somewhat swashbuckling tale, laid in Afghanistan."[27] When Howard received that issue, he wrote to Smith, "I got your paper and it's really good. Hurray for the 'Great Tiger!'"[28] Despite Howard's excitement, they never finished the serial.

Soon after, Howard created his own paper that he called the *Golden Caliph*, although he only produced one issue.[29] The sole edition featured a number of poems, including his own version of "Kublai Khan."[30] There was also a critique of jazz music and a list of heavyweight boxing champions.[31] Truett Vinson also published his own paper, which he called *The Toreador*, but by the end of the year all three papers had ceased publication.[32]

Back in Cross Plains, Howard was reunited with his friend Lindsey Tyson. They spent time together doing things such as hiking, and Tyson recalled one of Howard's peculiarities when he explained, "He would be walking along a path and he would suddenly stop, walk back maybe 15 or 20 feet and turn over a small rock or stick." Tyson never learned why he did this, but it does demonstrate at least his insatiable curiosity, if not his vivid imagination.[33] They would also go horseback riding since Tyson owned a horse named Gypsy, which he described as "a very spirited animal" that "wanted to run everywhere she went," although he did add that "Bob rode her very well."[34] Howard later recalled one of his experiences with Gypsy in a letter. Howard was riding with Tyson behind him, and they "were going lickety-split through the mesquite, the limbs of which occasionally smacked us gently in the face and removed pieces of hide," when he tried reining in the horse. Tyson apparently was not prepared for that move, so to keep from falling off the horse, he grabbed Howard, pinning his arms to his sides. Gypsy "instantly sensed something was the matter, and bolted," Howard wrote. "I yelled and cussed, and struggled but my friend evidently thought his only hope of salvation was to hold on to me." The only problem was they were heading for a large tree branch. "That limb hit me smack across the breast. And broke off," Howard recalled, believing, "That's the only thing that saved me from nine or ten crushed ribs."[35]

Howard apparently had numerous close calls with horses, for he wrote of having "horses running away with me and falling with me; one threw me and then jumped on me; one turned a complete somersault in mid-air and landed on her back which would have smashed me like a bed-bug if I hadn't been hurled over her head as she fell."[36] He also seems to have had a bad encounter while out possum hunting with his friends. Howard, Tyson, and Baker were with Tom Wilson, who recalled Howard was bitten by a possum they encountered and that it "bit hard enough that he had to kick his leg to get the animal off of him. It drew blood."[37]

Howard and his friends also passed the time roughhousing. In one letter to Smith he wrote, "We had quite an enjoyable time engaging in 'rough-and-tumble' wrestling," which he described as "No holds barred. Kick, knee, hit or gouge."[38] Howard scholar Jeffrey Shanks explains that "'Rough-and-tumble' fighting is a uniquely American style of unarmed combat that was prevalent in the South and on the frontier from the late 18th through the middle nineteenth century" and is "characterized by the use of brutal biting and gouging tactics."[39] Howard just called it "good exercise." When they became bored with that, they would play pranks on people. As Howard wrote, "We made a fool package and put it in the road and pretty soon here came the ex-mayor sliding along in his big car. He stopped, jumped out, read the writing on the package, sneaked back to his car and 'aired out.'" The words the mayor had read said, “Leave me lay where I can catch the next sucker.”[40] Howard also recalled going to the Cross Plains Picnic that summer, which he said was “bum,” although he did see “one fine fight and several minor scraps.”[41] He also spent time playing with the next door neighbors, when he began noticing the girls in the neighborhood. He wrote, “they are all nice girls and very good looking,” but he called Faustine Butler “the prettiest one.” Still, as he admitted to his friend, “I’m no lady’s man.”[42]

Howard enjoyed spending time visiting his friends in Brownwood. “He visited me for a few days during the middle of the summer,” Smith wrote, remembering how Howard used the mail hacks, “open, horse-drawn wagons with a top,” and the Brownwood North and South Railroad to get there.[43] When he went home, “Bob took the train to May, rode the mail hack from there to Rising Star, and transferred to another mail hack from Rising Star to Cross Plains,” which took “the greater part of a day’s journey.” While there, Smith reminisced how “we spent the time swimming, going to shows, visiting the library, taking short hikes, and talking.”[44] During those walk and talks, Howard often retold a story he had read or a movie he had seen. “Bob was one of the most brilliant people that I ever knew,” Smith once told an interviewer, “He could take a story book or a sorry movie, and by the time he got through retelling it, it would absolutely glow from his descriptions.”[45]

On one of these trips to Brownwood, Howard brought along his dog, Patch.[46] Smith remembered it because of a comment Howard had made about his dog. Howard was explaining his belief that “Humanity will probably destroy itself,” to which he added that at least “the animals will be able to enjoy themselves.” Scratching Patch’s back, Howard said, “Take Patch here. . . . He’s been around for years, and not once has he ever criticized me. He never has so much as implied that he is better than I am, and he never has corrected me about my manners. He doesn’t know anything about man’s inhumanity to man.” After a moment’s reflection, Howard concluded, “It’d leave a good world for the animals.”[47]

Sometime that summer Howard also became serious about his physical health and stature. He wanted to build himself up, so in addition to boxing and taking long walks, he began exercising.[48] “He got an old cotton sack,” a friend explained, “went to the creek, filled it full of sand, hung it in the barn and used it as a punching bag."[49] He also improvised by using logs. Leroy Butler remembered Howard beating on the log with a sledgehammer. "He'd take a twelve or fourteen-pound sledge hammer with a three-foot handle on it," Butler explained, "and stand out there and beat on the log for an hour . . . just pounding, bang, bang, bang, on that big old log." This memory left Butler to remark, "You know it takes a pretty strong man to do that."[50] And since there was no fireplace in their house, Howard gave away all of the split wood to his neighbors.[51]

Howard also began lifting weights.[52] Weightlifting was not a widely popular sport in the early twentieth century, and the equipment was not readily available, so, again, he often had to improvise. Eventually he found athletic equipment such as bands and barbells.[53] He kept these on the porch, where he would routinely lift weights as often as he could, a practice that became a life-long habit (assuming he could find the time).

Sometime after he began this regimen, his father took notice and finally asked him, "Robert, what's this all about?" Dr. Howard later wrote that his son had replied, "Dad, when I was in school, I had to take a lot because I was alone and no one to take my part. I intend to build my body until when a scoundrel crosses me up, I can with my bare hands tear him to pieces, double him up and break his back with my hands alone."[54] Howard later told a friend, "I work at weights and punching bags to increase my wind and harden my muscles," before explaining, "I feel that if it is possible, a man should try to give himself as much strength as possible, as well as developing his mind to the utmost."[55] It is unknown if Howard knew he was echoing the sixth-century BC Greek philosopher Thales or not.

Friends and neighbors recalled his serious dedication to this new endeavor. One neighbor said, "He took quite a lot of exercise" and "walked a lot, including to the post office every morning."[56] Tyson remembered him having "a powerful grip" and that he had "thick forearms like a blacksmith."[57] Still another added that after a year at this "he was pretty good-sized," and one more, "He was big enough and strong enough to have been an athlete himself."[58]

Although he had built himself up into an impressively muscular man, there apparently came a price with all of his exercising, for he later wrote what happened inside of a year. "As for myself, my only physical weaknesses, so far as I know—outside of flat feet!—is a bad heart," he explained. "I inherited a weakness of that organ, and about the age of eighteen suffered from what is commonly known as an 'athletic heart,' or dilation. After recovery, there was still a weakness that I occasionally notice now."[59]

Summer came to a close, and after Labor Day many of his friends moved on with their lives. Smith advanced to his junior year of high school; Austin Newton went to McMurry College in Abilene; Vinson enrolled at the Howard Payne Commercial School, where he studied bookkeeping; and C. S. Boyles attended Howard Payne College, joining the staff of the college newspaper, the *Yellow Jacket*, for which he asked Howard to contribute despite not being a student.[60] Although Howard continued writing for publication, with no success and in need of money, he was forced to find a job.

"I graduated from high school at the age of seventeen," Howard later shared with a friend, "and went to work in a tailor shop."[61] Howard's new employer was Settle's Tailor Shop located on Northeast Second Street, a half block east of Main, where he worked from September 1923 to June 1924, which Burke observed was "his longest tenure in any job other than self-employed author."[62] In a letter to Smith shortly after he started, Howard told him about the job: "Start work early in the morning and work until nearly night. I walk from five to fifteen miles a day, no exaggeration, soliciting clothes and delivering them and when I'm not doing that I wash and clean clothes. Not an overly pleasant occupation but I like it all right. I work on commission and ought to make about $40 per month, some months more."[63] He did not like the job for long, for as he later wrote, he had started the job "just as one terrific boom was dwindling out." The oil boom had brought in the usual camp of followers looking to profit from the oil workers, which included prostitutes. Howard did not fondly remember when the "harlots used to give me dresses to be cleaned." He explained the condition of those dresses: "Sometimes they'd be in a mess from the wearer having been drunk and in the gutter. Beautiful silk and lace, delicate of texture and workmanship, but disgustingly soiled—such dresses always symbolized boom days and nights, to me—shimmering, tantalizing, alluring things, bright as dreams, but stained with nameless filth."[64] Not long after, he wrote Smith about the oil workers themselves: "There was a merry old time when all the roughnecks got drunk. There was several fights and some knives and pistols drawn but no one was hurt much."[65] This was but one more reason Howard had said an oil boom "will teach a kid that life's a pretty rotten thing, about as quick as anything I can think of."[66]

Now that Howard had some money coming in, it proved to be a double-edged sword. He found himself with less time to write, but he now had money to afford the purchase of more pulp magazines and to attend the movies. "One of his favorite recreations was going to the movies," Tyson recalled, and Howard often wrote about those movies in his letters.[67] "Have you seen a good show lately?" asked Howard in a letter to Smith that fall, before proceeding to tell him about all the films he had recently watched.[68] As the film industry began producing more movies, the number of theaters available in which to watch them also increased. In Brownwood Howard attended films at the Lyric Theater, while in Cross Plains he first went to the Majestic Theater and then, after it burned down that spring, the newly opened Electric Theater.[69] One Cross Plains resident, James W. Nichols, recalled the popularity of these theaters: "You could go to the matinee for a dime and buy a sack of popcorn and a coke for a nickel each."[70] Although Howard saw many films, Tyson recalled that the one film "I remember his talking most about was 'The Hunchback of Notre Dame,'" to which he noted, "The role of the Hunchback was played by his favorite actor Lon Chaney."[71]

It was also that fall when Howard may have encountered his first real exposure to suicide. He wrote to Smith on October 5, 1923, "I see in the papers where Roy Guthrie committed suicide."[72] Howard would have known Guthrie from his year at Brownwood High School. The 19-year old boy lived on a ranch near Trickham in Coleman County, and on October 1, the newspaper reported, "The body was found about 5 o'clock by the father of the young man" and that "by the side of the body lay a .38 calibre pistol and . . . only one shot had been fired and it had pierced the heart."[73] Guthrie had left no note explaining why, leaving Howard to ask Smith, "Why, I wonder? Do you have any idea?"[74] Smith did not, but he later said of Howard, "The suicide had an impact on him."[75] Perhaps it was a good thing that he had family visiting at the time.

"I've had two cousins visiting me," Howard wrote Smith in the same letter, "who I hadn't seen for fifteen years."[76] They were Mary "Maxine" and Lesta Ervin from Big Spring, Texas, both of whom were well-read.[77] "They'd read the International Adventure Library," Howard told Smith, "and from what they said, Dracula is a hum-dinger. I'm going to order the set right away."[78] The series of hardback books from Caldwell and Company were a collection of the most popular adventure books up to that time and featured Bram Stoker's most famous creation.

As the calendar changed to 1924, Boyles paid a personal visit to Howard, encouraging him to write for Howard Payne's *Yellow Jacket*, at about the same time he learned that Smith had taken over as editor of Brownwood High's *The Tattler*.[79] Howard continued working at the tailor shop, although he took some time off in early April when he went to Brownwood to have his tonsils taken out. His job, however, was not looking very prosperous that spring. "I'm still working at the tailor shop," he wrote Smith in late April, "and haven't made very much money lately as another shop has been put in and three tailor shops are too many for a town this size."[80] Howard began looking for another job and was apparently offered one in Brownwood, so he quit his current job. Not long after, he told Smith, "The guy went back on it. Leaves me without a job. I've been heaving freight at the depot some but there's not much money in it."[81]

Now with fewer hours to work, he had more time for writing and visiting with friends. Vinson had graduated on May 21 with a diploma in bookkeeping.[82] On the same day, Smith was recovering from having his appendix removed the day before, after which he had to attend summer school to make up for some lost time.[83] Despite all the things going on in their lives, he still visited with them in Brownwood whenever he had the chance, and at least Smith visited him in Cross Plains.[84]

In between, he worked at odd jobs but found no steady employment. It is possible he had chosen against doing so anyway, for at some point Howard had decided to return to Brownwood that fall to take business courses like Vinson had done. Rather than bookkeeping, however, he chose to take classes with skills that might help him in his writing career, so he planned on courses in typing and shorthand.[85]

Before going to Brownwood, Howard took a trip with his parents south to the Rio Grande Valley.[86] While there, they crossed over into Mexico for a visit and unlike in America, where liquor was now illegal because of Prohibition, there were no such laws in Mexico. There is a strong likelihood Howard imbibed while there for in a piece of doggerel to Smith he wrote,

I went across the Rio Grande
And viewed the great Tequila land.
The Rio Grande I went across,
It cost just fifty centavos.
There is a bar on every street.
You get quite thirsty in the heat.
I am a temperance man, confound it,
Down with all liquor! So I downed it.[87]

This may have also been the trip when Howard picked up a hat that has been described as "a real Mexican sombrero with little balls dangling from its rim" and "the chin strap was a thin little strip of leather attached to the hat."[88] Smith recalled the hat and believed he had picked it up in the "lower valley." While visiting Howard, "I expressed a wish to wear it uptown while on one of my visits to his home," Smith later wrote, for he believed that "wearing the hat would have been a happy jest." Smith said that Howard had refused his request. "These people around here think I'm crazy as hell, anyway," Howard told him, "and I don't want to add to it."[89]

After the family returned from their vacation, they drove Howard to Brownwood, where he roomed with Tyson in a boardinghouse located at 417 Austin Avenue.[90] He then enrolled in Howard Payne Academy, which was separate from the college, for as Roehm explains, it "was designed to function like today's junior colleges," noting that it "even had its own building on the campus."[91] There were several programs within the academy, and Howard enrolled in the Commercial Department, headed by Professor James Edward Basham, who held a degree in accounting. He was described as "a slender man with white hair and a droopy graying mustache—very distinguished looking."[92] And it was in that program, Howard wrote, "I studied shorthand and typing."[93]

"And so I came to [Howard Payne] College and enrolled there as a student," Howard later wrote in an unfinished realism piece. "I felt strange and kinda caged and hemmed in—like everybody was looking at me and wondering at my poor clothes and uncouth language, and was laughing behind their backs."[94] His attempt at writing realism may have come about from his Brownwood friends. As he would later write in a novel, Smith had asked him, "Why don't you lay off the weird stuff and write about real life?" while Vinson had asked, "Why don't you write realism?"[95] This conversation may have been the impetus for Howard to attempt realism, and the result was one of the few novels he ever wrote in his lifetime. In addition to the encouragement of his friends, the writing of the novel may have also been influenced by Jack London, who had written his own semi-autobiographical novel, *Martin Eden*, one of Howard's favorites.[96]

Sometime after this conversation, Smith recalled Howard's plans for the novel. "On one of our rambles, Bob told me that he planned to write a modern novel," Smith explained, "It was to be titled *Post Oaks and Sand Roughs*."[97] Like the book's protagonist, Howard "had determined to write a tale of his own life."[98] Writing the novel in 1928, Howard substituted the names of real people, including his own, for fictitious ones. Howard became Steve Costigan. He also changed the names of places, such as Cross Plains becoming Lost Plains, and things, such as *Weird Tales* becoming *Bizarre Stories*. *Post Oaks and Sand Roughs* was never accepted for publication during his lifetime, and Smith believed the manuscript had been lost, but it was later found in 1966 by the literary agent of the Howard estate, Glenn Lord, and was eventually published.[99]

The novel, despite its fictionalization of events in Howard's life, appears to only change the names and occasionally rearranges timelines or compresses events to make the novel more readable. It is not until approximately three-quarters of the way through that it becomes entirely fictionalized. Many Howard scholars have demonstrated ample evidence to suggest that the events in the novel are real, covering the years from late 1924 through early 1928; they point out that nearly all of the pseudonyms have real people behind them.[100] For instance, the novel opens at a football game being played on the first day of Thanksgiving break, "Semple University from Abilene versus Gower-Penn College."[101] According to Roehm, this was a fictionalization of the actual game between Howard Payne College and Simmons College (today Hardin-Simmons). Because of this, Roehm stated more specifically that the game, and hence, the novel, "begins on November 27, 1924 around 7:00 p.m."[102] Still further, "Franey, the stocky, incredibly powerful captain of the Gower-Penn team" who "had run a full hundred yards through the center of the entire Semple team for a touchdown!" was also real.[103] According to the *Brownwood Bulletin*, at the actual game, the real "Captain Joe Bailey Cheaney" managed to run "100 yards in the early part of the first quarter for the Jacket's first touchdown."[104] Howard only moved the spectacular touchdown to the end of the game in his novel to add more drama.

In light of the autobiographical nature of the novel, the insights into Howard's life are indispensable for telling his biography and can therefore be used while still applicable—that is, before it becomes an entirely fictional story. To avoid confusion, brackets are used to denote a change from the pseudonym to the real name when passages of the novel are quoted.

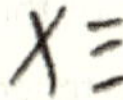

Howard may have had plans to write while he was in Brownwood, but there is little evidence he submitted anything to the pulps until late 1924.[105] He no doubt spent time with his friends but did little else, because between the cost of living in Brownwood and payment for his classes, he was left with little money. "[Howard] seldom had any money, and many of his nights were nightmares of hunger," he wrote in *Post Oaks*, "during which he was too ravenous to sleep and lay awaiting morning and breakfast." His pride prevented him from asking for a handout. He also wrote, "Once he found a dime in a pair of old trousers, and it was like a godsend. He bought two apricot tarts, and the fragrance and ambrosial tang of them remained a luscious memory as long as he lived."[106] Still, when *Weird Tales* hit the newsstands, he took what little money he had and bought a copy. The December 1924 issue he purchased on the newsstands the first of November was money well spent, for it proved to be the linchpin to his writing career.[107]

In that issue Howard would have read the caveman story, "With Weapons of Stone" by C. M. Eddy Jr., but it was when he reached the letter pages and read the editor's comment on that story that an idea formed in his mind. The editor, Farnsworth Wright, had written that the caveman story gave rise to a question: "Why has not someone written of a fight between a Cro-Magnon caveman and a Neanderthal man?"[108] Wright elaborated, "We get plenty of manuscripts dealing with fights between dinosaurs and pterodactyls on the one hand and cavemen on the other. . . . But Neandertalers and Cro-Magnons existed side by side, and waged relentless and savage warfare against each other." Wright then suggested a story be written of those two battling one another, "perhaps over a girl who has taken the fancy of the Neandertaler man."[109] After reading the editor's suggestion, explains Louinet, "This is exactly what Howard did in early November 1924, probably the very day he bought the latest issue of the magazine, faithfully following Wright's suggestion."[110] When he finished he titled the story "Spear and Fang" and sent it to the magazine. Then, he waited.

Sometime before November 27, he received a letter in the mail.[111] "I was with Bob when he got a notice," Tyson recalled, "*Weird Tales* Magazine had accepted his story."[112] "He was about the happiest man that I have ever seen," Tyson continued, and then he watched Howard do something rare: "Bob kneeled down by the bed and said I am going to thank my God for this. He said a silent prayer. He remarked that after this, maybe I won't have so much trouble selling my writings."[113] He had started writing at the age of 15, and now, three years later, he had his first professional sale.[114] He was to be paid sixteen dollars upon the story's publication.[115] Despite the fact Wright had accepted the story because he had, in fact, as Louinet stated, "specifically requested it," Howard had reached a decision.[116] He was going to drop out of the academy, go home after Christmas, and be a professional writer. There was only one problem, Howard wrote: "Christmas came, ushering in a whooping blizzard."[117] According to the newspapers, after a month of sunshine, "a mixture of wind, sleet, snow and ice gave us the most severe cold that has been experienced in 20 years."[118] His parents were supposed to pick him up, but "the blizzard prevented [it]" and so Howard "stayed on for several days after the rest left."[119] Little did Howard know, the storm would prove quite symbolic of what his next three years as a professional writer would be like.

Chapter 9

Weird Tales, 1925

There came to me a Man one summer night,
When all the world lay silent in the stars,
And moonlight crossed my room with ghostly bars.
It whispered hints of weird, unhallowed sight;
I followed—then in waves of spectral light
Mounted the shimmery ladders of my soul
Where moon-pale spiders, huge as dragons, stole—
Great forms like moths, with wings of wispy white.
—"Forbidden Magic"[1]

Once the roads were passable after the Christmas blizzard, Howard's parents picked him up from the boardinghouse in Brownwood and drove him home. "Back at [Cross] Plains he found a letter from [*Weird Tales*] awaiting him," Howard wrote in *Post Oaks*.[2] He had submitted another short story, "The Hyena," which the editor found "acceptable," offering him twenty-five dollars for it, and another story soon accepted was "In the Forest of Villefère," which Wright called a "gem."[3] "[Bob] was, of course, intoxicated by the pleasant aroma of success," he wrote in his semi-autobiography, because to the "penniless youth that he was, $25.00 looked like a million."[4]

Howard had also submitted a slightly longer story about his beloved Picts titled "The Lost Race," but the *Weird Tales*' editor asked him to revise it based on his recommendations. This was a first for Howard and one he did not especially like. Howard believed, "Once a story was completed, he was through with it," for he was "eager to start something else, and he wished to look on it again only in print." He also "doubted his ability to make the tale come up to standard, even with the editor's remarks to guide him, and dreading a second refusal, delayed several days before he made the changes."[5] It was a good thing he did, for the editor accepted it for thirty dollars, his highest payment for a story yet, although again, he would only receive it after the story was actually published.[6]

Howard did admit to a "foolish timidity" at submitting additional stories to *Weird Tales* magazine, for "It seemed like an imposition on a good natured editor who had already done more for [Bob] than the latter could ever repay." Yet, at the same time, Howard was now doing exactly what he wanted to do: write, which he called "Work of joy!"[7] And so, "He stayed at home," Howard explained in *Post Oaks*, "and wrote incessantly, fired by the increasing heights of success."[8]

"You know, sometimes it don't seem possible that I'm selling stuff to magazines," he told his mother. "I feel like I'll wake up some morning and find out it's all a dream." "You've got a good start," Mrs. Howard replied, "But remember, you're young yet. You may have to work a long time before you get full recognition." "With the start I got," he confidently told her, "I'd be a dub if I didn't succeed in a few years. Oh, of course, I don't expect to leap into fame overnight. But the first story is the hardest, and after that it's comparatively easy."[9] Comparatively, it did not get easier, it got harder. After three successful stories in a row, it would be three more years before he saw another acceptance.

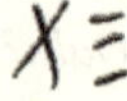

Weird Tales magazine would prove to be both Howard's salvation and his curse, but at this point in his writing career, it was simply his best hope. At that time the magazine had only been publishing for two years, and the strong reputation it would attain, partly due to Howard, was still some years in the future.

Weird Tales' mere existence "would not have been possible," explains pulp historian Sam Moskowitz, "without the direction, sympathy and approval of the magazine's originator and publisher, J. C. Henneberger."[10] Despite having created numerous magazines throughout his career, the one closest to Jacob Clark Henneberger's heart, the one he wanted to see succeed, was *Weird Tales*. He was certainly the man to make it happen, for one of *Weird Tales*' authors, Frank Belknap Long Jr., who knew Henneberger, described him as "highly energized in an extroverted, successful-businessman way," but "He was soft-spoken and had a cultivated, widely-read side to his nature."[11]

Henneberger was born on February 2, 1890, into a farming family who lived in Antrim Township in Pennsylvania.[12] His parents sent him to a military academy in Virginia when he was 16 years old, and while there he formed his love for the works of Edgar Allan Poe. "The English department was headed by one Captain Stevens," Henneberger recalled, "a hunchback who was a rather chauvinistic chap in that he favored Southern writers. One entire semester was devoted to Poe! You can imagine how immersed I became in him."[13]

After graduation Henneberger attended Franklin and Marshall College in Lancaster, Pennsylvania, beginning in the fall of 1909. There, he joined the fraternity Phi Kappa Psi and became fast friends with John Marcus Lansinger; they both developed interests in becoming writers.[14] Although Henneberger graduated in the spring of 1913, his best friend dropped out and became an assistant school principal.[15]

With college diploma in hand, Henneberger traveled to Portland, Oregon, where he lived with his brother and worked for the local newspapers.[16] When war broke out in 1917, he joined the navy and was sent to the Great Lakes Naval Training Station located just north of Chicago. From there he was sent to Naval Training School in Minneapolis, but a month later the Armistice was signed, and he found himself a civilian once more. He returned to Chicago, where he met his wife and began working for a weekly newspaper in Indianapolis.[17] It was there, Henneberger explains, "I met a map and atlas publisher who employed college students to sell their products during the summer months." The publisher was the National Map Company, and their work with college students gave him the idea for his first magazine.

As Henneberger relates, "I sold them on the idea of a national magazine for the college undergraduate to be called *The Collegiate World*." The first issue was dated February 1920, and it proved to be, according to *Weird Tales* historian Robert Weinberg, "a smashing flop."[18]

Henneberger, however, realized the error of his idea. The magazine was about all colleges and universities across the country and often featured one in each issue. The magazine only sold well to college students when their particular college was featured. "Henneberger showed his genius," explains Weinberg, "by changing the title and contents of the magazine to *College Humor*." The new format "sold out for twelve consecutive issues at the high price of 50¢ a copy. It was one of the great magazine success stories of the twenties."[19] Henneberger had a hit on his hands, and he knew he could have more. To do so, however, he decided to start his own publishing company.[20]

At the time, 1922, his friend John Lansinger had also found his way into the publishing world and was working for the magazine *Pictorial Review*. Henneberger pitched Lansinger the idea of going into partnership together and, after he agreed, they formed Rural Publications, Incorporated.[21] The first magazine they created was *Real Detective Tales and Mystery Stories*, and they hired Edwin Baird to serve as editor. Baird wanted to become a writer himself and sold stories to the Munsey pulps beginning in 1910. Although somewhat successful at first, he eventually went into the editing profession for a steady paycheck while continuing to write stories on the side.[22] He assumed the editorship of *Detective Tales* and ushered the first issue to the newsstands, where it landed in September of 1922.[23]

About that time Henneberger had been discussing the publishing world with four friends, all writers. "I discovered that all of them expressed a desire to submit for publication a story of the unconventional type but hesitated to do so for fear of rejection." They told him that "delving into the realm of fantasy, the bizarre, and the outré could possibly be frowned upon by publishers of the conventional."[24] Henneberger's love for Poe and similar types of stories motivated him to create Rural Publication's second magazine, which, as announced in December of 1922, would be titled *Weird Tales*.[25]

Henneberger added the new magazine to Baird's editorial duties, and Baird ushered this one to the newsstands as well. The first issue (dated March 1923) went on sale in February, was priced at twenty-five cents, measured six by nine inches, and was 192 pages long with twenty-four stories.[26] Baird wrote an editorial for the first issue in what would become the readers' forum—"The Eyrie." He wrote, "*Weird Tales* is not merely 'another new magazine.' It's a brand new type of new magazine—a sensational variation from the established rules that are supposed to govern magazine publishing. *Weird Tales*, in a word, is unique. In no other publication will you find the sort of stories that *Weird Tales* offers in this issue—and will continue to offer in the issues to come. Such stories are tabooed elsewhere."[27]

The first issue appears to have been successful with the readers, and the first letter to the editor, published in the next issue, was written by H. W. Sterling of Illinois. "*Weird Tales* seems to me to fill a long felt want in magazine circles. I have always delighted in stories of the 'Dracula' type and that Sax Rohmer stuff, and I never could understand why the editors didn't wake up. You, as a pioneer in the field, are giving them something to think about."[28] The new magazine, it seemed, was off to a good start.

There were problems, however, and they quickly began to mount. The first was the lack of quality submissions. Weinberg wrote that it was "lunatics and compulsive writers" who "filled the pages of the first thirteen issues of *Weird Tales*."[29] Certainly not high praise for the magazine's beginnings, but there were some promising authors among the lunatic fringe, including Otis Adelbert Kline, Seabury Quinn, Frank Owen, and H. P. Lovecraft.[30] The latter, however, only saw his stories accepted because Henneberger had discovered him in some of the small press publications he received.[31] Henneberger once explained, "I made it a point to read anything that Lovecraft submitted and it was published, sometimes over the objections of Baird."[32]

Henneberger's comment highlighted one of the many problems with Baird as editor. Weinberg called him a "less than an inspired editor," while *Weird Tales* author E. Hoffmann Price described him as "an idea man," for "once the magazine was going, he swiftly lost interest in it."[33] Baird was mostly publishing run-of-the-mill ghost stories, while Henneberger had envisioned the tales of Edgar Allan Poe.[34] To be fair, part of this was because of the poor submissions they received, which *Weird Tales* historian John Locke called "editor's hell."[35] Other problems included the fact that the pulp market had become saturated, the size of the magazine deviated from the industry standard and kept changing the first year, and while most pulps were selling for ten or fifteen cents an issue, *Weird Tales* was priced at twenty-five cents. Moreover, while they were trying to pay low rates to authors, such as one-third to one-half cent per word, some authors were receiving one cent per word. All of this culminated in the magazine not selling well, and by its first anniversary, it was approximately $40,000 in debt.[36]

Something had to change.

Henneberger first needed to deal with the debt in order to avoid bankruptcy. Since most of the debt was owed to the Cornelius Printing Company, Henneberger made a deal giving Cornelius control, with an agreement that if the debt was ever paid off, full ownership would revert back to him.[37] Next, Henneberger explains, "I sold *College Humor* and *Detective Tales* in order to clear up indebtedness and I stuck with *Weird Tales*."[38] He sold the two magazines to his partner, Lansinger, and so the company split into two.[39] As part of the deal, Baird was to go with Lansinger, so Henneberger now needed a new editor.

The first person he thought of was the author whose stories reminded him somewhat of Poe—H. P. Lovecraft.[40] Howard Phillips Lovecraft was born on August 20, 1890, in Providence, Rhode Island, in the family home on Angell Street. His father was a traveling salesman but suffered a mental breakdown and was committed to the Butler Hospital in Providence when Lovecraft was three.[41] Mr. Lovecraft never recovered and died on July 19, 1898, when Lovecraft was 8 years old. His mother lived on but was never quite the same after her husband's death, and two of Lovecraft's aunts, Lillian D. Clark and Annie E. Phillips Gamwell, as well as his maternal grandfather, Whipple Van Buren Phillips, helped raise him.

Lovecraft was a precocious child who recited poetry from memory at age 2, was reading by age 3, and was writing by age 7. He read voraciously and filled his hours with Grimm's fairy tales, the *Arabian Nights*, and Bulfinch's *Age of Fable*, becoming enamored with Greek and Roman mythology.[42] "Then," Lovecraft later recalled, "I struck EDGAR ALLAN POE!!

It was my downfall, and at the age of eight I saw the blue firmament of Argos and Sicily darkened by the miasmal exhaltation of the tomb!"[43] It was a pivotal moment in Lovecraft's life, for it helped launch his career writing supernatural horror.

Lovecraft received another blow to his family life when he was 14, for the grandfather who had helped raise him died. This also led to the loss of the family home, and Lovecraft's health began to decline. He attended school less and less, and in 1908, he, too, suffered a nervous breakdown. He withdrew from life for the next five years, never finished high school, and ceased writing during this period.[44]

Still, Lovecraft read, and it was during those five years that the pulp magazines began appearing on the newsstands, and he became an avid reader. This helped sustain Lovecraft through those dark years and because of this, in 1913, he became involved in amateur writing, from which, he confided, "I obtained a renewed will to live."[45] Through the encouragement of this literary circle, by 1917 he returned to writing weird tales. "I choose weird stories," he wrote, "because they suit my inclinations best," and they apparently suited Henneberger's inclinations as well, for he began reading Lovecraft during those early years.[46]

Perhaps because he was now writing, Lovecraft managed to endure his mother's nervous breakdown in 1919, her own committal to Butler Hospital for the next two years, and her final death from an unsuccessful gallbladder surgery on May 24, 1921. In fact, later that summer he attended an amateur writers' conference in Boston, where he met the widow Sonia Haft Greene, seven years his senior, and they eventually married on March 3, 1924. They moved into her apartment in Brooklyn, New York, and it was the first time Lovecraft had ever lived away from home. He was 34 years old.

After the first issue of *Weird Tales* appeared on the newsstands, Lovecraft's friends encouraged him to submit his work there.[47] He did so, and his story "Dagon" was accepted and published in the October 1923 issue. After the breakup of Rural Publications, when Henneberger needed a new editor, he wanted Lovecraft to fill the role, so he went to New York to offer him the job.[48] "He had tremendous admiration and respect for [Lovecraft]," recalled Tom Collins, "and would have made him editor."[49] Lovecraft himself explained later that Henneberger had told him the magazine would be "right in my line" and he wanted to know if "I would consider moving to Chicago to edit it!" He then exclaimed, "My gawd . . . bring the stretcher!"[50] Lovecraft had just married Sonia Greene and neither wanted to move to Chicago, so he declined the offer.

During this time Henneberger relied on two of *Weird Tales*' authors and manuscript readers who were local, Otis Adelbert Kline and Farnsworth Wright, to put together a "special anniversary issue" that would be dated May–June–July 1924[51] He hoped it would help buy the time he needed to settle both the financial and editorial issues of the magazine. Both of these men would continue to be associated with the magazine, but they also came to play a significant role in Robert E. Howard's life.

Otis Adelbert Kline was born in Chicago on July 1, 1891, and, like Lovecraft, was a precocious child, becoming an avid reader at age 5 "who enjoyed the adventure stories found in such magazines as *St. Nicholas* and *The Youth's Companion*."[52] He developed many interests in his childhood, including acting, singing, music, reading, writing, and illustrating, that left him unsure which career to pursue.[53] In the end he chose to follow his father into the business world.[54] His father worked for the company of Massey & Massey, the manufacturers of flavored syrups, especially those used for ice cream (today the company is known as Nielsen-Massey). After attending Brown's Business College, Kline married and joined the company. The job proved very flexible and, as Kline explained, "My evenings were my own. I decided to use them for the improvement of what I optimistically called my mind."[55] Having fallen in love with the stories of Edgar Rice Burroughs, Kline decided to try writing science fiction, submitting his first story to *Weird Tales* magazine, which Baird accepted for publication. Since he was in Chicago, Kline soon found himself involved on the publishing side of things by helping to read the slush pile of unsolicited manuscripts and editing the transition issue. Kline was evidently well liked, and people thought highly of him, for as fellow author E. Hoffmann Price once wrote, "Kline's expression and carriage indicated self-assurance. His manner, hearty and cordial, was that of a man who had been meeting life and the world with justified confidence, loving both."[56]

Farnsworth Wright was born in Santa Barbara, California, on July 29, 1888, to George Francis Wright and Genevieve Farnsworth Hard.[57] He was the third of four children, but not long after the last child was born, his father's lungs hemorrhaged, and he died on August 20, 1892. His mother began teaching music lessons to make ends meet, and the family moved to San Francisco in 1900.[58] In addition to developing a love of music from his mother, Wright became interested in writing, publishing, debate, languages, and acting while in school. When the Great San Francisco Earthquake struck on April 18, 1906, they were fortunate to be living outside of the city, but with the economy destroyed, his mother left for Reno, Nevada, while Wright stayed behind to graduate from high school in 1908. After graduation he joined the family in Reno and attended the University of Nevada, but after his mother remarried, Wright left for the University of Washington in Seattle to finish his degree.

In 1913 Wright faced several tragedies. The first came while swimming in the ocean with a friend who drowned, leaving him with survivor's guilt, and at the end of the year, he received a telegram that his mother had suddenly died.[59] However, he threw himself into his studies, and during his last two years in college, he served on the staff of the university newspaper, and in his final year, he was the managing editor. This opened doors, for after graduating in May of 1914, he went to work for the *Seattle Sun* and the following year became a reporter for the *Chicago Tribune*. Not finding the work of a reporter to his taste, Wright began working for the New York–based weekly *Musical America*, becoming their Chicago music critic. Because the job paid well and was not too demanding, he began writing stories for such publications as the *Overland Monthly*. When America became part of the Great War, Wright was called to serve in the American Expeditionary Force, and because of his ability to speak French, he was assigned as an interpreter.[60] He returned home to Chicago after the war, picking up where he had left off, although he did come down with what has been described as a "mild case of sleeping sickness," or encephalitis lethargica.[61] The disease was not well understood then or now, but like so many others who had sleeping disease at the time, Wright learned two years later he had Parkinson's Disease.[62] It did not, at first, inhibit him, and he continued to submit stories on the side, including one to *Weird Tales*, which Baird accepted, and because of his proximity, he too became a reader of the slush pile.[63]

The only other assistance available after Baird left was Bill Sprenger, the business manager of *Weird Tales*. He had been with Henneberger since 1919, and although he would have a long run with the magazine, it is said he never read an issue.[64] E. Hoffmann Price, who also knew Sprenger, once described him as "short, solid, all alive and alert, pleasant yet entirely business."[65] He did not help with the slush pile.

Together, they successfully put out the May-June-July 1924 issue, but the future of the magazine was still uncertain. Still, Kline put on a good face and wrote an editorial about the type of story the magazine published—"The weird story and the highly imaginative story"—and he suggested that *Weird Tales* would be around for the future.[66] Although Henneberger likely considered Kline for the editor position, he knew he could not compete with what he was making at Massey & Massey. So in the end Henneberger decided to replace Baird with Wright. "Farnsworth Wright was the ideal editor," Henneberger later explained, for "he combined a rare wit with a thorough knowledge of literature and understanding of writers especially those in whom he sensed a promise."[67]

Those who had come to know the *Weird Tales*' editor usually described him in the same manner. Wallace West recalled him as a "tall, charming man and as thin as a ghost," while Price remembered him as "tall, very tall, and somewhat stooped from bending low to deal with persons of ordinary height, a large framed, long legged man, conspicuously bald."[68] Another, Richard F. Searight, described him in the same manner but also added that he had "the typical hand tremor and facial expression of Parkinson's disease."[69] Wright, however, never let the disease bother him, at least not publicly, as demonstrated by Jack Williamson's approbation when he wrote of Wright, "I always admired the determination and the cheery courage with which he kept the magazine going in spite of that disabling handicap."[70] In fact, Wright was often remembered for his fondness for humor. "Wright's humor covered the entire spectrum," wrote Price. "Nothing was too subtle and nothing too bawdy."[71] His favorite, it seems, were puns, for he never passed up the chance to tell one, though, as Price commented,

"He never disputed the contention to the effect that puns were the lowest form of wit, and he never gave the impression of thinking them either clever or witty. They merely amused him." He also loved words, which is why the editor's position fit him so well.[72]

As editor John Pelan said, Wright "truly made *Weird Tales* 'the unique magazine,'" and developed a process for reviewing every story that came into the *Weird Tales*' office.[73] "It's really not necessary to read each dud to the horrible ending," he once said, for he believed, "If they don't come to life within the first two pages, they'll remain zombies to the finish."[74] If Wright felt the story had some merit, he would place a C on the manuscript cover and place it aside or take it home for a "careful read." If he still thought the story was good after doing so, he would accept it for publication. If he had any doubts, he rejected it. Wright estimated that only about two stories out of one hundred submitted were actually accepted, although there could be long stretches of time when no stories were accepted, and then he might find six acceptable stories in one day. And even though Kline, and later Price, assisted Wright by reading stories in the slush pile, Wright was the "sole arbitrator" and "from his decision there [was] no appeal."[75] While he had catholic tastes himself, Wright also showed deference to what the readers liked. "Often I buy a story because I like it," Wright explained, "but always, I am obliged to first consider whether my readers would like that yarn. Many a time, I've accepted things which I did not care for, but which I felt would please many of the readers."[76] And, like John Pelan once said, Wright had "an eye for talent."[77] He was instrumental in discovering numerous authors, including C. L. Moore, Henry Kuttner, Robert Bloch, Seabury Quinn, and Pulitzer Prize–winning author Tennessee Williams. His most important discovery, however, and the one he is still remembered for today is Robert E. Howard.

After Wright took over, his first issue hit the newsstands that fall. As the historian of *Weird Tales*' early years, John Locke, explains, "When readers rediscovered *Weird Tales* on the newsstands in October 1924, they found a completely reconfigured format."[78] The magazine now met the industry standard and, other than stylistic changes, remained the same under Wright's editorship.

One of the most challenging issues he faced was, of course, the debt. "When Sprenger and Wright took over," recalled Kline, "the magazine was so deeply in debt they wouldn't pay more than 1/2¢ a word to anybody," but "by careful selection of stories during the next few years, and by keeping all expenses down to a minimum while living on starvation wages themselves, Sprenger and Wright managed to pull the magazine out of its financial hole, and it started on a new era of prosperity, along about 1926."[79]

The other issue Wright faced was office space. They were then in the Baldwin Building in Indianapolis, Indiana, but they had to move into the Holliday Building when the other was torn down. In late 1926 the editorial office moved to Chicago, and resided at 3810 N. Broadway before settling into 840 N. Michigan, where they would remain during Howard's writing career. About the time Howard began publishing with *Weird Tales*, the magazine was starting to stabilize. And so, as Weinberg explains, "Under the steady hand of these two men, Wright and Sprenger, *Weird Tales* began to make progress."[80]

This certainly proved fortuitous for Howard, who had developed a deep respect for Farnsworth Wright as *Weird Tales*' editor. "You gave me my start in the racket by buying my first story," Howard wrote Wright, before adding, "I was eighteen years old at the time."[81] Howard also candidly told a fellow author what he thought of Wright, when he explained later in his career, "I have had dealings with many editors in the years I have been writing, and I have never encountered a squarer, fairer gentleman than he."[82] What he especially liked was the liberal policy for stories and poems under Wright, for Howard recognized, "You can build your own plot, scenery, characters, and everything; and you're not chained down by any limits."[83] He once sent Wright a purely psychological story, "The Fearsome Touch of Death," and told Smith he believed, "No other magazine except *Weird Tales* would publish such a story." Giving as his evidence, Howard offered, "I know because I tried most of them with this one."[84] He also praised Wright in the same manner for his acceptance of poetry, writing, "I find *Weird Tales* much more liberal regarding verse than most poetry magazines."[85] Howard summarized his appreciation for both Wright and *Weird Tales* when he stated, "It is the only magazine in the world, so far as I know, in which the writer can give full sway to his imagination."[86]

Howard was not the only *Weird Tales* author who spoke highly of Wright. Manly Wade Wellman once called Wright "the best editor I ever had" because "he was constructively critical."[87] Edmond Hamilton called him "the best fantastic fiction editor" primarily "because he uses catholic standards in judging a story."[88] Many of the authors appreciated his feedback on their stories, such as Greye La Spina, who called him the "finest editor I ever met," while explaining "his letters to me were enthusiastic and inspiring."[89] And even in the case of rejection, Mary Elizabeth Counselman said she appreciated the words he used in those letters, while Wallace West was left to comment, "Wright was one of the few editors I have known who could write a letter of rejection that bore no sting."[90] And like Howard, Frank Belknap Long was also given his start in the pulp magazines by Wright, and recalled Wright as "a powerful germinal influence from the very beginning."[91] Wright would create such a positive environment for *Weird Tales* magazine that Edmond Hamilton commented, "When I think of *Weird Tales*, I don't think of a magazine, or of the stories, but of people. People like Wright, earnest, grave, utterly devoted to literature and trying to get as good a quality of it as he could into the magazine."[92] This is exactly how historian Sam Moskowitz described Wright's abilities when he wrote, "Some magazines have a soul. *Weird Tales* was such a magazine. Few periodicals ever inspired such loyalty from its authors and such devotion from its readers."[93]

The letter column "The Eyrie" provided a place where readers could express their devotion to the magazine and its authors. As historian Brian Murphy wrote, it "offered stewardship, encouragement, and pruning. *Weird Tales* shaped and informed its writers' craft of creative minds, a creative community that fed off itself and drove one another to new heights of imagination."[94] Wright used the forum to share his editorial insights and to encourage his readers to send in their letters and votes for the best story of each issue. He kept track of the votes and reported the results two issues later, usually presenting what had been the top three stories.[95] And not only did Wright publish letters from the readers, but he also published letters from *Weird Tales* authors in which they shared their own insights into their favorite stories. In a sense it created a forum that attracted readers and writers in a setting where they could meet as equals. One *Weird Tales* author,

Hugh B. Cave, called this attraction the "Weirditis bug," when he wrote, "The Eyrie got me, and that settled it. In my doubtful opinion I think The Eyrie is the thing that magnetizes us. No other magazine makes such a point of discussing past stories and letting the authors know how their stuff is received."[96]

In addition to serving as a mechanism by which Wright could gauge reader reception of authors and stories, it also proved to be the well from which he could draw new authors, as he did through his commentary on a potential story that became Howard's "Spear and Fang."[97] When Wright first took over as editor, he had placed ads in many of the professional trade magazines, encouraging authors to submit their stories to *Weird Tales*, but within a year, as Locke explains, "The Eyrie became his one and only forum to attract new talent, from the only pool that mattered to him, the fans and readers of *Weird Tales*."[98]

Howard's "foolish timidity" caused him to submit stories to other pulp magazines in the hopes of opening up new markets for himself. "He wrote two stories about the prize ring that he submitted to a sports story monthly," he wrote in *Post Oaks*, "and a short tale of the West which he sent to a magazine dealing exclusively in Wild West stories." Roehm and Burke have identified the Western story as "44-40 or Fight," submitted to *Western Story*, and one of the prize ring yarns submitted to *Sport Story* was "The Fighting Dumbbell." "To his amazement," Howard continued, "all three tales were rejected with only stereotyped slips to explain the phenomenon." What Howard did not know at the time was that he was in the same situation as other *Weird Tales* authors. "Quite a few of my colleagues in that *Weird Tales* Club were in the same fix," Price explained.[99] "We made it with the readers of the 'Unique Magazine,' but we did not have what it took to crash the big time pulps."[100] Because of this, Howard "decided to return to [*Weird Tales*]."[101]

He submitted "The Trail of the Single Foot," "Drums of Horror," "The Streets of Grey-Beards," and "Windigo! Windigo!" to Wright in 1925. All were rejected. He would continue sending in more stories over the next two years, including "No Man Needs Three Hands" and "Vulture's Roost" in 1926 and "The Valley of the Golden Web" and "Sanctuary of the Sun" in 1927. Again, all of them were rejected.[102] Howard, no doubt, felt like his hero, Jack London, at the beginning of his writing career, who had voiced his own frustrations in *Martin Eden*: "He struggled in the dark, without advice, without encouragement, and in the teeth of discouragement."[103]

Howard's depression, however, had a brief reprieve in June of 1925, when the July issue of *Weird Tales* hit the newsstands, and he finally saw his name in print. Past the cover illustrating H. Warner Munn's "The Werewolf of Ponkert," and buried on page 111, with no accompanying artwork, was his story "Spear and Fang" with the subtitle "A Tale of the Caveman" and the byline "By Robert E. Howard."[104] "This was a pinnacle in [Bob]'s life," Howard wrote in *Post Oaks*. "He sat and stared at his name in print for hours at a time, thrilling to his finger tips. He could scarcely believe it, and at times feared that it was, after all, a gorgeous dream from which he would too soon awaken."[105]

Dr. Howard was certainly proud of his son, for as Leroy Butler recalled, when his stories first started appearing on the magazine rack in the drugstore where he worked, "Doctor Howard would come in [and] he'd leave, say, eight or ten on the rack, but he would buy all the rest of 'em."[106] And two months later, Howard would receive another thrill when his name appeared in "The Eyrie." "In casting about for a kind of mild sedative I ran across 'Spear and Fang' by Robert E. Howard—a good story of our remote ancestors before the dawn of civilization and intelligence, when man's reasoning powers were in the formative state."[107] Of course that thrill may have been mitigated somewhat because it had been written by his cousin Earl C. Comer at his request, but still, he had made "The Eyrie" for the first time.[108] It would not be his last.

Chapter 10

On Werewolves and Horror Yarns, 1925

There are strange tales told when the full moon shines
Of voodoo nights when the ghost-things ran—
But the strangest figure among the pines
Was Kelly the conjure-man.
—"Kelly the Conjure-Man"[1]

In July of 1925, when the August issue of *Weird Tales* hit the newsstands, Howard had a story in the magazine for the second month in a row. Not buried as deep in the issue as his first, but still with no illustrations, Howard's short story "In the Forest of Villefère" featured his name and noted he was "The author of 'Spear and Fang.'"[2] The story takes place in France and is an unusual werewolf tale, being one of the earliest to suggest a man afflicted with lycanthropy turns into a man with the features of a wolf, rather than a common wolf, when "the moon hovered close to her zenith."[3] These later became standard tropes in nearly all werewolf tales.

Earlier in the spring, after submitting stories to other publishers, Howard had returned to *Weird Tales*, but again, with little success. He sent five more stories to Wright, who rejected all of them. Howard "could not understand," as he wrote in *Post Oaks*. "Something was wrong here. The editor sometimes pointed out faults which seemed minor," but nonetheless Wright said they "did not suit." While Howard was trying to figure out what to do, he "came upon a short story he had written earlier and laid aside." It was "In the Forest of Villefère," and he sent the story to *Weird Tales*. When Wright replied that he was accepting it, Howard was "jubilant."[4] The month after it published, he received a check for eight dollars; the story had only been two-and-a-half pages long.

Howard encouraged Smith to write a letter to the editor about the story, which he did, and Wright later wrote Howard, telling him that he had received a letter from a "Clyde Smith" in Brownwood, praising the story before adding, "Personally I think it was a gem."[5] Motivated by Wright's praise, Howard set about writing a sequel he titled "Wolfshead," in which the same character, having contracted lycanthropy, struggles with the curse but ultimately redeems himself through an act of bravery resulting in his death.[6] This time Wright replied that the story "made the mark in great style," and he accepted "Wolfshead" for forty dollars. Howard wrote he "shot to dizzy heights of rapture" and "felt like a millionaire. Forty dollars! And all for a few hours' work on the typewriter. It seemed so simple—so much like a dream."[7]

These two yarns became his first published horror stories, a genre in which he wrote for the rest of his career, and one at which he excelled. Many of his stories outside the genre would still incorporate many of these same elements, especially his sword-and-sorcery stories, thus demonstrating the importance of his discovery of these tales at a young age.[8] Although the type of horror yarns he wrote changed over time, the source of his success proved mainly to come from the region in which he lived and the people who were closest to him.

One of Howard's early influences had certainly been "old Aunt Mary Bohannon," the family's cook when they lived in Bagwell. "Mary was a story-teller, well versed in the legend and lore of her African heritage," wrote Sharon Black, and although "she could not pass that lore to her own descendants, she could and did implant those legends into the mind of an impressionable Robert Howard."[9] At the same time, another Bagwell resident and former slave, Arabella Davis, who Howard had encountered as a local laundress and described as a "black philosopher," shared her stories with him as well. She told him tales of her conversion and the time she went into a ten-day trance in which "for four days she hung in the cobwebs of the gates of Hell, and the hounds of Hell bayed at her."[10]

He also recalled meeting Mrs. Crawford, who Howard described as "one of the old settlers of the country," writing that "many a time, as a child have I listened to her telling strange tales of old times." She shared many of the stories she heard throughout her life, "of doors in the old ranch-house that opened and closed without human agency, of an old chair rocking to and fro in the night in an empty room." Howard relished these stories and listened attentively, for he once wrote, "Any touch of supernatural always effected [*sic*] me as a child."[11]

The tales that gave him "the horrors," however, appear to have been those told by his grandmother, Louisa "Eliza" Howard.[12] A very genteel Southern lady who always wore her gloves when she was in public and carried her Bible to church every Sunday, she had gone blind in her later years after her cataract surgery failed.[13] "Her tales showed what a strange legion of folk-lore grew up in the Scotch-Irish settlements of the Southwest, where transplanted Celtic myths and fairy-tales met and mingled with a sub-stratem of slave legends," Howard explained, adding that she also "knew by heart all the tales and superstitions of the folks, black or white, about her."[14] Howard recounted the one story that scared him the most: "As a child my hair used to stand straight up when she would tell of the wagon that moved down wilderness roads in the dark of night, with never a horse drawing it—the wagon that was full of severed heads and dismembered limbs."[15]

There were others who influenced him later in life—the people he met who shared their stories, usually storytellers much older than him. One such person was his future girlfriend's grandmother, who beguiled Howard with her stories of life on the frontier, but he "was especially interested in the old ghost and witch stories she told. Those were a gold mine."[16] Howard once explained how "the world is full of unexplained incidents and peculiar circumstances," and he believed "the logical reasons for which are often so obscure and hidden that they are lent an illusion of the supernatural."[17] Regardless of their origins, however, it was the supernatural aspects of these stories that came to be a mainstay of his writing.

At first Howard drew on traditional legends for his horror tales, specifically those about lycanthropy, for werewolves filled his first two publications, while one more titled "The Hyena" featured a unique case of lycanthropy, a were-hyena. Although accepted for publication, it did not see print until 1928.[18] Soon after, his horror yarns were influenced by other authors.

"Most young writers are, of course, inclined to emulate other writers whom they admire or respect," explains Burke, "and Howard was no exception."[19] At first Howard fell for Welsh writer Arthur Machen's supernatural stories of "the little people," a lost race of subterranean dwellers, which is evident with Howard's story "The Little People," a yarn that went unpublished in his lifetime.[20] Later, as H. P. Lovecraft's cosmic-horror stories became popular, Howard wrote a number of tales in what has come to be known as the Cthulhu Mythos (chapter 20).[21] But it was after he returned to his roots that he began writing regional horror based on the stories he had heard in his youth.

"When we approach this 'regional' fiction," explains Burke, "we find that there are two distinct groups. One, the larger group of stories, we might term 'Texan' or 'Southwestern' fiction." He wrote these stories as a mixing of genres, a practice he would make into an art form, between his slightly more traditional Westerns and his horror stories (chapter 22). "The other, a smaller group," Burke continues, "might be termed 'Southern' or perhaps more specifically 'Piney Woods' tales."[22] These tales drew upon the stories he had heard growing up and included such titles as "Moon of Zambebwei," "Black Hound of Death," and "The Shadow of the Beast."[23] In these stories he wrote of the piney woods he had roamed during his Bagwell years, such as in the latter when he wrote, "There is no darkness in the world so utterly devoid of light as the blackness of the pine woods. The silent trees rose like basaltic walls about me, shutting out the stars. Except for the occasional eery sigh of an owl, the silence was as absolute as the darkness."[24] As Burke articulates, "Howard proves a master at describing a setting in a few words," for he could not only convey a description in those few scant lines, but also set a mood.[25] Howard once said to a friend, "Listen. Listen to the night sounds. I tell you . . . in sound is reality. As long as you can hear sound, you're alive," suggesting, as Burke points out, "If you hear sound, you're alive; if you hear silence, you're dead."[26] This captures not only how far Howard's ability as a horror writer would develop but also how he managed to capture the things he saw, heard, and experienced, and retell them in his own stories.

The Piney Woods tales were all written late in Howard's career, and his two most noted stories in this grouping, "Black Canaan" and "Pigeons from Hell," were both submitted in the latter half of 1934. The former was published in *Weird Tales*, dated the month he died, and was likely the last issue of the magazine he ever saw, while the latter was published posthumously. "Black Canaan" was based on the stories he had heard about the powers of the conjure-man while Howard was growing up; the conjure-man was a practitioner of voodoo magic, a figure well familiar to former slaves in the early twentieth century.[27] "Probably the most picturesque figure in the Holly Springs country was Kelly the 'conjer man,'" explained Howard in a letter, "who held sway among the black population in the [18]70s."[28] He described him as the "son of a Congo ju-ju man" who "dwelt apart from his race in silent majesty on the river."[29] Although Wright liked the story, he asked Howard to cut it down, for which Howard lamented, "I cut so much of the guts out of it, in response to editorial requirements, that in its published form it won't much resemble the original theme, woven about the mysterious figure of Kelly the Conjur-man."[30] Still, Lovecraft called the story "a clutchingly powerful picture of the horror that stalks through the moss-hung, shadow-cursed, serpent-ridden swamps of the far south," and the readers of *Weird Tales* found the story to their liking.[31] Gertrude Hemken of Chicago called it "perfect, the kind one reads with eyes popping and mouth agape," while Charles H. Bert of Philadelphia said it was "without a doubt the best story in the issue."[32] They were not alone, either, for the story was tied for first place in the reader poll.[33]

What has come to be recognized as Howard's "finest horror story" is assuredly "Pigeons from Hell."[34] The basis of the story was first told to him by Mary Bohannon and was one he had heard in many variations, including from his grandmother.[35] "Two or three men . . . travelling in a wagon through some isolated district," Howard explained, "come on to the ruins of a once thriving plantation at dusk, and decide to spend the night in the deserted plantation house. The house is always huge, brooding and forbidding, and always, as the men approach the high columned verandah, through the high weeds that surround the house, great numbers of pigeons rise from their roosting places on the railing and fly away."[36] In his own story, two young men, Griswell and Branner, come across the old, seemingly abandoned Blassenville Manor and decide to stop there for the night. Like the stories he had heard, Howard wrote, "They left the automobile beside the rutty road, and as they went up the winding walk of crumbling bricks, almost lost in the tangle of rank growth, pigeons rose from the balustrades in a fluttering, feathery crowd and swept away with a low thunder of beating wings."[37] Although pigeons may not seem horrific, as the story unfolds, Howard tells how the pigeons should not have been there at all, but that local legend believed that when they are seen, "the gates of hell are open, and the Blassenvilles fly out."[38]

Howard also incorporated the themes in the story that were told to him of the horrific background of the plantation houses "and the human or semi-human horror, with its severed head [which] was woven in the fiber of the myths."[39] And from his own background, Burke suggests that the Blassenville sisters in the story may well have been inspired by the Durel sisters he had met in New Orleans.[40]

When the story was finally published in May of 1938, it was well received by the readers. "The whole tale is too shuddery," wrote Hemken from Chicago, "one of those things that makes some folks have nitemares."[41] Donald Allgeier of Missouri wrote that it was a story "that really caused the goose pimples," while Margaret Warren of Columbus, Ohio, called it "just too scary" for she read it on a dark, rainy night, recalling, "I walked every stair with Griswell, and all night I heard steps in the hall and on the stairs."[42]

In addition to Howard's vivid descriptions and ability to set mood, one additional factor regarding his stories is demonstrated in his earliest, such as "Wolfshead," to his last, like "Pigeons from Hell": he was an adventure writer, and his characters, in the words of Burke, "refuse to give up or to run away, no matter how heavily the odds are stacked against them."[43] Many horror stories feature characters so gripped with fear that they become victims of their fate. Not so in a Howard story, for his characters almost always fought back. As horror scholar Dennis Rickard explained, Howard's "characters were 'doers' who put themselves in control of their fate, whose moments of fear of the unknown, if any, passed quickly into action."[44] And when all of these elements were put together, Howard created stories that placed him in a class nearly all by himself. H. P. Lovecraft saw this in Howard's writing, for he once wrote in a letter, "He was almost alone in his ability to create real emotions of fear and of dread suspense. . . . For stark, living fear . . . the actual smell and feel and darkness and brooding horror and impending doom that inhere in that knighted, moss-hung jungle . . . what other writer is even in the running with REH?"[45]

Despite having several stories accepted in *Weird Tales*, Howard began feeling a financial strain early in 1925 because the magazine did not pay until after publication. "Occasionally [Bob] went to the movies, but he did not always have any money," Howard wrote in *Post Oaks*. "His mother kept him supplied with small change, but the [Howard] family was poor, and it was a strain on their resources."[46] Because of this his parents suggested he look for a job, but as Howard explained, he "shook off the suggestion with irritation. Who would piddle with a one horse-job when he was about to burst into the golden glory of fame and fortune by means of his sapphire pen?"[47] However, by March, having not burst into glory, he began looking for that one-horse job.

On St. Patrick's Day, Howard wrote to Smith, "I'm writing oil news for a bunch of papers now. . . . Five bucks per column."[48] He worked out of the *Cross Plains Review* office, which then sent out the news he wrote to the "various Texas and Oklahoma papers."[49] In order to learn the language of the oil industry, Howard visited many of the drilling sites and talked with the roughnecks who did the work. Norris Chambers, whose family had recently moved back to Cross Cut, recalled some of Howard's visits to the family, who was experiencing an oil boom at the time. "Robert made several trips to our house, and we took him to drilling rigs where he was interested in finding out all he could about how drilling was done. He made notes about the terms used to describe the various tools and operations around the projects."[50]

Howard "worked at the newspaper game," he wrote in *Post Oaks*, and though he was writing and possibly publishing his oil-field news, it was not the type of story he wanted to compose, for he "hated all work except writing fiction." Moreover, because Howard "did nothing now except hammer the typewriter and hunt up oil news," he was no longer exercising or writing fiction but interviewing "roughnecks and arrogant promoters," which he despised.[51] Still, he was making the better part of one hundred dollars a month and was now able to contribute to the family, pay for niceties, and put a little money into savings.[52]

The only problem with the oil news position was it was dependent on activity in the oil business, which could wax and wane. By summer it was on the wane, so he began hunting for a new job, which he found in "packing a rod for a geologist."[53] Howard wrote about his experience in *Post Oaks*. "His duties were simple yet arduous. He carried a long narrow board hinged in the middle of convenience in carrying, and painted something like a flat barber's pole. This was called a rod. The object was to find a ledge of limestone, which was supposed to indicate oil, and follow it through its various torturous meanderings." On the first day, he recalled how all the hiking "rubbed great blisters on his heels which peeled off and never healed the two months he worked."[54] Each night, he would find his feet had been bloodied by the day's work, and he quickly came to despise this job more than writing oil news. After two months of this, on a hot summer day in Central Texas, he was trudging across the sunbaked landscape, thirsty, tired, and carrying all of the geologist's equipment, when his heart began troubling him. At that moment he thought "God, I'd pay high for an ice cream soda," and he knew he was done. "No more for me," he wrote in *Post Oaks*. "Geologizin' can go to hell. I'm goin' to get a job in town—in an office, where I can step out and get somethin' cold to drink when I'm thirsty."[55] So he quit and found the job he described, which was working in a law office.

Because Howard had typing and, ostensibly, stenography skills, he landed a job in an abstract office working as a stenographer for Paul V. Harrell, an attorney whose office was on the second floor of the Guaranty State Bank building.[56] "He was to get 30 dollars the first month, 40 the next, and so on, with a gradual increase in salary as he grew in usefulness," Howard wrote in

Post Oaks.[57] It also helped that he had a new typewriter, for his own, "originally a second-hand one, was worn out, and he bought another, spending all the money he had saved."[58] Once he began working, however, he soon found he "was a singularly inefficient stenographer," and he "made countless mistakes and was untidy and careless, and extremely absent-minded." It also did not help that "he hated the job and made no bones about saying so."[59] Fairly quickly, Harrell realized he needed to let Howard go, but he was kind in offering him office space to set up his own private enterprise "for typing other people's business letters, oil leases, and deeds."[60]

Not long after he started working there, Howard had the idea to play a practical joke on his friend Smith. Taking a page of legal stationary with the official letterhead "Paul V. Harrell, Attorney-at-Law," he set about typing up a fictitious court summons for Smith.[61] "The defendant CLYDE SMITH," it began, "minor of Brownwood, Texas is hearby [*sic*] summoned to appear before the Court of Brownwood Texas there to answer charges brought to and against said defendant. . . . Charge of Rape." On the next page, Howard wrote, "HAW! HAW! HAW! HAW! HAW! HAW! HAW! HAW! Old boy I bet you could hear the penitentiary doors clank behind you. Yes, *I'm* working in a Law office now."[62] He then placed the summons in the mail.

Smith apparently did not reply to the letter, and Howard became suspicious that he was going to pull something on him. On the weekend of July 10, Howard went to Brownwood to pay his friends a visit and, arriving late, he spent the night at Smith's house.[63] Smith told him that his girlfriend, Echla Laxson, wanted to meet him.[64] Naturally, that sounded suspicious to Howard.[65] Smith had known Laxson for several years, but they had only recently begun dating.[66] He was a senior at the time, and she a junior.[67] One person who knew them remarked that "they were always together," while another said that they were always so close to one another, "You couldn't have slipped a piece of paper sideways between them."[68]

The next morning, Howard, Smith, and Vinson went to pick up Laxson.[69] She was waiting on the curb when they drove up, and Howard observed she was "a slim passionate brunette [of] seventeen." After they were introduced, she remarked that she liked his stories, to which he coyly replied, "The inspiration of beautiful women." If she could play the part of seductress,

Howard could play his role, too. Because Howard himself admitted he was not a ladies' man, this no doubt took his friends by surprise.[70] Smith and Vinson made sure Howard and Laxson were sitting together in the car, no doubt "so they could talk," and they began driving. Suddenly, Laxson turned to Howard and asked, "Why are you afraid of women?" to which Howard responded by laughing, reaching out, and kissing her. He then told what happened next in *Post Oaks*, "She gasped. [Clyde] froze, [and Bob] felt a fierce wave of triumph."[71] Smith, "being a good loser," Howard explained "busted out laughing" and they later admitted to him that they had set him up. The plan had been for her to throw her arms around him and say, "You old dear, I've loved you all my life!" but Howard beat her to the punch.[72]

Howard went home on Sunday evening, July 12, and, having regrets for his actions, considered writing Smith a letter of apology. As he was typing, a fire broke out in town, and because, he wrote, "A fire was in the way of being a public entertainment," like everyone else, Howard went out to watch.[73] A garage and paint shop had caught fire, and soon the Cross Plains fire engine arrived on scene.[74] Howard wrote that they connected their firehose to the plug, "one of the two that the town boasted" and "the water was turned on," and then, "nothing happened."[75] There was little in the way of water in the Cross Plains supply and the building burned to the ground.

Howard returned to writing his letter but tore it up and started over. He mailed the letter the following day, when he also received a letter from Vinson, who told him, "You went too far," followed by a similar letter from Smith. Feeling despondent over the incident and not wanting to lose his friends, he went to his office on Main Street, sat down, and began writing a reply.[76]

"I got your letter," he wrote Smith, "I can't say that it made me feel cheap and mean because I already felt so much that way that nothing could have made me feel more so." He explained further, "I've hated myself ever since, the only extenuating principles being that it was absolutely unintentional and I didn't have sense enough to know that I was being a damn fool."[77] Howard was clearly in a dark mood. "I sat and thought," one passage began, "My thoughts ran, shall I live and continue to be a failure, to grind my life out and at least pass on, a failure, among failures *or*?" He explained the "or" in the next line when he wrote, "I really never expected to leave that office when

I entered it, alive."[78] He wrote of his "silent battle" that night but fortunately he did not succumb to his dark thoughts, for as he stated, "To have done what I considered would have been to admit that I was licked."[79] Still, it is likely the first time he had considered suicide as an option.

Smith called him on the telephone after receiving the disturbing letter. However, when they spoke, Smith inquired about things such as when he was coming back to Brownwood next and the status of his health. "Rather than resolve the issue," Burke explains, "it seems they settled upon the expedient of simply not mentioning it ever again."[80]

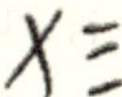

"Hot zowie, old topper, we've got the makings of another real oil boom," Howard wrote to Smith after learning of the likelihood that oil might soon be discovered in town. The possibility was made real in July of 1925, when "The oil boom struck [Cross] Plains overnight."[81] The oil field was discovered at the north end of town, and the excitement caused the population of Cross Plains to quickly double.[82] "If you come, you'll have a good chance of seeing a near–boom town for the townsite well I was telling you about came in for 400 barrels and everybody's oil-crazy," Howard told his friend. "Every big company in Texas has men in town and leases are changing hands so fast it makes you dizzy."[83] Suddenly, Howard found his typing services in demand, and for most of July he was working long days writing oil news and making some additional money typing for the oil companies. "The rush of the boom," Howard wrote in another letter, "People wild with oil, oil, oil! Working day and night, no sleep, little food."[84] And then, it was all over.

The townsite discovery had only been a small field, one-half square mile, so the oil quickly ran out.[85] Oil news became scarce again, and Howard found that his typing services were no longer needed, although they still wanted to make use of his typewriter. "These guys don't wait to hire me to write their stuff, they fight over the typewriter, figuratively speaking."[86] Once again, Howard found himself low on cash and looking for other job opportunities.

In late summer Howard was offered a job in the Cross Plains Post Office by the postmaster, Chess W. Barr. "The postmaster, a lanky dolt with a predilection for petty graft and loose women," Howard wrote in *Post Oaks*, who "offered to pay him $80.00 a month, providing he would work a month first to learn the business." The promise of steady money was too good for Howard, so he took the job, only to find out that after working one month for free, the postmaster then told him "he could pay only $40.00 a month."[87] Howard was incensed, writing Barr had made "a lifelong enemy," and he did not keep the job long. He then tried working for the local gas company, but he had to quit that job as well because, he explained, "I wouldn't kow-tow to my employer and 'yes' him from morning till night." He elaborated on his reasons later in a letter: "That's one reason I was never successful in working for people. So many men think an employee is a kind of servant. I'm good-natured and easy-going. I detest and shrink from rows of all sort, but there's no sense in a man swallowing everything."[88] Howard greatly treasured his freedom and independence and could not bring himself to become subservient to others. So he was back to working as a public stenographer and typist.

Throughout the summer business proved scarce, but it did afford him the opportunity to write. After Vinson brought back his amateur paper, *The Toreador*, Howard began publishing his own that he titled the *Right Hook.*[89] In his three issues, which were sent out between March and July of 1925, Howard wrote a variety of items on boxing, including short pieces on heavyweight champions such as John L. Sullivan and his favorite, Jack Dempsey.[90]

As fall settled in that year, Smith had now graduated from high school and enrolled at Daniel Baker College in Brownwood, where he intended on majoring in English.[91] Truett Vinson, near the beginning of summer, had secured a job with the Walker-Smith Company, a wholesale grocer, also in Brownwood.[92] Howard continued to visit with them as often as he could, and in between they exchanged letters. On one of his visits, Howard cowrote a story with Smith titled "Diogenes of Today" about a man who finds his city girlfriend a cheat and decides to go to the country, where he believes the girls are innocent; he finds out differently.[93] They sent it to *College Humor* and it was rejected.

Howard and his family also occasionally visited the Chamberses in Cross Cut. "Usually, just Dr. Howard and Robert would come," Norris Chambers recalled, "but sometimes all three would come on Sunday and eat dinner with us."[94] One of Howard's interests was shooting pistols, and people in Cross

Cut were less fickle about someone shooting targets in that town than in Cross Plains. Chambers recalled watching Howard on such occasions. "He would line up cans and shoot at them at a distance of about 75 to 100 feet. He could do pretty good by aiming the pistol, but in the fast draw type of shooting he very seldom hit a can. In this type of shooting (pointing without aiming) he often would shoot at a tree about the diameter of a man, and when he would hit it, which was pretty often, he would say 'Take that, you villain,' or something to that effect."[95]

Another pastime Howard took up was drinking alcohol. As he interacted with many of the roughnecks at the law office in Cross Plains, they often brought along various types of liquor and bottled beer despite it still being Prohibition. At first he "hesitantly experimented," but soon, he wrote in *Post Oaks*, he "drank a bottle of beer occasionally, and he learned the taste of redeye and thick white corn liquor, besides the fine Scotch which high-class bootleggers brought into [Cross] Plains and dispensed by the truckload."[96] In fact, that fall, when his mother went out of town for a few weeks to visit family, Howard tried brewing his own beer. Although he had promised his mother when he was very young that he would never touch alcohol, he wrote how he "felt no really great scruples in breaking it."[97]

By early October, with two stories published and two more accepted for future publication, Howard, feeling confident, packed in the public stenography job and brought his typewriter back home, intending to write full-time.[98] He submitted several more stories to Wright, but they were rejected, as were those he submitted to other pulp magazines.[99] When he finally received the proof pages for "Wolfshead," he started becoming despondent over what he had written. "After reading it," he admitted to Smith, "I'm not altogether sure I wasn't off my noodle when I wrote it. I sure mixed slavers, duelists, harlots, drunkards, maniacs and cannibals."[100] His low spirits eventually manifested in Howard writing a satirical take on the story that encapsulated his frustrations; he titled it "Wolfsdung."[101]

Christmas was soon upon the Howard family, and a few days later, Howard went to Brownwood to visit his friends. Smith's uncle allowed them to use his ranch for a get-together, so Smith, Vinson, and Howard drove to the ranch located just outside of town. They were also joined by someone none of them had yet met but who they had been corresponding with, Herbert Klatt.[102] Klatt lived in Hamilton County, Texas, with his parents, where he helped work their farm.[103] Being isolated, he had joined the Lone Scouts and through those contacts started corresponding with Vinson, and later Smith and Howard.[104] Although Klatt had shown literary aspirations like the rest, Howard was surprised when he found him to be "a stocky, diffident youth of medium height, with a strong German accent" who "did not appear worldly or sophisticated at all."[105] Klatt was also taken aback by his new friends, for he had probably envisioned literary discussions and almost immediately the rest of the group got drunk.[106] Klatt did not drink, so he was quite surprised when, "One of the party," wrote Howard, "was wild drunk on beer [Vinson] and another was stark crazy on raw jamaica ginger [Smith], with the obsession that he was a werewolf."[107] In little time, however, Smith and Vinson passed out, so Howard and Klatt sat up all night talking by the stove.[108]

The next morning they ate breakfast, went for a hike, and eventually left for home. The several-day retreat proved an enjoyable respite from their lives, and it quickly became a cherished memory that would reach mythical proportions in the retelling.

When Howard returned to Cross Plains, there was a letter awaiting him from Wright. Howard's story "Wolfshead" was to be featured with an illustration on the magazine's front cover. "By golly!" Howard thought to himself, "Think about it! I bet there's birds that toil for years and years and never get their stuff on the cover, and here this is the fifth story I've sold, and the third to be published, and they're giving it first place! I'll sure get a hand from the readers now—they always brag on the feature story."[109]

It was his first cover illustration, and it would not be his last, but publishing success remained elusive.

Chapter 11

"Ye College Days," 1926–1927

We walk a dim defined and mystic vale,
The mountains vaguely loom on either hand,
Groping we go and often lose the trail,
Compassed by demon shapes of Shadowland.
—"Futility"[1]

"I hope you have a carbon copy of *Wolfshead*. If so, will you please forward it to me at once by special delivery?" Wright wrote his plea to Howard at the beginning of the 1926 new year. He explained that because E. M. Stevenson (the artist for the cover illustration) lived in New York, Wright could not wait before sending him page proofs due to the turnaround time with the mail. So, to expedite things, he mailed Stevenson Howard's original manuscript. Stevenson received it and finished his first cover illustration for *Weird Tales* depicting Howard's story "Wolfshead," but he guiltily admitted to Wright that he had lost the manuscript. "I haven't got the [manuscript] to give to the printer," Wright continued. "If it should turn out to be lost, and you *haven't* a carbon copy, then Lord help us!"[2] It was too late to change the cover story for the April issue, which was due on the newsstands the first of March, and it had to get to the printer immediately to meet all deadlines.

Howard was "struck speechless," he wrote in *Post Oaks*, because "he had no carbon copy."[3] Howard had not thought to use carbon paper to make copies of his manuscripts as a backup. This was not an uncommon practice, for other authors, such as *Weird Tales*' Seabury Quinn, never made carbon copies of his manuscripts because, as Quinn explained, "they are a damned nuisance."[4] Still, there was a risk involved that Howard was now learning. As he grasped what the loss of the manuscript really meant, Howard explained his reaction in *Post Oaks*: "He cursed Fate and Life, seeming to see in the incident a master touch of that Destiny which he firmly believed had followed his trail ever since he first decided on his career."[5]

"I have no carbon copy of 'Wolfshead,'" Howard admitted to Wright. "I failed to make an extra copy." "I certainly hope the [manuscript] is not lost," he continued, "but am today beginning to re-write it from memory."[6] After mailing the letter to Wright, he rolled a blank sheet of paper into his typewriter and began typing, Then, as Howard explained in *Post Oaks*, "He rewrote the story from memory in a single night, and sent it, special delivery, to [*Weird Tales*]."[7]

A short time later, Wright mailed him another letter telling him that Stevenson had, in fact, found the manuscript, and it was off to the printer. It had been missing the front page, but with Howard's second copy, Wright was able to complete the manuscript. As a way of thanking Howard for his assistance, Wright told him he would be adding ten dollars to the price of the story for his troubles. Still, further, because Wright and Sprenger had *Weird Tales*' finances under control, he informed Howard that in the future he should be able to pay one cent a word for stories, rather than the one-third cent they had been paying.[8] This was good news for Howard, and he promised himself he would make copies of his manuscripts in the future.

When the April issue hit the newsstands, Howard was elated to find a copy of the magazine with his story featured on the cover. Wright had already written about the forthcoming story in the December 1925 issue, commenting, "In this tale Mr. Howard writes of werewolves from a viewpoint never before used in literature."[9] The werewolf in the story was not the usual man who turned into a true wolf; rather, Howard's werewolf has the head of a wolf with the body of a man, an image that Hollywood would later make its own.

Two months later, although there were no letters mentioning his story in "The Eyrie," Howard learned he had taken second place in the reader's poll, and one letter at the beginning of 1927 by Lennart Larson of Seattle claimed the best story for 1926 was "'Wolfshead' by Robert. E. Howard."[10] Despite what was clearly a successful story, Howard had little time to relish his achievement for he was too busy working full-time.

Howard had continued to write stories and submit them to pulp magazines in the fall of 1925, including *Adventure*, *Argosy All-Story*, and *Ghost Stories*, but all he ever received were rejection slips.[11] In addition, although "his parents did not murmur at boarding and clothing their grown son," as he wrote in *Post Oaks*, he was beginning to feel "callous and selfish" and "occasionally felt twinges of conscience as he saw how hard they worked—his father at his practice, his mother at her housework."[12] It was not until he received the advance proofs of "Wolfshead" that he decided to do something about it. "Reading it over," Howard later explained in a letter, "I was so depressed and discouraged that I went and got a job jerking soda in a drug-store."[13]

The drugstore was Dr. Robertson's, commonly referred to as Cross Plains Drug Store. Dr. Randolph Robertson first opened the store in the old town location along Turkey Creek in a "small raw-hide lumber shack on August 1, 1894."[14] When Cross Plains moved townsites, Dr. Robertson went with them, opening his storefront in 1911 two doors down from the bank building.[15] When Howard went to work there, Dr. Robertson was still around but was now retired, and his son, Buster, managed the store.[16] It was Buster, just a few years older than Howard, who had asked him to go to work for him, but Howard had demurred until the "Wolfshead" proofs came in. He then told Buster he would go to work for him as a soda jerk, sometime in late 1925 or early 1926.

A soda jerk worked behind the counter of one of the soda fountains located in drugstores across the country and was so named because of the jerking action of the handle on the soda water dispenser. Soda water had been listed in the *U.S. Pharmacopeia* in the early nineteenth century, but the entry was removed in 1831, and according to historian Anne Funderburg, it was transformed "from a drug to a treat."[17] The first known soda fountain in Texas was the one in Rio Grande City, for according to one settler's memoirs, there was a pharmacy there in 1858 "with a most pretentious soda water fountain."[18] By the turn of the century, soda drinks began gaining in popularity with the invention of soft drinks such as Dr. Pepper by pharmacist Charles Alderton in Waco, Texas.[19] Further, with the invention of malted milk and the ice cream soda that comedian Will Rogers called "the finest thing that you ever tasted in all your life," drugstores had become ever more popular.[20] According to Funderburg, in the year Howard was born, "30 companies manufactured soda fountains and related equipment" and in 1910, "Americans spent $500 million on carbonated drinks."[21]

The only places that surpassed soda fountains in revenue were bars that served alcohol, but all that changed on January 17, 1920. After Prohibition went into effect on that date, the *Ice Cream Trade Journal* was proud to proclaim that the soda fountain had become "the new American bar," while another trade magazine, *Drug Topics*, declared, "The bar is dead, the fountain lives, and soda is king!"[22] Funderburg explains, "The five industries that benefited most from Prohibition were, in order: savings banks, soft drinks, ice cream, motion pictures and candy," and the drugstores carried three out of the five. More specifically, local drugstores benefitted from the customers who had been regulars in the bars and now patronized their stores, in part, Funderburg points out, because "The prescription counter was the only legal place to buy liquor."[23] Throughout Prohibition, the local drugstore became the hangout of choice for most Americans.

Howard wrote of his experience as a soda jerk in *Post Oaks*, commenting that he felt like he had "entered a new world: The Other Side of the Counter." "He had never taken into consideration the thoughts, feelings, and emotions of those who had served him cold drinks," he continued, adding how "he learned many things."[24] As a new employee, he was making thirty dollars a month but was very quickly offered the position of "chief soda jerk at sixty dollars a month," although he soon found out why his pay had doubled. He wrote that "he worked seven days out of the week, from ten in the morning to closing time, which was anytime between ten at night and two in the morning."[25] "I often had the whole store on my hands," he added, "especially at night, when the main rush came." He elaborated that among his many duties were "to wait on throngs that absolutely crowded the store to capacity, to mix syrups, watch the cash register, sell patent medicines and 'handle the front,' wrangle with bellicose customers who wanted drink or dope and took refusal as an insult—to do the ten thousand things there is to do around a boom-town drug-store."[26]

He also quickly learned that he had little help from either of his coworkers, Dr. Robertson or Buster. He wrote of Dr. Robertson that he "stayed partly drunk most of the time, and most of his activities consisted in abusing the clerks for putting too much ice cream in the drinks." He described Buster as "a pot-bellied blond with a loud, empty laugh" who was supposed to help him manage the crowds but often would find them "too tough" and disappear, leaving Howard to fend for himself.[27] He had numerous difficulties with Buster as his manager at first, but explained, "We got along alright after I offered to tie my right hand behind me and beat his head off with my left."[28]

The customers, it seems, were not much better and were perhaps worse. "A soda jerk in a city is the object of considerable respect and reverence among the school girls, college boys, flappers, and the younger set in general," he wrote in *Post Oaks*, "but in a small town, he is generally an object of contempt—especially so in a tough oil town as [Cross] Plains was. A man who works all day or all night swinging a heavy sledge, clambering about on an eighty-foot rig, and in general doing work suitable for a giant, has scant respect for one who makes his living by doling out soft drinks."[29] Unlike the neighborhood customers, Howard described that in his town were "whores, bootleggers, gamblers, dope fiends, and yeggs, besides the general riff-raff of drillers, tool dressers and roustabouts."[30] He described how much he despised the job when he wrote how he hated being a soda jerk "worse than he had ever hated any task, and the contempt and apprehension which he felt toward the mass of oil field workers grew to a fear and venomous hatred of dangerous and abnormal size."[31]

The work was grueling, especially with its long hours, for Howard had little time for anything else. "He did not read or write," he wrote in *Post Oaks* and "scarcely had time to answer his correspondence. He had absolutely no time for recreation or even rest."[32] He did make a few friends among the roughnecks, as well as the man who delivered the ice to the drugstore, whom he referred to as Bill Murkin in his semi-autobiography but whose real identity remains unknown. Howard and Murkin enjoyed sparring, and they often went to the icehouse in town, where many of the other roughnecks would gather in the evening to drink bootleg beer and put on the gloves. "These roughnecks were different," Howard explained, partly "because they knew him, so there was no antagonism between them."[33] It also did not hurt that Howard was friends with Murkin and could hold his own in a boxing match with him. Apparently, Murkin had a reputation for having beaten everyone there.

It appears these were the few good memories from those months he worked as a soda jerk, for after they finished a bout in the icehouse, Howard would walk home shadowboxing and singing loudly, despite the late hour. One new neighbor did not take too kindly to this. Howard's friend Tom Wilson had left Cross Plains several years before but had recently returned with his wife. They were, at the time, living in Pauline Bond's house across the street from the Howards. Mrs. Wilson later recalled: "The first time I saw him was at night. Here he was, walking down the middle of the street in the moonlight, singing at the top of his voice, stopping every now and then to shadow-box with something." She succinctly stated, "I was afraid," but when she voiced her concern to Bond, she just laughed and replied, "Oh, that was just Robert Howard."[34]

Howard also took some days off to visit his friends in Brownwood, although one stay in either late April or early May of 1926 did not go very well.[35] He again stayed with Smith, and they engaged in their typical long walks and talks. When they went to bed, as usual, Howard had Smith tie his wrist to the bed so he would not wander in his sleep. Sometime later, Smith woke up to a primordial yell from Howard. In Smith's notes on the incident, he wrote that his parents also heard the yell, and "my mother said that Bob let out the most chilling scream she ever heard," while his father stated, "it was a fair-sized yell." Smith came out of bed and found Howard fighting with his steam trunk. Then suddenly, he dived "through the closed window and the screen," receiving a "deep cut on [his] right shoulder and some cuts on his face."[36] Howard then began wandering around the yard, evidently still in the grips of the sleep terrors he had been experiencing since childhood.[37] When he finally woke up, he remembered nothing but was no doubt somewhat embarrassed. Upon returning to Cross Plains, he wrote Smith, "My arm's all right. A fool experience. I have ridden nightmares over fences and down roads, but never through windows before."[38]

After his short visit, Howard was back at what he called his "lousy job."[39] He worked all day, and at night, he wrote, "I'd fall into bed and be asleep with fatigue before I landed, and the next morning I'd still be tired."[40] Then he would drag himself out of bed, walk to work, and repeat it all once more. He later invoked London's novel *Martin Eden* when he explained in a letter, "You remember how Martin used to get drunk on Sunday to forget the toil of the week. Well, I didn't work as furiously as Martin did, but I didn't get that day off, like he did. I worked harder Sunday than any day, except Saturday."[41] And like Martin Eden, he drank to cope with the stress of the job, for he explained to another correspondent, "The beer made it endurable, and quieted nerves that were jerking and twitching maddeningly."[42] Between the chronic fatigue, catching the flu, developing varicose veins, and dropping fourteen pounds, he wrote, "my health went on the rocks."[43] He could not keep at the endless job, and he wanted to write, so sometime that summer he made a deal with his parents.

While it was known that his mother was supportive of Howard's writing ambitions, there has been some speculation that his father was not as keen on his choice of careers.[44] It is possible he wanted his son to follow in his footsteps and become a doctor, or at least find a more respectable job than writer.[45] According to Smith, Dr. Howard had suggested his son become a newspaperman, to which he "received a cool brushoff," and when Dr. Howard suggested he go to New York to write, Howard told him, "I'll make the pulps, and not the slicks and I'll make them from here in Texas. I'm going to prove that a man doesn't have to live in New York to sell his stories."[46]

There were many famous authors with parents who did not approve of their career decision. Ernest Hemingway, born seven years before Howard, faced parents who "urged him to follow his father to Oberlin and pursue a career in medicine."[47] And J. D. Salinger, author of *The Catcher in the Rye*, who was born the year Howard moved to Cross Plains, was challenged by a father who "dragged him off" to "slaughter pigs" in Poland to break him of his writing notions and get him to take over the family meat import business.[48]

In order to overcome his father's concerns, Howard took a page from Jack London's book *Martin Eden*, when the title character told his girlfriend who hesitated to marry him out of concern he could not support them: "Give me two years. I shall succeed in that time, and the editors will be glad to buy my good work. I know what I am saying; I have faith in myself. I know what I have in me; I know what literature is, now; I know the average rot that is poured out by a lot of little men; and I know that at the end of two years I shall be on the highroad to success."[49] Howard asked his parents if they would support him for two years, one year to go back to college and earn his bookkeeping certificate and another year to write. If at the end of the two years he was not successful, he would find a job in bookkeeping.[50] They readily agreed to the plan. Of course, as he admitted in *Post Oaks*, "Bookkeeping had never appealed to him, but he felt too weary, mind and body, to take any but the easiest and most obvious route," and so at the age of 20, "He quit his job and made preparations to go."[51]

Howard made his way to Brownwood, where he enrolled in Howard Payne's Commercial School to continue the bookkeeping certificate he had started in the fall of 1924.[52] "Brownwood is enjoying a steady and reasonable rapid growth," declared the *Bulletin of Howard Payne College*, for since Howard graduated from high school in 1923, the city had grown by 1,000 residents and now stood at "a population of 12,000." There was commensurate growth at the college as well, including the enrollment in the commercial school. That same bulletin also touted the bookkeeping program in which Howard enrolled. "Our system of Bookkeeping is laid out along business lines, and includes buying, selling, shipping, consignments, partnerships, corporation, accounting, and banking," and it highlighted how "a thorough and practical knowledge of Shorthand and Typewriting offers unlimited opportunities for getting a start."[53] Classes commenced on September 6, 1926, and over the academic year, Howard wrote, "I studied such non-literary things as shorthand, typing, business arithmetic, commercial law, and the like."[54]

Although "he'd already been typing," Lindsey Tyson explained, "he learned a lot down there."[55] Tyson knew this well, for they once again shared a room in Brownwood, this time living in the Powell house located at 1214

Main Avenue, right next to the campus.[56] Howard had a less than memorable story regarding Mr. Powell, which he later shared with a friend. "The owner of a boarding house where I stayed always woke us up by trying to shake the liver out of us, regularly at six o'clock," he wrote. "He seemed to think it a great joke and some of the boys learned to wake up as he entered their room, and leap out of bed in a hurry." Howard did not appreciate Mr. Powell impinging on his freedom, but as he said, "I protested in vain." Howard then told how he finally asserted his independence. "One morning when I was awake," he began, "I heard him ascending the stairs, and I lay still, feigning sleep; as he bent over the bed and laid hold of me I gave him a smash under the heart that nearly laid him out. . . . After that, when he wanted to wake me up, he did so by calling from outside the doorway."[57]

As for rooming with Tyson, Howard wrote in *Post Oaks*, "They dropped back into the old easy comradeship with no effort at all," and he found that his good friend "was the same easy-going, good-natured fellow."[58] Since Tyson's family also still lived in Cross Plains, he recalled that "we'd come home, maybe, every two or three weeks; we'd make a trip home, and hitch-hike . . . sometimes my folks would meet us."[59]

Tyson recounted one anecdote during their time together in which he explained that "Bob Howard was a very honest kind of a person."[60] "I remember a time when he found a purse in Brownwood," he wrote. "This purse or billfold had among other things $50.00. Bob hunted the owner up with some difficulty, returned the billfold," for which "he received a $10.00 reward."[61] Howard later paradoxically remarked to Tyson, "See there, I make $10.00 for being honest, at the same time I lose $40.00 for being honest."[62]

Tyson also remembered Howard's work ethic and writing habits during the time they lived together. "He was the hardest—hardest worker that I ever saw," Tyson explained. "He'd write all day and all night and maybe all the next day. . . . He wouldn't go to bed, maybe, two days and a night. Maybe longer. I'd go to bed and go to sleep, and he'd just keep typing. . . . He wrote a lot when we were down in Brownwood."[63] Despite having a strong work ethic, there was only one problem. He was spending more time writing fiction than studying bookkeeping. "I studied hard at first," Howard wrote, "then my health came back and I spent most of my time writing verse and playing Seven-Up."[64] The card game, Howard explained, "was the abiding sin of the boarding house gang, and the devotees of the game kept it going with monotonous regularity."[65]

Howard had many other distractions from his studies as well, for he not only found himself "spending most of his time going to picture shows," but he also "began exercising slowly and carefully so as not to repeat his heart strain, and gradually worked harder."[66] As he wrote in *Post Oaks*, "His lean frame began to grow more supple and springy, his lean muscles harder and more resilient" and "a portion of his self-respect returned."[67] He also continued boxing and taking those long walks through town and the countryside.

Another reason Tyson witnessed Howard writing so much was because he had joined the staff of the Howard Payne newspaper, the *Yellow Jacket*. According to Roehm, "Before there was a *Yellow Jacket*, there was *The Prism*," for the newspaper was published under that name from 1915 to 1923, before changing names when Claude C. Curtis and C. S. Boyles Jr. took over as editors.[68] They were pleased to have Howard writing for them and wrote in their editorial, "The author is a writer for several national magazines" and noted how "Mr. Howard has consented to furnish the *Jacket* with stories from time to time."[69] The first two stories Howard decided to write about were experiences from his trip to the October 23, 1926, football game played on the Cotton Palace exhibition grounds in Waco, Texas, between the Baylor Bears and the Howard Payne Yellow Jackets.[70]

In order to travel to the game in Waco, Howard took a special train that had been arranged for the students. It left Brownwood at 12:30 a.m. and arrived in Waco at 9:00 in the morning on the day of the game.[71] According to Bob Roehm, Rob Roehm's father, a train aficionado, "Special trains were common during the railroad heyday." Despite the fact that it rained hard that day, the Howard Payne students had high hopes for their team to win, for they had a winning season thus far.[72] However, as Howard wrote a friend, "Muddy fields, fumbles, fumbles, fumbles—what would one expect," and continued with his description in this manner: "The Cotton Palace is the unmitigated applesauce; they soaked us every time we turned around."[73] Although they had started the game well, the Yellow Jackets lost by a score of 23 to 7.[74] The special train then left at 3:00 a.m. on Sunday, returning the students home by lunchtime.[75]

After arriving back in Brownwood, Howard wrote two stories about his experiences during the trip, and both were published in the October 27 issue of the newspaper.[76] His first was titled "Sleeping Beauty," about an "upperclassman" trying to sleep on the special train while the college co-eds were singing a repeated-verse song; by the "seventh-thousandth verse," the student asked the conductor, "Is there no chance at all for a train robbery, hold-ups, murders and all that you know?"[77] His second story, "After the Game," details returning to the train after the game in the rain only to find he had lost his ticket and was not being allowed to get back on board. Whether those things happened to Howard or not is unknown, but there is perhaps some basis in truth.

In a later edition of the paper, he wrote about attending the college football games in a piece he titled "Ye College Days." Howard wrote of the "ancient Grad" who fondly writes, "Now I don't believe there ever was a peppier flock of students than we were at Killem Kollege. Talk about class spirit!" "Back in those days," he continues, tongue-in-cheek, "there was intense rivalry between colleges. Ah, it would have done your soul good to have seen the preparation for a coming football game: the yell meetings, the cheering, the rifle practice, the sharpening of swords and greasing of pistols."[78]

As the end of 1926 drew near, his mother wrote him a letter that has been preserved. "My dear little boy," Mrs. Howard wrote on December 9 to Howard, who was 20 years old at the time. Ever the concerned mother she wrote of the "nasty weather" before pleading, "I do hope you keep your feet dry and warm. I am afraid you will expose yourself and take the flu. Please wear your overcoat, or at least your suit with coat and vest." She then ominously added, "I warned you." She shared some news about the family, a little town gossip, and informed him he still had $105.50 in his bank account. She also wanted to make sure he had paid the Powells up to December 18 before he came home but not to overpay them for the month. She also enclosed some money for him to pay for a train if they were unable to pick him up, and for him to buy some Christmas presents. She then signed off like a typical concerned mother: "Be sure & take care of your health. Love Mother."[79]

After New Year's Howard returned to Brownwood, and a few days later another letter from his mother arrived. This time she wrote "Dear Son" and said she was sending him clean clothes, encouraging him to "Please change your shirts every 2 or 3 days, also your handkerchiefs & so" and to "bring Lindsey & one of the other boys home with you on the 21st." Apparently Howard had contracted a cold over the break because she told him, "Son, be careful and don't take fresh cold and if you don't get rid of that cold go to Dr. Paige," She also warned him, "There are some cases of measles in Brownwood, and if you begin to feel bad, ache or feverish or anything, go to Dr. Fowler, Bailey or Snyder."[80]

Once classes started Howard settled into the routine of ignoring his studies, writing what he wanted to write, and playing Seven-Up with the other boarders. No sooner had he settled into this routine than Smith appeared one night and told him, "I've gotten myself in a hell of a jam!"[81] The girl he had been dating, the one Howard kissed, Echla Laxson, was pregnant.[82] Although in that era the right thing to do was for Smith to marry her, he apparently had decided he did not want to. "You mighta known things couldn't keep goin' on like they were. You want to dance without payin' the piper," Howard told Smith in *Post Oaks.* Howard reproved him, "You forget the human element," telling him, "Hell, you can't expect to use a woman for your pleasure and then throw her off and forget about her whenever you want to."[83] Howard told him the right thing to do was to marry her, and on March 17, 1927, Smith quietly did so, after which they disappeared from Brownwood.[84] They went their separate ways, he to New Mexico, her to Oklahoma, and on May 12 she filed for a divorce.[85] By the end of summer, Smith was back home living with his parents, and Howard wrote that he "found him bitter and more cynical than ever."[86]

Howard continued writing and found another reason to ignore his studies that spring, for the Howard Payne Press Club was sponsoring a journalism contest, and the winners would be entered into a statewide contest being sponsored by the Texas Intercollegiate Press Association.[87] The deadline was March 10, 1927, and Howard submitted a short story. That was also the day that saw Howard's last story published in the *Yellow Jacket* for the spring session.[88] And it seems his mother's concern over the cases of measles going around Brownwood had also been more than justified.

"The Powells we were living with," recalled Lindsey Tyson, "had a baby girl who got the disease."[89] Their daughter was 16-month-old Nelda June, and she had likely contracted it in late January. By February 12 it was reported that she was "quite sick at the family house."[90] The symptoms of measles appear one to two weeks after contracting the disease. Tyson wrote, "The Howards heard about the epidemic and came to take Bob home as he had never had the measles," but that Howard "did not want to go." According to Tyson, Howard said, "This time I dam sure will have this stuff," and "he went into a bathroom that the little girl had been useing, picked up a glass that the child had probably been useing, drank out of it, rubbed a towel over his face that he thought she had probably been useing."[91] Soon after, Howard was back home in Cross Plains writing a correspondent, "Measles! Can you feature a grown man being put into retirement for two months by measles?"[92] Howard had accomplished what he had set out to do.

Despite suffering some, Tyson wrote that Howard "came out without any bad effects."[93] Little Nelda Powell was not so fortunate. According to the *Brownwood Bulletin,* she "died at the family home Monday night," February 28.[94] The only inconvenience to Howard was that he missed the rest of spring classes and had to enroll in the summer session starting in June in order to finish his degree.[95] He also found out that he had won second place in the writing contest, not in person but while convalescing.[96]

Howard recovered by late May, and before classes started June 1, he and his other Brownwood friend, Truett Vinson, took a trip to Galveston. There is little doubt their objective was to be witnesses to the second annual International Pageant of Pulchritude and eighth Annual Bathing Girl Review over the May 21 weekend. They attended along with an estimated 250,000 other people.[97] "The day was hotter than a promise of Purgatory," Howard wrote in an autobiographical piece titled "Galveston Affair."

> We sat on the sea wall, with our backs to the gulf where a keen breeze was blowing, but the tiers of benches were so packed that not a breath of coolness could drift through. . . . Truett swore with an energy that I could not muster on account of the heat. We glared at each other without optimism. We had sat—and sat—and sat. Had we been merely waiting for some national hero to appear, we would have given it up

> and started a general slaughter as a diversion. But we were there to see legs, and legs we were going to see if we sat there till Hell froze over and the Devil took sleigh rides on the ice. . . . Bathing girls from all over the world. Their native lands had nobly sent them across the sea. Some were pretty, some had shapely forms. But as far as we were concerned, the weather was the only thing that was heated.[98]

The eventual winner of the contest, which featured young ladies from around the globe, was 19-year-old Dorothy Britton of New York City.[99]

Howard and Vinson returned to Brownwood, where Howard resumed taking classes and ignoring his studies. Howard never really took to college life and once wrote a friend that it was nothing but a "lot of narrow minded, musty old ideas dispensed by uninterested teachers to pupils who have come to college for athletics, because they considered it the stylish thing or to keep from going to work."[100] "I'm prejudiced against all colleges," he admitted, "to Hell with them."[101] Perhaps the thing that soured him the most were the college students themselves. "This hooey about the clean, honest college kids is all hooey," he declared. "The average college kid is a liquor-swillin', card-cheatin', skirt-pursuin' sap that thinks he is being a red-blooded he-man if he goes to the football games and yells 'rah' every time his college teams makes a touchdown. Bah!"[102] In the opinion of his roommate, Lindsey Tyson, the reason Howard did not like college and had never really wanted to go "was that he could not tolerate any degree of supervision. He was fiercely independent."[103] Of course, "Truth to tell," Howard wrote in *Post Oaks*, "one of his reasons for staying in school was that, while in college, he would not have to work."[104]

Nevertheless, after completing the last two courses over the summer, Howard graduated on August 3, 1927, with his bookkeeping diploma, having earned a B average and his freedom.[105] At least, that was, for one year. He had one year ahead of him in which he did not have to work and could write full-time in the hopes of never having to take another "real job" again. In fact, according to Tyson, Howard told him he was never going to labor at a job again, nor be a bookkeeper. "I will make my living doing what I like to do, writing, or I will be a tramp."[106] Again, Tyson explained that the real reason for this was because "Bob couldn't stand anybody telling him what to do. He was the most fiercely independent fellow you ever saw."[107] Howard agreed, for he once explained to his editor Farnsworth Wright, "Life's not worth living if somebody thinks he's in authority over you."[108]

Howard truly believed that freedom and writing were one and the same. "I've always had a honing to make my living by writing, ever since I can remember," he wrote Wright, explaining, "There's freedom in this game, that's the main reason I chose it."[109] And to Lovecraft he succinctly stated, "Writing has always been a means to an end I hoped to achieve—freedom." He continued,

> Personal liberty may be a phantom, but I hardly think anybody would deny that there is more freedom in writing than there is in slaving in an iron foundry, or working—as I have worked—from twelve to fourteen hours seven days out of the week behind a soda fountain. I have worked as much as eighteen hours a day at my typewriter, but it was work of my own choosing, and I could quit any time I wanted to without getting fired from the job. Yes, writing has been more of a means to an end then it may be with some.[110]

And so, with his newfound freedom, he returned home to Cross Plains to become the writer he knew he could be.

Chapter 12

The Anguished Poet, 1927

My soul is a blaze
Of passionate desire;
My soul is a blaze
That sets my pen on fire.
—"Poet"[1]

One of Mrs. Howard's greatest contributions to the development of her son as a writer came from her sharing one of her greatest joys in life. "She loved poetry," Dr. Howard wrote. "Written poetry by sheets and reams, almost books of it, was stored in her memory so that from Robert's babyhood he had heard its recital. Day by [day] he heard poetry from his mother."[2] In time his mother's love came to be equally shared by Howard, and it served to shape him as a writer of both his own poetry and his prose. Dr. Howard strongly believed that his son's abilities were a reflection of "his quiet, unassuming poetic mother," who "was a poet, although she never wrote poetry for publication."[3]

His father also deserves some of the credit, for he, too, shared his wife's passion for poetry. As a young boy, one neighbor, Larry McDonough recalled Dr. Howard often visiting their home for a meal accompanied by another physician, Dr. Dill, from Rising Star. "Both of them loved poetry," McDonough said, "and they'd come over to our house and mom would feed them and they would set there and right out of the blue sky quote poetry that I was having to read in school."[4] As Howard scholar Paul Herman explains, "A tradition of that time was that after dinner at a friend's house, the adults would retire to the sitting room and each take turns standing and quoting poetry from memory." Between growing up with his mother's recitations and this typical pastime, Herman explains that Howard "was steeped in the beauty of poetry, in all sorts of forms and styles."[5]

Howard had found someone who loved poetry as much as he, for Smith both read and wrote poetry. According to Burke, "It was an English teacher, Helen Post Wright, who kindled this interest in Smith," and she taught him "the intricacies of poetic diction."[6] Having found a kindred soul who loved poetry equally, Howard now had someone with whom he could share his interest. In their letters back and forth between Cross Plains and Brownwood, Howard and Smith shared their poetry, and Smith quickly became his poetical confidant. "You know there isn't half a dozen people who know I try to write the muck," Howard wrote Smith in April of 1926, "and you're the only friend I ever read it to."[7] In another letter Howard proved somewhat guarded in the quality of his own poetry, for he told Smith, "I never send any verse to any but close friends who know that I know my limitations and therefore, do not expect anything great from me."[8] It is true, some of Howard's early poetry is poor, but his genius shines through in some, and after doggedly pursing the art, he produced high quality poetry that stands the test of time.

Throughout their exchange Howard always considered Smith to be the better poet. "I read your verse again and again," Howard wrote Smith. "You are a poet and owe it to yourself to cultivate your talent."[9] Of his own poetry, Howard wrote, "You will doubtless read the stuff through courtesy, even though it bores you. However I never made any pretension toward poetry."[10] On his part, however, Smith enjoyed Howard's poetry, but like much of his writing, it always proved a greater joy to hear it recited in person. "It was an exceptional pleasure to hear him recite his verse, and the verse of other poets," Smith wrote. "His deep, booming chant would bring the words to life, complete with meaning."[11]

Although exposed widely to any number of poets, Howard knew who stood among his favorites. "I'm narrow in my literary likings," Howard wrote. "About the only poets and writers I can stand regularly are the British and American ones."[12] Among the British poets he wrote fondly of Rudyard Kipling and Lord Alfred Tennyson, and of British-Canadian Robert W. Service. Among the Americans he favored the likes of Edgar Allan Poe, Stephen Vincent Benét, and Henry Wadsworth Longfellow.[13] During this time in his life, he also developed new favorites, for he wrote of discovering "[Oscar] Wilde, [Charles] Swinburne, and [George] Viereck," in *Post Oaks*, after which he noted, "New vistas opened to him. He thrilled and expanded as he read. He sought poetry and more poetry."[14] In his letters he often voiced his admiration for certain poets more explicitly, such as when he said of contemporary poet Alfred Noyes, "Noyes is one of my favorites," explaining, "I like the music of drums and wind-harps that throb through so much of his poetry."[15] Howard also came to respect many of the poets published in *Weird Tales* magazine by Farnsworth Wright, another man passionate about poetry, to whom he would soon begin submitting his verse.

Howard also had an affinity for poetry of the lyrical type, especially folk songs from the Old World and those heard from early American times. At the beginning of 1925, he started corresponding with someone who shared this particular interest, Robert W. Gordon. About the time Howard began reading *Adventure* magazine, Gordon became a regular columnist with a feature titled "Old Songs That Men Have Sung," which shared the lyrics of many old folk songs. Gordon was a University of California (and later Harvard) graduate student who was conducting research to preserve these old songs, and the column was a reflection of his findings.[16] "I am sending you a few songs," Howard wrote Gordon; "So far as I know, they have not been printed. At least I have not seen them in print."[17] In the August 23, 1926, issue of *Adventure*, Gordon wrote in his column, "The next comes from Mr. Robert E. Howard of Texas. It is still a favorite and is sometimes known as 'The Green Bed.'"[18] The song was titled "Young Johnny." In one letter to

Gordon, Howard explained how he acquired his knowledge of folk song lyrics when he wrote, "I have a faculty of memorizing any song or poem as I hear it, many, especially the old Scotch and Irish ballads I heard my grandmother sing when I was but a child."[19]

The two men continued exchanging letters haphazardly over the next several years, and in the March 1, 1927, column, Gordon again published lyrics from among Howard's offerings, this time from the song "Sanford Burns."[20] Both the column and the correspondence ended after Gordon accepted a position as the first head of the Archive of American Folk Song at the Library of Congress in 1928.[21] Howard lamented the column's demise, writing to Gordon, "The *Adventure* handed themselves a slam when they discontinued your department and I'm writing them, protesting the movement—though I don't suppose what I could say would make any difference."[22]

It was also during this timeframe that Howard began writing poetry in earnest. As he wrote in *Post Oaks*, "[Bob] tried rhymes. He wrote a great deal of jingling, jangling verses on the order of Robert W. Service, for whom he entertained a regard second only to Rudyard Kipling."[23] He mentioned recalling his study of poetry and rhythm in school, "But he had forgotten most of what he had learned, and now could not give the technical name of a single foot, or form."[24] "Scanning verse," he later told one correspondent, "Scanning verse outside of iambics—or is it pentameter?—I never can remember which is which—is something that's entirely beyond me. I know nothing at all about the mechanics of poetry—I couldn't tell you whether a verse was anapestic or trochaic to save my neck." Howard explained that he actually wrote "the stuff by ear."[25] As he elaborated in *Post Oaks*, "Still, he could scan and could tell by the beat of the rhythm whether or not a line was metrical. He went by the music, not by the knowledge of set rules. His verse, while neither deep nor, in the last analysis, poetic, was naturally smooth and rhythmical. He rhymed by instinct, and while some of his verse was irregular in the number of feet, it would scan and, at least in meter, violated no great poetic principle."[26] Like his prose, which he composed while speaking out loud to hear how the written word sounded, his poetry was also composed in a similar fashion, with the intent that it should be not only read but also heard.

Howard found great joy in writing his poetry, and he wrote in *Post Oaks* that his "unspoken wish was to be a poet." He spent days, if not weeks, pouring his heart into his poetry, almost in a writing frenzy. "He read nothing those weeks but poetry," he wrote, "he thought nothing else. There were lines which made him freeze and burn, which caused goose flesh to rise all over him, and made him want to weep and laugh with the beauty and glory of the thing."[27] Howard had found a sense of freedom by writing poetry. On one occasion he wrote to Smith, "Funny, I've been trying to write poetry all day and literary work stimulates me sometimes just like wine."[28] "I'm no poet," he later wrote to another correspondent, "but I was born with a knack of making little words rattle together and I've gotten a bit of pleasure from my jingling."[29]

Much of the poetry Howard wrote was in the form of his letters to Smith and was often little more than doggerel, but he would just as equally turn his poetry more serious, such as when he wrote Smith a letter that included a poem about Smith, Vinson, and himself that he titled "Symbols."

Scarce had the east grown red with dawn
Or the moon-born day begun
Ere three of us went up a winding road
In the face of the rising sun.
One of us plucked a red rose
One of us plucked a white
One of us turned from the rising sun
And reached his hands to the night.[30]

Later, while attending Howard Payne College and having developed his "knack of making little words rattle together," he began writing poetry with the intent of submitting it at least to *Weird Tales* magazine, which under Wright's editorship had begun publishing weird poetry.[31] And then, "to his utter amazement," he wrote, Wright accepted two of his poems, "The Song of the Bats" and "The Ride of Falume."[32] Since the magazine paid 25¢ a line for verse, Howard was promised $3.00 and $4.50, respectively, for the poems. The first to be published was "The Song of the Bats" in the May 1927 issue, the first stanza reading:

The dusk was on the mountain
And the stars were dim and frail
When the bats came flying, flying
From the river and the vale
To wheel against the twilight
And sing their witchy tale.[33]

Although the measles had put a damper on his output, once he was back in Brownwood and ostensibly attending classes again, Howard wrote more poetry and submitted "The Gates of Nineveh" to *Weird Tales*. About the beginning of September, he wrote to Smith, "I received a letter from Farnsworth, offering me $4.00 for the dramatic and movie rights of 'The Gates of Nineveh.'"[34] The poem appeared in the July 1928 issue, and the last stanza read,

Cities crumble, and chariots rust—
I see through a fog that is strange and grey—
All kingly things fade back to the dust,
Even the gates of Nineveh.[35]

This was the first poem Howard published about which a reader, Arthur Downing of New York, sent a letter to "The Eyrie." Downing wrote, "Tell the author, please, how much I enjoyed *The Gates of Nineveh.*"[36] Not long after that poem was accepted, Howard received five more acceptances from Wright for "Crete," "The Moor Ghost," "The Riders of Babylon," and "Easter Island."[37] His poetry publications were proving popular, at least with Wright, and the flurry of acceptances no doubt increased his confidence in his writing, if not his income. "The verse I have written can only be reckoned by millions of lines," Howard wrote to Smith in January of 1929, reviewing his poetry accomplishments to date. "I sold my first rhyme in 1926 and since then have sold 13, aggregating $58.00, all to *Weird Tales*, that is, those for which I am supposed to receive money."[38] Despite the limited payment for poetry, Howard still came to be one of the most prolific poets of *Weird Tales* magazine, publishing a total of thirty-five poems in his lifetime.[39]

Howard did try submitting his poetry elsewhere with mixed results. In early 1928 he compiled some of his poems and titled it *Singers in the Shadows* and submitted it for publication with Boni & Liveright Publishing. "Thanks a lot for sending us the manuscript of your interesting poetry," came the reply in April of 1928, "but we are not including any poetry in our forthcoming list of publications."[40] Later, he tried submitting several poems to the Galleon Press for a book they were compiling to be titled *Modern American Poetry*. "When I submitted my stuff," Howard wrote, "They accepted these and asked me to buy twelve copies of the book. I told them I couldn't do it, and to send my stuff back. They wrote and told me they wanted to publish it anyway, and I didn't have to buy any copies if I didn't want to. I told them I'd take a couple of extra copies and see if I could sell them."[41] The book included Howard's poems "To a Woman" and "One Who Comes at Eventide."

In addition to book anthologies, Howard tried submitting to poetry magazines, but he found the formula was the same as the book publishers. In November of 1928, he submitted "Flaming Marble" to the *Poet's Scroll*. "A letter from the editor of *The Poet's Scroll* says he will publish my sonnet, 'Flaming Marble,' if I'll subscribe," Howard wrote. "Seems like no one but subscribers can get stuff published—subscription $3.00. It just amounts to paying for publication but I'm going to do it; I'd give that much to have the sonnet in print."[42] And so he did, and the sonnet was published in the January 1929 issue of the magazine. He submitted additional poems to the *Poet's Scroll*, including "Rebellion" (published in the February 1929 edition), "Dreaming on Downs" (published April 1929), "Empire's Destiny" (June 1929), and "Shadow of Dreams" (August 1929).[43]

Having now published in one poetry magazine, Howard submitted two poems, "Tides" and "Red Thunder," to another, sending them to Benjamin D. Musser in Atlantic City, New Jersey, who was himself a poet and was editing two magazines at the time, *Contemporary Verses* and *JAPM: The Poetry Weekly*, the latter of which sarcastically stood for "Just Another Poetry Magazine." "I don't know who you are," came Musser's reply to the submission, "forgive me but I never heard of you before; but by Jupiter the world will hear something of you in the future if you can build to greater heights the tower you are erecting in the special kind of theme treated in the poems you have submitted to me. These are superb!"[44] Musser accepted both, placing "Tides" in *Contemporary Verse* and "Red Thunder" in *JAPM*, both of which were published in September 1929.

Howard then received a surprise letter from Musser. As Howard wrote Smith, "[Musser] says he can't find Cross Plains in the atlas but wants to meet me when he comes to Dallas in October to lecture on modern poetry." Howard was not at all excited at the prospect. "All very nice, of course and I highly appreciate his kindness," Howard commented, but as he was his own worst critic, he told Smith, "Though I can't share his enthusiasm. The junk I write is pretty good rhyme, I guess, but Judas, I know in the heart of me I can never be a poet and the more people praise me the deeper the knowledge goes that my junk is like an empty shell—nice looking from without maybe, but when they stop and analyze it, I know they find there's not depth or solidity about it."[45]

Musser did present in Dallas, after which he traveled to Rising Star to meet another of his cherished poets, Lexie Dean Robertson. A native Texan, born and raised in Canton, she began writing poetry at a young age. After attending North Texas State Normal College (now the University of North Texas) and meeting her husband there, she settled down in Rising Star, where she served as a school principal. By this time Robertson had published her poetry in numerous magazines, including the two edited by Musser. She was also published in several popular mainstream magazines as well, and had just released her first collection of poems, *Red Heels*. Robertson's poetry came to be so popular she was later named Poet Laureate of Texas.[46]

Howard did attend the social at Robertson's home in Rising Star, located just a dozen miles east of Cross Plains, where he met Musser, but it seems the East Coast and Texas poets had very little in common. Howard wrote of their meeting, "I reckon I didn't come up to his idea of what a poet should be because he didn't write me, after he returned East, or even answer the letter I wrote him. I suppose he expected to meet some kind of an intellectual, and lost interest when he met only an ordinary man, thinking the thoughts and speaking in the dialect of the common people."[47] Howard also admitted that "after a part-day's conversation with him, I found relief and pleasure in exchanging reminiscences with a bus driver who didn't know a sonnet from an axle-hub."[48]

After that Howard soured on the poetry magazines and ceased submitting to them altogether for numerous reasons. "My best efforts were usually returned with lines by the editors, expressing appreciation for the rhymes, but requesting me to contribute verses less bitter or rebellious," Howard wrote. "My answer generally was that I refused to emasculate my stuff—poor as it was—for the empty honor of seeing my name in print. If poetry magazines paid for contributions it would be different."[49] In fact, it was the lack of payment and the usual request that he had to pay to become a subscriber in order to have his poetry published that turned him off. So Howard continued sending his poetry to those venues that paid, even if it was nothing more than for a prize in a poetry contest, such as when he won best poem for the May 1929 rendition of the *American Poet* with "Skulls and Dust." For his efforts he was awarded three dollars.[50] Mostly, however, he continued submitting his poetry to *Weird Tales* magazine.

It certainly did not hurt that Howard found a receptive audience in Farnsworth Wright, who once declared, "Robert E. Howard is a genius. I have no doubt of that at all, now that I have reveled in the sweep of his imaginative verse." Although it was certainly a far-reaching claim, Otis Adelbert Kline did not believe he made such statements lightly when he once explained, "Mr. Wright is an excellent judge of literary material, and I have never known him to offer a compliment where it was not deserved." Wright elaborated on his impressions when he wrote, "I read through the bale of manuscripts and feel intoxicated from a debauch of great poetry. I used the word great with full realization of its meaning; for I think Howard's voice is not that of a minor bard, but of sheer genius. Many of the poems seem to have been written under the inspiration of Kipling, but I think he has excelled his teacher; and his more imaginative poems reach a height that Kipling could never climb."[51]

Howard also received similar praise for his poetry from other authors of *Weird Tales* magazine who were themselves poets, including Frank Belknap Long, Clark Ashton Smith, and H. P. Lovecraft. "I am honored to know that Mr. Long and Mr. Clark Ashton Smith have noticed my efforts," Howard wrote Lovecraft. "Both are writers and poets whose work I very much admire, having carefully preserved all of their poems (as well as all of yours) that have appeared in *Weird Tales* since I first made my acquaintance with the magazine."[52] Lovecraft himself wrote Howard, "I don't know that I ever encountered a better natural ear for rhythm than yours" and later,

"Poetry is really a tremendous strong point of yours."[53] And after Howard's death, Lovecraft emphasized the importance of Howard as a poet when he wrote, "Mr. Howard's poetry—weird, warlike, and adventurous—was no less notable than his prose. It had the true spirit of the ballad and the epic, and was marked by a pulsing rhythm and potent imagery of the extreme distinctive cast."[54]

Despite the appeal of Howard's poetry to his editor and fellow *Weird Tales* authors, what truly mattered was how receptive the readers were to his poetry in the pages of their magazine. The response, it seems, was just as phenomenal. Mrs. Z. P. Gustafson of Miami, Florida, made a typical plea in "The Eyrie": "Please have more poetry by Robert E. Howard."[55] Howard S. Whiteside of Concord, New Hampshire, who thought his poem "Shadows on the Road" was "really a great piece of work," added, "If possible, print more poems by Mr. Howard in the near future."[56] Repeatedly, whenever a letter was received about his poetry, they used words such as "wonderful," "attractive," and "literature."[57]

Howard soon found uses for his poetic skills in his prose, for he often wrote poems with great effect that served as epigraphs for his stories.[58] By including his own poetical stanzas and denoting them as being derived from some historic epic poem or ballad, he brought verisimilitude to his stories, thereby presenting them with a touch of realism. In fact, many readers, such as William E. Springhorn of Chicago, often asked, "I would very much like to know if Robert E. Howard in his stories . . . composes the poetry himself or if it is taken from another author."[59] More often than not, it was written by Howard, for when a poem was composed by another author, he always gave proper credit.

Howard's use of poetry in his stories, however, went much farther than this, for his prose writing very often has the feel, timing, and cadence of poetry itself. This is because Howard's exposure to and mastery of poetry became part of his writing style, and its presence is commonly felt in most of his better stories. Howard's contemporary, Raymond Chandler (author of the detective Phillip Marlowe series), once said of writing good fiction, "It probably started with poetry; almost everything does."[60] But it was another contemporary, Ernest Hemingway, who understood it best when he told his wife, "Nobody really knows or understands and nobody has ever said the secret. The secret is that it is poetry written into prose and it is the hardest thing of all to do."[61] Howard knew the secret.

Howard also discovered a secret from poet G. K. Chesterton when he purchased a copy of *The Ballad of the White Horse*. Howard was already familiar with the poetry of Chesterton, especially his popular "Lepanto," but he was quite taken with Chesterton's long ballad. Howard told Smith, "It's great," and shared his favorite passages over two letters.[62] The epic poem tells the story of King Alfred bringing Britons, Anglo-Saxons, and Celts together to do battle against Norse and Danish invaders in the ninth century. Decidedly, the major theme was English Christians defeating the pagan hordes. In addition to reflecting Howard's own love for the "heroic poetic tradition," Chesterton's poetry also revealed a technique to him that he later employed in his own writing, and that is "telescoping history."[63] Chesterton's ballad is not an exact retelling of historical events, and he acknowledges this in his prefatory notes to the poem. Rather than adhere to historical facts, Chesterton wants to tell a story of, as Burke explains, "universal elements of human nature and historical patterns."[64] For as Chesterton himself wrote, "It is the chief value of legend to mix up the centuries while preserving the sentiment; to see all ages in a sort of splendid foreshortening," what he called telescoping history.[65] For a writer of poetry or prose, it is certainly less constraining on their storytelling abilities, and so it became for Howard. Chesterton's poem also motivated him to write his own epic poem a few years later titled "The Ballad of King Geraint," although in his case he wrote of the Celtic people of Britain joining together to fight the heathen English—Angles, Saxons, and Jutes.[66]

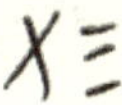

There is little doubt that although Howard is best known for his prose stories, he was a poet first, and it greatly influenced all of his writings. There have been many others who have recognized this in Howard's writing. Tevis Clyde Smith once wrote of Howard, "He was certainly, at the very first, primarily a poet."[67] Science fiction and fantasy historian Sam Moskowitz also recognized the importance of Howard's poetry in his writings when he explained, "Many of the great fantasy and science fiction writers who we particularly favor for the beauty of their style got that way because they were initially poets, which instilled in them a respect for the flow of words."[68] The first in his list of example authors was Robert E. Howard. And Howard biographer Rusty Burke noted this when he wrote, "Howard also brings to his work a gift of poetry, a talent for creating mood or atmospheric effects with just a few broad strokes, and a strong emotionalism that heightens the dramatic effects."[69] One of the strongest foundations for Howard's abilities as a writer had been laid down in his mother's love for poetry long before he took up his typewriter.

Despite his own love of poetry and the fury at which he wrote verse for several years, Howard continued to be frustrated by his attempts at being published. Poet Steve Eng has noted that one of Howard's frustrations came from the type of poetry he wrote. "Howard's tastes were traditional and romantic," he explained, with the problem being "he was ten or twenty years too late." Poetry had made a distinctive shift after World War I, moving away from the Romantic rhymed metrical verse of the nineteenth century that Howard favored to the more nihilistic poetry generally written largely in free verse, such as T. S. Eliot's *The Waste Land* (1922). "Since modern editors preferred the new poetry," Eng continued, "Howard's old-fashioned technique unsuited him for . . . publication."[70] There was also a larger cultural shift occurring as well, and Howard's fellow poet, Smith, understood this when he wrote, "It must be admitted that the true appreciation of poetry by a vast audience was probably all ready on the decline."[71]

It also had much to do with the often dark, brooding topics of Howard's poetry, uncommon among poetic circles at the time. Again, Eng highlights this when he writes, "The discernable concepts in Howard's poetry worth noting are: courage; barbarism; war; race; historicism; reincarnation; nihilism; carpe diem; determinism; wanderlust; beauty; and romanticism."[72] Although E. A. Townsend, editor of the *Poet's Scroll,* had accepted some of Howard's verse, much of it was rejected. Townsend's typical comment apparently was "because he said it was not rhythmic," but Howard believed, "he didn't have the guts to admit the real reason—which was that it was entirely too brutal for him and his pink tea laureates."[73] Howard's reaction to this was on full display in *Post Oaks* when he vented, "'I've tried to be a poet!' He exclaimed dramatically to himself. "I've made the Muse my goddess and I've worshipped at her throne. I've bruised my hands on her skirt hems, but from now on, she's a strumpet. I'll write what I damned please and put anything I want to in verse."[74] While he no doubt did so, it still did not help with publishing in the literary poetry magazines.

In the end, the primary reason Howard became the anguished poet was because poetry did not pay or pay well. "I wish I could give more time to verse," Howard wrote a friend, "but the necessity of making a living crowds it out."[75] He elaborated on this when he wrote, "I wouldn't hit the first key, or dip the pen in the ink, unless I knew there was a chance for me to get some money out of it, or publicity that would lead to money. That's why I gave up scribbling verse. I couldn't sell enough of it to justify me in dabbling with it."[76] Lindsey Tyson recalled Howard saying the same thing to him on numerous occasions when Tyson wrote, "He told me many times that he had rather write poetry than anything else, but there was no market for poetry. He always was interested in making a living, and the only way he was going to do that was by writing."[77] While Howard had found a sense of freedom in writing poetry, he knew in his heart he would not be free and independent if he continued. And so, after approximately two years, he all but gave up the writing of verse and returned to prose.

Howard continued to publish his poetry for the rest of his life, but as he admitted in a 1930 letter, "I've scarcely banged two lines together in years. The last verse I sold was stuff written years ago, and revamped; that is, pulled out of the unpublished archives and polished up a bit. Occasionally I go over rhymes I wrote a long time ago, and find I can iron out kinks that appeared impossible at the time of the original forging."[78] He occasionally entertained the idea of returning to "verse-writing," as he called it, but he also came to believe, as many do, that poetry is best left to the young. "I'm beginning to believe the poetry-business is a lot like the fight game," Howard wrote. "Most of the poets do their best work early in life."[79]

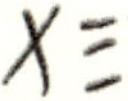

Howard finished the summer session at Howard Payne College and completed the courses that were interrupted by his attack of the measles.

On August 3, 1927, Howard Payne held their graduation ceremony at which the new and youngest governor of Texas, Dan Moody, delivered the commencement address.[80] Twenty-seven students received their bachelor of arts degrees, and sixteen their academy diplomas. Among the latter was listed "Robert Howard, Bookkeeping."[81] He had finally completed the program he had begun in the fall of 1924, but even more important to him, he was freed of classes and the associated responsibilities that went with them. Howard could now return home and concentrate on his writing over the next year under the agreement he had made with his parents. But first, he needed a vacation, so he and his friend Truett Vinson decided to take a trip to San Antonio together.

Chapter 13

"The Last Celt," 1927–1928

So come from your mists of the Northern Sea
Where the smoke-blue hazes melt.
Your dead shall lie where here I die,
The last unconquered Celt.
—"The Song of the Last Briton"[1]

As the summer of 1927 drew to a close, America recorded a number of important events, including Charles Lindbergh's successful solo flight across the Atlantic Ocean, Babe Ruth's sixtieth home run, which set a record that lasted for thirty-four years, and Alvin "Shipwreck" Kelly's world record for sitting atop a flagpole for twelve days.[2] Although not quite so sensational, Howard also had several important, life-changing events at the end of that summer, and they occurred when he and Truett Vinson decided to take a vacation to San Antonio and Austin after his graduation from Howard Payne College.

Howard enjoyed his visits to San Antonio, for he once wrote, "It is without question the most interesting and colorful city in Texas, possibly in the entire Southwest."[3] He was enamored "with the narrow river winding in and out all through it, with its broad plazas, old missions and cathedrals, and adobe houses shouldering modern buildings."[4] "Truett and I took our little jaunt to San Antonio," Howard later wrote Smith, "where we spent a delightful week and managed to get by without reaching the point where each waited for the other to go to sleep first—in the interests of safety."[5] In addition to their time in the Alamo City, Vinson and Howard agreed to drive up to Austin to visit a friend Vinson had been corresponding with but had not yet met. That friend was Harold Preece.

Born just days before Howard on January 16, 1906, in the small community of Bull Creek near Round Rock, Texas, Preece had been involved in the Lone Scouts, which was why he had been corresponding with Vinson. At the time they met, he was a student at Texas Christian University in Fort Worth and was home on summer break.[6] Preece's parents lived in Austin, and his father worked for the Austin State Hospital, where he "ran the institution's truck farm."[7]

Vinson, appropriately enough, sent Preece an Alamo postcard from San Antonio, dated August 20, 1927. On the back he wrote, "Bob and I will be in Austin Monday morning. Will call you up."[8] The following day Howard and Vinson took the train into the city and checked into the Stephen F. Austin Hotel, which had just opened its doors three years earlier. Evidently they called, for the next day Preece went to the hotel to meet them. "So with a hand rather tense," he recalled years later, "I rang the bell of the hotel room where the two were registered." He had no need to be nervous, for, as he wrote, "Instantly the door was opened. Instantly I was being welcomed with greetings as warm as the post-twilight hour outside."[9]

His first impressions on meeting his friends were that "both Bob and Truett stood approximately six feet." Vinson he described as "tall and handsome like movie idol Rudolph Valentino," while Howard he thought of "as a bulky lad of gracious manner . . . his arms and biceps were powerfully developed. His complexion was medium as I recall it. His movements were quick."[10]

The conversation that took place between them started as soon as Preece came through the door and lasted well into the night. And although it was Vinson and Preece who knew each other through their correspondence, as Preece wrote, "It was Bob Howard who set the mood [that] evening."[11]

"Bob took over the three-way conversation as I recall," Preece continued, "but by some easy, natural right of knowledge. Truett, I suppose, was used to being his willing auditor. I found myself eagerly listening."[12]

Since Preece also had literary aspirations, much of their conversation was focused on books, for he recalled, "Bob Howard's flow of tongue. Bob's range of knowledge. Bob's bent for books. These first impressions have never faded."[13] More specifically, Preece wrote, "I remember that Bob had bought several books during the trip, and they were in sight. One was a collection of verse by a talented child named Nathalia Crane, then making a splash in the American literary world. I had heard of Miss Crane, but not of Olive Schreiner, whose *Story of an African Farm* was also among Bob's purchases."[14] Nathalia Crane had only turned 14 that year, but the child prodigy already had four books of poetry, a novel, and an autobiography published, while the Schreiner novel, her most famous, had originally been published in 1883. The two books certainly demonstrated to Preece something about Howard's eclectic interests in reading.

The conversation also naturally turned to writing, especially because Preece had already read some of Howard's works, including his most recently published short story, "The Lost Race," about his beloved Picts. Preece recalled, "I had thought the piece a bit too outlandish . . . and was now telling the writer so in person. Bob's face flushed, then he proceeded to give me a lesson in anthropology. Little people—diminutive humans—once existed in Western Europe he told me. They had left their imprints most clearly upon the cultures of the Celtic countries—Ireland, Scotland and Wales."[15] This may well have struck up a common interest between the two men for all things Celtic-Irish.

"At one point," Preece wrote, as was natural for a small group of men, "the conversation veered toward women." "All of us may have commented about the scarcity of intellectual girl friends in church-dominated Texas," a trait it seems they all desired in a woman, but Preece was notably excited to have met such a young lady recently. "A few months ago, I met a very intelligent Dallas girl in Fort Worth and am corresponding with her. She's Maxine Ervin," Preece informed the others.[16] He had fallen in love after meeting her on the campus of Texas Christian University. "She was the first intellectual woman of my long romancing," he wrote of Ervin. "A large, charismatic sort of girl, she was in her early twenties. Her eyes were intense and haunting from nagging old sorrows. Rich dark hair crowned her medium dark face," and he noted "she was intensely individual."[17] She was then working for the *Dallas Times-Herald* and in addition to their correspondence, Preece had recently visited with her while in Dallas for a Lone Scout rally.[18]

Howard was surprised to hear the name Maxine Ervin, for he had not seen her since she and her sister, Lesta, visited Cross Plains in 1923.[19] "Maxine Ervin is my cousin," Howard told Preece, explaining, "My full name is Robert Ervin Howard."[20] There was no doubt shock at the strange coincidence, and Preece later remarked, "Oddly two kinspeople not close to each other became my most cherished friends."[21] Not long after, Preece recalled, "I wrote Maxine, expressing my pride in having met such a remarkable member of her family."[22] In addition, because Howard and Preece had a number of common interests, Preece also remembered how "week after week following the Austin session, I received a letter from Bob. Usually these were undated, written on two sides of a typed sheet, prefixed by an oriental greeting 'salaam.'"[23]

The meeting between the three men proved an important transition in Howard's life for two reasons, as Burke explains: "Howard's friendship with Preece . . . whose enthusiasm for Celtic lore fanned Howard's nascent interest into roaring passion; and the creation, in early 1928, of *The Junto*, a type-written-journal of one copy per issue which circulated among a small circle of Texans (and one or two out-of-staters) with literary aspirations."[24] These interests and endeavors still loomed in Howard's future, but both developed out of Howard's meeting with Preece.

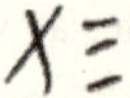

"I'm back at Cross Plains," Howard wrote Smith after his vacation with Vinson, "not working much just now, but will start to work soon. I still hate the damned place but sometimes I almost enjoy being here."[25] First, he returned to his routine of working out, having gained some weight over the summer months. He had weighed 170 pounds upon returning home, but by October he was able to write Smith, "I'm weighing 164 now and am developing my right arm.

I think I could knock a castle door off its hinges."[26] And so, as he wrote in *Post Oaks*, he "began to take on weight amazingly as a result of regular and systematic exercises, and for the first time in his life, began to assume really impressive proportions."[27] By the end of the year he weighed 180 pounds, which he proudly reported being "mostly solid muscle."[28]

Howard also resumed his writing with a determination to remain both free and independent by making his living as a writer.[29] He submitted many more stories and faithfully checked his lockbox at the post office daily for any correspondence from his editors, although he did become suspicious that the postal workers were reading his mail. To curb this he prefaced one of his letters to Smith with, "ARE YOU THE YOUNG MAN TO WHOM THIS LETTER IS ADDRESSED? ARE YOU ANY RELATION TO THAT WORTHY YOUNG MAN? YOU AREN'T? THEN WHY IN HELL ARE YOU OPENING HIS LETTERS?" He continued, "Having satisfactorily disposed of anyone who might open this letter by mistake, we will now proceed."[30]

On one trip to the post office that fall, Howard received a letter from *Weird Tales* editor Farnsworth Wright. Howard had been working on and off for a year on a short story called "The Shadow Kingdom," which he submitted to *Weird Tales* before his graduation. Wright offered him $100.00 for the story, the largest amount to date and a sum equivalent to approximately $1,500 in modern currency. As he wrote in *Post Oaks*, he "walked on clouds." It proved to be a turning point in his career, and it ended his nearly two-year dry spell. He showed the letter to his parents. "You're doing great," his father proudly told him. "Keep right on." And his mother, ever his biggest supporter, told him, "It looks as if you've finally landed in the game right."[31]

The acceptance of the story was significant for Howard, but because it would not be published until August of 1929, and payment sometime after, he still had a long road to travel before reaping the rewards of his success. Nevertheless, he was on the road to freedom. In the meantime, he continued to write, concentrating on his prose, for as he later wrote, "Since the summer of 1927, I've done little besides hammer out fiction."[32] And as the calendar gave way to a new year, his continued correspondence with Preece led to the first of the significant impacts their meeting had on his life, for in 1928 Robert E. Howard became decidedly Irish.

While Howard did have some Irish roots in his family tree, they were not omnipresent, and although he did demonstrate an interest in the history of the Celts at least as far back as 1919, it had never been at the forefront of his thoughts, words, and actions.[33] That all changed in 1928 when, as Howard scholar Patrice Louinet explains, "he began seeing himself as an Irishman." "He used every scrap of information and every chance he had," Louinet continued, "to *make* Irishmen of his ancestors OR TO *prove* their Irishness."[34] The friend responsible was Harold Preece, who later explained, "Bob Howard was the very first person with whom I could discuss intelligibly my avid interest in Celtica."[35] Just as Howard had found a confidant in Smith when it came to his interest in poetry, Howard found a similar fellowship with Preece in their shared love for all things Irish.

Preece did come to recognize that although "Bob was inalienably caught up in that powerful sweep of the Celtic legend . . . only by cancelling his very identity could he have subtracted himself from it."[36] Howard's last name was English and so were most of his father's ancestors, and although his mother was born an Ervin, that side of the family was at least as English as it was Irish, if not more so. Preece knew this because he once wrote how his love interest, Maxine Ervin, "would maintain to me privately that the family was of English descent, and express great admiration for the English society of fixed social classes which Bob so thoroughly despised."[37] While Howard helped foster Preece's interest in his heritage, Preece equally hoped "that I may have served a comparable purpose for him, with each having been the specialized audience of the other."[38] His hopes were fully realized.

The Celtic conversations between Howard and Preece came, in part, through their letters, although at first it appears only a scant topic; but over the next two years, it would subsume the content of their discussions. For instance, in one 1929 letter, Howard wrote of his heritage and craftily worded it so that he appears mostly of Irish descent. "As for their Norman blood, why, I wear a Norman name myself," Howard begins before claiming, "I am as proud of my close kinship with the Norman-Irish Martins of Galway as I am of kinship with the Dano-Irish O'Walsers and the pure Gaelic Ervins, Colliers and O'Terrals. The only English governor who ever treated the people right was Lord William Howard."[39] "The people," of course, were his people, the Irish.

Whenever they met, it seems their conversations were also crowded with talk of their Irishness. "During those years when I knew Bob Howard," Preece wrote, "our minds were fixed on the hills of Wicklow we had never seen, rather than those peaks of Callahan County we both knew."[40] It also became a shared topic of conversation whenever they got together with Vinson and Smith, for Preece also wrote fondly of "those legends of Ireland recounted by Bob when he, Truett Vinson, Clyde Smith, and myself gathered for night talk sessions in the woods around Pecan Bayou, near Brownwood."[41]

Howard embraced his newfound heritage in his letters to others as well. In an autobiographical sketch sent to Wright, Howard wrote, "By nationality I am predominately Gaelic, in spite of my English name—some three fourths Irish while the rest is a mixture of English, Highland, Scotch, and Danish."[42] While it did not reflect his true heritage, it does demonstrate just how far he was willing to go in his desire to make himself Irish. And by 1929 he began making use of the Gaelic language when he started signing his name "Fir Dun," for as he told Smith it was "Gaelic for The Brown Man," while he addressed Smith as "Fear Finn," meaning "The Fair Man."[43] In fact, Howard was "so fond of his Celtic heritage," Lovecraft once wrote another friend, "he has Gaelicised his middle name Ervin to Eiarbihn—as the fanatics in Ireland nowadays Gaelicise theirs."[44]

Christopher Dowd, a scholar of the Irish identity in American literature, once observed that "Howard's construction of his Irish identity went well beyond simply rehearsing an Irish narrative for himself in his letters; he always adopted supposedly Irish behaviors in his everyday life." One thing Dowd noted was how "he took to memorizing Irish poetry and Irish ballads, which he would recite and sing for friends."[45] Lindsey Tyson remembered this trait well when he wrote, "Bob was liked by all of his neighbors. He was especially kind and thoughtful of the elderly people who lived near him, made trips to town to get things needed by them, and just helped them any way possible. The fact that he would sometimes awaken them rather early in the mornings, singing about as loudly as he could some Irish song, did not seem to bother them. He had a rather good voice."[46]

Dowd also describes Howard's embrace of Irish ways through the continued cultivation of his love for boxing and the fact that he also took up drinking at this time in his life. Howard himself noted this fact in *Post Oaks* when he wrote, "Though he had taken to drinking, he was not extravagant, spending perhaps three or four dollars a month on wine elixir, alcoholic tonics, beer, and occasionally, bootleg whiskey. He did not drink as some drink, every day and all the time. When he drank, he got terrifically drunk, but between these debauches he seldom touched liquor of any kind. He liked beer as a beverage, but detested the taste of all other drinks."[47] Although "some scholars and biographers connect these interests to his efforts to assert a more masculine persona," Dowd believes they had become part of his Irish identity, "given common stereotypes of the Irish as hard-drinking pugilists and popular culture associations between fighting, drinking and Irish masculinity."[48]

Howard's Irishness also played to extremes as well. At one extreme he often described himself as suffering from dark moods. There is evidence that he already suffered from these prior to willing himself to become Irish, but now he could justify their presence in his life. "These moods," Howard wrote, "are hereditary, coming down the line of my purely Irish branch."[49] Although he had no pure Irish branch in his ancestry, Howard was now armed with a ready explanation when these dark moods prevailed; he could blame it on his ancestors. This would also include a suggestion that these dark Irish moods could play out in the greatest of extremes when he wrote that in his lineage "both men and women have been subject to black fits of savage brooding, which has been, in some cases, coupled with outbursts of really dangerous fury."[50]

On the opposite extreme, Howard could also be playful with his Irishness, such as when he started speaking in an Irish brogue with his mother. Being good-natured, Mrs. Howard played along. "She would use Irish words like 'Faith!' and 'Begorra!'" recalled Leroy Butler.[51] Evidently, she was so convincing with her contrived accent, Butler told one interviewer that he truly believed "his mother was Irish" because "she liked to use her Irish brogue."[52] Mrs. Howard was clearly just having fun, befitting her personality, for Butler's wife, Floyce, remembered her as a "humorous person," once saying "she was jolly."[53]

There are times, however, when Howard seemingly disparages the Irish-Celts, generally in his letters to Preece. In one such missive on St. Patrick's Day of 1929, Howard wrote, "I'm not worrying about my Irish past. What has my Celtic blood ever done for me but give me a restless and unstable mind that gives me no rest in anything I do? . . . Damn the Irish and damn the black Milesian blood in my veins that makes me like drift-wood fighting the waves and gives me no peace or rest waking or sleeping or riding or dreaming or traveling or wooing, drunken or sober, with hunger or slumber on me."[54] Around the same time the following year, Howard addresses a similar argument regarding the popular March celebration: "Saint Padraic's Day usually leaves me with a distaste for the whole Celtic Irish race. Simply because my last name isn't Gaelic, the shamrock I wear is sometimes the object of questioning glances. Well, anyhow I notice damn well that none of my bold tribesmen have tried to uphold Celtic integrity by jerking it off. I'll wear the green if I have to fight every damned Celt in the world."[55] In both these instances, and many others, while "Howard seems to be protesting against his heritage," Dowd explains that these kinds of statements "actually furthers his Irishness."[56] He elaborates that "by complaining about his 'Celtic blood,' he asserts that such blood exists and that it is the source for the defining features of his identity," so that "his criticism of the Irish is fundamentally an affirmation of his own Irishness; it is his way of staking an ethnic claim."[57]

As Howard's obsession grew, eventually it began to influence his writing. In fact, Burke observed that it became a pattern Howard would repeat throughout his career. In this case Burke explains that Howard's "Celtic Phase" led to the development of his "Celtic Persona."[58] Burke elaborates: "The pattern seems to work like this: he first begins reading about a subject; then he begins discussing the subject with his friends, adopting the point of view, even the speech and mannerisms, of this new *persona*; and when he has become comfortable with the new person he has, in effect, *willed* himself to become, he begins writing fiction from this point of view." Burke believes that "for Howard, the cultivation of these *personae* was an active—even if unconscious—process."[59] Howard himself demonstrates how taking on this Celtic persona influenced his writing, for after becoming a Hibernophile, he wrote a friend discussing his method of writing: "If I had a particular method, I suppose it should be Celtic, since the great part of my blood is of that race."[60]

As he developed this persona, his poetry became decidedly Celtic, and, by 1930, Burke explains, "Howard had become confirmed enough in his

Irishness, steeped enough in the history and lore of the subject, to begin writing fiction in this vein."[61] Howard was not alone in exploring his Irishness in literature, for there were other authors in the early twentieth century, including F. Scott Fitzgerald and Margaret Mitchell, who used their fiction to "explore the intersection of Irish and American cultures."[62] By so doing, Dowd explains, these authors, and Howard in particular, "believed he was anchoring his identity to something eternal, immutable, and authentic."[63]

Howard created two characters in 1930 who were both Irish reavers, Turlogh Dubh O'Brien and Cormac Mac Art.[64] He had limited success with the first character and none with the latter in his lifetime. The first story to result from his Celtic persona was "The Dark Man," written in early 1930 and featuring Turlogh Dubh O'Brien, who Howard described as "an Irish outlaw whose adventures are laid in the half century preceding the battle of Hastings."[65] The title of the story was likely derived from Nora Hopper's poem by the same name, for in January of 1930 he had written Smith about that very poem.[66] The story was one of Howard's darkest and most violent works, telling the tale of Turlogh's rescue of the Irish King Brian Boru's daughter from a Viking tribe.

Howard mailed the story to Farnsworth Wright for a new companion magazine to *Weird Tales* to have been called *Strange Stories*. Howard wrote Smith telling him the story had been accepted and that Wright "promised me $85.00 on publication." "The editor," Howard continued, "was kind enough to say it was a 'red blooded, he-man story.' Well, it has plenty of gore and action." Howard also wrote Preece, informing him, "I have submitted only one tale concerning this character, and it was accepted with an apparent relish, but I hope I can sell a series of stories on the same idea."[67]

To this end Howard set about writing a sequel to the story titled "The Gods of Bal-Sagoth," which was accepted for the impressive sum of $140.00, but his other efforts were either rejected or went unfinished. In the end only two Turlogh O'Brien stories were published in Howard's lifetime, and both saw publication in *Weird Tales* after the planned companion magazine failed to launch. And although "The Dark Man" was accepted before "The Gods of Bal-Sagoth," the latter appeared first in the October 1931 issue with the other following two months later. The stories received several positive comments, for A. V. Pershing, of Kenova, West Virginia, called "The Dark Man" "a masterpiece," while Charles D. Hornig, of Elizabeth, New Jersey, wrote of "The Gods of Bal-Sagoth," saying, "Its colorful scenes, so vivid in your mind's eye, and its quick daring action of the two enemies working for one purpose certainly make it Howard's best."[68]

Howard's other character was Cormac Mac Art, who, after being outlawed from Ireland, pursues a life of piracy by joining a band of Danes led by Wulfhere the Skull-splitter.[69] Howard wrote four stories with this character, only two of which were completed, and it is known that he submitted at least one, "Night of the Wolf," to Archibald Bittner, the editor of the pulp magazine *Argosy.* Although Holmes and Knight note it was "a breathless, blood-soaked, action-packed tale," Bittner responded to Howard with a one-line rejection letter on June 3, 1930: "I'm afraid 'The Night of the Wolf' is a lot too vague and slow moving for *Argosy*."[70] This led Morgan and Knight to call the rejection "the single most clueless of the Texan's prolific career."[71]

Although the two characters did not develop into consistent sales for Howard's fiction, the Celtic Persona influenced much of his writing and formed the basis for his most popular series character, Conan. It also greatly influenced the character of Robert E. Howard himself, for he had become Irish, as reflected in his thoughts, words, and deeds. Although he called "America, the land of his birth," Preece once wrote, he firmly believed that for Howard, Ireland was "the country of his heart." Preece also shared an anecdote that demonstrates just how deep this feeling ran in Howard.

> We were walking, and talking, across a grassy Brown County plain on a moonlit night during the last period of knowing each other well. I can recall his answer better than my words which prompted it. But I think I remarked that this was a night when our Old Folks might have gathered for some festivity or some battle, and of how I felt permeated by some mood emanating from some far-off age of theirs. Bob stopped still. I knew by his face that he was sharing the mood. "Yes," he said solemnly, "the last Celt should have died a thousand years ago."[72]

Robert E. Howard was the last Celt.

The other significant outcome of the Austin meeting was the creation of the one-copy literary paper they called *The Junto*.[73] Preece explains the idea developed as "friendships kept converging and, through letters, kept broadening." For instance, "Bob began writing also to my sister, Lenore, who was winning poetry prizes at the University of Texas, and to Booth Mooney, a Lone Scout."[74] "I told Booth of our fellow heretic, Bob Howard, Irish descended like ourselves," Preece recalled, and "afterwards those two began a cordial letter exchange."[75]

Booth Mooney was born in Wise County, Texas, in 1912, and from an early age he, too, had literary aspirations. He launched his writing career at the young age of 13 by covering local county courthouse news for the surrounding newspapers.[76] He later became a professional writer, authoring biographies of such notables as General Billy Mitchel, Sam Houston, and Lyndon B. Johnson, for whom he also served as a speechwriter during his senatorial years. At the time, however, he was a struggling 16-year-old aspiring author.[77]

It was Mooney and Preece who, while visiting together "on a cold rainy day in Decatur," developed the idea for the paper. They decided to call it *The Junto*, naming it "after Benjamin Franklin's coterie in Philadelphia," the debate club he had established in 1727.[78] There would only be one copy, and it would circulate through the mail in chain fashion, with comments added by each reader. The little paper was announced through their correspondence, such as when Howard wrote Smith, "I'm going to give your name to Booth Mooney as a possible subscriber to *The Junto*; a pretty good paper for that type. He seems to be a kindred soul."[79] The idea caught hold, for the first issue circulated in March of 1928.[80]

The little journal featured short essays, commentary, letters to the editor, poetry, movie reviews, anecdotes, and anything else the participants felt like writing. Most of what Howard submitted was his poetry, including such poems as "The King and the Mallet," "Nectar," "Age," and, perfectly in line with his Irishness, "Feach Air Muir Lionadhi Gealach Buidhe Mar Or." In addition, he wrote several autobiographical pieces, such as one describing his heritage and another regarding his trip to Galveston with Vinson to see the bathing beauties.

The other members made similar contributions, and many developed into heated arguments. For instance, in the July 1928 issue, Smith wrote an article titled "Collegiate" that was highly critical of college students and raised the ire of many of the members who were. Howard came to his defense, writing, "Let's have more by Smith; the rougher, the better; every man for himself and Hell for all." This left one member to comment, "There are only two objectionable features to *The Junto*—Clyde's 'college article' and [Howard's] opinion of it."[81]

In another case Preece had written a controversial essay called "Women; A Diatribe," in which he concludes there is no such thing as an intellectual woman, claiming there were only a few great women in history. Maxine fired back with indignation regarding his comments, but Howard also responded by writing, "I can't agree with you in your statement that the great women can be counted on the fingers of one hand. Men have sat at the feet of women down the ages and our civilization, good or bad, we owe to the influence of women."[82]

Smith also shared many autobiographical sketches, including one incident involving Howard.

> I remember that Bob Howard forcefully proved a point . . . [about] the instinctive will to live. A mutual friend, talking of the futility of existence, said life meant nothing. "Just the same, you'd jump like hell if I made a pass at you with this knife," said Bob. He was at the moment trimming his nails with one of his sabres; as the friend went ahead with his discourse, Bob slashed out at him with the cold steel . . . he missed, no doubt because the friend, in the midst of his eloquent desire for death, leaped out of the way and howled in a pale voice: "My God, you'd *kill* a feller!"[83]

After the first year, Mooney stepped down as the editor; Lenore Preece took over and saw it through to the end. The last issue is believed to have circulated sometime in the spring of 1930.[84] By that time all of the members, including Howard, were moving on with their lives, but when the literary endeavor began it provided each of them, and especially Howard, an opportunity to share their literary works among a close circle of like-minded friends.

Perhaps even more importantly, Preece later wrote, "I feel that it gave Bob a specialized, intimate, if small, sort of audience that he needed," an audience of "rebellious young intellectuals."[85]

Howard's writing career at the beginning of 1928 was showing evidence that he was right on the cusp of success.[86] "I have got a short story in the next *Weird Tales*," Howard wrote Preece, "and they hint that they will publish my stuff regular. I wish they would as I could use coin. I mean publish regular what I have already sold to them."[87] Again, the issue was that *Weird Tales* paid only after publication, not acceptance. Still, it was becoming clear to Howard, and evidently others, that his writing career was taking off.

One person who noticed was someone Howard had known from Cross Cut, R. Fowler Gafford. "The man was now past thirty and becoming somewhat settled in his habits," Howard wrote in *Post Oaks*, and "he had moved to [Cross] Plains and was in a sort of sketchy real estate business." Howard encountered Gafford one day in town; Gafford said that he, too, had decided to become a writer and that Howard should come read his stories. Hearing that he "now aspired to be a writer," Howard wrote, "amazed [Bob] as much as if a range bull had suddenly come into a haberdashery and demanded a silk hat and silk hose."[88] At first he did not take Gafford up on his offer, but as time passed, Howard became curious and acquiesced. After reading Gafford's yarns, Howard had to acknowledge "there was power there," but it was "struggling and halting, groping for life and expression, chained down by ignorance, stumbling over the stones of bad English."[89]

Gafford was well aware of his lack of education, for he explained to Howard that despite having written the great Western novel *West of the Rio Grande*, "a story of the modern West," it had been turned down by several publishers. "I can't seem to express myself as I'd like to," Gafford admitted; "I'm handicapped by my lack of grammar." He then proposed, "If you'll rewrite it for me, we will split it, fifty-fifty, all but the movie rights. I want the full dramatic rights."[90] Howard estimated it would only take him a week's effort, and so he agreed. After spending far more time on it than he felt he should have, Howard concluded, "The plot was good," but he felt his efforts did little to improve the novel, and he held out little hope it would ever be published.[91] It never was, and no copy of the manuscript is known to exist.[92]

What developed out of this seemingly futile exercise, however, was Howard's notion to write his own book. And so "he plunged into work with a zest," Howard wrote in *Post Oaks*, "determined to write a tale of his own life, seeking to instill an interest therein by a realistic account of the drabness, and sham of small town life, the futile and abortive gropings of humanity, and the failings and ambitions of such struggles as himself."[93] In a word, he was going to write realism.

The literary realism movement, the endeavor to represent reality in fiction stories, was born of the realist art movement of the late nineteenth century. It became popular with many early twentieth century authors and was epitomized by the works of two of Howard's favorites, Jack London and Jim Tully.[94] With a desire to write a novel that emulated his idols, Howard set about developing a new persona, one which, Burke explains, "would be a writer of 'realistic,' or mimetic, fiction, fiction drawn from or imitative of everyday life."[95] His letters throughout the spring and summer of 1928 were filled with discussions of realism, and he began experimenting with the style in his own writing. One such attempt was a short play titled "Irony," in which Costigan (the writer) is talking with former fellow employees of a confectionary store, no doubt a stand-in for the real drugstore at which Howard had worked as a soda jerk. In the play his alter ego rails against the small-town locals who harass him because he is a writer.[96]

Once he felt he was ready, Howard began writing the novel *Post Oaks and Sand Roughs*, telling autobiographical stories about real people only slightly hidden behind pseudonyms. "Time dragged into months, and still [Bob] toiled at his book," Howard wrote toward the end of his novel, but "as the book progressed, [Bob] realized that no publishing house in the world would buy it. It was too vague, too disconnected, too full of unexplained and trivial incidents—too much like life in a word."[97]

It is known that after Howard completed the novel, he sent it to at least one publisher, Dodd, Mead and Company. The only surviving correspondence regarding the novel comes from that publishing house, a rejection letter dated September 13, 1928.[98] As he had predicted the outcome and his reaction to it, "he was neither surprised nor very disappointed," because, he wrote, "He had enough artistic sense to know that his work had violated all rules of literature."[99]

Once again, Howard appeared to be engaging in another futile act, but by embracing this new persona, it greatly influenced his writing style. Although the realism movement itself eschewed stories having any fantasy or supernatural elements, Raymond Chandler understood that "fiction in any form has always intended to be realistic."[100] By embracing the tenets of this literary movement, Howard's writing became grounded in realism, imbuing them with a sense of verisimilitude. "Even his most chimerical flights of fancy are grounded in *realism*," writes Howard critic David A. Hardy, believing that "a sense of realism is a necessary companion of fantasy, one that allows for the willing suspension of disbelief."[101] This is what led another Howard critic, George Knight, to write, "The most interesting aspect of his fiction is not the fantasy but the realism—a realism springing from Howard's class, environment, beliefs, and the age in which he wrote."[102] This is not only what helped Howard sell stories but also one more thing that separated him from other pulp writers.

Chapter 14

Solomon Kane and Historical Fantasy, 1928

A wild moon rode the wild white clouds,
the waves in white crests flowed,
When Solomon Kane went forth again
and no man knew his road.
They glimpsed him etched against the moon,
where clouds on hilltop thinned;
They heard an eery echoed call
that whistled down the wind.
—"Solomon Kane's Homecoming"[1]

A friend once asked Robert E. Howard how he developed his characters, and he replied:

> To tell the truth, I don't know how a man gets a character for a story, anymore than I know how he falls in love. I don't know if his characters spring full-blown from his head, or if he sees a man walking down the street and recognizes him instantly. I doubt any writer knows for sure where his characters come from. . . . If somebody asks you where you get your characters, and they're sure to do that, you always say,

> "He's a combination of a lot of people I have known." That way, if your character is a damn fool, nobody will want to identify with him.[2]

Although how he developed his characters may not be clear, the type he liked writing about was. "It is the individual mainly which draws me," he wrote, "the struggling, blundering, passionate insect vainly striving against the river of Life and seeking to divert the channel of events to suit himself—breaking his fangs on the iron collar of Fate and sinking into final defeat with the froth of a curse on his lips."[3] His characters were the common man (and woman) who lived life on the frontier, not the culturally refined characters F. Scott Fitzgerald had recently made so popular with the publication of his novel *The Great Gatsby*. "This civilization is the hooey," Howard wrote Preece. "The characters I write about in my fiction are all primitive, see," and he described them as a "kind of combination of [boxer] Jack Dempsey, a Zulu chief and a prehistoric man," before adding in his best Irish pugilism, "To hell with these damned polished snobs—'sophisticated' hell."[4]

In addition to creating a new literary character, Howard knew full well that what was most attractive was to create a series character. From a simply self-serving standpoint, it meant the prospect for more regular payments. Yet Howard also knew that series characters were popular with the readers of the pulps, and it is what gets an author noticed and remembered. Farnsworth Wright once wrote about this in "The Eyrie": "A number of our readers have commented on the fact that the characters that appear in stories again and again are more interesting than heroes (or villains) whose exploits hold the stage for one story only. The characters who stride through weird adventures in more than one story, or in a series of stories, are welcomed by the readers as old friends." He then mentioned Robert E. Howard's "Solomon Kane, the dour Puritan fighting-man and redresser of wrongs" among the many beloved series characters.[5]

Although the first Kane story was started in late 1927, Howard had formulated the idea for the character sometime around 1922.[6] "Solomon Kane I created when I was in high school, at the age of about sixteen," he wrote, adding, "several years passed before I put him on paper." When describing how he created this character, he was evidently unsure, writing, "He was probably the result of an admiration for a certain type of cold, steely-nerved duelist that existed in the sixteenth century."[7] The first story he titled, appropriately enough, "Solomon Kane," and he finished it by early spring. When it came time for submission, Howard explained, "I wrote this story for the *Weird Tales* originally and then decided to try my luck with *Argosy-Allstory*, just as it was." It was not the type of story the editor at *Argosy* was likely to publish, and it was rejected, but as Howard wrote, "I got it back together with a long personal letter from the editor, written in pen and ink. Sure enough I did. He said in some places the story was 'very good' and in some places 'rotten!' He says that I have the 'stuff' if I 'get steered right' so therefore he is giving me the reasons it was turned down, in detail. He did, very concisely and very clearly . . . the main reason for non sale was 'unexplained miracles.'" This made sense, seeing as how such a story would be suitable for *Weird Tales*, his original intended audience. But, as Howard reasoned, "if a despised weird tale, whose whole minor tone is occultism, can create that much interest with a magazine which never publishes straight weird stuff, I don't feel so much discouraged."[8] Heartened by the editor's words, he submitted the yarn to Wright in late February.

"The *Weird Tales* took that [manuscript] the *Argosy* editor commented upon, offering me $80," Howard wrote Smith in March. "The *Weird Tales* editor took it in its original form, for I didn't change it any, in spite of the defects pointed out by the *Argosy* editor, and says that he thinks he'll give me front page and cover illustration." The first story with a new character receiving the front cover bode well for the possibility of a series. Wright, however, did have one request. "He asks me to change the title 'Solomon Kane,'" Howard wrote, before adding, "I can't seem to think of a good title." He managed to come up with one.[9] "Next month if nothing happens the *Weird Tales* publishes my 'Red Shadows,'" Howard wrote Smith in June.[10] He then quoted from the advertisement for the story in the July issue that announced "Next Month *Red Shadows* by Robert E. Howard."[11] "Red Shadows on black trails—thrilling adventures and blood-freezing perils—savage magic and strange sacrifices to the Black God the story moves swiftly and without the slightest let-down in interest through a series of startling episodes and wild adventure to end in a smashing climax in a glade of an African forest. A story that grips the reader and carries him along in utter fascination by its eery succession of strange and weird happenings." Howard then told Smith with total understatement, "The announcement does it a fair amount of justice I suppose."[12]

Fortunately for Howard, the August issue hit the newsstands on July 1 as scheduled. The cover illustration featured a woman in distress with a man standing over her dressed in clothing from the Renaissance, despite the fact that Howard's Solomon Kane wore the clothing of a Puritan. It did not matter. Howard's name was prominently featured on the cover, and he had launched his first successful series character.

Solomon Kane was indeed a Puritan, living in the late sixteenth and early seventeenth centuries, who wanders the world looking to mete out justice with his sword. Because of the supernatural elements and magic in the stories of Solomon Kane, they fall squarely in the genre of historical fantasy, mainly because the character is rooted in the real world.[13] Howard described him as "a tall man . . . clad in black from head to foot, in plain, close-fitting garments that somehow suited the somber face. Long arms and broad shoulders betokened the swordsman, as plainly as the long rapier in his hand. The features of the man were saturnine and gloomy."[14] In the opening Solomon Kane comes across a young girl who has been raped and stabbed. As he comforts her in his arms, she draws her final breath. Howard has his dark hero deliver one of his most memorable lines when he writes, "Slowly he rose, mechanically wiping his hands upon his cloak. A dark scowl had settled on his somber brow. Yet he made no wild, reckless vow, swore no oath by saints or devils. 'Men shall die for this,' he said coldly."[15] Despite the Puritan aspects of Solomon Kane's character, as Howard scholar Dierk Günther explains, "This vow demonstrates a decisive aspect of Kane's personality: an unrelenting thirst to mete out justice that can only be relinquished through punishment by the sword."[16] Kane's motivation is revealed after he finally tracks down the girl's murderer and the man asks why he has pursued him for killing a mere peasant girl. Howard wrote,

> All his life he had roamed about the world aiding the weak and fighting oppression, he neither knew nor questioned why. That was his obsession, his driving force of life. Cruelty and tyranny to the weak sent a

> red blaze of fury, fierce and lasting, through his soul. When the full flame of his hatred was wakened and loosed, there was no rest for him until his vengeance had been fulfilled to the uttermost. If he thought of it at all, he considered himself a fulfiller of God's judgement, a vessel of wrath to be emptied upon the souls of the unrighteous. Yet in the full sense of the word Solomon Kane was not wholly a Puritan, though he thought himself as such.[17]

"By branding him the 'fulfiller of God's judgement,'" Günther explains, "Howard adds a religious element to Kane's motivation."[18] This is clearly why Howard chose the name Kane, an alteration of the biblical Cain, who was cursed by God to be "a constant wanderer of the earth," and Solomon who was "a judge in God's name."[19]

Despite the fact the story held third place in the reader poll, no letters were published praising the story.[20] This did not stop Wright from accepting more stories from Howard featuring the wandering Puritan; "Skulls in the Stars" appeared in January and "Rattle of Bones" in June of 1929. With his fourth story, "The Moon of Skulls," he wrote a longer tale and tried submitting it to MacFadden Publications for their pulp magazine *Jungle Stories*, but after it was rejected, he sent it to Wright.[21] The first half of the story published in the June 1930 issue of *Weird Tales* was featured on the front cover, while the second half appeared in the following issue. One more story, "The Hills of the Dead," saw print in 1930, while "The Footfalls Within" was published in 1931, taking the number one ranking in the reader's poll for the September issue that year. The last Solomon Kane story published by Wright in 1932, "Wings in the Night," ended on a high note. It placed second in the reader poll and garnered the most praise of all his Solomon Kane stories in "The Eyrie."[22] Duke Williamson of Springfield, Massachusetts, wrote the story was "up to this author's highest standard, and that is saying a good deal," while fellow *Weird Tales* author H. Warner Munn wrote the yarn "made a deeper impression upon me than any other of the stories I have seen."[23] By the time it was published, however, Howard had not written a Kane story in two years.

Wright did not accept all of Howard's tales of Solomon Kane, for two others were rejected, "The Blue Flame of Vengeance" and "The Right Hand of Doom." Howard also tried submitting the former, a pirate-themed tale, to *Argosy* and *Adventure*, but they, too, sent rejection letters.[24] Moreover, Howard wrote three poems featuring the character, and although none were published in his lifetime, "Solomon Kane's Homecoming" has come to hold a special place in the hearts of Howard fans, especially those partial to the Puritan wanderer.

There were many readers in Howard's lifetime who also favored his first successful series character. It was not uncommon to read in "The Eyrie" such laments as the one by Robert L. Grantham from Ontario: "I wish we had more stories of Solomon Kane."[25] Even after the last story appeared in the July 1932 issue, readers continued to call for more Kane stories. In the January 1934 issue, Donald Allgeir of Springfield, Missouri, wrote, "I would like a revival of Solomon Kane," while in July 1935, J. Connell of Lowell, Massachusetts, wrote, "Have Howard bring back Solomon Kane—he was great."[26]

After Howard's death H. P. Lovecraft made note of the importance of the Kane stories for Howard when he wrote, "These tales . . . marked Mr. Howard's development of that skill and zest in depicting sanguinary conflict which became so typical of his work."[27] Others have since noted the importance of these stories to Howard, especially his first, "Red Shadows," for as *Weird Tales* historian Robert Weinberg wrote, the story was "destined to vault Robert E. Howard into the front ranks of authors" for the "unique magazine," while Howard biographer Mark Finn argued that with its publication "Howard became a literary force to be reckoned with."[28]

Out of all of the series characters Howard created, Kane proved to be the most complex, especially when it came to the character's driving motivations. This had much to do with Howard's own complexities and his personality. Lovecraft recognized this in a letter written after Howard's death. "Solomon Kane reflected another side of [Howard]," he wrote, "the brooding ethical sense which made him furious over injustices & oppressions."[29] It was not uncommon for Howard to rail against these in his letters such as when he complained of "the many injustices . . . of this country and system."[30] Kane's concern for the abused and oppressed was really nothing more than a reflection of Howard himself. This is what led his friend Smith to write, "He was

Solomon Kane, off paper," even going so far as to add, "even more than he was Conan."[31]

X≡

Over the summer of 1928, Howard spent some time on vacation, first going down to the Texas-Mexico border in June, to Eagle Pass, before crossing the Rio Grande River into Piedras Negras, Mexico.[32] There he sent a postcard to Preece depicting the customs house found in the Mexican border town and signing it with nothing more than his X-Triple Bar signature.[33] From his second-floor hotel room, Howard wrote a letter to Smith, complaining of the lack of creature comforts there: "Not even a movie in this god forsaken town."[34] He later informed another correspondent why people crossed the border when he wrote, "The main charm about those Mexican towns to most people is, of course, the liquor."[35] He evidently had taken full advantage of the legal liquor available there, for as he wrote Smith, "I've got the devil's disposition and a belly full of Sabinas and cognac."[36]

In a suggestive passage to his Brownwood friend, Howard mentioned the local women he saw there. "I didn't see such a hell of a lot of Eagle Pass but I saw Piedro Negras—and the hottest girl I've seen in many a day—a skirt in a Mexican whore house away out of the polite section. Also I learned several new vulgarities in Spanish. Some nice looking strumpets in what they name The Reservation across the border and most of them brazen as hell—five dollars."[37] There was, indeed, a section of Piedras Negras commonly known as Boys Town where not only liquor was legal but so, too, was prostitution. Whether Howard ever spent five dollars there is unknown, for he never explicitly states so, but it was not an uncommon practice and would remain so throughout the twentieth century.[38]

Howard also took a trip to Galveston with his friend from Cross Plains Lindsey Tyson. "We had a cabin near the ocean," Tyson recalled years later, and he held two vivid memories from the trip. The first, he explained, was "after I had gone to bed, Bob went down to the waters edge and wrote poetry all night—came back in at daybreak. He had written one poem" and Tyson noted, "it was a beautiful thing."[39] The poem, "The Call of the Sea," read in part:

White surf is beating
On the grey shore
Wave hordes, fierce meeting,
Savagely roar,
Where the white surf fiends
Screech evermore.
Now the tide surges
Far out to sea
Wave with wave merges
Where ocean-winds dree.
Hark to the wild wind,
Fierce, roaring, free![40]

The other memory Tyson held was a boat ride out into the Gulf. "We went out a lot, 10 or 12 miles on an excursion boat. I believe it was the only time he was on the sea. He liked the sea."[41] Tyson also recalled how Howard, ever the romantic, told him, "when he died he wanted someone to, after he had been cremated, to stand on the front of a ship and cast his ashes out over the water."[42]

Howard also visited Preece over the summer. "Glad you enjoyed our reunion in Fort Worth," Howard wrote him after the trip, "I sure as Hell did." Apparently on that visit and throughout the summer months, Howard had been indulging himself quite often, for his weight had shot up to 192 pounds.[43] "My appetites annoy me extremely," Howard wrote his friend. "I am trying to reduce and by superhuman efforts have gotten down to 185 pounds, and struggle against the temptation to gluttonize and guzzle."[44]

In addition to his vacations farther afield, Howard made many trips to Brownwood, where he still, evidently, continued to indulge himself. On one such visit with Smith, he recalled, they went for a drive up to Cross Cut "long enough to load up with ice, and beer at a bootleg joint." He continued, "We then proceeded along the road, halting to devour sandwiches and guzzle, and then took up our journey, considerably teed up. Additional beer increased our mood and you may visualize us racing along the road and blazing away at signs on each side of the road."[45]

On one such trip to Brownwood, believed to have taken place sometime in 1928, Smith wrote a realism play based on a conversation between himself and Howard on a bridge over Adam's Branch, a stream running through town. Clyde asks him in the play, "Well, tell me, are you having any luck? Or is it the same old story—rejection slips?" Howard replied, "There are too many of them—and, if I sell anything, I'm often forced to rewrite it three or four times."[46] Other than the sale of the first Solomon Kane story, Howard was still struggling to have his works accepted.[47]

On another trip in September, Smith, Vinson, and Howard spent several days on a ranch owned by Smith's uncle, located just outside of Brownwood. Smith wrote about one of their excursions to the ranch in *The Junto*.

> The Ford click, click clicks up the hill, down the hill, along a level stretch, across a gully. . . . Brakes grind, and yellow lamps throw a soft light on red gates. Three, two, one more to open, and beyond lies the ranch house huddled beneath the stars, half-hidden by the trees. . . . We troop merrily up the steps and Bob Howard yells, "Erin go Bragh," as I open the door. Truett Vinson lights the lamp, and we walk out upon the screened-in porch, and pump crystal-cold water from the cistern. We drink as horses drink: with relish and noise. Then we blow out the lamp, lock the house, and go for a ramble in the woods. Bob leads the way; he is naked to the waist, with a handkerchief tied around his head, and he assumes the grandeur of a pirate in our eyes. A romantic figure. We march in single file through the starshine. Into the woods . . . dark and gloomy, out again into a cleared space. Over rocks, boulders, mountains, the creek, briar bushes, and barb wire entanglements. Then back to the ranch house.

They talk long into the night before finally going to sleep. The next morning, Vinson gets a fire going in the kitchen stove, and, Smith writes, "We cook bacon and eggs, toast bread, make strong coffee. Then we set out for the caves. On the way, we stop at the swimming hole, where Bob and I take a plunge. Then we reach the caves."[48] They run around like cavemen, take some boxing pictures, and use "the cliffs as the Khyber Pass" to take several "Afghan photos." They take time out to read things of interest to each other before deciding it is time for dinner. "On the way back to the ranch house," Smith continues, "I recite several poems by Sassoon, Bob follows, chanting one of Jack London's verses." After dinner, they "lock the door once more, and tool homeward."[49]

Howard wrote Preece about their September visit to the ranch, telling him how "we sported hither and yon clad in innocence, purity and a loin cloth apiece—there being caves to explore and cliffs to climb."[50] They also drove up to the town of Cisco, for Howard also wrote, "At the dam at Cisco, the largest of its kind in the world, we stopped awhile and watched the bathers."[51] The dam had been constructed in 1923, and the pool, built at the base of the dam and considered the world's largest concrete swimming pool, opened to the public in 1927.

There were some occasions in which his friends came up to Cross Plains, but as Howard wrote about one such visit by Smith, "I have little entertainment to offer and we spent most of the time in idle conversation." The idle talk, however, proved to come in marathon sessions whenever they got together. As Howard wrote, "Our usual procedure is to drive or walk some miles out on a highway or some country road late at night and there sit and converse, varying this with strolls up and down in the vicinity, while our conversation ranges from metazoan to dinosaurs, and from prize fights to ancient religions. Sometimes we talk this way until three or four o'clock in the morning, sometimes until dawn. Quite often we stay up all night."[52]

Other times they walked along the highway in hopes that someone might give them a ride, although they had no particular destination in mind. On one such visit by Smith, they were picked up by a friend who drove them into Coleman, and the three of them, Howard wrote, "spent some time at a bootleg joint just outside the outskirts of town."[53] That location was likely the ranch owned by Charles G. Thorne, who ran the American Café in town with his wife, Kathryn. From their ranch they sold bootleg whiskey, or at least Charles did until April 1928, when he suspiciously died from a "suicide," and Kathryn took over the business. She then ran it for close to two years before running off to marry the notorious outlaw Machine Gun Kelly.[54]

Whenever he was not on vacation, visiting friends, or "gluttonizing and guzzling," Howard was either writing, helping out at home, or engaging in his favorite pastimes.[55] One of his interests was practicing with firearms and another was throwing knives. He had been collecting various weapons over the years, often purchasing them from the Sears Catalog or from the Francis Bannerman & Sons military goods mail order company operating out of New

York City.[56] Earl Baker remembered Howard's collection in an interview, "There were two swords, both sabers of Civil War vintage—one a battle saber, heavy and sharp; the other a handsome cross saber without an edge. There was a double-curved French bayonet of the late nineteenth century, modeled after the Turkish yataghan. There was a World War I trench knife, with a triangular blade and an iron knuckle-guard. There was a boomerang, and there were three or four heavy knives of various kinds."[57] Lindsey Tyson recalled Howard owning a .380 Colt Automatic and that one of the knives had "a five-inch blade." He carried it "in his hip pocket, and he could jerk that knife out of his pocket and open that blade at the same time. I never did know how . . . I couldn't do it."[58] To achieve this Howard worked hard at refining his skills, for Baker recalled a cedar post in his backyard and how "Robert practiced throwing knives at it until it was worn away in the middle to hardly more than half an inch thick."[59] Baker's sister, Vera, remembered watching Howard practice, commenting, "I was fascinated."[60] He also purchased a machete on one of his trips to Mexico and a sword from the Alamo gift shop in San Antonio.[61]

Howard still enjoyed going to see the silent films playing at the movie theater in town, or at the Lyric whenever he was in Brownwood. Over the summer of 1928, he informed Preece about two of his favorites when he wrote, "I saw *The Wizard* and thought it was red hot. Also *What Price Glory* which is in my opinion the nearest thing to a masterpiece ever filmed."[62] *The Wizard* was a 1927 silent horror film, now considered lost, and *What Price Glory* was a 1926 comedic war film about two veteran Marines. Both starred one of Howard's favorite actors, Edmund Lowe, and the latter also featured the actress Dolores del Rio, whom he found attractive. After seeing *The Bridge of San Luis Rey* in 1929, however, he came to believe Lily Damita was the most attractive actress ever. "My God, this Damita girl is a white hot flame," he wrote Smith. "She dances like a fanflare of sunfire blown before the wind—no, like a burning flame of moon-mist under the stars—Hell—see her for yourself. Some things can't be described. They have to be seen."[63]

Howard also enjoyed reading, but as he told Smith, "I haven't time to read for pleasure alone." He often found himself reading for work, gathering background information for a story he planned to write. When he did read for pleasure, he informed Smith, "I'd rather read straight action, Wild West stuff, than the insipid and bloodless muck handed out by most of the writers today."[64]

In addition to his professional writing, Howard also continued making contributions to *The Junto*, such as movie reviews, poems, or commentaries, including one on Charles Lindbergh's fame and the mob mentality of people.[65] In the fall of 1928, the editor of the paper, Booth Mooney, asked for contributor biographies, but Howard did not take too kindly to the idea. As he explained to Smith, "There are several reasons, the main one being that as several of my cousins receive it, my mother would be pretty near bound to hear about it and there are a good many things in my life that I don't want her to know about. Another thing, I don't care to have my inner self bared before the readers of the Junto because I have decided that some of them are crumbs."[66] Among the items he may not have wanted his mother to know about was "the diabolical blond."[67]

Howard had written to Mooney about a girl he liked, and he referred to her using that mysterious sobriquet. Though the letter does not survive, Preece explained, "By what Bob wrote Booth, he had not only started attending Sunday school—a rough shock to us debauched ones—but he had been elected vice-president of his Sunday school class. He mentioned the girl and his strong interest in her." Howard had apparently become smitten with a particular girl that fall and began attending Sunday school at the Methodist church, even going so far as to join the Epworth League, a young adult group at the church, all with the intent of being closer to the girl.[68] Word spread among the members of *The Junto*, who referred to the mystery woman as "The Sunday school girl," leaving them to gossip and ponder which of the revelations was more stunning: Howard going to church or pursuing a girl.[69]

Although Dr. and Mrs. Howard continued to attend church, Howard had fallen away. As Smith recalled, Howard had developed "an expressed detachment toward the Christian Faith, stating he did not know what he believed, adding that he supposed he was an agnostic."[70] So to suddenly begin attending the Methodist church took everyone by surprise. And his attitude toward women was usually rather neutral. "I notice this much," he wrote Preece that fall. "Truett or Clyde, together or alone, quite often are taken up by girls, but that the dames usually pass me up, even if they know me—and pass us all up when I am with the crowd."[71] In another letter he told his friend, "I am always courteous to the fair sex," but he concluded, "I cannot figure them out and I do not try."[72] So, again, to have gone so far as attending Sunday school to pursue a girl took everyone aback.

The true identity of the girl Howard himself referred to as "the diabolical blond," however, remains shrouded in mystery.[73] Howard's first biographer believed it may have been Ruth Baum, who lived across the street from the Howards, but in an interview she never recalled him saying anything to her, commenting, "He was a very quiet boy. Not an outward sort of person at all."[74] According to Roehm, there was one problem with Baum being the prime suspect; she was already married by the fall of 1928 and living in Brownwood.[75] Another possible candidate may have been Lindsey Tyson's sister, Elizabeth; however, she was away at college. Although his friends tried for several years to find out who she was, as Roehm concluded his research on the subject, "I think it's safe to say that we'll never know for sure."[76] Whoever she was, it evidently did not work out, and he soon dropped out of both associations by early the next year, for in March of 1929 he wrote Preece, "I've neglected the Epworth League and Sunday School lately."[77] Although it did not pan out, clearly Howard was beginning to pay more attention to the women around him as well as those on the silver screen.

If the ladies did not always take to Howard, he still had man's best friend. "Wherever Bob went, Patch went," Dr. Howard once wrote of Howard's relation with his dog. "Patch even shared Bob's food at the table and was a real companion."[78] The neighbors spoke of this as well. Floyce Butler recalled Patch being "a pretty black and white dog" that Howard "used to make bark" by teasing him.[79] Larry McDonough remembered Patch as "a friendly dog" and that he was always "chasing cats away or this, that and the other," and how "he didn't bark or anything, he'd just wag his tail."[80] That was, of course, unless Howard was teasing him.

Patch, however, suddenly became sick one day. As Dr. Howard later wrote, "When the dog was 12 years old, he sickened to die." They tried helping the dog recover, but it was no use, not even Dr. Howard's medicine could help the dog. Sadly, "Robert knew his dog was going to die." His reaction to his grief over this sobering realization was severe. "He packed his grip," wrote his father, "opened the gate, and walked out." As he proceeded to leave, he told his mother, "Mama, I am going," and then made his way to Brownwood.[81]

In his youth Howard developed a strong sensitivity toward animals. Even while out on hunting excursions with his friends growing up, he never participated in the kill, for as Dr. Howard explained, "You could not have induced him to have shot a bird or a jackrabbit or any kind of animal."[82] Howard himself often wrote about his sympathy toward animals, such as when he shared his feelings toward bullfighting: "That's one form of amusement I've never been able to induce myself to watch. I could stand the slaughter of the bulls but the disemboweling of the wretched worn-out horses would sicken me."[83] As Dr. Howard simply summed it up, "Robert loved animals of all kind."[84] And he proved to be very sympathetic toward them, for "when an old starved horse or dog came around [the] home, he fed them."[85]

Howard went to Brownwood while Patch lay dying in Cross Plains because he would not, could not watch a loved one die. He stayed with his friend Smith and "each morning he phoned and asked his mother if Patch was still alive."[86] For several days she said he was, and the conversation then turned to other things, but the situation weighed heavy on his heart. Patch's dying had put him in one of his dark Irish moods, moving him to consider his own mortality, and he opened up to Smith, his one true confidant in life. "Bob made the statement that he would do away with himself if it were not for his mother," Smith chillingly remembered. Howard then said to him, "My father is a man, and can take care of himself, but I've got to stay on as long as my mother is alive." As Smith explained, it was "as though duty kept him from doing away with himself" and that it was also this that "kept him pounding away on his typewriter."[87]

Howard's views on suicide had evidently changed over time, from his curiosity when he heard his high school peer, Roy Guthrie, had killed himself in 1923, to his despair over the Echla Laxson affair in which he kissed Smith's girlfriend then contemplated his own suicide in 1925.[88] Now, in 1928, he had seemingly resolved himself to the idea, with only his sense of duty preventing him from doing so. According to what he said to Smith, Howard no longer thought of writing as a means to freedom but a means to keep going while his mother was alive.[89] Perhaps had he known he had achieved success, his thoughts would have been different, but as there is often a lag between achieving success and reaping its rewards, as it was for Howard, the only means he saw for achieving true freedom now was suicide. If Smith's memory is accurate, Howard was now living on borrowed time; his mother's health—her very life—was the timepiece.

On Howard's fourth morning in Brownwood, the answer his mother gave to his question changed. "His mother," Dr. Howard wrote, "told him she thought the Patch dog would not last longer than 12 o'clock." After that, "he never inquired any more" about Patch, for "he knew the dog would soon die" and "therefore, he never spoke of him again."[90] Patch did die on the day of his fourth phone call, but the exact date is unknown as there are no specific dates associated with his death. Based on the circumstances and events surrounding the death of Howard's dog, as well as his age, Patrice Louinet estimates "the dog died in 1927 or 1928, but no later than that."[91]

Dr. Howard was left with the responsibility of burying Patch. "I had the dog buried in a deep grave in the back lot," he wrote, "then had the lot plowed deeply and then had them take a big harrow and harrow it deeply all over to destroy every evidence of the grave, so sensitive was he to the loss of the dog."[92] No marker was placed to show the location of Patch's grave, and the only remembrance was his entry in the family Bible, which simply stated, "(Patch) Robert Howard's dog, born Christmas 1917."[93]

Howard came home but did not talk about what had happened. He only mentioned the dog once more. "Mother, did you bury Patch under the mesquite in the corner of the lot on the east side?" he asked her. Mrs. Howard said, "Yes," and that was it. He never talked about Patch ever again, nor did he ever own another dog.[94]

As the end of the year approached, Howard did have some good news that certainly must have made his parents proud and likely surprised the citizens of Cross Plains. Most people around town already knew he was writing for *Weird Tales*, but most did not know he was also capable of writing Westerns.[95]

Beginning on November 2, 1928, the *Cross Plains Review* began serializing Howard's first commercially published Western, "Drums of the Sunset," and it ran for nine issues over the holiday season, ending on January 4, 1929. As Western author James Reasoner wrote, "The story is a good one, solidly in the tradition of Western fiction at the time, with a stalwart hero from Texas," and for his efforts Howard received twenty dollars.[96]

During the Thanksgiving holiday, the Howard house was busy. Howard's cousin Earl Lee Comer had left California and moved back to Dallas, so he spent the week of Thanksgiving visiting. In addition, Smith and Vinson came from Brownwood and spent the weekend with the Howards.[97] The gathering of his friends and cousin must have been memorable for him, because Howard left behind a sheet of paper with their names typed on it to which he added the word "life."[98]

After celebrating Christmas at home, Howard traveled to Brownwood for another gathering with his friends. For over two months, they had been planning a return trip to Smith's uncle's ranch outside of Brownwood. "I am heartily in favor of the get together," Booth Mooney wrote Smith in October, "of you, Preece, Truett, and Bob (and myself) sometime during the Christmas holidays. I believe that the days immediately following the twenty-fifth would be best."[99] As it turned out, Mooney was unable to attend, but the rest gathered together in Brownwood on Thursday, December 27, and drove out to the ranch.

Preece remembered the gathering fondly years later, describing the ranch as "a wooded ravine in Brown County," and how "the central personage of that reunion was . . . Bob Howard." Preece recalled their consumption of alcohol when he wrote that Howard's "tongue had been whetted by the bottle of liquor he'd been able to pick up from a drugstore as a 'medical prescription,'" and how at one point he was "bawling at the top of his voice a verse from an old Revolutionary song." Again, the conversation turned toward all things Celtic, particularly "fairies and leprechauns and all those diminutive humanoids of Celtic legend," and from Howard, Preece wrote, "I heard the first time some plausible explanations of the stories."[100]

"I had a wonderful time with you fellows," Preece later wrote Smith, "one that I shall always remember; and I deeply appreciate the hospitality which you and your family extended to me." The gathering had been a success, and after Smith wrote about it in *The Junto*, the other Juntoites became jealous. Lenore Preece suggested that they repeat the gathering at the end of 1929. Vinson voiced his agreement to the idea, writing that everyone is "welcome to any *shameful* gatherings which we may have in the future—*providing* a sense of humor, a gift of 'hooey,' and a bottle of liquor are all brought along!" Howard wrote he too agreed, adding, "And don't forget the liquor; that's the most important of the three; drunk, even Juntoites can stand each other."[101]

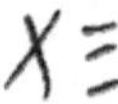

Although Howard would achieve success as a writer, beginning with the Solomon Kane series, he had yet to reap the benefits and was beginning to feel the strain. "Here I am, with seven years of hard work behind me," Howard wrote Smith, "and only some twenty five stories, articles and rhymes marketed to show for it." He also shared his concern that his only true outlet was *Weird Tales*, when he wrote, "Here am I, slugging away at a cheap, little known magazine which may already be bankrupt, weaving fanciful and impossible tales and absolutely unknown outside that magazine's limited clientele." And although he wrote somewhat disparagingly of himself, believing, "I am not a genius, neither am I clever, educated or especially intelligent," he at least added, "But I have faith in myself and a capacity for work."[102] He was certainly not afraid of work, but his first three years as a professional writer had proven lean ones. According to the former literary agent of the Howard estate, Glenn Lord, Howard's "annual earnings were: 1925, $24; 1926, $50; 1927, $37.50; and 1928, $186," to which he commented, "Not exactly an auspicious beginning for a man planning to earn his livelihood by writing."[103] Howard's earnings for 1928 were equivalent to approximately $3,000 in modern dollars, certainly not enough to live on. But Howard had another series character he was working on, and this time the outlet for the stories would not be *Weird Tales*.

you and your family extended to me." The gathering had been a success, and after Smith wrote about it in *The Junto*, the other Junto-ites became jealous. Lenore Preece suggested that they repeat the gathering at the end of 1928. [illegible] welcome [illegible] any more [illegible] gatherings which [illegible] the future [illegible] Howard [illegible] And [illegible] the most important of [illegible] can stand each other."

X

Although Howard would achieve success as a writer, beginning with the Solomon Kane stories, [illegible] was beginning to feel the strain. "Three [illegible] and seven years of hard work behind me," Howard wrote Smith, "and not [illegible] some [illegible] stories [illegible] He also [illegible] his concern that his only [illegible] outlet was *Weird Tales*, when he wrote: "Here am I [illegible] cheap, little known magazine [illegible] obscure and entirely unknown outside that magazine's limited circle. And although he wrote some [illegible] educated or especially intelligent," he at least added, "but I have faith in myself and a capacity for work." He was certainly not afraid of work, but his first three years as a professional writer had proven lean ones. According to the former literary agent of the Howard estate, Glenn Lord, Howard's annual earnings were: 1925, $24; 1926, $50; 1927, $37.50; and 1928, $186, to which he commented, "Not exactly an auspicious beginning for a man planning to earn his livelihood by writing." Howard's earnings for 1928 were equivalent to approximately $3,000 in modern dollars, certainly not enough to live on. But Howard had another series character he was working on, and this time the outlet for the stories would not be *Weird Tales*.

Chapter 15

Steve Costigan and the Boxing Yarns, 1929

The leather bursts and the hand gives way,
But it's the end of a perfect day.
He hasn't stirred at the count of ten,
The referee lifts my hand and then
I hear the yells of the crowd again.
—"In the Ring"[1]

When America welcomed in the New Year on January 1, 1929, the prospects for another great year were high. Herbert Hoover, who was soon to take the oath of office and become the thirty-first president of the United States, reflected this hope during his campaign, in which he promised "a chicken in every pot and a car in every garage," while one of the most popular songs of the day was "Ain't We Got Fun." Come October, however, with the stock market crash on Black Tuesday, America's high hopes turned bleak; promises faded, and so did the fun. For Howard, however, it was just the opposite. He entered the new year with bleak prospects for his future, but by the end of the year, he was beginning to realize the fruits of his labor, for he was seeing more stories accepted and published and new outlets opening up.

At the beginning of the year, Howard wrote a letter to his friend Tevis Clyde Smith in which he listed all of the stories he had submitted for publication, how much effort he had put into them, and whether they were accepted or rejected by the publishers. "This isn't the whole list of course," he wrote, "but I haven't forgotten more than four or five stories. Of course I started scores which I never completed, and completed several which I never sent off, but this list comprises the majority of those I did send."[2] While the list appeared to be a good start for the soon-to-be 23-year-old author, Howard recognized the main problem when he continued, "I have been harried for years by people who wanted to know what magazines were publishing my hokum. Up to a short time ago I would always reply apologetically, Only *Weird Tales*." Howard eventually found a better way to answer the question, for as he told Smith, "Now, having the Celtic ability to lie without telling a false hood, I reply as you may have noticed: *Weird Tales*, *Ghost Story*, *The Poet's Scroll*, *The Ring*, and various newspapers."[3]

The reality, however, was that the only magazine consistently publishing his works up to January 1929 was *Weird Tales*. Yet, by the end of the year, having taken on a new persona, he began writing boxing yarns that not only opened up new outlets for publishing but also saw the beginnings of a new successful series character, Sailor Steve Costigan, the character's name being the same one he had used for himself in *Post Oaks*. This is what led his friend Smith to later write, "1929 actually marks the beginning of arrival, with freedom from such drudgery as a soda skeet, which had followed other employment Bob liked even less."[4]

Howard had been born in the midst of a boxing craze. Although the "Sweet Science" had come to America from England in the late 1700s, it was not until a hundred years later that Americans had the leisure time in which to either participate in or be spectators of the sport.[5] With the development of the marquis of Queensberry's rules and the bombastic self-promoting first heavyweight champion, John L. Sullivan, boasting, "I can lick any son of a bitch in the world," America entered what is now known as the golden age of boxing. Sullivan, the first true professional boxer, galvanized a nation to the sport. The fact that boxing in the late nineteenth and early twentieth centuries was illegal in all thirty-eight states did not stand in his way.[6] Despite this prohibition also standing in Texas, the state's wide-open lands and proximity to Mexico made it the early bastion of the sport. So when Howard was born, not only was America in the throes of this craze, but his home state was ground zero.

By the time Howard was old enough to become aware of the sport, however, as biographer Mark Finn explains, he had "just missed what is generally thought of as the golden age of boxing, wherein one finds the legendary Jim Jeffries, James J. Corbett, John L. Sullivan and other such colorful personalities."[7] Yet Howard soon learned about every one of them, for as his friend Tyson recalled, "He knew all the fighters from along back, you know. He never forgot anything."[8] Still, he was fortunate to have been old enough to experience a resurgence in the sport. "Robert was just a teenager," Finn continues, "when Jack Dempsey won the heavyweight title from Jess Willard in 1919 and electrified the nation with his savage ferocity and charisma."[9]

Dempsey was referred to as "the million-dollar hobo" because that is exactly the lifestyle he led—riding the rails, working odd jobs, and participating in local prizefights—until he had the chance to fight the reigning heavyweight champion, Jess Willard.[10] Most people had never heard of Jack Dempsey until famous sportswriter and author Damon Runyon serialized his Jack London–like story in the newspapers in advance of the title fight.[11] Then, on July 4, 1919, the 6' 1", 187-pound Dempsey went up against Willard, who was 6' 6½" and weighed 245 pounds, a virtual David and Goliath confrontation, and Dempsey bested Willard by the fourth round, becoming the heavyweight champion of the world. His victory and kid-like smile captured the hearts of Americans and one particular Texan—Howard. The significance of this was highlighted by Finn when he wrote, "Dempsey's reign as champion was the beginning of the modern boxing era, the re-invigoration of the sport and, for Robert E. Howard, a headlong plunge into a deep reservoir of cultural inspiration that would save and sustain him through his entire writing career."[12]

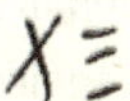

"No other subject is, for the writer, so intensely personal as boxing," wrote American author Joyce Carol Oates. "To write about boxing is to write about oneself—however elliptically, and unintentionally. And to write about boxing is to be forced to contemplate not only boxing, but the perimeters of civilization—what it is, or should be, to be 'human.'"[13] Boxing was, indeed, intensely personal for Howard, because, as Finn explained, it was "Howard's muse, his metaphor, his means to an end."[14] When he turned his writing to boxing, it afforded him yet another opportunity to write about the fighters he so loved, those on "the perimeters of civilization." But he was intimately familiar with his subject when it came to writing boxing stories. "[Howard] never led a sword-wielding army to victory against superior forces," Finn once wrote, "he was never a mercenary or a pirate, but he was a boxer."[15] This is why Howard boxing scholar Christopher Gruber accurately commented, "If there can be found in Howard's personality one absolute it is that he knew boxing."[16]

Growing up, Howard often sparred with his friends. Austin Newton recalled all the times they had done so sans gloves, as did Earl Baker and Lindsey Tyson.[17] Yet it was Smith, more than anyone, who motivated him to begin taking boxing more seriously. As Burke explained, "Howard describes at least two bouts with Smith, one in *Post Oaks and Sand Roughs*, the other in a . . . letter to Herbert Klatt: making allowances for hyperbole, Howard's comments lead us to believe that Smith was more than a match for him."[18] But when the roughneck he referred to as Bill Murkin in *Post Oaks* invited him to the Ice House when he worked as a soda jerk, Howard rose to a new level as he put on the gloves, stepped into the ring, and fought unofficial bouts with other men.[19]

Howard also enjoyed attending prize-fights.[20] "I'm not a fanatic on sports," he wrote, "but I'll admit, I get a good deal of enjoyment out of certain kinds. Boxing is my favorite." The reasons are reflective of the type of characters he liked to write about, for Howard explained, "I enjoy games that are mostly contests of brawn and endurance, with a certain amount of personal conflict a definite element, as in boxing . . . no game can interest me much unless there is plenty of violent action in it, the hurtling of man-power against man-power, muscular force pitted against muscular force."[21] Harold Preece recalled going to one such boxing match with Howard on July 13, 1928, in Fort Worth.[22] The match of most interest to Howard was a favorite, Art "Kid" Dula versus Duke Tramel in a ten-round bout.[23] "To me, the chief interest was in observing the reactions of the crowd," Preece wrote Smith after the fight, "but I thought, several times, that Bob was going to leap into the ring, and challenge Tramel himself."[24]

Howard also wrote about boxing, whether in his letters to his friends, in his short-lived newsletter, *The Right Hook*, or for the various school newspapers.[25] In 1926 he wrote a letter to the popular boxing magazine *The Ring* and offered, "Boxing reached its height between 1892 and 1905. That was the ring's Golden Era." He then proffered his opinion that "the culmination of perfection, the pinnacle of achievement, the greatest heavyweight of all time was James J. Jeffries," who held the title from 1899 until his retirement in 1904.[26] He also shared his boxing opinions with some of the local newspapers, including the *Fort Worth Telegram* and the *Brownwood Bulletin*. In one letter to the latter after the Dula-Tramel fight, he continued his advocacy for Dula, even though the middleweight had lost the fight. "Last Friday night a boy went through the baptism of blood and fire and emerged victorious," Howard wrote. "The decision went against him, but the moral victory was his." Howard then predicted, "Kid Dula is the next Middleweight Champion of the World."[27] However, as Howard scholar Brian Leno explained, "'Kid' Dula never became a champion."[28]

All of these things put together ultimately led Howard to the creation of what Burke calls his first major persona. Between 1925 and 1928, Howard not only had built himself up physically and engaged in amateur bouts himself but also had learned everything he could about professional boxing and had written on the subject.[29] He had gone so far as to have pictures of himself posing in a fighting stance or boxing with his friends. So "by the second half of 1928," explains Burke, "Howard [had] made himself a boxer, and something of an authority on boxing, and at last [began] to turn his hand toward this sort of fiction."[30]

Howard was not the only author who enjoyed boxing, and this fact was not lost on him. "Lord Byron was fond of boxing," he pointed out in a letter. "Jack London loved to box, fence and wrestle; Frank Harris was once a prizefighter, and so was Jim Tully; even the superior Mr. [Bernard] Shaw was once a clever boxer."[31] Howard's favorite author, Jack London, once explained his own interest in boxing, which aligned perfectly with Howard's own: "Ask people who know me today, what I am. A rough, savage fellow, they will say, who likes prizefights and brutalities."[32] There were others as well, for Gruber also mentions Hemingway and "even that cavalier of civilized refinement, Sir Arthur Conan Doyle," noting that all of these authors "felt the lure of boxing with a thoroughness that was out of character with their scholarly inclinations."[33] And while many embraced the sport, some also took up their pen—or like Howard, their typewriter—and wrote boxing stories.

Howard's first published boxing tale was, appropriately enough, a ghost story. He was testing the possibility of writing boxing fiction by incorporating boxing elements into the type of story he was already comfortable writing. After having a story rejected by a new boxing pulp and *Argosy*, he finally sold it to the magazine *Ghost Stories*, the first direct competitor to *Weird Tales* when it began publishing in 1926, though it never achieved great success; after sixty-four issues it folded in 1931.[34] Howard wrote the story using the pseudonym of John Taverel and submitted it as "The Spirit of Tom Molyneaux." The pseudonym Howard employed added to the story's realism because it is written from the viewpoint of Taverel, a boxing manager. The title's namesake was a renowned early nineteenth-century fighter who was born into slavery in the United States before migrating to Ireland in 1809. The following year he began his five-year run of bare-knuckle fights. The artist Douglas Guest captured the spirit of the fighter in a drawing, and John Young, an engraver, preserved the portrait of the boxer for posterity.

The other reason for employing Tom Molyneaux's name was because Howard had chosen a Black heavyweight contender by the name of Ace Jessel as the protagonist of the story, something certainly unique for the time period.[35] Unfortunately, the editor at *Ghost Story* changed the title and published it in April of 1929 as "The Apparition in the Prize Ring."[36] The story has Jessel contending for the heavyweight championship, but he reaches a point in the fight when he feels he cannot continue. It is then that Taverel shows Jessel the picture of his hero, thus giving him the willpower to continue. When Jessel stands up, Howard writes as Taveral, "*To my horror I saw that there were four men in that ring*!" Jessel, his opponent, the referee, "and the fourth—a short, massive black man, barrel-chested and mighty-limbed, clad in the long tights of another day."[37] It was the ghost of Tom Molyneaux standing beside him, and with his fighting spirit now up, Jessel wins the heavyweight championship. The story mixes Howard's growing expertise of writing the weird tale and his love for boxing and history; it allowed him to make the transition to writing straight boxing tales.

In July of 1929, Howard had two more boxing tales published: one, a straight boxing tale titled "Crowd-Horror," appeared in the July 20 issue of *Argosy All-Story Weekly.* Howard faced a problem with this submission, one he often encountered with editors, and that was the need to cut his stories down to a specific length. In this case the original submission was thirteen thousand words, but he had been asked to get it down to six thousand. As he wrote Smith, "I've worked myself into a state of nervous exhaustion and after rewriting and rewriting it's still 8,000 and if I shave it down any more it won't make sense. Therefore I guess I don't sell it."[38] He sent it back anyway, and although the editor said it was still too long, he told Howard he would do some more cutting, so the story was accepted for publication and Howard received a check for a hundred dollars. Alongside the story, it also included a short autobiography written by Howard in which he wrote of his lifelong interest in the sport, noting that "circumstances kept me out of the ring, which is probably a good thing for my health in general, but my desire to write materialized—to an extent anyway!"[39]

The other story published that July was in a relatively new pulp magazine dedicated entirely to boxing titled *Fight Stories*, which declared on each cover: "Fact and Fiction of the Ring." There was already a Street & Smith magazine with the more generic title *Sport Story*, which had launched in 1923 and had obtained a circulation of 150,000 copies sold each month. William H. Kofoed wanted not only to compete with the generic title but also to create a rival that would take advantage of the boxing craze reignited by Jack Dempsey.[40] "In 1928, I tried to sell George Delacorte on the idea of publishing a pulp called *Fight Stories*," Kofoed wrote, but the Dell publisher thought the title was too narrow and passed. "So," continued Kofoed, "I took it up to Jack Kelly, co-owner with Jack Glennister of Fiction House," and since "Kelly was a fight fan, he went for my *Fight Stories* right off."[41]

The new magazine hit the newsstands in May of 1928, and there is no doubt Howard was instantly aware of the magazine and its potential for him as a writer.[42] Its appearance, Louinet explains, "offered Howard the unique opportunity to write about a subject he loved probably as much as weird fiction."[43] More importantly, however, because Fiction House paid its authors on acceptance, not publication, it offered Howard a more lucrative market. He began writing boxing stories, such as the "The Spirit of Tom Molyneaux," and submitted them to *Fight Stories*, but they were rejected. In the span of just several weeks that fall, he submitted four more stories to the magazine, all of which were also rejected.[44] Then, in February of 1929, he created the character Steve Costigan, both boxer and sailor, whose stories were written with a sense of humor.

Howard once shared that the character Sailor Steve Costigan came to him "suddenly," but he was no doubt a combination of one of his favorite Jack London characters, Sailor Martin Eden, and the real Jack Dempsey, among others.[45] He was not alone in modeling his character off of the latter, for he once wrote, "It is not the Sailor Costigans alone, the wood-pulp heroes who emulate the terrific punch and iron man style of Dempsey. I have recognized him again and again in the more sophisticated type of stories that touched on fights and fighting men."[46] Howard made his character more unique, not only among the many Dempsey imitators but also among his own as well. "Costigan," notes Finn, "is unlike other Howard characters with his fists of iron, his heart of gold, and his head of wood."[47] The stories are told in the first person and Costigan is an unreliable narrator who shares his versions of the events that happened to him at many a port of call throughout the South Seas. The humor is very much in the same vein as Damon Runyon's Broadway Tales, the first of which, "Romance in the Roaring Forties," had just published in *Cosmopolitan* the month before Howard's.[48]

"The Pit of the Serpent" was quickly accepted and appeared in the July 1929 issue, hitting the newsstands in June.[49] "My story 'Pit of the Serpent' came out in *Fight Stories* this month," Howard wrote Smith, telling him, "Get a copy and read it." He was evidently quite proud of his first Costigan tale for he told Smith, "The style and form are not much, but the mechanics are perfect. Writing is a lot like architecture. The whole structure has to suit—each piece has to be in place. A master of the game, like Kipling, for instance, or Jack London, always places the pieces right. A dub like me stumbles on to the right combination once in every five hundred stories he writes. But as I say, the architecture of this story is more nearly perfection than any other I ever wrote."[50] The yarn certainly had its merits, for right from the opening paragraph, the story introduces the cast of characters, sets the tension, and delivers it with a touch of humor. "The minute I stepped ashore from the *Sea Girl*, merchantman, I had a hunch that there would be trouble. This hunch was caused by seeing some of the crew of the *Dauntless*. The men on the *Dauntless* have disliked the *Sea Girl*'s crew ever since our skipper took their captain to a cleaning on the wharfs of Zanzibar—them being narrow-minded that way. They claimed that the Old Man had a knuckle-duster on his right, which is ridiculous and a dirty lie. He had it on his left."[51] Although *Fight Stories* did not have a reader forum for Howard to assess how fans reacted to his Costigan yarns, he was happy enough with the editor's quick acceptance, payment, and publication that he began writing more boxing tales. The editor was certainly pleased upon hearing Howard was planning to write more stories about his new character, as he wrote, "I am glad to hear that Steve Costigan is going to swashbuckle his way across more pages of *Fight Stories*. All of us here are for him."[52] And with that Howard clearly had a successful series character.

The next story, "The Bulldog Breed," was not published until February of the following year, but it was the first to introduce Costigan's white bulldog, Mike. For personal reasons this was an important addition to the stories for Howard. "At the time he was writing this story," explains Louinet, "Howard's dog Patches had been dead for several months, and it makes little doubt that the strong affection—one could write bond—which exists between Costigan and Mike mirrors the one that existed between Howard and Patches." The entire cast of characters were now together: Sailor Steve and his bulldog, Mike, along with the Old Man on their ship the *Sea Girl*—in a sense a family not unlike his own, for as Louinet continues, "Howard was apparently recreating some sort of ideal family on a boat, a family Costigan leaves at times for his boxing and drinking bouts, but where he systematically returns to as his only home."[53] If Costigan was Howard and Mike was Patches, then, allegorically speaking, the Old Man was Dr. Howard, and the one thing that held the family together was the *Sea Girl*, a representation of Mrs. Howard.[54]

Howard's success with the character continued with "Sailor's Grudge" the following month and "Fist and Fang" in May, but the story Howard considered his finest, with which critics readily agree, was "Iron Men," which was changed to "The Iron Man" and published in June 1930. Named for the type of fighter Howard liked, those who could endure all manner of punishment and still stay in the fight, he told Smith in a February letter, "This is by far the best fight story I ever wrote. In many ways the best story of any kind I ever wrote. I guess my destiny is tied up with the Costigan family." He then explained, "This tale isn't humorous like the others. It's harsh and brutal," adding his worries: "I don't know whether the readers will like it or not."[55] Fiction House liked it enough to give it the issue's cover that month, and he received a check for two hundred dollars.[56]

Despite his belief in the story, it did make him somewhat frustrated with the editors, and it revealed another common problem Howard found in pulp publishing. "*Fight Stories* was kind enough to give me the cover design this month," he wrote Smith. "But they changed the title and the chapter headings and made quite a number of changes throughout the story which seemed not only needless to me, but in some places entirely distorted the original meaning. I think some of the changes must surely have been mistakes in printing."[57] They were not. Rather, they were the result of tampering by the editors. As Louinet explains, "Fiction House was notorious for altering authors' words, deleting passages, and adding whole paragraphs to a manuscript without consulting the author."[58] Despite the cuts it remained a good story, "but most Howard scholars agree," Louinet writes of the original submission, "that this is probably Howard's best serious boxing story, and his best illustration of the fascination those atavistic boxers with a granite jaw held for the Texan."[59]

Howard continued sending in Sailor Costigan yarns to the boxing pulp, and more were accepted, with some being published in another Fiction

House magazine, *Action Stories*. But not all of the Costigan stories were accepted. In December 1930 he wrote Smith, "I'm having no luck with *Fight Stories*. They rejected one story some time ago, and since then they've had another over a month and haven't reported on it at all. I somehow feel that they've soured on me."[60] And even when he did sell them another story in the series, the pay was sometimes below standard rates. After sending the editor one Costigan yarn, Howard wrote Smith, "He only offered me $75 when I expected to get $90 or $100 if I sold it at all."[61] Part of the problem may have been that Howard was running out of ideas, for he admitted to a friend in 1931, "I've written so blamed many of them I'm hard put to work up new plots and situations."[62] The other problem was the deepening realities of the Depression, for by the early 1930s, the entire pulp industry was beginning to feel the effects of the economic turmoil. The reduced rates may have been a cost-saving measure in light of the limited funds available from banks that were taking "holidays" or permanently closing. By April of 1932, Howard wrote Smith that he had received a notice from Fiction House "that *Fight Stories* had been—or was going to be—taken off the stands."[63] It was. The magazine that had proven a boon to Howard went on hiatus with the April issue, along with eleven other Fiction House titles.[64]

Still, Howard knew he had a good thing going, for Fiction House had published thirteen of his Sailor Costigan yarns before suspending operations. Therefore, he began casting about for a new outlet and found it in *Jack Dempsey's Fight Magazine*. In May 1934 Dempsey had his own boxing magazine and served as editor—in name only, of course. Still, Howard was pleased with the idea and wrote a friend, "I am particularly gratified to have been given a niche in Dempsey's publication for he was one of my boyhood heroes, and I still entertain a deep admiration for him."[65] The real editor behind Dempsey's name was William Kofoed, who had contacted Howard directly to solicit stories from him. Howard responded immediately, for Louinet writes, "In a matter of weeks, he wrote and sold seven new tales to the new magazine, only one of which was not a Steve Costigan tale."[66] Howard appeared in every issue of the magazine, but, unfortunately, the magazine folded after only three issues. Not even this "Iron Man" could stand up to the Depression.

Howard also became innovative by changing the character's name in some of his rejected stories, turning Steve Costigan into Dennis Dorgan, the bulldog Mike into Spike, and the *Sea Girl* into *The Python*, but otherwise making no other changes. He also created another character, Kid Allison, for *Sport Story*.[67] And while he did manage to find several more outlets for these yarns, *Fight Stories* had proven his best outlet and Sailor Steve Costigan his best series character, for he wrote more stories about his exploits than any other character.[68] Fiction House managed to stay alive through the depths of the Depression and restarted many of their titles, including *Fight Stories*. This was, unfortunately, in the spring of 1936, not long before Howard's death.

The Sailor Steve Costigan stories are unusual for most readers who are familiar with Howard's weird tales and horror stories, and they are often surprised by the boxing tales, especially when it comes to their humor. But, as Gruber states, "Don't be fooled by the slapstick nature of the stories," because "the theme of love, responsibility, sacrifice, and honor churn just beneath the surface of the rugged, burlesque humor."[69] Yet it was his humorous stories that sold well, paid well, and often saved him financially throughout his career, and in the case of *Fight Stories*, on which Finn once commented, it had "appeared at exactly the right time in the young author's life."[70] His boxing tales were highly personal for him, not only for the intimacy of family but also for his love and familiarity with boxing, which is why, Finn wrote, when reading his boxing yarns, "you feel every punch, smell the sweat, and taste the blood as if you were in the ring."[71]

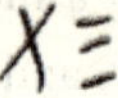

As his writing career began to take off and success was becoming a reality, it also meant he was busier than he had ever been before, but he still managed to find time to visit with his friends, though with less frequency. Perhaps because of this, his friends came to Cross Plains several times in the first half of 1929. Smith and Vinson visited with him in late January, and after Preece moved to Brownwood to work on the city directory there, all three of them came up to visit Howard in July.

Outside of visits with his friends, Howard was hoping to travel more that year and was planning another trip to Mexico that did not happen.[72] Instead, he had to settle for more local trips. "I went to San Antonio soon after I got back from Waco," Howard wrote Smith in April. "The Battle of Flowers and the fiesta was a lot of hokum although Zeus knoweth it must have cost up in the hundred thousands of dollars to stage it. There were about a hundred thousand visitors there from other towns . . . it's an old Texas institution and even if it is a lot of hokum, I'm might glad I saw it."[73] The Battle of Flowers parade began in 1891 to honor the heroes of the Alamo, Goliad, and the Battle of San Jacinto.[74] When Howard went they were celebrating the festival's thirty-eighth year, which the *Waco News* reported as "the most brilliant battle of flowers parade in the city's history [as it] wound its way through the heart of the downtown district for an hour and a half, through a crowd of spectators estimated at 150,000 persons."[75]

The most surprising event for Howard that spring may well have been when he learned that his father was planning to relocate. Norris Chambers once noted, "The Dr. talked of doing many things that he never did," especially when it came to moving someplace, but it seems in this case it was not all talk.[76] Not only had Dr. Howard spoken of moving to Spur, Texas, approximately 150 miles to the northwest of Cross Plains, but he also had actually taken steps to do so.

There has been much speculation regarding why Dr. Howard suddenly desired to move.[77] It simply may have been his wanderlust returning, but there is the possibility he was once again hoping to follow a potential boom. Jack Scott, still the future *Cross Plains Review* editor in 1929, once stated his belief that "the reason for [Dr. Howard]'s stay in Spur was a cotton boom in that region, which he thought would give him a chance to make some money."[78] That may be likely, for the prices of cotton that spring had hit new highs, and the area around Spur in Dickens County was known for the fiber plant.[79]

Regardless of why, what is known is that on May 1, 1929, Dr. Howard left Cross Plains for Spur. The *Cross Plains Review* would report two days later, "Dr. I. M. Howard left on Wednesday of this week for Spur, Texas, where he has gone with a view of tentatively locating there for the practice of his profession," while the Spur newspaper, appropriately named the *Texas Spur*, reported on the same day, "Dr. Howard and family, of Cross Plains, are moving to Spur. Dr. Howard will be with the City Drug Store and engage in the practice of medicine."[80] The Spur newspaper did mention that "if the climate of that locality is more agreeable to his health he may make it a permanent location," which may possibly have been more about his wife's health, because Spur is located on the semiarid plateau of the Texas Panhandle, the type of environment often recommended for tubercular patients.[81]

Dr. Howard returned to Cross Plains but left again for Spur on May 8, and the two newspapers detailed his comings and goings throughout the month.[82] The *Texas Spur* noted that Dr. Howard was planning to have two offices in town, one in the City Drug Store, the other in the office building over the Piggly Wiggly grocery store, and that on the May 20 trip, he had brought his wife with him.[83] The next month, in the June 7 issue of the paper, the editor proudly declared, "Dr. and Mrs. Howard are excellent citizens and we welcome them to Spur."[84] It seemed they had made themselves at home. As for Howard, he was reported to have gone to Brownwood "visiting relatives."[85]

Then, Mrs. Howard's health apparently took a turn for the worse, and Dr. Howard returned her to Cross Plains. The *Texas Spur* reported that a Dr. Gibson had taken over Dr. Howard's practice "during his absence with his wife who is in ill health."[86] Although the Spur paper continued talking about the good doctor settling there, on July 5 the *Review* headlined the news, "Dr. Howard Moving Back to Cross Plains."[87] If it had been motivated by Dr. Howard's wanderlust, the outcome may have been what put an end to any future plans to relocate the family. What it may have also done, however, was motivate Howard to take that one last step toward total freedom—moving out of his parents' home.

Chapter 16

King Kull and the Birth of Sword and Sorcery, 1929

Before the shadows slew the sun
the kites were soaring free,
And Kull rode down the forest road,
his red sword at his knee;
And winds were whispering round the world:
"King Kull rides to the sea."
—"The King and the Oak"[1]

"About Atlantis," Howard wrote Preece, "I believe something of the sort existed."[2] Like many romantics Howard was fascinated with the lost continent of Atlantis, which was believed to have once existed before perishing into the ocean's deep, the result of a cataclysmic earthquake.[3] He apparently did not, however, subscribe to the popular belief that Atlantis had once been a perfect utopian society. "I do not especially hold any theory about a high type of civilization existing there," he continued, "in fact, I doubt that. But some continent was submerged away back, or some large body of land, for practically all peoples have legends about a flood."[4] Howard was certainly not alone in this belief, for the notion had already existed for several thousand years, and the theory had gained new traction in the late nineteenth century.

The story of Atlantis has its origins in Plato's dialogues dating back to approximately 360 BC. In the opening to Plato's *Timaeus*, the Athenian Critias provides the background on this island continent. "Now in this island of Atlantis," Critias explains, "there was a great and wonderful empire which had rule over the whole island and several others, and over parts of the continent, and, furthermore, the men of Atlantis had subjected the parts of Libya within the columns of Heracles as far as Egypt, and of Europe as far as Tyrrhenia." After a war between the city of Athens and the Atlantean Empire, however, "There occurred violent earthquakes and floods," and Atlantis, Critias continues, "disappeared in the depths of the sea. For which reason the sea in those parts is impassable and impenetrable, because there is a shoal of mud in the way; and this was caused by the subsidence of the island."[5] And with that, the legend of Atlantis was born.

There were many ancient writers who read the story as intended—a fictional metaphorical myth—but there were others who believed it to have been historically based. In time the myth grew, and the island became a romantic story that depicted the perfect example of a utopian society, all despite the fact Plato had simply employed it to depict a city-state becoming a belligerent power. It was Ignatius L. Donnelly, a US congressman, who greatly popularized the belief that the lost continent was real with the publication of his 1882 book, *Atlantis: The Antediluvian World*.[6] Donnelly's book sold well, and his theory that the sinking of Atlantis occurred as a result of the biblical great flood became a mainstay of popular literature throughout the twentieth century. Howard may have been familiar with the publication, or he had, at least, read of the theory.

In his letter to Preece in which he discussed Atlantis, Howard even broached the possibility of his having a personal Atlantean connection. "An occultist of my acquaintance," he wrote, referring to his Marlin friend Frank Thurston Torbett, "who has gone deeper in the matter than any man I ever knew, says I have a very ancient soul, am a reincarnated Atlantean, in fact!" Howard does wonder if it might even be true. "Sure I live in the dust of the past and my dreams are seldom of present or future," he writes, "but I am ever treading roads of the dim ages and strange are some of the figures whom I meet and strange the shapes who stare at me."[7] Regardless of his true beliefs, his fertile imagination would conjure up a new character who did have Atlantean roots.

In 1926 Howard created his character King Kull, born in Atlantis but who later gained the crown of Valusia.[8] In an autobiographical sketch in which he explained the creation of his many characters, Howard wrote, "King Kull differed from these others in that he was put on paper the moment he was created, whereas [the others] existed in my mind years before I tried to put them in stories."[9] The first yarn Howard wrote had no known title but was later referred to as "Exile of Atlantis" by Glenn Lord, the literary agent for the Howard estate.[10] It features three characters, Am-ra, Gor-na, and Kull. At the beginning of the story, it is Am-ra who appears to be the main character of the story, but while Kull "was intended to be a minor character," Howard explained, "I had not gone far before he was dominating the yarn."[11]

Although the short story was never published in Howard's lifetime, nor is it known if he ever submitted it, the story proved to be an important step in Howard's writing.[12] Not only had Howard switched the lens from Am-ra to Kull, but he had also switched the story's focus from Atlantis to Valusia.[13] Atlantis was still believed by some to have existed, and so the legend and lore built up around the sunken continent made the setting a historical backdrop, in a manner of speaking; Valusia, however, was entirely created from Howard's imagination. His first successful character, Solomon Kane, had existed in the real world, making those stories historical fantasy, while Kull was born on a continent believed to have once existed but ruled in one entirely fantastical.[14] Howard had subtly changed the type of stories he wrote. "In a nutshell," explains Louinet, "he stopped writing 'historical' tales in favor of fantasy tales."[15] In so doing he opened up newfound freedoms in his writing, for he was no longer constrained by the facts of history.

The first publication of a King Kull yarn came after "The Shadow Kingdom" was accepted by Farnsworth Wright for *Weird Tales*. It had taken Howard a long time to write the story, which he described in *Post Oaks*. In the fall of 1926, while in college, when he had been writing primarily poetry, he recounted how "he wrote very little prose, though he did begin a wild fantasy entitled 'The [Shadow Kingdom],' which he laid aside partly finished and forgot about."[16] Then, in the spring of the following year, Howard continued, "[Bob] again discovered 'The [Shadow Kingdom],' rewrote it, and again laid it aside."[17] Finally, as the summer session ended in 1927, before graduation, Howard wrote, "He at last sent 'The [Shadow Kingdom],' to [*Weird Tales*]," and he explained what happened next. "Then a letter came, offering $100.00 for 'The [Shadow Kingdom].'"[18] Soon after, he wrote Smith telling him, "I don't know when it will be published or whether you'll like it or not," before noting, "I enjoyed writing it more than any piece of prose I ever wrote."[19]

Despite the quick acceptance by Wright, Howard would not receive the one hundred dollars until approximately two years later; "The Shadow Kingdom" was not published until August 1929.[20] Perhaps as a reminder of the story's acceptance, Howard wrote Wright the following year, detailing his views on Atlantis, "which," he wrote Preece, "I expect will be published as a foreword to that story."[21] It was not, nor was it included in "The Eyrie." The story was published without much notoriety, featuring only a title illustration, and ran for seventeen pages before being continued in the back pages of the magazine. Still, the effort Howard put into the story was demonstrated through his prose, and the impact the story had would prove to be far-reaching.

King Kull is introduced in the first pages of the story, with him mounted on a horse as he watches his soldiers pass in review. "A brave sight," Howard wrote, "and a sight which aroused a fierce thrill in the soul of Kull, king of Valusia. Not on the Topaz Throne at the front of the regal Tower of Splendor sat Kull, but in the saddle, mounted on a great stallion, a true warrior king. His mighty arm swung up in reply to the salutes as the hosts passed. His fierce eyes passed the gorgeous trumpeters with a casual glance, rested longer on the following soldiery."[22] In those pages and throughout the rest of the story, it becomes clear that because Kull is Atlantis-born, he is an outsider, and though they recognize him as king of Valusia, he only has enemies of varying degrees, for as Howard writes, Kull is "a man against a nation."[23]

The story forces Kull to ally with the hated Picts because an ancient race of reptile men who have the ability to change their appearance have infiltrated the king's own people, including his closest advisors. Howard draws on his fascination with races, Louinet explains, especially lost races, and the confrontation between them, so that ultimately the story pits an ancient, civilized society of reptile men against the modern barbaric race.[24]

Howard's prose in the story demonstrates a mastery of language, showing evidence of having been greatly informed by his poetry. Highlighting this fact are several passages in the story that read like prose poems. For instance, when Kull is being escorted back into the city after a nearly all-night meeting with the Pict's chieftain, Kull rides through the "city's antiquity," which "was more than ever apparent beneath the bent, silver moon." Kull's "imaginative mind is then inspired by the weird grandeur of the scene" and "the palaces and the temples and the shrines" speak to him. "How many kings have we watched ride down these streets before Kull of Atlantis was even a dream in the mind of Ka, bird of Creation? Ride on, Kull of Atlantis; greater shall follow you; greater came before you. They are dust; they are forgotten; we stand; we know; we are. Ride, ride on, Kull of Atlantis; Kull the king, Kull the fool!"[25] While certainly not the typical prose found in *Weird Tales*—or any pulp, for that matter—his unique style, derived in part from his poetical sensibility, is what began to set Howard apart from the other pulp writers.

This story also set him apart for another reason. When "The Shadow Kingdom" appeared in print in the August 1929 issue, Louinet explains, "Neither Howard nor Wright could imagine that in the years to come the story would be widely considered as the first of a new genre."[26] The overarching genre was fantasy, and the subgenre Howard created is generally referred to today as "sword and sorcery."[27]

XΞ

Brian Murphy, the author of *Flame and Crimson: A History of Sword-and-Sorcery*, describes the larger genre of fantasy as being "a type of literature characterized by tales of adventure and quest in realms of faerie, populated by wizards, warriors, and monsters, in which magic works."[28] Examples of early fantasy can be found in the traditional myths, folklore, and fairytales of many cultures, as well as famous works such as the *Epic of Gilgamesh*, Homer's *Odyssey*, or Virgil's *Aeneid*.[29] However, George MacDonald's *The Princess and the Goblin,* published in 1872, which itself was influenced by fairytales, is generally considered the first modern fantasy novel.[30] As the genre developed, it was, at first, commonly associated with children's fantasies, such as Lewis Carroll's *Alice in Wonderland*, J. M. Barrie's *Peter Pan*, and L. Frank Baum's *The Wonderful Wizard of Oz*. In time subgenres began to grow that were more adult-like, such as the Lost World subgenre, as signified by works such as H. Rider Haggard's *She*, Sir Arthur Conan Doyle's *The Lost World*, or Edgar Rice Burroughs's *The Land That Time Forgot.* The pulp magazines of the early twentieth century, however, are what truly opened up the publishing of fantasy stories and made Howard's new subgenre a possibility.

According to Murphy, sword and sorcery "has a distinctive aesthetic and conventions." He describes the elements that allow for a story to be identified as belonging to this classification. "While no story is likely to contain all these elements," he explains, they often consist of men (and women) of action, having personal and/or mercenary motivations, fighting enemies wielding dark and dangerous magic; are inspired by history but are not historical; have horror influences and outsider heroes; and are typically short, episodic stories.[31] Regardless of the combination of elements, editor and author Jason Waltz believes all sword-and-sorcery stories are at their root about "an indomitable will with a passion to live . . . at any and all costs even in the face of unbalanced or unnatural odds, no matter what."[32]

Many have suggested that the subgenre developed out of the style of storytelling found in historical adventure tales.[33] And still others have identified it as having brought a gritty realism to fantasy world stories—men living in a savage world having to take up arms to defend their way of life and their very lives against evil monsters or wizards.[34] This is similar to the changes in detective fiction in the 1920s, when that genre was brought out of the armchair, English intellectual tradition popularized by Sir Arthur Conan Doyle's Sherlock Holmes and placed squarely on the mean streets of modern America.

"The Shadow Kingdom," Murphy writes, "is the first story in which Howard assembled all the elements that would constitute classic sword-and-sorcery:

a barbaric hero on the civilized throne of Valusia, beset by a race of serpent-men plotting overthrow, disguised and masked by dark sorcery."[35] Kull is an outsider to Valusia, having been born in Atlantis, who must defend both his throne and his life, and the story is a synthesis of adventure, the fantastic, and horror, particularly gothic horror. In fact, many believe it was out of the latter that Howard developed this subgenre.

Howard scholars such as Charles A. Gramlich argue that he "mined the gothic and mixed it with history and fantasy to create sword-and-sorcery."[36] "The Shadow Kingdom" is essentially a gothic horror story, for it draws upon gothic themes such as dark and passage-filled castles, ancient evils, mysterious villains, and foul sorcerers, with good ultimately triumphing over evil in the end.[37] Gothic horrors were, at first, predominately written by Europeans, and Horace Walpole's *The Castle of Otranto*, first published in 1764, is generally considered the first such novel. It was the writings of Nathaniel Hawthorne and Edgar Allan Poe that brought the genre to America. Gothic horror grew in popularity in the late nineteenth and early twentieth centuries, as marked by such novels as Bram Stoker's *Dracula,* Robert W. Chambers's *The King in Yellow*, or Gaston Leroux's *The Phantom of the Opera.* Howard's story, however, is unlike any gothic story written up to that point in time, for gothic characters typically started as victims and ended as heroes or, generally in the case of the gothic romances, heroines. They do so, however, only through rational thought, assistance of some kind, or by virtue of an ancient relic or religious symbol.[38] "The Texan" changed all this, explains Louinet, for he "took what was an essentially European genre in its value and style, and Americanized it."[39] Never had the genre seen a character engage the evil head-on with force delivered through the might of a sword. What he had done, Louinet continues, was to get rid of gothic horror's "chivalrous aspects, flowery language, and stilted personalities" by "writing violent tales in a realistic style that reflected Howard's environment and that of his readership."[40] And that was what really mattered the most: how his readers reacted to this new subgenre story.

After the issue appeared on the newsstand in July, letters began arriving at the *Weird Tales* office. Wright's editorial in the October issue said it all. "It is the consensus of our readers that the August *Weird Tales* was a little bit better than any previous issue of the magazine. *The Shadow Kingdom*, by Robert E. Howard, evoked enthusiasm that in some cases bordered on delirium." One such letter was written by Mrs. Joseph C. Murphy of New York City, when she asked, "Please reprint in every following W. T. the story in the last one entitled *The Shadow Kingdom*. I thought it a beautiful tapestry of words, also weird, also with warm human interest, also unique." Fellow *Weird Tales* author E. Hoffmann Price effusively praised Howard when he wrote, "That is a story for you! Weird, fantastic, but peopled with real men who think and act as we conceive the thoughts and acts of men. And good fighting stuff. Howard very nicely refrained from slowing his combat stuff by technicalities of the sword. . . . Weird enough and then some; and savage and hairy-chested!"[41] Perhaps the most complimentary praise came from Abraham Merritt, who had already established himself as an author of fantastic fiction with the publication of *The Moon Pool*, *The Ship of Ishtar*, and *Seven Footprints to Satan*, and was very familiar to the readers of *Weird Tales*, having already published the most popular story ever printed in the magazine's history, "The Woman of the Wood."[42] Merritt simply wrote, "*The Shadow Kingdom* is told beautifully."[43]

The popularity of Howard's story with readers is best understood by Wright's succinct statement. "*The Shadow Kingdom,* by Robert E. Howard," he wrote, "was the most popular story in the August issue."[44] He made no mention of a second or third place. And so, with this yarn, Howard had achieved the top tier of *Weird Tales* authors, taking his place alongside the popular Seabury Quinn and H. P. Lovecraft.[45]

Between the birth of King Kull in the fall of 1926 and into 1930, despite writing ten additional stories of the ruler of Valusia (not to mention three more he started but did not finish, as well as one poem), Howard only managed to sell one more story in which Kull appeared as the lead character—"The Mirrors of Tuzun Thune"—which was published in the September 1929 issue of *Weird Tales*.[46] Written in September 1927, it, too, was quickly accepted for publication by Wright, although because the story was much shorter, Howard would only receive twenty dollars for his efforts.[47] Once again, Howard demonstrated the influence of his poetic writing, for the very opening reads as a prose poem, establishing Kull's dark mood.

> There comes, even to kings, the time of great weariness. Then the gold of the throne is brass, the silk of the palace becomes drab. The gems in the diadem and upon the fingers of the women sparkle drearily like the ice of the white seas; the speech of men is as the empty rattle of a jester's bell and the feel comes of things unreal; even the sun is copper in the sky and the breath of the green ocean is no longer fresh. Kull sat upon the throne of Valusia and the hour of weariness was upon him.[48]

The reaction to this story was—and remains—laudatory. As Howard's friend Smith fondly remembered, "I received intense enjoyment from my original reading, when I was introduced to the tale in manuscript form on one of my many visits to Bob. Time has not changed the story's enchantment." Smith described it as "probably his best prose, if such poetry can be called prose. More than likely it can, for prose and poetry intertwine, and all good prose is really poetry, either in imagery, or flow of words. 'The Mirrors of Tuzun Thune' has both."[49]

Weird Tales' readers also praised the story. "My congratulations," wrote Mrs. Murphy again, "on the continuation of the King Kull series by Robert E. Howard. That is unique stuff; it makes me feel like the *Idylls of the King*, filled up with thrills."[50] Another reader, K. W. Hill of Chicago, also equated it to the world's greatest literature when writing to express his "pleasure in Mr. Howard's writing"; "his tales have a certain lilt in the telling that one finds in the Harvard Classic translation of the *Odyssey*."[51] There is also a strong consensus among modern scholars, such as when Howard's first literary critic, Don Herron, wrote of the opening to the story, "Such extracts consider Howard at his best."[52]

Having two quick acceptances back-to-back, Howard knew he had a successful character, so over the next fourteen months, he wrote King Kull yarns.[53] He started a serial-length story, but abandoned that in favor of another short story, originally titled "Delcarde's Cat" but changed to "The Cat and the Skull" for submission. Wright rejected the story.[54]

Howard then wrote "The Screaming Skull of Silence" and submitted it, but it, too, was rejected. Howard wrote more: "The Striking of the Gong," "The Altar and the Scorpion," "By This Axe I Rule!" and "Swords of the Purple Kingdom."[55] Each was rejected in turn. His prospects for a new series character had turned bleak.

The main impediment to additional stories being published was Farnsworth Wright. As neither of the two accepted stories had been published during this writing and submission frenzy, the editor had no way to gauge reader reaction to the King Kull series. Therefore, he could only rely on his read of the stories, and, despite some being strong, he accepted none. Wright may have also felt that no other Kull story ever lived up to the first, for after Howard's death, he wrote Dr. Howard, "I don't think anyone has ever written a more powerfully imaginative story than 'The Shadow Kingdom.'"[56]

Still, Wright was not alone in his assessment of at least some of the stories, for Howard tried submitting them to other magazines, such as "By this Axe I Rule!" which he sent to both *Argosy* and *Adventure*, where it was again rejected.[57] Fortunately, Howard placed all of these stories in his trunk for possibly revisiting them one day. Although Howard did later return to the Kull character, bringing him into one story featuring another series character that was published, nothing else featuring the king of Valusia ever saw print in his lifetime.

The labor Howard put into writing stories and the difficulties of rejections reveal an interesting trait about Howard. He seldom ever admitted how hard he worked. H. P. Lovecraft had praised Howard's King Kull yarns to him and to others, such as when he wrote, "Of all R. E. H.'s work I think I like the 'Kull' stories most."[58] Howard had written in reply, thanking him for the kind words but stating, "I doubt if I'll ever be able to write another." He explained that the King Kull stories he had published "seemed almost to write themselves, without any planning on my part; there was no conscious effort on my part to work them up. They simply grew up, unsummoned, full grown in my mind and flowed out on paper from my finger tips." He then suggested that because the stories had been written through some supernatural means and that ability had not returned, "To sit down and consciously try to write another story on that order would be to produce something the artificiality of which would be apparent."[59] What Howard never mentioned was all of the effort he had put into writing the King Kull stories, including those subsequently rejected.[60] This may possibly have been out of a desire to avoid discussing his personal failures, but it is more likely he wrote those words because he simply preferred spinning a good yarn.

As for the readers, they continued pleading for more King Kull stories. In the May 1932 issue of *Weird Tales*, Donald Jones of Chickasaw, Arkansas, wrote, "Give us more of Robert E. Howard's stories about King Kull."[61] Fellow author Donald A. Wollheim wrote in the April 1934 issue, "Get Robert E. Howard to write a few more about Kull of Valusia. That was his best character, and besides, those stories were his weirdest."[62] In December 1935 Donald Allgeier from Springfield, Missouri, likewise pleaded, "Couldn't Howard revive King Kull?" and as late as April 1936, six years after the last Kull yarn was published, Mrs. John A. Heller of Long Beach, California, wrote in favor of "further stories about King Kull."[63] After his death the pleas changed from new stories to reprints of the originals, and as late as May 1937, Gordon R. Pugh of Ontario, Canada, wrote, "Why not reprint some of the great Howard's King Kull stories? How about it, fans?"[64]

It never happened.

Although unable to sell any additional stories of his Atlantean-born character, Howard was not done with Atlantis.[65] He began writing a longer yarn, his first novella, titled "Skull-Face," in the second half of 1928, which Howard scholar Richard Lupoff described as "swashbuckling from beginning to end, with aura of the Gothic hovering over it."[66] Howard used a variation of his favorite character name, Stephen Costigan, as the main protagonist, although this was not Sailor Steve the boxer.[67] The title comes from a description of the main villain, Kathulos, who controls an eastern criminal syndicate plotting to overthrow the world. The mysterious title figure only appears masked or disguised throughout much of the story and is heard speaking in a sibilant voice. Only brief glimpses of his true nature are revealed as Costigan and his friend John Gordon race through this fast-paced tale of weird menace battling what they believe is possibly an Egyptian mummy. Toward the end of the story, Kathulos himself reveals his true nature when he tells Costigan:

> They knew me in the old days! I reigned in the dim misty sea lands ages and ages before the sea rose and engulfed the land. I died, not as men die; the magic draft of life everlasting was ours! I drank deep and slept. Long I slept in my lacquered case! My flesh withered and grew hard: my blood dried in my veins. I became as one dead. But still within me burned the spirit of life, sleeping but anticipating the awakening. The great cities crumbled to dust. The sea drank the land. The tall shrines and the lofty spires sank beneath the green waves. All this I knew as I slept, as a man knows in dreams. Kathulos of Egypt? Faugh! *Kathulos of Atlantis*!"[68]

The villain likely developed directly out of two of the King Kull stories that did not sell, "The Cat and the Skull" and "The Screaming Skull of Silence," since the former contained a near-skeletal slave Kuthulos and the latter a near-identical villain.[69] The basis for the story, however, is clearly derived from Howard's enjoyment of Sax Rohmer's fast-paced tales in which Sir Denis Nayland Smith and Dr. Petrie battle the insidious villain Dr. Fu-Manchu.[70]

The lead story in Rohmer's popular series, "The Zayat Kiss," first saw publication in America in the February 15, 1913, issue of *Collier's* magazine, and was an instant success spawning additional stories, story collections, novels, and movies for the next forty-five years. The centerpiece of all the tales was the sinister Dr. Fu-Manchu, who personified the Yellow Peril genre of adventure fiction. He is described in the first story when Smith tells Dr. Petrie, "Imagine a person, tall, lean, and feline, high shouldered, with a brow like Shakespeare and a face like Satan, a close-shaven skull, and long, magnetic eyes of the true cat green. Invest him with all the cruel cunning of an entire Eastern race, accumulated in one giant intellect, with all the resources of science past and present. Imagine that awful being and you have a mental picture of Dr. Fu-Manchu, the yellow peril incarnate in one man."[71] Howard's description of Kathulos is quite similar, for his face was a skull that was "hideous yellow instead of white," whose "eyes glimmered deep in the sockets and the jaws moved as if in speech," while "the body, except for the high, thin shoulders, was vague and indistinct, but the hands . . . were like the hands of a mummy, long, lean and yellow, with knobby joints and cruel curving talons."[72] Likely the real difference between Rohmer's Dr. Fu-Manchu and Howard's Kathulos is the fact the former is very much alive, while the latter is very much dead.

When Wright received the submission for the more than thirty-three-thousand-word story in late 1928, he no doubt recognized the story's nod to Sax Rohmer, and knowing how popular the tales were among readers, combined with Howard's excellent writing, he accepted it, offering him three hundred dollars, upon publication, the most he had yet been offered for a story.[73] This set Howard up well for 1929, for in addition to some poetry, Howard published the Solomon Kane stories "Skulls in the Stars" and "Rattle of Bones" in January and June, and the two King Kull stories in August and September. As Howard wrote to Smith, he believed Wright was "paving the way to publish the serial I sold him," though never sure when anything would actually see print, he added, "Of course I may be wrong. He may not publish that for years, if at all."[74] Nevertheless he did. Wright broke up "Skull-Face" into three parts, and it published as a serial in the October, November, and December 1929 issues.

Despite the strength of the story and the popularity of the Dr. Fu-Manchu character in America, "Skull-Face" was published with no cover treatment and poor interior illustrations, and only the first installment was placed near the front of the magazine.[75] Nevertheless, it was a hit with many of *Weird Tales*' readers. The Rohmer-Howard connection was immediately noted by Ernest H. Ormsbee of Selkirk, New York, who wrote to "The Eyrie," "If Robert E. Howard keeps up to the level he has set in *Skull-Face*, he will be hailed as the new Sax Rohmer. This story *is* a Sax Rohmer story. I had to turn back to the title-page when this installment was half read to convince myself that the Old Master of the Oriental tale had not returned to us."[76] N. J. O'Neail from Canada put Howard on notice after the second installment: "Please warn Robert E. Howard that the majority of readers will never forgive him if Skull-Face turns out to be a mere human being, instead of a bona-fide mummy."[77] O'Neail and others were no doubt pleased with the outcome, for they were effusive after the last installment, with one reader, John Lawrence Taylor of Fort Worth, Texas, pleading for a sequel.[78] Howard did begin a sequel to "Skull-Face," but he left it unfinished.

Among the most complimentary missives he received, long after the serial had finished, was from A. M. D. Pender of England, who wrote, "Robert E. Howard is certainly a worthy successor to Sax Rohmer. His yarns are always reliable," and in the June 1933 issue, Frank Harrison Cunningham of Roanoke, Virginia, thought it should be made into a film, believing Boris Karloff "would have been a wow in Howard's 'Skull-Face.'"[79]

The readers decidedly enjoyed the novella, for after the first installment, Wright informed readers, "Your votes have given first place among the October issue stories to *Skull-Face*, by Robert E. Howard."[80] And the ending was clearly satisfactory, for again Wright wrote, "The last installment of *Skull-Face*, Robert E. Howard's romantic and fascinating serial about a mummy that came up out of the sea and attempted to rule the world, was easily the first choice of you, the readers, among the stories in the December issue." What he wrote next, once again, said it all: "Howard is rapidly becoming a prime favorite with *Weird Tales* readers."[81]

Around the time the two King Kull stories hit the newsstands, Howard left Cross Plains and moved to Brownwood. He visited the larger town several times that summer while his friends visited him mid-July in Cross Plains, but made the move sometime in late July or early August.[82] The exact date is unknown mainly because two of his correspondents—Smith and Vinson—lived there, so there was no need to write.[83] In his publication *Pecan Valley Days*, Smith mentions that Howard lived most of his life in Cross Plains, only having lived in Brownwood to attend Howard Payne and "several months here while he worked at his writing."[84] This could have been those months in the fall of 1929. The better evidence comes from the August issue of *The Junto*, an extant letter written to *Thrills of the Jungle*, a new pulp magazine which only lasted one issue, and the typescript to the unpublished story "The Voice of the Mob," for all bore the mailing address of 816 Melwood Avenue, a boardinghouse in Brownwood.[85]

There has been much speculation regarding why Howard decided to make the move at that time in his life. "The most probable hypothesis," Louinet surmises, "is that Howard was now considering himself a full-time professional and wanted to fly on his own wings. Brownwood was the logical choice, as it wasn't far away, had all the facilities a writer needed, including large libraries, and this was where Vinson and Clyde Smith lived." And, like every youth desiring to leave home, "it would be easier for Howard to be who he was in Brownwood."[86] There was also no longer a concern for his mother, since Dr. Howard had firmly reestablished his practice in July after having toyed with the idea of moving to Spur.[87] And, as Roehm suggested, "It was a good time to move there: Tevis Clyde Smith graduated from Howard Payne on August 7."[88]

Smith had returned to college in the 1927–1928 academic year but had enrolled at Howard Payne rather than Daniel Baker.[89] After taking some final credits in the summer of 1929, he received his diploma at the commencement ceremony. The timing of his graduation was not a good one. "Our speaker assured us, in so many words, that the world was our oyster—all we had to do was open it," Smith wrote, but "eighteen days later, rumbling reached us from the Eastern States. Before too much longer, the Depression had hit our part of the Country."[90] Still, to celebrate having earned his English degree, he got together with his friends Vinson, Preece, and Howard. "I can remember, that night after Clyde Smith had graduated," Preece later recalled, for Howard and Smith "celebrated by repeated dives on a children's slide in a local park, with Truett and myself being their audience."[91]

Smith had briefly entertained the idea of becoming, like Howard, a writer. However, after submitting to both the slicks and the pulps with nothing more than rejection slips to show for his efforts, he followed in his father's footsteps and became a salesman.[92] By September he was gone, having moved to Carlsbad, New Mexico, for his new job.[93]

Howard remained in Brownwood, where he continued writing and spending time with his friends. Lindsey Tyson came down to Brownwood to visit, and Howard occasionally traveled to Cross Plains for visits with family and friends.[94] Oddly enough, it appears he spent more time with his Cross Plains friends while living in Brownwood, for Smith and Vinson were busy with work and their own lives. "My old gang was over here a day or so ago from Cross Plains," Howard wrote Preece in September, telling him, "A fair is going on and we took it in."[95]

Despite enjoying his new level of freedom, it did not work out. Once again, the reason for his return home is unknown. It likely resulted from the reality Smith had mentioned regarding the promises made by his commencement speaker. The stock market had peaked on September 3, and the day after began rapidly declining before crashing on Black Tuesday, October 29. This would have been further exacerbated by the fact that, despite having sold so many stories, he still had yet to be paid on those awaiting publication in *Weird Tales*. Cash flow may have made his financial situation in Brownwood difficult, and the true constraint on his freedom.

Whatever the case may be, sometime in the month of December, Howard wrote Smith, "Here I am doing business at the old stand or trying to. I don't know if I'll be able to write worth a damn here or not."[96] He found a way and closed out the year, despite the stock market crash, having made $772.50 in sales, nearly $12,000 in today's dollars.[97]

Chapter 17

"Lovecraft, One of the Greatest Writers of Our Time," 1930

Fingers turn the hidden Keys,
Looting wealth from lair and hold;
Cast what shapes in what dim mold?
Question now the Eternities.
But who is Grandpa Theobold?
—Letter to Smith, October 1931[1]

H. P. Lovecraft once shared where he was when he first learned the name Robert E. Howard. He told a correspondent, "I first became conscious of him as a coming leader just a decade ago," he wrote in 1936, "when (on a bench in Prospect Park, Brooklyn) I read 'Wolfshead.'" He then added, "I had read his two previous short tales with pleasure, but without especially noting the author. Much as I admired him, I had no correspondence with him till 1930."[2] That year the two men began what quickly developed into a long, frequent, and voluminous correspondence.

While Howard was becoming a *Weird Tales* reader favorite, Lovecraft was already one of the most popular authors, and his stories continued to see publication in the "unique magazine."[3] "Robert E. Howard is on the up-grade," Lovecraft wrote to Wright in 1930, although he did add his belief, "If he will avoid popular catering, he will turn out important stuff in the future."[4] Despite the admonishment, however, Howard's star began to rise with the readers of *Weird Tales* and other pulps, partly because he did cater to popular, mainstream audiences, which Lovecraft refused to do.

Like the other readers of *Weird Tales* magazine, Howard was also familiar with Lovecraft's stories, and he effusively praised them. After reading his "The Call of Cthulhu" in the May 1928 issue, Howard sent a letter to Wright, which was published in "The Eyrie." "Mr. Lovecraft's latest story," Howard wrote, "is indeed a masterpiece, which I am sure will live as one of the highest achievements of literature."[5] Howard further added, "He has the gift of making the unreal seem very real and terrible, without lessening the sensation of horror attendant thereto."[6] Even eight years later, before his death, Howard continued to praise Lovecraft's writing. When asked to offer criticism of one of his stories in 1936, Howard wrote, "Frankly, I don't feel capable of criticizing any of Lovecraft's stories. I see no flaw in them, as weird stories and works of art, and if I seemed to see a flaw, I'd hesitate to call it such, for I concede him a vastly greater knowledge and skill in constructing fantasies than I could ever attain."[7] This is the very reason he once called Lovecraft "one of the greatest writers of our time."[8]

Lovecraft built his reputation in the early issues of *Weird Tales*. Once he discovered the magazine, he began submitting stories and poems, all of which were accepted by Edwin Baird, no doubt prompted by Henneberger's fondness for Lovecraft's writing. "By late January [1925]," writes historian John Locke, "Lovecraft couldn't be ignored, having grown into a major force among *Weird Tales* contributors, accounting for nine stories." One of those submissions was "The Rats in the Walls," for which Henneberger personally wrote Lovecraft informing him it was "the best tale *Weird Tales* ever received."[9] It was for these reasons that Lovecraft was considered as the replacement editor for Baird during the magazine's reorganization. Lovecraft, however, turned Henneberger down for the position because neither he nor his new bride had any desire to move to Chicago.

Lovecraft and his wife, Sonia Greene, were living in her Brooklyn, New York, apartment at the time of Henneberger's proposal. Things may have looked promising at the start of their marriage, for Greene owned a hat shop, and Lovecraft's stories were selling, but by the end of the year, things had turned bleak.[10] Greene lost her hat shop and became ill, and Lovecraft could not find adequate work, although he was trying to help make ends meet. By the beginning of 1925, Greene was living in Cincinnati, having found employment there in a department store, while Lovecraft moved into a small, one-bedroom apartment in the poorer section of Brooklyn Heights in New York City.[11] He lived there, unhappily, alone for the majority of the year. The relationship with Greene had failed, and by early 1926 his aunts were encouraging him to come home to Providence. He did, and never left again. Greene filed for divorce in 1929, but when Lovecraft received the papers, he simply ignored them.

Although Lovecraft went home to Providence, he did not return to the life of a recluse, for he continued writing stories and fostering his circle of correspondents, many of whom wrote for *Weird Tales* magazine. He also traveled frequently, typically visiting those with whom he corresponded. In the summer of 1927, he met fellow writer H. Warner Munn, who later recalled his first meeting with Lovecraft: "I beheld a tall, lean man—his face almost cadaverous in aspect—with high cheekbones, a long, bony jaw, and thin lips compressed in a rather stern expression."[12] By this time Lovecraft had become a frugal man who lived on the meager earnings he made from his writing. His production, however, proved as meager as his earnings, for he did not quickly produce a high volume of stories as did most pulp writers at the time. This had much to do with the manner in which he wrote, preferring to craft them in longhand rather than using the faster typewriter that he despised. He was also a meticulous writer, which no doubt slowed his progress, but, in turn, this contributed highly to the quality of his writing. Still further, in order to make additional income, Lovecraft began doing work for hire, editing and rewriting others' works, as well as occasionally ghostwriting for additional income.

By 1930 Lovecraft continued appearing regularly, though not frequently, in the pages of *Weird Tales*. He found Wright to be a far more fickle editor than Baird had ever been, for Wright rejected many of the stories he submitted, such as "The Shunned House" and, at least initially, "The Strange High

House in the Mist." Despite this, Lovecraft remained a fan favorite among the magazine's readers, generally ranking alongside such notables as Henry S. Whitehead and Seabury Quinn. Also, by that year Howard had become a regular and fan favorite in the pages of the "unique magazine," and it was not uncommon to see Lovecraft and Howard's names invoked together in "The Eyrie." One longtime reader, Carl Belknap of Corpus Christi, Texas, provides a good example in 1933: "Ever since 1924, I have read every issue of *Weird Tales*, and as do most constant readers of any magazine, found and followed my favorite authors. Two men made the greatest impression on my mind in those days: [Henry S.] Whitehead and Lovecraft. Today I find Robert E. Howard's type of yarn has an almost irresistible appeal. There is a quality about his type or his approach that lifts something dead out of the reader's mind and replaces it with an exhilarating alcohol."[13] Other readers wrote of their favorite type of stories appearing in the magazine, such as C. H. Osborn of Fulton, New York, who shared that he liked "STORIES of strange races who lived and fought with gargantuan monsters, behemoths and elementals and worshipped forgotten gods, when the earth was young," before stating, "Lovecraft is a master of this type of story; so also is Howard."[14] It is perhaps not all too surprising then that these two authors should strike up a correspondence in the summer of 1930.

Lovecraft's story "The Rats in the Walls" was originally published in the March 1924 issue of *Weird Tales* under Baird's editorship. It was then reprinted in the June 1930 issue. The story tells of an American who loses his son during World War I and decides, as the last descendant of his ancestral line, to return to the family home in England, where he begins hearing rats moving behind the walls. Upon discovering the true nature of the rats, he descends into madness. Lovecraft truly became a professional writer with this story, for as literary biographer John Haefele explains, "In every respect, it exhibits sudden, tremendous growth in Lovecraft's literary skills."[15]

Reader reaction to the first publication is unknown, for there were no letters published regarding the story, but we do know Henneberger favored the story. When it was reprinted, many readers saw it for the first time, and it received so much attention that Wright wrote in the August issue, "The most popular story in our June issue, as shown by your votes, was *The Rats in the Walls*, by H. P. Lovecraft, which was reprinted from *Weird Tales* of six years ago."[16] Not only was it popular then, but scholars also continue to cite it as one of Lovecraft's best, such as pulp historian Robert Weinberger, who called it "one of HPL's most powerful tales."[17]

Near the end of the story, when the American descends into madness, he undergoes a sort of atavistic fit in which his mind rapidly reverts back through his ancestral heritage. In order to show this mental regression, Lovecraft has the man speak at first in an older English diction, then go back to Middle English, archaic Latin, and Gaelic before finally devolving into prehistoric guttural sounds.[18] The passage reads: "Curse you, Thornton, I'll teach you to faint at what my family do! . . . Sblood, thou stinkard, I'll learn ye how to gust . . . wolde ye swynke me thilke wys? . . . *Magna Mater! Magna Mater!* . . . *Atys* . . . *Dia ad aghaidh's ad aodaun* . . . *agus bas dunach ort! Dhonas's dholas ort, agus leat-sa!* . . . *Ungl* . . . *ungl* . . . *rrrlh* . . . *chchch* . . ."[19] "This sentence," Lovecraft later wrote a correspondent, "was what brought me into correspondence with Robert E. Howard."[20]

Because Lovecraft was not familiar with ancient languages, he had lifted the passage from a story he had previously read, "The Sin-Eater," by Fiona Macleod. First published in an 1895 collection by William Sharp, a Scottish writer who often employed the Macleod pseudonym when writing romantic stories of Celtic lore, he has a character speak a passage in Gaelic: "*Dia ad aghaidh's ad aodann . . . agus bas dunach ort! Dhonas's dholas ort, agus leat-sa!*" The passage translates as "God against thee and in thy face . . . and may a death of woe be yours. . . . Evil and sorrow to thee and thine!"[21] There was only one problem with Lovecraft employing Gaelic; it was the wrong language.

Since the story takes place in England, the ancient people of that land spoke Cymric, not Gaelic. The Gaelic language was primarily spoken in Scotland, and it had its influences on the Irish language. Lovecraft actually knew this. "The only objection to the phrase," he wrote not long after composing the story, "is that it's *Gaelic* instead of *Cymric* as the south-of-England locale demands." Despite this, Lovecraft figured it did not matter all that much for, as he noted to his correspondent, "with anthropology—details don't count. Nobody will ever stop to note the difference."[22] One person, however, did, and he lived in Cross Plains, Texas.

After reading the reprinted story, Howard set about typing a letter to Wright. "I have long looked forward to reading Mr. Lovecraft's 'The Rats in the Walls' and it certainly comes up to all expectations," he wrote. "I was amazed by the sweep of his imagination . . . because of the strange and unthinkable by-path into which he has wandered in this tale. There, assuredly, he has taken a road never before traversed, or even dreamed of, by any writer or thinker, ancient or modern. He has painted an incredible word picture." Howard also wrote, "The climax of the story alone puts Mr. Lovecraft in a class by himself."[23] It was the climax, though, that he wanted to address.

"I note from the fact that Mr. Lovecraft has his character speaking Gaelic instead of Cymric," he told Wright, believing Lovecraft, by "denoting the Age of the Druids, that he holds to Lhuyd's theory as to the settling of Britain by the Celts."[24] Edward Lhuyd was a seventeenth-century Welsh scholar who believed, wrongly, that the Brythonic language (that of the ancient Britons) was Gaelic in origin.[25] "This theory," Howard continued, "is not generally agreed to, but I scarcely think that it has ever been disproved, and it was upon this that my story 'The Lost Race' was based—that the Gaelic tribes preceded the Cymric peoples into Britain, by way of Ireland, and were later driven out by them." However, he informed Wright that despite his story, "Personally, I hold to the theory of Cymric precedence." Still, Howard did concede that "every man is entitled to his own view and a writer has the right to use any and all theories, no matter how conflicting, in his stories."[26]

Howard's ability to recognize the Gaelic being used for what should have been Cymric no doubt came from his fascination with all things Irish and his study of Celtic history and language. More specifically, it has been found to derive specifically from his ownership of *An Irish-English Dictionary*.[27] As a result, he was curious as to Lovecraft's views on the matter, but not knowing his personal address, he sent the letter to their mutual editor at *Weird Tales*.

Wright promptly sent the letter to Lovecraft, who read it with great interest. He, in turn, sent off several letters to fellow authors informing them of the curious letter he received from Howard.[28] "Wright has recently sent me a letter from the W. T. author Robert E. Howard," he wrote to one of his correspondents, "praising my 'Rats in the Walls' & giving me incidental remarks on Celtic Britain. Howard seems to be a rather erudite person—& I am dropping him a line." He added that he liked "some of his work—especially the 'elder world' stuff," but again admonished him for being "woefully prone to spoil his tales by concessions to the cheaply romantic element."[29]

After Howard's death Lovecraft wrote to a friend about how the correspondence had begun, and he was a little more specific with details. He noted that Howard did not realize the source from which he had derived his Gaelic, "but his sharp eye for Celtic antiquities told him it didn't quite fit—being a *Gaelic* (not *Cymric*) expression assigned to a South British locale." Lovecraft believed Howard "too charitable to suspect me of ignorant appropriation, he came to the conclusion that I followed a now-discredited theory whereby the Gaels were supposed to have preceded the Cymri in England."[30] So Lovecraft wrote Howard, "telling him I had merely picked a phrase with the right meaning from a note to a Scottish story while perfectly well aware that the language of Celtic South-Britain was really somewhat different."[31]

Howard wrote back on July 1, 1930, sharing much of the knowledge he had gained since becoming a Hibernophile. Lovecraft was amazed and once again wrote to his two correspondents about the lengthy and detailed letter. "Had another letter from Robert E. Howard, who seems to be a really profound student of Celtic philology & anthropology," wrote Lovecraft. "I wonder that a scholar of his calibre makes so many concessions to popular taste. He has a theory that the early Irish legends contain a greater substratum of truth than we are commonly inclined to concede. His middle name, apparently resurrected from Celtic dawns, is *Eiarbhin, Robert Eiarbhin Howard* . . . can you beat it?"[32] Lovecraft was clearly impressed with Howard's knowledge, and although the first letter and Lovecraft's initial reply are nonextant letters, most of the others in this nearly six-year exchange have been preserved.

At the time Lovecraft already had an extensive circle of correspondents to whom he wrote, and his letters, written in longhand, tended to be lengthy. According to Howard and Lovecraft scholar Bobby Derie, "Lovecraft's epistles (both letters and postcards) numbered in the tens of thousands."[33] The letter exchange between Howard and Lovecraft would number well over a hundred; often the letters were as long as ten to twenty pages and are today contained in a two-volume set numbering close to one thousand pages.[34]

Lovecraft often employed affectionate nicknames for his many correspondents, and he would do the same for Howard. Over the next two years, Lovecraft began referring to Howard by many of his "now-famous nicknames," continues Derie: "Bran Mak Morn, King Kull, REH, 'our Master of Massacre' and Conan the Reaver, Two-Gun Bob, Sagebrush Bob, 'the Terror of the Plains,' Conan, Brother Conan, and Longhorn." The one he favored, and "by far the most common to appear in Lovecraft's letters," was "Two-Gun Bob."[35] Howard did, after all, live in Texas and wrote of his penchant for guns.

Lovecraft's personal preference, and the name he often used when referring to himself, was Grandpa Theobold. Howard, at first, did not know this, so when Lovecraft sent him one of his stories, "At the Mountains of Madness," for feedback by his circle of friends, Howard was familiar with the other nicknames on the circulation list, but not Grandpa Theobold. Not knowing to whom the name referred, in a letter to Smith, Howard wrote a poem questioning the identity of this old man.

At the beginning of their correspondence, however, they remained far more formal by referring to each other as "Mr. Howard" and "Mr. Lovecraft." The first surviving letter is the one written by Howard dated July 1, 1930. After his formal salutation, he opens with words that make Howard sound almost awestruck by the fact he was writing and corresponding with Lovecraft: "I am indeed highly honored to have received a personal letter from one whose works I so highly admire. I have been reading your stories for years, and I say, in all sincerity, that no writer, past or modern, has equalled you in the realm of bizarre fiction." Lovecraft had evidently praised Howard's writing in his first letter, likely not mentioning his concessions to popular taste, and Howard wrote in return, "I am indeed gratified that you have liked my efforts in Weird Tales, and I thank you very much for your kind comments on them."[36]

In ensuing letters both writers are laudatory of each other's work and knowledge and spend most of their time agreeing with one another, such as when Lovecraft wrote, "You are right, too, I think, in believing that early Irish legendry ought to be carefully examined for its historic significance," or Howard writing, "I believe, like you, that civilization is a natural and inevitable consequence, whether good or evil I am not prepared to state."[37] Despite this early politeness, Howard recognized their differences from the very beginning. After receiving Lovecraft's first letter, Howard wrote Smith, informing him, "I got a long letter from Lovecraft. That boy is plenty smart. And well read too." Howard then continues by highlighting the differences he noted with Lovecraft. "He starts out by saying that most of my arguments seem logical enough and that he is about on the point of accepting my views—and then follows with about three or four closely written pages with which he rips practically all my theories to shreds." Howard then wrote how he felt about their differences: "He's out of my class. I'm game to go the limit with a man my weight, but me scrapping with him is like a palooka climbing into the ring with a champion."[38] So Howard told Smith his plan for continuing the letter exchange: "I think I'll ask him a lot of questions about things when I write him, instead of presenting my own views."[39] Still, Howard wanted to make clear to Smith how he really felt about Lovecraft's way of thinking when he stated, "That don't mean, understand, that he's convinced me to his way of thinking. Not at all; I still think I'm right."[40]

It did not take long before the politeness of their letter exchange developed into an often-heated debate, and Howard proved himself more than worthy to rebut Lovecraft's positions and advance his own. Howard was no palooka. Still, at the beginning they typically wrote more about their biographical differences, such as the environments in which they lived, their culture and history, and their upbringing and heritage. There are early mentions of some of the key topics of their future discussions, one of the most important being their debate on civilization versus barbarism and the freedoms attendant therein, but in the early letters, they spend most of their time getting to know one another.

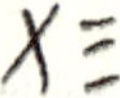

Howard traveled some in the first half of 1930, taking trips to Mineral Wells and Brownwood and an impromptu trip to San Antonio in June.[41] He shared his activities on the latter trip with Smith. "Last Monday Pink Tyson and Slue-foot Cross came around before I was up," Howard wrote. The Monday was June 9, and "Pink" was the nickname for Lindsey Tyson, while "Slue-foot" was Aud Cross, a friend from Brownwood.[42] Cross was on vacation, and he had come to Cross Plains to entice his two friends to join him for some fun. "We went to San Antonio that evening and spent the night in a tourist camp," Howard wrote, and the next night they took in the local boxing matches.[43] The following morning, Howard continues, "We went through Kerrville and Junction and camped on the Llano some ten miles out of Junction." There, they went fishing, but as Howard wrote, "As we had absent-mindedly omitted to bring anything that looked like bait, the fishing wasn't much of a success. We got some frogs but an eel kept stealing our bait and we caught one fish—a pound and a half cat which we later tossed back into the river. I don't get much kick out of fishing but I did enjoy rowing up and down the river. We made several miles altogether in the rowboat."[44]

Although his friends wanted to continue their ramblings, Howard decided he needed to get back home to continue writing. Another incentive was to listen in on the heavyweight boxing champion match between Max Schmeling and Jack Sharkey airing on the radio. Former heavyweight champion Gene Tunney had retired after his last fight, so the title was currently vacant. Howard missed most of the match; he wrote, "Getting here just in time to hear Schmeling declared winner on a foul. Phooey. I despise Sharkey but it looks like he gets some rotten breaks."[45] Sharkey had been contending for the title since his contest with Jack Dempsey, but when he delivered the low blow, Schmeling became the first boxer to win the title on a technicality.[46]

Outside of these short trips, Howard spent most of his time now in Cross Plains writing. He did appear to be growing somewhat more disgruntled with the town, for it certainly did not have the conveniences or the entertainment opportunities that Brownwood or San Antonio afforded. "This is a lousy town," Howard wrote Smith. "Not even any matinee shows and I've gotten so I'd rather go in the afternoon than at night."[47] Going to the movie theater remained a favorite pastime for Howard, but to see a matinee, he either had to go up to Cisco or down to Brownwood. Among the films he had recently seen were *Montana Moon* with Joan Crawford and John Mack Brown, *The Benson Murder Case* with William Powell, and the popular adaptation of Owen Wister's novel *The Virginian*, starring Gary Cooper. He liked the latter "fairly well. . . . But Judas," he wrote, "it was full of hokum."[48]

There was one major change in town that June and it came to the local newspaper, for Jack Scott had returned to the area, taking over ownership of the *Cross Plains Review*. "I started running that paper in 1930," Scott later recalled in an interview; "I was 20 years old."[49] Scott was born on September 14, 1909, in Baird, Texas, to George B. and Adelia Scott, and he had two older sisters.[50] He attended school mostly in Baird, but after his father took over the First State Bank in 1922, the family moved to Cross Plains, where Scott continued his schooling. As with Howard, he had to go elsewhere to finish his education, but rather than going to Brownwood, Scott finished his education at the West Texas Military Institute in San Antonio before he enrolled in the journalism program at Simmons University in Abilene (later Hardin-Simmons University). While attending college, he served as the editor of the school newspaper.

After graduating on June 4, he returned home to Cross Plains.[51] "I got out of college one day," Scott recalled, "and took over the newspaper here the next."[52] The newspaper was in dire straits, and the bank that held the note on it was eagerly willing to sell. The problem at the time was, of course, the Depression. "Couldn't get a job anywhere," explained Scott. "That was tough times. You had more guys with BA degrees pullin' a cotton sack, more than ever in Texas history. You couldn't get a job teaching school. Nobody. It was rough. So, I came down here, assumed that note and took over this paper. And it was broke." Still, Scott understood the importance of running a small-town paper. "A country newspaper is different," he once stated. "About the only thing more widely read is the Bible." For the majority of his working years, he maintained some affiliation with the *Cross Plains Review*, serving as owner, manager, reporter, print specialist, columnist, and any other job required to keep the paper running. "I enjoyed it," he once remarked, though he did note that the occupation was "not the most remunerative field."[53]

Of the Howard family, Scott came to know the doctor the best. Dr. Howard had served as the Scott family physician, and because he was a Cross Plains professional, he was often a source of town news. Summing up his feelings about the good doctor, Scott once told an interviewer, "I just did love that ole man." As for Mrs. Howard, he once commented, "You know for the life of me, I can't remember Mrs. Howard." And regarding Howard himself, Scott admitted, "I didn't know Robert Howard as well as a lot of people."[54]

Part of the reason for this is the three years difference in their ages. "When I first met Robert E. Howard," Scott said, "I was about twelve years old." Howard was 15 at the time. "I would speak to him and he would speak to me," Scott continued, "but we never had very much in common."[55] And although initially he remembered him as "skinny," he said that eventually, "Robert was a big, strong, robust guy," and he would often liken him as "a cross between Jack London and Edgar Allan Poe."[56]

Scott observed that before taking over the newspaper, there had really been little time to come to know Howard. In addition to his year in Brownwood for high school, Scott explained, "Howard left here and went to Howard Payne, [while] I went to a military school [which] took two more years before I went to college." So, he admitted, "Our time in school didn't overlap much."[57] Because of this, he remarked in one interview, "What I know about him is mainly what I wrote through the newspaper."[58]

Scott remembered him primarily from the 1930s, when Howard was a writer. And despite both men being writers in their fashion, that did not appear to create any sort of social bond between them. "I don't think he liked anybody in the newspaper business," Scott believed, though he did add, "I don't think he disliked me, but there was no camaraderie between us."[59] Scott did, however, develop a good relationship with Dr. Howard, and through him and others, like any good small-town newspaper editor, he would have been familiar with both the activities of the son and the gossip.

Howard did not have a personal relationship with Jack Scott or many of the folks in town. His occupation was different from theirs, as were most of his interests. This resulted not only in people seeing Howard as different, but also in him believing they acted differently toward him. "The people in this town treat me in several manners," Howard wrote Smith, "contemptuously ignore me, which doesn't bother me any; go out of their way to start trouble with me, which does; and assume a story of monkey in a cage attitude." Howard then described the situation with those who saw him as something of a spectacle: "Those who deign to notice me at all, are forever on the lookout for some peculiarity, some difference that will stamp me as an eccentric. The infernal fools can't seem to understand that a man can make his living some other way besides dressing tools or selling stuff and still be an ordinary human being with human sensations. The more money I make at my trade the more strangely they eye me."[60] While no doubt many of the people of Cross Plains read the pulps, most likely the Westerns, few could imagine or understand the lifestyle of the people who actually composed those stories.

Other than not having employment like most other men in town, it was the nature of the writing occupation that made Howard peculiar. One aspect of this had to do with the hours Howard kept. Many authors, Celia Blue Johnson wrote in her book *Odd Type Writers*, have been labeled odd, weird, and crazy because of the strange hours they kept, working far outside the norm of the rest of society.[61] She highlights how some, such as Friedrich Schiller, "wrote at night to ensure that no one descended on his doorstep while his pen flew." Simply not wanting to be interrupted, "He'd work for hours while the stars were up and potential visitors were fast asleep."[62] Another author, J. D. Salinger of *The Catcher in the Rye* fame, also worked well into the night and did so from the very beginning. "At night in bed, under the covers," while he was in military school, "with the aid of a flashlight, he began writing stories."[63] Perhaps the most unusual of these late night writers was Robert Frost, who was "driven by creative forces to write at night," despite the fact he had, from earliest childhood, "a deep-rooted fear of the dark." Johnson explains, "This phobia haunted Frost throughout his life," so much so that "it drove him to sleep in his mother's room as a teen."[64]

For many authors it was not so much that they had a penchant to write at night or did not want to be disturbed; rather, they felt a need to write a story straight through. Franz Kafka composed his famous short story "The Judgment" "in one great gust, from 10 p.m. until 6 a.m.," as he noted in his diary. He explained, "Only *in this way* can writing be done." Jack London, one of Howard's favorite authors, was also known for writing in long stretches, for when he "first attempted to launch his career," Johnson explains, he "toiled for fifteen hours every day," and Salinger was known to "spend up to sixteen hours straight writing and revising in the concrete bunker behind his home in Cornish, New Hampshire."[65] The French writer Alexander Dumas, famous for his novels *The Count of Monte Cristo* and *The Three Musketeers*, also "worked up to sixteen hours a day."[66] "During these intense work periods," Johnson notes, "he had meals delivered to his study so he wouldn't have to break from writing."[67]

It was no different for Robert E. Howard, for he was known for writing through the night. In an interview J. H. Child recalled how Howard "made a racket, big racket. He typed all night long."[68] This is what many people remembered about Howard, for as Burke explained, "Leroy Butler and others reported that when Robert was typing, in addition to the incessant clatter of keys, he talked his stories out in a booming voice, without particular regard for the hour."[69] Even Jack Scott once recounted how "Robert Howard wrote into the night," explaining, "There was no air conditioning and he raised all the windows, to let the air in. Robert would be writing over there and he would keep all his neighbors in houses nearby awake."[70] Howard also noted the long hours he kept in a letter to Lovecraft when he wrote, "I have worked as much as eighteen hours a day at my typewriter."[71] Norris Chambers recalled how "Dr. Howard would sometimes say, 'Robert's been writing for two days and two nights, now.'" Like a good father, "He'd worry about it," Chambers explained, but they all knew that Howard would "get started and he'd just keep going."[72]

Still, most of the people of Cross Plains at the time did not understand this, and so Howard remained strange, eccentric, and, in Johnson's word, odd. Howard did acknowledge the realities of the situation, for he summed it up as the nature of his chosen profession when he concluded, "It's the price a man pays for being any way different from the mob." However, his frustrations still shone through when he added, "Well, damn the mob."[73] The only problem was, sometimes they damned him back.

Late in life, Dr. Howard wrote of one such example in his son's life. "Robert was a lonely man," the doctor wrote, "because the people around him understood little of his life and the character of the man. His writings little appealed to those around."[74] When Howard first began publishing in *Weird Tales*, Dr. Howard had been proud the magazine was being sold in town, but that soon changed.[75] "The newsstands carried the magazine which carried his stories for a time," he continued, "but quit altogether handling the W. T. and other magazines carrying Robert's stories."[76] This was probably because Farnsworth Wright, knowing the old adage that "sex sells," began commissioning front covers that were gradually becoming more lurid, featuring scantily clad women who, in some cases, were topless. By 1930 the type of pulps that Howard published in were being removed from the racks. This forced Howard to either purchase the magazines with his stories in them while visiting Brownwood and elsewhere, or ask his friends to send him copies as he did Smith in one letter: "Say, bring me a June *Weird Tales*, will you? I can't get the dam thing here and I haven't seen the latest one. Thanks."[77]

Despite becoming successful in his profession, it was turning him into an enigma in his own hometown.

Chapter 18

Bran Mak Morn and the Picts, 1930

How can I wear the harness of toil
And sweat at the daily round,
When in my soul forever
The drums of Pictdom sound?
—"The Drums of Pictdom"[1]

"Had I grown into the sort of man, which in childhood I wished to become," Howard once wrote, "I would have been short, stocky, with thick, gnarled limbs, beady black eyes, a low retreating forehead, heavy jaw, and straight, coarse black hair—my conception of a typical Pict." Howard was no doubt intrigued by the ancient North Britain race ever since discovering them in the "Canal Street library" in New Orleans.[2] Why this is the case, however, is not clear, for as Burke once expressed, "The reasons for Howard's fascination with the Picts are undoubtedly as complex as the man himself."[3] Howard tried several times to explain it to Lovecraft in his letters, but even he seemed unclear as to their specific allurement to him. "There is one hobby of mine which puzzles me to this day," he wrote. "That is my interest in the people . . . I have always designated as Picts. . . . To me

'Pict' must always refer to the small dark Mediterranean aborigines of Britain. This is not strange, since when I first read of these aborigines, they were referred to as Picts. But what is strange, is my unflagging interest in them."[4] In a follow-up letter, Howard wrote how he first saw the name on several maps, but that it was always placed outside the borders of the Roman Empire. "This fact aroused my intense interest," Howard explained, for it "suggested terrific wars—savage attacks and ferocious resistance—valor and heroism and ferocity," three traits found in the characters he wrote about.[5] It is not all too surprising, then, that he began writing about the Picts not long after his discovery of them.

The Picts first made an appearance in some of his earliest handwritten stories, including one essay he possibly wrote for school.[6] Howard explained that after the "great Celtic invasion . . . the Picts could not stand before the race of warriors skilled in the work of metals and the make and usage of weapons . . . so they fled to the northern mountains" (the highlands of Scotland).[7] Louinet points out that the Picts are also "the only fictional creations to appear throughout Howard's writing career," and that rarely did a year go by that Howard did not include them in some story he wrote.[8] The Picts played a major role in the first King Kull story published, "The Shadow Kingdom," and were mentioned in the second, "The Mirrors of Tuzun Thune," but his first published story featuring the Picts was "The Lost Race."[9]

Howard wrote the story in the fall of 1924 and submitted it to Wright, who returned it requesting revisions. After sending it back in December, the story was accepted on January 7, 1925, for thirty dollars upon publication.[10] It was his second professional sale, after "Spear and Fang," but it was not published in *Weird Tales* until January 1927.[11] The story takes place shortly after the Britons had driven out the Gaels from South Britain, and one of them encounters the Picts living in a cave. He hears their story about how they had come into the land from the south but were driven underground when the Celtic Gaels invaded.[12]

In a letter to Howard in August 1930, Lovecraft recalled reading the story and noted that "for fictional purposes it is perfectly proper—perhaps even *best,* on account of the dramatic simplicity of the idea—to attribute the

British legends to forgotten races in the British Isles themselves."[13] This was in response to Howard having explained to Lovecraft that his story was based on the idea "that the Gaelic tribes preceded the Cymric peoples into Britain, by way of Ireland, and were later driven out by them."[14] Lovecraft then noted that what Howard had done, "is what Arthur Machen has done with such marvelous skill and potency."[15]

Arthur Machen, born Arthur Llewellyn Jones, was a Welsh author of supernatural horror and fantasy and a contemporary of Howard and Lovecraft. Although born long before either of them in 1863, he would outlive them both. Among the stories Machen was best known for were those he wrote of the little people, an atavistic race of small, bestial men who lived underground and on the fringes of society, not unlike Howard's Picts. Machen first wrote of them in 1895, when "The Shining Pyramid" was published in *The Unknown World.* According to Howard scholar Jeffrey H. Shanks, when Machen's tales of the little people were reprinted in the United States in the 1920s, they "were an important influence on many of the *Weird Tales* writers, especially Lovecraft and Howard."[16] Machen was considered by Howard to be the greatest author of the weird (alongside Poe and Lovecraft), once writing of him, "I have always been fascinated by his work."[17]

"The Lost Race" was clearly influenced by the works of Machen, and Howard emulated him again, in his own fashion, when he wrote another story, "The Little People," which was not published in his lifetime. Written sometime in 1928, Shanks calls the story an "overt homage to Machen," and the tale makes a direct reference to "The Shining Pyramid" when a character calls Machen's story "a masterpiece of outré literature."[18] But it was another of Howard's early character creations in which his thinking about the Picts began to develop and change, growing into something wholly unique; it came in his stories of the last Pictish king, Bran Mak Morn.

Howard once explained that his character Bran Mak Morn "was the result of my discovery of the Pictish race, when reading some historical works in a public library in New Orleans at the age of thirteen."[19] Unlike the Picts he read about in the library who were "sly, furtive, unwarlike, and altogether inferior to the races which followed," Howard wrote, "I made them a strong, warlike race of barbarians, gave them an honorable history of past glories, and created for them a great king." Howard claimed, as he so often did, that Bran Mak Morn "leaped full-grown into my mind—a pantherish man of medium height, with inscrutable black eyes, black hair and dark skin." He also explained how he had derived the name. "I named him Bran, for another favorite historical character of mine—the Gaul Brennus, who sacked Rome. The Mak Morn comes from the famous Irish hero, Gol Mac Morn. I changed the spelling of the Mac, to give it a non-Gaelic appearance."[20]

"I first put Bran on paper," Howard wrote, "in a long narrative rhyme which I never completed."[21] The poem is "A Song of the Race."[22] The earliest prose writing comes in the form of three handwritten pages Howard titled "Bran Mak Morn," believed to have possibly been written in his high school days as early as 1922.[23] The following fall Howard was evidently writing a novel featuring his new creation, for he wrote Smith in October, "I'm writing a book which doubtless would make you tired and would sound like a lot of fool stuff to most folks, but as I am writing it for my own amusement, the opinion of other people about it don't interest me."[24] Two chapters from the novel survive, though they only frame the story and present background, so Bran Mak Morn does not appear in the writing.[25]

After becoming a professional writer, Howard began composing another Mak Morn story in the fall of 1925 that he submitted to the "unique magazine." "I thoroughly enjoyed 'Men of Shadows,'" Wright replied, "but I fear I can not use it in *Weird Tales*. It is too little of a 'story,' despite the vigorous action in the opening pages. It is rather a chronicle of a tribe, a picture of the evolution of a race; and thereby it lacks the suspense and thrill that a story of individual conflict and hopes and fears and drama would have."[26] In that story Howard describes Bran Mak Morn as a "chief" with a pure Mediterranean bloodline, while the misshapen Picts are degenerates of the race.

Howard laid the character aside and focused on other stories for a while, including the tales he wrote of King Kull. After receiving numerous rejections for stories about the king of Valusia and no acceptance letter for his king of the Picts, Howard decided to bring the two of them together in one story in February of 1930.[27] The tale is told from the point of view of an Irish prince, Cormac of Connacht, but is decidedly a Bran Mak Morn story. Facing an impending battle against the Roman legionaries, Mak Morn calls upon magical forces that bring King Kull forward in time to help unite divided forces into one in order to save the Pictish kingdom.

Howard sent the story to Wright's new publication *Strange Stories*, because he had received a letter from his editor announcing that the magazine would begin appearing on the newsstands that summer.[28] This was good news, for it meant a new publishing outlet for Howard. "I'm hoping to just about double my income from his company when that magazine comes out," he informed Smith, and so he submitted "Kings of the Night" to the new magazine.[29]

In March Wright accepted the story for $120.[30] "I rather expected him to take it for the new magazine," Howard wrote Smith. "However he accepted it for *Weird Tales*; possibly because the central figure is Kull of Atlantis."[31] It was actually because the new magazine was never launched over a dispute with another publishing company.[32] Still, Wright saw merit in the story. "It was rather a new line for me," Howard continued, "as I described a pitched battle," though tentatively adding, "I think I handled it fairly well."[33] That fall, just before publication, he again wrote Smith, "Some ways this is the best I ever wrote. Nothing very weird about it, but good battle stuff, if I do say so myself."[34] The short story was published in the November 1930 issue of *Weird Tales*, and it was the last King Kull story published in his lifetime, as well as the first one published featuring his character Bran Mak Morn.

The response to the yarn was fulsome; it received more votes for most popular in an issue than any other story Howard ever wrote for *Weird Tales*.[35] "Never did I read a more thrilling account of a battle than that portrayed in Robert E. Howard's *Kings of the Night*," wrote H. F. Scotten of Indianapolis, calling it "a masterpiece unsurpassed by anything ever written on a like subject."[36] Because of this story, many even claimed Howard as "my favorite author" and the "greatest writer of the Twentieth Century."[37] And still two years later, Frederick John Walsen of Denver, Colorado, wrote to "The Eyrie," "The best story that you have ever published was one by

Robert E. Howard, a fine author, called *Kings of the Night*."[38] All the praise led Wright to declare, "To judge by the enthusiastic letters that you have written to this department commending Robert E. Howard's latest story . . . *Kings of the Night* easily took first place in the voting for favorite story in the November issue."[39]

By the time the story's praise appeared, however, Howard's conceptualization of his beloved Picts had changed as a result of his correspondence with Lovecraft. His friend from Providence acknowledged, "It's true that the Celts share most vigorously the myth cycle of *fairies, gnomes*, and *little people*, which anthropologists find all over western Europe," that he explained were attributed "to vague memories of contact with the Mongoloids." However, he continued, "Since these fair Nordic Celts found a smaller, darker race in Britain and Ireland, there is a tendency . . . to assume that the 'little people' legends allude to contact with *those* dark aborigines."[40] In other words, Shanks explains, "Lovecraft agrees that the pre-Celtic people of Europe . . . were Mediterraneans." What Lovecraft was arguing, however, (according to Shanks) was "that they were *preceded* by the diminutive Turanian/Mongoloid race and that it was the latter that gave rise to the tales of fairies, dwarfs, and elves, not the former."[41] The little people were of Mongoloid origin, whereas the Picts were originally Mediterranean.

After this exchange Howard's stories began to reflect this idea, for he depicted the Mongoloid people as being the little people who were driven underground by the Mediterranean Picts, who themselves were later overrun by the Celtic Britons.[42] The first yarns he wrote with this in mind, however, only mentioned Bran Mak Morn. In one, "The Dark Man," the king, long dead, has come to be considered a god, while another, "The Children of the Night" refers to the few Picts left as "The Bran cult."[43] Still another yarn that does not mention the last king of the Picts but embraces the new idea is "People of the Dark."[44] It was this idea, Burke explains, that "served as the genesis of what most fans regard as Howard's finest story of Bran Mak Morn and the Picts (and one of his very best, period)."[45] This story was "Worms of the Earth."

Written in the last weeks of 1931 and the beginning of 1932, Howard crafted a story that was wholly unique.[46] After witnessing the crucifixion of a fellow Pict by the Roman governor and wanting to protect his people against further atrocities, Bran Mak Morn vows his vengeance against the man. Subsequently making a deal with a witch, he learns the means by which he can use the race of creatures driven underground by his own ancestors to kill the powerful governor. Not only had Howard employed the new idea of two separate races, but he also took a different perspective in his writing. "In a long narrative rhyme which I never completed," Howard explained to Lovecraft, he told the story "through a Roman centurion on the Wall" (Hadrian's Wall, which had been built by the Romans as fortification against the Picts). "[In] my first Bran Mak Morn story," Howard continued, "I told the story through the person of a Gothic mercenary in the Roman army. . . . In 'The Lost Race' the central figure was a Briton; and in the 'Kings of the Night' it was a Gaelic prince. Only in my last Bran story, 'The Worms of the Earth' which Mr. Wright accepted, did I look through Pictish eyes, and speak with a Pictish tongue!"[47] The story was all the more powerful for that very reason. Wright clearly thought so, too, for in his acceptance letter, dated March 10, 1932, he wrote, "I want to schedule 'Worms of the Earth' soon, for that is an unusually fine story."[48] After its publication in the November 1932 issue of *Weird Tales*, Howard once again had a hit on his hands. Readers praised the story in "The Eyrie," including one unknown reader from Newport, Kentucky, who wrote, "Robert E. Howard's 'Worms of the Earth' is a story that has *everything*—vividly drawn characters—intense, sustained, powerful atmosphere—it is utterly different from anybody else's stories—perfect illusion from first sentence to last—and he even manages to inject admiration for a character into a weird story. I definitely admire this man's passionate feeling that his subjects are his children and he's in honor bound to be loyal to them. This story is a perfect thing."[49] And once all the letters and votes were tabulated, Wright declared it "the most popular story in the November issue."[50]

Fellow *Weird Tales* authors also praised the story, with Lovecraft personally writing Howard, "Another recent thing which impressed me as tremendously fine . . . 'Worms of the Earth.' The subtle way in which you *suggest* the abysmal horror of those retrograded *things* is truly inimitable."[51] Modern critics have praised it as well, such as *Weird Tales* historian Robert Weinberger, who called it one of Howard's "best works."[52] Literary critic John Clute wrote that with these two Mak Morn stories, Howard "had become perhaps the most word-perfect, consistent, unrelenting, irresistibly succinct narrator of violent action ever to write in English."[53]

Louinet also suggests that there may well have been an autobiographical representation of Howard in his character Bran Mak Morn. "More so than any of his characters," he wrote, "Bran feels the heavy weight of personal responsibility for his people, much as one suspects Howard must have felt toward his aging parents, especially his sickly mother."[54] While his mother's ailing health was true, the autobiographical aspects are left to speculation.

Despite the success of both Bran Mak Morn stories, however, Howard never wrote another story featuring the last king of the Picts. Although the character was well received by the readers of *Weird Tales*, they were the last Bran Mak Morn stories published in his lifetime. He would still, however, continue writing about his beloved Picts.[55]

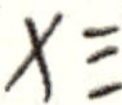

By the latter half of 1930, Howard was spending practically all of his time writing. He was working on additional stories that included his series characters Solomon Kane, King Kull, and Bran Mak Morn in the hopes of having another sale. In addition, he was still composing and selling his boxing stories that showcased Sailor Steve Costigan. In the midst of the many King Kull and Bran Mak Morn stories being rejected, not to mention Costigan stories as well, he tried developing another series character, Cormac Mac Art, about a renegade Gael, cast out by his own Irish people, who joins with a Danish Viking, Wulfhere the Skull-splitter.[56] He started several stories but only managed to finish one that he sent to *Argosy.* It was rejected, as Howard predicted. He had written Smith sometime after submitting it in May of 1930. "I am confronted with the enigma of editors," Howard began. "They say they want action-stuff. Well, I have a story with *Argosy* which I am as certain they will reject as I am that I'm sitting here. Yet it bristles with fast, well-written action. There is a perfect shimmer of swords from the opening scene. . . . By golly, whatever else they may say about that story, they can't kick about the action. I consider it my best attempt of the sort, to date. But will I sell it? Like Hell I will."[57] Howard was feeling the same frustrations with the many rejections he received from Wright. And there were still more disappointments when new outlets and new opportunities fell through, such as the planned companion magazine to *Weird Tales*, or when Howard was informed by Wright that radio station WTAM had begun dramatizing the magazine's stories, only to receive a later missive telling him the radio series was discontinued.[58] Both of those new opportunities had held out the possibility for increased sales.

Howard also found himself frustrated from his lack of travels. "I envy you," he wrote Lovecraft in September 1930. "It has been so long since I have taken a trip of any kind, I feel as if I were taking root. For instance, it has been two years since I have been across the Mexican Border."[59] He wanted to travel, but he was hamstrung by two things. "I should like very much to go prying around in out-of-the-way places, redolent with the musk and decay of antiquity," he continued, "but I've never had the time or money."[60] Writing took time, and he wrote for money, but with so many rejections, it took up more of his time but earned him less money.

Because he was working longer hours, he had stopped exercising, and without traveling, he was not getting away from his work. His lifestyle was beginning to take a toll on his health. He admitted as much to Preece in a letter that fall. "I put on the gloves the other day for the first time in months, and, for the first time in my life, found myself staggering and holding on to avoid being knocked out, and unable to inflict any punishment on my opponent. My legs never failed me before, but this time—well, I've slipped a long way, in every way. I'm just a shell of a man."[61] He was suffering from physical and mental exhaustion. The only problem was, at the time this was little understood by most people in and especially out of the medical field. Howard had a problem, but he did not understand its source.

Howard complained to his father of several physical problems he was having in mid-October, and Dr. Howard, evidently unsure of the proper diagnosis, referred him to a clinic in Temple, possibly King's Daughters Clinic and Hospital. Howard presented with the complaint of a "varicocele," or an enlarged vein in his scrotum. The doctor noted that Howard had "first noticed varicocele about 3 years ago," but two weeks before the appointment, he "did quite a bit of walking" and had been experiencing pain.[62]

According to John Hopkins Medicine, varicoceles are "very common" and they "are not dangerous." However, they can cause three main problems: "impaired fertility, decreased testosterone production in the testis, or scrotal discomfort."[63] Howard had been experiencing the latter, and, likely from information gathered from his father, he was concerned about the former.

The doctor also noted in the personal history section of his report, "He says that he has been slow in developing," and was concerned "that his penis is not of normal size." Between his slow development through puberty and possibly knowing of the associated problems with a varicocele, Howard was naturally concerned for his manhood. In addition, the doctor recorded a third concern of his patient: "He has quite a bit of gas in his stomach and belches quite a bit."[64]

The doctor began a physical examination of Howard and made numerous notations of his health, finding no cause for any physical concerns. Essentially, he concluded Howard was in good health, declaring him "a well developed white male 25 years of age not acutely ill." The doctor did ask about his sexual development, writing that his "sexual impulse did not seem to develop until he was 19 or so," but that he now had "normal desires."[65]

In the end the doctor recorded his working diagnosis of Howard's underlying problem as "sexual neurasthenia," a term that was then outdated and no longer widely used by the medical community.[66] According to medical historian Francis G. Gosling, this diagnosis was originally defined in the post–Civil War era and was at first associated with Civil War soldiers suffering from fatigue, anxiety, headaches, heart palpitations, and depression. However, it was not only many of the soldiers who were suffering from what would be called post-traumatic stress disorder today; so too were the wives who were left behind to tend the farms and plantations on their own. As America quickly industrialized in the late nineteenth century, similar symptoms and diagnoses were found among overworked businessmen as well as busy women in high society. In other words, the diagnosis of sexual neurasthenia, or, by the twentieth century, neurasthenia, was an ailment of modern man.[67]

In an age when Charles Darwin's theories of evolution had developed into the mindset that there existed a natural social Darwinism by extension, there came a continual race for the top. "Competition, insecurity and ceaseless striving," explain medical researchers Marijke Gijswijt-Hofstra and Roy Porter, "made for an exhausting schedule, as Americans battled to make good and prove themselves in a market place whose law was the survival of the fittest."[68]

In the post–Civil War era, it was Dr. George Beard who became the first leading authority on this ailment and titled his book *Sexual Neurasthenia (Nervous Exhaustion)*. "The causation," he explained, "as of all other clinical varieties, and of modern nerve sensitiveness in general, is not single or simple, but complex; evil habits, excesses, tobacco, alcohol, worry and special excitements, even climate itself—all the familiar excitants being secondary to the one great predisposing cause—civilization."[69]

One of the excesses of modern man Dr. Beard found was that they were overworked; a person in the habit of working sixteen-hour days, sitting at his typewriter until he was too exhausted to continue, would be a good example of a person who had reached the state of "nervous exhaustion."[70] And since one of the effects of this exhaustion can be the loss of sexual desire, the term was thus known as "sexual neurasthenia."[71]

One of the most famous people diagnosed with neurasthenia was William James, a Harvard professor who is often referred to as the "father of American psychology."[72] He had been diagnosed in early adulthood with sexual neurasthenia and came to know many people with the same ailment. "The number of people in James' circle of relatives and friends," historian Kim Townsend explains, "who suffered from what was generally labeled neurasthenia—literally a weakening of the nerves, otherwise everything from gastric problems to impotence to listlessness to pathological depression—is legion." He wrote that among these men, the "hold on their lives seemed tenuous, the line between sanity and insanity far from clear" and that it was found "especially among the highly educated." James suffered deep bouts of depression brought on by overwork that often led to his contemplation of suicide. The year after his famous lecture, "Is Life Worth Living?" James wrote offhandedly, "I take it that no man is educated who has never dallied with the thought of suicide."[73] Townsend also noted that by the time James was in his 30s, he struggled with his relationship with women, for "his conception of his own body and his conception of women and of his relation to them was integral to his idea of the kind of man he wanted to become—even as he feared he was not physically sound enough to win the hand of the woman he loved."[74]

Howard, like James, was experiencing gastric problems and bouts of depression, had contemplated suicide, and was wrestling with his relationship with women, most likely brought on by his work habits. Both his physical ailments and any psychological problems he was having were most likely due to his work.

The diagnosis of neurasthenia by the twentieth century is considered to have reached its peak in its first decade.[75] The First World War marked its retreat as a common diagnosis, and it became obsolete within the medical community. It was Sigmund Freud and the opening of the field of psychiatry who took over writing on the psychological disorder caused by modern stress, and by the end of the century it would be more commonly referred to as "chronic fatigue syndrome." The likely reason it was still referred to as sexual neurasthenia by the doctor examining Howard was because the new field was slow to be accepted and in places like rural Texas, it remained a common diagnosis.[76]

"We are herewith mailing you Robert's examination records," the Temple physician wrote to Dr. Howard on October 23, 1930. "We do not think there is anything wrong with Robert. We can find no varicocele of any consequence, his organs are normally developed and he tests out good in every respect." The doctor then concluded that "his trouble, in our judgment, is due to him thinking there is something wrong. After he has dispelled this thought from his mind he will be in fine shape."[77] The only problem with that was he did not dispel the thought, nor did he do the things necessary to commonly overcome the illness with diet, exercise, and time away from work—by relaxing.

The end of the year found Howard still suffering, for he wrote Smith of his listlessness, "I don't know what I'm going to do next, or where I'm going. Probably nothing and nowhere." When talking about one thing that may have actually served him well, traveling, he told Smith, "I've been sketchily considering a trip to Mexico City but I won't go. There's no particular reason why I shouldn't, I suppose, except that the thought of bestirring myself and making the effort is one that well-nigh overwhelms me. I have money enough to go anywhere in the Western Hemisphere, but the thought of going anywhere is as repellent as is the thought of staying here." And when it came to his work, it was the same thing. "I have done nothing recently," Howard continued. "I have a number of manuscripts that are practically ready to be sent off, and a number more which lack only a little work to be completed. Some would probably sell, but I have been too lethargic. The game is hardly worth the candle."[78]

Howard was in trouble, but neither he nor anyone around him understood. The same behaviors the people of Cross Plains looked askance at Howard for were the very same behaviors that were causing his illness. He was living the life of a modern man surrounded by people who still lived the small-town, rural, agrarian life. The doctor was unfamiliar with the ailments of a modern man, although he came close to perhaps diagnosing Howard in the correct manner. Labeling his ills with an outdated term, the prescription offered by the doctor was not going to address the underlying causes, and Howard was left to suffer on his own.

Despite the difficulties of numerous rejections and poor health, according to Lord, Howard's "sales for 1930 rose to $1303.50."[79] This was the equivalent of slightly more than twenty thousand in modern dollars. It was an attractive sum for someone living in the early throes of the Great Depression. But it came with a price.

necessary to commonly overcome the illness with diet, exercise, and time away from work—by relaxing.

The end of the year found Howard still suffering, for he wrote Smith of his illness: "I don't know what I'm going to do next, or where I'm going, probably nowhere." When talking about one thing that may have actually served him well, travel, he told Smith [illegible] contemplating a trip to Mexico City but I won't go. There's no earthly reason why I can't, I suppose, except that the thought of packing myself and making the effort is one that well-nigh overwhelms me. I have saved enough to go anywhere in the Western Hemisphere, but the thought of going anywhere is as repugnant as the thought of staying here." And when it came to his work, it was the same thing: "I have done nothing lately," Howard continued. "I have a number of manuscripts that are practically ready to send off, and a number more which lack only a little work to be completed. Some would probably sell, but I have been too lethargic. The cause is mostly [illegible]."

Howard was in trouble, and neither he nor anyone around him understood. The same behaviors the people of Cross Plains looked askance at Howard for were the very same behaviors that were causing his illness. He was living the life of a modern man surrounded by people who still lived the small-town, rural agrarian life. The doctor was unfamiliar with the ailments of a modern man, although he came close to perhaps diagnosing Howard in the correct manner. Labeling his illness with an outdated term, the prescription offered by the doctor was not going to address the underlying causes, and Howard was left to suffer on his own.

Despite the difficulties of numerous rejections and poor health, according to Lord, Howard's sales for 1930 rose to $1703.50. This was the equivalent of slightly more than twenty thousand in modern dollars, a rather attractive sum for someone living in the early throes of the Great Depression, but it came with a price.

Chapter 19

Oriental Stories, The Magic Carpet, and Historical Fiction, 1931

The dust is deep along the trail,
Yet stars gleam on the way;
It knows no worldly hill nor vale,
The Road to Yesterday.
—"The Road to Yesterday"[1]

One of the many reasons Howard held such a deep interest in the lost race of Picts was due to his insatiable passion for history. "I am almost consumed by curiosity concerning the immemorial past," Howard wrote, adding the lament that he was "irritated beyond measure to think that that curiosity will never be satisfied!"[2] Throughout his life Howard read widely in the field of history and listened to the oral histories of his elders. He discussed and debated historical topics with family and friends and regaled them with many historical stories. But Howard could live the history he so loved by writing historical fiction.

"Even in my earliest childhood," Howard wrote, "I read more history than anything else, partly because I lived in the country and textbooks came more easily to my hand, and partly because of a natural inclination that way."[3]

One story is told that while on a visit with his grandparents, Howard "spotted a set of history books and looked through it the entire time."[4] And, like most people, he had his favorite historical subjects. "I will admit that my love of history and historical novels is limited to some boundaries," after which he declared, "The main part of my historical and traditional love and lore centers on the British Isles." The main motivation for this had much to do with his interest in genealogy, for he explained, "There is not one foot of British ground, not one handsbreadth of soil in England, Scotland, Ireland, and Wales that has not been drenched with blood—my own blood—the same that courses through my veins."[5]

Howard loved talking about history nearly as much as he enjoyed reading it. "He was really a conversationalist," Dr. Howard recalled. "He loved to talk in his home to me and his mother, and often in our rides I had but to suggest some historical theme, and he looked it up and talked interestingly and revealed a wide knowledge of history of which I had only a smattering acquaintance. And on and on until he seemed to exhaust every bit of everything written about that particular bit of history. Robert had a wonderful memory as well as a vivid imagination."[6] His good friend Smith recalled, "Our discussions always included history, and Bob was excellent in his presentation of this subject." Smith also remarked, "He had picked most of it up through his own personal reading, and not in school."[7] Another friend remembered how he had had regaled her with the story of Genghis Khan, whom he called "my favorite barbarian," and explained how Howard had brought the man to life in her mind.[8] "I felt every emotion Jenghiz Khan felt. I reacted with intense feeling toward things he did. I was repelled when he took his sword and ripped open a man's belly, spilling his guts in the dust and heat of the desert. But I saw another side to Jenghiz Khan, too. I saw his gentleness with his horse. I marveled at his respect and admiration for his mother. I saw him cross verdant valleys with no fences."[9]

When she asked how he knew so much about Genghis Khan, he replied, "I was there, girl. I rode with Jenghiz Khan."[10] She could little argue the veracity of that statement, for Howard's oratorical gifts for recounting history left her to comment, "No one had ever made history so alive and glowing."[11]

Even Lovecraft was amazed at his command of history, and commented not long after Howard's death, "I always gasped at his profound knowledge of history—including some of its more obscure corners." He was still more impressed with Howard's ability to bring history alive through the written word. "[I] admired still more," Lovecraft continued, "his really astonishing *assimilation* and *visualization* of it. He was almost unique in his ability to *understand & mentally* inhabit past ages."[12] When Howard wrote history, his words spoke as if he had had lived it himself.

Howard's affinity for history also proved to be beneficial to him as a writer. Once chided by a friend who asked him if he thought he owned enough history books, he replied, "No. You never have too many histories. They pay off. About a year ago, I bought a history—paid twenty-five dollars for it. Sounds like a lot, but I sold five or six hundred dollars worth of yarns based on what I learned from it."[13] This profitable investment had come after the launching of a new pulp magazine, *Oriental Stories*, that was intentionally open to historical fiction.

After the companion to *Weird Tales* failed to launch, Wright developed another magazine.[14] He named it *Oriental Stories*, and its content would consist of adventure and historical tales. "Just before I left Cross Plains," Howard informed Smith in June of 1930, "I got a letter from Farnsworth saying he was starting an Oriental magazine and asking me to send him some Oriental tales." The trip had been the one with Tyson and Aud Cross on which Howard enjoyed paddling up and down the Llano River. He explained to Smith the reason for his early departure: "The more I thought of it, the more I decided that if I delayed too long he might get mad at me and turn to some other louse for the stuff, so the next morning, after our night on the river, I told my bold comrades that I was going to clap on sail for Cross Plains."[15]

Howard also shared the type of story Wright wanted for the new magazine with Smith: "I especially want historical tales—tales of the Crusades, of Genghis Khan, or Tamerlane, and the wars between Islam and Hindooism." Unlike *Weird Tales*, Wright continued, "Each story will be complete in one issue, and we will use no serials. The longer lengths are preferred—that is about 15,000 words."[16] However, like *Weird Tales*, the magazine would only pay upon publication. Still, once safely home in Cross Plains, Howard immediately set about writing his first short story for the new magazine.

Oriental Stories had not come about in the same manner as its older companion, for publisher J. C. Henneberger really played no role in its creation. "The Indianapolis printer lost several of his publications," he explained, "and suggested to Wright that they start several new magazines of the pulp variety."[17] The main force behind the creation of the new magazine was Wright, based on reader feedback in "The Eyrie." As early as October 1925, Wright had mentioned in that forum how "the few Oriental stories that have been published in *Weird Tales* during the past year were popular with you, the readers, far beyond expectation, considering the proportion they bear to other stories."[18] At first he increased the number of such stories in the pages of the "unique magazine," but after noting how well they continued to be received, he seized on the opportunity to create a new magazine dedicated to these historical tales.

Instead of writing a historical tale, Howard opted instead to write his first story as an adventure with elements of history forming its background. He titled it "The Voice of El-Lil," the story of two men's venture into Somaliland where they find a lost civilization of Sumerians. Howard had an interest in these ancient people, for as he once wrote, "When I think of the ancient world, my thoughts leap instantly and subconsciously to the valley of the Tigris and Euphrates and the fertile lands of Mesopotamia."[19] That interest, his imagination, and some research resulted in the story. It also afforded Howard the opportunity to ease into the writing of historical yarns by composing the type of story he was already familiar with writing: an adventure tale. This was similar to what he had done with "The Spirit of Tom Molyneaux," a boxing tale written in the guise of a ghost story that allowed him to make the transition to writing in a new genre. Still, the research he had to do for the story's historical elements took time, which led him to write Smith, "It was the very devil to write," though he did add that, in the end, "I rather like the thing."[20]

The following month Howard wrote to Smith, "Well, me bauld buccaneer, I sold 'The Voice of El-Lil' to Farnsworth for $95.00 being about the first story I ever sold that I had to batter out by pure force of study. He says it's to appear in the first copy of *Oriental Stories*, which will come out about September 15."[21]

Dated October–November 1930, the premier issue hit the newsstands as promised, and Howard's name appeared alongside those of many of Wright's other *Weird Tales* authors, including Otis Adelbert Kline. Howard's story was placed near the back pages of the magazine, which ended with its own version of "The Eyrie," redubbed "The Souk." In his first column, Wright addressed the focus and intent of the new magazine when he wrote, "It will be the purpose of *Oriental Stories* to present in fiction the glamor and mystery of the East. There seems a genuine need for such a magazine to fill a want that has long been felt. The Orient makes a romantic appeal to the imagination that no other part of the world can equal."[22]

Although the magazine was only planned to appear every other month, the prospect of another paying outlet opened new opportunities for Howard. "I'm very well pleased with the magazine," he wrote Preece after seeing the new publication with its bright, vivid art deco cover drawn by artist Donald von Gelb. In that letter Howard also praised his editor, who was now pulling double duty with two magazines, when he wrote, "One of the main things I like about Farnsworth Wright's magazine is you don't have to make your heroes such utter saints."[23]

Reader feedback in "The Souk" was good, and Wright personally wrote Howard informing him, "'The Voice of El-Lil' is tied for first place with 'Strange Bedfellows,'" a novelette by S. B. H. Hurst, "in the letters and votes received so far for the first issue of *Oriental Stories*."[24] One reader, Wallace West of New York City, wrote that the story was "out of the ordinary" and he believed it was "as good as H. Rider Haggard's best."[25] Lovecraft had his usual mixed views on the story when he wrote to another correspondent, "Robert E. Howard's 'Voice of El-Lil' has possibilities—he has a certain sense of *unholy antiquity* in mysterious jungle-found cities & piles of masonry, but which would be marvellously effective if freed from the popular-adventure background which he always tacks on."[26] Yet, again, this is the type of story Howard enjoyed writing, and they were clearly well received by those who counted the most—the readers. As Howard wrote Lovecraft, "What I write for 'Oriental Stories' will be purely action, and romance—mainly historical tales." Although he did admit, "I greatly fear that my Turks and Mongols are merely Irishmen and Englishmen in turbans and sandals!"[27] There is some truth to that statement, for Burke explains, "While the stories were set during the Crusades, or periods of Mongol or Islamic conquests, they inevitably featured Celtic heroes."[28]

The next story he composed was an unusual one, for he collaborated with Smith on "Red Blades of Black Cathay." Smith later explained how they had worked together on the story: "I did the research and Bob did the writing."[29] This may have been to encourage Smith to write for *Oriental Stories*, considering his own interest in history, but it may also have been to obtain some assistance with the more detailed research the story entailed. Smith's easy access to resources in Brownwood helped as well.

It seems Howard also had some additional assistance in the construction of the story. Author Howard Andrew Jones explained, "It is the only Howard historical that can truly be said to read like a Harold Lamb pastiche."[30] Lamb was one of Howard's favorite authors from the pages of the pulp magazine *Adventure*, and he wrote Cossack, crusader, and Asian/Middle-Eastern historical tales. Jones believes "Red Blades of Black Cathay" is a reworking of many of Lamb's story elements, though still resulting in something very Howardesque.

The story, submitted to Wright in June of 1930, follows crusader Sir Godric, who assists the Black Cathayans against Genghis Khan. "I am very well pleased with 'Red Blades of Black Cathay,'" Wright responded the following month, "and may use this as the cover design story for our third issue of Oriental Stories. We can offer you $118 on publication for it."[31] The story was, indeed, the magazine's front cover, another vividly colored art deco drawing of Genghis Khan by von Gelb, and the February–March 1931 issue prominently featured the byline of "Tevis Clyde Smith and Robert E. Howard." Howard had graciously given the lead to his good friend. Wright even announced the story in his editorial when he wrote, "The first of our historical tales, *Red Blades of Black Cathay*, appears in the current issue," but to keep the idea of a historical tale from turning off any readers, he added, "These stories will be selected not because they are historical, but because they are corking good stories, replete with thrills and fascinating interest, and filled with the flavor of the Orient."[32]

The next issue of the magazine did not appear until the summer, for by then the magazine had gone to a quarterly format; however, it was instantly clear that the collaboration had paid off. Reader response was laudatory. Howard even had several fellow *Weird Tales* authors commend the story, such as Henry S. Whitehead, who wrote it was "as good an action-adventure yarn as I've ever read in my life . . . and the authors are to be congratulated. It is a real corncracker!" It was the many comments like this that led Wright to state in "The Souk," "Your favorite story in the February-March issue, as shown by your votes and letters, was that vivid action-story of Genghis Khan, *Red Blades of Black Cathay*, by Tevis Clyde Smith and Robert E. Howard."[33]

Howard's next two stories were written and researched on his own in the fall of 1930 while he was suffering from neurasthenia. "I lately sold a tale to *Oriental Stories*," he wrote Preece that October, "in which I created the most somber character I have yet attempted. The story is called 'Hawks of Outremer,' and I got $120 for it. The character is called Cormac FitzGeoffrey." Hoping for a successful series, Howard created the crusader character whom he described as half-Norman and half-Gael.[34] After submitting the story to Wright, he set about composing a second tale of FitzGeoffrey at a time when he was suffering the most with his illness. "The title, 'The Blood of Bel-Shazzar,' referring to a jewel," Howard wrote Smith in December, "was the only thing interesting about it. The plot was hackneyed and sketchy, the action labored and artificial. Only once in the entire story did I evoke a slight spark of the fire that has smoldered out in me." Despite his own disappointment with the story, Wright accepted it for $115, and it was voted the most popular story of the issue.[35]

Howard attempted one more FitzGeoffrey story but quickly abandoned it. As Louinet explains, "He soon realized that the times, places, and historical events that held his interest were far too numerous and scattered for a single character."[36] This was very true, for in a letter to Smith, Howard wrote of all the things he wished to write about, including, "Babar the Tiger who established the Mogul rule in India," "the final destruction of Christian

Outremer by Al Kalawun," and "the first Crusade." Howard then wrote just how passionate he had become about writing historicals: "Ye gods, I could write a century and still have only tapped the reservoir of dramatic possibilities. I wish to Hell I had a dozen markets for historical fiction—I'd never write anything else."[37] That turned out not to be the case.

His renewed excitement led Howard to create some of the finest historical yarns he ever composed. "If Howard had stopped with the FitzGeoffrey tales his historical work would only be an interesting sideline in the adventure writer's career," Jones wrote, but "instead, he found his comfort level and sat down to write masterpieces."[38]

Howard's next two yarns were "The Sowers of the Thunder" and "Lord of Samarcand," published in the winter and spring of 1932, respectively. They would both be voted the most popular story of the issue and led Jack Darrow of Chicago to write, "I don't think I'll ever tire of reading stories by Robert E. Howard. Can't you manage to have one in each issue?"[39] Jones, writing about the former, described it as "a long, bloody thrill ride" in which "kings and kingdoms have fallen and loves have been lost." He called it "a masterful performance."[40] Regarding the latter, he described it as "an epic threaded with tragedy" in which "the prose is gilt everywhere with words that are crystal clear and descriptive, beautiful even when it describes the fall of cities and the death of men."[41] Writing to Smith about that tale, Howard told his friend, "It's the sort of thing I like to write—no plot construction, no hero or heroine, no climax in the accepted sense of the word, all the characters complete scoundrels, and everybody double-crossing everybody else."[42] These were surely sweeping historical tales that, by the very nature of the writing, were far ahead of their time.

"Lord of Samarcand" also managed to spark a debate in "The Souk." Howard had written of Muslims consuming alcohol in the story, a practice expressly forbidden by their religion. Francis X. Bell wrote to Wright noting that while he enjoyed Howard's historical tales, in regard to Muslims imbibing he was "wrong—dead wrong."[43] Wright himself penned an editorial response, explaining his views of the history on this subject, and readers shared their own. As for Howard himself, he wrote a letter to Wright that was published in "The Souk," thanking him for "the remarks and quotations," before diplomatically adding that "criticisms of this nature promote discussions helpful and instructive to all."[44]

The summer 1932 issue of *Oriental Stories* proved to be the magazine's last, though fortunately for Howard, it returned in January 1933 with a new name, the *Magic Carpet Magazine*. The focus of *Oriental Stories* had been too narrow, limiting stories only to the Orient. With the title change, stories could now be set in other locales, including far-off planets, which they were. Howard, however, continued writing his historical tales, including "The Lion of Tiberias," which he sent to Wright in June of 1932. In the interestingly dated letter of June 31, Wright replied, "'The Lion of Tiberius' has the makings of a splendid story, but it is not satisfactory in its present form." His complaint was in regard to the beginning of the tale, telling Howard, "From page 10 on the story is magnificent."[45] After revisions it was published in the third issue of the retitled magazine, dated July 1933.

Howard's next historical yarn proved wholly unique for the time period, for in addition to creating a complete scoundrel of a character, Gottfried von Kalmbach, he allied the man with a red-haired woman who fights at his side. He called her Red Sonya of Rogatino, and the historical backdrop of the story is the Siege of Vienna. "I'm curious to know how the readers will like Gottfried von Kalmbach, one of the main characters in a long historical yarn I sold Wright," Howard wrote Lovecraft. He described Gottfried as a "wastrel, drunkard, gambler, whore-monger, renegade, mercenary, plunderer, thief, rogue, rascal," before happily noting, "I never created a character whose creation I enjoyed more." Howard also suggested how the story brought history alive for him, when he wrote, "Gottfried and his mistress Red Sonya seem more real to me than any other character I've ever drawn."[46]

The story was published in the January 1934 issue of the *Magic Carpet Magazine*, but Howard never learned how the readers perceived von Kalmbach, for the magazine folded with that issue. He was fortunate that Wright also included a Sailor Steve Costigan yarn in the issue, one that had been reworked into a Sailor Dennis Dorgan story. To avoid the industry taboo of having an author's name appear more than once in a single issue, the byline was changed to "Patrick Ervin." Yet the "Coming Next Issue" announcement at the back of the magazine declared there would be two more Howard stories in the spring edition, "Gates of Empire" and "Sailor Dorgan and the Jade Monkey" under the Patrick Ervin byline. The stories were sent back, earning him no money, and neither were published in his lifetime.

With the demise of the magazine, Howard lost yet another outlet for his writing and the main one for his historical fiction. This had to have been a great disappointment for Howard, for just months before he had written Lovecraft, "There is no literary work, to me, half as zestful as rewriting history in the guise of fiction. I wish I was able to devote the rest of my life to that kind of work. I could write a hundred years and still there would be stories clamoring to be written, by the scores."[47]

Despite the loss, Howard was not entirely done with historical fiction. He had been fascinated with the concepts of reincarnation, ancestral memories, and the nature of dreams at least since reading Jack London's *The Star Rover* and developed a deep desire to have lived in the past himself. [48] "I have often wished strongly that I had lived on the ancestral plantations in the Deep South, in the days before the Civil War!" he wrote. "I particularly wished this in earlier days, when dragging a cotton-sack through the morning dew or swinging an axe in the face of a blue blizzard."[49] This is likely why his dreams were so filled with history, for he told his Providence friend, "Long narrative dreams are fairly common with me, and sometimes my dream personality is in no way connected with my actual personality."[50] He then detailed a long list of the people he had become in his dreams including "a prehistoric man," "a yellow-haired Italian of the Renaissance," and "a weird-eyed flowing-bearded Gothic fighting man." He also wrote, "I believe that many dreams are the result of ancestral memories, handed down through the ages."[51] Howard had grown up hearing of the many theories about reincarnation from his father.

According to Louinet, "Dr. Isaac M. Howard, was all his life interested in mysticism, yoga and hypnotism" and he had "annotated his copies of *The Hindu Science of Breath* and *Fourteen Lessons in Yogi Philosophy* by Yogi Ramacharaka."[52] During America's Progressive Era, people were generally open to new ideas of health and healing through the power of the mind, and believed such actions were possible through such things as mysticism, made popular by the writings of the self-proclaimed mystic Madame Blavatsky, the founder of Theosophy, a mixture of Eastern and Western mystical traditions that advanced the theory of reincarnation.[53] This also led many charlatans to capitalize on the movement, such as William Walker Atkinson, who fed this fascination with his numerous publications using various pseudonyms, including the mystical sounding name of Yogi Ramacharaka. Norris Chambers recalled his father and Dr. Howard having long discussions about the practice, which included the belief that "after souls attain a certain degree of development, they become conscious of the process of reincarnation, and are thereafter conscious of past lives, and preceding a rebirth may take a conscious part in selecting the environment and surroundings."[54] As to whether Howard actually believed in reincarnation, there is some debate, but nonetheless, it led to the development of a new character who, like London's Standing, could mentally project himself into his past lives lived.[55]

Unlike his many characters who lived in the past, Howard placed his new creation, James Allison, in his own present-day Texas and confined him not to a straitjacket, as London had done, but to the body of an invalid. Allison has the ability to project himself into the past lives of his ancestors, to actually live their lives. He writes in one of the Allison stories, "Why I can remember is the strangest tale of all; but as I lie here . . . my previous lives are shaken out before my eyes, and I see myself in many forms and guises."[56] He then becomes his ancestor Niord, and he uses the phrase "I am" to state he is not dreaming. "I am James Allison no less than I was Niord."[57]

Despite the combined joy of writing history and emulating one of his favorite authors, Howard proved mostly unsuccessful with this character. His first story, "Marchers of Valhalla," and others were rejected and never published in his lifetime. His only success was with "The Valley of the Worm," which Wright accepted for *Weird Tales* and published in the February 1934 issue. The story was well received by many readers, such as B. M. Reynolds of North Adams, Massachusetts, who called the story "his greatest," or the soon-to-be *Weird Tales* author Henry Kuttner, who wrote, "combining weirdness with excellent style of narrative," he believed it to be "his best."[58] The only other Allison story published in Howard's lifetime was the Wright-rejected "The Garden of Fear," which he gave to the fan publication *Marvel Tales* at no cost.[59]

Another opportunity for Howard were two new pulp magazines from the Clayton Publishing Group. "I see where the Claytons are bringing out a new magazine dealing with weird subjects and another dealing with historical tales of romance and adventure—two cents a word on acceptance and up," Howard wrote Smith, adding, "If I can't make both of them I oughta be ham-strung."[60] The former was *Strange Tales of Mystery and Terror*, while the latter was *Soldiers of Fortune*. Having a second outlet for both genres, ones that paid better and upon publication, boded well for Howard.[61]

"I'm deeply interested in the intention of your company to bring out a new magazine devoted entirely to historical tales," Howard wrote editor Harry Bates in June of 1931.[62] Along with the letter, he submitted a historical tale, "Spears of Clontarf." Bates, who later became famous for his short story "Farewell to the Masters" (which formed the basis for the popular movie *The Day the Earth Stood Still*), rejected it. Howard then tried submitting to both *Adventure* and *Argosy*, only to have them reject it as well. He tried adding a weird element and rewriting the story under the title of "The Grey God Passes" before sending it to Wright for *Weird Tales*. Wright rejected the story, writing Howard, "The story itself, the plot, seems very slight, and the weird element is not as strong as I would like it to be."[63]

Howard next tried sending a rejected *Oriental Stories* yarn to Bates, but in a letter to Smith, Howard wrote, "They turned down 'The Road of Azrael' for Soldiers, and I seemed to sense a hint of irritation in the letter of rejection, as if they suspected I'd never read the magazine. Which I haven't. But I hope to make it eventually."[64] He never did. *Soldiers of Fortune* folded after four issues.

One other historical bit of writing that was entirely unusual for Howard was his one published nonfiction article, "The Ghost of Camp Colorado." As Howard explained, the camp "is situated some twenty-five miles southwest of this town and was one of a string of army posts which was literally the Southwestern frontier in the 1850s."[65] The impetus for writing the story actually came from Lovecraft, who had written to one of his many correspondents, Wilfred Blanch Talman, in October of 1930, informing him, "Howard is the chap who can give you the colour—the sweep of the oil camps across the primal Texas plains, and the pageantry and social developments connected with them."[66] Talman wrote to Howard about his editorship of the *Texaco Star*, the oil company's magazine published "For Employees of The Texas Company," and asked him for a special interest story about his home state. "I've received a letter from Talman," Howard wrote Lovecraft, "regarding contributions to his paper; he says you suggested my name to him, and I wish to express as much as I can, my sincere appreciation of that fact."[67]

Howard set about doing research for the article, much as he had done with his fiction. He already had a penchant for listening to the stories of his elders, for as one friend recounted, Howard "made it a point to seek out old settlers to listen to their stories. They gave him an understanding of the times and emotions of the people; they were the inspiration for many of his own stories." And because he also enjoyed learning about historical events, as well as "the *place* the events happened," Howard was primed to learn all there was to know about the old military encampment.[68]

Commenting on Howard's visit to Camp Colorado, Cross Plains resident D. C. Lee recalled "Robert . . . and some friends had spent some time there while Robert was researching the article."[69] Howard went with his friend Dave Lee in the winter of 1930/1931 to the old camp, and he brought along his camera to snap some pictures. There was little left to see there, only the cemetery and what Howard called "a substantial ghost, built of square cut stone and sturdy timber, but just the same a phantom, rising out of the ruins of a forgotten past."[70] The remains Howard spoke of was the old guard house Henry Sackett had incorporated into his modern home.

The article was published in the April 1931 issue of the *Texaco Star*, and it featured the photos Howard had taken with his camera, including one of Dave Lee. It was also reprinted in another Texas magazine, *Frontier Times*, that June. In a reply letter to Talman after the article's publication, Howard wrote, "I'm very glad that my article was well received, and hope that future articles which I intend to submit, will be as well liked. I am indeed honored that, as you mentioned, the Director of Publications should praise my work before the Company officials; I am the more gratified because this is the first article of the sort I ever submitted to any publication, having devoted practically all my time to fiction."[71] Sadly, Howard never published another nonfiction article in his lifetime.

During the flurry of writing historical fiction, Howard continued submitting to *Weird Tales*, but even this pulp magazine was beginning to feel the impact of the Great Depression. "Farnsworth tells me that he is going to make *Weird Tales* a bi-monthly like *Oriental Stories*," Howard wrote Smith in December of 1930, "cutting my already slim market in half. He says he's stocked up on *Weird Tales* stories for the present."[72] Howard conveyed his greatest fear in a letter to Lovecraft when he wrote, "I hope the magazine isn't discontinued."[73]

Weird Tales was facing serious financial issues, and according to pulp historians Marshall Tymn and Mike Ashley, "A sudden bank closing, freezing nearly all of the magazine's cash assets late in 1930, brought about a minor crisis early in 1931."[74] Although having gone bimonthly with the February/March issue, by summer the magazine's assets were unfrozen and their cash-flow had been restored.[75] Howard heard the good news through the author grapevine, for he wrote Smith, "By the way, Lovecraft told *me* that August Derleth told *him* that Farnsworth told *him* that the first of June *Weird Tales* goes back to the monthly basis. I gather that writers and readers whooped with rage at Farnsworth; I hope the finances are as good as I hope they are."[76] Wright announced that decision in the April/May issue, never mentioning the financial troubles, only noting that the move to bimonthly had "evoked a chorus of protest from you, the readers."[77] So, with the August issue, the magazine resumed publishing monthly.

As for the readers of *Weird Tales* and Howard, evidently a rumor had started about his personal background.[78] "I also note with considerable amusement," Howard wrote Lovecraft, "that a rumor has been circulating pertaining to me being a professor."[79] In "The Eyrie" for the June/July issue of the magazine, Earl Morgan of Detroit, asked the question, "Is Robert E. Howard a professor of history at the University of Southern California? (I have heard this)." Wright's reply to the question was "No, Robert E. Howard is not a professor of ancient history, and he lives in Texas instead of in California."[80] Howard found the idea preposterous, for he wrote Lovecraft, "As for being a professor of history in a great university, that's beyond the pale of possibility—I never even attended college as a student."[81]

In addition to writing in a new genre he enjoyed, Howard also helped himself out of the doldrums by spending more time with friends and doing some traveling. His Brownwood friends were busy with their lives, so he saw them less frequently. Smith had good news, for he informed Howard he was publishing a book on the history of Brown County to be titled *Frontier's Generation*.[82] "Congratulations on your history book," Howard wrote Smith in March. "I'm sure glad you've decided to put it out and believe you'll make some money on it. Let me have the honor of buying the first copy, autographed."[83]

As for Truett Vinson, Howard learned that his father had died on March 3, just one day past his 62nd birthday.[84] Howard sent Vinson a letter of condolence. Then the man who wrote for a living expressed his frustrations in composing that letter to Smith, "There isn't anything anyone can say, really. Anything like that is past words. Words are such damned weak and futile things any time."[85]

Howard spent most of his time with Lindsey Tyson. As he wrote Smith, "Pink and I went over to Forth Worth to see the Dula-Freeman fight and it was a hummer."[86] Tyson recalled how the two of them did spend a lot of time watching sports: "We went over to a lot of football games together. We went to Fort Worth and Dallas and prizefights. Football and prizefighting was about the only sports."[87] And in March, after a heavy bout of rain in the area that put Howard in a "desultory manner," Howard declared to Smith, "Heigho for sunny San Antonio."[88]

Howard took along his mother for the much-needed break in the Alamo City. He spent his time seeing a number of picture shows, including the Edward G. Robinson film *Little Caesar*, attended some of the local prize fights, did some genealogy research in the library, and celebrated his Irish roots on St. Patrick's Day. He wrote Lovecraft a letter informing him that "tomorrow begins a week-long fete marking the opening of the old Spanish governor's palace, closed and vacant for generations."[89] The restoration of the historic site had been the idea of Adina Emilia De Zavala, the same lady who had rescued the Alamo from being razed, and it opened on March 4, 1931. "I got a big kick out of going through the place," Howard wrote Smith; "it looks just like scenes from swash-buckling movies."[90]

Howard also ran across Preece several times during his visit. "Well, I was in the library the other day," Howard wrote Smith, "when I heard a sort of bellow or roar and looking up saw Harold Preece towering over me."[91] Preece also wrote Smith later that month informing him, "I saw Bob twice during his stay in San Antonio, lunching once with his mother" and "I ran across him wearing a big shamrock, in front of the Alamo, St. Patrick's Day."[92] The friends Preece were hanging around with by that time and his strong Communist leanings had evidently become a turnoff for Howard, so he spent little time with him while in San Antonio.[93]

In June Howard again did some traveling. He had considered going to New Orleans but only got as far as Fort Worth and Waco.[94] He spent a week in Marlin, taking his mother to the Torbett Sanatorium for the water treatments offered there, which consisted of hot baths and mineral waters. Howard spent his time writing and visiting with his friend Thurston Torbett, who recalled how they mostly walked and talked. He found Howard to be "blue and depressed" during that visit, whereas normally he always found Howard to "have a very good disposition," describing him as "kind hearted, affable and [having] a very likable personality."[95] Torbett enjoyed their conversations and thought of Howard's mother as "a very intelligent woman," though he noted that Mrs. Howard was "not in the best of health."[96]

Mrs. Howard was about to turn 61 that year, and her tuberculosis was beginning to affect her health more in recent years. It is difficult to mark just when her decline began, but sometime starting around 1930, as her health grew worse with each passing year, she would require more and more assistance from her son.

Cross Plains was the hub of activity on Saturdays in the 1920s and 1930s. This photo of the downtown was taken Saturday, January 3, 1925. Photo courtesy of the *Cross Plains Review.*

This 1922 photo of Cross Plains downtown is looking north. Note the road is still not paved. Photo by J. R. Rogers and courtesy of the Dublin Historical Museum.

This 1922 photo of Cross Plains downtown is looking west. Howard worked for a short time at the law office located on the second floor of the bank building on the left. Photo by J. R. Rogers and courtesy of the Dublin Historical Museum.

An early photo of Dr. Howard circa 1908. Photo courtesy of the Robert E. Howard Foundation.

A studio photograph of Dr. Isaac Mordecai Howard. Photo courtesy of the Robert E. Howard Foundation.

A studio photograph of a young Hester Jane Ervin with one of her nephews. Photo courtesy of the Robert E. Howard Foundation.

Hester Jane Ervin Howard in Exeter, Missouri. Photo courtesy of the Robert E. Howard Foundation.

A childhood studio portrait of Howard at a young age alleged to have been found in his mother's scrapbook. Photo courtesy of the Robert E. Howard Foundation.

A young Howard playing Indian. Photo courtesy of the Robert E. Howard Foundation.

From the earliest of ages, Howard was earning Lovecraft's favorite sobriquet for him: "Two-Gun Bob." Photo courtesy of the Robert E. Howard Foundation.

Damaged snapshot of Howard in the front yard of his house with Patch in a rare Texas event: snow. Photo courtesy of the Robert E. Howard Foundation.

From a young age, Howard enjoyed boxing as both a spectator and participant. Photo courtesy of the Robert E. Howard Foundation.

The Howard family (*left to right*): Robert "Bob" Ervin, Mrs. Hester Jane Ervin, and Dr. Isaac Mordecai Howard. Photo courtesy of the Robert E. Howard Foundation.

Leroy Butler (*left*) and Howard (*right*) striking a combat pose as Faustine Butler officiates the "duel." Photo courtesy of the Robert E. Howard Foundation.

Left to right: Leroy and Faustine Butler and Howard, striking a memorable role-playing pose for the camera. Photo courtesy of the Robert E. Howard Foundation.

THE PECAN

BEATRICE BUCHER
Spanish Course; Glee Club '21, '22, '23; Camp Fire '21, '22.

HERVEY MAYES
Latin and Science Course; Football '23; Tattler Staff; Heels Club; W. O. N. Club; Oratory Club '23; Swimming Club.

ANNE GREELEY
Spanish and Science Course; Glee Club '21, '22, '23; Swimming Club.

TRAVIS B. CURTIS
Latin and Science Course; Cadet Corps '22, '23; Pecan Staff; Oratory Club '23; Heels Club.

ROBERT HOWARD
Science Course; Heels Club.

ALLYNE EASTERLING
Spanish Course; Literary Society; Oratory Club; Camp Fire.

Page 28

Howard's picture in the Brownwood High School Yearbook, 1923. Photo courtesy of the Robert E. Howard Foundation.

A common display of the pulp magazines on newsstands throughout the 1930s. Photo by John Vachon and courtesy of the Library of Congress.

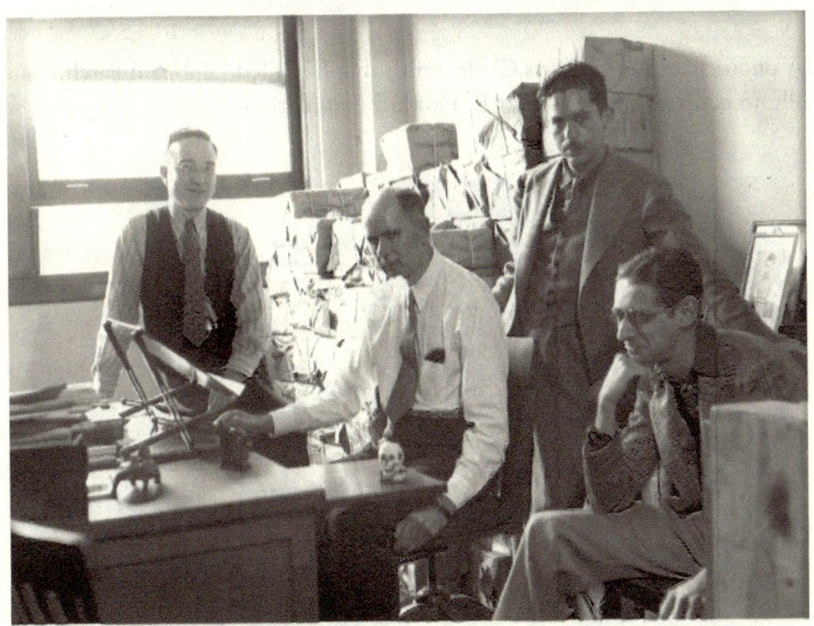

Weird Tales editorial office in Chicago with (*left to right*) William R. Sprenger, Farnsworth Wright, and two of their writers, Henry Kuttner and Robert Bloch. Photo courtesy of the Wisconsin Historical Society.

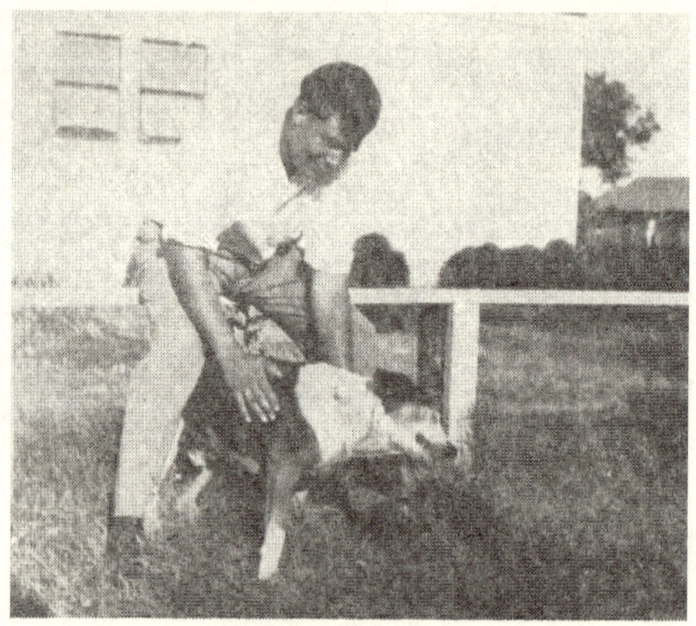

A photo snapshot by Tevis Clyde Smith that he called "Bob and Patch." Photo courtesy of the Robert E. Howard Foundation.

Mrs. Hester Howard and Robert E. Howard's dog, Patch. Photo courtesy of the Robert E. Howard Foundation.

Picture of Howard and his friends (*left to right*): Howard, Lindsey Tyson, and Tevis Clyde Smith. Photo courtesy of the Robert E. Howard Foundation.

The Three Musketeers (*left to right*): Howard, Truett Vinson, and Tevis Clyde Smith. Photo courtesy of the Robert E. Howard Foundation.

A 1930 picture of Howard's friend Harold Preece. Photo courtesy of the Robert E. Howard Foundation.

Howard (*left*) and his friend Tevis Clyde Smith in a boxing pose for the camera. Photo courtesy of the Robert E. Howard Foundation.

Truett Vinson and Howard (*right*) striking a fight pose for photographer Tevis Clyde Smith while at the Cisco Dam. Photo courtesy of the Robert E. Howard Foundation.

Howard (*left*) and Dave Lee in a boxing pose. Photo courtesy of the Robert E. Howard Foundation.

Howard (*left*) and Truett Vinson posing in a fight scene. Photo courtesy of the Robert E. Howard Foundation.

Howard's Cross Plains friends Dave Lee (*left*) and Lindsey Tyson. Photo courtesy of the Robert E. Howard Foundation.

The icehouse where Howard boxed with many of the local roughnecks. Photo courtesy of the *Cross Plains Review*.

Tevis Clyde Smith and Howard (*right*) playacting a combat scene, possibly from Howard's first professional sale, "Spear and Fang." Photo courtesy of the Robert E. Howard Foundation.

Howard and his friends took frequent hikes, often walking all night. Tevis Clyde Smith took this picture of Howard on one of those hikes. Photo courtesy of the Robert E. Howard Foundation.

Howard holding his hat. This picture was featured in the fan magazine the *Fantasy Fan* in 1934. Photo courtesy of the Robert E. Howard Foundation.

The front cover of *Weird Tales*, September 1934, by Margaret Brundage for Howard's Conan story "The People of the Black Circle."

The cover of the June 1930 issue of *Fight Stories* featuring Howard's story "The Iron Man."

The cover of the February–March 1931 issue of *Oriental Stories* featuring "Red Blades of Black Cathay" by Tevis Clyde Smith and Robert E. Howard.

Howard showing off his impressive physique from lifting weights, boxing, and hours spent chopping wood. Photo courtesy of the Robert E. Howard Foundation.

Weird Tales author H. P. Lovecraft, whom Howard called "One of the greatest writers of our time." Photo by Lucius B. Truesdell and in the public domain.

Howard sent this photo to H. P. Lovecraft writing, "Ruins of Fort McKavett, July 9, 1933; I like this snap; it makes me feel kind of like a Vandal or Goth standing amidst the ruins of a Roman fortress or palace." Photo courtesy of the Robert E. Howard Foundation.

Howard sent this picture postcard to E. Hoffmann Price, writing on the back, "Schlitz didn't pay a penny for this endorsement—and probably won't." Photo courtesy of the Robert E. Howard Foundation.

Lovecraft once wrote of this picture, "Yes—I have the hat-in-hand, horizon-gazing snapshot which you mention, and really like it . . . [it] ought really to be the standard likeness to be remembered, since it represents the aspect of REH during the greater part of his writing career." Photo courtesy of the Robert E. Howard Foundation.

Robert E. Howard in 1934. Photo courtesy of the Robert E. Howard Foundation.

Howard sent this picture postcard to H. P. Lovecraft, writing on the back, "This isn't to flaunt my homely countenance, but to serve as an illustration of the luxuriant plant-life in South Texas; note rubber-plant, cactus, hibiscus, and banana-tree all growing together, Robert E. Howard—Feb. 1932." Photo courtesy of the Robert E. Howard Foundation.

Howard's only girlfriend, Novalyne Price. Photo courtesy of the Robert E. Howard Foundation.

This photo has become the iconic image of Howard despite his distaste for the hat. Photo courtesy of the Robert E. Howard Foundation.

Howard (*right*) in front of the Lincoln County Courthouse, Lincoln, New Mexico, made famous by the Lincoln County War and Billy the Kid's escape. Photo courtesy of the Robert E. Howard Foundation.

A picture postcard of the Torbett Sanitarium in Marlin, Texas, where Mrs. Howard often went for treatment. Photo courtesy of the Texas Medical Association.

Howard dressed liked one of his character creations, El Borak. Photo courtesy of the Robert E. Howard Foundation.

The last known picture of Howard (with mustache) at the Cross Plains railroad depot with bales of cotton behind him. Photo courtesy of the Robert E. Howard Foundation.

The Howard family headstone in the Greenleaf Cemetery, Brownwood, Texas, as it appears today. Photo by author.

Chapter 20

The Cthulhu Mythos, 1931

Drowsy and dull with age the houses blink
On aimless streets the rat-gnawed years forget—
But what inhuman figures leer and slink
Down the old alleys when the moon was set.
—"Arkham"[1]

After reading H. P. Lovecraft's "The Call of Cthulhu" in the February 1928 issue of *Weird Tales*, Robert E. Howard was so impressed with the short story that he wrote a letter to "The Eyrie." Howard declared the story a "masterpiece" and wrote how he firmly believed it "will live as one of the highest achievements of literature."[2] Two years later Howard was now corresponding with the author of that masterpiece and seized upon the opportunity to ask him something that had long mystified him. "I have noted in your stories you refer to Cthulhu, Yog Sothoth, R'lyeh, Yuggoth, etc.," he prefaced his question. "Would it be asking too much to tell me the significance of the . . . names or terms? And the Arab Alhazred, and the Necronomicon. The mention of these things in your superb stories have whetted my interest immensely. I would extremely appreciate any information you would give me regarding them."[3]

Like so many other Lovecraft readers, Howard wanted to know the sources for these fantastic names, and when he asked his questions about "The Call of Cthulhu," Lovecraft had already published another story, "The Dunwich Horror," which appeared in the April 1929 issue of *Weird Tales.* The yarn featured the same names, as well as two sonnets from his "Fungi from Yuggoth" sequence. While Lovecraft began writing what later came to be known as the "Cthulhu Mythos" as early as 1919, it was "The Call of Cthulhu" that solidified his concepts of a connected cosmic horror featuring the "Great Old Ones," a pantheon of powerful deities who had once ruled earth but had long since fallen asleep. As for the *Necronomicon*, Lovecraft described it as a rare ancient book of magic written by a worshipper of these deities, the Mad Arab Alhazred, and it reveals many dangerous secrets of the Old Ones. These stories were also typically set in the fictional town of Arkham, Massachusetts, a city replete with its own sanitarium and university, the latter of which he called Miskatonic.

Lovecraft is believed to have created his fictional universe from many sources, ranging from Alfred Tennyson's sonnet "The Kraken" to the writings of Lord Dunsany and ancient Babylonian mythology.[4] In addition to writing his own stories and poems about the Old Ones, often when he ghostwrote or edited stories for others, he incorporated some of these same elements into their manuscripts. Still further, he encouraged his fellow writers through his correspondence to include these elements in their own stories. As a result, the legend of Cthulhu grew, and its mythos added more names to its pantheon, as well as the names of other ancient tomes, locations, and creatures through the scores of additional tales set in Lovecraft's fictional universe.[5]

"Regarding the solemnly cited myth-cycle of Cthulhu," Lovecraft wrote in reply to Howard's question, "let me confess that this is all a synthetic concoction of my own, like the populous and varied pantheon of Lord Dunsany." Lovecraft also made note that the reason some of the names were being found in other authors' works were because, as he wrote, "I think it is rather good fun to have this artificial mythology given an air of verisimilitude by wide citation."[6]

Howard was seemingly disappointed with Lovecraft's reveal, for he soon wrote Smith, "I got a letter from Lovecraft wherein he tells me, much to my chagrin, that Cthulhu, R'lyeh, Yuggoth, YogSothoth, and so on are figments of his own imagination."[7] Howard even echoed this disappointment later when he wrote, "Concerning the *Necronomicon*, etc. . . . It's really a pity these diabolical tomes exist only in imagination."[8] Howard was not the only person likely disappointed to learn the names had no historical basis, for many *Weird Tales* readers wrote to Wright and "The Eyrie" hoping to obtain more information on the deities or where they could read the horrifyingly dangerous *Necronomicon*. For instance, in the August 1932 issue, André Galet of New York City practically pleaded, "If you are really sincere in your desire to please us (the readers) and if it is humanly possible, why not publish in your reprint department . . . the *Necronomicon* by Abdul Alhazred?"[9] In an attempt to not ruin this belief in the myth for all readers, Wright once explained, "I answer such letters personally, for it would be a shame to destroy the illusion of reality by broadcasting in the Eyrie."[10]

Intrigued by the idea of contributing to the myth Lovecraft had propagated, Howard decided he, too, would join in on the fun. From the fall of 1930 and throughout 1931, he began incorporating these elements into his own stories. Ironically, many readers felt he had already done so with his popular serial "Skull-Face." The main villain in that story had been Kathulos, whose name sounded similar to Lovecraft's Cthulhu. One reader, N. J. O'Neail of Toronto, asked about this in "The Eyrie": "I was very much interested in tracing the apparent connection between the characters of Kathulos, in Robert E. Howard's *Skull-Face*, and that of Cthulhu, in Mr. Lovecraft's *The Call of Cthulhu*. Can you inform me whether there is any legend or tradition surrounding that character?"[11] While it is true Howard had read Lovecraft's tale before writing "Skull-Face," he had earlier used a version of that name while writing his King Kull yarns. Howard informed Lovecraft of this in an August 1930 letter, to which he replied, "It would be amusing to identify your Kathulos with my Cthulhu—indeed, I may so adopt him in some future black allusion."[12] The following year, in his story "The Whisperer in Darkness," Lovecraft mentioned "L'mur-Kathulos" alongside the name "Bran," no doubt a nod to Howard in "good fun."[13]

The first story in which Howard incorporated these elements was in "The Children of the Night."[14] Inspired by what Lovecraft had written "regarding the Mongoloid aborigines and their relation to the fairy tales of western Europe," Howard adopted the idea that this race of little people were different from his beloved Picts, and they formed the basis of the story.[15] Howard also employed the familiar Lovecraftian elements, for he mentions Cthulhu and Yog Sothoth, as well as the *Necronomicon*. Howard takes it even further by adding new elements, such as the deity Gol-goroth, and another mysterious tome, Von Junzt's *Nameless Cults*, for which a character in the story comments, "There's a book to keep you awake at night!" Moreover, Howard even mentions Lovecraft by name in the story when the same character identifies three books—"Poe's *Fall of the House of Usher*, Machen's *Black Seal* and Lovecraft's *Call of Cthulhu*"—which he declares are "the three master horror-tales."[16]

After completing the story in less than two months, Howard sent it to Wright, who accepted it for publication in October 1930.[17] Howard then wrote Lovecraft, informing him, "I recently sold *Weird Tales* a short story, 'The Children of the Night,' in which I deal with Mongoloid-aborigine legendry, touch cryptically on the Bran-cult, and hint darkly and vaguely of nameless things connected with Cthulhu, Yog-Sothoth, Tsathoggua and the Necronomicon."[18] Lovecraft's reply letter is nonextant, but he wrote another correspondent, letting him know, "I feel flattered by our adoption of some of this background," and how "the more these synthetic daemons are mutually written up by different authors, the better they become as general background-material!"[19]

The story was published in the April–May 1931 issue of *Weird Tales*, leaving at least one reader, Wilford Allen of Sanger, California, to declare it "splendid."[20] The judges of the O. Henry Memorial Prize also felt it was a deserving story, for it was mentioned under the category of "Stories ranking second" in their annual publication of the year's twenty best short stories in the United States and Canada.[21]

Howard then moved quickly beyond the mere mention of Cthulhu elements by writing a story built around his contributions to the mythos. The yarn, titled "The Black Stone," expanded upon his own hideous tome, naming it Friedrich von Junzt's *Nameless Cults*, or the "so-called Black Book," and introduces the mad poet Justin Geoffrey, who, five years earlier, had been driven insane by his exploration of the monolith and died "screaming in a madhouse." The nameless narrator of the story recounts finding the Black Stone himself, but unlike Geoffrey, he bears witness to the Midsummer Night's annual rite with all its attendant horrors.

Howard submitted the story in December of 1930 and wrote Smith that it was "a short one that brought $64," and though he felt it was "marred by a clumsy style and too melodramatic development," he believed it was "the best attempt at bizarre literature that I have yet sold."[22] Howard evidently felt worse about the story after it was published in the November 1931 issue, for he wrote Lovecraft soon after, "As for 'The Black Stone' . . . since reading it over in print, I feel rather absurd. The story sounds as if I were typing, in my feeble and blunderingly cruel way, to deliberately copy your style. Your literary influence on that particular tale, while unconscious on my part, was none the less strong."[23] Although the story was well received by the readers of *Weird Tales*, Howard felt he was struggling to make the transition from writing action stories to the cosmic horror tales of Lovecraft.[24] Howard scholar Morgan Holmes believes this is evident, for he once remarked, "Howard's handling of Lovecraftian concepts was awkward at first, as he attempted to ape Lovecraft's convoluted writing style."[25] Even Howard recognized this fact, for after writing the Solomon Kane yarn "Wings in the Night," he informed Smith, "It's about the poorest story I've ever sold, marking a distinct transition in my development as a writer—a sort of half-way mark between pure action stuff and the cosmic horror tale, to which style I have at last managed to achieve, but I feel that I may eventually gain some recognition in that field. Of course, I'll never equal Lovecraft, but I believe I can do at least as well as most of the other *Weird Tale* writers do in that line."[26]

With the next story he wrote, Howard believed he had finally written a decent yarn in this vein. "I have a still shorter and better story," Howard informed Smith, " 'The Thing on the Roof,' which I have not yet sent Farnsworth and which I may not send him, since he says he is stocked up. But this story is by far the best thing I have ever written and one which I am really inclined to believe approaches real literature, distantly, at least."[27]

Howard first sent the story to *Strange Tales* less than a week after sending Bates "Spears of Clontarf," but it, too, was rejected. After trying *Argosy* with no luck, he was forced to sit on the story as his main outlet, *Weird Tales*, was then moving to a bimonthly format. Wright had plenty of accepted stories on hand for the time being. Howard changed his mind and submitted it in early 1931 only to have Wright reject it. However, in August that year, after the magazine had returned to publishing monthly, Wright was now in need of more stories and so wrote Howard asking him if he could see it again. "In his latest letter," Howard wrote Smith, "[Wright] accepted it for $40."[28]

It was published in January 1932, and Lovecraft wrote Howard, "I enjoyed 'The Thing on the Roof.' That carried the sort of kick I enjoy! Before long I mean to quote Justin Geoffrey and von Junzt's 'Black Book' in some story of my own."[29] Lovecraft did end up using some of these names in his own works when he mentioned von Junzt in "The Dreams in the Witch House" (1932), "The Thing on the Doorstep" (1933), and "Shadow Out of Time" (1934–35).

Lovecraft had also come to the realization that Howard's "Nameless Cults" had a fictitious author who was German. "Robert E. Howard invented the mythical von Junzt opus," Lovecraft wrote one of his correspondents, "but did not give it a German name—since he is as ignorant as I of German. I thought it would be more convincing to have one." Writing *Weird Tales* author August Derleth, who was of German descent, he inquired as to what he thought the translation of "Nameless Cults" would look like, and he "responded with *Unaussprechlichen Kulten*."[30] Lovecraft informed Howard of this to which he replied, "Thanks for the German of 'Nameless Cults', which I'll use in referring to it. Though I've lived adjacent to Germans for many years, I know nothing of the language—and neither do a lot of them."[31]

For his next Cthulhu mythos story, Howard set his sights on finally breaking into the pulp *Strange Tales*. Having already received two rejections from Bates, Howard tried again that summer by writing a story that not only featured the elements he had developed within the mythos but also included the Mongoloid race of little people, his favored theme of reincarnation, and a character named Conan the Reaver.[32] He submitted the story in September and finally received a positive response from Bates.[33] "The originality of your story, 'The People of the Dark,' appeals to me. I liked it better than anything of yours I have yet seen," Bates wrote, but he believed, "The chief fault that I found in the story was that there was too much fighting and chasing and maneuvering within the body of the story" because it "spoils the rounded reincarnation effect which is the chief merit of the piece." He then asked Howard to cut the story by at least one-third, if not in half.[34]

At the same time, Howard also received a request for revisions on a boxing yarn he had submitted, and, as he wrote Smith, "I acceded to both requests, practically rewriting the stories, at least once, some parts more." Howard still found the revision of stories laborious, especially when forced to cut a story's length, and he was always disappointed with the outcome. "I feel that my revised jobs will be turned down because I sent them off without corrections, without even reading them over for mistakes. When I finished them, I'd been working so long and so hard I wasn't in any shape to hunt for mistakes. I tried to read the stuff over, and the sentences didn't make sense to me."[35] Fortunately, Howard was wrong, and Bates did accept it; at last he had a new outlet for his weird fiction, one that paid upon acceptance, in this case $134.[36] "I finally made Clayton's *Strange Tales*," Howard wrote Lovecraft after the story appeared in the June 1932 issue, "with a yarn called 'The People of the Dark' a tale of reincarnation, pre-Roman Britain, Mongoloid aborigines, yellow-haired Britons, Irish pirates, and anything else I could lug in."[37]

Howard did compose two additional tales within the Cthulhu mythos, "The Fire of Asshurbanipal" and "Dig Me No Grave," writing two endings for the former story, one making it an adventure tale while the other included a weird element. Neither story was published in his lifetime. The only other Cthulhu mythos writing that Howard saw published was his one-stanza poem "Arkham," about Lovecraft's fictional town.[38] After sending the poem to Lovecraft in December of 1931, it was published in *Weird Tales* the following year. After that Howard abruptly stopped writing tales in Lovecraft's genre.[39] The reason he abandoned these stories, Burke explains, was because Howard "ultimately realized this wasn't his natural style."[40] Nonetheless, this brief experiment with Lovecraftian writing informed his own, and he incorporated aspects of cosmic horror into his own future writing to great effect.[41]

As Howard began experiencing the effects of the Great Depression with his publishing outlets, Cross Plains experienced it directly in 1931 from its two local banks, the Farmer's National Bank and the First State Bank. They both faced the problem of maintaining enough assets to cover all of their depositors' accounts. However, while other banks across the country began failing (starting in early 1930), the two Cross Plains banks had managed to stay afloat.[42] That came to an end in 1931.

Farmer's National Bank was Cross Plains' first victim when it closed its doors on July 12, partially due to the bank's vice president embezzling $800.[43] The bank liquidated its assets and only paid depositors approximately "two and one-half cents on the dollar."[44] Then, four months later, there was a run on First State Bank, and it too was forced to close. "Cowardly selfish creatures placed their second stigma in less than four months upon Cross Plains Wednesday," Jack Scott wrote in a vituperative editorial on October 3, blaming the "yellow-bellied skunks [who] got their lying tongues to waggling and circulated fear causing heavy withdrawals from the First State Bank."[45] As was happening across the country, fear of a bank closure led so many depositors to overwhelm a bank with demands on their money, it rapidly depleted the bank's assets, causing the inevitable closure. Fortunately, First State Bank was able to reorganize, shore up its assets, and over the next two years slowly provided its depositors with their money. Although they never fully recovered their funds, the citizens were no doubt at least somewhat mollified to have received some of their money rather than none.

As the banks closed, it also brought about a cascading effect on the town's businesses, for without access to their deposits, they too were forced to close. Scott estimated that approximately half of the businesses in town went broke and closed shop. "Higginbotham's got along better than everyone else," Scott noted, "because they were well financed. But times were tough here in Cross Plains. Anybody who had $150 a month job had a good one."[46] If Scott's estimate is correct, Howard was making decent money from the sales of his stories. According to Glenn Lord, Howard closed out 1931 having earned $1,500.26, thus making on average $125 a month.[47] So although not at Scott's threshold, he was, at least, holding his own.

The Depression, along with Howard's commitment to his profession, limited his travels somewhat that year. "I've wandered about a little in the last few months," Howard wrote Lovecraft in August, "though my journeys are hardly worth the name, since I havent left the state," before noting, "You can cover a good deal of territory, though, and still stay in Texas."[48] This also may have been the year when he took a trip with just his father, for Dr. Howard wrote in late 1936, "Robert and I drove over that country [Southwest Texas] some five years ago."[49] He continued, "His mother did not go with us at the time. It was the only time that she ever failed to go, and he, she and I went many times to San Antonio and to the valley, and many times he and his Mother went to San Antonio and I did not go."[50] It also proved to be the last trip father and son would take together by themselves, for as Howard biographer Finn explains, "In the last four years of his mother's illness, Howard was put in the position of staying close to home and looking after her; a task he willingly took on."[51] Moreover, Howard also took the time to drive his mother for her treatments and stayed there, often for a week or two, such as when he took her to Marlin for therapeutic treatment in November that year.[52]

His own health seemed to ride the tide of his writing commitments, for he noted that after revising the two stories and writing one more, "I went all to pieces."[53] And there were always disappointments along the way, including the many rejections he still continued to receive and two more book projects that fell through. One had been an anthology of weird stories that was to have included his King Kull yarn "The Shadow Kingdom," and the other was a collection of poetry, consisting of works by him, Tevis Clyde Smith, and Lenore Preece. In both cases they were unable to find a publisher willing to move the book to print.[54]

In addition to the stress of editors and the publishing industry, Howard's occupation was also placing a great strain on his eyes.[55] "My own optics have been giving me a good deal of trouble," Howard wrote Lovecraft in October, "I ought to wear glasses all the time, but I dread the idea . . . though

I'm grateful to their aid in reading and writing." His concern was because, outside of the home, "There's always so much chance of somebody smashing them in your eyes."[56] He also continued experiencing his vivid nighttime dreams and sleepwalking, so much so that he still tied a cord around one foot and connected it to the bedpost in order to keep himself from wandering around at night. Yet even that proved somewhat hazardous, for in one dream that fall, Howard wrote Smith, "[I] bounded out of bed and on account of the cord on my foot, did a neat nose-dive onto the floor which skinned my face somewhat."[57] Outside of this and thunderstorms, as he reported to Lovecraft, "I can sleep through almost any other sort of disturbance," including the largest earthquake ever to hit West Texas. The Valentine Earthquake, named for the town upon which it centered, occurred on August 16, 1931, and was felt across the entire state. "I was slightly intoxicated when I retired, besides being tired from wrestling with the huge foreman of the local ice factory," Howard continued, "so I slept more soundly than usual and knew nothing at all about the earthquake until next morning."[58]

Despite his ups and downs with the writing profession and his health, Howard's brand of biting humor still shone through in his letters. In one missive to Lovecraft, he wrote of spending a night in Rockport, "a little port not very far from Corpus Christi." Both the town and the hotel had experienced damage from a recent hurricane, but when the potential threat of another hurricane in the future was posed, Howard reported, "The proprietor of the hotel waxed irritable at the suggestion." He then proceeded to state that "Rockport was in no more danger from the elements than any other town in the country." Howard explained what he had to say to this next. "Not wanting to antagonize the man, I agreed with him, commenting on the peril of oceanic inundation of Denver, Colorado, and the risk of tropical storms run by the inhabitants of Butte, Montana, and Madison, South Dakota. But he seemed to suspect a hint of irony in my innocent remarks, and thereafter treated me coolly."[59]

On another occasion Howard received what appeared to be an official mailing from the military. "This morning I took out a big registered envelope with a 'War Department' letter-head," he wrote Smith, "I had visions of me shouldering a Springfield already, but it was from a gentleman named Barlow, at Fort Benning, Georgia, asking me for my autograph."[60] The 13-year-old Robert Hayward Barlow, explains Derie, was "the precocious younger son of an army lieutenant colonel, and lived with his family at Fort Benning, Georgia."[61] A fan of *Weird Tales*, he wrote to many of the pulp's authors asking for their autograph, and later for their typescripts and any original illustrations they may have received from the magazine's artists.[62] Had he not been such an avid, not to mention tenacious, fan, collecting the manuscripts and typescripts of Howard's short stories and poems, many of these might have been lost forever.

Despite his humorous side, Howard also had a temper. He shared with Lovecraft one such anecdote in October, after they had received a torrential downpour. "Somewhat past midnight, at the height of the down-pour," he explained, "I sallied forth to rescue a small but pestiferous pig from the flood which was threatening to drown him in his pen." Still having a deep concern for all animals, he went out into the severe weather to save the pig. "Did you ever," Howard asked Lovecraft, "pursue a yammering pig around a muddy pen at midnight, with the rain driving down in torrents, the wind howling in gusts, and the thunder and lightning splitting the heavens?" When he finally caught the pig, it "yelled bloody murder" and he "dumped him into a shed with greatest of disgust," leaving him to remark, "I'll admit I was completely disgusted with live stock in general."[63]

Mrs. Virginia Sargent also shared an anecdote about Howard's "hot temper." She only met him once on a visit to Cross Plains, but his actions made an impression upon her. They had gone "to a boarding house for supper," she recalled in an interview. "There were two vacant chairs with a man between them. Robert asked the man to move so he could take a chair. The man ignored him. He asked again. The man kept [eating]. He asked a third time. The man just kept chewing away. Whereupon Robert just jerked the chair out and dumped the man on the floor and proceeded to sit himself down in the chair and began to eat."[64] As Jack Scott once remarked, "He just didn't give a damn for a lot of things that other people do."[65]

As 1931 came to a close, despite the grip of the Great Depression growing stronger, Howard was still making a decent income for the time period though experiencing the stress of his profession. "Besides Wright's magazine," Howard wrote Talman, "I've sold stuff to *Fight Stories*, *Action Stories*, *Ghost Stories*, *Argosy*, and of course *Sport Stories*." Although he believed it was "not a very impressive number of markets," that was not what mattered to him the most. "I don't have to keep regular hours and have somebody holding a stopwatch to me," he continued, "which is what I always detested about regular jobs."[66] He sought and struggled to obtain his freedom, and despite all the odds being against him, from the limitations of writing in Cross Plains to the worldwide Depression, he had obtained success; he had obtained his freedom. "There's freedom in this game," he wrote Wright earlier that year, informing him, "That's the main reason I chose it."[67] Over the next four years, however, that freedom began to ebb away, and the game itself would become a trap.

Chapter 21

Westerns both Strange and True, 1932

Poets and novelists have sung of me;
Made me a bronzed-faced Centaur, leather-girt.
The real man they all have failed to see;
A weary, ignorant man in an unwashed shirt.
—"Cowboy"[1]

"When men began to write of the West," Howard wrote Lovecraft in 1931, "it was to exploit its more lurid aspects for sensational purposes. Hence, rose the 'cowboy' tradition, the 'Wild West' tradition."[2] Howard was referring to the dime novels of the late nineteenth and early twentieth centuries, in which writers from the east, who had never been west, wrote fictionalized accounts of real frontiersmen such as Kit Carson and Buffalo Bill, or famous outlaws like Jesse James and Billy the Kid.[3] Howard called it "an absolutely criminal distortion" of the real men behind the myths they had created, and he lamented that their fiction all but ignored the literary stories of regional writers who lived and wrote in the west and how it kept all but a few good authors from writing on the subject.

Still, he was encouraged by the changes he had witnessed over his lifetime. "Now thinking people all over America are beginning to realize the truths of the pioneer West," he explained, "with the resultant boom in good Western literature—which I hope spells the doom of the Wild Bill dime-novel."[4] It certainly had, for the dime novels were replaced by the pulps, and Western novels were being published by the score.

The Westerns that Howard speaks of were, in many ways, actually tales of the American frontier that had their beginning with James Fenimore Cooper's Leatherstocking Tales, including *The Pioneers* and *The Pathfinders*.[5] As America moved west, so too did the story settings with the early pathfinders becoming backwoodsmen, plainsmen, and mountain men. In time these stories glorified the cowboy's life, and with the advent of Jack London, the frontiersmen moved north to Alaska and farther west to the Pacific islands. It was Owen Wister's *The Virginian* (1902), however, that endeared an American audience to the Western cowboy tale as literature and paved the way for Zane Grey to soon became a household name. Grey's novels were beloved by millions, including Howard, who once remarked after reading some of modern journalist H. L. Mencken's works, "I'd rather read Zane Grey the rest of my life."[6] The early pulps, such as *Argosy* and *Adventure*, did publish Westerns, but the first magazine dedicated to them came in 1919 when Street & Smith started their first pulp in the genre, *Western Story Magazine*. Countless others soon followed.

These stories almost always featured the common trappings that made them Westerns, including the cowboy hat, boots, and six-shooters, as well as horses and a pretty girl. Shootouts, fistfights, and chase scenes always rounded out the action. In his study of the Westerns, Lee Clark Mitchell notes these trappings were really just the elements that made up a typical Western. Underlying this, Mitchell states, is the man of action who confronts problems because what "we recognized as a Western are a set of problems recurring in endless combination": "The problem of progress, envisioned as a passing of frontiers; the problem of honor, defined in a context of social expediency; the problem of law or justice, enacted in a conflict of vengeance and social control; the problem of violence, in acknowledging its value yet honoring occasions when it can be controlled; and submitting all, the problems of what it means to be a man, as aging victim of progress, embodiment of honor, champion of justice in an unjust world."[7] These underlying themes were not only identical to those Howard enjoyed reading; they were also the ones he wrote about. All of his stories were, in a manner of speaking, tales of the frontier. So, since he enjoyed writing about the frontier in his other stories, it is not surprising that he would also adopt the common elements of the Western and write his own yarns in that genre.

Howard had already been writing Westerns off and on throughout his life, and some of his earliest were "'Golden Hope' Christmas" and "West Is West."[8] His first attempt at a professional sale was "Bill Smalley and the Power of the Human Eye," which had been submitted to the pulp magazine *Western Story* when he was 15.[9] He tried again in 1925 with one story and, later, assisted Gafford with his "great western novel," *West of the Rio Grande*, but neither were accepted for publication. His first professional sale of a Western actually came with his submission of "Drums of the Sunset" to the *Cross Plains Review*, which sold for twenty dollars in 1928 and appeared as a serial in nine parts.[10] Despite continuing to write the occasional Western for submission, however, he remained unable to sell to one of the pulps. Therefore, Howard did what had worked for him in the past: he wrote a Western in the guise of a genre that he was already comfortable and successfully writing in—the weird tale.

Just as Howard had created the genre of sword and sorcery by mixing gothic, adventure, and horror, he also created the weird Western by mixing elements of horror with the traditional frontier tale.[11] "By juxtaposing horror and supernatural elements, such as vampires, animated corpses, lost races, and Native American mysticism with traditional Old West settings and stock characters," explain Shanks and Finn, "Howard subverted the genre expectations of his readers and, in doing so, created a new iteration of the weird tale."[12] And as he had done when writing a boxing yarn in the guise of a ghost story, Finn explains, he was able to create "hybrid stories to transition from weird or horror stories to traditional westerns."[13] His first successful publication within this new genre was "The Horror from the Mound," which he sold to *Weird Tales* and was published in the May 1932 issue.

The mound featured in the story was a commonly known sight in East Texas, the burial mounds of the Caddo Indians. In the story a cowboy turned farmer notices his old Mexican laborer avoids the mound on his property out of superstition. When the cowboy decides to break into the mound, he awakens the horror, a vampire buried there since the days of the conquistadors, and in true Western fashion, the cowboy fights against the creature and defeats it.

The story, generally considered his best in this new genre, as well as one of his best stories overall, received mixed reviews upon publication.[14] Lovecraft immediately praised the story to at least one correspondent before writing Howard himself.[15] "I must praise in particular your 'Horror from the Mound' in last month's W.T. That is a magnificent piece of work, and gave me a shiver of the genuine sort which is not often obtainable from popular magazine material. The suspense and atmosphere are admirable—a brooding charnel pall seems to hover over the whole scene."[16] Howard was appreciative of the praise for, as he wrote Lovecraft, "Some of my friends weren't much impressed with it." He had first sent it to Bates at *Strange Tales* only to have him reject it. "Thank you for your comments . . . your remarks . . . encourage me," Howard replied, adding, "Your comments revive my confidence."[17]

When the July issue hit the newsstands, there were two comments regarding the story. The first came from fellow *Weird Tales* author August Derleth, who praised the story when he wrote, "Howard's *Horror from the Mound* was also first rate." However, he diminished this compliment somewhat when he commented, "though I didn't care too much for the fight between the vampire and the narrator." Derleth was not fond of Howard's style of story, believing, like Lovecraft, it was a concession to popular taste. "Nevertheless," Derleth continued, "Howard did a good job on it and made me swallow it and like it."[18]

The truly critical feedback came from those who took issue with Howard for altering accepted vampire lore. Just as he had changed the commonly held tradition of the werewolf being a man who turns into a wolf to that of a human with the features of a wolf, or his creation of the female zombie in "Pigeons from Hell" that he called a *zuvembie*, Howard also broke with some of the common tropes regarding vampires.[19] Harold Dunbar of Chatham,

Massachusetts, wrote a practically seething reaction to the story, published in "The Eyrie":

> *The Horror from the Mound* was the single poor effort in the issue, containing as it did not less than four flagrant breaches of accepted vampire tradition. Are we to believe, simply because Mr. Howard so informs us, that vampires can now remain alive for years, underground, without their customary nightly feast of human blood? Or they can be confined to their graves by a mere slab of rock? Or that they now find it necessary to engage in rough-house wrestling bouts with their prospective victims? Improvements are always in order, but Mr. Howard's new type of vampire is certainly no improvement![20]

Howard also received a similar missive mailed directly to him in Cross Plains from a crank who signed his letters as "Olson." He had been writing other *Weird Tales* authors, taking issue with aspects of their fictional stories, although his comments often made little sense.[21] Howard wrote Smith about the letter he received in May 1932: "I've gotten some more letters from the fool Olson, in Iowa. I could endure his lunacy, but his illiteracy gets on my nerves. This time he's frothing at the mouth on account of my 'Horror from the Mound.' He lashed himself into a perfect frenzy because I said a vampire was really dead. He says that there is no death in the first place, and that Christ was a vampire. Also that a vampire is in 'reallity' an idealist, with an earth-gravity of 50 per cent. Whatever the hell that means."[22] When Howard wrote Lovecraft about Olson's letter, he responded that another *Weird Tales* author, Clark Ashton Smith, had also received the same treatment from Olson over his own, "disrespectful treatment of vampires."[23]

Howard continued writing weird Westerns and also sent his next story, "The Valley of the Lost," to Bates at *Strange Tales*.[24] That April he wrote Lovecraft that he had sold the yarn that he described as "a horror tale in an early Texan setting," explaining, "I'm trying to invest my native regions with spectral atmosphere, etched against a realistic setting."[25] For this story Howard played on one of his key historical interests—the violent family feud.

Howard's letters to Lovecraft and others detailed the "Texas feuds," which he said tended to be "short and bloody," unlike those in Kentucky that had a habit of "drag[ging] on through the generations."[26] He regaled his correspondents with a recounting of several Texas feuds, including those of the Sutton-Taylor and Lee-Peacock families, along with the famous Hatfield-McCoy feud of Kentucky. One of the reasons this particular aspect of history may have held such a strong interest for him can be gleaned from a statement about humanity he made to Lovecraft: "We remember our friends long, but we remember our enemies longer."[27]

Despite the successful sale of "The Valley of the Lost," *Strange Tales* folded before the story was published. *Weird Tales* remained his main outlet for such stories, and he successfully saw "The Man on the Ground," another feud story, published in July and another weird Western, "Old Garfield's Heart," in December of 1933. The latter story takes place in the post oak country of Central West Texas, in a town he called Lost Knob, which is really a stand-in for his own Cross Plains.[28] He enjoyed writing the story, for as he told one correspondent, "The background and environment were realistically drawn," and although he felt like "I oughta sit down and write a lot of yarns laid in this country," he was afraid "I wouldn't be able to sell them."[29] Howard did write one additional weird Western using the feud theme "The Dead Remember," but it was not published in his lifetime, being sold posthumously to the pulp magazine *Argosy*.[30]

Having at least some success with his weird Westerns in 1933, Howard began writing traditional Westerns the following year, which was, as Glenn Lord noted, "a scant two years before his death."[31] "What I feel is one of the best stories I've ever written was a 30,000 word Western," Howard wrote of "The Vultures of Whapeton." Having composed it in the fall of 1934, he continued, "I knocked [it] off in two and a half days," though he lamented, "I have my doubts if anybody will accept it."[32] As Burke explained, "Howard's assessment was correct," for the manuscript did have a "hard time finding a home."[33] The story was submitted to multiple pulp magazines in both the Western and adventure lines without success. Eventually, an agent in New York City had the manuscript and found interest from a new pulp magazine, *Smashing Stories*. The magazine hit the market as a low-paying outlet for pulp yarns in May 1936, which afforded it the ability to publish for fifteen cents versus the typical quarter most pulps cost at the time.[34] The only problem was that the offer he received in early June 1936, a mere week before his death, was for one-half cent a word. Howard responded in one of his last missives, "½ cent is O.K. if you can't get more; I think this yarn has been turned down by most of the better paying mags, anyway."[35] The story was published posthumously that December.

Despite his disappointment in never seeing it in print, the story is an important work for Howard. As Western writer James Reasoner explains, not only was the tale important for Howard's transition to writing a traditional Western, but it was also important "in the overall history of Western pulp fiction. Its moral complexity, especially in the hero, Steve Corcoran, puts the story in the forefront of a movement away from what pulp editors called the 'gun-dummy' story and toward more realistic Western fiction."[36] As opposed to the morally simplistic characters who were either good guys or bad guys, Howard's story imbued his characters with a moral complexity that was not commonly found in the typical Western of the time period. As literary critic John Clute explained, "The tale systematically strips every character (except the protagonist) of any pretense that their 'civilization' is anything but a sham, then kills them off." The analogy he offers for reading the story is "like watching a train wreck, but a train wreck in a magic realist dream: every detail of the disaster fixes in the eye like poison."[37]

So, satisfied with the story, Howard set about writing a shorter yarn titled "Vulture's Sanctuary." The sanctuary to which he referred was the Guadalupe Mountain chain between Texas and New Mexico. He sent the story to John F. Byrne of Fiction House in late 1935, because they were planning to restart their line of pulps that had been suspended in 1932. Byrne sat on the story, trying to find a way to use it, but decided to send it back. After Howard received no response, he sent an inquiry to which Byrne replied, "I was under the impression that this story had been returned to you with explanations some time well before Christmas," but despite this he did remark, "This is a well told, well motivated yarn."[38] After Byrne was recruited away by *Argosy* to become their editor, the manuscript was again sent to Byrne, and he accepted it. "Vulture's Sanctuary" was also published posthumously that fall.[39]

Howard did have one Western published before his death, the originally titled "The Last Ride," appearing as "Boot-Hill Payoff" in *Western Aces*, in October of 1935. The unique thing about this story, however, was it was not originally Howard's. Chandler Whipple, who wrote under the pseudonym Robert Enders Allen, had originally written the story. In a letter to Glenn Lord, he explained how Howard became his coauthor: "As I recall, that was the first long western I ever wrote. It kicked around for a time, almost but not quite selling." It was then suggested that he send it to Howard to see if he could make the story publishable, and as Whipple explained, "I did not know Bob Howard, but did know him as a good western writer. He did a good job on the collaboration, for the piece sold the first time out, I believe, and we split the proceeds fifty-fifty."[40]

Howard wrote additional Westerns that were not published until years, sometimes decades, after his death, including "Gunman's Debt" and "Wild Water."[41] The former was both a cattle drive and feud story that Burke calls a "truly 'Howardian' western."[42] The latter is also of note because it uses a backdrop with which Howard was intimately familiar. "They're building a huge dam in Brown county," Howard wrote Lovecraft in January of 1932, "at a cost of several million dollars, where a couple of rivers join and run through a broad, steep-walled valley. It will be the biggest artificial lake in Texas, with a shore-line of 145 miles."[43] The dam was located south of Howard, about halfway between Cross Plains and Brownwood, where the Jim Ned Creek met the Pecan Bayou. Once flooded, the area would form Lake Brownwood. Howard wrote that "the engineers had predicted that two years at the least would be required to fill it," but that a terrific Texas downpour "filled Lake Brownwood in twenty-four hours."[44] The Army Corps of Engineers had, in fact, estimated that since the area received 25.9 inches of rainfall annually, it would take three years for the lake to fill. However, on June 30, 1932, it began to rain, swelling the creeks so much so that by July 3, when the torrential downpours deluged the already full waterways, the lake had filled overnight.

Overall, Howard proved more successful with the weird Western in his lifetime than he did the traditional Western. In part this was because by the time he made the transition from weird to traditional, he had simply run out of time. Reasoner also suggests that in addition to his stories being morally complex, "Howard's stories were simply too offbeat and often too violent for a magazine like *Western Story*, which on the cover of every issue boasted of featuring 'Big Clean Stories of Outdoor Life.'"[45] As Holmes elaborates, Howard crafted Westerns diametrically opposed to those of the genre's top gun, Frederick Faust, who wrote under his most popular pseudonym, Max Brand. "Faust wrote the mythic West," continues Holmes, while "Howard wrote the historical West. Faust wrote in a smooth style, while Howard's was rough and hard."[46] Had he only waited a few years, Holmes and Reasoner believe Howard would have found more receptive markets for his style of Western, for the very reason Burke explains, "several years after his death . . . the bleak worldview and the protagonist whose hat isn't white would come into their own in the western magazines."[47] Howard had simply been ahead of his time.

As the world ushered in 1932, the future looked bleak. The year would witness the greatest depths of the Depression and the specter of what awaited America in its near future loomed great. "The samurai is lifting his crest after his enforced submission to the West. . . . And in Germany the steel helmets are goose-stepping," Howard wrote that year, "The nations are heaping up the coals and stirring the fires; the pot's simmering and when it explodes the whole world is going [to] rock."[48] From Cross Plains, Texas, Howard sensed the danger of a looming war with both Germany and Japan. In regard to the former, he lamented the possible outcome of the upcoming presidential election there. "I note that in Germany, by the way, the citizenship of Hitler has been questioned to the extent of forcing him to withdraw from the presidential race," Howard wrote. "I hope Von Hindenburg carries the election. During war days I would cheerfully have lighted a torch to burn him at the stake, but now I think he is one of the strongest stabilizing factors in Europe, and that his reelection would be to the advantage of not only Germany, but the entire world."[49] That did not come to pass, and Howard knew that eventually Hitler would have to be stopped. Howard was not alone, for among most people in a state emerging from frontier life, Texans were acutely aware of such threats. "A barbarian awareness of true danger can be an asset to any society," historian T. R. Fehrenbach wrote, "as well as a barbarian willingness to believe that straight action, not interminable moral confusion, is sometimes required. A majority of all classes in Texas believed that eventually Hitler must be destroyed."[50]

The immediate and pressing threat to most Texans in the spring of 1932, however, was the crushing economic crisis. Yet despite the loss of many jobs and the rising number of farmers who were losing their land, most managed to survive fairly well. Howard explained the reasons why to Lovecraft in January that year: "I mentioned to you before the tendency of the people of Texas to live at home. This of course has been a necessary move, but it's a good one, I believe. I never saw so little money and so much food in the country in my life. Most of the barns and granaries are filled with grain, and the cattle are fat."

In describing his own situation with their "small piece of land," Howard told Lovecraft, "We have enough to keep a little stock and raise a garden. Right now we have far more than we need of greens, radishes, turnips, and the like...We have milk from our own cow, and plenty of meat. We had a whole calf canned—its surprizing how much meat a good fat calf makes. . . . And you ought to see the pork we have. . . . We dont have to pay out much money for food."[51] Howard did highlight, however, the greatest problem faced by rural farmers when he explained, "Of course, the catch in that is so much land, crops and livestock are mortgaged, and so many bank failures have caused the collection of notes and debts and the like."[52] When the debt collectors came, they wanted cash, not grain, meat, or produce in payment. Still, being not so far removed from the frontier life or the land itself, meant most Texans managed to survive. It was those dependent on industries, corporations, and banks for their livelihoods who suffered the most, including Howard, who was dependent upon the pulp magazines for his.

"God knows I need the money," Howard wrote Smith in May. "Markets are cracking every day. The depression is beginning to lick the wood-pulps."[53] As historian Ed Hulse explains, by 1932 there was little in the way of disposable income, and discretionary spending was plummeting, meaning people often had to dispense with purchasing their favorite pulp magazine, or they bought fewer and shared them more often. Regardless, it had an impact on the industry's bottom line. As a result, Hulse explains, titles were "put on hiatus or canceled outright" and although "Industry-wide, 27 new pulps will come to market during the year. . . . Only a half dozen will make it to 1933. Even the best books in the field experience[d] precipitous drops in circulation."[54] Howard wrote Smith what he was seeing from his vantage point: "I see *Sport Story* is offering 1¢ per word instead of 2¢. Also Bates writes me that *Astounding Story* is going on the bi-monthly basis, while *Strange Tales* will be made a quarterly. Also that both magazines are well stocked on material. If this keeps up, I'm s.o.l., but what the hell. A writer either starves or works himself to death. Often both."[55] Howard also knew of one pulp author, E. Hoffmann Price, who had lost his full-time industrial job and had decided to turn to writing full-time. "Hundreds of part-time authors have been dumped on the market," Howard informed Smith, "and that makes competition tougher."[56]

Howard's greatest fears, however, had to do with his first and best outlet for his writing, *Weird Tales*. "Too bad the magazine field is getting curtailed—but that's the universal story in depression days," he wrote Lovecraft. "I hope *Weird Tales* will be able to carry on. It ought to if any weird magazine does, for it is the first and most deeply entrenched of all the periodicals in its field."[57]

Besides the fear of the magazine folding, Howard also faced the frustrations of receiving more rejections from Wright, and he had received additional criticism for his Turlough Dubh O'Brien story featuring Bran Mak Morn titled, "The Dark Man." Paul S. Smith of Orange, New Jersey, had written a letter published in February 1932's "The Eyrie" in which he argued that while the story was "well written . . . it is not the least bit weird," so it did not belong in *Weird Tales*.[58] Howard believed letters like this were hurting him. "The yammerings and droolings of Paul S. Smith of Orange and his breed begin to bear fruit," he complained to Smith. "Farnsworth rejected four out of the last six stories I sent him, and almost invariably the reason was given was not weird enough." Bates at *Strange Tales* was also rejecting Howard's stories, as was John F. Byrne for both *Fight Stories* and *Action Stories*. "Byrne rejects my tripe—with reason," Howard wrote before explaining, "I'm slipping on action stories. Rather, I've already slipped."[59]

And if all of this was not frustrating enough, his typewriter, the very instrument of his livelihood, was giving him fits. "Now my damnable typewriter is going to pieces," Howard wrote Smith. "I broke the left margin catch off it, and the letters are out of line, and in order to write at all I have to swing on each key like I was punching a bag." When not striking hard enough, it left only a faint mark on the paper, making it difficult to read, which left Bates to complain that he could barely read the typescript produced by Howard's typewriter. "So, I'm going to cut this letter short," Howard wrote Smith, "and see if I can fix the blasted thing."[60]

Howard set about trying to alleviate some of his frustrations, particularly those with his editors and manuscript rejections, and his first step in that direction came when he applied for membership in a writers' interest group that spring. "I've recently joined the American Fiction Guild," he wrote Lovecraft in May, "which looks like a pretty good thing. If you are not already a member, and would care to look into it, I'll have them send you some literature regarding it."[61] The guild was based out of New York City and was a consortium of some of the top pulp writers in the field, including *Weird Tales* authors Arthur J. Burks and Paul Ernst, who served as the president and treasurer, respectively, along with Erle Stanley Gardner, the creator of the powerhouse lawyer Perry Mason, who held one of the many vice president positions. According to the guild's bulletin, the organization's purpose was to provide pulp authors with timely information through their weekly bulletin, as well as the monthly magazine *Author & Journalist*, which Howard called "the best publication of its kind extant."[62] In addition, the guild provided an array of services, including legal and expert, and in time of need, they could provide emergency funds from a "woefully inadequate" reserve.

One of the key recommendations made by the guild was for its authors to secure an agent. In so doing they could free themselves from the repetitious submission of rejected manuscripts, and it saved them the demoralizing effect of receiving such notices. Further, because the agents knew and were in contact with magazine editors, they had more timely information on the need for specific types and lengths of stories and could easily meet this need from an author's unsold manuscripts. Howard had inquired with fellow

Weird Tales author Henry S. Whitehead about his agent, but after receiving a letter from him criticizing the man, Howard decided to look elsewhere.[63]

Howard certainly needed some sort of reprieve, for once again he was experiencing chronic fatigue syndrome, which some still called neurasthenia.[64] Faced with the stress of limited and closing markets, he was working harder and longer hours without much sleep and little to no exercise.[65] "My health is poorer than it's been in some time," he wrote Smith that May, "though you wouldn't think so to look at me; I weighed just awhile ago and kicked the beam at 208."[66] In addition to gaining weight, he was having problems with his eyes again. "Mine are beginning to give me trouble; I don't know whether they'll stand up to the strain of continuous work or not. I've been averaging at least six hours a day, seven days out of the week, recently. The more work I do, the less I seem to sell. My markets are shot and so am I." He then ominously reminded Smith of one of their earlier conversations, "I told you years ago that I didn't intend to slave my whole life away for a bare living," before stating, "If my eyes hold up, though, I'm going to slave for another year."[67] In a postscript, however, after receiving still more rejection letters, he amended that declaration: "I've changed my mind about that year business. But I'll work for another six months, if I'm able to."[68]

Howard did, at least, manage to make a trip to Fort Worth shortly after writing Smith, but the lethargy and depression brought on by fatigue was on full display in his letter. "Well, here I am back at . . . Fort Worth. I could have gone on to East Texas, but I didn't have the energy. The thought of the exertion the trip entailed appalled me. The fact that travel repels instead of fascinating me as formerly, causes me a vague apprehension. . . . This is not indolence; it is merely that life has so far lost its tang that nothing I can do is worth the stress of the effort."[69] In the same letter, he told Smith, "In the event of my death, I wish you'd drop a line to each of the following," after which he named, among others, Farnsworth Wright and H. P. Lovecraft.[70] There is little doubt that Howard's chronic fatigue had once again brought back his thoughts of suicide.

There is a strong possibility that two events helped bring Howard out of this particular low point. One may have been the purchase of his own vehicle.[71] Before Howard owned a car, Dr. Howard once explained that his son generally got around by rides from friends or hitchhiking, noting "[I] have known him to start hitchhiking to Fort Worth or Brownwood to see a fight before he owned a car of his own."[72] He also briefly owned a horse he called Gypsy.[73] Dr. Howard owned a car, first a Model T and later a 1926 Essex, but he never taught his son how to drive.[74] Yet despite the steep learning curve, Howard certainly had reasons to want his own vehicle. Texas historian T. R. Fehrenbach explained one of those possible reasons. "The automobile, in a very real sense, replaced the horse in both social function and symbology," he wrote, for "Texas went from a horse culture to something resembling an automobile culture in one swoop."[75] The fact that in the depths of the Great Depression Howard had the cash to afford the purchase of a car certainly went a long way toward the "symbology" of the purchase; it was a demonstrable fact he had made it as a writer in Cross Plains.[76] The other, no doubt, was the level of freedom it would afford him.

Dr. Howard drove his son and Lindsey Tyson to purchase the two-door Chevrolet Coach, believed to have been "Dark Green" in color.[77] As Tyson recounted, "Bob, Dr. Howard and I went to Arlington, Texas, in about 1932 and Bob bought a used 1931 model Chevrolet. I drove the car home for him and then taught him to drive, after he learned to drive, he had a lot of fun driving on short trips around the country. I can not understand why Dr. Howard had never taught him anything about driving a car. And by the way Bob gave $350.00 for this car, about a year old."[78] Howard's friend and next-door neighbor, Leroy Butler, also recalled Howard's purchase of the vehicle with Tyson's assistance and how, afterward, "they'd go out in the country together in his car and just ride around."[79] They would drive and talk, much like they used to walk and talk, though it did not make Howard an attentive driver. "He's not the best driver in the world," one friend noted; "He gets too interested in what he's talking about."[80] Evidently, that was not surprising to many people who knew the family, since Dr. Howard was not recalled as being a good driver either.[81]

The other event that may have helped Howard through the low point was what came out of a trip he made south into the Rio Grande Valley.

The vacation took place in February 1932, before he experienced his bout of chronic fatigue syndrome that May, but if Howard's recollection is accurate, what happened down there changed his life and how he is remembered forever. "I reckon you got my postcard from the Valley," he wrote Smith upon his return. "Only went down the valley from Mission as far as McAllen once; and did the rest of my exploring up the river—west of Mission, in Starr County."[82] While stopping in the "little border town" of Mission, population five thousand, and situated "on the lower Rio Grande," Howard's most famous and immortal character, he explained, "simply grew up in my mind."[83]

Chapter 22

"Hither Came Conan, the Cimmerian," 1932

What do I know of cultured ways, the gilt, the craft and the lie?
I, who was born in a naked land and bred in the open sky.
The subtle tongue, the sophist guile, they fail when the broadswords sing;
Rush in and die, dogs—I was a man before I was king.
—"The Road of Kings"[1]

"I've been working on a new character," Howard wrote Lovecraft in April of 1932. "Wright rejected most of the series, but [I] did sell him one—'The Phoenix on the Sword' which deals with the adventures of King Conan the Cimmerian, in the kingdom of Aquilonia."[2] That sale marked the beginning of Howard's most famous and immortal character, who, he claimed, "simply grew up in my mind when I was stopping in a little border town."[3] Although the imagery of Conan coming to life in his mind fully formed makes for a good yarn, the truth is a little more complex.

In many ways Conan had already been gestating in Howard's mind for years. Over the course of his lifetime, he had been adding the threads that wove this character to life. By February of 1932, Howard had already created the genre of sword and sorcery. He had written of both men and kings, personal grudges and large-scale battles, and heroes armed with swords and daggers or simply their wits and their fists. He had mastered writing historical fiction, discovered its constraints, learned to telescope history from G. K. Chesterton, and pounded out yarns on his typewriter set in many historical and pseudohistorical lands. He had composed realism pieces that, despite having little commercial value, led Howard to imbue even his most fantastical characters with a genuine personality, a central compelling figure with real thoughts, motivations, and feelings that permeates his stories with a sense of verisimilitude. And the easiest way he had discovered to do this was to write himself into each of his characters, sharing with them his personal love for freedom by writing tales of frontier life—writing tales of barbarism.

While Howard's passion for barbarism had long existed, his correspondence with Lovecraft helped to illuminate this devotion.[4] Their debate regarding civilization versus barbarism was still in its infancy at that time, but it was forming as Lovecraft waxed eloquent on the classical civilizations of Rome and Greece, for which Howard showed little interest.[5] After Lovecraft's criticism of the "Dark Ages," calling it a "lapse into ignorant Barbarism," Howard had enough and informed him, "I am unable to rouse much interest in any highly civilized race, country or epoch."[6] "When a race—almost any race—is emerging from barbarism, or not yet emerged, they hold my interest. I can seem to understand them, and to write intelligently about them. But as they progress toward civilization, my grip on them begins to weaken, until at last it vanished entirely, and I find their ways and thoughts and ambitions perfectly alien and baffling." Howard then succinctly stated, "My study of history has been a continual search for newer barbarians, from age to age."[7] In Mission, Texas, Howard's imagination created both a new barbarian and a new age. Knowing the limitations of writing stories firmly entrenched in historical settings, by using the technique of telescoping history, Howard could envision a new era, one he realized he personally could not have. "What I want is impossible," he wrote Lovecraft. "I want, in a word, the frontier—which is compassed in the phrase, new land, open land, free land—land rich and unbroken and virgin, swarming with game and laden with fresh forests and sweet cold streams, where a man could live by the sweat of his hands unmarred by taxes, crowds, noise, unemployment, bank-failures, gang-extortion laws, and all the other wearisome things of civilization."[8] Although he could not have this in his own world, Howard could create it for Conan's, and he called it the Hyborian Age. Set between the sinking of Atlantis and before the great cataclysm that created the modern world, Howard now had free rein to populate this world, *his* world, with, as Burke states, "the barbarians he so loved to study."[9] Unlike the creation of an entirely fantastical world, Howard could root his age in things that both he and his readers already knew: the names, history, and legends of our world without the constraints of writing true history. "By telescoping history and geography to create a universe that was new and yet familiar," Louinet explains, "Howard was deliberately striving for efficacy and stereotype, a technique that allowed him to create an exotic background with a minimum of description."[10] Howard's Conan would roam free through the lands of a supercontinent, not unlike Pangea, in the years of the Hyborian Age, later reasoned to have been set around 10,000 BC.

The proximate causes for Howard's creation of Conan in the little Texas border town, however, may have had more to do with his financial situation. Louinet explains that the reason he was able to make the trip to the Rio Grande Valley in February 1932 was because of the sale of "People of the Dark" to Bates at *Strange Tales*. Since that magazine paid on acceptance and also paid better, Howard received a check for $278 before it appeared in print, thus affording him the ability to take a vacation. The break then gave him the opportunity to let his imagination wander without the pressing demands of his writing, and he was likely thinking of trying to develop another series character like Kane, Kull, or Bran. Because Howard had already created a character called Conan of the Reavers for "People of the Dark," Louinet suggests that "perhaps this became the genesis for his popular Conan story."[11]

After returning to Cross Plains, Howard set about writing the tales of Conan the Cimmerian. In later years there would arise some confusion over the pronunciation of the character's name, just as there had been confusion over Edgar Rice Burroughs's titular character, Tarzan of the Apes. When it came to the proper pronunciation of that name, Norris Chambers recalled how "Robert was pretty particular about that," for "he would say, 'It's not supposed to be TAR-zun. It's Tar-ZAN.'"[12] When Howard scholar Don Herron interviewed Chambers, he asked about Howard's pronunciation of Conan. Chambers replied, "CO-nun I believe is the way he always said that. At least I never heard him correcting anyone for saying it like that."[13] Howard's future girlfriend also confirmed the pronunciation when she later told an audience, "I am very happy to hear . . . some of you saying KO-nun, because . . . that's what he called him. It was not ko-NAN, it was KO-nun, you know, with that West Texas drawl."[14] Smith also confirmed this as the proper pronunciation.[15]

Howard set about creating Conan to be as authentic a character as he could make him. "It may sound fantastic to link the term 'realism' with Conan," he wrote, "but as a matter of fact—his supernatural adventures aside—he is the most realistic character I ever evolved." Howard further elaborated that what made Conan so realistic was that he was "simply a combination of a number of men I have known," for he believed, "some mechanism in my sub-consciousness took the dominant characteristics of various prizefighters, gunmen, bootleggers, oil field bullies, gamblers, and honest workmen I had come in contact with, and combining them all, produced the amalgamation I call Conan the Cimmerian."[16] And although he did not mention his own self in the list, Lovecraft well knew that Conan was also the embodiment of Howard. As he wrote, "'Two-Gun Bob' will never be a hack because he puts so much of himself into his work—even his most ostensibly mercenary work. He *is* King Kull or Conan or Bran—or whatever may form the subject of any given tale."[17]

Howard's first writing of the Hyborian Age came with his poem "Cimmeria," which he explained to a correspondent was "written in Mission, Texas, February 1932; suggested by the memory of the hill-country above Fredericksburg seen in a mist of winter rain."[18] The poem opens with the words, "*I remember*," signifying a remembrance of a past life lived, or reincarnation, just as the story featuring Conan of the Reavers had been.[19] And unlike most of his poetry, "Cimmeria" is more akin to modern blank verse rather than the traditional rhyming poems he commonly wrote.[20] Specifically describing the land of Conan's birth, the poem echoes passages from both Plutarch's *Lives* and Homer's *The Odyssey*, when he describes the northern country as a "land of Darkness and the Night."[21]

When it came to Howard's first Conan story, however, he did not so much write something new as rewrite his image of King Conan into the Wright-rejected King Kull story titled "By This Axe I Rule!"[22] Retitled "The Phoenix on the Sword," Conan would now rise out of the ashes of a character from that long dead series. And while both kings shared characteristics, such as Kull with his "great shoulders" and Conan with his "broad shoulders," or both being described as having "steel spring muscles," there were differences between the two. Kull was described as having a face "dark and immobile," while Conan had "sun-browned skin." Kull's eyes were "narrow" and "grey," while Conan's were "smoldering blue." And though Kull's eyes "gloomily eye the man who stood before him," Conan fixed his blues "enviously on the man." The difference in character was that although Kull always proved brooding, dour, somber, Conan was more outgoing, adventurous, always embracing life. Kull was Howard in one of his dark moods, whereas Conan was Howard rambling carefree through South Texas with $278. Still further, as Louinet explains, "By dropping the love-interest of the former story and adding a weird touch to his revision," he ensured that "the first Conan tale was tailored specifically to meet *Weird Tales'* requirements."[23]

As soon as he was satisfied with the revisions, Howard immediately began writing more stories, for he explained, "Episode crowded on episode so fast that I could scarcely keep up with them. For weeks I did nothing but write of the adventures of Conan. The character took complete possession of my mind and crowded out everything else in the way of story-writing."[24] He next wrote "The Frost Giant's Daughter," a short story featuring Conan in his youth confronting the northern siren of the title, as well as her twin frost giant brothers. Louinet believes the idea for the story may have come from Howard's copy of Thomas Bulfinch's *The Outline of Mythology*.[25] When later asked by two fans why he did not write the Conan stories in a linear fashion, he wrote in reply, "In writing these yarns I've always felt less as creating them than as if I were simply chronicling his adventures as he told them to me. That's why they skip about so much, without following a regular order. The average adventurer, telling tales of a wild life at random, seldom follows any ordered plan, but narrates episodes widely separated by space and years, as they occur to him."[26] It is likely Howard also relished the freedom he would have in not being pinned down to one period of Conan's life.

Once the second story was finished, the two were packaged together and sent to Wright in early March. Howard received a reply shortly thereafter, dated March 10, 1932, that opened with, "I am returning *The Frost Giant's Daughter* in a separate envelope, as I do not much care for it." Wright continued, "But *The Phoenix [on] the Sword* has points of real excellence," though he did ask Howard to make some revisions. Wright believed the first chapter "uninteresting" because it featured too much exposition trying to orient the reader, and while the second chapter opened well, he believed it "sagged from too much writing."[27] Wright also suggested the last page be "re-written with advantage," because he did not feel it ended strongly enough.

Despite being one of the most popular Conan tales today, "The Frost Giant's Daughter" was later given by Howard to the nonpaying amateur publication *The Fantasy Fan* for their March 1934 issue. Howard changed the title of the story to "The Frost King's Daughter," for by then Conan was a popular character, thus motivating him to change his name.[28] It was eventually published as "Gods of the North."

The fate of "The Phoenix on the Sword," however, is legendary. After rewriting the story according to Wright's wishes, Howard still wanted to orient his readers to the Hyborian Age in which Conan roamed. In order to do so without taking up as much space, Howard wrote the famous preamble, "The Nemedian Chronicles," which began "Know, oh prince," and reads like prose poetry. Wright accepted the story, promising $85.00 upon publication.[29] That occurred when it quietly appeared in the December 1932 issue, where it was placed about the middle of the magazine. Despite this, it would make history.[30]

When the feedback to the first Conan story began appearing in "The Eyrie," the readers were highly pleased. "*The Phoenix on the Sword* fairly took my breath away with its fine intrigue and excellent action and description," wrote Frederick John Walsen of Denver, Colorado. "It was a magnificent story. Mr. Howard never writes but that he produces a masterpiece." Claude H. Cameron of Toronto, Canada, praised the story, stating, "Howard has that certain something that makes a good weird tale," while John H. Bate of Philadelphia was clearly pleased when he declared, "Welcome to Conan the Reaver, Mr. Howard's picturesque fighting man."[31] The first Conan adventure received second place as the most popular story of the issue.[32]

Before Howard heard back from Wright in early March, he was already at work on his third Conan yarn, "The God in the Bowl." The story features a Conan not much older than he was in "The Frost Giant's Daughter," and depicts him now as a thief caught up in a murder mystery—a murder he did not commit. It took Howard three drafts before he was finally satisfied with the story, so it was not until early April when he mailed it to Wright.[33] Once again, Wright did not care for the tale and sent it back.[34]

Before immediately chronicling Conan's fourth adventure, Howard took the time to develop his Hyborian Age on paper. Having now written three stories, he had experimented enough with Conan's environment that he needed to keep track of it.[35] Louinet, who has made a study of the timeline of Howard's writings, believes that "in all probability, Howard first drew the maps."[36] The map of the supercontinent features the names of the countries and their political boundaries. The country of Conan's birth, Cimmeria, was placed to the north and center, while the land in which he would later become king, Aquilonia, was to its immediate south.

Howard also began setting down some of his ideas in an essay format that he titled "The Hyborian Age." Louinet explains that the essay started "out as a brief two-page outline," but that through "four successive versions . . . it soon developed into an 8,000-word essay, enriched with each successive version."[37] Howard later explained why he had done this: "When I began writing the Conan stories a few years ago, I prepared this 'history' of his age and the peoples of that age, in order to lend him and his sagas a greater aspect of realness. And I found that by adhering to the 'facts' and spirit of that history, in writing the stories, it was easier to visualize (and therefore to present) him as a real flesh-and-blood character rather than a ready-made product."[38] This ambitious endeavor gave Conan's world coherence, and because each country and its people were based on those from our own, past and present, it afforded Howard the ability to quickly describe both. As Burke explained, Howard "used words that you already have a meaning for, in your head, so that he doesn't have to slow down the story to explain things to you."[39] And Lovecraft recognized this because, he wrote, Howard "possesses a panoramic vision which takes in the evolution & interaction of races & nations over vast periods of time," and thus "gives one . . . large-scale excitement."[40] J. R. R. Tolkien would later do the same thing with his own Middle Earth, and the practice is commonly known today as "world-building."[41]

Armed with a map and a two-page outline of "The Hyborian Age," Howard set about writing Conan's next adventure in April 1932.[42] With only one Conan story accepted and two rejected so far, he knew it had to be good if he was going to secure an ongoing series character that outlasted Kull or Bran. "Wright took another of the Conan the Cimmerian series, 'The Tower of the Elephant,'" he reported to Lovecraft at the end of April, adding that "the setting of which is among the spider-haunted jeweled towers of Zamora the Accursed, while Conan was still a thief by profession, before he came into his kingship."[43] The story, despite being the second accepted, was actually published third in March 1933, earning him $95 and a first-place tie for most popular story of the issue.[44] The tale that was published second, coming the month after Conan's first appearance, was "The Scarlet Citadel." Louinet surmises that because it was a King Conan tale, Wright decided it would be less likely to confuse the reader.[45] Howard had started the story at the end of April and finished it in May, earning him $140 and the top spot, for as Wright noted in "The Eyrie," it "received more than twice as many votes as its nearest competitor."[46]

And then, not surprisingly, Howard began experiencing burnout, for this was the May in which he once again suffered from chronic fatigue. The flurry of writing not only so many Conan adventures but also other stories had taken its toll.

By the time he recovered and could return to writing Conan, it was August of 1932. Howard knew at this point he had at least found the beginnings of a successful character, one that Wright embraced, for he now had three stories accepted, although at the time the first to appear in print was still four months off. Nevertheless, he set about writing "Queen of the Black Coast," one of his most famous yarns, which took place during Conan's pirate days and featured his first important female character in a Conan yarn, the pirate Bêlit.[47] Although accepted in August of 1932, it did not publish until May of 1934 and was well received. Lovecraft called it "veritably a prose poem" after he read it, and Conan's speech regarding his personal beliefs is undoubtedly one of the reasons why:[48]

> In this world men struggle and suffer vainly. . . . Let me live deep while I live; let me know the rich juices of red meat and stinging wine on my palate, the hot embrace of white arms, the mad exultation of battle when the blue blades flame and crimson, and I am content. Let teacher and priests and philosophers brood over questions of reality and illusion. I know this: if life is illusion, then I am no less an illusion, and being thus, the illusion is real to me. I live, I burn with life, I love, I slay, and am content.[49]

The story netted him the issue's cover, $115, and a second-place finish for the issue.[50]

The first story meriting the front cover was "Black Colossus," the last Conan story he wrote before seeing the first in print. In addition to the $130 he earned when it appeared in June of 1933, it was voted the most popular story of the issue.[51] It also seems the cover, featuring a naked woman in supplication before a statue, proved quite popular as well. "The cover design by M. Brundage seems to have caught the fancy of our readers," Wright reported in "The Eyrie," "we were unprepared for the flood of approval that greeted the cover of the June issue, illustrating Robert E. Howard's fascinating story."[52] Howard was impressed as well.[53]

The artist, Margaret Brundage, was born in Chicago in 1900, and according to pulp historian Robert Weinberg, was "the youngest student ever to attend the Art Institute" and "later completed her art education at the Chicago Academy of Fine Arts."[54] She became a fashion artist in the late 1920s, for which there was little need during the Depression. With an invalid mother and a son to care for, she had to take what jobs she could find. As Howard began writing his stories of Conan, Brundage began looking in the phone directory for local publishers, thinking she might be able to make extra money doing artwork for the pulp magazines. Since the office of *Weird Tales* was located in her hometown, she decided to pay them a visit and brought along some sample art. Because "Wright and Sprenger were impressed by one picture of an oriental woman done in pastel chalk, [she] was commissioned to do the cover for the short-lived companion to *Weird Tales*, *Oriental Stories*."[55] Her first cover appeared in the spring 1932 issue of that magazine, and she was paid ninety dollars.[56] In the depths of the Depression, it proved a godsend.

Brundage was soon doing regular artwork for both magazines and quickly settled into a routine. "She would stop by the offices and pick up the story that was to be the lead for the issue being prepared," Weinberg explains. "After reading the story, Mrs. Brundage would pick those scenes that stood out as the most dramatic occurrences in the story. She would sketch these incidents and show them to Wright and Sprenger." As Brundage recalled, "They would always pick the one that showed a girl with the least amount of clothing. They felt that those pictures were best for the covers."[57] Wright fully understood that both shocking and sensational covers, not to mention sex, sold magazines. Brundage would then return home and begin drawing the selected scene on canvas using pastel chalk. She tacked the finished piece onto a wooden frame, then personally delivered it to the *Weird Tales* office.[58] Wright once told readers that Brundage's final products "are so delicate that we are afraid even to sneeze when we have a cover design in our possession, for fear the picture will disappear in a cloud of dust; and we are always glad when it is safely in the hands of the engravers."[59] It made for a good story, but Brundage explained, "Once the pictures were framed under glass, they could last forever without any real damage or fading."[60]

For Howard's "Black Colossus," Wright and Sprenger, as usual, selected the nude in supplication pose as their choice for the final artwork. After bringing the finished piece back, "They were so impressed by the cover," Brundage recalled, "that they brought it to the best engraver in Chicago."[61] Wright informed her months later that it had "generated the most mail ever for a cover for *Weird Tales*."[62] It most certainly helped, too, that she became a fan of Howard's writing. As she told an interviewer late in life, "Howard was my favorite author. I always liked his stories the best."[63]

By late fall of 1932, as the impact of the Depression grew worse, Howard found himself in need of cash. Knowing that Wright was now accepting nearly all of the Conan stories he wrote, Howard set about writing them in quick succession. In November and December he wrote "Iron Shadows in the Moon," "Xuthal of the Darkness," and "The Pool of the Black One." Wright accepted all three but changed the first title to "Shadows in the Moonlight" and the second to "The Slithering Shadow." In an attempt to also capture more covers, Howard included scenes assured to pique Wright's interest, and it worked, for the story published as "The Slithering Shadow" took the cover that depicted one seminude woman whipping another.[64] Also, to ensure Wright continued accepting his Conan stories, Howard had his mother, Hester Ervin Howard, write a letter to "The Eyrie" as H. J. Ervine from nearby Coleman, Texas, praising the "Shadows in the Moonlight," and voicing her opinion: "I hope Mr. Howard will write more Conan stories. They are great."[65] Howard's flurry of stories secured him two first-place finishes in a row for "The Slithering Shadow" in the September 1933 issue and "The Pool of the Black One" in October's issue.[66] Howard had certainly found a formula for Conan that worked.[67]

Once the Conan stories saw print, Howard began receiving much praise. "The Conan stories by Howard," Walter W. Miller of Madison, Wisconsin, wrote, "I sure get a kick out of the swashbuckling soldier of fortune. The fearless way he does things grips one right up to the end of the story."[68] Howard was fast becoming known as a writer who spun a good yarn, for S. G. Gurwait of Chicago wrote, "Robert E. Howard, too, is one of my favorites. What a smash he packs!"[69] As more stories were published, more praise was heaped upon him by fans such as S. Y. Bryant of South Bend, Indiana, who asked, "How does Howard manage to bring Conan to us so often and still keep him so interesting? The man must be a genius."[70] Even Howard's fellow *Weird Tales* authors were heaping praise on his Conan adventures, including Clark Ashton Smith, Carl Jacobi, and Jack Williamson.[71] Burke suggests the reason for the "appeal of Robert E. Howard's Conan stories lies in his gifts as a storyteller," for he is "unsurpassed in his ability to sweep the reader up and bring him *into* the story."[72]

Fans also began writing to him directly. Robert Barlow wrote requesting his original "typescripts" for the Conan stories, to which Howard complied, and other readers wrote inquiring about the wonderful poetry at the beginning of his stories, such as "The Road of Kings," asking where they could find a copy of the poem.[73] Howard only wrote the lone stanzas as epigraphs for his stories, often attributing them to some poem with a pseudo-title to give the story more verisimilitude. He did, however, lament having to write these fans back, for as he told Lovecraft, "I was sorry to have to tell them that it didn't exist."[74]

Not everyone had such high praise for Conan. Margaret Sylvester of Denver believed he was "beginning to sound like Edgar Rice Burroughs" and his Tarzan stories, which she evidently did not care for.[75] Sylvia Bennett of Detroit wanted to know when Howard would stop "writing his infernal stories of 'red battles' and 'fierce warfare'?" noting that she for one was "becoming weary of his continuous butchery and slaughter."[76] Even Howard pondered how far he could go with the barbarity of his character when he wrote Lovecraft in August of 1932, "I wonder how much barbarity the readers will stand for," lamenting that "one problem in writing bloody literature is to present it in such a manner as to avoid a suggestion of cheap blood-and-thunder melodrama."[77]

The greatest criticism, however, came from future *Weird Tales* writer and author of psychological horror Robert Bloch, of *Psycho* fame. At the time he wrote to the magazine, Bloch was merely a reader, but in one letter to "The Eyrie" he hoped that Howard would drop "Conan the Cimmerian Chipmunk" and in another he wrote, "I am awfully tired of poor old Conan the Cluck."[78] Wright added a postscript to the last letter, writing, "Sharpen your axes, you loyal supporters of the Conan tales, for anon we shall publish a short story by Mr. Bloch."[79] Bloch's words did spark a heated debate, with most heaping criticism on him and defending Howard, so it did make for a rocky start to Bloch's publishing career.[80] However, he did note that he liked Howard's writing and his other characters; what he objected to was the character of Conan. In later years, when Bloch penned his autobiography, *Once Around the Bloch*, he recalled how the incident "taught me a valuable lesson" and "from that point on and to this very day I have avoided public criticism of my fellow writers."[81]

Despite there being some criticism, Howard's Conan had gone beyond the point of either his King Kull or Bran Mak Morn series and was paralleling his run of acceptances with Solomon Kane. In the end, as pulp historian Ron Goulart points out, Conan "became the most popular character *Weird Tales* ever got hold of."[82] Howard had a successful series and had written some of the best Conan tales in 1932, but he was not yet finished, and some would argue the best was yet to come.

In the summer and fall of 1932, despite the ups and downs of the Depression, the pulp industry, and his moods, Howard did find time to partake of the things he enjoyed in life. He continued making trips south to Brownwood to visit his friends or to get his mother out of Cross Plains to do some shopping, and on occasion his father accompanied the family.[83] In August he and his friend Lindsey "Pink" Tyson took a short vacation to Galveston. "Shortly after getting your letter," Howard wrote Smith, "Pink and I went down to Galveston for a week-end. We had a good time."[84] Howard attended the Cross Plains annual picnic that summer, although he was disappointed in not seeing any fights there. "Well, the picnic came and went, and no violence," he wrote Lovecraft. "That's the forty-ninth picnic of its kind to be held in this town, and if there ever was another one that didn't have a few fights, I never heard of it."[85] He believed the event was peaceful because no carnival had been invited that year.

Howard also frequented the local movie theaters, seeing everything from comedies to dramas. He watched all four of the Marx Brothers films to date, with his favorites being *The Cocoanuts* (1929) and *Animal Crackers* (1930). He also enjoyed the comedies of the little remembered vaudeville duo Wheeler and Woolsey, with his favorite being *Hold 'em Jail* (1932). One of the melodramas that impressed him was the movie *Skyscraper Souls* (1932), starring Warren William and Maureen O'Sullivan (who had earlier that year appeared as Jane in *Tarzan of the Apes*). The film depicted the tragic lives of people living in a fictional high-rise building in New York City. "The morals of the people in the picture disgusted me," he wrote to Smith. "They—some of them—were of the class that considers itself salt of the earth, and they acted like a herd of swine. I enjoyed it—and marveled." But the one film that hit him the hardest was *Back Street* (1932) starring Irene Dunne and John Boles, depicting the tragic life of a kept woman. "*Back Street* was powerful, to my mind, and most damnably harrowing," he wrote Smith, "I wept bitterly. That's no lie." Howard also noted how he became irritated when the man in front of him took notice. "While weeping some yegg in front of me turned around to make a smart crack, I gave him a murderous glare, wiped away my tears and drew back my right to mash him for the insect he was, but he made no comment and turned around again." The film itself clearly angered him, for Howard continued, "It really tore me up. The thought of an intelligent and talented woman wasting all her years on a low-lifed son-of-a-bitch and sacrificing herself and living in the shadows, it gave me the jitters."[86] He also added that it made him so angry he wanted to take a club and beat someone. Fortunately, he did not.

Howard did, however, find release for his pent-up anger through sports, especially by watching a boxing match or a football game, not to mention his occasional forays to watch the ladies. He tried explaining this to Lovecraft, to no avail, when he stated, "After a hard day's work I feel far more like seeing a prize-fight or a leg-show than I feel like delving into questions of science and philosophy." Lovecraft had a great love for his intellectual pursuits and could not understand how a person, especially one as intelligent as Howard, could engage in these pastimes. Howard tried to elaborate further when he wrote, "I am only saying that the average man, like me, simply lacks the brains to find his pleasure and thrills in purely intellectual followings."[87] It was one more thing that highlighted their differences and fostered their debates.

Howard and Lovecraft did share at least one common trait between them—their love for food. Lovecraft's palate was somewhat limited by his gastrointestinal problems, while Howard appeared to have none of those issues. "I'm a big eater and I get a real kick out of gorging," Howard wrote his Providence friend. "Any kind of meat—fish, fowl, beef, turtle, pork; practically any kind of fruit; I'm not much of a vegetarian." He also loved milk. "I see people coaxing children to drink milk, and I can't understand their dislike for it," he continued. "I always drank it in huge quantities, and believe its one reason I was always so healthy."[88] He also loved cheese, all kinds, though his favorite was Swiss.[89] There were also certain meals for which he had a particular liking. "Give me limburger cheese, German sausage and beer and I'm content," he shared in one letter, and in another, "Liver is a favorite dish of mine, especially when fried with onions."[90] Among the few things he did not like was spinach, and he was not fond of cakes, preferring pies and homemade ice cream.[91] Lovecraft shared this particular love, for he was known to walk into an ice cream shop and order one scoop of every flavor.[92] Ice cream was apparently easy on his stomach.

With regard to religion and politics, Howard had decidedly established his beliefs on both by this point in his life. "I guess an Agnostic is what I am," he wrote of his religious beliefs to Lovecraft, having explained, "I've never heard a theological argument which convinced me beyond the shadow of a doubt in the existence of a Supreme Being; nor have I ever heard a scientific argument that convinced me that such a Being did not exist."[93]

Howard was far more engaged in politics, for he avidly followed the news. "Robert read the newspapers," Dr. Howard later recalled. "He was keenly interested in the pageant of both nation and state in which he lived. At election time I've known him to sit by the radio far into the night listening to election returns."[94] Like so many other Texans of that time period, he embraced the Democratic Party and the New Deal, voted for Franklin D. Roosevelt, and hated Republican Herbert Hoover, once writing, "I'd cut my throat before I'd vote for Hoover."[95] T. R. Fehrenbach once explained that this was not uncommon, for "the Texas Democratic Party was folk-conservative in thought and tone," but he also noted that "almost all Texas voters agreed in regulating the powerful, 'foreign' railroads, and in singling outside capitalists, or anything else touched with a Yankee taint."[96]

Despite voting for the Democratic party, however, Howard was truly, Burke explains, "a thorough-going populist." This is what Burke believes was one of the driving factors behind his debates with Lovecraft, stating that their barbarism versus civilization debate "might better be categorized as a 'populism vs. progressivism' debate."[97] Historian Richard Slotkin once defined a progressive as one who "idealizes centralization and efficiency," while the populist values "decentralization, idealizes the small farmer-artisan-financier, and either devalues (or opposes) the assumption of a

Great Power role or asserts that the nation derives both moral and political power from its popular character."[98] Lovecraft was the progressive, Howard the populist. And the driving force for Howard was, once again, freedom. "In the last analysis," he explained to Lovecraft, "I reckon, I have but a single conviction or ideal, or whateverthehell it might be called: individual liberty. It's the only thing that matters a damn. I'd rather be a naked savage, shivering, starving, freezing, hunted by wild beasts and enemies, but free to go and come, with the range of the earth to roam, than the fattest, richest, most bedecked slave in a golden palace."[99] Freedom was Howard's center of gravity. It was what drove him. It ordered his thoughts, it was the source of his love for the frontier, and it is found in each of his character creations. "By God, I demand freedom for myself," he succinctly declared to Lovecraft, "and if I can't have it, I'd rather be dead."[100]

Thoughts of death still came upon him from time to time, whenever he found himself in one of his dark moods, likely brought on by overwork. In November 1932 he wrote a letter to Lovecraft apologizing for his last missive, which had found him in one of these ill tempers. "I wrote while in the grip of one of the black moods which occasionally—though fortunately rarely—descend on me," he explained. "With one of these moods riding me, I can see neither good nor hope in anything, and my main sensation is a blind, brooding rage directed at anything that may cross my path." He also wrote, "At such times I am neither a fit companion nor a gentlemanly correspondent."[101] The person who knew this best was his closest friend, for Smith recalled, "This bitterness was, at times, depressing to his companions," but he also noted, "at other times, when in real, rare moods, he was one of the most entertaining persons one could hope to find."[102] As was typical of Howard, he blamed it on his Celtic line, when he wrote Lovecraft, "These moods are hereditary, coming down the line of my purely Irish branch," reinforcing his Celtic heritage and explaining it away.[103]

Then, with the holidays nearing, Howard found himself in a more cheerful mood. On Thanksgiving he and Tyson drove to Brownwood, checked into a hotel, had their Thanksgiving dinner at a friend's—a meal he so dearly loved—and after helping unload some steers, went to watch the Howard Payne College versus Southwestern University football game for the championship of the Texas conference. "I don't know when I enjoyed a holiday more," he wrote Lovecraft.[104] His Christmas was a little more low-key affair as he stayed at home. "It was pretty quiet in these parts, nothing out of the ordinary occurring," he wrote. "I did about as usual—ate too much rich food, drank a good deal of whiskey, and shot a few holes in the air, by way of celebration. But it was all mighty tame."[105]

As 1932 came to a close, Howard saw a slight drop in his yearly sales, no doubt because of the Great Depression. Still, he managed to make $1,067.50—the equivalent of about $22,000 in modern dollars.[106] Although he had learned that *Strange Tales* had folded, by the end of the year he now saw two of his Conan stories in print, and with six accepted the new year looked promising. What Howard did not know, however, was that *Weird Tales* was beginning to experience serious problems resulting from the devastated economy and was in danger of folding itself, and that it was he who was about to save them. This was not made known until 1961, when *Weird Tales* author E. Hoffmann Price revealed that "Farnsworth Wright and others of the *Weird Tales* inner circle told me that the Howard-Conan combination had many a time staved off disaster."[107] As pulp historians Holmes and Knight once stated, "Conan is a major reason the magazine survived during the Great Depression."[108]

Chapter 23

Steve Harrison and the Detective Yarns, 1933

The blind black shadows reach inhuman arms
To draw me into darkness once again;
The brooding night wind hints of nameless harms,
And down the shadowed hill a vague refrain
Bears half remembered ghosts to haunt my soul—
Like far-off neighing of nightmare's foal.
—"The Voices Waken Memory"[1]

"Until recently—a few weeks ago in fact," Howard wrote Lovecraft in June of 1933, "I employed no agent."[2] He had been considering the idea for some time, but it was not until May of that year that he finally secured a literary agent. The person he hired for the job was fellow *Weird Tales* author Otis Adelbert Kline.

Originally starting out as a part-time author, Kline turned to full-time writing by the late 1920s but did not find it to his liking.[3] "Otis couldn't make the grade as a full-time fictioneer," E. Hoffmann Price explained, because although "he sold all he wrote," Kline could not "produce the volume which his life-style required."[4] He soon returned to writing part-time with his full-time occupation becoming the management of his own literary agency. "Some years ago," Kline explained in his short biography, "[I] started to do some agenting for a writer friend. He liked it and told others, and the business grew by this method until it took a great deal of time and attention."[5] Eventually, Kline advertised his services in the American Fiction Guild's publications, which is likely where Howard saw the ad. In addition to his knowledge of the publishing industry in Chicago, Kline also knew many of the agents in New York City; thus, he could expand the market for his writers. Yet one of Kline's greatest strengths as an agent came from his many European contacts, where he could sell first European rights for his clients, thus opening up an entirely new market for not only his authors' stories but also his own.[6]

Howard contacted Kline, and they soon struck a deal. Howard would send Kline all of his manuscripts except for those he sent directly to *Weird Tales*. Howard retained the right to continue submitting directly to Wright since that relationship had long been established. Howard scholar Bobby Derie explains how Kline handled the manuscripts and received his commission: "Kline waived reading fees and worked on a straight commission: 10% of whatever the story sold for went to the agency. Kline, who was centered in Chicago, also had associates in other cities: if he couldn't sell a story himself, Kline would send it out to an agent. If that agent sold a story, he or she got a 5% commission. The checks generally went directly from the publisher to Kline, who subtracted his (or his associates') commission, then cut a check to Howard." This arrangement worked greatly to Howard's advantage. Up to this point, Howard could only submit to magazines he was aware of through what appeared on the local newsstands, those he learned about through his correspondence, or the calls for stories in the American Fiction Guild's magazine *Author & Journalist*.[7] Having Kline as his agent helped in the marketing of his stories to magazines he was unfamiliar with. It also helped him because while Kline kept Howard informed about the status of his manuscripts, according to Roehm, he also "offered tips and strategies to more effectively produce those stories."[8] But perhaps most importantly, Howard no longer had to spend the time repeatedly mailing out his manuscripts until he made a sale or receiving any more of those demoralizing rejection slips.

The earliest known letter from Kline as Howard's agent is dated May 11, 1933, and he already mentions being in possession of four of Howard's stories that he was trying to market.[9] And although Kline is said to have "initially struggled to market Howard's fiction," Derie notes that "as the years went on Kline was selling a greater and greater percentage of the work that Howard sent him."[10]

As to whether Howard thought Kline was a good literary agent, there appears to be some mixed sentiment, perhaps depending on Kline's success at the moment of Howard's comment. To one aspiring author, Emil Petaja, Howard wrote of his agent, "I have found him very satisfactory in every way, and do not hesitate to recommend him."[11] However, to a friend who asked him if Kline was a good agent, Howard is said to have replied, "So-so . . . sometimes I think he might work a little harder for me. Chances are that I could sell my stuff as well as he can, but selling things myself takes too much time." Although he added "I'm thinking about trying someone else," he never did.[12] The one thing about Kline that Howard appreciated the most was the fact he "agreed with him that editors were all bastards," but, nevertheless, "you had to deal with them."[13]

It was Kline who encouraged Howard to consider writing detective stories, since he was aware of the many markets and the high demand for these stories at the time. Writers such as Hugh B. Cave recognized this as well. "Detective fiction is the best bet in the pulps right now," he wrote, noting that "Western stuff is good but the big western writers have the market pretty well padlocked. *The Weird Tales* market is shot to hell."[14] In need of new markets, Howard set about creating his first character in the detective genre.[15]

It was Edgar Allan Poe who created the genre when he penned "The Murders in the Rue Morgue," featuring his fictional detective C. Auguste Dupin, who was modeled on real-life French detective Vidocq.[16] Despite being an American invention, however, detective stories quickly became the purview of English authors including Charles Dickens and Wilkie Collins who helped establish the literary genre. It was, however, Sir Arthur Conan

Doyle who popularized the genre with the creation of the most famous fictional detective character of all time, Sherlock Holmes. With the publication of "A Study in Scarlet" in *Beeton's Christmas Annual of 1887*, Doyle's stories were "flung like a bombshell into the field of detective fiction," writer Vincent Starrett once wrote.[17] The English detective soon became the model for all literary detectives, that of the aristocratic gentleman who uses the power of his mind to solve crimes, often from the comfort of an armchair. Some of the more famous English detectives that followed included G. K. Chesterton's Father Brown series, Dorothy L. Sayers's Lord Peter Wimsey, and Agatha Christie's Hercule Poirot. The model would largely remain unchanged for a generation.

As with the weird stories, it was the creation of the pulp magazines that opened up a new genre of detective fiction. In this case it was the pulp magazine *Black Mask*. First published in April 1920, the magazine initially billed itself as "five magazines in one," claiming to be "the best stories available of adventure, the best mystery and detective stories, the best romances, the best love stories, and the best stories of the occult." That all began to change after Carroll John Daly published the first hardboiled detective story, "Three Gun Terry," in the May 15, 1923, issue, followed by his series featuring the character Race Williams. "Detective fiction as we see it has only commenced to be developed," wrote editor Joseph Shaw in 1927. "All other fields have been worked and overworked, but detective fiction has barely been scratched."[18] The plan was to move *Black Mask* toward being an all-detective fiction magazine, and although Daly created the new type of story in the genre, it was author Dashiell Hammett who led the way.

The creator of the nameless private investigator referred to as the Continental Op and the detective Sam Spade, Hammett blended two stock dime novel characters—the detective and the outlaw. "The hard-boiled detective," explained historian Richard Slotkin, "is both an agent of law and an outlaw who acts outside the structures of legal authority for the sake of a personal definition of justice."[19] This was not the aristocratic armchair detective of the English world but a streetwise American who was willing to get his hands dirty. As creator of the popular detective Philip Marlowe series, Raymond Chandler, once explained, Hammett did not write his stories for the upper-class intelligentsia but "for people with a sharp, aggressive attitude to life. They were not afraid of the seamy side of things; they lived there. Violence did not dismay them; it was right down their street."[20] These were detectives the common pulp reader could understand, and as pulp historian DeForest wrote, it "had injected a badly needed dose of realism in the genre."[21] Hammett was likely the best author to do this, for he had worked as an operative for the Pinkerton Detective Agency prior to his writing for *Black Mask*.

There is little indication that Howard had any interest in this genre, even when he began writing his own version. The closest he had come was when he wrote his detective parodies for the amusement of his friends and fellow students when they were published in the school newspaper.

As was Howard's forte, he relied on mixing genres for the first detective story he sent Kline. "Talons in the Dark," a tale of weird menace, featured a Sailor Steve Costigan–like character as a detective who is described as looking somewhat like a college professor. After mailing the story in July, he wrote Smith that October: "Kline cracked me into a new market—*Strange Detective Stories*; don't know how it will pan out."[22] The magazine was a revamped continuation of *Nickle Detective*, with the new iteration attempting to mix the two genres.[23] Although most certainly compatible with Howard's type of detective story, the magazine only lasted four issues. Published as "Black Talons" in the December 1933 issue, it proved to be Kline's first sale for his new client, and after taking his commission, he mailed Howard a check for $55.25.[24] "Kline has been a big help in teaching me the technique of detective story writing," Howard wrote Lovecraft before cautiously adding, "whether I am able to profit by his teaching remains to be seen."[25]

Howard created another detective team, this time Butch Gorman and Brent Kirby, but because neither of the two stories sold, he moved on to creating another character by the name of Detective Steve Harrison. Howard wrote nine stories featuring his new character, but only four sold in his lifetime. Steve Harrison's status as a detective is never fully established by Howard in the stories, although he seems to be working through some unknown arrangement with the city police in the dangerous waterfront district of River Street. Similar to his popular story "Skull-face," these detective yarns show a distinct Sax Rohmer influence, for they are primarily tales of Asian menace.[26]

Two Harrison stories that Howard sent Kline, "People of the Serpent" and "The Teeth of Doom," were sold to *Strange Detective Stories*, earning Howard $77.25 and $85.00, respectively. The editor decided to publish both stories in the February 1934 issue, but to avoid having two stories by the same author, "Teeth of Doom" was attributed to the pseudonym Patrick Ervin and Steve Harrison's name was changed to Brock Rollins. Still further, the titles were then changed to "Fangs of Gold" and "The Tomb's Secret." And as if that was not confusing enough, according to Roehm, at some point during production, the new titles were somehow switched, making their publication history ever more murky.

The magazine continued to create confusion about Howard's stories. After Kline secured another sale for "Lord of the Dead," featuring the archvillain Erlik Khan, it was scheduled for publication in the March issue.[27] The magazine, however, folded, and the manuscript was sent back to Kline.[28] In the meantime Howard had written a sequel to the story titled "Names in the Black Book," also featuring the same nemesis. Kline sent the story to *Super Detective Stories*, which accepted it for publication in their May 1934 issue, meaning the sequel published before the original story. Nevertheless, Howard received a check from Kline for eighty-five dollars.[29] The only other sale from his detective series in Howard's lifetime was "Graveyard Rats," which featured Steve Harrison investigating a case in the town of Lost Knob, Howard's fictional version of Cross Plains.[30] It appeared in the February 1936 issue of *Thrilling Mystery.*

Although Howard tried writing in the detective genre per Kline's encouragement, he found it extremely frustrating. In the fall of 1933 he wrote one correspondent, "Lately I've been trying to write detective yarns, something entirely new for me, and haven't had much success," and to another, "I don't have the feel for detectives that I do for weirds."[31] After *Strange Detective Stories* folded, he wrote yet another: "Of late I haven't been doing much in the detective line."[32] And by June of 1935, Howard simply declared, "I've given up trying to write detective yarns—a job I despise anyway."[33]

Raymond Chandler once observed, "The detective story, even in its most conventional form, is difficult to write well."[34] The main reason, he said, was because the typical detective story had certain requirements. "There were rules about the story itself," according to detective historian Julian Symons, who specifically noted the "insistence that the writer must play fair with the reader."[35] Readers wanted to play detective right alongside the story's fictional sleuth, using their own powers of deduction to solve the case based on the clues given along the way. These were not, however, the stories Howard liked writing, for as he once told Lovecraft, "When my fictional characters can't slash and slug and litter the pages with one another's carcasses, I'm an utter flop as a tale-spinner."[36] Despite his dislike for the genre, however, many critics still believe Howard's detective yarns hold their own. As detective fiction scholar Don Herron once observed, "For someone who detested detective fiction, . . . against the typical hard-boiled crime fiction of the period the writer from Cross Plains holds up pretty well indeed."[37]

At the beginning of 1933, Howard continued his frenzy of writing Conan yarns with "Rogues in the House," which he sent to Wright. It was accepted for one hundred dollars and published in the January 1934 issue to little acclaim. He followed in February with "The Vale of Lost Women," but it is unknown whether he even submitted the manuscript to Wright; if he did, it was rejected.[38] And despite two additional starts to other stories featuring the Cimmerian, he soon turned his attention to other characters, stories, and pulp magazines. Although he may have been burned out from having written so many Conan yarns back-to-back, it likely had to do with the *Weird Tales* payment policy. By the time he wrote the last story, he had only seen two Conan tales in print. Seven more were awaiting publication, and until they appeared in the magazine, he did not get paid. As a result Howard took a break from writing any further Conan adventures and did not return to the fictional character until the fall of 1933. By that time three more stories had been published, two with covers, and his character was clearly popular with *Weird Tales*' readers.[39]

When he did return that fall, his next story, "The Devil in Iron," followed some of the same storyline as his previous "Iron Shadows in the Moon." Louinet explains, "It was apparently taking Howard some time to re-immerse himself in the Cimmerian's world after a long absence."[40] He finished the story in October and sent it to Wright, and it was published in the August 1934 issue. Despite being somewhat similar to the earlier story, *Weird Tales* readers did not seem to mind, and it was voted "The most popular story in the August issue."[41] The yarn also led Alvin Earl Perry of Rockdale, Texas, to comment, "Howard held me enthralled throughout his masterpiece" and "with each succeeding tale Howard becomes better; his unique character, Conan, is the greatest brain-child yet produced in weird fiction."[42]

It was sometime in 1933 that family friend Norris Chambers took some part in the writing of the Conan yarns. "I saw some of those writer's magazines," he later recalled in an interview, "and they were full of ads with people willing to type manuscripts. Some of them were thirty-five cents per thousand words . . . so I put an ad in one of those. And I put twenty-five cents, and that included a carbon copy. Double-spaced." When he showed the ad to Howard, he was said to have replied, "Well, I've got some typing you could do," and so Chambers began typing the revisions of the Conan stories.[43]

As Chambers now had more interaction with Howard, Don Herron and Leo Grin asked him what Howard sounded like when he spoke. "When he talked," Chambers explained, "it sounded just like a book, like somebody reading out of a book. He just had that pronunciation, and his composition was just like as if he had written it." Chambers deemed it "very precise talk." Others recalled that he had a good "bass voice," that he talked "real slow," and "his voice was kind of like Humphrey Bogart's."[44]

In addition to the prospects of Conan being a continuing series and his opening up new markets with his detective yarns, Howard had some other good prospects that year as well. After "The Valley of the Lost" was returned to him when *Strange Tales* folded, he submitted it to *Astounding Stories*. Although the magazine no longer took such weird tales, Howard was encouraged to write science fiction instead.[45] "Whether I'll be able to make the market or not is doubtful," he wrote a correspondent, "it is an entirely new field for me, and . . . there is so little of the scientist about my nature that I feel no confidence in my ability to write convincingly on the subject."[46]

Another prospect came from England when Hugh G. Schonfield of the Denis Archer publishing company wrote inquiring if they could have permission to reprint his two stories from *Strange Tales.* The executive also requested a sampling of his best weird stories in consideration for publishing a book collection. Howard readily agreed to the first and complied with the second, sending him eight stories, including a tale each of Solomon Kane, Bran Mak Morn, King Kull, and Conan.[47] Although hopeful, he was also realistic, for as he wrote Lovecraft, "Literary success is a persimmon that hangs out of my reach."[48]

The correspondence between Howard and Lovecraft continued throughout 1933, highlighting ever more their differences. One marked divide had to do with the physical versus the mental. Howard embraced the former, while Lovecraft the latter, setting up one of their many debates. Howard had spoken of his physical abilities, to which Lovecraft had replied in January, "It is *no distinction at all* for you to be able to lift a certain weight, knock down a certain man, or carry a bale of hay. A bull gorilla could do more. But it *is* a rare distinction for you to be able to write a story like 'Worms of the Earth.'" "The physical," Lovecraft then stated, "means nothing whatever in relation to your excellence as a person."[49] To Howard, however, it did, for which he wrote in reply, "You should realize that I live in a sphere entirely different from that in which you live. The fact that I make my living with my typewriter certainly doesn't mean I have no other work to do. I don't live on a farm, but it's almost like one. Specifically, I milk cows, clean our pig-pens and stalls, dig ditches, behead chickens, and unload feed wagons when necessary."[50] Howard summed it up by stating, "I wrote the story because I needed the money; I unloaded the wagon because it was necessary to do it in order to save money. Exactly the same motive was behind both endeavors."[51] He then concluded in words that were clearly directed at Lovecraft, "Of all the snobberies, the assumption that intellectual endeavors, attainments and accomplishments are the only worth-while and important things in life, is the least justifiable."[52]

It seems Lovecraft could simply not grasp the concept, so he accused Howard of being truculent. "When you seem to read hostility towards literature in my remarks," Howard wrote in reply, "remember this: that I was first to light a torch of literature in this part of the country, however small, frail and easily extinguished that flame may be. I am, in my way, a pioneer. To the best of my knowledge . . . I was the first writer of the post oak country." Howard was no doubt proud of his accomplishments, but he again had to clarify that, unlike Lovecraft who wrote as an end, for Howard,

> Writing has always been a means to an end I hoped to achieve—freedom. Personal liberty may be a phantom, but I hardly think anybody would deny that there is more freedom in writing than there is in slaving in an iron foundry, or working—as I have worked—from twelve to fourteen hours seven days out of the week behind a soda fountain. I have worked as much as eighteen hours a day at my typewriter, but it was work of my own choosing, and I could quit any time I wanted to without getting fired from the job.[53]

In another unsent letter, Howard stated it more succinctly: "My desire for personal freedom has been the ruling passion of my whole life."[54]

In addition to his frequent correspondence with Lovecraft, Howard also began writing two other *Weird Tales* authors, August Derleth and Clark Ashton Smith. Both were already part of Lovecraft's circle, and although he shared many of the things Howard wrote in his letters with them, he encouraged them to also communicate with Howard directly.[55] Derleth was the first to do so in December of 1932.

Born on February 24, 1909, in Sauk City, Wisconsin, Derleth was a fan of Poe's stories, and upon the appearance of *Weird Tales,* he began submitting his own.[56] His first acceptance came on October 15, 1925, and Derleth went on to write 139 stories for the "unique magazine," mostly filler ghost stories, but he later became well-known for his Sherlock Holmes pastiche (using the character name Solar Pons) and regional fiction about his home state. His most important contribution to literature, however, may have resulted from his cofounding Arkham House Publishing with fellow *Weird Tales* author Donald Wandrei, which set about publishing the works of H. P. Lovecraft after his death.

The other author, Clark Ashton Smith, began corresponding with Howard in the summer of 1933.[57] Born on January 13, 1893, in Long Valley, California, Smith spent nearly his entire life in the area and helped his father build a log cabin in 1902 where his parents, and later he, died.[58] For Smith it was the discovery of Poe's poetry that motivated him to write. With the publication of his first collection of poetry, *The Star-Treader and Other Poems* in 1912, the local papers hailed him "the Keats of the Pacific Coast." In time he followed it with *Odes and Sonnets* (1918) and *Ebony and Crystal* (1922).[59] Having become aware of Smith's poetry, Lovecraft was soon corresponding with him and suggested Smith submit his poetry to *Weird Tales*. His first poem appeared in the July–August 1923 issue.[60] By 1930, with ailing parents and in need of cash, Smith turned to writing prose for *Weird Tales*, producing forty-five stories over the years 1930 through 1935.[61] "Smith's best tales," according to *Weird Tales* historian Reginald Smith, "were set in such imaginary lands as the medieval region of Averoigne, the lost continent of Hyperborea, and an area of the far future named Zothique."[62]

Ever the lover of poetry, when Howard began corresponding with Clark Ashton Smith, he purchased a copy of *Ebony and Crystal*. After finishing it he wrote Smith, "I can hardly find words to express the pleasure—I might even say ecstasy—with which I have read, and re-read your magnificent *Ebony and Crystal*. Every line in it is a gem."[63] Howard's effusive praise took Smith aback, for he soon wrote Lovecraft, "Howard is a rather surprising person, and I think he is more complex, and is also possessed of more literary ability, than I had thought from many of his stories. The Conan tales, in my opinion, are quite in a class by themselves. H[oward] seemed very appreciative of my book of poems, *Ebony and Crystal*, and evidently understood it as few people have done."[64]

In the spring of 1933, while on a visit to Brownwood, his friend Tevis Clyde Smith told Howard there was someone who wanted to meet him. Her name was Novalyne Price. Smith had met her in the seventh grade, and they were friends throughout high school and even started college together.

They did not, however, graduate together, or at the same time. Smith had transferred to Howard Payne and completed his degree on time. Price could not afford to do the same, so she worked one year and attended classes the next. He had graduated in 1929, and she was just about to do so.[65] Although they had been dating in recent years, it seems they were really just friends who enjoyed talking about books and their literary aspirations.[66] She had heard Smith talk often about Howard, and because he was a real author, she wanted to meet him.[67]

Howard agreed to the visit, so the two of them drove to the farm where she lived just outside of Brownwood. "I was sitting on the front porch with my physics book in my lap, trying to absorb some of the uninteresting facts in it," Price wrote in her diary that night, "when I heard a car stop by the two big oak trees in our front yard." She continued, "After a minute, I heard a car door slam. I didn't get up. On the farm, you don't have too many visitors. Clyde Smith came down the walk to the porch." The first words out of his mouth were, "Didn't you say you wanted to meet Bob Howard?"[68] She said she did, and he told her to come with him to the car.

Lindsey Tyson later recalled Price as "nice-looking," explaining she was "not real pretty, but she was nice-looking."[69] Jack Scott remembered her as being "a weeny bit skinny," and described her as "a brunet" with "real brown eyes," and a "nice complexion." He found her to be "an attractive girl," and noted she "was more intellectual than most."[70]

Novalyne Price was born on March 9, 1908, to Etna Reed and Homer Hall Price.[71] Her parents divorced when she was 4, and it formed one of her earliest memories. "Our furniture was loaded on a wagon drawn by two mules, and we went . . . to my grandmother's house. She lived on a small ninety acre farm. Big oak trees bordered the road along the field across from her farm."[72] Her grandmother, referred to as "Mammy," ran the farm located near Bangs, Texas, west of Brownwood, with the help of her son. In 1915 mother and daughter moved to Brownwood so Price could attend the Coggins Ward School, but after World War I broke out, she and her mother returned to Mammy's home again because her uncle had been drafted. Her mother remarried in 1920, and the following year she moved in with her stepfather's parents, who lived in Brownwood, so she could attend the local high school. That was when she first met Smith, who was in the same grade as she was.

During her high school days, Price developed an interest in expression, today known as speech, and she began reciting poems and delivering readings. She soon began taking private lessons, although the cost placed a burden on her family, but she was eventually able to give younger children lessons, thereby affording her own. She evidently became quite accomplished, for the school paper called her "the best reader Brownwood High has ever had," and she won first place in an oratorical contest.[73] She carried this interest into her college career at Daniel Baker, where she majored in expression and became involved in the drama program.[74] She continued to impress the college editors, and in one of its articles she was described as "truly one of Brownwood's most gifted and popular readers and is well deserving of the splendid reputation she has acquired."[75] Price was now set to graduate in May.[76]

"Bob Howard was sitting in the front seat of the car!" she wrote excitedly in her diary that night. "He got out as soon as we came toward it. This man was a writer! Him? It was unbelievable. He was not dressed as I thought a writer should dress. His cap was pulled down low on his forehead. He had on a dingy white shirt and some loose-fitting brown pants that only came to his ankles and the top of his high-buttoned shoes. He took off his cap and I saw that his hair was dark brown, short, almost clipped. He ran his hand over his head." She described him as standing six feet tall and weighing about two hundred pounds, and she was evidently fascinated by his eyes. "They were blue," she wrote, "or gray. Deep. Shadowy. I couldn't tell from their expression whether he was happy or unhappy . . . I'll always remember his eyes and this meeting."[77]

"Howdy," Howard greeted her. "I liked his voice," she wrote, "It was pleasant. Not too high. Not too deep. Pleasant."[78]

They decided to go for a ride, and Price sat up front with Smith driving, while Howard climbed into the backseat. They talked about her attending Daniel Baker College and her forthcoming graduation. Howard then joked with her, "I was too dumb for college."[79] The conversation then turned to her greatest interest in him, how he started writing. Howard told her of the many jobs he had held and hated and decided to go into writing to get out of working. She asked him if writing was not work, and he replied, "Well, not by the sweat of your brow at any rate. You can stay home. All you have to contend with is a typewriter and it just puts down what you want it to. It doesn't swear at you when you do something wrong. If it does, you can whip it."[80] Price then told him she, too, had been writing recently and submitting to the confession magazines, but lamented that all she ever received were rejection notices with only an occasional word or two written on them. Howard fully understood and said, "We live on words of encouragement."[81]

They talked more about Howard's writing and Smith asked him, "Do you try to write like the guys who write for the magazines you write for?" Howard quickly replied, "Hell, no! I let them try to write like me." He then explained how he went about it: "After I read a lot of issues of a magazine to get the feel of what the readers want and of the things the editors look for, I sit down at my old trusty typewriter and bang out a yarn I think fits the pattern. Then I send 'em off. Some of 'em come back. If they've been the rounds, I throw 'em in an old trunk I have. Someday, they'll sell, and I'll be rich and famous." Curious as to how he started his stories, Price asked him, "Do you begin with a character or with a description of a place or with a plot?" Howard thought about it some and replied, "Every way, but mostly with a character, I suppose." Finally, the conversation turned to his latest character creation, and Howard told her, "That Conan's the damndest bastard I ever saw. He gets himself into all kinds of scrapes. I sure don't try to give him advice when he tells me all that junk. I just sit back and listen." Price likely gave Smith a curious glance, because he interpreted for her, "He's telling you that a real character has a mind of his own, even in a story."[82]

Eventually, Howard explained that he had to get back to take his mother somewhere, and they brought Price home. That night, she recorded everything in her diary, beginning with "I met Bob Howard today!"[83]

Howard often brought his mother to Brownwood with him, as he did when he took the month of April off that year. "I went south in the latter days of March," he wrote Lovecraft, "taking my mother with me, because I wanted her to escape the discomforts of a dry spring in this country which is always accompanied by stormy clouds, high winds and sand storms." They spent a few days in Austin before continuing to San Antonio. Texas began experiencing high temperatures at the beginning of May that would eventually bring drought to the area, so they returned home. "I wish we could have stayed longer," he continued, "because my mother has many congenial friends in San Antonio, and enjoys her visits there."[84]

When sharing information about his home state and some of his travels with August Derleth, Howard wrote, "There are hundreds of places in my own state I've never seen, though I've roamed over a goodly portion of it."[85] He did just that in 1933, for after his visit to San Antonio, he also made trips to Fort Worth and Dallas, as well as some of the smaller towns such as Waxahachie and Decatur.[86] The new Brownwood Lake became a frequent spot for him to visit, and he wandered around the many surrounding counties, including one visit to Fort McKavett in Menard County, where he had his picture taken standing among the fort's old ruins.[87]

The traveling appears to have been helping him fight off his chronic fatigue, as did his continued exercise program of "a daily short walk of eight or ten miles" and his "usual work with weights."[88] Howard also took up a particularly grueling form of exercise when he contracted for someone to cut down an oak tree and deliver the logs to his backyard between the house and the garage. "He would go out there in the afternoon," his neighbor Larry McDonough recalled, "with pants on a little below the knee and a T-shirt and . . . he would take the spike driving axe and sledge hammers and spikes and split those oak trees up. . . . Every damn day!" After cutting the log into firewood, he gave it to his neighbors; the Howards had no fireplace.[89] Despite some complaints of rheumatism and his continuing claims of a weak heart, Howard's health seemed to be faring well in 1933.[90]

Sometime that fall, Howard learned that Smith was to be married, so he and his friends got together to celebrate. "I well remember the last riot we went on before he got married," Howard later wrote Lovecraft. "He, Tyson, Vinson and I started to go somewhere to a movie, or some other innocent pastime, but we started drinking whisky, and that called for beer, and along about midnight we found ourselves in a den of iniquity in a county-seat town about fifty miles east of here. The beer was punk and the girls were worse—well, there was one I remember with pleasure, a blond with a figure like—well, no matter."[91] Smith married Rubye Barkley on November 17 in Lawton, Oklahoma.[92] Having been born on February 4, 1907, the new Mrs. Smith was a year older than her husband. As for Howard, it appears it was the marriage that began to erode their strong friendship.[93] "Hell, I aint' seen ol' Clyde in several months," Howard told a friend in December of the following year. "I kinda have the feelin' that his wife ain't got no hankerin' to have Clyde's drinkin' friends hangin' around."[94] The bacchanal before the wedding was one of the few remaining times Howard would see Smith before his death.

As the year came to a close, Vinson came to Cross Plains to spend Christmas there, and they drove to nearby Cisco and Ranger to see some of the latest movies.[95] After Vinson left Howard drove to Brownwood with his friends Lindsey Tyson, Dave C. Lee, and Bill Calhoun to attend the Golden Gloves boxing tournament.[96] On the way back, it was a dark and misty night and, as Howard later wrote Derleth, "I wound up the old year by wrecking my car and acquiring another scar."[97] As he explained in detail to Lovecraft, "We passed through a small town about fifteen miles from Cross Plains, where a steel flag pole was planted in concrete in the middle of the street. The pole was painted grey and was practically invisible. None of us saw it until we had hit it, head-on."[98] According to Roehm's photographic research, the pole in question was most likely a streetlamp.[99] Tyson later confirmed the accident "was not because of Bob's driving, none of us saw the thing before we hit it," and he noted that since they were traveling slow because of the weather conditions, "none of us were seriously injured."[100] Howard, of course, never one to let a good yarn go unspun, wrote his many correspondents about the incident, telling Clark Ashton Smith, "The fellow on the seat with me went through the windshield and I went partly through it, being checked by the steering wheel which was bent double on my breast bone." He then described their wounds, writing, "He got a bad gash on his head, and I got my jaw ripped open. A little lower and it would have been my jugular."[101] To Lovecraft he gave a highly detailed account that soon spread and grew through Lovecraft's many correspondents, so that in May of 1934, *The Fantasy Fan* reported on the accident, stating, "Robert E. Howard sustained some very painful injuries, severe cuts, crushings and wrenchings in an auto accident a few months ago . . . it would have killed anybody less tough than Howard."[102]

The repairs to the vehicle, if any, would not have helped his finances, for his sales were down from the previous year, totaling $962.25, approximately $22,000 in today's dollars.[103] The Depression continued to impact the publishing industry, and Howard lamented to Derleth, "I've seen so many of my hopes, plans and ambitions go up in smoke that I'm beginning to get fatalistic."[104] There was at least a glimmer of hope. "A few months ago," he told Derleth, "an old stand-by of mine, *Action Stories*, returned to the wars on a bi-monthly basis, but I've been so busy trying to learn to hammer out detectives that I haven't given it the consideration I intend to."[105] The pulp had published many of his Sailor Steve Costigan yarns before it went on hiatus, and, fortunately, in the new year, Howard did give it some consideration. In doing so he created one of his most successful characters ever: Breckenridge Elkins.

Chapter 24

Breckenridge Elkins and the Tall Tale Yarns, 1934

"I'm a whole blamed army by myself alone,
"I'm a straight hurricane and a twistin' cyclone!
"I can lick any guy from the Gulf to Powder River,
"Look a grizzly in the eye and make him shiver!"
—"Modest Bill"[1]

The beginning of 1934 brought both good and bad news for Howard. In addition to the last issue of *Magic Carpet* being released, he received a letter from the British publishing company regarding his short story collection. "The difficulty that arises about publication in Book Form," editor Hugh G. Schonfield explained, "is the prejudice that is very strong over here just now against collections of short stories."[2] He was, therefore, sending back the manuscript. The persimmon still hung too high in the tree.[3] His editor did, however, hold out some hope when he added "that any time you find yourself able to produce a full-length novel of about 70000–75000 words along the lines of the stories," he would be able to "sell a first edition of 5,000 copies."[4]

The truly good news was that the impact of the Depression on the pulp industry was beginning to ease. "Markets are opening up," Hugh B. Cave wrote. "New sheets are being planned for fall publication and old ones are boosting their present low prices and increasing their size. . . . Some of those old Fiction House titles will be revived, too."[5] One new magazine announced was *Jack Dempsey's Fight Magazine*, while Fiction House was starting up *Action Stories* again, and they were looking for manuscripts. Howard had been too busy trying to write detective stories, but as he had told Derleth the month before, he was going to consider it, writing, "I hope to work out a series, as I used to in the past with Steven Costigan, the fighting sailor."[6] It certainly proved beneficial to Howard that he did, for the series he developed was his most successful and profitable, featuring the larger-than-life Breckenridge Elkins. As Morgan Holmes explains, "From 1934 on, Fiction House's *Action Stories* was Robert E. Howard's main market, not *Weird Tales*."[7]

Howard had a penchant for telling tall tales, especially having grown up listening to his father and other older men share theirs. "Story telling was a favorite entertainment in the old days," Norris Chambers recalled, "and you never knew how many to believe. The old timers would talk for hours about the comic happenings around a country syrup mill."[8] It became a favorite of Howard's as well, for as Lindsey Tyson reminisced, "He could tell some tall tales, all right."[9]

One example of this can be found in a letter Howard wrote to Harold Preece in which he recounted testing his strength on a penny arcade grip machine he found in a hotel lobby. "I strode into the largest hotel in the town and without speaking a word to anyone," Howard wrote, "caught hold of the grip machine which was on a steel stand." He then explained what happened next: "I nearly tore it apart and lifted the stand clear off the floor and slid it around. Everybody gaped at me and a man asked me not to shake the hotel down, but I cowed him with a glare and stalked silently out, followed by the amazed stares of the humans who crowded the lobby." He was disappointed with the results, however, because, "Damn it to hell," he wrote, "I lacked a pound of making the record," all because of a "cut on my finger."[10] Howard was certainly good at telling these tall tales, for as he wrote of another author,

"Ten to one he was a damn liar in a lot of respects which is what makes a good story teller!"[11]

It was Howard biographer Mark Finn who first pointed out that folklorist Mody C. Boatright's essay "The Art of Tall Lying," published in the 1949 autumn issue of *Southwest Review*, is highly indicative of Howard's form of storytelling.[12] Boatright wrote in the essay, "The tall tale has come to be accepted as one of the most characteristically American forms of folk humor."[13] It is epitomized by the tall tales of fictional characters such as Pecos Bill and Paul Bunyan, and the fictional exploits of real people such as Davy Crockett and Buffalo Bill. Boatright explains that in America, "westward-moving men . . . were essentially realists," but that "their heroic literature took a comic turn; and in keeping with nineteenth-century ideals, their comedy was the comedy of exaggeration."[14] A good tall tale, Boatright believed, was rooted in realism for it must begin "plausibly and build carefully up to a climax," before turning into a tall lie, for "like all good burlesque," it "rests on a solid foundation of truth."[15]

Although the Texan Pecos Bill, created by Edward Sinnott "Tex" O'Reilly for the *Century Magazine* in 1917, seems the likely candidate for Howard's exposure to the literary tall tale, he once admitted to Derleth, "You mentioned Pecos Bill. I don't know much about that mythical hombre."[16] What he did know, however, were the popular Western tall tale stories written by W. C. (Wilbur Coleman) Tuttle that appeared regularly in his favorite pulp magazine *Adventure*.[17] Tuttle's stories were "out and out comedy Westerns," explains James Reasoner, "set in the towns of Pipe Rock and Blue Nose and populated by characters with colorful monikers such as Magpie Simpkins, Dirty Shirt Jones, and Telescope Tolliver."[18] Like all good tall tales, they were always "told in the first person and thick with vernacular and dialect."[19]

The first story in the Breckenridge Elkins series was titled "Mountain Man" and was published in the March–April 1934 issue of *Action Stories*. The style of the yarn and its sense of humor are evident from its very beginning:

> I was robbing a bee tree, when I heard my old man calling, "Breckenridge! Oh, Breckenridge! Where air you? I see you now. You don't need to climb that tree. I ain't goin' to larrup you."
>
> He come up, and said, "Breckenridge, ain't that a bee settin' on yore ear?"

> I reached up and sure enough, it was. Come to think about it, I had felt kind of like something was stinging me somewhere.[20]

Although generally agreed upon that humor is the hardest thing to write, Howard proved highly successful with the series.[21] While *Action Stories* had no forum by which to gauge reader reaction, the fact that from the publication of the first story through the October 1936 edition Howard appeared in every issue for a total of seventeen issues straight, with one more published in January 1937, is evidence of their popularity at the time.[22] And even when *Action Stories* rejected one Elkins yarn, Howard changed the character's name to Bearfield Elston and sold the story to *Star Western.* Still further, when Jack Byrne left Fiction House and took over as editor of *Argosy*, he asked Howard if he would be willing to write some Elkins-like tall tales for him. He was, and Howard created the character Pike Bearfield from Wolf Montana, Texas, who was featured in three more stories.[23] One last iteration was Buckner J. Grimes of Knife River, Texas, who appeared in two more tall tales published in *Cowboy Stories*.[24]

Fellow *Weird Tales* author E. Hoffmann Price, who enjoyed the series immensely, once commented to Howard that the Breckenridge Elkins dialogue sounded so real.[25] Howard was said to have replied, "Well, that's the way these ignorant bastards out in this part of the country just naturally think and talk and act. They don't know any other way, and I don't, either."[26] It seems Howard was good at self-deprecating humor as well.

"An English firm, after keeping a collection of my short stories for months, finally sent them back," Howard wrote Derleth, informing him they "suggested that I write a full length novel for them. But I'm not overly enthusiastic about it, for I've been disappointed so much. Of course, I'll do my best."[27] First, however, Howard had another Conan yarn to write, "The People of the Black Circle." Written over the months of January and February, the longest of the Conan stories to date came in at thirty-one thousand words. He sent the yarn to *Weird Tales* and, as Louinet elucidates, "Farnsworth Wright must have been impressed with it since less than five months elapsed between its acceptance and the publication of the first part of the serialization."[28] Appearing in the September, October, and November issues of the "unique magazine," Howard/Conan fans were elated. Harold F. Keating of Quincy, Massachusetts, said the serial "promises to be up to Howard's usual high standard," while Fred Anger of Berkeley, California, called it "Robert E. Howard's triumph," and Claude H. Cameron of Canada believed the "serial will make history for W[eird] T[ales]."[29] The most prolific letter writer, Jack Darrow, stated, "I'm glad to see Conan in a long story," and even his own mother, "Mrs. Jane Howard" of "Marlin, Texas," wrote that the serial "is one of his very best."[30] The first installment was voted the most popular story of the issue, while the serial's conclusion came in second.[31] Now Howard could reach for that persimmon once more.

According to Louinet, Howard's first attempt at a novel was the science fiction yarn titled *Almuric*.[32] Perhaps motivated by the *Astounding Stories* editor's suggestion that he try his hand at writing "pseudo-scientifics," or by Kline, his agent, who himself wrote Edgar Rice Burroughs–like planetary romance novels, Howard set about writing the tale of the troubled Esau Cairn of Earth. Teleported to the planet Almuric, the Conan-like Cairn battles to civilize his new home world.[33] Despite a flurry of writing for two weeks, Louinet continues, "he abandoned this idea and decided to make the novel a Conan yarn, for there had been some in the original proposal to Archer and, if it was rejected, he could always submit a Conan tale to Wright."[34] So *Almuric* was placed in his trunk and forgotten, but its ultimate fate was to be sold and published posthumously as a three-part serial in 1939. It also proved to be his last original publication to appear in *Weird Tales*. The novel was well received by readers, and the first installment was voted the most popular story of the issue.[35]

Howard next set about writing *The Hour of the Dragon*, the only Conan novel he ever wrote. Beginning the story on Saint Patrick's Day, March 17, and writing his submission letter on May 20, Howard wrote the novel in only two months.[36] What helped speed up the process of writing was that he engaged in a practice common in the writing industry at the time, what Raymond Chandler later called "cannibalizing."[37] Authors such as Chandler, who had made it an art form, drew upon the characters, plot devices, and descriptive passages from earlier works and combined them to create the single narrative of a novel. In this case Howard drew upon both "The Scarlet Citadel" and "Black Colossus" to begin the novel, before it eventually becomes a quest story as Conan seeks the jewel artifact known as "The Heart of Ahriman."

Despite having two stories to draw upon, Howard still spent long days writing and rewriting the novel, for in the end, according to Louinet, "Howard wrote five versions of his story, with several parts of these rewritten two or three times."[38] Although Howard liked to lay claim to the Conan stories coming so easily to him, that was a tall tale unto itself, for Howard worked incredibly hard on his stories, this novel especially. He then sent the manuscript to Schonfield and waited. He finally heard from him later that year, and it was not good news. "Just got a letter informing me that the English company which had promised to bring out my book had gone into the hands of the receiver," he wrote Derleth in October. "Just my luck. The yarn's in the hands of the company which bought up the assets, but I haven't heard from them." As Glenn Lord explained, "If he ever heard from the firm that bought up Denis Archer's assets, it was a negative answer."[39]

Fortunately, Howard's decision to write a Conan novel that could be sent to Wright in the event it was not accepted for book publication paid off. In late 1934 he submitted it to *Weird Tales* and Wright accepted it for publication, writing Howard that it was his "best Conan story so far," and Howard agreed with that assessment.[40] The novel premiered in the December 1935 issue and was serialized over a total of five issues, ending in April 1936. The first installment received overwhelming praise and was voted the most popular story of the issue.[41] One fan, Gertrude Hemken of Chicago, wrote that "*The Hour of the Dragon* has a gripping start—with an eye-flashing interest—Conan is just too grand—a reg'lar he-man."[42] Throughout the serial's publication, praise for each installment came in, and when its conclusion was published, that installment tied for first place in the April issue.[43] Reflecting the views of many *Weird Tales* readers, Hemken then wrote of the end of the tale, "And then I laid down my WT after having read the conclusion of *The Hour of the Dragon*—with a sigh of satisfaction—as of accomplishing a thing well done. The whole story was brimful of excitement, fun, eye-widening horror—it's just about the best

I've ever read in WT. Mr. Howard certainly created a dynamic character when he introduced Conan."[44]

He still, however, did not have a bound book publication to his name, and Howard doggedly tried again. "Perhaps not wishing to spend too much time on a venture that was shaky at best," Louinet explains, on his next attempt, "Howard simply took nine of his Elkins tales—stories already written, sold to, and published by *Action Stories*—and added a love element to string them together, writing four new tales to bridge the gaps and create some sense of continuity."[45] Later known as a fix-up novel, the book was episodic in nature, but because the stories sold well in the pulp market, Howard believed the novel might appeal to a book publisher.[46]

Once finished, he sent *A Gent from Bear Creek* to Kline, who received it on August 31, 1935.[47] The manuscript, only recently rediscovered in the early 2000s by Howard's first literary critic, Don Herron, is approximately 81,500 words in length with editorial marks for its preparation.[48] Kline first sent it to Caxton publishers, but as he wrote Howard on October 8, "I recently had an inquiry from an English publisher on four Western novels submitted to him some time ago. It has occurred to me that it might be well to offer them a carbon copy of your novel *A Gent from Bear Creek*. The American publisher who is considering the original has not yet reported."[49] After the novel was turned down by Caxton on November 9, Kline sent the manuscript to the English publisher Herbert Jenkins Limited.[50] There was a delay in sending it because Kline's agency needed to have a clean copy prepared, so it was not actually submitted until June of 1936. It was accepted in December of that year, six months after Howard had died, and published posthumously in 1937.[51] The actual number of copies printed remains unknown, but as of this writing only nineteen copies are known to exist.[52]

Howard had finally been able to reach the fully ripe persimmon, but he was just never able to enjoy it.

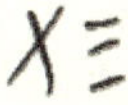

In early April of 1934, Howard received guests when E. Hoffmann Price and his wife, Wanda, came to Cross Plains for a visit. Howard had been familiar with Price's stories in *Weird Tales* beginning in 1929, and both had praised each other's works in "The Eyrie." When Howard learned that Lovecraft was visiting New Orleans in 1932, he sent a telegram to both Lovecraft and Price, helping to arrange a meeting between the two men.[53] "Price proved delightful," Lovecraft wrote Howard afterward. "I am surely indebted to you for putting him in touch with me." In the letter Lovecraft described Price as "a dark, handsome, rather small, wiry man of 34, with a small moustache." They apparently enjoyed each other's company because they met over three days for "25½, 10, and 9 hours each," Lovecraft noted. He then briefly detailed Price's background, telling Howard he was a "West Pointer, war veteran, Arabic student, Persian rug connoisseur, chess expert, fencing-master, abstruse mathematician, amateur coppersmith and ironworker," but having recently lost his job because of the Depression, he was now attempting to write full-time.[54] Therefore, when Lovecraft learned Price was going to visit Cross Plains, he wrote Howard, "I envy him the opportunity to call at the palace of Conan the Cimmerian."[55]

Price and his wife were traveling to California in his 1928 Model A Ford, which he affectionately referred to as "Juggernaut."[56] They made a number of stops along the way, the last being in Oklahoma, before they left for Cross Plains on the evening of April 7, 1934. "I drove down from Pawhuska, Oklahoma, by night," Price later recalled, "so that my 1933 license plates would be less conspicuous: my writing, augmented by work in an auto repair shop, had not been profitable enough to pay for current plates!"[57] They then drove 545 miles to Cross Plains on the dusty county highways of the time period. Despite Price's best-laid plans for avoiding the police, Howard explained how "Price was stopped at the Red River crossing by men with guns in their hands, looking for the famous outlaw Clyde Barrow, who was working in those parts at the time. As I told him, it was fortunate that his car was loaded with objects that evidenced his innocence, for Barrow was about his size, and was, like him accompanied by a blond young lady: Bonnie Parker."[58] It was a month later, on May 23, that Bonnie and Clyde were gunned down.

When they finally arrived late that evening, Howard was not there; he was out getting drunk with his friends while attending a football game. "When I got home, late that night," Howard explained, "the Prices had arrived, and

Ed, after waiting up for me for hours, had at last retired, so my drunk did me out of a few more hours of very enjoyable conversation."[59] Meanwhile, it had been Dr. and Mrs. Howard who welcomed the Prices into their home.

"His father, Isaac Mordecai Howard, M.D., welcomed us," recalled Price, while "Robert's mother was a soft voiced lady whose welcome made me feel that after a long trip, I had unexpectedly come home. One didn't feel like a guest."[60] Knowing "that Wanda must be dead tired," Mrs. Howard "hustled her off to rest."[61] The Howards had given up their front bedroom, which is where Mrs. Howard took Mrs. Price.[62]

Dr. Howard, meanwhile, ever the conversationalist, ushered Price into the living room. "Left without an ally," Price wrote of the doctor, "I had no chance with that parcel of concentrated energy." The good doctor immediately began asking questions. "I faced a grilling regarding *Weird Tales* and each one whose name had ever appeared on the magazine's letterheads."[63] "They are robbing my son," Dr. Howard then complained, before asking Price, "What do you think of those sons of bitches?" "Doctor," Price replied, "they rob us all, so I am getting into other [pulps], and so is Robert."[64]

As the doctor continued his grilling, Price began considering the man before him. "At times I got the notion that Dr. Howard rather than his son must have been the author," he reflected. "I mean the doctor looked the part. I can not ever remember having met another man who had such intent and penetrating blue eyes." He believed there was something in both his speech and appearance that "concealed something which made his son a writer."[65] Finally exhausted beyond measure, Price begged off to join his wife in slumber.

The following morning, "after tucking home a farm style breakfast," Price wrote, "I met Bob."[66] His first impressions of Howard were that "he was broad and towering, with a bluff, tanned face and a big, hearty hand, and a voice which was surprisingly soft and easy, not at all the bull-bellow one might expect of the creator of Conan."[67] Price, a native of California, was fascinated by his speech. "His was typical Texas talk, and he knew his medium: salty, rugged, volcanic, colorful—shot with whimsy, and set off with phrases of scriptural simplicity."[68] Price found it interesting how both father and son "from time to time garnished their speech with the quips and phrases I had already, or would later read in the published adventures of such autocratic heroes as Buckner J. Grimes of Knife River."[69] He did recall some oddities in his speech, noting how "he always pronounced the 'w' in 'sword,' very clearly; and 'wound'—that which Conan inflicted so prodigiously and lavishly—was invariably pronounced to rhyme with 'sound.'"[70] Howard's friends also recalled these oddities in Howard's speech, though Novalyne Price remembered having also been taught the same pronunciation of the word wound in school.[71]

After presenting gifts to one another—a bottle of sherry and Aguardiente from Price and a case of beer from Howard—they headed out for the day.[72] "Howard drove my wife and me to Brownwood, combining shopping and sightseeing," wrote Price, recalling how "it was fascinating to hear him tell the traditions and the anecdotes brought to mind by each landmark. More and more, I began to understand why his western burlesques were so convincing." Price began to realize that "Howard's material came from the land and the people of his childhood and his manhood."[73] What he could never seem to reconcile, however, were the stories with the man before him. His writing was "packed with whimsy and poetry which rang out in his letters, and blazed up in much of his published fiction," but "his face was boyish" and his blue eyes "had a wide-openness which did not suggest anything of the man's keen wit and agile fancy." Despite this, Price was steadfast in his belief that "the first picture persists—a powerful, solid, round faced fellow, kindly and somewhat stolid."[74]

There was one anecdote Price shared that puzzled both him and his wife. "We were driving . . . and were fascinated by Howard's yarns," Price explained, when "Suddenly, he took his foot off the throttle, cocked his head, idled down. We were approaching a clump of vegetation which was near the roadside. He reached across us, and to the side pocket. He took out a pistol, sized up the terrain, put the weapon back again, and resumed speed." Then, "in a matter of fact tone," Howard told them, "I have a lot of enemies, everyone has around here. Wasn't that I figured we were running into anything but I had to make sure."[75]

Price believed he was not kidding but could only attribute it to his imagination. When his good friend Tyson was asked about this, he replied,

"I do not believe that Bob had any real enemies that would like to do him harm. I believe that a vast majority of people who knew him, liked him."[76] Novalyne Price would recall a similar incident the following year in which they saw two men changing a tire, and Howard sped right by them without stopping to help. When asked about this he replied, "You have to be careful out in this country. You never know when you see a car like that whether it's someone needing help or someone ready to hold you up and take your life and your money."[77] Although his girlfriend thought it just an "act," Howard was not exaggerating about this. When the oil booms hit, many profit seekers took to hijacking and robbing people by posing as stranded motorists on the side of the road.[78] For instance, one Texas oil worker from that time period, Bill Ingram, later recalled in an interview one close call he had: "I'm comin' through that East Texas field and they tried to hold me up one time . . . just before daylight, a fella run out and flagged us. . . . We just drove right on. But it wasn't 100 yards till another 'un jumped right out, see. And I says, 'Hit that son of bitch, Bill; hit him!' . . . but he got outta the way. See you could tell—this one that was there, he thought I'd stop and the other one'd run up."[79] Howard may well have been exaggerating the incident, to tell a good story, but that story was rooted in reality.

Another anecdote came from later that day when Howard abruptly turned to Price and told him, "Ed, I am God-damn' proud to have you visit me." Price replied, "Hell, Bob, I don't see what *you've* got to be proud about."[80] In Price's opinion, between the two of them, Howard was the more important writer.[81] "It's this way," Howard tried to explain. "Nobody thinks I amount to much, and so I am proud to show these people that a successful writer thinks enough of me to drive a thousand miles to hell and gone out of his way to visit me."[82] Price came to understand the difficulties Howard faced as a writer in Cross Plains.[83]

On the way back home, Price learned that Howard did not smoke or drink hard liquor. "The lowest bastard I know," Howard explained, "goes for whiskey and tobacco, so to show my contempt for him and all his breed of stinkers, I turn down drinking and smoking." Price said his stern face then showed signs of a grin before he heard him emit a low chuckle. "Sure, I know I am inconsistent." Howard then said, "That low down skunk breathes, and so do I. Sometimes you've got to compromise in matters of principle."[84]

The following day, because Price was working on an oil field story, he was hoping to gain some insights into the local drilling operations. Howard drove Price out to an oil lease not far from Cross Plains, where they met an engineer who answered all his questions. On the way back home, Howard asked Price, "You sure he told you everything you wanted to know? Didn't hold out or cut you short?" Before Price could answer, Howard continued, "I'll go back and give him hell, none of these bastards can snub my friends!"[85] Price also came to understand just how deep Howard's feelings of persecution by the locals ran.

The Prices left for home on the morning of April 11, and over the summer Howard wrote to his many correspondents about their visit. "Yes, I did enjoy Price's visit here," he wrote Lovecraft, "my only regret was he was unable to stay longer. I hope to meet him again some time." As for Price, in years to come, one of his claims to fame became the fact he was the only author ever to meet Robert E. Howard.[86]

In June Truett Vinson accompanied Howard on a vacation to Carlsbad Caverns, New Mexico. "Vinson had his vacation and he spent a week with me," Howard wrote Lovecraft. "We had a most enjoyable time. I had an unbroken case of Sterling bock all ready when he arrived."[87] As Howard had previously explained to Derleth, "We had a county election for beer; Beer now flows freely in Cross Plains."[88] When Prohibition ended, the county had initially voted to go dry, forcing Cross Plains to do the same. The vote in May changed all that.[89] That was what they did the first night, drive around and drink beer.

"We were up early the next morning and on our way," Howard wrote of their trip. "I can not remember a more enjoyable day than that one, spent in whirling across the wind-whipped, sun-baked plains the direction I love best to go—southwestward."[90] They crossed the Pecos River in the afternoon, and "Carlsbad was reached well before sun-down." Howard described it to Lovecraft as "a beautiful little town, with broad streets over which giant cottonwoods, planted by the first settlers, form lofty green arches."[91]

The next morning they entered the caverns, and Howard was left speechless. "I can not describe the fantastic wonders of that great cavern," he wrote. "You must see it yourself to appreciate it." He tried, however, the best he could: "The entrance of the Cavern is gigantic, but it is dwarfed by the dimensions of the interior. . . . In the Cavern natural laws seem suspended; it is Nature gone mad in a riot of fantasy. . . . The coloring is really subdued, somber rather than sparkling. . . . We moved through a wonderland of fantastic giants whose immemorial antiquity was appalling to contemplate. God, what a story you could write after such an exploration!"[92]

To Howard the caverns were the highlight of the trip, for afterward they spent a short time in El Paso with an excursion across the border into Mexico. "I like El Paso," he wrote, "but Juarez is disappointing."[93] They then drove to the small town of Van Horn, where they spent the night, and the next day drove on to Fort Stockton, San Angelo, and finally Cross Plains, after which Howard noted, "The speedometer showed 1137 miles for four days travelling."[94]

Once Vinson left, Howard settled back into writing and, as he had told Price, he resumed "looking after" his parents.[95] He also took care of many things around the house, including milking the cow. "The cow, Delhi," whose name Tyson confirmed was "pronounced dell-high," was described by Howard as being "wild as a kite."[96] And he also took care of any stray cats that happened to wander by. "There was an addition of three to the feline community while Price was here," Howard wrote Lovecraft, "and since then a fourth kitten has wandered in from somewhere and been adopted."[97] Tyson explained he did enjoy feeding Delhi's milk to the cats, "to which he gave names like 'Mussolini' and 'Stalin.'"[98]

His health in early 1934 seemed to be good, for as he wrote Derleth that June, "I've turned out my usual amount of work, and have even gained several pounds. I started the spring weighing 194 and now tip the beam at 207."[99] What worried him, however, as always, was making sales and bringing in money. "My own prospects are, as always, shadowy, uncertain and nebulous," Howard wrote at the time. "I am doing a great deal of work but markets are unstable and checks are slow."[100] The pulp magazine that was notorious for paying slowly was *Weird Tales*, which is what prompted Dr. Howard to call the people at the magazine "robbers." Howard was not the only *Weird Tales* author owed payment for published stories; so, too, was Hugh B. Cave. "This business of waiting months and months for money isn't conducive to good work," he wrote, a sentiment no doubt shared by Howard.[101] This was what had motivated Howard to create the series character Breckenridge Elkins for *Action Stories*, as it was when he began writing the exploits of his childhood creation, El Borak. He needed outlets that paid.[102]

Chapter 25

El Borak and the Adventure Yarns, 1934

The night primeval breaks in scarlet mist;
The shadows gray, and pales each silent star;
The eastern sky that rose-lipped dawn has kissed
Glows crimson o'er the hills of Kandahar.
—"The Hills of Kandahar"[1]

"Lately I've been trying to break into some new markets," Howard wrote Lovecraft, particularly aiming his sights on those "specializing on the adventure angle."[2] Howard set about doing so by reviving one of the characters he had created in his childhood. "The first character I ever created was Francis Xavier Gordon, El Borak," he explained, and although he could not recall the basis for the character, he did know "he came to life in my mind when I was about ten years old."[3] The character may have filled his mind in 1916, but if he ever recorded any of his exploits that early, they have been lost to the ages. What has survived are a dozen fragments written in the early 1920s, when he was around the age of 16.[4] In this iteration of the character, he is simply named Frank Gordon, a Texan who seems to be a man of the world in pursuit of treasure and is referred to as "El Borak," which is

Arabic for "The Swift."[5] While the character may have been influenced by the novels of Sir H. Rider Haggard, three of which he owned, there is also the possibility the story ideas were heavily influenced by the tales of Talbot Mundy, who was appearing regularly in the pulp magazine *Adventure* with his exploits of a similar character he called Jimgrim.[6] Of these early efforts, it is known that Howard submitted at least one story, "The Iron Terror," to *Cosmopolitan*, which was rejected.[7]

When he began "splashing the field," a phrase he learned from E. Hoffmann Price (meaning to try to open up new markets), Howard revived and updated El Borak.[8] The new iteration was a "more fully-realized character," explains Howard scholar David A. Hardy, for "it is obvious that Howard the professional writer had somehow provided the later tales with a solid core of realism, based on research, that the younger Howard's work had lacked."[9] Gone was the man of the world, for Gordon's new background was that of a former gunslinger with strong Irish roots who had come from around the Texas border. Also gone were the treasure-seeking yarns, replaced with more mature tales focused primarily on issues of duty and justice.[10] Now, more flamboyantly named Francis Xavier Gordon, El Borak finds himself in Afghanistan, having gone native, not too unlike a British officer by the name of T. E. Lawrence.[11]

Thomas Edward Lawrence, more popularly known as Lawrence of Arabia, may well have served as the role model for the character's update. Lawrence had been trained as an archaeologist and, having studied Arabic, joined the British Army after World War I broke out in 1914. Due to his education, he was assigned to the Arab bureau of military intelligence, but it was Lawrence's involvement in the Arab Revolt of 1917/1918—an uprising of Arab forces against the Ottoman Empire with British support—that led to his fame. Between his successful strategies and bold exploits, he established himself as a leader of men, but he fell into disfavor with the British government when they learned he had gone native, especially in his advocacy for Arab independence. Lawrence wrote of these years in his 1927 book, *Revolt in the Desert*, a book that Howard owned.[12]

The first of the new tales were likely begun sometime in the summer or fall of 1933, and Howard submitted them to his agent once the stories were completed. Kline found a home for them in a new outlet for Howard, *Top-Notch.* The pulp first published in 1910, being one of Street & Smith's early forays into the pulp-paper magazines. Despite having in its pages stories by such authors as Jack London and Theodore Roosevelt, *Top-Notch* did not live up to its name for the most part.[13] What changed all that was some behind-the-scenes fallout from the Great Depression. After Clayton Publishing went bankrupt, one of its editors, F. Orlin Tremaine, began looking for work elsewhere. Finding employment with Street & Smith, he served as the editor of a number of magazines, including *Top-Notch.* According to Holmes, "Tremaine immediately began bringing in the best writers from other magazines," which included Clark Ashton Smith, H. P. Lovecraft, and Robert E. Howard.[14] The timing proved fortunate for Howard since his El Borak yarns tended to be longer than most pulps wanted, but it was exactly the length Tremaine was looking for. Kline began making sales with *Top-Notch* on Howard's behalf, but in the end, it was not an El Borak story that published first. Rather, it was that of another character Howard began writing about the same time—Kirby O'Donnell.

In some ways Howard split the early 1920s character into two, for unlike El Borak, Kirby O'Donnell is an Irish-American in Afghanistan who, disguised as a local Kurdish merchant, was seeking treasure. Howard first sent "Gold from Tartary" to Kline in November 1933, and soon after, in January 1934, its sequel, "Swords of Shahrazar."[15] Tremaine received both, but after passing on the first, he asked for revisions on the second story. As an editor he was evidently a stickler, for he asked Howard to make revisions twice before the story was finally published in the October 1934 issue of *Top-Notch.* Howard received $124.90 for it. The first O'Donnell story was then bought by *Thrilling Adventures* and retitled "The Treasures of Tartary." It was published two months later in the January 1935 issue and earned Howard $42.50.

Howard only wrote one other O'Donnell story, "The Trail of the Blood-stained God," which he sent to his agent in the fall of 1935. Kline sent it to an unknown number of editors, but it was rejected by *Thrilling Adventures* and possibly *Top-Notch.* Howard revised the story and sent it again to Kline, who received rejections from *Dime Adventure*, *Short Stories*, *Adventure*, and

Argosy. Its publication would have to wait another forty years. Fortunately, Howard had better luck with El Borak.

Only a few days before sending Kline his first O'Donnell tale, Howard had sent his agent "Swords of the Hills," his first Francis Xavier Gordon yarn. Like his last O'Donnell story, it, too, would have to wait another forty years to see publication. His second tale of El Borak, "The Daughter of Erlik Khan," received by Kline at the very end of 1933, met with greater success.[16] Tremaine accepted the story and published it in the December 1934 issue of *Top-Notch*, and after Kline took his agent fee, Howard received a check for $195.50, the equivalent of just over $4,000 in modern dollars. With its publication Hardy writes that after a long incubation period, Howard's El Borak yarns had reached maturity, for the story includes "a beautiful woman, a horde of bandits, heaps of treasure, and bloody battles to the death," and that "Howard juggles all these elements with skill and ease."[17]

Kline sold two more of Howard's El Borak adventures to *Top-Notch*, "Hawks of the Hills" and "Blood of the Gods," published in June and July 1935, respectively, and the former earned him the front cover. He sold one more, "Sons of the Hawk," to *Complete Stories*, which was published posthumously in August 1936 as "The Country of the Knife," and another to *Thrilling Adventures*—"Son of the White Wolf," which was also published posthumously in December of that year. Although the latter was his last written story of El Borak, one which Hardy calls his "most violent" and similar to Lawrence's novel, Howard had written one other yarn that he doggedly tried to get published without success.[18]

Howard originally wrote the adventure "Three-Bladed Doom" as a forty-two-thousand-word novella and sent it to Kline, who was unable to secure a sale. Howard then shortened the story to twenty-four thousand words, returning it in November 1934. The story would still not sell, and Howard tried rewriting it at least twice, but in the end six different pulp adventure magazines rejected it.[19] Despite this, the story contains an excellent description of El Borak's motivations. "One of the most persistent legends in circulation about Gordon was that he was an enemy of the English," Howard wrote, which he immediately reveals is not the case. Howard explains that Gordon "had no reverence for authority which bedecks itself in pomp and arrogance and arbitrary worship of precedence, and he did have an abiding contempt for certain types of officials, whether civilian or military."[20] The sentiment was certainly one Howard shared with his first character creation.

Although he was trying to splash new markets, *Weird Tales* remained Howard's steadfast publisher, and Conan, as he saw it, was his "bread and butter."[21] Before the end of spring 1934, Howard wrote one more tale of the Cimmerian titled "A Witch Shall be Born."[22] With this story, Louinet writes, "Howard was growing extremely confident with his creation as testifies the strength of the tale."[23] The boldest content of a Conan story up to that point in time most certainly had to be that yarn's depiction of Conan's crucifixion. Despite the automatic association with the crucifixion of Jesus Christ, the form of punishment had been used as a means of criminal execution, as well as for those deemed political or religious agitators, in many cultures and religions, and in pre-Roman times. Howard used the imagery to demonstrate Conan's dogged determination to fight while he still drew breath, for as Conan hangs on the cross, vultures begin circling down toward the dying man. Howard powerfully wrote,

> One dipped—dipped—lower and lower. Conan drew his head back as far as he could, waiting, watching with the terrible patience of the wilderness and its children. The vulture swept in with a swift roar of wings. Its beak flashed down, ripping the skin on Conan's chin as he jerked aside his head; then before the bird could flash away, Conan's head lunged forward on his mighty neck muscles and his teeth, snapping like those of a wolf, locked on the bare, wattled neck. Instantly the vulture exploded into squawking flapping hysteria. Its thrashing wings blinded the man, and its talons ripped his chest. But grimly he hung on, the muscles starting out in lumps on his jaws. And the scavenger's neck bones crunched between his powerful teeth.[24]

Consisting of such powerful scenes as that, "It was accepted with relish by Farnsworth Wright," states Louinet, and it was "published on the heels of four consecutive issues of *Weird Tales* starring the Cimmerian, and once again won the cover."[25]

After censoring several of the passages, Wright published it in the December 1934 issue and included a sidebar about the story's author.[26] "Back in 1925, when Robert E. Howard was a college student, specializing in anthropology," it erroneously began, Wright wrote how "many thousands of readers eagerly buy any magazine that features one of Mr. Howard's stories." Wright then effusively praised him when he continued, "He has the faculty of making real characters of his heroes, not mere automatons who act as they do merely because the author pulls the strings . . . these are literary creations that fairly live and breathe, so graphically does the author portray them." Writing in praise of "A Witch Shall be Born," Wright claimed, "Mr. Howard is at his best in the strange and thrilling—and at time blood-chilling—novelette."[27] The readers of *Weird Tales* agreed.

Letters received by Wright and published in "The Eyrie" noted the story "was a humdinger" and "the most exciting WT novelette in a long while."[28] Julius Hopkins of Washington, DC, called it one of Howard's "best Conan tales" and wrote, "His description of Conan on the cross causes one to feel the agony suffered by the giant barbarian."[29] Alvin Earl Perry of Rockdale, Texas, more colorfully wrote, "Every blood-dripping line of every heroic page in this latest Howard orgy is delightfully 'disemboweling,' so to speak; in other words, I think the yarn is swell!"[30] And fellow *Weird Tales* author C. L. Moore sent a letter directly to Howard writing, "That 'Witch' story was pretty strong meat, but perfectly grand. Such a lustiness about your stories when you want them that way. And the witch herself was gorgeous. O dear, I'm consumed with jealousy."[31] Two months later Wright declared that it was the favorite story of the December issue, and it was the only story he mentioned.[32] As Louinet rightfully commented, "Howard had every reason to be confident."[33]

Howard, it seems, also felt confident enough in his finances that he decided to purchase a new car, a 1935 Chevrolet Standard. Little is actually known about when and where he purchased the new vehicle, but based on Roehm's research, it was probably in the late summer or beginning of fall from the Anderson Chevrolet Company in Cross Plains. The Standard was a four-door automobile with "suicide doors" in the back, meaning the hinges were placed toward the back of the car.[34] It described what could happen in an age of faulty door latches with the possibility of the wind opening up the door while the car was in motion. To close the door in that situation with no seatbelts available could, indeed, prove suicidal. The Standard also had a square top and no front-end suspension, making for a rough ride over dusty country roads. Nearly everyone recalled the vehicle as having been black in color.[35]

James Cross, the manager of the Magnolia Service Station in town, next door to Anderson Chevrolet, spoke of Howard and his 1935 Standard in a later interview. "He was a good customer," Cross recalled. "I washed & lubricated his car; he got gas there all the time."[36] When Howard went there to fill up his tank, he evidently always went alone, for Cross never remembered him having anyone in the car with him. He did share with the interviewer, Charlotte Laughlin, one anecdote about Howard. "One day he stepped out of his car and slipped on a greasy spot. His feet went straight out from under him, and he landed on his behind, but he practically bounced back to his feet as 'quick as a cat.'" "I ought to sue this goddamn place!" Howard roared, before starting to laugh, commenting to Cross on how fast he managed to regain his feet: "That just goes to show you what a good boxer I am!"[37]

In November 1934 Leroy Butler and his wife, Floyce, moved back into the family home next door to the Howards, after having lived in Brownwood for the previous six years. Although they stayed less than a year, they did share some memories of Howard and his father from that time. Mrs. Butler remembered all the "arguments" between "father and son."[38] Dr. Howard loved to argue and debate, and because his son had strong opinions, too, there were many evenings spent debating and arguing particular points.[39] She also recalled, however, that after some of those exchanges, "I'd hear Doctor Howard coming out whistling. He could really whistle."[40] As far back as their time spent in Cross Cut, neighbors recalled Dr. Howard whistling.[41] One neighbor in Cross Plains, Larry McDonough, who was 10 years old in 1934, also later recalled, "He could whistle, beautiful music." He remembered hearing the doctor whistling when he would walk over to their house for a meal. "We'd hear him coming and mom would start putting on meat and he wanted two big slabs of pork and four eggs," and then with a chuckle he added, "He ate a huge amount. And you'd hear him coming whistling."[42] Tyson also shared one anecdote about the doctor's whistling. One morning, upon hearing the doctor walking up the street whistling loudly, Tyson commented to him, "Dr. Howard, you must be very happy this morning." He remembered him replying, "Lindsey Tyson, when you hear me whistling like that you will know that I am a mad S.O.B."[43] Angry, hungry, or in a good mood, it seems, regardless, friends and neighbors remembered Dr. Howard for his whistling.

As the end of the year approached, the Howards celebrated Christmas together. "I had a very quiet Christmas," Howard wrote Lovecraft, adding, "I didn't even have anything to drink." Before the holiday Howard had given a friend a much-needed ride, and he repaid his kindness with a fresh turkey. The Howard family had the gift for Christmas dinner and Howard recalled, "I believe it was the fattest, finest turkey I ever set tooth in."[44]

As the year closed, Howard assessed his financial status from sales that year and he found himself quite pleased. "My income for the year of 1934 has been a considerable improvement over 1933," he wrote Derleth, but he was unsure what the next year would hold, approaching it with "scanty optimism."[45] It had clearly been a prosperous year, for Howard had been able to pay cash for a new vehicle primarily because he had nearly doubled his earnings from 1933, earning the equivalent of over forty thousand in modern dollars.[46]

There had been one other significant event in Howard's life in the fall of 1934, and that was when Novalyne Price came back into his life.

Chapter 26

Novalyne Price, 1934–1935

I have felt your lips on mine
Your hair has veiled my eyes
When my blood was wild as singing wine
And star-gold flecked the skies.
—"Love"[1]

Having graduated from Daniel Baker College in May of 1933, Novalyne Price found a position teaching English in a rural school near Abilene.[2] The following year, however, she was going to have to teach home economics and that, as she wrote, "really scared me!" She hated home economics and personally professed to be a truly bad cook. She was elated, then, when her cousin Enid Gwathmey informed her of an opening where she was teaching—the Cross Plains High School. "My cousin Enid," Price wrote, "saved my life!" Because she still wanted to be a writer, English was certainly a better subject to be teaching, but there was another reason that appealed to her, for she wrote, "Cross Plains! Cross Plains, Texas. Bob Howard's home town."[3]

Because even aspiring writers need to write, Price kept a journal during the time she lived and taught in Cross Plains, from 1934 to 1936.[4] "These diaries and journals are good practice," she wrote after having written in them for several months. "They are filled with my thoughts, my fears, my hopes, things I love, and things I hate, how the weather affects me."[5] They remained a private affair until 1986, when she published the entries dealing with her relationship with Robert E. Howard. She titled the book *One Who Walked Alone*, because of something Howard had said to her. After regaling Price with stories of Alexander the Great, Howard told her how he had declared himself a god but after that, "He became very lonely, and it was the beginning of the end for him." Howard then turned to her and said, "But remember this, girl. The man who chooses to follow a dream to its bitter and ultimate end, walks alone."[6] As it proved a prescient statement, she chose it for the title of her book.

On August 27, 1934, Price went to Cross Plains to interview for the position before the high school board of trustees. The superintendent of the Cross Plains schools, Nat Williams, asked Price about courses in English she had received and her experience in teaching public speaking. She told the board about her background in both, including having taught children expression in order to pay her way through college.[7] Price wrote how awkward she felt during the interview and that she was unsure if the board would offer her the position. When the interview was finished, Williams told her that the board would be meeting that afternoon, and she could return at four o'clock to learn their decision.

Price and her cousin spent the intervening hours in downtown Cross Plains. "On any other day, I would have loved Bob Howard's town," she wrote of her nervousness in the journal, for "It was a typical southwest town. Quiet. Sprawling. Nice, well-kept yards with trees and a profusion of flowers. On any other day, I would have loved the rows of stores bordering the wide, wide main street that cuts through the town and led straight to the school yard. Today, I didn't love anything. We ate lunch at a little café next door to Smith's drugstore and across from the post office. After lunch, we crossed the street to Higginbotham's."[8] Upon returning to the high school at four o'clock, Price learned she had had little to worry about; Mr. Williams informed her that she was to be the new teacher of public speaking in the English department.[9]

Price moved to Cross Plains at the beginning of September for the new school year, which was set to open on September 10, 1934.[10] She moved into a room at Mrs. Hemphill's house, a new brick home located near the school, where she had a roommate. It was a flurry of activity, between the moving, attending meetings, and preparing her lessons plans, so Price had little time to think of "Bob Howard." Once she settled in, however, that all changed.

Price, her cousin, and some of the other teachers went to Smith's drugstore for lunch one day. The City Drug Store had been purchased by Mr. and Mrs. Jesse Peyton Smith in 1932 and was a popular establishment in town.[11] As they sat around talking, Price noticed when "an elderly man came out from a little room in the back of the drugstore and walked toward the front." She recalled him being a "big man" with a "loping gait" who tipped his hat to the ladies at the table and said, "Good evening." She asked Mrs. Smith who the man was and she replied, "That's Dr. Howard." Price then asked Mrs. Smith if she knew Bob Howard, and that set the ladies at the table into a flurry of conversation. One of the teachers commented, "Well, I think he's kind of a freak," and another added, "I've heard he's crazy."[12]

Price, ignoring them, asked Mrs. Smith if Howard ever came into town to hang out, and she replied, "Oh, Lord, no. Sure. I see him go across the street at the post office. Sometimes, he comes downtown with his mother, but Lord, no, I never see him hanging around town."[13] While the others continued making derogatory comments, Mrs. Smith made an attempt at being more civil, stating, "I don't think he's crazy, but he is a little peculiar. Personally, I don't care much for the things he writes either. Dr. Howard brought one of his stories to the store once, and I read it. It was all about men fighting and killing each other. I didn't enjoy it much."[14]

Incensed by the treatment of Howard by her cousin and fellow teachers, Price became defiant and stated she had met Howard and was going to call him on the telephone. When she did so, much to her friend's amusement, Mrs. Howard answered the phone. When Price asked if Bob Howard was there, she replied, "No. Robert isn't here." After telling Price he was in

Brownwood, Mrs. Howard added she had no idea when he would return. Price then boldly asked her, "Is he still writing?" and Mrs. Howard replied, "Of course, he's still writing," for which Price noted in her diary, "She sounded shocked."[15] Price then asked her to let Howard know she called; after hanging up the receiver, she realized the phone call had not quite gone as she had anticipated.

Howard never called back, and after trying again, and again, and again, only to be told he was still not there, that he was in Brownwood, Price decided she would pay a personal visit to see for herself. Her cousin, along with some fellow teachers, gave her a ride one evening to the Howard home, telling her they would wait for her. Price approached the house, writing that night in her diary, "A thousand impressions impinged on my mind as I went down the walk. The house was average. A white frame house in need of paint. The walk was average. The yard was average, no better than the yards next door. Nobody here had done anything spectacular about the place he lived in." She climbed the steps to the porch, and it was then, she wrote, "I could hear the sound of a typewriter and someone talking at the very top of his voice. It sounded as if somebody were reading from a book while someone else typed. I stood still at the door, listening. Bob was writing and talking at the top of his voice as he wrote."[16] "Conan was as much a part of this wilderness as Balthus was alien to it," she might have heard,

> The Cimmerian might have spent years among the great cities of the world; he might have walked with the rulers of civilization; he might even achieve his wild whim some day and rule as king of a civilized nation; stranger things had happened. But he was no less a barbarian. He was concerned only with the naked fundamentals of life. The warm intimacies of small, kindly things, the sentiments and delicious trivialities that make up so much of civilized men's lives were meaningless to him. A wolf was no less a wolf because a whim of chance caused him to run with the watch-dogs.[17]

It was the combination of hearing how others spoke of Howard and how he composed his stories that quickly led Price to understand why the townspeople had come to alienate him so much. "Bob doesn't fit the pattern people have cut out for Dr. Howard's son," she wrote. "A lot of people laugh and say he's crazy, but that doesn't make him crazy. By whose standards do you judge a man?" She knew a town set certain standards and "if you break those standards, the town thinks you're crazy," so that in Howard's case, she wrote, the town claimed, "You can't be a writer. You can't sit at a typewriter all day pounding out pulp yarns. If you do, you're lazy and good-for-nothing." The problem, she realized, was that no one ever stopped to consider or accept the idea that writing for the pulp magazines was a legitimate profession.[18]

Price knocked on the door and waited. The door opened and Dr. Howard, she wrote, grunted, "Yeah?" She asked to see "Bob Howard," but Dr. Howard did not open the door. Price asked again, noting that the typing had stopped. Dr. Howard, she wrote, then turned and called out, "Mamma. There's somebody here to see Robert. She can't see him, can she?" From somewhere inside the house, Price heard Mrs. Howard beginning to say he was busy, as Howard himself came and opened the door. "In a friendly way," she recalled, he said, "Come in."[19]

Ushered into the living room, she noted it was rather "ordinary," a fact that seemed to continue surprising her about a professional writer. Mrs. Howard joined her husband, and Price noted that his father was "more painfully shy than Bob," while his mother's "hair was nearly white, short, and parted on one side, not stylish," and that "she got up with a great effort and stood leaning slightly to one side."[20]

After introductions were made, Price said she only really had a few minutes, since her friends were waiting for her. Howard suggested that he could give her a ride home, so Price went out to tell her cousin not to wait. The ladies were certainly quite shocked, but departed nonetheless. When Price came back, Howard asked, "Were they afraid to leave you in my tender care?" She laughed it off saying they just did not want it to cause any trouble, to which Howard replied, "Trouble? No trouble. A man doesn't get a chance to take a pretty girl home every moonlit night. It's the harvest moon, you know, a time of great rejoicing and honor to Ceres."[21]

Price then began asking Howard about his writing. They talked, and he told her, "I'm working on a Conan yarn now. I don't know whether it will sell or not, but I'm working on it. I figure the law of averages will give you sales if you keep pounding them out."[22] The Conan story was to become one of his most popular, "Beyond the Black River." "He's my bread and butter," he told her. "I do bang out a western or adventure yarn now and then, but, mostly, I go along with Conan."[23]

Howard asked her if she would like to go for a ride, and Price readily agreed. After telling his parents, Price heard Mrs. Howard comment, "That's all right, honey. You go right ahead. Forget about me if you can!"[24] He came back out, took Price's hand, escorted her down the front steps, and opened the car door for her. "I felt very happy," Price wrote that night, "comfortable, very much at ease."[25]

Perhaps it was her comfort that led her to comment that he had had been in Brownwood a lot lately. "Brownwood?" he replied, "Hell, I haven't been to Brownwood in months." Despite knowing that Mrs. Howard had lied to her, she pressed the issue, which Howard claimed must have been a misunderstanding. Perhaps realizing his family needed an explanation, Howard told her, "My family. . . . They're damn good to put up with me staying around home writing all the time. Everybody in this town thinks I ought to be out working at some kind of job. That's hard on my family. And so I just tell them to hell with what people think. When I'm writing, I'm working. You know I'm working. To hell with everybody else. So when I get going on a yarn and somebody calls me, just tell them I'm working, or something like that."[26] Mrs. Howard had at least partly been protecting Howard's time writing, knowing full well that for him to be productive he could not be disturbed. Other writers have also guarded their writing time closely, such as fellow Texan Katherine Anne Porter, who once wrote that when she was writing, "I don't want to speak to anybody or see anybody. Perfect silence."[27] The other reason was likely Price's aggressive manners, for calling a man on the telephone or calling upon him at his home were not the things a proper lady did according to Mrs. Howard's upbringing.

In the end Howard proved to be quite a charming man on the car ride. Noting the moon he said to her, "That's a beautiful harvest moon, if I do say so myself." She laughed and commented, "I suppose you're responsible for the moon," to which Howard replied, "By all means. That moon was designed especially for you." She then coyly queried, "You knew I was coming?" to which Howard responded, "Oh, yes, I was going along with 'ol Conan and all that cr—stuff, and, all of a sudden, you popped up out of the typewriter." Reaching over, he took her hand, saying, "Yes, sir. You popped up out of the typewriter, and I said, 'Now, Bob Howard, you big, ugly lummox, there's a girl who's going to appreciate your moonlight.'" He continued, "Here I am, pounding out words and poems and singing to high heaven and looking up and ordering moons, and do you know anybody who can appreciate them? Of course, Novalyne Price could," and he told her, "You're one in a million girl. One in a million."[28] As she recalled much later in life, Howard certainly had the "ability to be compassionate, witty, and charming."[29]

Although their outing seemed to be going well, Price was surprised when Howard turned the car around and began heading back into town. Howard explained to her, "I—I have to give my mother a dose of medicine. It's time for it now. Do you mind if I stop and run in and give it to her? Then I'll take you home." She had little choice but to agree and after Howard did so, she asked him why Dr. Howard did not give the medicine to his mother. Again, Howard found he had to explain himself, "Well, it's my job. My dad is gone a lot of the time. When he's home, he has to try and get some sleep. No telling when somebody will knock on the door for him to get up and go take care of a sick baby, man, or woman."[30]

After arriving at Price's boardinghouse, Howard did pose one serious question to her, and that was about her and Smith. Despite the fact Smith was now married, he wanted to make sure she still did not carry a torch for him. She explained they were just friends, and so, pleased with the answer, he asked her out on a date the following night, to which she readily agreed. Before he left, he told her, "And about that moon. That's a beautiful moon, if I do say so myself. I'll order another one tomorrow night."[31]

Their first official date proved a rather rocky affair. Price had dressed up in a dress, gloves, and hat, so imagine her surprise when Howard came in wearing, "No coat! No tie! . . . a dingy white shirt, open at the collar!" and his hands "clutching an old floppy cap, turning it round and round." One look at Price and Howard stammered, "Well—Well—I—I didn't know—"[32]

Recovering, Howard remembered he had brought her a gift. "You said you'd like to read some of my stuff," he reminded her, "so I—I brought you a copy of this magazine that's just come out . . . it's—it's got a yarn of mine in it. I thought you might like to look at it." The magazine he handed her was the August 1934 issue of *Weird Tales*, sporting a cover by Margaret Brundage of Howard's hero Conan fighting a giant serpent that coiled itself around him, while at his feet, on her knees, was a half-dressed, blonde-haired woman leaning back and looking up at her defender. "My eyes bulged," she wrote later that night.[33] Sensing her discomfort, Howard turned the conversation to their plans for the evening. "I didn't think about going to a show or anything," he told her. "I just thought maybe we'd drive around a little while." That did not go over well either, but he did add, "Ride around with a pretty girl, that is," which did.[34] In many ways this became endemic of their relationship. Howard managed to do and say things that caused both a negative and positive response with Price, sometimes in the same sentence. Howard never professed to understand women, and Price was, after all, his first girlfriend.

They drove north to the town of Cisco, where they stopped at a drugstore for a soda. The conversation was predominately about writing and eventually turned to his newly published Conan yarn, "The Devil in Iron." Out of this came a discussion of civilization versus barbarism. She wanted to write of civilization, but he wrote of barbarism, so he tried to explain, "The people who read my stuff want to get away from this modern, complicated world with its hypocrisy, its cruelty, its dog-eat-dog life. They want to go back to the origin of the human race. The civilization we live in is a hell of a lot more sinister than the time I write about. In those days, men were men and women were women. They struggled to stay alive, but the struggle was worth it."[35] The topic would arise time and again in their discussions and debates, for which Howard told her, "In this civilization we live in, they get more depraved and demonic all the time. I'll tell you, girl, it's a hell of a world we live in. . . . Greed. Corruption. Selfishness. That's our civilization."[36] And on another occasion, he told her, "When a civilization begins to decay and die, the only thing men or women think about is the gratification of their body's desires. They become preoccupied with sex. It colors their thinking, their laws, their religion—every aspect of their lives."[37] Looking back over her lifetime in a later interview with Rusty Burke, she told him, "[Howard] predicted the evils, the grossness that civilization would fall into" and how "the abnormal becomes normal," leaving her to conclude, "It seems to me he was pretty prophetic."[38]

They drove around some more, and Howard regaled her with many stories. He was certainly a different man than the ones she had previously dated, and she could not help but admit he had certain qualities she found attractive. "I watched Bob's face in the dim light," she wrote, "He was a good-looking man . . . aloof . . . accustomed to being alone a lot, but now enjoying immensely the pleasure of a good listener." She liked his voice, for it was "vibrant, full, pleasant, rising and falling with the excitement of battle, or racing across changing terrain" and she noted how, "he spoke with authority." She listened avidly to his descriptions she felt were so vivid they left her "amused. Fascinated. Uncertain."[39]

On their next date, Howard adjusted to Price's disappointments with their first. He brought no magazine with a lurid cover, and he had donned a suit and was wearing a fedora. As she recalled, "At one-thirty on the dot, Bob's car stopped in front of the house. I peeped out the window of my room and nearly fainted! I honestly didn't know that good-looking man who got out of the car and started toward the house. He had on a nice brown suit with a vest and tie, a tan hat settled debonairly over his right eye. I was so excited when I opened the door, it was all I could do not to throw my arms around his neck and hug him." Instead, she told him he looked "swell," to which he grinned and replied, "This fool hat kinda bothers me. It's not the kind of hat I ought to be wearing." She asked what kind of hat he should be wearing, and he replied, "Well, you take these hats the Mexicans wear—sombreros. Now, there's a hat for you. It's the kind of hat you need in this part of the country. Keeps the sun off real good."[40] She laughed and commented it was a pretty day, to which he told her, "For a fall day. This is a bad time of year, girl. A dying time of year. Things are in their sere and yellow leaf."[41] She did not realize until later that he had been quoting from Shakespeare's *Macbeth* (act 5, scene 3), in which the bard had written, "My way of life is fall'n into the sere—the yellow leaf," a metaphor for old age.

As they headed to his car, he complimented her on her dress and perfume, and still amazed at how handsome he looked all dressed up, she told him, "I hope you'll have your picture made for me in that outfit."[42] He did, including one while wearing the hat, despite the fact, as he told Lovecraft, "I detest the thing."[43] Nevertheless, that photograph has become the most iconic image of Robert E. Howard.

The picture pleased her to no end, as did many things about Howard while they were dating, at least in the first five months. "I've never before dated a man who can talk on so many different subjects nor one who uses words so beautifully," she wrote of his storytelling. "Let him describe a scene from history, or a cowboy riding these Texas hills in search of adventure, and I hear English spoken at its best. I think, then, I could fall in love with him."[44] She liked how at the end of the day he would point out to her, "Look at that sunset. Just you look at that sunset! Only in Texas do you ever see a sunset like that." As she wrote in her diary, "No other man I'd ever known had stopped to look at a beautiful sunset."[45]

Price also shared Howard's love for reading and for poetry. She recalled how on one date he quoted some lines, rather "badly," from Rudyard Kipling's "The Ballad of East and West." Howard had hit upon Price's expertise, which was expression, for she then recited the ballad from memory, along with several others. Impressed, Howard told her she "could recite poetry better than any woman he'd ever heard, except his mother."[46] The praise pleased her; the mention of his mother riled her.

Howard later shared some of his own poems with her, including "To a Woman" and "One Who Comes at Eventide," of which she wrote, "both of them leave me rather speechless." She elaborated, "I am speechless because they tie in with some of the things he keeps talking about. They also tie in with another thing I feel deep inside him, a thing he tries to hide from himself."[47] These were glimpses of Howard's dark side, of which she pondered but realized, "It is not even necessary to remind myself that Bob is a good man, a kind and thoughtful man, a little troubled perhaps."[48]

She loved his kindness. "Underneath the waving, and ranting, knocking the steering wheel all around," she knew, "he was a very kind man. Very, very sweet, kind man."[49] She loved his openness to her, for he would often preface things he would say to her with, "I'll say this to you, but I wouldn't say it to anybody else . . ."[50] And she loved how he wrote letters to her, even though they lived in the same town, as well as the pet names he had for her. It had started when he called her, "My Cherished Little Bunch of Onion Tops" or "My very dear Beans, Cornbread and Onions," because she had eaten beans with little green onions and cornbread before one of their dates, and he told her every man should address his girl with the names of things "close to his heart—his stomach."[51] And she loved his humor, recalling one anecdote that after receiving several of the envelopes with his letters unsealed and he confirmed with her he had sealed them, his next letter was addressed, "Dear Novalyne and Members of the Cross Plains Post Office Staff."[52] He made her laugh.

She also loved the attention he gave her, once writing how happy it made her feel and how "it's great to have a friend you can depend on."[53] And she loved the attention he gave both her mother and grandmother. "I loved the way he was at ease when I introduced him," she wrote in her diary, adding, "I liked the way he gave his attention to Mother and Mammy."[54] He asked them many questions and would listen intently to the stories they told.[55] Howard especially enjoyed listening to the stories Mammy told of the Civil War, its aftermath, and the tales of witches and ghosts she recalled from her childhood.[56] "It amuses me and always makes me want to hug him," she wrote of those visits, for she knew, "He makes Mammy feel just his age and all the time she's talking about something that happened more than seventy years ago."[57]

Still, there were many things about Howard she did not like. She once complained that "Bob swears an awful lot. Every other word is either 'damn,' or 'hell,' or 'goddamn,' or some other swear word."[58] She did not like the fact he could be rather shy, and how he refused "to go where he'd have to be around a large group of people."[59] She also complained that while "Bob was so willing to take me to Brownwood, . . . he wouldn't go anywhere in Cross Plains with me, not even to a high school football game."[60] And while she loved to hear him tell stories, he would get so wrapped up in the telling she felt he "had forgotten me."[61]

She also did not like what he did when he "got an idea for a whopping fight yarn," for he would commence "shadow boxing as he walked down the street," accompanying "the shadow boxing with words!"[62] This was one of his behaviors that led many town residents to call him "a nut" or a "crazy man," and it left Price embarrassed or, at least, embarrassed for him.[63] Howard was not the only author who exhibited such behaviors, for literary historian Celia Johnson wrote of other authors who did similar things, including William Butler Yeats when he was composing poetry. "The poet would barrel through city streets like a tornado," she explained, and "he'd wave his arms and mutter as he walked, so absorbed in his musings that he lost track of the world around him."[64] Johnson, of course, knew that such "quirks are great fodder for gossip and can morph into gross exaggeration when passed from one person to the next," concluding there is simply "no way to escape the self-mythologizing particularly when dealing with some of the greatest storytellers that ever lived."[65]

Price could relate to this type of behavior to a point, for she did recall an incident in which she was rehearsing a scene in a play, using hand gestures while she was driving down the street. Price, however, wrote that, "When I saw that somebody was watching me, I stopped rehearsing immediately and turned my car in the opposite direction." "Bob," on the other hand, would keep "on shadow boxing, telling himself that he didn't care what people thought of him." Of course she did not believe him. "I knew he did care, very much," she wrote, "but was just too stubborn to admit it."[66]

One other thing Price did not like much about Howard were his parents. She usually wrote that when she did have contact with Dr. Howard, he was gruff, mumbled, and cussed a lot. It was Mrs. Howard, however, with whom a tension had been present at the very beginning and continued to build. She did not perceive Howard's mother as being as sick as she claimed, clearly not understanding the nature of her illness. She also felt Mrs. Howard was too protective of her son, and that he was too tied to his mother. There were certain incidents that reinforced this for Price. As she later learned from Mrs. Smith, there had been an exchange between Dr. and Mrs. Howard on the first day she went to visit Howard at the house. "Dr. Howard told me," explained Mrs. Smith to Price, "that when you and Robert left for him to bring you home, he looked at Mrs. Howard and said, 'Mother, are we going to lose our boy?'" Mrs. Howard was said to have replied, "No. Don't worry about that. We're not going to lose him."[67]

On another occasion Howard told her of a question his mother had asked about Price: "My mother asked me if you didn't have a lot of Indian blood, maybe as much as half-Indian." He explained that his mother had once lived in Oklahoma, and she felt they were all "dirty, thieving rascals who came around at night, stealing, burning, murdering." Price, incensed at the line of questioning, wrote in her diary that night, "I thought: well, that woman! She doesn't like Indians. She doesn't like me."[68]

And there was another odd encounter the day after Christmas that year when she had gone to the Woolworth's in Brownwood. While at the store counter purchasing some items, she happened to look up and saw, as she wrote in her diary, "Mrs. Howard was standing there, looking at me." Howard had not seen her, but Mrs. Howard had. Price recounts what happened next: "Mrs. Howard was standing straight and tall. We looked at each other and neither of us gave any sign of recognition, but she knew me and I knew her! She said something to Bob; he looked up, smiled, and spoke. I spoke, got my change, the things I'd bought and beat it out of there. I'd never had any woman stare at me with such malevolence before."[69] It was an awkward situation for sure, and one that continued to foster the tension between the two women in Howard's life.

Soon, almost any mention of his mother caused Price to bristle. Howard had made the statement once, "Any man who reaches greatness reaches it because of his mother," and Price wrote in her diary that night, "I resented that statement."[70] And when he had to cancel a date because of his mother, she could not understand him. "I thought of the way he did things for her," she wrote after once such cancellation, "always putting her interests ahead of his own. How had she bound him so close to her?" Yet it was her next statement that demonstrates the fundamental change Howard had undergone. "Most young men his age would demand their freedom," she wrote, before magnanimously commenting, "How great a sense of duty!"[71] Howard, more than perhaps most young men his age, truly did demand his freedom, for it was the preeminent value in his life. Yet, he had decided to make it subservient to his mother's needs, for at least as long as she was still alive. As such, he was prone to defend her.

Price complained on one date with Howard that she still wanted to write but that whenever she tried to do so, she found herself constantly interrupted.

"The more you talk," he then told her, "the more I can see how lucky I am. My family understands. If the phone rings or somebody comes to the house, Mother makes sure that I'm not disturbed until I finish." Again, mentions of his mother seemed to irritate her for she wrote that night, "When he said that about his mother, I figured she had other reasons in mind also, but I didn't say it."[72]

All of these things, both those she liked and disliked about Howard, led her to see him in a very different light. She came to realize that Howard was "a man of adventure. But a man in chains. A man shackled by his own gentleness of nature. He was held firmly to a small town, to a chair at a typewriter, bound by the chains of love and duty to an old, sick woman while he dreamed of another life, another time, another exciting world."[73] Her mixed feelings toward him were, perhaps, best summed up in the next line she wrote in her diary: "I looked at him with love and pity."[74]

As Howard and Price continued to date, the New Year brought about a change in their relationship. Howard was breaking more dates with her because of his mother's illness, and Price became more critical of the situation, writing things such as "I wonder why Dr. Howard can't take care of his sick wife" and "The truth is I doubt she's really sick."[75]

She also noticed that when they did go on dates, his disposition was growing gloomier, and he was sharing more of his problems with her. "I wouldn't have any troubles, if editors paid me what they owe me," he complained of the pulp writing industry. "I wouldn't have any troubles, if I could sell all of the stuff I bang out. Damn sorry editors keep a yarn till they wear it out, then they send it back to you and tell you they don't want it. Sorry bastards. They don't have to worry about where their next meal is coming from."[76] The lack of payment by such magazines as *Weird Tales* was also compounding his problems. "I could put up with my living hell," he continued, "if my mother wasn't sick and needing things I can't give her. If the damn editors paid me what they owe me, I could see that she got better treatment. I can't give her the things she needs. She's got to have an operation and, even with the professional discount my father gets, I'll have a hard time making it." And then his anger at the world spilled forth: "It's hell to be old and sick. I don't see how a just God can punish people like that. My mother has never harmed anybody in her whole life, and look at all the things she has to suffer. It's not right! Not a damn bit right. Her life is hanging by a thread, and it seems a damn shame to me that life should be taken from her. Life is all old people have. When it's miserable and painful, it makes me so damn mad I want to tear up the whole damn universe."[77] It must have been a sobering experience for Price to listen to Howard's despair, especially since she had been so critical of Mrs. Howard and her relationship with her son.

Howard did pull out of his dark mood; they began talking of other things, and he even managed to get his sense of humor back. Price had shared with him an interesting fact she had recently learned, that the last Indian killed in Brown County had been killed on Mammy's farm. An old Texas Ranger had told her mother the story. It had been a raiding party of Indians out of Oklahoma who had stolen some horses, and when the men tried to rescue the livestock, one Indian shot at the Rangers and they returned fire, killing him. Howard looked at Novalyne and said, "That crazy Indian. That was the damndest fool Indian I ever heard of." Confused at his response, Price asked why. "He didn't have a bit of sense," Howard replied.

> A few weeks ago, I talked to an old man up in Cross Cut. He told me positively that the last Indian killed in Brown County was killed a couple of miles west of Cross Cut. While I was in Brownwood, I lived close to an old man who'd been one of the first cowboys in this part of the country. He was with the Rangers, too, and he swore to me that the last Indian killed in Brown County was killed around Indian Creek. When ol' Clyde was working on his history of Brown County, he said the last Indian was killed over on the Sears place. Now, you tell me he was killed over there, close to the railroad on your grandmother's place.

Price just stared at Howard, baffled. Then, as she wrote, "he spoke softly, lightly, whimsically," when he added: "That damn fool Indian didn't do a thing but go around getting himself killed all over the damn county."[78]

By late February, however, his dark moods had returned. He told her that he was going to be taking his mother to Temple, Texas, where she would have an operation, something serious at her age and with her health. She was 64 years old. He seemed to get better as they drove and talked, even laughed, but on the return to Cross Plains a pall came over him once again. He began talking, saying things that made no sense to her. "He talked now of wanting to live and to come back again," she wrote, "See the spring come again."[79] She wondered if he was going somewhere. Price continued, "He began to thank me for all the times I'd given him. He said there were very few women whom he had known who let a man talk about his dreams and his work the way I did. He wanted me to know he thought I was a very unusual woman, and he appreciated knowing me." Now she was really confused and "began to feel nervous," she wrote, "for he sounded as if he'd never see me again!" He did not elaborate or explain what he meant, leaving her to close that evening's entry with, "I wondered if there would ever be a time when I would understand all the things he'd talked about today."[80]

Sadly, there would be.

Chapter 27

Dark Moods, 1935

Were I like this forever
You'd but too little to give,
But here tonight we sever,
For life loves life to live.
—"To A Woman (3)"[1]

Late one afternoon in March of 1935, Novalyne Price stepped into Smith's Drugstore and ran into Dr. Howard. She asked him, "How is Mrs. Howard?" and he replied, "She is holding her own. We believe she is going to get better." Price could sense the weariness in his voice, but was taken aback when he added, "Robert will be all right now, I think."[2] Confused over this declaration she asked him, "Has he been sick, too?" and Dr. Howard told her, "No. Not sick. He is very close to his mother."[3] It proved an awkward conversation that left her puzzled, as did her trip to the post office where she once again found no letter from Howard.

Mrs. Howard's health began to seriously decline in early 1935, and she was in need of an operation. As Howard later explained to Lovecraft, "It was necessary to remove my mother's gall-bladder, and reduce adhesions resulting from an old appendicitis operation."[4] Dr. Howard and his son took her to Kings Daughters Hospital in Temple, Texas, where she underwent surgery. It proved "a very serious operation," Howard wrote, "especially for a woman of her age and state of health."[5] Afterward, her surgeon Dr. McKelvey, as Dr. Howard recalled, "expressed a fear that she would not recover," and Howard had told Lovecraft, "She had a very bad time of it."[6]

Howard remained at her side for a month while she was recovering, leaving him no time to write. When she was released from the hospital, they tried to make the trip home as comfortable as possible. "My father and I fixed a bed out of blankets and cushions and quilts," Howard wrote, because "Temple is about a hundred and ninety-odd miles from Cross Plains." Unfortunately, the trip did not go well. Howard had some work done on the vehicle while in Temple, but it had been a shoddy repair. "We'd hardly gotten into the hill country," Howard continued, "perhaps thirty-five miles from Temple, when the clutch broke all to pieces and left us stranded." A farmer pushed their car into the next town, where the clutch was repaired, but they were forced to spend the night there. The next day they did not get much farther when "the differential broke all to pieces," necessitating another repair and a night in a hotel.[7] They finally made it home the following day.

The month-long ordeal certainly took a toll on Mrs. Howard and the family, but it impacted Howard financially, physically, and mentally. "My expenses, naturally, were great," Howard wrote, noting, "You can imagine the licking my pocket-book took, with all that car trouble."[8] In addition, there were the extra expenses of lodging and meals the mechanical problems had necessitated and the time he lost in writing. Yet the greatest expense had certainly been the month-long stay in the hospital. "But for the professional discount on the operation, my father being a physician," Howard continued, "I do not know how we would have been able to meet the expenses. As it was they were great, considering the hospital expenses, special nurses, etc., and my own expenses, though I cut these as closely as I could by staying in the cheapest rooming house I could find and skipping meals with such regularity that I lost fifteen pounds during that month." The return home, however, did not alleviate the strain, for "an abscess developed in the operation wound, which necessitated her staying for several days in a hospital at Coleman," and Howard then had to make the trip there "every few days in order to have her wound dressed and cleansed."[9] And the person who bore all of the cost was Howard.[10]

Outside of these struggles, it had been the thought that his mother might die that placed the greatest strain on him. After Dr. McKelvey informed both father and son that Mrs. Howard might not recover from the operation, Howard told his father things no man should ever hear from his son. "He began to talk about his business," Dr. Howard wrote Lovecraft after his son's death, "and I at once understood what it meant. I began to talk to him, trying to dissuade him from such a course."[11] Lindsey Tyson, many years later, explained it more succinctly in a letter when he wrote, "It was on this trip that Bob told his father that he did not wish to live any longer after his Mother was gone."[12] As Howard saw it, his mother was the only thing standing between him and freedom.

Howard had written many times before that the driving motivation in his life had been "individual freedom."[13] He cherished it more than anything, once going so far as to say, "By God, I demand freedom for myself, and if I can't have it, I'd rather be dead."[14] His ideas about suicide had evidently grown stronger over time, and he began to see it as a solution to those things that impinged upon his freedom: his dependence on fickle editors and lack of payment for stories he had sold or, in the case of *Weird Tales*, that had finally published. And whenever he suffered from neurasthenia—chronic fatigue—or when one of his dark moods was upon him, he must have seen suicide as a solution to the demons that denied him absolute liberty. And yet the one thing now standing in the way of such freedom was his mother, because he felt a strong sense of duty for her, motivated by a son's love.

"This feeling of responsibility for a parent, a sister, or brother," Price explained in an interview, "was not unusual in the 1930s. In fact, when a relative needed help 'to be taken care of' a family member accepted the responsibility." Howard had accepted that obligation with his mother, even making it subservient to his one driving ideal in life, because of "his love for her," Price said. When there was the possibility that his mother might not live though the operation, Howard realized that he would have no more responsibility, and so no sense of duty stood in his way for achieving that ideal. There was, of course, still his father, but it was Howard's belief that "a man could take care of himself, but a woman needed someone to take care of her" as he had once told Price, something that she asserted "he believed intensely."[15] He saw, selfishly, that his father had his work as a physician to sustain him if he were gone. As such, he felt he did not bear the same duty toward his father as he did to his mother.

As it turned out, Howard's obligation would continue, for Mrs. Howard slowly began to recover. And "as immediately as she began to improve," Dr. Howard would write of his son, "he became cheerful and no more was said."[16] It was, however, only a temporary reprieve, for as Glenn Lord explained, "She never fully recovered her health" and would spend the next year in and out of hospitals and sanitariums.[17] As one neighbor, Larry McDonough, recalled during that time period, her health declined, and "She started getting punier."[18] Sadly, Mrs. Howard was slowly dying, but Howard did everything he could to comfort her, even going so far as purchasing some goats because, according to Burke, Mrs. Howard "apparently loved goat's milk."[19] It was not enough, however, and Mrs. Howard's operation would prove to have been the beginning of the end, not only for herself but also for her son.

"Bob is coming home," Price recorded in her diary at the end of March. "I had a card from him, saying that his mother was getting better, and he was bringing her home."[20] Price was not only ecstatic for Howard coming home, but she was also elated by the fact the high school speech team she had been working with since September was beginning to be recognized. Her team swept the awards at a competition held at Abilene Christian College, and they managed to beat out students from larger towns such as Brownwood, Breckenridge, and Abilene. She was also in charge of the student drama club, and they were to perform a one-act play at a competition in Breckenridge. Between teaching during the day, supervising these many after-school activities, and traveling for their competitions, Price was beginning to burn the candle at both ends, so much so that she fell ill at the play contest, vomited and passed out, and had to be taken to the local hospital.

The only explanation offered for her collapse was that she had become so busy with the play, she had forgotten to eat. And Price, who reported her normal weight as having been ninety-nine pounds, entered the hospital weighing only eighty-five. She remained there for several days before going home to Cross Plains, where she was under Dr. Howard's care. She asked him about his wife and son, and having heard that the *Cross Plains Review* had voted Dr. Howard "Man of the Year," she tried congratulating him, but as usual, she wrote, their conversations did not go very well.[21] The good doctor, believing that Price needed better care, advised her to go to Brownwood and be treated by Dr. Jewel Daugherty at the Central Texas Hospital. She did so and remained there for a week.

By the end of her stay, she was able to eat and was feeling much better, at which point Dr. Daugherty confronted her. "You starved yourself almost to death!" he told her, and he wanted to know, "What made you do a thing like that?" She tried to explain she had just been so busy she forgot to eat, but the doctor was having none of it and, having spoken with Dr. Howard, abruptly asked her, "What about that young man you're going with—Dr. Howard's son, Robert? Are you in love with him? Are you trying to starve because of him?"[22] She was flabbergasted and did not know what to say. It did not matter, for Dr. Daugherty did all the talking, lecturing her on many things.

When he was finally finished, she looked him in the eye and spoke. "Dr. Daugherty, I am going to say this again and don't you forget it," she began. "I am sorry, very sorry I don't love Bob Howard. When a girl gets twenty-seven years old and isn't married, all the good men she meets are either married like Nat Williams, or they're jackasses like Bob Howard."[23] This time it was the doctor who was flabbergasted.

Once he recovered, he began to explain his concerns. Dr. Howard was a friend of his, and they had many conversations about his son. He eventually asked her, "Has Robert ever said to you that he didn't want to live after his mother dies?" Howard evidently had, but Price did not think it was that serious, just Howard talking out loud. "Dr. Daugherty, when I was a kid and got mad at Mother, I thought about killing myself to make her sorry," she said.

"Bob still makes stupid remarks like that once in a while, but it's all baloney. He just wants me to sympathize with him and try to talk him out of it. I used to do that; but the last time he said anything like that I agreed it might be a good idea, and he shut up about it mighty quick."[24] The conversation then shifted to their relationship, and in an indirect way, Dr. Daugherty was inquiring if she was considering marriage. Price succinctly answered the question when she wrote in her diary, "I wasn't thinking about marrying Bob."[25]

Howard's friends Smith and Tyson remembered that whenever their talk of marriage came up, Howard would always quote from Rudyard Kipling's poem "The Winners": "Down to Gehenna or up to the Throne / He travels fastest who travels alone."[26] For the sake of his freedom and writing, he had no desire to marry. So whenever the topic was brought up by Price, Howard would say things like, "A wife would handicap a man," or "A woman puts chains on a man."[27] There were times he evidently thought about it, such as when Price said she really liked her job, and Howard asked her, "What about marriage? Ever think of that?" to which Price replied, "I don't see why I can't get married and still keep on teaching school." She wrote in her diary that he then banged on the steering wheel, became short with her, and said, "No, I suppose there's no reason you couldn't."[28]

Howard and Price, it seems, were never in agreement on the topic. "Marriage often entered their minds," Burke once wrote, "but the two never entertained the same feelings at the same time."[29] As Price put it when Burke interviewed her, "Usually, when he was thinking about love, I was dreaming about another man. When I was thinking about love, he was thinking about the obligations he had." She knew Howard also believed a good wife filled the traditional role of cooking and keeping house, which she had no intention of doing.[30] Yet despite these things, the greatest impediment for Howard was, as he told her, "Marriage with a man who dreamed of freedom wouldn't last, you know. A woman ties a man down, and a man's got to be free. He's got to get out and do a man's work. He's got to go. He'd have to leave her behind. So it's better for a man to stay free, never hinder himself with a wife. A man can't stand the ropes, the chains of marriage." To which Price had replied, "Well, don't worry about it, Bob. I wasn't planning to ask you to marry me any time soon. I like to be free too."[31]

Dr. Daugherty, in the end, told her that his best advice for her was to leave Cross Plains. Price did mention that she had read two books on speech by professors at Louisiana State University, and she had considered going there to study. The doctor encouraged her to do so, and that in the meantime, to take a tonic, eat three meals a day, and to "stop seeing Bob Howard!"[32] Price agreed she would and told her mother the same thing, but then wrote in her diary, "Bob and I were right for each other. I had lied to Mother and Dr. Daugherty when I said I didn't care for him. I had lied to myself. I love Bob."[33] Price was conflicted.

When she returned to Cross Plains, Howard and Price resumed dating, but things did not go well. His dark moods were upon him once more, brought on by the strain and expense of his mother's operation. She asked about his mother and, as she wrote in her diary, "That set him off."[34] She tried offering some consoling words or talking about his father's award, and to everything she said, he exploded.[35] Yet on the next date, he seemed to be fine, but then, "After a happy date with Bob," she would write of the next, "A near disaster."[36] As his dark moods returned, his behaviors were becoming erratic. "He was a moody kind of fellow," Tyson would later explain, recalling how "he was capable of being very happy and also capable of being very low."[37]

Price also noticed that in addition to his mood swings and angry outbursts, he was showing physical signs of depression as well: "He kept wiping his hands across his forehead as if his head hurt. But he denied it when I asked him if he had a headache. He moved constantly, but without the exuberance and vitality with which he usually moved. Something was wrong; yet he had talked of everything, except whatever it was that troubled him."[38] Howard was clearly suffering, once again, from depression, and it was steadily getting worse.[39] This is unfortunately a very common trait found among many professional writers, for as literary historian Celia Johnson points out, this was also the case for such famous authors as Mark Twain, Emily Dickinson, F. Scott Fitzgerald, Tennessee Williams, and Howard's favorite, Jack London.[40] It is not just the artistic personality that contributes to ten times the rate of clinical depression among writers; it is also caused by the writing industry itself.[41]

"Writing for pulp-paper magazines never can be anything but a trade," admitted the editor of *Writer's Digest*, declaring that "Writers should face it as such."[42] Despite having gone into writing as a means to freedom, Howard had come to recognize that it, too, was just another form of slavery. An anonymous writer, believed to have been Victor Rousseau, a contemporary of Howard's who wrote for the pulps including *Weird Tales*, exposed the reality in the *American Mercury* in March of 1936. Whether Howard read the contribution is unknown, but he likely would have agreed with the sentiment. "The pulps are now an industry," Anonymous wrote, detailing the mass production of words that had to happen in order for a pulp writer to survive.[43] He wrote that it was rare for such a writer to escape the market by breaking into the better paying "slick" magazines, and that "the writers who fail to escape face sorry prospects." Anonymous explained that, "First, the rates of payment are extremely low: the average pulp pays from one to two cents a word; some less than a cent. A few writers receive more than two cents: they are the successes . . . but they are surprisingly few in number."[44] Howard was not one of them.

Another problem Anonymous pointed out was that the magazines had their own problems, especially "cash newsstand sales," which often necessitated responding to submissions with rejections. The bottom line was, "If a writer's product sells the magazine, his stuff is bought," but if the stories do not appeal to the readers, "he is out of luck."[45] Still another problem was the reality that "the pulpster does not earn more money by trying to secure higher rates," as authors in other writing industries would, but with the pulps, "he must do it by selling more words."[46] It becomes a matter of production, for the more an author writes, the more they might sell, and the more they sell, the more they make. However, Anonymous also pointed out that (as in the case of Howard not writing while in Temple caring for his mother) "when production stops, earnings stops."[47] All of these were reasons Howard no longer felt freed by his writing but rather enslaved.

"I have to produce a great deal in order to make a living at all," Howard wrote Lovecraft, admitting to him, "I sell so little."[48] When it did sell, he was mostly making the industry standard. And while he no longer had to peddle his stories to the editors, because Kline had taken over that duty, he was still stretched thin for time. When he created a dependable series character that sold, such as Conan or Breckenridge Elkins, he had to continue writing those yarns while at the same time writing for other magazines to try to break into new markets. "My time is divided between trying to make new markets to replace defaulting old ones and trying to persuade old ones to pay me what they owe me," he wrote Price. And if the editors no longer bought the stories of a dependable character, he would have to start all over again with that magazine and create a new series the editor would accept and the readers would like. Perhaps the most frustrating issue remained failure to receive payment for stories accepted and published, making further submission to those magazines highly questionable and necessitating, as Howard wrote, "breaking into new pastures."[49] It was the nonpayment for tales published in *Weird Tales* and his need for money to care for his mother that motivated Howard to make a personal plea to Wright.

The expenses the family incurred had exhausted the savings of both father and son, and it forced Dr. Howard to move his practice into his home; therefore, patients were there both night and day, which made writing more difficult for Howard.[50] When looking at how much *Weird Tales* owed him as of May 1, 1935, Howard discovered the total now stood at approximately $860. The magazine was experiencing its own cash flow problems, so earlier that year it had resorted to sending out "half-checks," partial payments for moneys owed to its authors.[51] If Howard could have received the full amount owed him, most of his problems would have been solved, and his mother could get the care she needed. So on May 6 Howard swallowed his pride and put a sheet of paper into his typewriter and began his missive to Wright. "I always hate to write a letter like this, but dire necessity forces me. It is, in short, an urgent plea for money."[52]

Howard tried to explain that his expenses in March and April had been great, that he had continuing expenses, and that they were "forced to hire a woman to do the cooking and most of the house-work." His mother was unable to work, his father needed to tend to his patients, and Howard needed to write. There was no one left to do any of the other things that needed to be done. Succinctly he wrote, "Whether my mother ever recovers or not possibly depends on the kind of care and attention I am able to give her, and that in turn depends on the money I am able to earn."[53]

He then got to the matter at hand, that for months he had been receiving and surviving on half-checks, "But this month, at a very time when I need money so desperately bad, I did not receive a check. Somehow, some way, my family and I have struggled along this far, but if you cut off my monthly checks now, I don't know what in God's name we'll do."[54] He wrote that he did not believe he was being unreasonable in his request, and that he had worked hard and was dedicated to *Weird Tales*, but that "To a poor man the money he makes is his life's blood, and of late when I write of Conan's adventures I have to struggle against the disheartening reflection that if the story is accepted, it may be years before I get paid for it." He closed by saying he meant no offense with his request, but that a check meant "the difference between a life that is at least endurable—and God alone knows what."[55]

Writing this letter was no doubt hard on Howard, because he was having to admit that someone had power over him, and his love of freedom would never have allowed him to do so if it were not for the needs of his mother. The true travesty was that his Conan yarns were some of the most popular stories in *Weird Tales* magazine at the time, and if the account is accurate, he had saved the magazine from going under during the Depression. Yet he still could not get paid for his work, especially at a time when he needed it most. Despite the fact Howard swallowed his pride and wrote the letter, he received no emergency funds from the *Weird Tales* office, for they were having their own financial problems brought on by the continuing pressures of the Depression. There was, however, one distinct difference between both men's plight. Wright was trying to save his magazine; Howard was trying to save his mother's life.

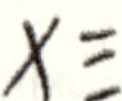

In May, before the end of the school year, Price went home for the weekend to visit her mother and Mammy. She decided to make a trip into Brownwood, and while she was shopping downtown, it began to rain. Stepping into a bookstore, she ran into Howard's good friend Truett Vinson. They began talking, mostly about books, and after lingering for some time, Vinson asked her out to a picture show that evening. Price said yes, and he picked her up at the farmhouse. After seeing the movie and spending time talking, he took her home. It was there he asked her, "Are you still going with Bob?" She wanted to avoid answering the question, but she finally said, "Yes."[56] Vinson then wanted to know if she was going to tell Howard, and she claimed that he would not mind them dating because they were "just friends."[57] Yet Price had known exactly what she was doing, for she had written in her diary that day: "Clyde Smith, Robert Howard, and Truett Vinson. Three close friends. Three friends who liked to read, talk, and try to solve the problems of the world. Now, when I dated Truett, I will have dated all three!" She may also have been motivated by his looks, for she did add that Vinson was "definitely the best looking one of the three."[58]

Vinson remained concerned about Howard knowing of their relationship, yet Price seemed less troubled, for she wrote in her diary, "I didn't want to marry anybody. I just wanted to date Truett while I was in Brownwood, and Bob while I was in Cross Plains. I didn't want any complication."[59] The next time she was on a date with Howard, however, she only admitted to having seen Vinson, but said nothing about their date. Each date after that it was the same thing. She wanted to tell him but never did.

When the school year finished, Price moved home to Brownwood for the summer and did just as she had hoped: she continued to date Vinson. Howard did come down to visit in early June, but his time was limited. Now that they had someone to cook, clean, and help tend to Mrs. Howard, he could leave the house more often, but he needed to be home writing in order to pay the bills and their new caretaker. Mrs. Kate Merryman, whom Dr. Howard and his son hired for the job, was a nearby neighbor they had known since living in Cross Cut.[60]

Price finally decided to tell Howard she had seen Vinson again, and that was when things turned strange. She tried telling him, albeit in a feeble manner, but Howard chose simply to ignore her. Vinson and Howard also got together in early June, yet according to Price, when Vinson tried telling his friend he was dating her, Howard ignored him as well. The reason they had gotten together was because they were planning a late June trip to Santa Fe,

New Mexico, together, which, under the circumstances, certainly must have made for an awkward vacation.

Howard's true motivation for the trip, as Tyson explained, "was to learn more about the outlaw 'Billy the Kid' and his association with a feud, 'The Lincoln County Wars.'"[61] Howard had long been interested in both topics, and the trip presented an opportunity for him to visit the location he had read so much about. "Vinson and I left Cross Plains early the morning of the nineteenth," Howard wrote of his trip, "and followed the Bankhead Highway westward to the Pecos."[62] Their first stop was in Roswell, New Mexico, where he sent Price a postcard, writing on the back, "Dear Novalyne. The weather is good but the beer is lousy. Hoping you are the same."[63] She laughed at his humor.

They arrived in the town of Lincoln the next morning. "We rounded a crook in the meandering street," Howard wrote, "and it burst upon us like the impact of a physical blow. There was no mistaking it. We did not—at least I did not—need the sight of the sign upon it to identify it."[64] Howard, along with Vinson, visited many of the locations in town and even had his picture proudly taken in front of the county courthouse, from which Billy the Kid had orchestrated his escape from the second-floor jail. "Lincoln is a haunted place," was the impression the town left upon Howard. "It is a dead town; yet it lives with a life that died fifty years ago."[65]

They moved on through Carrizozo, Socorro, and Albuquerque before finally making it to Santa Fe. There he sent another postcard to Price. This one featured the picture of a rattlesnake swallowing a rabbit whole. She did not like the picture, but she found the back side humorous. All it read was, "Dear Novalyne" and "Cordially, Bob."[66] As she said in a later interview, Howard "could be devastatingly sarcastic when he wanted to be."[67]

"We stayed only one night in Santa Fe," Howard wrote, despite the fact that "it had been my intention to stay longer." Vinson, Howard explained, "got in a swivet to get home, for some reason which he never made entirely clear, but which seemed so important to him that I didn't press the matter."[68] No doubt it was the tension between the two men that had to have been building on the trip.[69] And so they returned to Cross Plains by the same route.

Howard next corresponded with Price on Independence Day. "I take my typewriter in hand to write to you a letter on this grand and suspicious—I mean auspicious occasion—when the zoom of the horse-race and the rodeo is heard in the land," he began the letter before closing with: "I trust you and Truett had a good time."[70] Howard must have heard from someone that they were seen together at the Texas Cowboy Reunion, an annual rodeo held in Stamford, Texas. Price was unsure how to take the letter, so she invited Howard to pay her a visit in Brownwood. "Thank you for your invitation to call," Howard replied, "but you honestly can't expect me to enjoy ridicule and contempt so much that I come back for another dose." He was also quite succinct when he wrote in the lengthy letter, "You understand me, I think, but I'll make myself clear so there won't be any chance of misunderstanding. It's simply that you and Truett haven't played fair with me, in concealing the fact that you were going together—and you know you haven't."[71] The relationship had soured. Howard had been hurt.

Although Price tried replying, Howard simply sent the letter back. Then, just before the beginning of the new school year, Howard sent Price a letter saying he was coming to visit the next day. There was no time for her to decline, so he arrived wearing his everyday clothes, neither the suit or the hat she had grown accustomed to, and he was sporting a mustache, something she detested, which he knew. He took her to a picture show and ushered her to the right front section of the Lyric where he knew Vinson had a habit of sitting. Price was mortified when she saw Vinson stand up and walk out of the movie theater. She demanded several times that evening to be taken home, which Howard ignored, and when he did, he walked her to the door, kissed her passionately, and left.

The next time she saw him was in Cross Plains, not long after Labor Day, but what she saw caused her to write in her diary, "I nearly dropped dead." He was walking downtown wearing the hat he had purchased in Mexico, which Price described as "a real Mexican sombrero with little balls dangling from its rim. The chin strap was a thin little strip of leather attached to the hat. It came down and was tied under his chin." He still had the mustache, which she noted "was longer and droopier than ever."[72]

When Howard saw her, he removed his sombrero, bowed low, and said to her, "Miss Price, imagine meeting you here!" She stormed off, running across the street to the drugstore from which Dr. Howard was exiting. "What is he trying to prove?" she desperately asked him. "I don't know," his father replied. "I really don't know."[73] Price said later in an interview that she believed, "He wore the hat to tell me that what the world thought of you didn't really matter."[74] The world—or at least the people of Cross Plains—thought he was crazy, and Howard had ceased to care.[75]

Despite Howard's conduct, they did go on the occasional car ride together that fall, but it was never the same. The intimacy in their relationship was gone.

"A freak windstorm which swept down on Cross Plains from the East shortly after five o'clock Friday afternoon, unroofed buildings, broke windows, snapped trees and demolished several outbuildings," the *Cross Plains Review* reported on July nineteenth.[76] Howard recalled it as "the hottest day of the year" but did not think the clouds forming would cause it to "rain much." However, when he went to close the windows in his room, he wrote that "with suddenness the wind rose to a scream, the rain turned into slashing sheets, and the tornado struck!"[77] They hastily closed all the windows in the house and were fortunate there was no damage. Many homes and businesses in Cross Plains were not.

The storm, coming like that in July of 1935, seemed emblematic of Howard's life that year, and not just regarding his relationship with Price. His correspondence with Lovecraft also became tempestuous. Their letters back and forth had become increasingly more argumentative over the years, and Howard was tired of the accusations Lovecraft heaped on him. Sitting down at his typewriter that July he wrote, "Recalling off-hand the charges you have made against me, I remember that at various times you have accused me of being: Exalter-of-the-Physical-Above-the-Mental; Enemy of Humanity; Foe of Mankind; Apostle of Prejudice; Distorter of Fact. . . . Emotionalist; Defender of Ignorance; Sentimentalist; Romanticist."[78] He then concluded the long litany by writing, "If I were guilty of all the things of which you've accused me, I not only wouldn't be fit to live; I wouldn't have sense enough to live."[79] Howard did take the high road the following month, writing Lovecraft, "There is nothing personal in anything I may say about a certain sort of attitude or method," and concluded that their disagreements arose from "a lack of common language or set of association-patterns."[80] In December Lovecraft agreed, believing it "merely a clash of opposing cultures."[81]

There were also many bittersweet things for Howard that year as well. He saw the publication of more Conan tales, such as "The Servants of Bit-Yakin," which was published as "Jewels of Gwahlur" in the March 1935 issue of *Weird Tales*, and "The Man-Eater of Zamboula," published as "Shadows in Zamboula" in November's issue. Both were well received by the readers, and the latter earned second place in the reader poll.[82] In fact, both Howard and his character were continually praised by the readers. For instance, Annabelle Lantz of Chicago wrote to "The Eyrie," "My one request is that we have more Conan stories. I never tire of them." Wright's reply to her: "You'll have them."[83] And Howard earned $155 and $120 for the stories, respectively. Yet, again, it must have been frustrating to know that it would be months on end after their publication when he would receive payment.[84]

His relationship with his Brownwood friends also became strained that year. Not only was Vinson now dating his girlfriend, but Howard also had little contact with Smith. The last time he saw him was in January of 1935.[85] And although he was visited by E. Hoffmann Price once more in October as he made his way back east, Howard lamented to Lovecraft, "They stayed only three days before they left for Mexico City, which disappointed, as I had hoped to entertain them for a week at least."[86]

The real storm, however, was in the home, as he tried to keep his mother alive while at the same time attempting to write stories to bring in more needed cash. Although Mrs. Howard had long enjoyed getting out of the house and visiting other people, especially for church socials, she was no longer physically capable.[87] She spent most of her time resting in bed, trying to gain her strength back. Howard began caring for his mother when her caretaker was not around, doing most of the grocery shopping and some of the cooking.[88] During these last months of Mrs. Howard's life, Mrs. Merryman recalled that Howard "was devoted to her" and "just couldn't bear for her to be sick."[89] Vera Baker echoed this sentiment when she recalled, "One day I saw him kneeling by the bed holding her hand. I have no idea if he was praying, but it impressed me that he was devoted." Merryman also remembered how his moods began to reflect the condition of his mother's health, for she later said in an interview, "When she was up, he was up. He was up in the air and singing, and when she went down, he quit."[90]

Becoming desperate to find some means to help his mother improve, Howard and his father decided perhaps she needed to get out of Cross Plains and that a different climate might prove therapeutic. They decided to take a trip into the Texas Panhandle. "My parents and I went to Amarillo in the latter part of July," Howard wrote Lovecraft. "None of us had ever been to that city, and I wanted to see if the high altitude, 4500 feet, might help a persistent cough that had been bothering my mother." They fixed up the backseat with the bedding to make the ride more comfortable for her and traveled first to the cereal king's utopian town of Post, where they had dinner, before moving on to Lubbock and finally Amarillo. As he informed Lovecraft, "My mother had not regained her strength from her operation, but she stood the trip remarkably well." They also went to see the Canadian River and Palo Duro Canyon before making their way to San Angelo and home. According to Howard, they drove "nearly 1000 miles in about three days."[91] Despite his positive outlook on his mother's endurance, it had to have been taxing on her health all the same.

Finally, in November, with her health still declining, Howard and his father took her to the Torbett Sanatorium in Marlin, where, he wrote E. Hoffmann Price, Mrs. Howard had "more than a gallon of fluid drawn off the pleura [the lining that envelopes the lungs]."[92] When her tuberculosis caused the pleura to fill again, she was not able to return home right away. "When I learned that my mother would have to stay in Marlin for a few weeks," Howard wrote, "I came back to Cross Plains, to bring my father home, and to get my typewriter." After returning, Howard stayed there a week while he wrote several more stories.[93] Dr. Howard then came to Marlin to bring his wife home, having fixed up his backseat with the bedding she needed.[94]

Mrs. Howard was only home two weeks when her pleura had filled once more. This time father and son rushed her to the hospital in San Angelo, where the fluid was again drained. "After a few days, then we put her in a sanatorium about seventeen miles northwest of San Angelo," Howard wrote, referring to the Texas State Sanitorium in Carlsbad, Texas, where she would remain for the rest of the year.[95]

As 1935 came to a close, Howard took a look at his sales for the year and informed Derleth, "I haven't done quite as well this year as last, partly because of a difficulty in making regular collections. But I've managed to get by somehow."[96] According to Glenn Lord, although Howard's 1935 records are incomplete, he estimates that his "sales were probably slightly over $2000."[97] That would be the equivalent to just over forty thousand in modern dollars. Despite having to find time to write where and when he could, Howard would still manage to splash several new markets, one being the more lucrative (not to mention, lascivious) line of pulps known as the Spicys.[98]

to Marlin to bring his wife home, having fixed up his breakfast with the [illegible] he needed."

[illegible] was only the two weeks when her pleurisy had filled once more [illegible] time [illegible] and [illegible] rushed her to the hospital in San Angelo when the fluid [illegible] drained. [illegible] a few days [illegible] not have a [illegible] miles northwest of San Angelo," Howard wrote, [illegible] to the Texas State Sanatorium in Carlsbad, Texas, where she would remain for the rest of the year.

As 1935 [illegible], Howard took a [illegible] his sales for the year and [illegible]. The overall conclusion [illegible] this year [illegible] because of [illegible] in making [illegible] to get by somehow." According to [illegible], although [illegible] is incomplete, his estimate that his sales were probably slightly over $2,000. That would be the equivalent to just over forty thousand in modern dollars. [illegible] when he could. He [illegible] would [illegible] new markets, one being the [illegible] [illegible] known as the Spicys."

Chapter 28

Spicy Pulps and Shudder Stories, 1936

"Turn out the light." I raised a willing hand
And plunged the room into the silken, cool
Darkness in which the deeper passions rule;
Your tresses snared me with each moon-lit strand,
Your soft breasts sent warm raptures through my hand.
—"Desire"[1]

In early January 1936, Novalyne Price returned to Cross Plains after the break to resume teaching at the high school. She also resumed dating Howard. "Bob was busy telling me about a yarn he'd just completed," she wrote in her diary after their first date in the new year, "Not a Conan yarn. One for *Spicy-Adventure* magazine."[2] The Spicys were a relatively new line of pulps featuring scantily clad women on the covers and risqué stories that found many new and innovative ways to quickly undress their female characters. Although highly suggestive, these pulps never directly addressed sexual anatomy or acts and would be considered mild fare by modern standards.[3]

Pulp editor Frank Armer, who had a background in publishing romance and love magazines, formed the intentionally named company Culture

Publications with partner Harry Donenfield to begin producing this new line of pulps. Mixing sex with a traditional pulp genre, Armer created the first title to appear in April of 1934, *Spicy Detective Stories*, and two more followed in July: *Spicy-Adventure Stories* and *Spicy Mystery Stories.*[4] Armer added one more title, *Spicy Western Stories*, in 1936, and the entire line was priced at twenty-five cents per issue rather than the typical ten or fifteen cents most publishers charged.[5] Despite the higher price, the magazine sold, no doubt based on the old adage "sex sells."

Howard had been acutely aware of society's obsession with sex, once telling Price, "I can tell you the demand is growing for more and more sex." He then predicted, "In a few years, there won't be anything held back. It'll all be sex, and since language plays a part in sex, the language will become the language of dirty men talking about sex."[6] She tried to argue against him on this particular point, but he was relentless in his beliefs. "You'll live to see what ol' Bob is telling you," he told her and then further predicted, "Pornography will be the order of the day, and the good men—if there's a damn one left—will feebly attempt to do something about it for a while; but they'll give up, and the depraved, as you call them, will take over. Enough good men will keep silent."[7] Ever conscious of the struggle between civilization and barbarism, Howard believed American society had reached its zenith and was now witnessing a slow and steady decline. "You see, girl, when a civilization begins to decay and die, the only thing men or women think about is the gratification of their body's desires. They become preoccupied with sex. It colors their thinking, their laws, their religion—every aspect of their lives."[8] Price remembered the conversation for the rest of her life, and with the benefit of hindsight in her sere and yellow leaf, wrote that she believed, "He displayed what I have since thought was a rare gift of prophecy."[9]

Howard had already been moving in the direction of including sex in his stories, beginning at least as far back as the publication of "People of the Dark," for *Strange Tales* in 1932.[10] Where it is perhaps most evident are his Conan stories, for as he admitted to Price in April of 1935, "My Conan yarns are filled with sex."[11] Yet with the opening up of the Spicys and knowing they paid on acceptance, Howard decided to break into this new line of pulps.[12]

"Now, I'm going to have to work to catch up with the market," Howard told his girlfriend. "I can tell you the demand is growing for more and more sex."[13] She told him she did not think a good and decent man should stoop to that level, and Howard started to reply, "But if you're trying to make money—" to which she cut him off by telling him, "Making money is not everything. Doing the right thing is important, too." Howard then turned to her and said, "Girl, you make it hard for a man to earn a living."[14]

In October of 1935, Howard inquired with his agent about writing for the Spicys, and Kline suggested he use a penname. When Howard asked if people had anything against his own name, Kline replied, "No, I don't think anyone has any prejudice against your name; however, I do think it wise for you to use a pen name on sexy adventure stories, since you are identified with the straight adventure and Western field under you own name."[15] Kline was familiar with the common practice of using a penname when writing for magazines that were considered to be the more inferior of the trade in order to avoid tainting the readers' views of a favorite writer. Fellow *Weird Tales* authors used pseudonyms when writing for the Spicys. Hugh B. Cave wrote as Justin Case, while E. Hoffmann Price sometimes used Hamlin Daly, so Howard picked the name Sam Walser, which he called "a rugged, upright, forthright typical American name," as his own.[16]

Howard then had to learn the formula for the stories, as well as what was—and was not—acceptable. The instructions for potential authors written by Armer began, "On account of the attitude of certain groups of people in different parts of the country, it is necessary that we use great discretion in the amount of sex we have in the stories run." Although he admitted it was hard to have definitive rules, there were some prohibitions. "There are several words which must never be used," he continued, "such as 'nipples,' 'buttocks,' etc. In describing breasts of a female character, avoid anatomical description of the points of the breast. If it is necessary for the story to have the girl give herself to a man, do not go too carefully in the details." Still further, when it came to dress, Armer encouraged authors to "avoid complete nudity of the female characters," but having a girl "strip to her underwear, or transparent negligee, or nightgown" was perfectly acceptable, if not highly encouraged. He then concluded, "The idea is to have a very strong sex element in these stories without anything that might be interpreted as being vulgar or obscene."[17]

"In my efforts to make new markets," Howard wrote Lovecraft in December of 1935, "I've been 'splashing the field' as Price calls it. One market I tried was *Spicy-Adventures* . . . I sold the first yarn I tried, but doubt if I could make that market regularly, as it requires a deft, jaunty style foreign to my natural style."[18] His first yarn featured the last character he would ever create, Wild Bill Clanton, who Howard himself described as "a pirate, gun-runner, smuggler, a pearl-thief and slaver, and carefully avoids all moral scruples in his dealings with the ladies."[19] He finished the first story in early October and sent it to his agent. "Your story 'The Girl on the Hell Ship,'" Kline wrote back, "seems to be pretty close to what Frank Armer wants for *Spicy-Adventures*, although it may not be quite hot enough for that book. However, I am trying it on Armer and will let you know his reaction."[20] He apparently had a positive one, for he immediately accepted it for publication, earning Howard $48.60 after Kline's fee.[21]

The title of the story was changed by Armer to "She Devil," for the sole reason he had a stock cover painting he wanted to use and the change, he felt, complemented it better.[22] The story published in the April 1936 issue and did appear under the byline Sam Walser. Howard would write five more yarns of Wild Bill Clanton, with four of them published in *Spicy-Adventure*, although only one would appear on the newsstands while he was still alive—"Desert Blood" in the June 1936 issue.[23]

Despite his concerns about the style of publication, he found "that sort of yarn is easy to write."[24] In fact, as he told Price, he had discovered a method for writing the stories: "A favorite formula is for the hero to accomplish what only the villain attempts in conventional yarns" and "to strip the heroine gradually—she loses part of her clothes in one episode, some more in the next, and so on until the climax finds her in a state of tantalizing innocence." The only real issue he had with the stories was their length. "The main handicap," he wrote, "is the necessity of keeping the wordage down—they take nothing over 5500 words."[25] Because there were fewer words, there was less pay, but as Price said in an interview, "He could just sit down and dash those things off without thought, without work."[26] One fellow pulp author agreed when he wrote, "If I needed money (and I generally did), I could take them a story in the morning, come back and get a check in the afternoon."[27] The money was important to him, for as Louinet explains, the Spicys came "at a time when Howard was desperately trying to secure money so as to meet the expenses incurred by his mother's declining health," adding that sales "did help keep the bank account positive."[28]

Howard once reflected on the yarns he wrote for *Spicy-Adventure* in which he made yet another prediction. "He foretold a time when the yarn he'd written," Price explained, "would appear harmless and innocent compared with the accepted writings of the day."[29] It seems, once again, he was right, for Hugh B. Cave once said the stories in the Spicys "were considered quite sexy in their day," but from a late twentieth century perspective, in reality, "No one ever did anything sexy."[30] As for Howard's yarns, E. Hoffmann Price praised them, but noted they "depended far more on gusty humor and whopping extravagance of phrase than on the 'spice,' the sex-appeal which was supposedly the *sine qua non*. In a word, he wrote a 'clean dirty story.' "[31]

Howard had only a short run with *Spicy-Adventure*, and he never made any of the other magazines in that line of pulps. He had simply run out of time. The magazine published the three other Wild Bill Clanton yarns posthumously, and the magazine's own demise came not long after, as interest in the Spicys began to wane. In 1943 the word "Spicy" was dropped and replaced with the new titillating word of the day: "Speed."[32]

At the beginning of the new year in 1936, *Weird Tales* was still running Howard's only Conan novel, *The Hour of the Dragon*, and the praise from readers was effusive. The five-part series would earn him the most praise published in "The Eyrie" for one of his stories, and letters lauding his achievement continued publishing well into the summer. Conan had definitively become the most popular character in the "unique magazine." Fans such as Edgar Hurd of Sacramento exclaimed, "Conan is one of my favorite characters. May we have adventures of Conan until doomsday, I'll never get tired of him."[33] Elleanor Layton, of Washington, DC, stated, "Howard gets better and better; Conan is superb, magnifique, and more!" while E. A. Taylor of West Asheville, North Carolina, declared, "Robert E. Howard with his tales of Conan the Barbarian is by far your finest author."[34] Some fans were also writing Howard directly, such as P. Schuyler Miller and Dr. John D. Clark, who sent Howard their outline of Conan's life and a map of his world. "I feel indeed honored that you and Dr. Clark should be so interested in Conan as to work out an outline of his career and a map of his environs," Howard replied. "Both are surprisingly accurate, considering the vagueness of the data you had to work with. I have the original map—that is the one I drew up when I first started writing about Conan—around here somewhere and I'll see if I can't find it and let you have a look at it."[35]

Although Howard was no doubt appreciative of the praise, it was also somewhat disheartening, mainly because he was not receiving money owed for the stories already published. He did, at least, receive one check over the holidays for $99.00 from *Weird Tales* for his short story "The Grisly Horror," which he called "a pleasant surprize," but still he was owed nearly $1,000.[36] Because of this he told E. Hoffmann Price in February, "I haven't submitted anything to *Weird Tales* for many months." He explained his dilemma to Lovecraft when he wrote, "I would hate to abandon weird writing entirely, but my financial needs are urgent, immediate and imperious. Slowness of payment in the fantastic field forces me into other lines against my will."[37]

One of those lines was his boxing tales, which were not being accepted like they once were. Still, he was hopeful, since *Fight Stories* had resumed publishing. He did manage to place one boxing yarn with *Dime Sports Magazine*. "I finally crashed the Popular magazines, in the shape of a prize-ring novelet bought by *Dime Sport*," he wrote E. Hoffmann Price. "Bloomfield expressed an interest in my work and a desire to see more of it," although he did voice some concern when he added, "But I'm haunted by a conviction that I've written myself out on prize-fight yarns, a narrow field at best."[38] The story was originally titled "Fists of the Desert" but was published as "Iron-Jaw" in the April 1936 issue. Another line was the most prestigious of the Munsey pulps, *Argosy*.[39] Howard's editor at Fiction House, Jack Byrne, became the new editor of *Argosy*, and he wanted Howard to write for him. Howard sold him a weird Western, "The Dead Remember," as well as several Western comedies using the Pike Bearfield character. Despite opening up these new lines, however, his sales to the pulps were becoming as erratic as his relationship with Price and his mother's health.

Although they had resumed dating after Price returned to Cross Plains, Howard had little time for her. He still wore the mustache she detested and continued to dress in his own manner, rather than the style she so adored. "He just will dress some crazy way," Price complained to her new roommate about his sombrero. "I hate it, even though I know why he's doing it." She believed Howard was "trying to tell people he's a writer and writers have a right to be odd. Since they think he's crazy anyway, he'll show them just how crazy he can be."[40] And then, she did not hear from him.

Just prior to Valentine's Day, Price decided to write Howard a letter, and he responded on that saint's day. He told her about his writing and sales, joked about the traditions of that particular day, and defended his mustache against her "sinister insinuation regarding my whiskers."[41] He then signed off, "I'll be seeing you, I hope. Your bearded friend."[42] He included a drawing of himself sporting a full-sized mustache and wearing the sombrero hat. Price wrote of her reaction to the letter in her diary: "To me, the letter is as delightful as the big gump himself."[43]

She saw him ten days later, as she was walking back to her boardinghouse from the high school. He pulled his car beside her, and they talked, joking about his mustache. She noticed he was unsure of himself in her presence, for she recalled his "drooping shoulders, the uneasy mouth, and I could read the questions in his eyes!"[44] Unsure of what to make of him, she agreed to go for a drive. He opened the door for her, and they drove east along the dirt road heading toward Rising Star. They talked about her work and squabbled over his mustache, before Price asked about his mother. "She's not doing at all well," he answered. "Everything is falling in on me at once. I'm going to do all I can to get her to hang on and get well." He talked about taking her back to Marlin, where she had received helpful treatment in the past, and because, he explained, "I can't write or do anything else but take care of her. A week or so in Marlin may straighten us both out." With the doctors attending to her needs, it would provide him a break and the opportunity to write. Price, however, could not understand why Howard could not write at home, and he explained, "Mother requires almost constant care night and day. . . . She has these terrible night sweats. Her nightgown and bed get wet, really wet. I changed her bed and gown three times last night."[45]

That last statement drew a strong, visceral reaction from Price, for that night she wrote in her journal, "I don't know why that simple statement nauseated me."[46] Her immature response may be forgiven for more than just her youth. She had never been in a position to be a caregiver for anyone but herself, and not only was her mother in good physical health, but so too was her grandmother.[47] The difference, however, was that neither of them was dying. She recognized this several weeks later when she reflected, "My trouble, I suppose, is that Mammy will be seventy-nine years old next July, and she can take care of herself." "Consequently," she added, "I don't understand Bob."[48] She did come to understand in time, but when Howard needed a more sympathetic ear, she did not offer any empathy.[49]

"You could get a nurse who is trained to do the job better than you can," Price suggested, as if the Howards had not already done so.[50] They had hired help; the problem was, they could not keep them. "Woman after woman we hired," he explained in a letter, "and they quit, either worn out by their work, or unwilling to do it, though my father and I did most of it. Sometimes when we could get a couple of good women we'd get a short breathing spell. Again there were times when we couldn't get anybody, and I not only took care of my mother, while my father handled his wide practice, but did all the housework, washing, and cooking."[51] The only one who stuck with the Howard family to the end was their neighbor, Kate Merryman, but she could not be present twenty-four hours a day and came mostly during the daylight hours, necessitating Dr. Howard and his son to care for her at night.[52]

Even after explaining the nurse dilemma, Price could not let her discomfort go. "You change her gown and bed? Where is your dad?" she asked, before telling him, "For God's sake, Bob, that's not your job."[53] He turned on her abruptly and said, "I do it because I have to. It's my job. Damn it, you do what needs to be done. You can't let her stay there, wet and uncomfortable. You do the damn best you can."[54] It sparked a heated exchange. Price could not understand why it had to be him, especially when he should be working.

"My God, Bob, you're not required to give up your whole life, your writing and everything."[55]

Howard slammed on the brakes, bringing the car to a halt. He again turned on her and yelled, "What's work? A man can do any kind of work. Work is not worth a damn, unless you work for somebody you love. All my life I've loved and needed her. I'm losing her. I know that. Damn it to hell, I know that. I want to live. You hear that?"[56] Once again, Howard had spoken words she did not understand, leaving her even more confused. In hindsight, those words signify that Howard had set himself on a course of action that was now inexorable.

He then did something that both angered and frightened her. He grabbed her, and shaking her violently said, "I want to live! I want a woman to love, a woman to share my life and believe in me, to want me and love me. Don't you know that? My God, my God. Can't you see that? I want to live and to love."[57] Howard, in his own way, was trying to tell her he loved her and needed her. Price, who was no longer in love with Howard, felt trapped.

Howard pressed the issue, asking her if she still loved him. She struggled for a response, but it was not the one he wanted to hear. "Bob, your work. I do believe in you," she feebly replied. "I know you're brilliant, and you've got a great talent." He then asked her if she still loved Vinson and crying, she replied, "I don't love anybody. Not anybody at all."[58]

Once regaining her composure, Price then told him what she had been keeping from him for some time. "I'm going to Louisiana State University this summer to begin work on my master's degree," and "I've already been accepted." A silence came over Howard, as well as a look of defeat. "You'll make a good teacher," he finally said, "You'll do anything you set your mind to."[59]

He drove her back to her boardinghouse in silence, punctuated by awkward and stilted conversation. After arriving, he let her out, asking if she was free the following day. She said yes, and he drove away. "The last rays of the setting sun shone on the car illuminating his big, ungainly body," she wrote later in her diary. "His shoulders sagged. He looked beaten. He was staring straight ahead into the empty street."[60] That night she thought of all that had happened as she recorded the events, but the one thing she could not forget were the words he had once told her: "For life to be worth living, a man must have either a great love or a great cause. I have neither."[61]

Howard did not show up the next day, for he took his mother to Marlin instead. He left a letter for her that opened with an apology before laying bare his soul. "I have thought a great deal about our date yesterday," and stated, "It seems incredible that I, in the blackest hours of my life, should have occupied half an hour in a childish squabble over a mustache!"[62] He told her he had looked forward to the date, for he thought it would afford him a chance to forget all his troubles, but that had not happened. "How could I? What chance did you give me to enjoy it?" He questioned her,

> I was already punch-drunk with grief, worry and trouble; but, with my mother's life ebbing away before my eyes, with my father breaking and aging before me with the worry and strain we both labor under, and I myself faced with the wreckage of all my life's plans and labors, and the utter ruin of my career—I found myself, in the brief period I had stolen in the vain hope of forgetting my miseries for a little while, forced into the same petty altercations. My God, arguing over a mustache when my whole life is crumbling to powder under my hands![63]

Price read the letter twice and then, she wrote, "I went into the bathroom, sat down and cried with anger and frustration."[64] It had been all but the end in their relationship, and as she would write over forty years later, "He was never the same after that."[65]

Mrs. Howard was still at the Texas State Sanatorium run by Dr. Joseph Banning McKnight for tubercular patients in Carlsbad, Texas, at the beginning of the year.[66] "We thought in our innocence," Howard later explained to E. Hoffmann Price, "she'd get better care [there] than we could give her during the harsh winter months."[67] As Howard explained to Lovecraft, "This has been the worst winter since 1929, one blizzard after another, combined with dust storms bringing epidemics of sickness, and sleets and snows, but no rain, no real moisture," leaving him to declare, "the outlook is grim."[68] It was the same for his mother.

Howard and his father moved her back to the San Angelo hospital, where she stayed for twelve days. Because fluid continued to build up in her lungs, both the sanatorium and the hospital tried to drain the fluid with "frequent aspirations," that Howard knew were "painful, weakening and dangerous."[69] Medical historian Thomas Dormandy agreed when he explained that the use of a needle to draw off fluid in the pleura was "both dangerous and painful," and that "the procedure could be frightening as well as exhausting for a patient."[70]

The prognosis was not good. The doctors did not believe she would live much longer. All the time she was there, according to Dr. Howard, his son was "driving back and forth daily from San Angelo to home." The doctor, writing Lovecraft after his son's death, explained how the prognosis once again raised the specter of his suicide. "One evening," the doctor wrote, "he told me I would find his business, what little there was to it, all carefully written up and in a larger envelope in his desk. Again I begged him not to do it, but he positively did not intend to live after his mother was gone."[71]

Mrs. Howard did not die in the San Angelo hospital, but neither was her health improving, so finally it was decided they would bring her home on the first of February.[72] Once again this put them in the position of having to find someone to help care for her at home. "First one woman and then another we hired to help wait on her has been taken sick herself," Howard wrote Lovecraft, "so the job of nursing my mother has been done largely by my father and myself."[73] They did everything possible to make her comfortable, but still, she did not improve.[74] Frustrated, Howard wrote, "There seems to be little we or anyone can do to help her, though God knows I'd make any sacrifice, including my own life, if it could purchase her any relief."[75]

Finally, in late February, running out of options, they decided to take her back to Marlin for treatment. Once more, circumstances prevented her from receiving treatment that helped. "The head of the place left for Detroit just after we got there," he wrote Lovecraft, "leaving his conceited jackass of a son in charge." Apparently, Dr. Torbett's son had his own ideas about how Mrs. Howard should be treated, and these practices differed from past treatment by his father, leaving Howard to feel she was being neglected.

Dr. Howard confronted the idealistic son and set him straight. "Meeting somebody he couldn't bully seemed to be a new and rather terrifying experience to him," Howard wrote. "Anyway . . . following my father's orders, he did improve her condition enough for us to bring her home," although the two-hundred-mile trip back to Cross Plains over rough country roads left Howard pondering, "How my mother in her weakened condition stood it, I don't know."[76]

As was the culture of the time, people did not talk openly about their illnesses or medical conditions.[77] Never once did Dr. Howard or his son ever write that Mrs. Howard had tuberculosis. Howard had not even spoken that dreaded word to his girlfriend in all the time they were dating. Like Novalyne Price, many people in Cross Plains had wondered if Mrs. Howard had not simply been feigning her illness, perhaps as a means of garnering attention from her son. Yet research has clearly indicated Mrs. Howard had contracted tuberculosis, and both her decline and treatments were in accord with that diagnosis.[78] "In the final analysis, her detractors were wrong," Howard scholar Leo Grin wrote; "she hadn't been faking the severity of her illness," rather, "she had been dying a miserable and painful death all along."[79]

Chapter 29

Future Texas Laureate, 1936

For days they ringed us with their flame,
For days their swarming soldiers came,
The battle wrack was gory.
We perished in the smoke and flame,
To give the world their traitor shame
And our undying glory.
—"The Alamo"[1]

In 1890 the US Census Bureau declared the American frontier was closed. There were no longer any tracts of land across the country that were not settled. Three years later historian Frederick Jackson Turner delivered his influential thesis before the American Historical Association titled "The Significance of the Frontier in American History." It was his conclusion that "four centuries from the discovery of America, and the end of a hundred years of life under the Constitution, the frontier has gone, and with its going has closed the first period of American history."[2] And along with moving from American experience to American history, the frontier also moved into the pages of American literature, firmly establishing itself there in the first two decades of the twentieth century. This transition was important, for as literary professor Jay B. Hubbell wrote in 1925, "The frontier gave to American literature . . . two very important things. It gave our writers a vast field of unexploited literary material, new backgrounds, new types of characters, and a wealth of romantic incident," while at the same time it also gave them "a new point of view."[3] Such was the case for those authors living in the state of Texas, because their point of view became the land itself.

One of the state's first literary authors, Texas folklorist J. Frank Dobie, understood this well when he wrote, "Great literature transcends its native land, but none that I know ignore its soil."[4] While Texas authors were not likely to ignore their beloved state, they almost always wrote of it with a strong nostalgic sensibility. The noted Texas historian Walter Prescott Webb recognized this when he acknowledged, "There has been a tendency on the part of writers to mix a good deal of sentiment with their history of the West," and Texans were likely to mix far more than any other author from another region.[5] Perhaps the one author who understood this best was novelist and Texan Larry McMurtry, who had a longer view of this practice than either Dobie or Webb, for he wrote in the 1960s, "Everyone who writes from Texas feels this to be his own, his native land, and no one yet has had a soul so dead that it would allow him to write about the state unsentimentally."[6] Howard was certainly no exception.

Born, raised, and living nearly all his life in rural Texas, Howard had strong ties to the state. "I really have no connection with the early history of Texas," he wrote Lovecraft in 1930, "though I was born here. Still, because of birth and environment I feel more closely knit to Texas than to the Old South."[7] In Howard's formative years Texas was certainly in transition; it was not fully frontier, yet not fully settled. This was not uncommon for the rural parts of the state, for as late as the 1940s, McMurtry asserts, "The hem of the garment of the Great Frontier could still be touched in rural Texas," and Howard most certainly felt it at times, such as when he recalled riding along the Nueces River in a covered wagon in the fall of 1909.[8] He wrote in earnest to Lovecraft, attempting to explain his personal connections to the Texas frontier.

> Let me point out to you that I was born in a region that had suffered Indian raids less than thirty years before my birth, and range-wars less

> than ten; a region of whose population a large percent still consisted of the original settlers. That from my very birth I have listened to first-hand narrations and descriptions of the pioneering era by the people who made that era. That as a child I had at least a child's part in the last great pioneering movement of the southwest—the settlement and development of the Great Plains and the Lower Rio Grande regions. That my entire life has been spent among pioneers and their children and grandchildren.[9]

As evident, most of his associations to the frontier were not his own lived experiences but rather those of his elders. Yet he still had touched the hem of the garment more so than those who would follow him.

Howard was also keenly aware that the Texas frontier was quickly disappearing around him. "The old Texas is gone or is going fast," he wrote. "All the plains are fenced in, where in my childhood I've ridden for a hundred miles without seeing a foot of barbed wire. I can't remember when I've heard a coyote."[10] And when Lovecraft questioned him if Texas was in a state of transition, Howard realistically replied, "Transition? Why, heavens, there's never been anything else in Texas!" He elaborated that "less than a generation before I came here, it had changed from a cattle country to a farming country" and he believed that "a generation after I am gone, it will change again into a land of irrigated gardens and intensified stock farming."[11] Yet despite this practical point of view, as the Texas literati noted, Howard the Texan could still be quite sentimental about his home state.

This sentimentalism was on full display in many of his letters when he wrote of his desire to have lived on the frontier in the early 1800s. "I yearn for the days of the early frontier," he wrote Lovecraft, "where men were more truly free than at any other time or place in the history of the world, since man first began to draw unto himself the self-forged chains of civilization."[12] His romantic notions of helping to forge the state of Texas led him to wish he had "fought through the Texas Revolution, and taken part in San Jacinto," and had "served as a soldier in the war with Mexico."[13] He saw it as a more noble time and one that afforded a man more freedom than the age in which he lived. "Maybe that's why I like the study of history so well," he opined to Lovecraft. "I'm unable to orient myself with this complicated age and understand it."[14]

Despite having grown up on a Texas frontier in transition and having both realistic and sentimental views of his home state, the land and its people shaped Howard in a much more fundamental way. Texas historian T. R. Fehrenbach wrote in his magisterial history of the state that "the long barbarism of the frontier created something akin to a barbarian ethos in parts of Texas" in which "the strong were respected, even if they might be hated," while "the weak, or late-comers clamoring for 'their share' tended to be despised."[15] In his upbringing Howard had absorbed this ethos from both the land and from his elders. It had shaped him as a person, and it formed the "tough-minded writer" he had become.[16] As such, the stories he wrote, whether of the Texas or Pictish frontiers, were highly imbued with this barbarian ethos; they were imbued with the culture of frontier Texas.[17]

By early 1936 Howard had already written a number of stories that featured a Texas setting. Some of his horror stories were set in the Lone Star State with Texans as protagonists, including "The Horror from the Mound," "The Man on the Ground," and "Old Garfield's Heart."[18] He had also written several Western yarns that were set in Texas, such as "The Vultures of Whapeton," that was now in the hands of his agent. Even some of his fantasy stories, including several of his Conan stories, had essentially been set in Texas or the Southwest, although in these cases, the stories were transported to the Hyborian Age. The most explicit of these, and considered one of his best Conan yarns, was "Beyond the Black River."

"I sold Wright a yarn," Howard told Price in early 1935. "I'm damned surprised he took it. It's different from my other Conan yarns . . . no sex . . . only men fighting against the savagery and bestiality about to engulf them. I want you to read it when it comes out."[19] Composed in October of 1934, it was published as a two-part serial in *Weird Tales* over the May and June 1935 issues. "I was afraid he wouldn't take it, but he did!" Howard excitedly told Price. "By God, he took it!"[20] In her memoirs she explained, "He was excited about it because it was about this country and it sold!"[21]

Howard elaborated on this to Lovecraft when he wrote the serial was really, "a frontier story." "In [this] Conan story I've attempted a new style and setting entirely—abandoned the exotic settings of lost cities, decaying civilizations, golden domes, marble palaces, silk-clad dancing girls, etc., and thrown my story against a back-ground of forests and rivers, log cabins, frontier outposts, buckskin-clad settlers, and painted tribesmen."[22] Howard had already spelled out the premise of the story to Lovecraft three years before he had written it. "A student of early Texas history is struck by the fact that some of the most savage battles with the Indians were fought in the territory between the Brazos and Trinity rivers," he explained, before detailing how "in the old times the red-skins held the banks of the Brazos. Sometimes they drove the ever-encroaching settlers back—sometimes the white men crossed the Brazos, only to be hurled back again, sometimes clear back beyond the Trinity. But they came on again—in spite of flood, drouth, starvation and Indian massacre."[23] As Howard scholar John Bullard explains, Howard had, in reality, written a story set in the wilderness between the Trinity and Brazos Rivers of Texas, changing the names to the Thunder and Black Rivers, while the Picts became the Hyborian stand-ins for the American Indians. Because "Howard used his knowledge of Texas's history and people, as well as his family's history," Bullard believes it made "the story as realistic as possible in a fantasy setting."[24] It had given the story a sense of realism.

Part of that realism may well have been derived from that fact that Howard put not only himself in the story but also his dog Patch. Many scholars believe that the character Balthus in the story is Howard's own persona who, accompanied by his dog Slasher, meets Conan in the Pictish wilderness.[25] In the end, after both die, Conan states, "He was a man," before honoring both of them when he lifts his leather jack saying, "I drink to his shade, and to the shade of the dog, who knew no fear."[26]

Howard also approached the story through his lifelong interest in the relationship between civilization and barbarism. "He also said another thing most emphatically," Price later recalled in an interview. "A story had to express some philosophy or belief in life." She then explained that Howard "believed that since the barbarian lived a simpler life, expressed his deepest emotions of love and hate honestly in a world that was unhindered by false trappings of civilization, the barbarian would ultimately triumph." This, she explained, was "the basic idea in his beautiful story,

'Beyond the Black River.'"[27] The last lines of the story convey Howard's deep belief when he wrote, "Barbarism is the natural state of mankind. Civilization is unnatural. It is a whim of circumstance. And barbarism must always ultimately triumph."[28]

The serial's publication proved to be a well lauded story, not only by the readers of *Weird Tales* but also by his fellow writers. It even led Lovecraft to declare there was "no question but that you and Clark Ashton Smith are the twin pillars of the institution."[29] Howard also received some unexpected praise from another reader, Natalie H. Wooley, who wrote an article titled "The Adventure Story" for a small literary publication called *The Californian.* In the article she alludes to the following short passage from "Beyond the Black River": "Valannus shuddered. Turning, he walked to a casement and stared silently out over the river, black and shiny under the glint of the stars. Beyond the river the jungle rose like an ebony wall. The distant screech of a panther broke the stillness. The night seemed pressing in, blurring the sounds of the soldiers outside the blockhouse, dimming the fires. A wind whispered through the black branches, rippling the dusky water. On its wings came a low, rhythmic pulsing, sinister as the pad of a leopard's feet."[30] Wooley then succinctly stated, "There, my friends, is writing." She continued by explaining her assessment for why Howard's writing was of such high quality. "A paragraph of less than a hundred words, yet combining description, menace, and a hint of action to come. Each word is carefully chosen. Note the artfully worded last sentence, with its intimation of impending conflict; sustaining the readers' interest through what otherwise might be a rather colorless bit of description. Mr. Howard, well known adventure-fiction story writer, is one of a few who do not sacrifice beautiful narrative style for the action demanded in such stories, but combines the two masterfully."[31] The words of one who could appreciate the quality of Howard's writing ability, who wrote her analysis while Howard still lived, have been echoed through the years by Howard fans, scholars, and other writers, especially when it came to this Texas-based Conan story.[32]

Howard liked the story so much, he first wrote a quasi-sequel to it, "The Black Stranger," featuring Conan in opposition to the Picts, with many autobiographical details, but it did not sell and was rewritten as a pirate tale featuring the character Terence Vulmea.[33] He then set about writing what would become his last written Conan yarn, "Red Nails," a story that more deeply explored the conflict between civilization and barbarism.

"The last yarn I sold to *Weird Tales*—and it well may be the last fantasy I'll ever write," Howard explained to Lovecraft in July of 1935, "was a three-part Conan serial which was the bloodiest and most sexy weird story I ever wrote."[34] The reason Howard posited it might be his last fantasy, his last story of Conan, was, once again, due to finances.[35] As it turned out, his belief was well founded, for according to Howard scholar Patrice Louinet, "no evidence exists that Howard ever wrote anything about the character after that date."[36]

Howard described the story as his "grimmest, bloodiest and most merciless story of the series so far," but defended it by writing, "I merely portrayed what I honestly believe would be the reactions of certain people in the situations on which the plot of the story hung."[37] The yarn takes place in a lost city, whose once great civilization had declined and decayed into a murderous blood feud. Like "Beyond the Black River," Howard transported a part of historic lore, this time in the Southwest, into the Hyborian Age.

The story was motivated by his visit to Lincoln, New Mexico, with Vinson, where a violent blood feud had resulted in the Lincoln County War. "It was during this visit," writes Louinet, "that Howard found the last elements he needed to write 'Red Nails.'"[38] "After returning home from that trip, in late June 1935," Louinet continues, "Howard at last sat down to write the story which had been germinating in his mind for so many months."[39] The story dispensed with the clash between civilization versus barbarism by allowing Conan to witness the results of a civilized society that had completely decayed.[40] He was writing of his own belief about what was happening around him as he began to witness America's own decline.[41] "I had always felt," Price wrote Burke, "that 'Red Nails' described Bob's rotting, decaying end of civilization perfectly. The abnormal has become accepted as normal in that decadent city."[42]

The first installment of "Red Nails" may have been seen by Howard since it hit the newsstands in June 1936, but otherwise, the last Conan yarn was published posthumously over the July, August/September, and October issues of *Weird Tales*, and proved a bittersweet ending to the series for the magazine's readers. Gertrude Hemken of Chicago, always a reader with colorful expressions, wrote to "The Eyrie" after the first installment exclaiming, "My! It's exciting already; strange, possibly unexplored places. Goody—I'm so-o-o happy, I could gurgle!"[43] Because readers did not yet know that Howard had died, letters such as the one by Robert A. Madle of Philadelphia would prove sadly tragic in hindsight: "Robert E. Howard's latest Conan adventure takes first place. I have yet to be displeased by Howard, and I hope he never stops writing for *Weird Tales*."[44] Readers continued to praise the three-part serial over the course of its run, while at the same time learning of his demise, and both parts one and two would be voted the most popular story of their issue.[45]

"I want to make a prediction," Howard wrote to Farnsworth Wright in 1931, "that the Southwest is entering what I believe will prove to be a gigantic literary boom, and the next generation will see this section of the country fictionalized, dramatized, and glorified generally."[46] Howard was at least already familiar with such writers as Dobie and Webb, who were working toward solidifying this in their nonfiction work, but Howard understood it would also be the case for fiction.[47] After all, he continued, "the history of the Southwest is rich in drama."[48]

At least as far back as 1930, Howard had considered writing a sweeping history of his home state. "By the way," he wrote Smith that year, "I'm going to write a history of early Texan days some time, entitled: An Unborn Empire or something like that."[49] And to Lovecraft he wrote, "I hope to some day write a history of the Southwest that will seem alive and human to the readers, not the dry and musty stuff one generally finds in chronicles. To me the annals of the land pulse with blood and life, but whether I can ever transfer this life from my mind to paper, is a question. It will be years, at least."[50] In his voluminous letters to Lovecraft, Howard often informed him of his state—its lands, peoples, and culture. Lovecraft, never a complete fan of Howard's stories, found himself both fascinated and amazed by Howard's writings of his home state. Soon after their letter exchange began, Lovecraft wrote to Derleth, "Have just heard more from Howard—a highly interesting character, & *much* superior to his work. He has a poet's sense of the epic sweep of Texas life & history, & really ought to link up more with this native & lifelong soil of his. Perhaps he will some day—I shall certainly encourage it."[51] Lovecraft not only encouraged Howard in his own letters, but he also wrote to his many correspondents about Howard's descriptions of Texas, once calling them "literature in the truest sense of the word."[52] Because of the mix of his own desires and this encouragement, Howard set about creating the most natural persona he had yet created for himself, one which Burke calls "The Texian."[53]

"Of late," Howard wrote Derleth in 1933, "I have confined my wanderings almost entirely to the hill country in this region."[54] Howard was beginning to seek out local history and personal narratives to provide background and the impetus for his stories.[55] After he began dating Price, he regaled her with stories of Texas past, about which she bristled slightly. "He's always wanting to tell me something about Texas history," she wrote in her memoirs, "as if I had moved here from somewhere else."[56] He encouraged her and his friend Smith to also consider writing regional yarns, telling the latter, "Now is the time to write historical Texas stuff, because the Southwest is entering a big literary boom."[57] Writing to Derleth in late 1935, Howard reflected, "I'm seriously contemplating devoting all my time and efforts to western writing, abandoning all other forms of work entirely; the older I get the more my thoughts and interests are drawn back over the trails of the past; so much has been written; but there is so much that should be written."[58]

Howard was writing about Texas at this time, but he had another dream. He wanted to write the great Texan novel. "I wouldn't say this to anybody but you," Howard told Price on one of their dates, "but, by God, I know what I can do. I love this country, and I know damn well I can write about it. I know damn well I can write a novel that will move, be about people facing real odds."[59] She explained in her memoirs that he wanted to write "a novel depicting the settlers' fear as they tried to carve out a new life, and the Indians' fear as they tried to hold on to a doomed country."[60] Unfortunately, he never did. As Price later commented in an interview,

"Although he said he put something of Texas in everything he wrote, I'm still very sorry that he didn't give himself time to write the novels about Texas he wanted to write."[61]

Howard had certainly been well positioned to do so. Both Dobie and Webb had tried writing fiction, but they gave it up to write nonfiction. Howard could have easily filled that gap. When it came to translating the true stories of history into literature, several of Texas's premier laureates understood the difficulty. Larry McMurtry lamented that it was unfortunate that "great raconteurs who are also writers are all too often sloppy when they go to write down the stories they tell so well," explaining that "At heart they are usually impatient with the written word and feel that it is a weak substitute for the human voice."[62] J. Frank Dobie himself admitted as much, when he wrote, "It's the despair of a writing man who has known the best of storytellers that he cannot translate their oral savor into print."[63] There is little doubt this would not have been an impediment for Howard's Texas stories had he written them. His friends certainly agreed, for like Lovecraft had written, they believed, "His knowledge of its history and folkways was profound, and the descriptions and reminiscences contained in his private letters illustrate the eloquence and power with which he would have celebrated it in literature had he lived longer."[64]

Howard himself had come to believe that this was how he would make his mark in literature. "I have always felt," Howard wrote Lovecraft in his last letter to him, "that if I ever accomplished anything worthwhile in the literary field, it would be with stories dealing of the central and western frontier."[65] Given time, Howard may well have become a future laureate of the state he loved so dearly. Larry McMurtry, a Texas laureate in his own right, likely would have agreed, for he once wrote of Howard that he was "one of the few Texas writers of the 30s who is still being read today outside of Texas" and that "Howard, of course, was a pulp-writer, far and away the best pulp-writer that the state produced."[66]

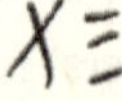

Having brought Mrs. Howard home from Marlin at the beginning of March, Dr. Howard and his son took care of her as best they could.[67] At this point she was not eating, so the purchase of the goats had been fortuitous; Howard wrote Lovecraft, "She lives mainly on their milk."[68] Dr. Howard spent more time with his wife, who had become his number one patient, while at the same time still trying to manage his practice. The Howards' neighbor, Larry McDonough, recalled in an interview that in those last months of Mrs. Howard's life, "I was going over there all the time," and he described her as having "got real puny." He also explained how, "Doc Howard . . . rented, or bought or something, a hospital bed," and Mrs. Howard, "would be in the front bedroom in [the] hand-cranked, hospital bed" and she "had two nurses that would come in and bathe her [and] change her clothes." He also recalled Dr. Howard "doing his work" while his son "was in this room here next pounding the typewriter."[69] Each in their own way was now simply trying to survive.

Dr. Howard's care of his wife did appear to be helping at first. "She seemed to be improving a little," Howard wrote Lovecraft, but then tragedy struck again for, "she had an attack of acute pleurisy on her right side."[70] It was not uncommon for tubercular patients to experience such inflammation in the thin layers of tissue between the lungs and chest, but because of their condition, it was a dangerous complication of the disease and if left undiagnosed or treated, could be life-threatening.[71] "My father handled that," Howard continued, "and she was definitely on the mend, although the sweats never ceased."[72]

Not long after they settled back home in Cross Plains, Dr. Howard ran into Novalyne Price in the City Drug Store. He updated her on Mrs. Howard's condition and about the around-the-clock care she now needed. While they were talking, they both saw Howard drive up to the post office across the street and mail a letter. Price noted he was nicely dressed and had shaved his mustache. Despite both of them seeing Howard, neither said a word about him. It was an awkward situation.

After both Howard men had departed, Price crossed the street and retrieved the letter he had sent her. Howard apologized for not seeing her earlier letter because his mail had not been forwarded to Marlin, and for the fact that she had found herself under "such a bitter strain." He then told her, "It's hard, in the last analysis, to blame anyone for anything. We are all caught in a mesh of circumstances we cannot break." Although he did not like giving anyone unsolicited advice, he explained that, in this case, he thought he would. "I feel that the main source of your unhappiness lies in the very point you brought out in your letter, when you said you are always trying to change things." He then cautioned her,

> You cannot change things or people, and you only make yourself miserable when you try. Life is necessarily a continual series of compromises. No one is perfect, nor is anything perfect nor can anything or anyone be perfect. If one is to live at all, one is forced to accept the faults of life along with the virtues. . . . If we demand perfection in all things, and try to bend all things into our particular pattern of belief, we only hurt ourselves. You cannot change people, because they cannot change themselves; they were cast in an inflexible mold of heredity and circumstances, long before you ever saw them. You beat against an iron wall and hurt yourself and embitter your life.[73]

The letter, as Price said, hurt her, but "I hurt for Bob, not for myself."[74] Price saw his attitude as being far too fatalistic and the letter was written by a man who had given up hope. Price still had a lot of fight in her and a future to look forward to. Howard, on the other hand, was exhausted from the fight—the fight with editors, nonpayment for stories, keeping his mother alive, and meeting expenses—and on the course he had set for himself. With his mother dying, Howard knew he had no future.

Chapter 30

"In the Realization That I Must Die," 1936

Drums of glory are lost in the ages,
Bare feet fail on a broken trail—
Let my name fade from the printed pages;
Dreams and visions are growing pale.
—"Lines Written in the Realization That I Must Die"[1]

During the spring of 1936, Hester Howard's condition did not improve. While she had rarely left the house in her last years, by this time, Marie Baker recalled, "She was always in bed, as far as I remember. Always in bed."[2] Howard explained in a letter to Lovecraft that his mother was "very weak and weighs only 109 pounds," indicating that her normal weight was 150, and that "very few kinds of food agree with her."[3] The worst, however, were the night sweats she had been experiencing since January, generally an indication that the body's level of infection is very high.[4] "Many a night," Howard wrote, "she had to be changed six or seven times, and that many times a day—sometimes more."[5] It was not just the inconvenience of Mrs. Howard's nightclothes becoming saturated but also the pain accompanying the night sweats that often proved unbearable. "Disturbed nights turned into nightmares," medical historian Dormandy states, describing how "no pain-killer, not even laudanum or later morphine, could entirely cope with them."[6] For Howard, who often stayed up tending to his mother regardless of whether nurses or other help was available, it had to have been a traumatic experience watching his mother suffer so, for as Bynum, another medical historian, describes the experiences of caregivers: "Sitting up with a consumptive patient, onlookers heaved a sigh of relief when the feverish tossing and turning, at its worst between two and four in the morning, finally ceased."[7]

Then, in early April, Mrs. Howard's health took a troubling turn. Howard described how "the worst dust storm I ever saw in my life" swept through Cross Plains.[8] The southwestern Great Plains had been suffering from drought since the beginning of the decade, causing the overgrazed and over-farmed lands to simply blow away. As the Callahan County Agent would chide the farmers in the April 17, 1936, edition of the *Cross Plains Review*, "You have not been saving or rebuilding enough wood lots to serve as wind-breaks against dust storms and to keep good soil rooted down."[9] And when the dust storms blew through, despite all attempts otherwise, the dust was everywhere. As Caroline Henderson recalled in her memoirs, "Dust to eat, and dust to breathe and dust to drink. Dust in the beds and in the flour bin, on dishes and walls and windows, in hair and eyes and ears and teeth and throats, to say nothing of the heaped up accumulation on floors and window sills after one of the bad days."[10] The problem for Mrs. Howard was dust in her already suffering respiratory system, and because of this, Howard wrote, "She developed pneumonia in the right lung." After suffering through this added ailment, she did recover by the end of April, but all Howard could write of her condition at that time was, "She is a little better, but is very weak and suffers a great deal of pain."[11]

His constant care of his mother left Howard with far less freedom than he was accustomed to, causing his writing, correspondence, and time away from home to become infrequent and sporadic. On one occasion, likely when there was enough hired help to watch his mother, Howard drove to Fredericksburg, Texas, to purchase a particular bottle of port wine his mother enjoyed, likely in the futile hope that it would improve her health, if not, at least, her spirits.[12]

On occasion he still asked Novalyne Price out on dates, although their outings were more as friends rather than lovers, for Price admitted to him she had started dating a fellow teacher at work.[13] On one such date in April, Howard wanted to show Price an old, abandoned house he had discovered. As they explored the rooms together, despite knowing she had committed to a life of teaching, he encouraged her to continue writing, and that perhaps she could write of the people who had once dwelled in the empty house. She pointed out that he kept talking about her writing but not about his. "I can't write anything anymore," Howard told her. "No time. Never any time. I get started; I have to stop."[14] On another date he elaborated that even when there was help, he was constantly being interrupted with questions about how to do certain things, leaving him exasperated.[15] He also continued making cryptic comments to her, ones she could not understand. She wrote in her memoirs that in April that he told her, "When his burden was lifted, things might seem different, he didn't know." Puzzled, but not curious enough, she added, "I didn't ask what burden he meant."[16]

The following month, after several weeks had lapsed since their last date, Howard asked her out again. After picking Price up at her boardinghouse, they drove southwest toward Coleman. Since the end of the school year was drawing near, he asked her if she was still planning to attend Louisiana State University. Price told him she was and shared her excitement for the opportunity. "Now you be sure to write to me," Howard told her. "You have my address, old Lock Box 313, Cross Plains, Texas. I ain't likely to be anywhere else for a good while yet."[17]

After teaching her last classes on Friday, May 8, and attending graduation on the twenty-second, Price packed her belongings from Mrs. Hemphill's boardinghouse.[18] Her mother had come to drive her home for a visit before she left for Baton Rouge. In packing her things, Price discovered she still had one of Howard's books she had borrowed and was not sure what to do with it. Mrs. Hemphill suggested she drop it off at Dr. Howard's office, which they did on the way home. In so doing she did not bid Howard goodbye, the man she had so enthusiastically wanted to meet just a few short years before.

Upon receiving the book from his father, Howard sat down at his typewriter and wrote what would be his last letter to her. It was dated May 27, 1936.

"You needn't have bothered about returning the book," he wrote, "I intended for you to keep it, if you wanted it. I hope you enjoy your vacation, and that you'll find Louisiana all you hope it to be. I'm sure the courses of study you're taking will be interesting and helpful. With the best wishes for your health, prosperity and success, I am, as I always was, Your Friend, Bob."[19]

Despite having little time to write and being under so much strain caring for his mother, Howard still managed to find a way to keep publishing his stories.[20] "Naturally, my work has had to be neglected," he wrote Derleth in mid-April, "though I've managed somehow to keep up the Breck Elkins series. I've made three new markets since writing you last: Dime Sport, Cowboy Stories, and Complete Stories—the latter with a 24000 [word] novelet of the El Borak series."[21] *Dime Sports* had published his boxing tale "Iron-Jaw" in April, which was apparently well received by the readers. "So many of you fans seemed to like Robert E. Howard's fight novelette 'Iron-Jaw,'" the editor wrote in the June issue, "that we asked Mr. Howard to step up and introduce himself. Here's what he says:"[22] Howard wrote of his Scotch-Irish ancestry, peripatetic childhood, and various occupations, before writing, "In case anybody's interested I stand a little less than six feet, weigh a hundred and ninety-five pounds, like fried liver and onions washed down with lager, and my favorite pastime is holding down a ring-side seat and watching a good fight-card."[23]

In addition to his Breckenridge Elkins series, which was continuing to be published in *Action Stories*, the pulp magazine *Cowboy Stories* had accepted his Buckner J. Grimes comedic Western yarn, "A Man-Eating Jeopard." And since Jack Byrne had moved over to Munsey Publications, the editor had requested a similar character for their flagship magazine, *Argosy*, and Howard wrote him, "I have in mind a new character, Pike Bearfield, of Wolf Mountain, Texas, about as big, dumb, and ludicrous as B. Elkins."[24]

By the beginning of June, Howard had sold two of the Pike Bearfield stories to *Argosy*, along with a yarn to *Spicy-Adventure* and numerous others, all seemingly in record time.[25] The reason for this sudden increase in sales was actually thanks to Otto O. Binder, a fellow pulp author who wrote with his brother Earl under the name Eando Binder. He had started working for Kline at the end of 1935 as his representative agent in New York City.[26] Quite pleased with Howard's work, Otto wrote his brother Earl at the beginning of June, informing him, "The business is beginning to pick up a bit at that, though I wish all our authors were like Robert E. Howard. Since I've been here, I've sold $700 worth of his stuff, getting him into *Argosy*, and into *Star Western*, and *Complete Stories* [Street & Smith]. He's thirty years old and has sold 22 different magazines and over 125 stories altogether. I've seen his picture—he's a rough and ready Texan."[27] In fact, according to Binder's biographer, Bill Schelly, the reason for his elation over Howard's work was because it "had constituted about a fourth of the sales that Binder had made to this point."[28] Howard was helping Binder stay afloat in his new job.

Perhaps most pleasing to Howard, however, may have been that *Weird Tales* had returned to paying regularly—no more half-checks—so there was hope he would be able to profit more from the stories of his that had already published. At that point in time, they owed him approximately a thousand dollars in back payment, the equivalent of twenty-two thousand in modern dollars.[29] It was likely these payments that motivated Howard to consider resuming his writing for the "unique magazine." "I haven't written a weird story for nearly a year," Howard wrote Derleth in early May, "though I've been contemplating one dealing with Coronado's expedition on the Staked Plains in 1541. A good theme if I can develop it."[30] Howard did manage to partially develop the story, leaving behind an untitled fragment that Glenn Lord later titled "Nekht Semerkeht." According to Burke "this was likely Howard's last writing and reflected some of his innermost thoughts at the time, for in the story the protagonist contemplates the idea of suicide."[31]

Howard tells the story of the aged conquistador Hernando de Guzman, who, attacked by Apaches in the desert, is left horseless and knows "a man afoot was a man as good as dead."[32] Howard then writes that while the "will to live burned fiercely in his breast," Guzman also believed "that the game was not worth the candle." Howard continued, "He did not try to deceive himself into believing that there was any intellectual reason why he should not give up the agonizing struggle, place the muzzle of the pistol to his head and quit an existence whose savor had long ago become less than its pain."[33]

For Howard, writing and publishing in the pulps, something he once savored, had in many ways long ago become less than its pain. He evidently was not alone in this belief. Fellow pulp author Victor Rousseau, who published his article as "Anonymous," wrote of the stress caused by the industry. "My career started ten years ago, and I am still working for the same magazines. My stepping-stone became my biggest step. Here I am, God help me, still a pulpster."[34] Although Howard was opening up new markets, he had not crossed over into the slicks, and the prospects for a book publication remained bleak, so, like Rousseau, he remained a pulpster.

"The greatest hazard outside the writer himself," Rousseau continued, "is the constant change in editorial policies."[35] Much of this, he explained, resulted from the fickleness of readers and the idiosyncrasies of continually changing editors. It also came from a steady supply of new authors so that "the relatively steady seller is always crowded by rivals." As an author in the game as long as Howard had been, it meant, Rousseau wrote, "As an average writer, I have no security. I can never pause to rest. No matter how I feel, I must keep at the machine in relentless, merciless, deadening toil. The toll on my energy will be inevitably fatal to my work, as it has been to others. Added to this, making my future more uncertain, are those minute variations I have mentioned. They are cumulative, and over a decade prove tremendous. As I grow older it will be progressively more difficult for me to adapt myself to new policies."[36] Rousseau then detailed the impact that writing for the pulps had on many of his colleagues, including burnout, alcoholism, and (he hinted) suicide.[37] Howard knew this was the case, for he had once written to Wright, "Every now and then one of us finds the going too hard and blows his brains out," concluding, "it's all in the game, I reckon."[38]

Writing for the pulp industry clearly took a toll on its authors, which is why pulpster Wyatt Blassingame once said, "Short story writing is a young man's game."[39] Howard was no longer the young man of 19 who first saw his name in print in the July 1925 issue of *Weird Tales*. He was now 30 years old, and the pressure of writing for the pulps was starting to catch up to him, for as he told Lovecraft, "The year that brings me into middle age has so far been a rather stormy one."[40] Howard was under a lot of stress not only in his personal life but also in his professional one.[41]

Then, as May gave way to June, Hester Howard's health began to decline rapidly.[42] Even then, Dr. Howard recalled, "She was the bravest woman I've ever seen," for he wrote, "During the months and years of intense suffering, no word of complaint was ever heard more than this (Oh dear)."[43] His son, however, had become ever more distressed over his mother's turn for the worse; Dr. Howard witnessed the change in his countenance, writing, "I saw the awful worry that came over him."[44] Merryman, whose assistance was now needed more than ever, also recalled the change in Howard when she said in an interview, "He walked a lot. Just walked the floors." She also remembered, "He'd go in there and stay with her," and said that Mrs. Howard, putting on a brave face for her son, "pretended to be better than she was."[45] Looking for anything that might help his mother's situation, Howard made several purchases. "My son," Dr. Howard wrote, "ordered an invalid's wheel chair," as well as "a long rubber cushion for seat and back." Mrs. Howard's health had declined so much, however, that she never left her bed. "The chair came, was unpacked, but never used."[46]

Several days later, without any signs of his mother's health improving, Howard came to the realization that his mother might not recover this time. "I haven't time to write much," he wrote to his friend E. Hoffmann Price. "My mother is very low and I fear cannot survive."[47] In light of this, Dr. Howard later wrote that his son "had purchased a burial lot."[48] The lot that was ultimately selected was number thirteen, block twenty-five, in Brownwood's Greenleaf Cemetery.[49] However, according to the cemetery's records, it was Dr. Howard who purchased the lot, not his son.[50] There is the possibility that Howard may have found and suggested the location to his father or perhaps even had gone so far as to reserve the plot, but it could also be that Dr. Howard was simply mistaken.

The days now began to pass interminably. "I would set up all night, one night," Merryman recalled, "and Robert would set up the next night." Merryman was getting little sleep because in addition to frequently staying overnight with Mrs. Howard, she still had to attend to things around the house during the day, including her own.[51] As for Howard, even when

Merryman was attending to his mother at night, he did not sleep well, for he kept the window between their rooms open so he would be able to hear if his mother needed assistance.[52] There were also more people in the house, for Dr. Howard had called upon his friends and fellow doctors to help care for his wife. Again, Merryman recalled, "Doctor Dill stayed there an awful lot of time, while Mrs. Howard was sick. All the doctors just come in there and stayed there. One would stay a while, and then they'd leave and another would come."[53]

On Wednesday, June 10, Mrs. Howard slipped into a coma.[54] Dr. Dill did not leave, and two nurses, Miss Green and Mrs. Speller, and a cook were brought in to assist. In addition, Merryman's sister, Alice Younglove, also came to help.[55] Howard sat with his mother throughout the day, and "in the afternoon," Merryman recalled, "he asked his daddy if he thought his mother would ever regain consciousness." Dr. Howard told him, "[He] didn't think so."[56]

Later that evening, Drs. Howard and Dill were sitting on the front porch swing while the latter's nephew, Larry McDonough, sat on the steps. Howard was with them as well, still walking, pacing back and forth. Alice Younglove recalled that on the front sidewalk, Howard "walked out to the end of it, and he'd come back and face the porch, and he'd stop and look at Doctor Howard. Then he'd go back and walk some more; and every time he'd come up to the porch, though, he'd just stop and look at his daddy."[57] The doctors, meanwhile, were discussing "an accident over at Rising Star" about which McDonough explained, "Somebody was using a big circular saw cuttin' logs and when they cut one of the logs there was a rock in the crotch of the tree . . . and, there was a kid over there around where they were sawing and this saw when it hit this rock . . . broke off, went out and hit in the kid's head." Dr. Dill had been called to the scene, and he rushed the boy to the Cisco hospital, where he and the other doctors operated. They managed, McDonough noted, to get "that blade outta that kid's head—saved him." McDonough then remembered how "Robert sorta perked up" upon hearing this story and morbidly "asked my uncle, a person who was gonna kill themselves, whereabouts in the head, if that blade went in . . . whereabouts would they do it."[58] Howard's thoughts of suicide now prevailed.

Dr. Howard was well aware of his son's intent to kill himself when his mother died, for his son had told him that fact on several occasions. Each time, he wrote, "I tried to persuade him from this and talked to him a great deal."[59] Knowing this, Dr. Howard stated that in those last few days, "I was following him and watching him closely." Still, in light of his own grief for the woman he so loved, the doctor would have been hard pressed to maintain his vigilance over his son. In addition, Dr. Howard explained, "I did not think that he would kill himself before his mother went," for if there were any truth in his statements, he would wait until she passed. He admitted, "I was mistaken," for he later came to the realization that his son "never intended to see his mother die."[60]

Yet despite Howard's dark mood over the past several weeks, a change came over him that night. Dr. Howard later recalled how "he assumed an almost cheerful attitude," while Mrs. Merryman told an interviewer that he "seemed to change markedly" for "he grew cheerful," which was "quite a contrast to the dour, concerned expression he usually bore when [his] mother was serious ill."[61]

It was during this change in behavior that he approached his father, who was sitting quietly crying in the living room, and did something entirely unexpected. Dr. Howard later wrote that his son came up to him, put an arm around him, and said, "Buck up, you are equal to it; you will go through it all right."[62] Merryman said that he then left the room singing.[63] If she did not think that behavior odd enough, Howard later came into the kitchen for coffee. As she and others knew, "He never drank it before." When she asked if he wanted cream and sugar, Howard told her, "Well, I don't know. I just want something to keep me going."[64] He drank it black.

That night, Howard spent most of his time going through his papers, leaving it a mess.[65] As Dr. Howard recalled, "Each time his mother began to get in a bad way and death was expected, Robert would begin to set his house in order."[66] This time, he placed two manuscripts in a large envelope with instructions for where they were to be sent, most likely to Wright, for Howard had earlier made arrangements with Kline concerning what to do with his stories in the event of his death. The two manuscripts were "The Fire of Asshurbanipal" and "Dig Me No Grave," both written sometime before the spring of 1936 and later published posthumously in *Weird Tales*.[67] Howard had also made one other fateful arrangement shortly prior to his mother slipping into a coma: he borrowed a .380 Colt Automatic from his friend Lindsey Tyson.[68] Howard never told his friend why he wanted it.

The next morning, June 11, was exceptionally warm and would turn out to be one of the hottest days of the summer.[69] The cook had returned to the house, and after helping with the breakfast, Merryman returned to her own home.[70] After all but Howard had eaten, the cook began to clear the dishes from the dining room table and set about washing them in the kitchen sink.[71] Dr. Dill was still present, keeping his friend Dr. Howard company more than anything, and there were two nurses present, one who remained at Mrs. Howard's bedside. At this time, having been awake ever since his mother had gone into a coma, Howard went into his mother's room. According to his father, Howard then asked the "nurse if she thought his mother would ever regain consciousness enough to know him."[72] In an apparent effort to be honest with him, "the nurse told him she feared not."[73] Howard then left the room.

He walked through the house, exiting by the back door. According to some neighbors, he was talking loudly at the time, which attracted their attention, and they saw him get into his 1935 Chevrolet Standard.[74] The car was parked in front of the garage, which was visible from the kitchen, and "the cook standing at the window at the back part of the house, saw him get in his car" as well.[75] He closed the door.[76] Dr. Howard later wrote Lovecraft that the cook "thought he was fixing to drive to town as he usually did."[77] What happened next shocked everyone who heard.

Howard took the .380 Colt Automatic, likely stored in the glove box, and placed it to his right temple. He then pulled the trigger. The bullet entered his right temple, traveled through his brain, and exited on the left side before passing through the metal strip above the driver's side window.[78] As Howard had written in his poem about suicide, titled "The Tempter," he "saw the world fade swift away."[79]

Despite the suddenness of killing himself after learning that his mother was likely to soon die, his suicide had not been a rash act.[80] Since Howard had learned that a classmate had committed suicide when he was 17 years old, Tevis Clyde Smith explained that Howard had become ever "more constant in defending the right of self-destruction, dropping hints of the value of such an ending."[81] Howard told his father, his girlfriend, and several of his closest friends, including Smith, that he had no intention of living after his mother died.[82] It only came as a surprise because no one believed he would actually carry out this horrific act. Howard's suicide had clearly been a premediated act.[83] The natural question that follows then is why?

There are many attendant reasons for Howard's suicide, but the most immediate was most certainly his mother's impending death. This has long been held as the singular cause for Howard's suicide since at least the release of the first Howard biography by authors L. Sprague de Camp, Catherine Crook de Camp, and Jane Whittington Griffin.[84] Howard scholar Patrice Louinet, however, addressed this conventional wisdom when he wrote, "That Howard was close to his mother is indisputable, but her death was obviously not the cause of his suicide." He argues that it merely "*provided the occasion* Howard had been waiting for."[85] Again, because the evidence suggests it was premeditated, one has to look elsewhere for the true cause.

There were other proximate causes, more than just his mother dying. The increasing stress he was facing with his work should be considered, as well as the depression brought on by watching his mother die, the fact that he was exhausted from a lack of sleep, or even his being overstimulated from drinking coffee all night. Yet, again, because the act was premeditated, these factors likely only made the final act easier for him to carry out but provide little explanation for the real cause.

The personal relationships in his life at the time of his death should also be considered. His relationship with his first and only girlfriend had recently ended, and even maintaining a friendship with her was no longer possible, for she had left the state. With regard to male companionship, as Leo Grin explained, "Howard watched his friends get married and find jobs and move away."[86] Because of this he was finding himself ever more alone in the world.[87] In addition, despite having made a successful career as a pulpster, respected by readers and fellow authors alike, the people in his own community looked down on him and his chosen profession.[88] In fact, the general consensus appears to be that they all thought he was crazy. Moreover, he was not keen on the larger society he lived in, for as Price recalled, "He said he didn't want to live in a rotting civilization," and this statement led her to believe that "he may have used this philosophy to make his suicide possible . . . ending it all before he had to face that final decay, rot and failure."[89]

There is also his lack of self-confidence, as evidenced in his belief that, while not entirely a failure, he had not proven to be as successful as he had hoped to be with his writing. "I have not been a success," he wrote Lovecraft, "and probably never will be."[90] He also told Price on several occasions that he was nothing more than a "hack" writer.[91] And it certainly had not boosted his confidence when, writes Grin, "He watched now-forgotten writers thriving in high-end markets he had never been able to break."[92] For Howard, all of this must have seemed like the prediction he had made to Smith eight years earlier coming true: "Surely . . . by the time I have gained the heights of success I will be old and hardened so by life that the taste of success will be as dust and ashes in my soul—a man without hope, without joy and without friends."[93] While this may have been a contributing reason, it was not the primary cause. The true cause of Howard's suicide originated from his lifelong passion for freedom.

"I want as much personal freedom as is possible under this system," Howard had written Lovecraft, before stating, "If I can't have at least as much as I have now, I don't want to live at all."[94] Burke once explained that Howard "was not at all enamored with life for its own sake, seeing it only as weary, grueling toil at the behest of others, with scant chance of success and precious little freedom."[95] Just as Howard had seen his writing as a means to freedom, he had come to believe that suicide would offer him the ultimate freedom he so desired. Yet the one thing that had kept him from doing so before June 11, 1936, was his mother. "Duty kept him from doing away with himself," explained his closest friend, Tevis Clyde Smith, believing "that this sense of duty kept him pounding away at the typewriter when everything else would have failed."[96] Yet now, believing his mother was going to die, Howard was free of this duty. "At the moment he learned, not that she was dead, but that she no longer needed him to look after her," explains Louinet, "Howard found himself master of his fate again, and in a position to do what he had been considering for months at the very minimum, and probably for years."[97] As Burke succinctly states, "His mother's death liberated him from the necessity of staying alive."[98] Now he could truly be free.[99] And, so, like his characters, all men of action who chose their own fate, he walked out to his car, closed the door, and pulled the trigger.

"When she heard the muffled sound of the gun," Dr. Howard wrote of the cook, "she saw him fall over the steering wheel." She screamed, turned, and ran into the dining room.[100] Both doctors were there talking while Dr. Dill drank a cup of coffee. They immediately rushed outside to the car. Upon opening the door, at first they "thought that it was a death shot," but it was not.[101] They quickly realized Howard was still breathing.[102] The doctors moved him to "the larger sleeping porch," for where "Dr. Howard slept there was a half bed and a large bed."[103] Howard was placed on the smaller bed.[104]

Dr. Dill began working on Howard, and a call was made for additional help. The young nurse who was not attending Mrs. Howard immediately went to assist him.[105] Someone went after Mrs. Merryman, for she recalled, "I had just left, but they come after me."[106] Then her sister, Mrs. Younglove, was also sent for, and she later recalled the scene: "I just felt badly when he was dying. He was suffering so . . . the two nurses were still there, you see. And one of them nursed Robert . . . every breath was a moan."[107] Dr. Dill, overwhelmed by the situation, summoned Dr. Edward to come to his assistance.[108] After his arrival, it was he who attended Howard, while Dr. Dill watched over his close friend. All three doctors knew there was no chance Howard would ever recover. There was now little anyone could do but wait until he passed.

The commotion at the house had naturally brought out both concerned and curious neighbors. When the *Cross Plains Review* editor Jack Scott heard the news, as he recalled in an interview, "I got my car and ran there and the yard was full of people. All the neighbors were around."[109] Gathering the facts of what happened and talking with Dr. Edward, Scott rushed back to the office to write the story, for he wanted to make sure it was put on the wire in time for it to appear in the afternoon papers.[110] One paper, the *Brownwood Bulletin*, printed the sensational news and reported on Howard's prognosis, "Attending physician said this afternoon they expected him to live only a short time."[111]

After the commotion settled down, those inside the house began what must have seemed like a long death watch. Dr. Howard, overwhelmed by his grief, called on his friend Calvin Baker of Burkett to come to the house to be with him. Baker brought along his son, Bob, who later recalled his experience of seeing Howard that afternoon. "[I] went into the house where Robert was lying on a small bed in the back of the house," Baker recalled. "I looked at him and a doctor, name unknown, told me not to look at a dying man."[112]

From the time he had pulled the trigger, Howard lingered for eight more hours.[113] E. Hoffmann Price later speculated why he believed Howard lived so long after such self-induced trauma when he wrote to a friend, "I do feel justified in hazarding the guess that uncommon vitality was necessary to stave off the shock, and for such a period resist a fatal wound."[114] In his last letter to Lovecraft, Howard had, after all, written, "Anyway my health is splendid, my muscles are harder than they've been in years."[115] But that, too, was the way Howard had wished to die. In his last letter to Derleth, he told him, "I want to die when my time comes, quickly and suddenly, in the full tide of my strength and health."[116]

Sadly, he did just that.

"He died, without ever showing the least return of consciousness," Dr. Howard wrote Lovecraft shortly after, "at four o'clock, June 11, 1936."[117] Howard was only 30 years old.[118]

Epilogue

"All Fled, All Done"

All fled—all done, so lift me on the pyre—
The Feast is over and the lamps expire.
—Robert E. Howard[1]

Hester Howard never regained consciousness. Perhaps it was just as well, for she never had to learn that her son had committed suicide. After remaining in a coma for thirty-one hours, she passed away at 10:30 p.m. on June 12, 1936.[2] Her death record stated she died of "chronic ulcerative tuberculosis" and "anemia."[3] She was 65 years old.

The ambulance, having already come for Howard's body the night before, arrived only twenty-four hours later to take Mrs. Howard's body away. The following day, Kate Merryman recalled, "They brought both of them back home," and as was customary of the time period, their open coffins were placed on display in the living room of the Howard residence.[4] Friends and neighbors could then pay their respects to the dead and offer their condolences to the living.

"Fate dealt me a blow," Dr. Howard wrote of his situation, "leaving me alone in the midst of this tragedy."[5] In two days he had lost his beloved wife and his only son. The doctors, nurses, and other help became greatly concerned for him. "We were all uneasy about the Doctor," Merryman explained, "as he would go in the bathroom where the guns were kept." Howard's small, eclectic weapons collection was stored in a bathroom cabinet. "So, two of the men went in there," Merryman recalled, "and handed them out the window and they were taken to a neighbor's house."[6]

On the morning of June 14, the coffins were moved to the Baptist Church in preparation for the funeral later that morning.[7] It was believed to have been the first double funeral ever to take place in Cross Plains.[8] As Jack Scott would later recall, "His funeral was one of the biggest things I have ever seen here."[9] He continued, "It was held in the tabernacle, there were about four or five hundred people, and every seat was taken because Dr. Howard had a lot of friends here. There were some friends of Robert, and many of Dr. Howard who had delivered five hundred babies in this country."[10] One other estimate put the number of people in attendance even higher, believing approximately one thousand people had come to pay their respects.[11]

The services began at ten o'clock that morning with the Rev. B. G. Richbourg presiding. Dr. Howard had asked the former pastor of the Cross Plains Baptist Church to officiate the funeral, while local pastors J. C. Mann, S. P. Collins, and V. W. Tatum assisted. However, according to Norris Chambers, Dr. Howard "didn't think they'd preached the kind of sermon they should have."[12]

When the service ended, the pall bearers carried the coffins out to the waiting hearse. Dr. Dill was among the men who carried Mrs. Howard, while Dave Lee, Lindsey Tyson, Winfred Brigner, Russell McGowen, Earl Baker, Mack Underwood, Jap Adams, R. Elliot Bryan, Dr. T. G. Edwards, Dr. J. Henry McGowen and J. C. Huntington, a mix of Howard's and his father's friends, escorted Robert E. Howard's body out of the church. As friend and pallbearer Dave Lee later recalled, "It was the saddest funeral I've seen in my life."[13]

The funeral party then traveled to Brownwood for the internment at the Greenleaf cemetery located on the southside of the city.[14] When the service was finished, the two caskets were lowered into the grave, where they would rest side by side. There was also ample room for Dr. Howard's body to join them later. When the headstone for the family was finally placed, it included each of their names, birth and death years, and a biblical passage from 2 Samuel 1:23, which reads, "They were lovely and pleasant in their lives and in their deaths they were not divided." A year later, out of concern for the standing water over the graves after several heavy Texas downpours, Dr. Howard paid to have the caskets exhumed and placed in steel vaults.[15]

After returning home to Cross Plains, the doctors and nurses who were no longer needed left the house. Merryman, however, stayed with Dr. Howard for the next two weeks to help cook, clean, and organize things, as well as to keep him company.[16] Because Howard had left his room in a mess, one of the things Merryman and the doctor worked on during this time was sorting Howard's papers. Out of this came the discovery that Howard had left behind a will, although this event is highly questionable. According to Merryman, there was a letter written in longhand that left all of his property to his Cross Plains friend Lindsey Tyson.[17] "Doctor! Look at this!" Merryman is reported to have shouted, upon which Dr. Howard took the paper and read it. She then recalled that he turned to her and said, "Don't say anything to anybody about this!"[18] As she explained in a later interview, he left the room with the will, and it was never seen again.

Lindsey Tyson himself picks up the story when he told the same interviewer, "A few days after the suicide, on the street in Cross Plains, a lawyer said to me that Bob had made a will leaving everything to me; but Dr. Howard destroyed the will."[19] The person the lawyer had most likely heard this from was Merryman, for if Dr. Howard had indeed destroyed the will, there would have been nothing for him to gain by mentioning it to anyone, much less a lawyer. If the will did exist, Dr. Howard may have destroyed it out of concern for his own financial situation. It had been months since he had been able to practice medicine, but even so, it had never brought in enough cash, which he would need to pay the funeral expenses. Because of his age (65 years old at this time) and not being as able as he once had been, he may possibly have destroyed the will out of concern for his future. There is also the possibility the will never existed and was only the product of small-town gossip.[20]

Regardless, on June 15 Dr. Howard swore in Callahan County court that Howard had died intestate.[21] He became the temporary administrator of his son's estate the following day.[22] It was estimated that Howard's property was valued at $3,000, approximately $66,000 today.[23] The majority of this consisted of his 1935 Chevrolet, valued at $350, the $702 he had in a First National Bank account, and $1,850 held in "Postal Deposits."[24] These deposits, held in the Brownwood Post Office, were part of the Postal Savings System established by Congress in 1910 that allowed citizens to hold money in what amounted to a certificate of deposit earning modest interest in a government-backed account rather than a private bank. "Although bankers first viewed the Postal Savings System as competition," according to the US Postal Service, "they later were convinced that the Postal Savings System brought a considerable amount of money out of hiding from mattresses and cookie jars" because the law directed those with such holdings "to redeposit most of the money in the system in local banks."[25] While the court's proceedings in this matter would take a long time to clear up, Dr. Howard eventually became the sole heir of his son's estate.

In addition to the will, there was one other questionable event that occurred in the weeks following the funeral. Jack Scott later claimed in many interviews that the morning after Howard had shot himself, he had rushed to the Howard residence to report on the events in time to get the article out on the wire and make the afternoon papers. While there, he claimed the justice of the peace asked him to come into the house, where he showed him the sheet of paper in Howard's typewriter. He stated there were four lines of a couplet typed on them: "All fled, all done / so lift me on the pyre / The feast is over / and the lamps expire."[26] He then rushed back to the *Cross Plains Review* office to write the article. Oddly, Scott never made mention of the couplet in his article that day or for the one appearing the following day in his own weekly newspaper.[27]

Another unusual aspect of this story is the presence of the justice of the peace in the house so soon after Howard had shot himself.[28] In Texas the justice of the peace serves as a coroner to declare a person deceased. At the time, Howard was still alive, so there would have been no reason to have called for the justice of the peace. So unless he came of his own volition, his presence in the house that morning is questionable.

The first actual mention of what has become the famous couplet is actually found in a letter to E. Hoffmann Price that Dr. Howard wrote on June 27, in which he stated in a postscript: "I herewith append the last words that he ever typed, which I am sure was only a few minutes before he shot himself. It was found written on a white slip of paper in his bill folder in his hip pocket."[29] Dr. Howard then relayed the words found in the couplet that Howard had cribbed from a poem titled, "The House of Caesar" by Viola (Taylor) Garvin. In the poem she repeats two similar lines at the end of each stanza, but the one closest to the words Howard had typed were, "All fled, all done—a Caesar's brief desire—The Feast is over and the lamps expire!"[30]

That Howard typed these words is not disputed, but where they were found is questionable.[31] Dr. Howard claimed he found the words typed on a small piece of paper sometime before June 27, which he states was in his son's billfold, not his typewriter. This likely occurred in the days after the funeral, while he and Merryman were going through Howard's effects. When asked later if she had seen the lines of poetry in the typewriter, she reported, "I didn't see that."[32]

Scott did not write of the couplet in the June 12 edition of his newspaper, nor in the following week's June nineteenth edition, in which he wrote of the suicide and the double funeral. It was not until July 3, twenty-three days after that fateful morning, and at least one week since Dr. Howard's discovery of the words on a piece of paper in Howard's billfold, that Scott wrote of the poem in his newspaper.[33] In a small box at the bottom of the front page, Scott wrote, "Just before walking from his home to his automobile . . . Robert E. Howard, talented Cross Plains writer, dashed off the following poem."[34] According to the nurse, upon hearing his mother would not survive, Howard immediately left the house. No one mentioned him stopping to compose something on his typewriter.

Howard, knowing what he had intended to do, likely appreciated the sentiment of the repeating lines in the poem, so he retyped them as he saw fit and placed the piece of paper in his wallet. Sometime after finding the slip of paper, Dr. Howard possibly shared the discovery with Scott, who then told the apocryphal story in his newspaper and continued telling it for the rest of his life.[35]

During the weeks following the funeral, Dr. Howard also had additional assistance from Norris Chambers. "I was out hoeing peanuts," Chambers explained, when he first learned of both deaths. Recalling in an interview, Chambers reminisced, "Mama came down there. Someone had come and told her that Robert had killed himself and Mrs. Howard had died." He and his father, Dr. Chambers, drove up to Cross Plains. On Sunday morning Chambers said, "I went to the funeral. We all went to the funeral." Afterward Norris Chambers stayed with Dr. Howard for several weeks. He also remembered how badly the doctor suffered. "He was *stricken* with it," for it had been, "a *terrible* blow to him." Regarding his son's death, Chambers told how Dr. Howard "thought that he maybe could have done something that he didn't do," saying things like, "Maybe it was *my* fault. Maybe I didn't raise him right. Maybe I should have done this, or maybe I should have insisted that he do something else."[36] Chambers listened, which may have been all the doctor really needed.

Chambers also helped around the house in other ways. Dr. Howard had decided that because his son's car was only a year old, it was more practical for him to keep that car and sell off his old one. Chambers had the difficult job of driving Howard's car in for repair. "I drove it down to the wrecking yard down on the corner," Chambers explained, "to have it fixed where the bullet had gone up through the top there."[37] It was James Cross, however, who had the truly gruesome job, for he was the one who cleaned up the car and patched the hole.[38]

Chambers also assisted Dr. Howard with gathering up all of his son's books and magazines, which he donated to the Howard Payne College in Brownwood. Some representatives of the library drove up to Cross Plains to receive them, and they were to be maintained as the Robert E. Howard Memorial Collection.[39] The librarian there found the magazine covers too lurid and locked them away. After Dr. Howard learned of this, he asked for them to be returned.

In time Chambers returned home to Cross Cut, and Merryman stopped coming over daily. Dr. Howard was on his own, and from that time forward, he lived off the generosity of his former patients and neighbors and the earnings from Howard's sales, which his agent, Kline, continued handling.

"I once had a good practice," Dr. Howard wrote Farnsworth Wright of his situation that fall, "but sickness in my home caused me to lose it all. Today I am bereaved of my family, I have lost my business and I see myself an old man standing within the ruins of it all with hardly a meal ticket, and at times an agony of grief indescribable."[40] Dr. Howard remained in Cross Plains for another five year, but after World War II broke out, there developed a shortage of doctors, and his friend Dr. P. M. Kuykendall in Ranger asked him to come out of retirement and help him run the West Texas Clinic. He did so, and died there on November 12, 1944, of coronary thrombosis.[41] As a final act of kindness, Dr. Howard left the rights to his son's estate to Dr. Kuykendall.

After traveling home to Bangs, Texas, Novalyne Price made the move to Louisiana. She felt bad about the way she had left Cross Plains without seeing Howard or saying goodbye. To make up for her transgression, she was determined to write to him. Once arriving on the campus at Louisiana State University, however, she became incredibly busy. While studying in the library there in mid-June, she decided to go back to her dorm room and finally write that letter to Howard. When she entered the dormitory, the receptionist told her she had a telegram. She was also informed that there had been a delay in the delivery. She should have received it several days previous. Price looked at the telegram and saw it was from Pat Allen, the teacher she had last been dating in Cross Plains. Opening the telegram, she read the words, "Bob Howard killed himself this morning. His mother very low."[42] The telegram was dated June 11, 1936.

Price made it back to her dorm room, and as the shock wore off, she became angry at Howard, then angry with herself, but then everything Howard had ever said came flooding back to her, and though she now understood his words, it still made no sense. In one of his recent tirades, when they had argued about who should be taking care of his mother, he had told her, "I guess you'll never understand that life without her isn't worth living."[43]

Letters continued arriving, filling her in on the circumstances of the suicide, Mrs. Howard's death, the double funeral, and the burial in Brownwood.

She struggled through the summer, for everything reminded her of Howard—books, the rain, sunsets—and she thought often of Howard's statement, "Life is not worth living unless you have a great love or a great cause, and I have neither." "He could not believe in a woman's love," she wrote in her memoirs, at least "no woman's except his mother's." As for finding a cause in a dying civilization, she also understood. "He turned to books, read them, loved them, and understood them." What he did not understand and did not know was "how to live the common, everyday life he dreamed about."[44]

It took Price many years to overcome her guilt, for as she explained in an interview, even by 1947, "I just hadn't gotten over the feeling of guilt. It's a feeling that I think everybody who knows a friend or a family member who commits suicide feels."[45] That year, however, she married and became Novalyne Price Ellis and was later the head of the speech department at Lafayette High School, a nationally recognized program. She published her memoirs, *One Who Walked Alone* (1986), covering the years she knew Howard, which was later turned into the film *The Whole Wide World* (1996). She passed away on March 30, 1999.[46]

When asked in an interview to reflect on the type of person Howard was, Price replied, "I would sum up that he was a good man, a fine man, a compassionate man. A man who was willing to encourage anyone who needed encouragement, who would stand by friends." She then shared what she wanted the world to know. "I would like for people to know that he was a good man, and I think, a good writer. That he was capable of kindness."[47] Tevis Clyde Smith, in the foreword to Price's memoirs, believed she had truly come to know Howard, even if she did not always understand him, for he wrote, "Novalyne saw Bob's devotion to his mother and his sense of duty to her. She also saw the true gentleman behind his bluff exterior. She saw his brilliance and his genius."[48] His other friends echoed these same sentiments, for Lindsey Tyson once stated, "The most admirable thing was his honesty and straightforwardness," while Frank Thurston Torbett wrote, "His was a powerful personality, of a type that can never be forgotten. I never knew a man more devoted to home and family, or more loyal to his friends, or more honest and upright."[49]

Just as Howard's death had stunned Novalyne Price, so too did it shock his fellow authors when they first learned of the tragedy. "When Robert

Ervin Howard died, June 11, 1936, we could not believe the news," wrote E. Hoffmann Price. "We fought against belief, until there was no fight left in us." He explained that after sharing their condolences to Dr. Howard, "we authors wrote to each other, as though each needed the other's sympathy. No doubt each did!"[50] Lovecraft had first learned of the suicide from fellow *Weird Tales* author C. L. (Catherine Lucille) Moore, who had learned the news from her mutual friend Frank Thurston Torbett.[51] Lovecraft, shocked and overcome with grief, wrote his fellow authors. One of the first missives was to E. Hoffmann Price, informing him in a letter he had already been composing. "This loss will probably seem a more acute bereavement to you than to the others, since you are the only one of the group to have seen R E H in person," Lovecraft wrote, "But if you can feel worse than I do about it, you'll be going some. Damnation, what a loss!"[52] Price immediately replied, "Last page your letter hit me between the eyes. I don't know what to say."[53] Clark Ashton Smith replied to Lovecraft's notification in a similar manner when he wrote, "Howard's death startled and shocked me as it must have shocked everyone else. It is understandable but infinitely tragic and regrettable."[54] No one really knew what to say, but all mentioned their last correspondence with Howard, and while knowing he was under a lot of strain, they had not detected anything unusual in what he wrote.[55]

Lovecraft felt Price should be the one to write Howard's obituary since he was the only writer who met him. "Perhaps it might be easier for those who never met him at all," Price wrote back. "A complex and baffling personality one can't—couldn't—get all at once." He tried listing all of the impressions of Howard he had been left with, but could only conclude, "hell—I can't begin to tell you what a man this Howard was."[56] It was Lovecraft who ended up writing the obituary, "In Memoriam," published in *Fantasy Magazine* that fall. Lovecraft chose to focus on the one thing most readers were familiar with—Howard's stories. "It is hard to describe precisely what made Mr. Howard's stories stand out so sharply," Lovecraft, as previously mentioned, wrote, "but the real secret is that he himself is in every one of them."[57] This included his most popular creation as well, for Howard, he continued, "suggested more than casually his own famous character—the intrepid warrior, adventurer, and seizer of thrones, Conan the Cimmerian."[58]

Tragically, Lovecraft himself soon followed Howard in death. After beginning to feel poorly in January of the following year, ever plagued by stomach problems, he was in constant pain by the end of February and died of stomach cancer on March 15, 1937.[59] And although he lived to the age of 68, Clark Ashton Smith all but stopped writing fiction after the deaths of Howard, Lovecraft, and his parents. He reverted to writing poetry and taking up sculpture. In just over a year's time, *Weird Tales* had lost three of its most popular writers.[60]

The staff of the "unique magazine," were also stunned by the news. Margaret Brundage later recalled in an interview, "When I learned of Robert E. Howard's death I was very upset. I came into the offices one day and Wright informed me of Howard's suicide. We both just sat around and cried for most of the day. He was always my personal favorite."[61] At about that time, the August/September issue of *Weird Tales* was about to go to press in order to be on the newsstands by July 1. Wright included a quick notice in "The Eyrie." "As this issue goes to press," he wrote, "we are saddened by the news of the sudden death of Robert E. Howard at Cross Plains, Texas." He wrote that Howard had become "one of the most popular magazine authors in the country" and how "He was master of a vivid literary style," "possessed an inexhaustible imagination," and that "His poems were works of sheer genius." He concluded with an expression widely shared by all who knew him and read his stories: "His loss will be keenly felt."[62]

Wright himself felt a personal sense of loss, for he could, after all, claim that Howard "was one of my literary discoveries," and because he believed he had come to know Howard through their twelve-year correspondence.[63] He continued working with Dr. Howard and Otis Adelbert Kline, publishing some of Howard's remaining yarns and poems. But Wright was not long for the world either. The financial situation, never having been good, caused *Weird Tales* to be sold, and the magazine moved to New York.[64] Wright made the move with the magazine, but by that time, as one *Weird Tales* author personally knew, he was unable to "walk without assistance."[65] After the March 1940 issue, he was no longer the editor. Some said he resigned, others that he was let go because of his disability, while Otto Binder claimed he had simply been "cold-bloodedly fired."[66]

He died on June 12, 1940.[67] The magazine changed direction under the new editor, Dorothy McIlwraith, and it folded after publishing its last issue in September of 1954.

The greatest number of people affected by the news of Howard's death most certainly had been his readers, especially those in *Weird Tales*. "No one knows better than I how useless words are in a situation like yours," C. L. Moore wrote to Dr. Howard after hearing the news. The reason Moore understood more than others was because four months earlier, the man she was to marry had committed suicide. "But it does help a little to know," she continued, "all over the United States men and women in every walk of life are grieving with you over so great a loss not only to his father and his friends but to all of us who read his stories, and indeed to the world of literature in general."[68] The truth of her words can be seen in the high volume of letters that would continue to pour into the *Weird Tales* office for the next several years regarding the loss of Howard. "Letters about Robert E. Howard's untimely death continue to come in to the editor's desk," Wright explained in "The Eyrie" of January 1937. "They are letters of appreciation of his genius," he continued, "and of sympathy and condolence."[69]

"I was very sorry to hear of the death of Robert E. Howard," wrote Dr. John D. Clark of Pittsfield, Massachusetts, in one such letter, stating, "He will be missed."[70] Another, B. M. Reynolds, from the same state, wrote to "The Eyrie," "It was with deep regret that I learned of Robert E. Howard's sudden and untimely death. A great favorite with all of us, I know that he and his work will always be remembered. . . . We, the readers of *Weird Tales*, will never forget you."[71] Many, like Bernard E. Schiffmann of Laurelton, New York, told of being hard hit by the news when he wrote, "It was with deep sorrow indeed, that the tragic death of Robert E. Howard affected me. It was not merely that a fine author had passed on, but that I myself had lost something personally."[72] Many others also wrote of their first reaction upon hearing the news. "I want to weep on your editorial shoulder about what, to me, as to hundreds of other readers is an acute personal loss," while another, Miss V. Frank of Gloversville, New York, admitted to doing just that: "I want to say I actually cried over Robert E. Howard's untimely death."[73]

Many, like Robert A. Madle of Philadelphia, understood what his passing meant for an entire genre when he wrote, "Howard's death is certainly a blow to weird fiction," while others recognized the impact it would have on the "unique magazine," such as Fred C. Miles of New Providence, New Jersey, who wrote, "It fills one with an almost nameless dread to contemplate future issues of *Weird Tales* without the name of Robert E. Howard gracing its pages."[74] Yet the keenest loss for most was that of his popular, and what would become most famous, character. "I have just read about Robert E. Howard's death," wrote Margaret Warren of Columbus, Ohio, "What a pity! He was among your best. To think we never will have Conan again! How I always loved him."[75] A. H. McDonald of Little Rock, Arkansas, echoed this same sentiment when writing, "It is a sad thought to know that I can never again follow Conan through his strange lands."[76]

As the letters continued coming into the *Weird Tales* office, many readers requested reprints of Howard stories in future issues, whether for a specific story or series character, particularly Conan. As late as the January/February 1940 issue, readers like Donald V. Allgeier of Licking, Missouri, were asking, "Why wait so long to reprint early stories by Howard? The Eyrie is demanding them."[77] Although Wright would acknowledge that reprints of Conan stories were forthcoming, the only Howard story he ever reprinted in *Weird Tales* was "Worms of the Earth" in the October 1939 issue.[78]

Another repeated request in "The Eyrie" was for the publication of a Howard collection. In the November 1936 issue, Julius Hopkins of Washington, DC, wrote, "In view of his untimely departure from our material world, I suggest that you print a collection OF his best works, selections to be made by the readers."[79] Robert Oberon of Denmark, Maine, wanted even more when he wrote, "Let me add my plea for an edition of the works of Robert E. Howard, only make it his complete works," for he believed "it would be a 'best seller' among us readers."[80] Although J. R. Delt of Vancouver Barracks, Washington, dreamed, "Some day, I will have the pleasure of purchasing a bound volume of Howard's stories," it did not happen through *Weird Tales* publishing, and only years later.[81]

There were also many calls for another author to be selected to continue writing stories of Howard's characters. This sparked a controversy, for while there were many who liked the idea, some were more realistic, such as N. W. Siringer of Lakewood, Ohio, who believed, "The death of Robert E. Howard . . . leaves a gap that will be hard to fill."[82] There were some who were entirely against it, such as Charles H. Bert of Philadelphia, who definitively stated, "Howard is *irreplaceable.*"[83] *Weird Tales* author H. Warner Munn chimed in when he wrote, "I believe that would be a mistake," and explained that "a character is the author's own child, and must die with its creator."[84] Wright put an end to this idea, however, when he wrote after one such plea, "Sorry to deny your request for some other author to carry on the Conan stories of the late Robert E. Howard. His work was touched with genius, and he had a distinctive style of writing that put the stamp of his personality on every story he wrote. It would hardly be fair to his memory if we allowed Conan to be recreated by another hand, no matter how skillfully."[85] Like the idea of a bound Howard collection, Conan pastiche would also have to wait for the future.

Out of all the letters of tribute to Howard, the most eloquent printed in "The Eyrie" came from Reginald A. Pryke of Kent, England, who wrote:

> Howard the great, the incomparable, the master. Howard, whose tales were breathless sagas snatched vibrant with life from the mouths of the scalds of old. Howard, who lifted his characters out of the dust and decay of times long forgotten, breathed eager, lusting, laughing, fighting life into them tramping the witch-haunted, battle-strewn roads; men, every one, reveling in life and its joys, wine, women and the mad exhilaration of combat. Howard is dead. Solomon Kane, King Kull, Conan the Barbarian who set a crown upon his black head and defied all the world and the next to deprive him of it. Three real literary achievements, three who will live now that he is gone and the hand writes no more.[86]

Despite only being on this earth for thirty years, Howard left behind a legacy so immense that it is far too expansive to cover in these pages; it would require its own book. Had his writing not been so good and so well loved by the readers of *Weird Tales*, his legacy may have died with the magazine itself. However, after Martin Greenberg returned from World War II, he established Gnome Press to reprint many of the old pulp stories he grew up with.[87] In 1950 he fulfilled the fans' request to finally see Conan printed between bound covers when he published *Conan the Conqueror*, reprinting Howard's *The Hour of the Dragon*. Four more books followed, and soon fans had another request fulfilled, for after Howard's Conan stories were all reprinted, two books with Howard pastiche were released. These books all sold but did little to renew the character. That did not happen until the 1960s.

At that time J. R. R. Tolkien's *The Hobbit* and *The Lord of the Rings* had become fantastically popular with high school and college students. This caused a resurgence of interest in adult fantasy. And while Tolkien provided one aspect of this genre, often called high fantasy, Howard provided an entirely different one that would come to be known as sword and sorcery. Conan quickly became the Howard estate's key commodity, and reprints of his stories and new pastiche novels sold well. After Marvel began producing a Conan comic in 1970, and Hollywood produced the movie *Conan the Barbarian* (1982) with actor Arnold Schwarzenegger in the titular role, Howard's character crossed over into popular culture, becoming a household name. As with other characters such as Sherlock Holmes, Tarzan, and James Bond, whose media portrayals widely diverged from their literary source, so, too, had Howard's character, Conan of Cimmeria.[88]

In time the commercial value of all of Howard's characters grew, with everything from films, role-playing games, comics, and video games being produced. At the same time, the Robert E. Howard Foundation has worked to preserve his legacy, ensuring that all of Howard's writings—whether short stories, poems, or letters—are published and available. And each year fans gather in Cross Plains, Texas, to celebrate Robert E. Howard Days and walk through the Howard home to see where their favorite author wrote nearly all of his imaginative stories. "This little house is going to be a shrine some day," Dr. Howard once predicted. "People are going to come here."[89] He said this because he had truly come to believe, he told Norris Chambers, "Robert'll be famous someday."[90] Despite his strong assertions, Dr. Howard never could have known just how famous Robert E. Howard has become.

Yet behind all of this was the young man with a thirst for freedom and a dream to write, who grew up in a Texas not long removed from life on the frontier. He lived and wrote from a rural part of the state, in a small town, in a small house, in a room no larger than a walk-in closet by today's standards, yet his imagination was as wide as the Texas sky. He was dedicated to his family and friends, was highly talented, and proved to be one of the most literate authors of the pulp magazines. Although some have come close, no author has ever been able to write like Robert E. Howard, and it cannot be said that there has been a man like him since. In a letter written not long after learning of Howard's suicide, H. P. Lovecraft wrote E. Hoffmann Price, exclaiming, "Good old Two-Gun! We shall not look upon his like again."[91] Lovecraft was echoing a line from Shakespeare's *Hamlet*, which summarizes Robert E. Howard well:

> He was a man—take him for all in all,
> I shall not look upon his like again.[92]

Acknowledgments

"I will be kind to my biographers," Howard once wrote in an autobiographical essay, "for assuredly the day will come when some lined-faced scrivener will be glad of this information, rambling and trivial as it may seem."[1] Although that particular essay strayed far from telling his own story, I am glad for all the information he left behind—letters, essays, poems, and stories—that formed the basis of this biography.

I never thought I would one day become that "line-faced scrivener," when I first discovered Howard soon after my parents divorced in early March of 1979. Finding those Frazetta-cover Conan collections in a mall bookstore, however, set me on a path that has resulted in the biography you now hold in your hands. I am not the first Howard biographer, nor shall I likely be the last, but what I wanted to do was begin the process by starting from scratch, incorporating first Howard's own words and then those of his closest friends. From there I added the recorded interviews with people who knew "the greatest pulp writer that ever lived," and, finally, I leaned heavily on all of the biographical research that has been done to date.

Despite my efforts, which you, the readers, are the best judges of how I fared, I cannot help but agree with his closest friend, Tevis Clyde Smith, when he wrote:

> The best that any writer can do is bring Bob Howard to the public second hand. No man can transmit the vitality of the man: his gusto, his hates and rages, his moments of calm appraisal, his many moods ranging from depression to high spirits, his brilliance of mind, his cleverness, his keenness of wit. It would have been necessary to have known Bob to have that knowledge, to have walked and talked with him all night long on pleasant summer nights . . . through the narrow, sandy lanes toward the highway, out of the post oaks, eerie with their shadows as the moon hung low over East Peak. There was to be found the real Bob Howard.[2]

I wish I could have "walked and talked with him all night long on pleasant summer nights," but as that is not possible, I can only hope that I at least achieved some success in bringing Robert E. Howard to the public secondhand.

Being little more than a line-faced scrivener, there were many who helped make this biography possible. First and foremost was a man I never met: Glenn Lord, the literary agent of the Robert E. Howard Estate. Lord was instrumental in finding and preserving Howard's letters, stories, and poetry, and everyone I have ever met who knew him always said he was a kind and gracious man. There have been others who have worked diligently to preserve Howard's legacy, such as the many people behind the Robert E. Howard Foundation, and I must acknowledge their significant contribution to this biography. They include Rusty Burke, Rob Roehm, Paul Herman, and John Bullard. If not for them, Howard's letters and poetry would not have been so readily available. I must also acknowledge my special gratitude for Rusty and Rob, who agreed to review the manuscript and keep me from making too many mistakes; and for Rob agreeing to write the foreword.

I would also like to thank the other Howard scholars whose work was instrumental in my writing this biography, including Dr. Patrice Louinet (who earned his PhD with a dissertation on Howard); Mark Finn, a fellow biographer who writes in a style I love but would never be able to imitate; Dr. Morgan Holmes, whose knowledge of the pulps is incredibly vast and who was welcoming at my first Pulpfest; and Lee Breakiron, whose collection makes any fan of Howard envious, and who was always willing to share.

There are so many others I want to thank for keeping Howard alive, and they include Bill Cavalier, long time editor of the Robert E. Howard United Press Association (REHupa); Arlene Stephenson, who heads up Cross Plains Project Pride, the group responsible for preserving the Howard House as a museum and who graciously welcomes fans to the annual Howard Days celebration in Cross Plains every year; and all of the people and groups who were helpful in my research: the *Cross Plains Review*, especially Teri Brown and Phyllis Pancake; the Cross Plains Public Library; Texas A&M Cushing Library; the University of Texas Ransom Center; the University of Texas Dolph Briscoe Center; and the Newton Gresham Library's Interlibrary Loan office, especially Sarah Greenmyer for always finding me copies of all those esoteric publications.

A special thank you is extended to my favorite copyeditor, Ronda Harris, who more importantly has become a good friend, and now admirer of Robert E. Howard. Your work on my two biographies has been outstanding and greatly appreciated. To my external reviewers, Jonas Prida and Patrick Burger, thank you for your critical but positive reviews of both the proposal and final draft, as well as catching yet more of those pesky mistakes I have a tendency to make. And everyone at the University of North Texas Press, including Amy Maddox and Joe Alderman, but especially the director, Ronald Chrisman, a Howard fan himself, who believed in this project.

Finally, as always, I have to thank Judy, my beautiful wife, for allowing me the ability to take on such an incredibly difficult project, putting up with my incessant talk about Howard, and listening to me read my finished drafts out loud. God was looking out for me in the fall of 1986.

Willard M. Oliver
Huntsville, Texas

Endnotes

Notes for Prologue

1. Howard, *The Collected Poetry of Robert E. Howard*, 2nd edition, 3 vols., ed. Paul Herman (Plano, TX: Robert E. Howard Foundation Press, 2023), 1:145 (hereafter TCP).
2. Howard, *The Collected Letters of Robert E. Howard*, 2nd ed., 3 vols., ed. Rob Roehm and John Bullard (Plano, TX: Robert E. Howard Foundation Press, 2021), 2:422 (hereafter TCL).
3. H. P. Lovecraft and Howard, *A Means to Freedom: The Letters of H. P. Lovecraft and Robert E. Howard*, ed. S. T. Joshi, David E. Schultz, and Rusty Burke (New York: Hippocampus Press, 2017), 91 (hereafter AMTF).
4. Glenn Lord, *The Last Celt: A Bio-Bibliography of Robert E. Howard, the Creator of Conan* (New York: Berkley Windhover Books, 1976), 84 (hereafter LC).
5. Christopher Long, "Callahan County," *Handbook of Texas Online*, updated October 19, 2020, https://www.tshaonline.org/handbook/entries/callahan-county.
6. TCL, 2:423.
7. TCL, 2:423.
8. Howard, *Post Oaks and Sand Roughs & Other Autobiographical Writings*, ed. Rob Roehm (Plano, TX: Robert E. Howard Foundation Press, 2019), 55 (hereafter POSR2).
9. TCL, 3:282.
10. TCL, 2:422.
11. TCL, 2:422–23.
12. Howard, *Swords of the North* (Plano, TX: Robert E. Howard Foundation Press, 2014), 53 (hereafter SotN).
13. TCL, 3:302.
14. National Oceanic, "Global Summary."
15. *Cross Plains Review* (hereafter CPR), February 26, 1932.
16. Rusty Burke, *Robert E. Howard in Cross Plains: A Guide for the Howard Fan* (Washington, DC: Rusty Burke, 2006), 13.
17. CPR, February 26, 1932.
18. Jack Scott interview, March 12, 1981, Oral Histories, Southwest Collection, Texas Tech University, Lubbock, TX (hereafter SWC); Ann L. Beeler, *Footsteps of Approaching Thousands* (Cross Plains, TX: Cross Plains Public Library, 2011), 66.
19. Jack Scott interview, March 12, 1981, SWC.
20. CPR, March 18 and 25, 1932.
21. CPR, March 18, 1932.
22. CPR, March 18, 1932.
23. CPR, March 18, 1932.
24. CPR, March 25, 1932.
25. CPR, March 18, 1932.
26. CPR, March 25, 1932.
27. TCL, 2:422.
28. CPR, March 25, 1932.
29. CPR, March 18, 1932.
30. CPR, March 25, 1932.
31. CPR, March 18, 1932.
32. CPR, February 26, 1932.
33. CPR, March 18 & 25, 1932.

34. TCL, 3:9.
35. TCL, 2:422.
36. Howard, *The Last of the Trunk*, ed. Patrice Louinet (Plano, TX: Robert E. Howard Foundation Press, 2007), 433 (hereafter TLT).
37. Leroy Butler interview, July 20, 1977, L. Sprague de Camp and Catherine Crook de Camp Collection, Harry Ransom Center, University of Texas at Austin, Austin, TX (hereafter LSdC).
38. Beeler, *Footsteps*, 43.
39. Leroy Butler interview, July 20, 1977, LSdC.
40. Floyce Butler interview, July 20, 1977, LSdC.
41. Leroy Butler, interview by Daryl Lane, Science Fiction Radio Show Collection, Science Fiction Oral History Association Archives (hereafter SFOHA).
42. Leigh Brackett, "Introduction," in *The Sword Woman*, by Robert E. Howard (New York: Zebra Books), 10–11.
43. Paul Herman, "Interview of Larry McDonough by Paul Herman," *Another Thought*, no. 1 (June 2001), http://www.robert-e-howard.org/AnotherThought1.html.
44. Jack Scott interview, April/May 2001, SWC.
45. Leroy Butler interview, SFOHA.
46. Novalyne Price Ellis, *One Who Walked Alone: Robert E. Howard: The Final Years* (West Kingston, RI: Donald M. Grant Publishers, 1986), 45 (hereafter OWWA).
47. Howard, *The Coming of Conan the Cimmerian* (New York: Del Rey, 2002), 21 (hereafter CC).
48. Ben Friberg, "Margaret McNeel on Robert E. Howard," *YouTube*, January 14, 2012, video, 5:09, https://www.youtube.com/watch?v=MxveGf1-cpI
49. Burke, *Robert E. Howard*, 7, 9.
50. CC, 22.
51. OWWA, 47.
52. Howard, *The Best of Robert E. Howard*, vol. 2, *Grim Lands* (New York: Del Rey, 2007), xv (hereafter BO2).
53. John W. Clark, *Early English: A Study of Old and Middle English* (New York: Norton, 1964), 41.
54. John Clute, "Introduction," in Robert E. Howard, *Heroes in the Wind: From Kull to Conan* (New York: Penguin Books, 2009), x–xi.
55. Norris R. Chambers letter, October 28, 1978, LSdC.
56. Novalyne Price Ellis, *Day of the Stranger: Further Memories of Robert E. Howard* (West Warwick, RI: Necronomicon Press, 1989), 11 (hereafter DOTS).
57. J. H. Childs interview, October 18, 1978, LSdC.
58. Norris R. Chambers interview, July 22, 1977, LSdC.
59. Leroy Butler interview, SFOHA.
60. TCL, 2:276; Alma Baker King interview, August 26, 1978, LSdC.
61. Leroy Butler and Jack Scott interviews, SFOHA.
62. Tevis Clyde Smith, *"So Far the Poet . . ." & Other Writings*, ed. Rusty Burke and Rob Roehm (Plano, TX: Robert E. Howard Foundation Press, 2010), 255 (hereafter SFTP).
63. TCP, 3:5.
64. TCL, 3:248.
65. AMTF, 126.
66. TCL, 3:269; Patrice Louinet, "The Birth of Conan," *Dark Man: The Journal of Robert E. Howard Studies*, no. 4 (May 1997): 2.
67. TCL, 3:143.
68. TCL, 3:143, 338.

69. OWWA, 20.
70. TCL, 3:97.
71. Louinet, "Robert E. Howard, Founding Father of Modern Fantasy for the First Time Again," *Contemporary French and Francophone Studies* 15, no. 2 (March 2011): 164.
72. CC, 11.
73. CC, 436.
74. Howard, *Kull: Exile of Atlantis* (New York: Del Rey, 2006), 161 (hereafter KULL); CC, 11; Karen Joan Kohoutek, "By the Phoenix on This Sword I Rule!," *On An Underwood No. 5*, July 22, 2018, http://onanunderwood5.blogspot.com/2018/07/by-phoenix-on-this-sword-i-rule-by.html.
75. CC, 436.
76. LC, 374.
77. CC, 432.
78. CC, 7.
79. *Weird Tales* (hereafter WT), December 1932.
80. Mark Finn, "Robert E. Howard," in *Conversations with Texas Writers*, ed. Frances Leonard and Ramona Cearley (Austin: University of Texas Press, 2005), 173.
81. WT, February 1933.
82. WT, February 1933, 262.
83. WT, February 1933, 262–63.
84. LC, 102.
85. Lovecraft, "In Memoriam: Robert Ervin Howard," *Fantasy Magazine*, no. 38 (1936).
86. OWWA, 107.
87. CC, 433.
88. Rusty Burke, "Toward Other Lands: An Approach to Robert E. Howard," *Dark Man: The Journal of Robert E. Howard Studies*, no. 1 (August 1990): 17.
89. POSR2, vii.
90. OWWA, 121.
91. LC, 16.
92. Lovecraft, *Selected Letters: H. P. Lovecraft*, 5 vols., ed. August Derleth and Donald Wandrei (Sauk City, WI: Arkham House, 1965) 5:31–32 (hereafter SLL).
93. LC, 87–88.
94. Finn, *Blood and Thunder*; Mody C. Boatright, "The Art of Tall Lying," *Southwest Review* 34, no. 4 (Autumn 1949): 357.
95. POSR2, vii.
96. DOTS, 15.
97. Leroy Butler interview, July 20, 1977, LSdC.
98. AMTF, 548–49.
99. AMTF, 604–5.
100. TCL, 2:165.
101. TCL, 1:276.
102. Isaac M. Howard, *The Collected Letters of Doctor Isaac M. Howard*, ed. Rob Roehm (Plano, TX: Robert E. Howard Foundation Press, 2011), 54 (hereafter IMH).

Notes for Chapter 1

1. TCP, 1:46.
2. TCL, 2:156.
3. AMTF, 87.

4. TCL, 3:151.
5. Wallace C. Howard interview notes, July 22, 1977, LSdC.
6. TCL, 2:201–2.
7. AMTF, 224.
8. LC, 34.
9. TCL, 2:5.
10. TCL, 2:28.
11. TCL, 2:278.
12. TCL, 2:164.
13. Christopher Dowd, "Irish-American Identities of Robert E. Howard and Conan the Barbarian." *New Hibernia Review* 20, no. 2 (Summer 2016): 15–34.
14. T. R. Fehrenbach, *Lone Star: A History of Texas and the Texans* (1968; repr., New York: Tess Press, 2000), 87–88.
15. POSR2, vxii.
16. Dowd, "Irish-American," 17.
17. POSR2, vxii.
18. Roehm, "Virginia Howards."
19. Family Search.
20. Rob Roehm, "The Earliest Howards," *Howard History: The Life and Times of Robert E. Howard*, January 18, 2019, https://howardhistory.com/2019/01/18/the-earliest-howards-part-1/.
21. TCL, 2:156.
22. Rev. C. Kingsley, *Hereward the Wake: Last of the English* (London: Macmillan, 1866).
23. TCL, 2:156.
24. AMTF, 89.
25. Roehm, "Oglethorpe, County GA," *Howard History: The Life and Times of Robert E. Howard*, February 13, 2019, https://howardhistory.com/2019/02/13/oglethorpe-county-ga/.
26. Roehm, "The Virginia Howards," *Howard History: The Life and Times of Robert E. Howard*, January 22, 2019, https://howardhistory.com/2019/01/22/the-virginia-howards/.
27. Family Search.
28. Roehm, "Virginia Howards."
29. Roehm, "Oglethorpe"; see also Roehm, "Earliest Howards."
30. Roehm, "Virginia Howards."
31. Roehm, "Oglethorpe"; see also Roehm, "The First Isaac M. Howard," *Howard History: The Life and Times of Robert E. Howard*, October 10, 2019, https://howardhistory.com/2019/10/10/the-first-isaac-m-howard/.
32. POSR2, 10.
33. Roehm, "Oglethorpe."
34. Roehm, "Upson County, GA," *Howard History: The Life and Times of Robert E. Howard*, February 21, 2019, https://howardhistory.com/2019/02/21/upson-county-ga/.
35. Roehm, "William Benjamin Howard," *Howard History: The Life and Times of Robert E. Howard*, August 23, 2020, https://howardhistory.com/2020/08/23/william-benjamin-howard/; Roehm, "Upson County."
36. *Thomaston Herald*, May 6, 1876.
37. *Middle Georgia Times*, July 24, 1880.
38. Family Record, LSdC; Roehm, "Earliest Howards."
39. POSR2, 10.
40. Roehm, "William Benjamin."
41. H. W. Brands, *The Age of Gold: The California Gold Rush and the New American Dream* (New York: Anchor Books, 2002).
42. *Constitutionalist*, January 31, 1849.

43. Brands, *Age of Gold.*
44. *Constitutionalist*, January 31, 1849.
45. AMTF, 89.
46. Roehm, "Earliest Howards."
47. TCL, 2:164.
48. AMTF, 174.
49. POSR2, 10–11.
50. AMTF, 89.
51. Roehm, "Earliest Howards."
52. Roehm, "William Benjamin."
53. POSR2, 11.
54. AMTF, 89; see also Roehm, "Squire."
55. TCL, 2:304.
56. Roehm, "Family Legend."
57. Roehm, "Squire James Henry," *Howard History: The Life and Times of Robert E. Howard*, December 3, 2020, https://howardhistory.com/2020/12/; e.g., AMTF, 596.
58. POSR2, 11.
59. AMTF, 832–33; Ben Friberg, "Howard Family," *YouTube*, June 30, 2015, video, 38:15, https://www.youtube.com/watch?v=H-RkpZsaPhc.
60. AMTF, 832–33.
61. AMTF, 832–33; POSR2, 12.
62. Roehm, "Earliest Howards"; POSR2, 12.
63. TCL, 3:138.
64. Roehm, "Earliest Howards"; Roehm, "William Benjamin."
65. POSR2, 10–12; Roehm, "William Benjamin."
66. Friberg, "Howard Family."
67. AMTF, 89.
68. Roehm, "William Benjamin."
69. Roehm, "Henry's Will," *REHupa*, no. 252 (April 2015): 1–4.
70. AMTF, 111; Roehm, "William Benjamin."
71. National Park Service, "3rd Regiment, Tennessee Cavalry (Forrest's)," *National Park Service: The Civil War*, November 9, 2021. https://www.nps.gov/civilwar/search-battle-units-detail.htm?battleUnitCode=CTN0003RC
72. Ollie Lorene Davis interview notes, September 9, 1978, LSdC; Roehm, "William Benjamin," "First Isaac."
73. Roehm, "William Benjamin."
74. Family Record, LSdC; Beeler, *Footsteps*.
75. AMTF, 89.
76. Patrice Louinet, "The Long Road to Dark Valley," *REH: Two-Gun Raconteur*, January 18, 2013, https://web.archive.org/web/20150907100640/www.rehtwogunraconteur.com/the-long-road-to-dark-valley-introduction/"; Arthur M. Schlesinger, "Patriotism Names the Baby," *New England Quarterly* 14, no. 4 (December 1941): 611–18.
77. TCL, 2:156.
78. POSR2, 3.
79. According to the Rowman County Marriage Bonds, North Carolina, County Marriages, p. 181, Robert's last name is listed as "Erwin," while Jenny's name is spelled "Jenney."
80. POSR2, 3–4.
81. POSR2, 3–4.
82. POSR2.
83. POSR2, 4.

84. TCL, 3:151.
85. Louinet, "Long Road"; 1880 US Census.
86. POSR2.
87. AMTF, 111.
88. AMTF, 224.
89. AMTF, 111.
90. POSR2, 5–6.
91. POSR2.
92. AMTF, 639.
93. Louinet, "Long Road."

Notes for Chapter 2

1. TCP, 3:153.
2. TCL, 3:151.
3. Roehm, "The Road to Cross Plains," REHupa, no. 261 (October 2016): 8; IMH, vxii.
4. Family Record LSdC.
5. IMH, xvii; US Census, 1880, "Isaac M."
6. IMH, ix.
7. IMH, ix.
8. IMH, ix; Jim Tom Barton, *Eight from Decatur: Growing up in North Texas* (College Station: Texas A&M University Press, 1980), 110.
9. Roehm, "Road"; "Training Dr. Howard," *Howard History: The Life and Times of Robert E. Howard*, September 17, 2020, https://howardhistory.com/2020/09/17/training-dr-howard/.
10. Roehm, "William Benjamin Howard," *Howard History: The Life and Times of Robert E. Howard*, August 23, 2020, https://howardhistory.com/2020/08/23/william-benjamin-howard/; "Road."
11. IMH, x.
12. POSR2, 12.
13. *Biographical and Historical Memoirs of Southern Arkansas* (Chicago: Goodspeed Publishing, 1890), 674; IMH, x.
14. Roehm, "Isaac M. Howard in the 1880s," *REH: Two-Gun Raconteur*, October 18, 2012, https://web.archive.org/web/20130121130544/http://rehtwogunraconteur.com/?p=20488; "Road," "Training Dr. Howard."
15. Mark Caldwell, *The Last Crusade: The War on Consumption, 1862–1954* (New York: Atheneum, 1998), 152.
16. Edward Livingston Trudeau, *An Autobiography* (Garden City, NY: Doubleday Page, 1916), 37–38.
17. Caldwell, *Last Crusade,* 152.
18. Abraham Flexner, *Medical Education in the United States and Canada: A Report to the Carnegie Foundation for the Advancement of Teaching* (New York: Carnegie Foundation, 1910), 53.
19. IMH, x; Medical Board of Examiners document, April 19, 1899, LSdC.
20. Chester R. Burns, "Health and Medicine," *Handbook of Texas Online*, updated November 5, 2020, https://www.tshaonline.org/handbook/entries/health-and-medicine.
21. IMH, x-xi; Roehm, "Road."
22. Freestone County, July 20, 1899, LSdC.
23. IMH, x–xi; Roehm, "Road."
24. IMH, xi; Roehm, "Willie and Oscar," *REHupa*, no. 293 (February 2022): 1–4.

25. Remarks by Fannie Dell McClung Adamson, April 1978, LSdC.
26. Roehm, "Willie and Oscar."
27. IMH, xi.
28. Remarks by Fannie Dell McClung Adamson, April 1978, LSdC.
29. IMH; Palo Pinto County, January 8, 1902, LSdC; Roehm, "The Howards Are a Moving People," *Howard History: The Life and Times of Robert E. Howard*, December 13, 2019, https://howardhistory.com/2019/12/13/the-howards-are-a-moving-people/.
30. POSR2, 12; Louinet, "Long Road."
31. AMTF, 379–80.
32. Jack Scott interview, March 12, 1981, SWC.
33. Ibid; see also Jack Scott interview, July 19, 1977, LSdC.
34. Jack Scott interview, July 19, 1977, LSdC.
35. E. Hoffmann Price letter, September 2, 1979, LSdC.
36. Annie Newton Davis interview, January 21, 1981, SWC.
37. Jack Scott interview, March 12, 1981, SWC.
38. Herron, "Robert'll Be Famous," 16.
39. Jack Scott interview, July 19, 1977, LSdC; Herron, *Famous Someday.*
40. Norris R. Chambers letter, May 22, 1978, LSdC.
41. Howard O. Newton letter, July 9, 1978, LSdC.
42. L. Sprague de Camp, Catherine Crook de Camp, and Jane Whittington Griffin, *Dark Valley Destiny: The Life of Robert E. Howard* (New York: Bluejay Books, 1983); Rusty Burke, *REH: A Short Biography of Robert E. Howard* (New York: Cross Plains Comics, 1999).
43. J. H. Childs interview, October 18, 1978, LSdC.
44. Herron, *Famous Someday.*
45. Jack Scott interview, July 19, 1977, LSdC; see also Jack Scott interview, March 12, 1981, SWC.
46. Jack Scott interview, July 19, 1977, LSdC.
47. Annie Newton Davis interview, January 21, 1981, SWC.
48. AMTF, 379–80.
49. Jack Scott interview, July 19, 1977, LSdC.
50. Deoma Morgan interview, March 6, 1978, LSdC; "Dr. Isaac M. Howard," *Texas State Journal of Medicine* (February 1945): 560.
51. Herbert C. Klatt, *Lone Scout of Letters*, ed. Rob Roehm (Lancaster, CA: Roehm's Room Press, 2011), 154 (hereafter LSOL).
52. Herron, *Famous Someday.*
53. Interview with O. G. Lawson, July 28, 1952, Oral History of the Texas Oil Industry Collection, 1952–1960, Dolph Briscoe Center for American History, University of Texas at Austin, Austin, TX (hereafter OIL).
54. J. Gordon, Bryson, *One Hundred Dollars & A Horse: The Reminiscences of a Country Doctor* (New York: William Morrow, 1965), 77.
55. Ann Anderson, *Snake Oil, Hustlers and Hambones: The American Medicine Show* (Jefferson, NC: McFarland, 2000); Boyle, *Quack Medicine: A History of Combating Health Fraud in Twentieth-Century America* (Santa Barbara, CA: Praeger, 2013).
56. Lewis E. Newton interview, September 13, 1983, SWC.
57. Howard O. Newton letter, no date, LSdC.
58. AMTF, 380.
59. Barton, *Eight from Decatur*, 103; Ora Lewis Bradley, *The Country Doctor's Wife* (New York: House of Field, 1940), 1.
60. Bradley, *Country Doctor's Wife*, 1.

61. Bradley, *Country Doctor's Wife*, 84.
62. Howard O. Newton letter, July 9, 1978, LSdC.
63. Barton, *Eight from Decatur*, 102.
64. SFTP, 259.
65. Bradley, *Country Doctor's Wife*, 93.
66. Herron, *Famous Someday*; see also Norris R. Chambers interview, July 22, 1977, LSdC.
67. Jack Scott interview, March 12, 1981, SWC.
68. Jack Scott interview, July 19, 1977, LSdC.
69. Jack Scott interview, July 19, 1977, LSdC.
70. AMTF, 379–80.
71. Howard O. Newton letter, July 9, 1978, LSdC; Herman, "Interview."
72. Bryson, *One Hundred Dollars*, 98.
73. Wallace C. Howard interview, July 22, 1977, L. Sprague de Camp notes from Leroy Butler interview, July 20, 1977, LSdC.
74. Jack Scott interview, March 12, 1981, SWC; Herman, "Interview."
75. POSR2, 7.
76. Family Record, LSdC.
77. Louinet, "Long Road"; Roehm, "A Question of Birth," *REHupa*, no. 238 (December 2012): 1–2.
78. Roehm, "Question," 2.
79. Louinet, "Long Road."
80. *Dallas Daily Herald*, June 3, 1874
81. Louinet, "Long Road."
82. POSR2, 8.
83. Louinet, "Long Road."
84. *Dallas Daily Herald*, May 22, 1877 & August 18, 1880; *Galveston Daily News*, April 14, 1878.
85. Roehm, "The Rise and Fall of Robert T. Ervin," *REHupa*, no. 286 (December 2020): 1; see also Louinet, "Long Road."
86. IMH, 148–49.
87. AMTF, 839.
88. Roehm, "The Lost Ervin Mine," *Howard History: The Life and Times of Robert E. Howard*, October 18, 2019, https://howardhistory.com/2019/10/18/the-lost-ervin-mine/.
89. POSR2, 9.
90. Roehm, "Lost Ervin Mine"; *El Paso Times*, July 17, 1888.
91. *Lampasas Leader*, November 24, 1888, December 29, 1888.
92. *Lampasas Leader*, April 20, 1889, May 25, 1889.
93. Louinet, "Long Road."
94. POSR2, 9–10.
95. Roehm, "Lost Ervin Mine."
96. Louinet, "Long Road."
97. Roehm, "Ervins in Oklahoma," *REH Two-Gun Raconteur*, June 21, 2012, https://web.archive.org/web/20130121131150/http://rehtwogunraconteur.com/?p=19789; Louinet, "Long Road."
98. Roehm, "Ervins in Oklahoma"; *Muskogee Phoenix*, December 24, 1891; December 22, 1891, with 1892 handwritten at top of page.
99. *Muskogee Phoenix*, February 16, 1893.
100. Leo Grin, "In Defense of Hester Jane Ervin Howard," *Cimmerian*, October 2, 2008, https://web.archive.org/web/20110708132217/www.thecimmerian.com/in-defense-of-hester-jane-ervin-howard/.

101. Barbara Barrett, "Hester Jane Ervin Howard and Tuberculosis (Revised)," *REHupa*, no. 250 (December 2014): 1–68.
102. Barrett, "Hester Jane Ervin," 6.
103. Thomas Dormandy, *The White Death: A History of Tuberculosis* (Washington Square: New York University Press, 2000), 22.
104. Helen Bynum, *Spitting Blood: The History of Tuberculosis* (Oxford: Oxford University Press, 2012), 95.
105. Dormandy, *White Death*, 246–47.
106. Thomas M Daniel, *Captain of Death: The Story of Tuberculosis* (Rochester: University of Rochester Press, 1997); Caldwell, *Last Crusade*.
107. Caldwell, *Last Crusade*.
108. Dormandy, *White Death*, 41.
109. Dormandy, *White Death*, 148.
110. Caldwell, *Last Crusade,* 74.
111. Bynum, *Spitting Blood*, 131.
112. Dormandy, *White Death*, 261.
113. Frank Ryan, *The Forgotten Plague: How the Battle against Tuberculosis Was Won—and Lost* (Boston: Little, Brown, 1992).
114. "Leading Causes of Death, 1900–1998," *Centers for Disease Control*, February 13, 2020, https://www.cdc.gov/nchs/data/dvs/lead1900_98.pdf.
115. Bradley, *Country Doctor's Wife*, 99.
116. Louinet, "Long Road."
117. *Abilene Reporter*, June 30, 1899; POSR2.
118. Louinet, "Long Road."
119. "History," *Crazy Water*, October 22, 2020, http://drinkcrazywater.com/crazy-water-history/.
120. LSOL, 154; Truett Vinson letter, June 29, 1977, LSdC.
121. Truett Vinson letter, June 29, 1977, LSdC.
122. Don Herron, "The Last of the Baker Kids: A Talk with Marie Baker Andrews," *Cimmerian* 3, no. 3 (March 2006): 26.
123. Lewis E. Newton interview, September 13, 1983, SWC.
124. Grin, "In Defense."
125. POSR2, 9–10.
126. Some have suggested Frank Ezell as the man Hester dated, but the source of her relationship comes from Annie Newton Davis, who cared for Hester on her deathbed and is a questionable source. See Annie Newton Davis interview, October 18, 1978, LSdC.
127. Roehm, "Howards"; *Jacksboro News*, April 13, 1905.
128. IMH, xii; Ben Friberg, "Travels with Ol' Two-Gun: with Rob Roehm," *YouTube*, June 26, 2017, Video, 29:37, https://www.youtube.com/watch?v=-_jaJPxgovQ; "Dark Valley Creek," *Handbook of Texas Online*, updated December 1, 1994, https://www.tshaonline.org/handbook/entries/dark-valley-creek; Mary Whatley Clarke, *The Palo Pinto Story* (Fort Worth: Manney Company, 1956).
129. John Dean McClure and W. H. Green interview, July 16, 1977, LSdC.
130. John Dean McClure and W. H. Green interview, July 16, 1977, LSdC.
131. John Dean McClure and W. H. Green interview, July 16, 1977, LSdC.
132. Clarke, *Palo Pinto Story*, 37–38.
133. Clarke, *Palo Pinto Story*, 38–39.
134. Allen H. Moore, *Mustard Plasters and Printer's Ink: A Kaleidoscope of a Country Doctor's Observations about People, Places and Things* (New York: Exposition Press, 1959), 122.
135. Moore, *Mustard Plasters*, 121.

136. Moore, *Mustard Plasters*, 122.
137. Grin, "In Defense."
138. IMH, xi.
139. Ira Carleton Chase, ed., "Copy of Report of Committee Appointed by the Medical Association of Arkansas," *Texas State Journal of Medicine*, no. 4 (June 1908): 37.
140. Roehm, "Road," 4.
141. Chase, "Copy of Report," 38.
142. Roehm, "Howards."
143. Wallace C. Howard interview, July 22, 1977, LSdC.

Notes for Chapter 3

1. TCP, 2:241.
2. POSR2, 13.
3. AMTF, 542.
4. AMTF, 387.
5. Fehrenbach, *Lone Star*, 633.
6. Leo Grin, "Hail to the King," *Cimmerian* 3, no. 1 (January 2006): 3.
7. Family Record, LSdC; Ben Friberg, "Howard Family," *YouTube*, June 30, 2015, video, 38:15, https://www.youtube.com/watch?v=H-RkpZsaPhc.
8. Robert E. Howard Birth Record.
9. Roehm, "Road."
10. Roehm, "Howards."
11. State Board of Medical Examiners, May 12, 1905, LSdC.
12. IMH, xii.
13. TCL, 2:202.
14. Jon R. Vandagriff, *The Story of Parker County, Texas* (Virginia Beach: Donning Company, 2010), 74.
15. Roehm, "Peaster, Texas," *REHupa*, no. 245 (February 2014): 1; Vandagriff, *Parker County*, 73.
16. AMTF, 190.
17. John Dean McClure and W. H. Green interview, July 16, 1977, LSdC.
18. *Weatherford Weekly Herald*, February 22, 1906.
19. TCL, 2:202.
20. AMTF, 94–95.
21. John Dean McClure and W. H. Green interview, July 16, 1977, LSdC.
22. Wallace C. Howard interview, July 22, 1977, LSdC.
23. IMH, xiii.
24. Questions for Mrs. Merryman, September 30, 1978, LSdC.
25. Kate Merryman interview, July 18, 1977, LSdC.
26. Roehm, "Howards," "Road."
27. Chris Cravens, "Weatherford, Mineral Wells and Northwestern Railway," *Handbook of Texas Online*, updated March 5, 2019, https://www.tshaonline.org/handbook/entries/weatherford-mineral-wells-and-northwestern-railway.
28. Wallace C. Howard interview, July 22, 1977, LSdC.
29. Lindsey Tyson interview, March 7, 1978, LSdC.
30. Howard, *The Savage Tales of Solomon Kane* (New York: Del Rey, 1998), 393–94 (hereafter SK).
31. IMH, xiii–xiv.
32. TCL, 1:342.

33. Bryan Burroughs, *The Big Rich: The Rise and Fall of the Greatest Texas Oil Fortunes* (New York: Penguin Press, 2009), 1.
34. Burroughs, *Big Rich*, 2.
35. Burroughs, *Big Rich*, 4.
36. Burroughs, *Big Rich*; Fehrenbach, *Lone Star*.
37. TCL, 2:165.
38. AMTF, 91.
39. Barfield interview, OIL.
40. Rust interview, OIL.
41. SK, 394.
42. OWWA, 80.
43. TCL, 2:202.
44. Howard, *West Is West & Others*, ed. Rob Roehm and Alex Runions (N.p.: Roehm's Room Press, 2006), 153–54.
45. AMTF, 385.
46. AMTF, 948–49.
47. John Dean McClure and W. H. Green interview, July 16, 1977, LSdC.
48. IMH, xiii.
49. *Enterprise*, January 3, 1908.
50. Roehm, "Mary, Mary, Quite Contrary," *REHupa*, no. 251 (February 2015): 1.
51. *Enterprise*, January 3, 1908.
52. *Enterprise*, January 24, 1908; Roehm, "Mary, Mary."
53. POSR2, 378.
54. IMH, xiii.
55. Dormandy, *White Death.*
56. POSR2, 13; Roehm, "Road."
57. AMTF, 92.
58. AMTF, 283, 181.
59. POSR2, 13.
60. Roehm, "Road."
61. IMH, xiii; Roehm, "Road."
62. Craig Alan Drone, "On to the Orient: The History, Restoration, and Preservation of the Kansas City, Mexico, and Orient Railway Depot in San Angelo, Texas" (PhD diss., Texas Tech University, 1990), 86.
63. AMTF, 293.
64. POSR2, 378.
65. Roehm, "Down the Nueces," *Howard History: The Life and Times of Robert E. Howard*, December 9, 2018, https://howardhistory.com/2018/12/09/down-the-nueces/.
66. AMTF, 91.
67. Roehm, "Down the Nueces," "Willie and Oscar."
68. Fannie McClung Adamson interview, October 16, 1978, LSdC.
69. AMTF, 199.
70. AMTF, 216.
71. AMTF, 281.
72. AMTF, 199.
73. Roehm, "Road," 6; Roehm, "We Spent the Winter in San Antonio," *Howard History: The Life and Times of Robert E. Howard*, December 10, 2018, https://howardhistory.com/2018/12/10/we-spent-the-winter-in-san-antonio/.
74. Roehm, "Down the Nueces."
75. IMH, 133.

76. TCL, 2:202; Roehm, "Road."
77. Roehm, "Road," 6.
78. AMTF, 542.
79. AMTF, 877.
80. TCL, 2:86.
81. TCL, 2:202; Roehm, "Road."
82. Roehm, "The Mystery of the Wichita Falls Country," *Howard History: The Life and Times of Robert E. Howard*, May 1, 2019, https://howardhistory.com/2019/05/01/the-mystery-of-the-wichita-falls-country/.
83. AMTF, 92.
84. Bertha McKee Dobie et al., *Growing Up in Texas* (Austin: Encino Press, 1972), 32.
85. Louinet, "Pigeons from . . . Bagwell," *Dwelling in Dark Valley*, no. 4 (Spring 2002), http://www.robert-e-howard.org/Louinet/dwelling4a.htm
86. TCL, 2:202.
87. POSR2, 13.
88. "Dr. Willis Commodore Stephens," *Find-A-Grave*, accessed December 3, 2024, https://www.findagrave.com/memorial/36844321/willis-commodore-stephens; Louinet, "Pigeons"; Rusty Burke, "A Deep Dark Current Flows Forever," *REHupa*, no. 200 (August 2006): 1–19.
89. POSR2, 13; Roehm, "Road," 6.
90. Roehm, "Road."
91. Burke, "Deep Dark," 3.
92. Lee Somerville letter, October 22, 1978, LSdC.
93. Burke, "Deep Dark," 3.
94. AMTF, 544.
95. Louinet, "Pigeons."
96. Walter S. Deffenbaugh and Ward W. Keesecker, *Compulsory School Attendance Laws and Their Administration* (Washington, DC: Government Printing Office, 1935).
97. Sharon Stephens Black, "Mary Bohannon of Bagwell, Red River Co., Texas," *Red River County Texas Genealogical Society Quarterly* 19 (Spring 2002): 4.
98. Louinet, "Pigeons."
99. William Manire, *Buggies to iPhones: A 96-Year-Old Man Remembers His Youth in Roanoke, Texas* (Roanoke: Manire, 2019), 17.
100. Louinet, "Pigeons."
101. Lee Somerville letter, November 27, 1978, LSdC.
102. TCL, 3:127.
103. LC, 32.
104. AMTF, 43.
105. Black, "Mary Bohannon," 3.
106. Black, "Mary Bohannon," 4.
107. AMTF, 45–46.
108. AMTF, 44.
109. Burke, "Deep Dark," 9.
110. Black, "Mary Bohannon," 3.
111. POSR2, 13.

Notes for Chapter 4

1. TCP, 2:10.
2. POSR2, 13.

3. TCL, 3:282.
4. Robert H. Williams, *Joyful Trek: A Texan's Times and Travels* (Lubbock: Texas Tech University Press, 1996), 5.
5. IMH, 205.
6. POSR2, 13.
7. Roehm, "Road," 7.
8. CPR, January 29, 1915.
9. Friberg, "Travels: Roehm"; Roehm, "1915," *REHupa*, no. 256 (December 2015): 1–4.
10. Howard, *School Days in the Post Oaks: Cross Plains and Brownwood in the 1920s*, ed. Rob Roehm (Plano, TX: Robert E. Howard Foundation Press, 2011), 1 (hereafter SD).
11. Norris Chambers, "Old Time Fishing," *Norris Chambers Old Timer's Tales,* February 23, 2021, http://www.norrisc.com/fish.html.
12. Dorothy C. Ashton, "Cross Cut, TX," *Handbook of Texas Online*, updated December 1, 1994, https://www.tshaonline.org/handbook/entries/cross-cut-tx.
13. Chambers, "A Brief History of Cross Cut, Texas," *Cross Cut, Texas; Presented by Norris Chambers*, February 22, 2021, https://www.norrisc.com/crosscut/xcut.html.
14. TSHA, "Cross Cut."
15. Chambers, "How We Built a Steam Engine!" *Norris Chambers Old Timer's Tales*, February 22, 2021, http://www.norrisc.com/steamengine.html.
16. Chambers, "Brief History."
17. Lois Garrett letter, November 13, 1978, Lilburn Leonard and Deoma Morgan interview, March 6, 1978, LSdC.
18. CPR, June 11, 1915, July 2, 1915.
19. Lois Garrett interview, October 18, 1978, LSdC.
20. Deoma Morgan letter to Jane W. Griffin, n.d., LSdC.
21. Annie Newton Davis interview, January 21, 1981, SWC.
22. Deoma Morgan letter to Jane W. Griffin, n.d., LSdC.
23. Annie Newton Davis interview, October 18, 1978, LSdC.
24. Annie Newton Davis interview, January 21, 1981, SWC.
25. Deoma Morgan questions, November 22, 1978, Austin Newton letter, n.d., LSdC..
26. John Limmer, "The Chambers," *Norris Chambers Old Timer's Tales*, May 20, 2021, http://www.norrisc.com/crosscut/xcutchamb1.html.
27. Norris R. Chambers interview, July 22, 1977, LSdC.
28. Herron, *Famous Someday*; Herron, "'Robert'll Be Famous Someday': An Interview with Norris Chambers," *Cimmerian* 3, no. 10 (October 2006): 4–24.
29. Elsie Byrd interview, February 16, 1983, SWC.
30. Elsie Byrd interview, February 16, 1983, SWC; Annie Newton Davis interview, January 21, 1981, SWC.
31. Deoma Morgan letter, June 12, 1978, LSdC.
32. Norris R. Chambers interview, July 22, 1977, Deoma Morgan letter, n.d., Lilburn Leonard Morgan interview, March 6, 1978, LSdC; Annie Newton Davis interview, January 21, 1981, SWC.
33. Norris R. Chambers interview, July 22, 1977, LSdC.
34. Deoma Morgan letter, n.d., LSdC.
35. CPR, June 23, 1916, November 9, 1917.
36. Raymond De Busk interview, February 3, 1979, LSdC.
37. Deoma Morgan interview, March 6, 1978, Deoma Morgan letter, n.d., LSdC.
38. Annie Newton Davis interview, October 18, 1978, LSdC; Elsie Byrd interview, February 16, 1983, SWC; Austin Newton interview, April 2, 1978, LSdC.
39. Deoma Morgan interview, March 6, 1978, LSdC.

40. Deoma Morgan interview, March 6, 1978, LSdC; Damon Sasser, "I Knew Robert E. Howard," *R.E.H. Two-Gun Raconteur*, August 8, 2011, https://web.archive.org/web/20111114171638/http://rehtwogunraconteur.com/?p=6126.
41. Annie Newton Davis interview, January 21, 1981, SWC.
42. Raymond De Busk interview, February 3, 1979, Kate Merryman interview, July 18, 1977, LSdC.
43. Raymond De Busk interview, February 3, 1979, Annie Newton Davis interview, October 18, 1978, LSdC.
44. Elsie Byrd interview, February 16, 1983, SWC.
45. Annie Newton Davis interview, October 18, 1978, LSdC; Elsie Byrd interview, February 16, 1983, SWC.
46. Lois Garrett letter, November 13, 1978, LSdC.
47. Annie Newton Davis interview, January 21, 1981, SWC.
48. AMTF, 171.
49. Friberg, "Memories of Robert E. Howard," *YouTube*, February 18, 2010, video, 7:12, https://www.youtube.com/watch?v=8r6HASJNcpk.
50. Austin Newton letter, n.d., LSdC.
51. Roehm, "Austin, Who?" *REHupa*, no. 231 (October 2011): 1.
52. Deoma Morgan interview, March 6, 1978, LSdC.
53. Austin Newton letter, n.d., LSdC.
54. LSdC, Austin Newton interview April 1, 1978.
55. LSdC, Austin Newton interview April 1, 1978.
56. Limmer, "The 3 R's," *Norris Chambers Old Timer's Tales*, May 20, 2021, http://www.norrisc.com/crosscut/xcutschoolsite.html.
57. Austin Newton letter, n.d., LSdC.
58. AMTF, 390.
59. Lindsey W. Tyson letter, October 10, 1977, LSdC.
60. Roehm, "The Comer Connection," *REHupa*, no. 240 (April 2013): 1–4.
61. "Big Spring Troop 1," *West Texas Scouting History*, October 20, 2020, https://www.westtexasscoutinghistory.net/troop_bigspring_troop1.html.
62. Roehm, "Comer Connection," 3.
63. Roehm, "Comer Connection," 3.
64. TCL, 2:297.
65. *Austin Daily Statesman*, March 30, 1912; Alex Palmer, *The Santa Claus Man: The Rise and Fall of a Jazz Age Con Man and the Invention of Christmas in New York* (Guilford, CT: Lyons Press, 2016).
66. TCL, 3:146.
67. Chambers, "Railroad Remembrances," *Norris Chambers Old Timer's Tales*, February 22, 2021. https://www.norrisc.com/train.html.
68. Herron, *Famous Someday*.
69. Roehm, "Road."
70. Deoma Morgan questions, November 22, 1978, LSdC.
71. Chambers, "Railroad Remembrances"; Norris R. Chambers interview, July 22, 1977, LSdC; Herron, *Famous Someday*.
72. CPR, March 29, 1918.
73. Roehm, "Comer Connection," 3.
74. IMH, xiii; Roehm, "1918," *REHupa*, no. 263 (February 2017): 1–4.
75. Herron, *Famous Someday.*
76. Barton, *Eight from Decatur*, 76.
77. Lois Garrett interview, October 18, 1978, LSdC.

78. Austin Newton interview April 1, 1978, LSdC.
79. Deoma Morgan letter, n.d., LSdC.
80. AMTF, 608.
81. AMTF, 118–19.
82. TCL, 3:185.
83. Herron, "Last," 24.
84. Earl Baker interview, n.d., LSdC.
85. Alma Baker King interview, August 26, 1978, LSdC.
86. Alma Baker King interview, September 12, 1978, Earl J. Baker interview, October 16, 1978. LSdC.
87. Lilburn Leonard Morgan interview, March 6, 1978, LSdC.
88. TCL, 2:202.
89. Deoma Morgan interview, March 6, 1978, LSdC; OWWA, 217.
90. CPR, July 10, 1936; IMH, 75.
91. Deoma Morgan interview, March 6, 1978, LSdC.
92. Lois Garrett interview, October 18, 1978, Alma Baker King interview, August 26, 1978, LSdC.
93. T. A. Burns and Merrill Burkett, *History of Coleman County and Its People* (San Angelo, TX: Coleman County Historical Commission, 1985), 126–27.
94. AMTF, 119; see also Francis Edward Abernethy, *Texas Toys and Games* (Denton: University of North Texas Press, 1989), 123.
95. Abernethy, *Texas Toys and Games*, 298–99.
96. Abernethy, *Texas Toys and Games*, 319.
97. AMTF, 319; OWWA, 220; see also SFTP, 223–24.
98. Austin Newton interview April 1, 1978, Deoma Morgan letter, n.d., LSdC; Jack Scott interview, March 12, 1981, SWC; for more information see Rusty Burke, "Bob Howard and the Bullies," *Iron Harp* 2, no. 1 (March 2002), http://www.robert-e-howard.org/Iron-Harp3.html.
99. John Myers Myers, *The Westerners: A Roundup of Pioneer Reminiscences* (Lincoln: University of Nebraska Press, 1969), x.
100. Randolph B. Campbell, *Gone to Texas: A History of the Lone Star State* (New York: Oxford University Press, 2003), 353.
101. POSR2, 14.
102. POSR2, 14–15.
103. TCL, 3:127.
104. TCL, 2:176.
105. *Coleman Democrat-Voice*, April 25, 1935.
106. TCL, 3:127.
107. Family Record, LSdC.
108. IMH, 206.
109. IMH, 206; LSdC, Lois Garrett letter, November 13, 1978, LSdC.
110. IMH, 206–7.
111. Jane W. Griffin interview notes from Leroy Butler interview, July 20, 1977, LSdC.
112. CPR, July 10, 1936; IMH, 74.
113. *Coleman Democrat-Voice*, April 25, 1935.
114. CPR, July 13, 1917, January 28, 1919.
115. CPR, May 2, 1919; POSR2, 16.
116. Herbert Asbury, *The French Quarter: An Informal History of the New Orleans Underworld* (New York: Thunder's Mouth Press, 2003), 318.
117. POSR2, 19; TLT, 418.

118. POSR2, 19; TLT, 418.
119. Gary Krist, *Empire of Sin: A Story of Sex, Jazz, Murder, and the Battle for Modern New Orleans* (New York: Broadway Books, 2015), 2.
120. Miriam C. Davis, *The Axeman of New Orleans* (Chicago: Chicago Review, 2018).
121. POSR2, 19; TLT, 418.
122. Davis, *Axeman*, 155.
123. POSR2, 19; TLT, 418.
124. POSR2, 18; TLT, 479.
125. AMTF, 122; Rusty Burke, "Robert E. Howard in New Orleans," parts 1 and 2, *REHupa*, no. 241 (June 2013): no page numbers; *REHupa*, no. 243 (October 2013): no page numbers.
126. AMTF, 381.
127. POSR2, 17; Burke, "New Orleans."
128. AMTF, 255.
129. G. F. Scott Elliot, *The Romance of Early British Life: From the Earliest Times to the Coming of the Danes* (London: Seeley, Service, 1909); Howard, *Bran Mak Morn: The Last King* (New York: Del Rey, 2005), 344–46 (hereafter BMM).
130. Eric W. Curtis, "Two Victorian Botanists: Professor Roger Hennedy and Professor George Francis Scott Elliot," *Glasgow Naturalist* 25, part 2 (2009): 49–55.
131. AMTF, 255.
132. Elliot, *Romance*, 80.
133. Elliot, *Romance*, 318, 81.
134. Neil Oliver, *A History of Scotland* (London: Weidenfeld & Nicolson, 2009), 35–36.
135. Oliver, *History*, 44.

Notes for Chapter 5

1. TCP, 3:277.
2. LC, 29.
3. IMH, xiii.
4. TCL, 2:422.
5. Beeler, *Footsteps*; Jack Scott interview, March 12, 1981, April/May 2001, SWC.
6. Beeler, *Footsteps*, 1.
7. Beeler, *Footsteps*, 2.
8. TCL, 2:422.
9. Texas Central Railroad, *Eighteenth Annual Report of the Texas Central Railroad Company for the Year Ending June 30, 1910* (Waco: Hill Printing and Stationery, 1910), 10.
10. Beeler, *Footsteps*, 3.
11. Ernest Haycox Jr., *On a Silver Desert: The Life of Ernest Haycox* (Norman: University of Oklahoma Press, 2003), 123.
12. Beeler, *Footsteps*, 6.
13. Jack Scott interview, March 12, 1981, April/May 2001, SWC.
14. Beeler, *Footsteps*, 53.
15. Beeler, *Footsteps*, 40–41.
16. Jack Scott interview, March 12, 1981, SWC.
17. Beeler, *Footsteps*, 66.
18. Teri Brown, *Cross Plains Remembered* (Cross Plains, TX: Barbarian Festival Committee, 2011), 25.
19. Jack Scott interview, April/May 2001, SWC.
20. AMTF, 172–73.
21. Beeler, *Footsteps*, 112.

22. AMTF, 173.
23. CPR, February 20, 1920.
24. Jack Scott interview, March 12, 1981, SWC.
25. Brown, *Cross Plains Remembered*, 70.
26. Beeler, *Footsteps*, 113.
27. Burke, *Robert E. Howard*, 5.
28. Beeler, *Footsteps*; Jane W. Griffin notes from Leroy Butler interview, July 20, 1977, LSdC.
29. CPR, October 24, 1919.
30. Jane W. Griffin notes from Leroy Butler interview, July 20, 1977, LSdC.
31. Jane W. Griffin notes from Leroy Butler interview, July 20, 1977, LSdC.
32. Jane W. Griffin notes from Leroy Butler interview, July 20, 1977, LSdC; see also Norris R. Chambers interview, July 22, 1977, LSdC.
33. Floyce Butler interview, July 20, 1977, LSdC.
34. Jane W. Griffin notes from Leroy Butler interview, July 20, 1977, LSdC.
35. "Sleep," *Reclamation Record* 12, no. 12 (December 1921): 566.
36. James H. Kingman, "Tuberculosis in Some of Its Aspects," *Atlantic Medical Weekly: A Journal of Reform and Progress in the Medical Sciences* 4, no. 19 (November 9, 1895): 294; "Treatment of Tuberculosis in General," *Southern California Practitioner* 16, no. 11 (November 1901): 414.
37. Leroy Butler interview, July 21, 1977, Norris Chambers interview, July 22, 1977, LSdC. Note: Family members who occupied the home after the Howards recalled it as a door.
38. Celia Blue Johnson, *Odd Type Writers* (New York: Perigee, 2013), xix.
39. Jane W. Griffin notes from Leroy Butler interview, July 20, 1977, LSdC.
40. Beeler, *Footsteps*, 20.
41. Brown, *Cross Plains Remembered.*
42. Brown, *Cross Plains Remembered*, 132–33.
43. Beeler, *Footsteps*, 20.
44. Lindsey W. Tyson letter, October 10, 1977, LSdC.
45. TCL, 2:202.
46. AMTF, 173.
47. AMTF, 120.
48. Alma Baker King interview, September 12, 1978; Vera Baker Nichols interview, March 8, 1978, LSdC.
49. Alma Baker King interview, September 12, 1978; Earl J. Baker interview, October 16, 1978; Earl J. Baker interview, n.d., LSdC.
50. *Empire-Tribune*, July 29, 1984.
51. Vera Baker Nichols interview, March 8, 1978, LSdC.
52. Earl Baker interview, April 2, 1978, LSdC.
53. Jack Scott interview, April/May 2001, SWC.
54. 1910 US Census.
55. Lindsey W. Tyson letter, February 2, 1977, LSdC.
56. Lindsey W. Tyson letter, October 10, 1977, LSdC.
57. Lindsey Tyson interview, March 7, 1978, LSdC.
58. Lindsey W. Tyson letter, October 10, 1977; Lindsey W. Tyson interview notes, August 13, 1977, LSdC.
59. Lindsey W. Tyson letter, October 10, 1977; Lindsey W. Tyson letter, October 10, 1977, LSdC.
60. Lindsey W. Tyson letter, September 27, 1978, LSdC.
61. Lindsey Tyson interview, March 7, 1978, LSdC.
62. LSdC, Tom Ray Wilson interview, August 13, 1977.

63. Lindsey W. Tyson letter, September 27, 1978, LSdC.
64. Lindsey W. Tyson letter, n.d., LSdC.
65. Estill Franklin Allen, *Cross Plains-Burkett, Texas, Methodists* (Cross Plains, TX: First United Methodist Church, 1985), 4–5.
66. Lindsey W. Tyson letter, October 10, 1977, LSdC.
67. Leroy Butler interview, July 20, 1977, LSdC.
68. Leroy Butler interview, SFOHA; Leroy Butler interview, July 20, 1977, LSdC.
69. Leroy Butler interview, SFOHA.
70. TCL, 2:304.
71. TCL, 3:15.
72. Mrs. D.K. Woolridge interview, February 3, 1979, LSdC.
73. Lois Garrett letter, November 13, 1978, LSdC.
74. Leroy Butler interview, SFOHA.
75. CPR, December 26, 1919.

Notes for Chapter 6

1. TCP, 1:141.
2. AMTF, 607.
3. AMTF, 607.
4. AMTF, 608.
5. AMTF, 608; see also H. P. Lovecraft, *Letters to E. Hoffmann Price and Richard F. Searight*, ed. David E. Schultz and S. T. Joshi (New York: Hippocampus Press, 2021), 275 (hereafter LPS); Glenn Lord, ed., *The Howard Collector: By and about Robert E. Howard* (New York: Ace Books, 1979), 195.
6. AMTF, 608; see also LPS, 275.
7. AMTF, 607.
8. Deoma Morgan letter, June 12, 1978, LSdC.
9. AMTF, 548.
10. Paula Bond interview, August 13, 1977, LSdC; Herron, "Last," 24.
11. Norris R. Chambers interview, July 22, 1977; Deoma Morgan interview, March 6, 1978, LSdC.
12. Lindsey W. Tyson interview notes, August 13, 1977, LSdC.
13. Preece, "Chapter II," Harold Preece Papers, 1922–2017, Dolph Briscoe Center for American History, University of Texas at Austin, Austin, TX (hereafter HP); LC, 99.
14. IMH, 274; POSR2, 23.
15. AMTF, 101; see also David A. Hardy, "Indomitable Wildness, Unquenchable Vitality," *Cimmerian* 3, no. 4 (April 2006): 4–20
16. WT, May 1926, 715.
17. AMTF, 81.
18. AMTF, 510.
19. AMTF, 592.
20. TCL, 2:381.
21. SFTP, 224.
22. TCL, 1:166; see also L. Sprague De Camp, *The Spell of Conan* (New York: Ace, 1980); Lovecraft, "In Memoriam."
23. AMTF, 550.
24. Louis L'Amour, *Education of a Wandering Man* (New York: Bantam, 1989), 21.
25. Oliver, "Robert E. Howard and Jack London's *Martin Eden*: Analyzing the Influence of Martin Eden on Howard and His Semi-Autobiography," *Dark Man: The Journal of Robert E. Howard and Pulp Studies* 11, no. 1 (June 2020): 6–32.

26. Jack London, *The Star Rover* (Orinda, CA: Seawolf Press, 2018).
27. TCL, 2:90.
28. De Camp, *Spell of Conan*, 30–31; Brian Murphy, *Flame and Crimson: A History of Sword-and-Sorcery* (n.p.: Pulp Hero Press, 2019), 80.
29. Frank Belknap Long, *Howard Phillips Lovecraft: Dreamer on the Nightside* (Cabin John, MD: Wildside Press, 2016), 175–76.
30. Roehm, "The Birth of a Writer," *REHupa*, no. 280 (December 2019): 1–4.
31. AMTF, 608–9.
32. Morgan Holmes and George Knight, "Conan the Argonaut," *Cimmerian* 5, no. 4 (August 2008): 7.
33. Charles Beaumont, "The Bloody Pulps," *Playboy* 9, no. 9 (September 1962): 90.
34. Mary Noel, *Villains Galore: The Heyday of the Popular Story Weekly* (Berkeley: University of California, 1954), 3.
35. Tony Goodstone, *The Pulps: Fifty Years of American Pop Culture* (New York: Bonanza Books, 1970), xii.
36. Tim DeForest, *Storytelling in the Pulps, Comics, and Radio: How Technology Changed Popular Fiction in America* (Jefferson, NC: McFarland, 2004), 26.
37. Mike Ashley, *The Time Machines: The Story of the Science-Fiction Pulp Magazines from the Beginning to 1950* (Liverpool: Liverpool University Press, 2000); Goodstone, *Pulps.*
38. *Argosy All-Story Weekly*, July 20, 1929, 286.
39. Ashley, *Time Machines*; Ron Goulart, *Cheap Thrills: The Amazing! Thrilling! Astonishing! History of Pulp Fiction* (New Rochelle, NY: Arlington House, 1972); Goodstone, *Pulps.*
40. Rusty Burke, "Robert E. Howard and Edgar Rice Burroughs," *Pavilion Blog*, September 1, 2020, https://www.thedarkmanjournal.org/the-pavilion-blog/robert-e-howard-and-edgar-rice-burroughs.
41. Goodstone, *Pulps*, xii.
42. Goulart, *Cheap Thrills*, 12.
43. Goulart, *Cheap Thrills*; DeForest, *Storytelling*; Brian Murphy, "From Pulps to Paperbacks: The Role of Medium in the Development of Sword-and-Sorcery Fiction," *Journal of American Culture* 43, no. 1 (March 2021): 43–53.
44. DeForest, *Storytelling*, 11.
45. Dobie et al., *Growing Up*, 97.
46. Richard Bleiler, "A History of *Adventure* Magazine" *Galactic Central*, July 28, 2022, http://www.philsp.com/articles/magazines/adventure.html.; Goulart, *Cheap Thrills*, 13.
47. Goulart, *Cheap Thrills*, 32; Brian Taves, "An Author in Search of His Genre: Talbot Mundy's Earliest Stories," in *The Best of Blood 'N' Thunder*, ed. Ed Hulse (Morris Plains, NJ: Murania Press, 2013), 211.
48. Bleiler, "History of *Adventure*."
49. Burke, "The Robert E. Howard Bookshelf" *Howard History*, December 28, 2020, https://howardhistory.com/the-robert-e-howard-bookshelf/#l007; Brian Leno, "When Yaller Rock County Came to Chawed Ear," *Cimmerian* 5, no. 5 (October 1928): 4–13; Howard, *The Adventures of Breckenridge Elkins*, 2 vols. Plano, TX: Robert E. Howard Foundation Press, 2016) vol. 2 (hereafter ABE); DeForest, *Storytelling*; Howard, *El Borak and other Desert Adventures* (New York: Del Rey, 2010), 533 (hereafter EB).
50. AMTF, 592.
51. Murphy, *Flame and Crimson*, 39.
52. Howard, *Sword Woman and other Historical Adventures* (New York: Del Rey, 2011), 518 (hereafter SW).
53. Earle Labor, *Jack London: An American Life* (New York: Farrar, Straus and Giroux, 2013), 119; see also Johnson, *Odd Type*.

54. Robert Weinberg, "Introduction," : The Long Journey of the Morning Star," in Harold Lamb, *Swords from the West* (Lincoln: University of Nebraska Press, 2009), xiii; AMTF, 609.
55. AMTF, 609.
56. Jack London, *Martin Eden* (New York: Penguin Books, 1984), 115.
57. Patrice Louinet, "'The Wright Hook' (Or, The origin of 'Spear and Fang')," *REH: Two-Gun Raconteur*, October 25, 2016, https://web.archive.org/web/20170417100627/http://www.rehtwogunraconteur.com/the-wright-hook-or-the-origin-of-spear-and-fang/.
58. AMTF, 603.
59. Roehm, "A Little History . . .," *REHupa*, no. 201 (October 2006): 1.
60. Howard, *Sentiment: An Olio of Rarer Works*, ed. Rob Roehm (Plano, TX: Robert E. Howard Foundation Press, 2009), xii (hereafter *Sentiment*).
61. Burke, *Robert E. Howard*, 6.
62. *Sentiment*, xiii.
63. AMTF, 606.
64. J. Frank Dobie, *The Flavor of Texas* (1936; repr., Austin: Jenkins Publishing, 1975), 7.
65. Fehrenbach, *Lone Star*, 716.
66. Lindsey W. Tyson interview notes, August 13, 1977, LSdC.
67. Paula Bond interview, August 13, 1977, LSdC.
68. Roehm, "Back to School," *Howard History: The Life and Times of Robert E. Howard*, September 24, 2018. https://howardhistory.com/2018/09/24/back-to-school/.
69. POSR2.
70. POSR2, 249–50.
71. POSR2, 251.
72. LC, 365.
73. Howard, *Pictures in the Fire: Remaining Weird Tales and Esoterica* (Plano, TX: Robert E. Howard Foundation Press, 2018), 414.
74. Howard, *Pictures*, 415.
75. HP, "Chapter III."
76. Lindsey Tyson interview, March 7, 1978; Paula Bond interview, August 13, 1977, LSdC.
77. February 11, 1921, December 2, 1921, CPR; IMH.
78. Beeler, *Footsteps*.
79. Paula Bond interview, August 13, 1977, LSdC.
80. Roehm, "Comer Connection."
81. *Big Spring Herald*, January 7, 1921.
82. Burke, *Robert E. Howard*, 6.
83. Roehm, "My Name Is Earl," *REHupa*, no. 229 (June 2011): 1–5; Lindsey W. Tyson letter, October 10, 1977, LSdC.
84. Leroy Butler interview, SFOHA.
85. AMTF, 606.
86. CPR, July 16, 1920.
87. AMTF, 348.
88. Todd B. Vick, "The Carnival , The Girl, and The Smitten Teenager," *On An Underwood No. 5,* October 6, 2019. http://onanunderwood5.blogspot.com/2019/10/the-carnival-girl-and-smitten-teenager.html.
89. Harold Preece, "Women and Robert Ervin Howard," *Fantasy Crossroads* 1, no. 3 (May 1975): 21.
90. Preece, "Women," 22.
91. CPR, May 12, 1922.
92. CPR, May 19, 1922.
93. Roehm, "Class of '22," *REHupa*, no. 241 (June 2013): 1.

Notes for Chapter 7

1. TCP, 2:350.
2. *Brownwood Bulletin*, March 10, 1923 (hereafter BB).
3. Mark Odintz, "Brownwood, TX," *Handbook of Texas Online*, updated September 20, 2023, https://www.tshaonline.org/handbook/entries/brownwood-tx.
4. BB, May 22, 1923.
5. Brownwood Public Library.
6. John F. Worley, *Brownwood City Directory, 1923* (Dallas: John F. Worley Directory, 1923), 140; Charlotte Laughlin letter, July 26, 1978, LSdC; SD, 13.
7. Roehm, "Austin, Who?," 1.
8. BB, September 21, 1922, October 2, 1922, November 21, 1922, December 11, 1922.
9. SD, 13.
10. CPR, July 28, 1922; Roehm, "Good Ol' Boys," *Howard History: The Life and Times of Robert E. Howard*, September 24, 2018, https://howardhistory.com/2018/09/24/good-ol-boys/.
11. SD, 13; Roehm, "Austin, Who?"
12. Roehm, "Brownwood High School," *REH Two-Gun Raconteur*, April 21, 2010, https://web.archive.org/web/20100722021701/http://rehtwogunraconteur.com/?p=3842.
13. AMTF, 606.
14. BB, September 12, 1922.
15. AMTF, 606.
16. Austin Newton letter, no date, LSdC; SD, 13.
17. AMTF, 239.
18. Austin Newton letter, no date, LSdC; SD, 13.
19. BB, November 21, 1922, December 11, 1922.
20. Tom Ray Wilson interview, August 13, 1977, LSDC.
21. Howard Waldrop, "Journey to Cross Plains," in *The Robert E. Howard Reader*, ed. Darrell Schweitzer (Berkeley Heights, NJ: Wildside Press, 2010), 158.
22. Charles Duhigg, *Power of Habit: Why We Do What We Do in Life and Business* (New York: Random House, 2014), 253.
23. Duhigg, *Power of Habit*; Antonio Zadra and Robert Stickgold, *When Brains Dream: Exploring the Science & Mystery of Sleep* (New York: W. W. Norton, 2021).
24. Duhigg, *Power of Habit*, 254.
25. Duhigg, *Power of Habit*, 255.
26. Zadra and Stickgold, *When Brains Dream.*
27. SD, 13.
28. SD, 18.
29. Howard, *Western Tales* (Plano, TX: Robert E. Howard Foundation Press, 2013), 482 (hereafter WEST).
30. SD, 13.
31. BB, December 22, 1922.
32. SFTP, 222; Roehm, *The Brownwood Connection: A Guide for Robert E. Howard Fans.* Plano, TX: Robert E. Howard Foundation Press, 2010), 8.
33. SD, 33.
34. BB, January 2, 1923.
35. SD, 39.
36. Roehm, "Hawkshaw & Howard," *Howard History: The Life and Times of Robert E. Howard*, February 2, 2018, https://howardhistory.com/2018/02/02/hawkshaw-howard/.
37. SD, 54.

38. Bobby Derie, *Weird Talers: Essays on Robert E. Howard and Others* (New York: Hippocampus Press, 2019), 268.
39. SD, 13.
40. Roehm, "The Vinson Papers," *Howard History: The Life and Times of Robert E. Howard*, October 19, 2021, https://howardhistory.com/2021/10/19/the-vinson-papers-part-1/.
41. AMTF, 198.
42. Truett Vinson letter, June 29, 1977, LSdC.
43. Roehm, "Robert E. Howard and the Lone Scouts," *Dark Man: The Journal of Robert E. Howard Studies* 7, no. 1 (December 2012): 45–57.
44. Janice A. Petterchak, *Lone Scout : W. D. Boyce and American Boy Scouting* (Ann Arbor: Legacy Press, 2003).
45. Roehm, "Lone Scouts"; although Preece believed Howard joined the Lone Scouts, Roehm has found no evidence for that assertion. See Preece, "Quest for Books," *Fantasy Crossroads*, nos. 10–11 (March 1977): 46–47.
46. SFTP, 241.
47. SFTP, xi.
48. SFTP, ix–x.
49. AMTF, 549.
50. SFTP, 246.
51. Tevis Clyde Smith, *Report on a Writing Man & Other Reminiscences of Robert E. Howard*, ed. Rusty Burke (West Warwick, RI: Necronomicon Press, 1991), 5 (hereafter RWM).
52. Roehm, "Lone Scouts"; Truett Vinson to Tevis Clyde Smith, June 6, 1921, Robert E. Howard Collection, Texas A&M University, College Station, TX (hereafter TA&M); LSOL, 151.
53. SFTP, 217.
54. SFTP, 219.
55. SFTP, 241.
56. DOTS, 7.
57. SFTP, 246.
58. SFTP, xii.
59. RWM, 6.
60. DOTS, 7.
61. Lord, *Howard Collector*, 234.
62. Patrice Louinet, *The Robert E. Howard Guide* (Tallahassee, FL: Skelos Press, 2018), 45.
63. AMTF, 544–45.
64. TCL, 2:202.
65. AMTF, 544–45.
66. AMTF, 606.
67. TCL, 3:175.
68. OWWA, 51.
69. OWWA, 157.
70. AMTF, 544–45.
71. TCL, 1:39.
72. SD, 97; *Sentiment,* 527.
73. Roehm, "Footnotes #2," *Howard History: The Life and Times of Robert E. Howard*, November 1, 2018, https://howardhistory.com/2018/11/01/footnotes-2/.
74. BB, May 10, 1923.
75. BB, May 19, 1923.
76. AMTF, 606.
77. TCL, 2:202.
78. BB, May 26, 1923.

79. *Sentiment*, 521.
80. SD, 97; *Sentiment*, 527.
81. TCL, 1:6.
82. Roehm, "Footnotes #2."
83. *Commerce Journal*, May 25, 1923; Roehm, "A Little History."
84. TCL, 1:6.
85. CPR, June 29, 1923.
86. AMTF, 606.
87. SFTP, 217.

Notes for Chapter 8

1. TCP, 2:173.
2. CPR, June 1, 1923.
3. SD, 99; Roehm, "The Summer of '24," *REHupa*, no. 246 (April 2014): 1–2; Norris R. Chambers interview, July 22, 1977, LSdC.
4. SFTP, 224.
5. TCL, 1:303; Louinet, "Wright Hook."
6. Labor, *Jack London*, 118.
7. SFTP, 225.
8. SFTP, 218.
9. TCL, 2:165.
10. Lindsey W. Tyson letter, February 2, 1977, LSdC.
11. LC, 84.
12. OWWA, 114.
13. DOTS, 28.
14. Roehm, "508 Coleman Street," *REH: Two-Gun Raconteur*, April 3, 2015. https://web.archive.org/web/20150907153854/http://www.rehtwogunraconteur.com/508-coleman-street/.
15. J. W. Torbett Sr., *The Doctor's Scrapbook* (Marlin, TX: Torbett, 1947), 20, 43.
16. Torbett, *Doctor's Scrapbook*, 46.
17. Torbett, *Doctor's Scrapbook*, 51.
18. Torbett, *Doctor's Scrapbook*, 59.
19. Torbett, *Doctor's Scrapbook*, 64.
20. Torbett, *Doctor's Scrapbook*, 94.
21. TCL, 1:3.
22. BB, June 7, 1923; TCL, 1:3.
23. CPR, June 22, 1923; TCL, 1:6.
24. SFTP, 217.
25. SFTP, 262; Roehm, "Vinson Papers."
26. SFTP.
27. SFTP, 217.
28. SFTP, 9.
29. Derie, *Weird Talers*, 270; Roehm, "Lone Scouts," 55.
30. TCP, 3:143.
31. LC, 380.
32. LSOL, 152; Roehm, "Vinson Papers."
33. Lindsey W. Tyson letter, October 10, 1977, LSdC.
34. TCL, 3:46.
35. TCL, 3:45.

36. TCL, 3:183–84.
37. Tom R. Wilson letter, March 4, 1978, LSdC.
38. TCL, 1:10.
39. Jeffrey Shanks, "Gouged Eyes and Chawed Ears: The Rough-and-Tumble World of Breckenridge Elkins," *REH: Two-Gun Raconteur*, no. 15 (Summer 2011): 47–52.
40. TCL, 1:10.
41. TCL, 1:10; SFTP, 10.
42. TCL, 1:17.
43. Roehm, *Brownwood Connection*, 64, 19.
44. SFTP, 246.
45. *Dallas Times Herald*, August 8, 1981.
46. SFTP, 219; CPR, September 27, 1923.
47. SFTP, 219.
48. Howard, *Post Oaks and Sand Roughs* (Hampton Falls, NH: Donald M. Grant, Publishers, 1990), 103–4 (hereafter POSR1); Herron, *Famous Someday.*
49. DOTS, 42.
50. Leroy Butler interview, July 20, 1977, LSdC; see also Leroy Butler interview, SFOHA.
51. Burke, *Cross Plains*, 6.
52. POSR1, 103–4.
53. Friberg, "Memories."
54. IMH, 207.
55. AMTF, 491.
56. Kate Merryman interview, July 18, 1977, LSdC.
57. Lindsey Tyson interview, March 7, 1978, LSdC; Herron, *Famous Someday.*
58. Norris R. Chambers interview, July 22, 1977; Jack Scott interview, July 19, 1977, LSdC.
59. AMTF, 447.
60. Vinson to Smith, April 26, 1925, TA&M; Roehm, "Austin, Who?," 1; SD, 99.
61. TCL, 2:202.
62. Burke, *Cross Plains*, 14.
63. TCL, 1:19.
64. AMTF, 111.
65. TCL, 1:21.
66. POSR1, 371.
67. Lindsey W. Tyson letter, September 27, 1978, LSdC.
68. TCL, 1:21.
69. Beeler, *Footsteps*, 75.
70. James W. Nichols, *On the Banks, of Turkey Creek*, (Cross Plains, TX: 1st Book Library, 2003), 31.
71. Lindsey W. Tyson letter, September 27, 1978, LSdC.
72. TCL, 1:21.
73. BB, October 1, 1923.
74. TCL, 1:21.
75. SFTP, 246.
76. TCL, 1:21.
77. Roehm, "Mary, Mary."
78. TCL, 1:21.
79. SD, 100; Derie, *Weird Talers*, 268.
80. TCL, 1:29.
81. TCL, 1:30.
82. Roehm, "Vinson Papers."
83. BB, May 21, 1924; TCL, 1:30.

84. CPR, August 23, 1924.
85. SFTP, xvii.
86. Roehm, "The Missing Mexico Trip," *Howard History: The Life and Times of Robert E. Howard,* October 19, 2018, https://howardhistory.com/2018/10/19/the-missing-mexico-trip/; CPR, September 19, 1924.
87. TCL, 1:32.
88. OWWA, 249.
89. SFTP, 225.
90. Lindsey W. Tyson letter, n.d., LSdC.
91. Roehm, *Brownwood Connection*, 22.
92. Charlotte Laughlin letter, July 26, 1978, LSdC.
93. TCL, 2:202.
94. TLT, 466.
95. POSR2, 184.
96. POSR2, x; Labor, *Jack London*, xiii; London, *Martin Eden.*
97. SFTP, 225.
98. POSR2, 212.
99. POSR1, 5.
100. POSR1, 6.
101. POSR2, 97.
102. Roehm, "Post Oaks and Football," *Howard History: The Life and Times of Robert E. Howard*, February 1, 2018, https://howardhistory.com/2018/02/01/post-oaks-and-football/.
103. POSR2, 97–98.
104. BB, November 28, 1924.
105. SD, 100.
106. POSR2, 114.
107. Louinet, "Wright Hook."
108. WT, December 1924, 176.
109. WT, December 1924, 176–77.
110. Louinet, "Wright Hook."
111. Roehm, "Birth," 2.
112. Lindsey Tyson interview, March 7, 1978; Lindsey W. Tyson letter, n.d., LSdC.
113. Lindsey W. Tyson letter, n.d., LSdC.
114. AMTF, 603.
115. POSR2, 99.
116. Louinet, "Wright Hook."
117. POSR2, 114. Roehm, *Brownwood Connection.*
118. *Liberty Vindicator*, December 26, 1924.
119. POSR2, 115.

Notes for Chapter 9

1. TCP, 1:77.
2. POSR2, 116.
3. POSR2, 116, 120; TCL, 1:38.
4. POSR2, 117.
5. POSR2, 117.
6. POSR2, 117; TCL, 1:38.
7. POSR2, 102.
8. POSR2, 117.

9. POSR2, 117.
10. Sam Moskowitz, "The Forgotten Creator of Weird Tales: An Introduction," in *Worlds of Weird*, ed. Leo Margulies (New York: Pyramid Books, 1965), 10; John Pelan and Jerad Walters, eds., *Conversations with the* Weird Tales *Circle* (Lakewood, CO: Centipede Press, 2009), 712.
11. John Locke, *The Thing's Incredible! The Secret Origins of Weird Tales, 1923–24* (Elkhorn, CA: Off-Trail Publications, 2018), 160 (hereafter TTI); see also Pelan and Walters, *Conversations*, 133.
12. TTI, 12.
13. Robert Weinberg, *The Weird Tales Story: Expanded and Enhanced* (n.p.: Pulp Hero Press, 2021), 1 (hereafter WTS).
14. TTI, 12; Weinberg, WTS, 1.
15. TTI, 13.
16. WTS, 1.
17. TTI, 15.
18. WTS, 1.
19. WTS, 1.
20. TTI, 25.
21. TTI, 19.
22. TTI, 22; Locke, *Pulpwood Days*, vol. 1, *Editors You Want to Know* (Castroville, CA: Off-Trail Publications, 2007), 79, 81.
23. WTS, 2; TTI, 21.
24. WTS, 1.
25. TTI, 26; Lin Carter, *Imaginary Worlds* (New York: Ballantine Books, 1973), 53.
26. WT, March 1923.
27. WT, March 1923, 180.
28. WT April 1923, 180.
29. WTS, 29.
30. Reginald Smith, Weird Tales *in the Thirties* (Santa Ana, CA: Reginald Smith, 1966); WTS.
31. Pelan and Walters, *Conversations*, 713.
32. Weinberg, *WT50: A Tribute to* Weird Tales (Oak Lawn, IL: Weinberg, 1974), 4.
33. WTS, 2.
34. WTS, 29.
35. TTI, 33.
36. IMH, 176–77; TTI, 125.
37. TTI, 125; WTS, 2–3.
38. Weinberg, *WT50*, 6.
39. TTI, 166; WTS, 3.
40. WTS, 3.
41. S. T. Joshi, *I Am Providence: The Life and Times of H. P. Lovecraft* (New York: Hippocampus Press, 2013), 21.
42. Joshi, *I Am Providence*, 21.
43. Joshi, *I Am Providence*, 44.
44. Joshi, *I Am Providence*, 44.
45. Lovecraft, *Miscellaneous Writings* (Sauk City, WI: Arkham House, 1995), 452.
46. Lovecraft, *Miscellaneous Writings*, 113; Pelan and Walters, *Conversations*, 713.
47. TTI.
48. John D. Haefele, *Lovecraft: The Great Tales* (n.p.: Cimmerian Press, 2021), 152; TTI, 160.
49. Pelan and Walters, *Conversations*, 133.
50. TTI, 157.

51. IMH, 175–76; WTS, 3.
52. Kraft, *OAK Leaves*, hereafter OAK, 12; TTI, 58.
53. TTI, 59.
54. TTI, 63.
55. TTI, 64.
56. E. Hoffman Price, *Book of the Dead: Friends of Yesteryear: Fictioneers & Others (Memories of the Pulp Fiction Era)* (Sauk City, WI: Arkham House, 2001), 27.
57. TTI, 38–39; Julius Schwartz, "Titans of Science Fiction: Farnsworth Wright," *Science Fiction Digest* 1, no. 7 (March 1933): 3.
58. WTS, 19.
59. TTI, 43–44.
60. TTI, 48.
61. WTS, 3; John M. Barry, *The Great Influenza: The Epic Story of the Deadliest Plague in History* (New York: Penguin Books, 2004).
62. "Wright, Farnsworth to Lovecraft, H. P.," Howard P. Lovecraft Collection, Brown University Library, Providence, RI.
63. Pelan and Walters, *Conversations*, 520.
64. Pelan and Walters, *Conversations*, 713; Price, *Book of the Dead.*
65. Price, *Book of the Dead*, 10.
66. WT, May-June-July 1924, 1.
67. Moskowitz, "Forgotten Creator," 12.
68. Weinberg, *WT50*, 41; Price, *Book of the Dead*, 10.
69. LPS, 315.
70. Pelan and Walters, *Conversations*, 562.
71. Price, *Book of the Dead*, 18.
72. WTS, 12.
73. Pelan and Walters, *Conversations,* 524.
74. WTS, 17.
75. Schwartz, "Titans," 3–4.
76. Price, *Book of the Dead*, 13.
77. Pelan and Walters, *Conversations*, 520.
78. TTI, 200.
79. IMH, 176–79.
80. WTS, 5.
81. TCL, 2:165.
82. TCL, 2:421.
83. POSR2, 185.
84. TCL, 2:11.
85. AMTF, 81.
86. AMTF, 118.
87. Pelan and Walters, *Conversations*, 360.
88. Pelan and Walters, *Conversations*, 506.
89. Pelan and Walters, *Conversations*, 701.
90. Weinberg, *WT50*, 41.
91. WTS, 163.
92. WTS, 169.
93. Moskowitz, "Forgotten Creator," 9.
94. Murphy, "Pulps to Paperbacks," 44.
95. WT, October 1926, 574.
96. Hugh B. Cave, *Magazines, I Remember* (Chicago: Tattered Pages Press, 1994), 14.
97. Louinet, "Wright Hook"; Roehm, "Birth."

98. TTI, 205.
99. POSR2, 102.
100. Weinberg, *WT50*, 9.
101. POSR2, 102.
102. Roehm, "Birth"; WTS.
103. London, *Martin Eden*, 162.
104. WT, July 1925, 111–15.
105. POSR2, 122.
106. Leroy Butler interview, July 20, 1977, LSdC.
107. WT, September 1925, 417.
108. POSR2, 132.

Notes for Chapter 10

1. TCP, 1:227.
2. WT, August 1925.
3. WT, August 1925, 187.
4. POSR2, 120.
5. TCL, 1:67.
6. WT, April 1926; WTS, 39.
7. POSR2, 147.
8. Howard, *The Horror Stories of Robert E. Howard* (New York: Del Rey, 2008), xix (hereafter HS).
9. Black, "Mary Bohannon," 7.
10. AMTF, 45.
11. AMTF, 220.
12. AMTF, 44.
13. Fannie McClung Adamson interview, October 16, 1978, LSdC.
14. AMTF, 44.
15. AMTF, 44–45.
16. OWWA, 226.
17. *Fantasy Fan*, December 1933, TA&M.
18. WT, March 1928; Charles Hoffman, "'The Shadow Kingdom' and the Origins of Gothic Horror in Robert E. Howard's Heroic Fantasy," *Skelos*, no. 2 (Winter 2017): 84–97.
19. HS, xviii.
20. HS, xviii, 145; AMTF, 171; Bobby Derie, "Conan and the Little People: Robert E. Howard and Lovecraft's Theory," *On An Underwood No. 5*, January 13, 2019, http://onanunderwood5.blogspot.com/2019/01/conan-and-little-people-robert-e-howard.html.
21. HS, 145; AMTF 171; Howard, *Nameless Cults: The Cthulhu Mythos Fiction of Robert E. Howard* (Oakland, CA: Chaosium Book, 2001).
22. Rusty Burke, "The Old Deserted House: Images of the South in Howard's Fiction," *Dark Man: The Journal of Robert E. Howard Studies*, no. 2 (July 1991): 13.
23. Burke, "Old," 14.
24. HS, 97.
25. Burke, "Old," 16.
26. OWWA, 241; Burke, "Old," 15.
27. Willard M. Oliver, "Ghosties, Haunts, and Conjure-Men: Robert E. Howard and the Yarns of Mary Bohannon," *REHupa*, no. 191 (October 2021): 15–46.
28. AMTF, 109; see also TCL, 3:283.
29. AMTF, 109.
30. TCL, 3:402.

31. Lovecraft and Clark Ashton Smith, *Dawnward Spire, Lonely Hills: The Letters of H. P. Lovecraft and Clark Ashton Smith*, ed. David E. Schultz and S. T. Joshi (New York: Hippocampus Press, 2020), 644 (hereafter DS); see also Lovecraft, "In Memoriam."
32. WT, August/September 1936, 251, 254.
33. WT, August/September 1936, 256.
34. HS, xxiii; Stephen King, *Danse Macabre* (New York: Gallery Books, 1981), 240.
35. AMTF, 45.
36. AMTF, 44.
37. HS, 425.
38. HS, 429.
39. AMTF, 44.
40. Burke, "New Orleans."
41. WT, July 1938, 122.
42. WT, July 1938, 124, 126.
43. HS, vxii.
44. Don Herron, ed., *The Dark Barbarian: The Writings of Robert E. Howard: A Critical Anthology* (1984; repr., Berkeley Heights, NJ: Wildside Press, 2000), 68.
45. HS, xvii.
46. POSR2, 103.
47. POSR2, 120.
48. TCL, 1:49.
49. TCL, 2:202.
50. Norris R. Chambers letter, n.d., LSdC.
51. POSR2, 123.
52. POSR2, 125.
53. TCL, 2:248–49; POSR2, 375.
54. POSR2, 125.
55. POSR2, 126–27.
56. TCL, 2:202–3; POSR2, 375; Burke, *Cross Plains*, 14; Beeler, *Footsteps*, 61.
57. POSR2, 128.
58. POSR2, 128; Louinet, *Howard Guide*, 156–57.
59. POSR2, 128.
60. Burke, *Cross Plains*, 14.
61. Roehm, *Brownwood Connection,* 26.
62. TCL, 1:53–54.
63. Roehm, *Brownwood Connection*, 26.
64. Roehm, "Tell of Gloria's Life," *REHupa*, no. 273 (October 2018): 1–8.
65. POSR2, 131.
66. SFTP, xiv.
67. Roehm, "Gloria's Life," 3.
68. SFTP, xiv.
69. POSR2, 133.
70. POSR2, 134.
71. POSR2, 134–35.
72. POSR2, 136.
73. POSR2, 139.
74. BB, July 13, 1925.
75. POSR2, 139.
76. POSR2, 141.
77. TCL, 1:58.
78. TCL, 1:59.

79. TCL, 1:59–60.
80. SFTP, xv.
81. TCL, 1:51.
82. Brown, *Cross Plains Remembered*, 71; CPR, October 16, 1925.
83. TCL, 1:57.
84. TCL, 1:59.
85. Brown, *Cross Plains Remembered*, 71; CPR, October 16, 1925.
86. TCL, 1:57.
87. POSR2, 147–48; Beeler, *Footsteps*, 60.
88. TCL, 2:203; POSR2, 375.
89. Roehm, "Vinson Papers"; "Dating the Right Hook," *Howard History: The Life and Times of Robert E. Howard*, February 1, 2018, https://howardhistory.com/2018/02/01/dating-the-right-hook/.
90. Roehm, "Dating"; Howard, *Fist of Iron: The Collected Boxing Fiction of Robert E. Howard*, 4 vols., ed. Patrice Louinet, Christopher Gruber, and Mark Finn (Plano, TX: Robert E. Howard Foundation Press, 2019), vol. 1 (hereafter FOI).
91. SFTP, xv. Note: Daniel Baker later merged with Howard Payne College.
92. Roehm, "Vinson Papers."
93. POSR2, 112; SFTP.
94. Norris R. Chambers letter, January 7, 1978, LSdC.
95. Norris R. Chambers letter, October 28, 1978, LSdC.
96. POSR2, 131–32.
97. POSR2, 132.
98. POSR2, 149.
99. POSR2, 152.
100. TCL, 1:66.
101. *Sentiment*, 318–19.
102. LSOL, xiii.
103. LSOL, vii–viii.
104. POSR2, 128; Glenn Lord, "Herbert Klatt," *Dark Man: The Journal of Robert E. Howard Studies*, no. 1 (August 1990): 24.
105. POSR2, 159.
106. POSR2, 161.
107. AMTF, 173–74.
108. LSOL, 102.
109. POSR2, 163.

Notes for Chapter 11

1. TCP, 2:417.
2. IMH, 5.
3. POSR2, 168.
4. Bobby Derie, "A Letter from Seabury Quinn," *On An Underwood No. 5*, March 22, 2020, http://onanunderwood5.blogspot.com/2020/03/a-letter-from-seabury-quinn-by-bobby.html.
5. POSR2, 168.
6. TCL, 1:81.
7. POSR2, 169.
8. POSR2, 169.
9. WT, December 1925, 848.

10. WT, March 1927, 421.
11. Derie, "Wolf Prints (or, The legacy of 'In the Forest of Villefère')," *Weird Beginnings* (2019): 21.
12. POSR2, 163–64.
13. TCL, 2:203.
14. Beeler, *Footsteps*, 25.
15. Burke, *Cross Plains*, 13; Brown, *Cross Plains Remembered*, 15.
16. POSR2, 170.
17. Anne Cooper Funderburg, *Sundae Best: A History of Soda Fountains* (Bowling Green, OH: Bowling Green State University Popular Press, 2002), 21.
18. Funderburg, *Sundae Best*, 33.
19. Funderburg, *Sundae Best*, 67.
20. Funderburg, *Sundae Best*, 51, 58.
21. Funderburg, *Sundae Best*, 101.
22. Funderburg, *Sundae Best*, 103.
23. Funderburg, *Sundae Best*, 123.
24. POSR2, 169–70.
25. POSR2, 172.
26. AMTF, 341–43.
27. POSR2, 170.
28. TCL, 2:203; POSR2, 375–76.
29. POSR2, 169–70.
30. POSR2, 172.
31. POSR2, 170.
32. POSR2, 172.
33. POSR2, 178–79.
34. Tom Ray Wilson Interview, August 13, 1977, LSdC.
35. SFTP, xvii.
36. SFTP, 254.
37. Duhigg, *Power of Habit*, 255.
38. TCL, 1:95.
39. TCL, 2:203; POSR2, 375–76.
40. AMTF, 341–43.
41. TCL, 3:132; London, *Martin Eden*, 198.
42. AMTF, 341–43.
43. TCL, 2:203; POSR2, 172.
44. Alma Baker King interview, August 26, 1978; Lindsey W. Tyson letter, October 10, 1977, and interview, March 7, 1978, LSdC.
45. Alma Baker King interview, August 26, 1978, LSdC.
46. SFTP, 224–25.
47. Jeffrey Meyers, *Hemingway: A Biography* (New York: Harper & Row, 1985), 20.
48. Kenneth Slawenski, *J. D. Salinger: A Life* (New York: Random House, 2010), 21.
49. London, *Martin Eden*, 238–39.
50. SFTP, xvii; IMH, 189.
51. POSR2, 182.
52. SD, 183; SFTP, xvii.
53. *Bulletin of Howard Payne College*, June 1927, TA&M.
54. AMTF, 544; Roehm, *Brownwood Connection*, 34, 37.
55. Lindsey Tyson interview, March 7, 1978, LSdC.
56. Roehm, *Brownwood Connection*, 35; POSR2, 182–83.

57. AMTF, 200.
58. POSR2, 182–83.
59. Lindsey Tyson interview, March 7, 1978, LSdC.
60. Lindsey W. Tyson letter, n.d., LSdC.
61. Lindsey W. Tyson letter, n.d., LSdC; CPR, December 23, 1927.
62. Lindsey W. Tyson letter, n.d., LSdC.
63. Lindsey Tyson interview, March 7, 1978, LSdC.
64. TCL, 2:203.
65. POSR2, 187.
66. POSR2, 197–98.
67. POSR2, 184.
68. Roehm, "Yellow Jacket," *REH: Two-Gun Raconteur*, September 17, 2010, https://web.archive.org/web/20150911051745/http://www.rehtwogunraconteur.com/yellow-jacket/.
69. *Yellow Jacket*, October 27, 1926; SD 198.
70. *Yellow Jacket*, October 13, 1926; SD 190.
71. *Yellow Jacket*, October 13, 1926; SD 190.
72. Bob Roehm in Roehm, *Brownwood Connection*, 69.
73. TCL, 1:110; SD 184.
74. *Yellow Jacket*, October 27, 1926; SD 198.
75. TCL, 1:110; SD 184.
76. SD, 183.
77. SD, 199–200.
78. *Sentiment*, 358–59.
79. SD, 279–80; IMH, 6; POSR2, 363.
80. SD, 280–81; IMH, 7–8; POSR2, 364.
81. POSR2, 187.
82. SFTP, xviii.
83. POSR2, 188.
84. BB, March 19, 1927; Roehm, "Gloria's Life."
85. Roehm, "Gloria's Life," 7.
86. POSR2, 200; SFTP, xviii–xix.
87. *Yellow Jacket*, March 10, 1927.
88. Roehm, "Yellow Jacket."
89. Lindsey W. Tyson letter, October 10, 1977, LSdC.
90. BB, February 12, 1927.
91. Lindsey W. Tyson letter, October 10, 1977, LSdC.
92. TCL, 1:117.
93. Lindsey W. Tyson letter, October 10, 1977, LSdC.
94. BB, March 2, 1927.
95. *Yellow Jacket*, May 24, 1927.
96. *Yellow Jacket*, May 5, 1927.
97. *Galveston Daily News*, May 23, 1927.
98. POSR2, 33.
99. *Galveston Daily News*, May 24, 1927.
100. TCL, 1:114.
101. TCL, 1:236.
102. TCL, 1:167.
103. Lindsey W. Tyson letter, October 10, 1977, LSdC.
104. POSR1, 124; POSR2, 197–98.
105. SD, 272; Bill Celis, "REH: College Fictioneer," *Weird Adventures* 1, no. 1 (May 1978): 14–16.

106. Lindsey W. Tyson letter, October 10, 1977, LSdC.
107. Lindsey Tyson interview, March 7, 1978, LSdC.
108. POSR2, 371.
109. POSR2, 371.
110. AMTF, 604.

Notes for Chapter 12

1. TCP, 3:23.
2. IMH, 205.
3. IMH, 149.
4. Herman, "Interview."
5. Herman, "Introduction," in *A Rhyme of Salem Town and Other Poems*, by Robert E. Howard (Plano, TX: Robert E. Howard Foundation Press, 2006), 1.
6. SFTP, xv.
7. TCL, 1:92.
8. TCL, 1:154.
9. TCL, 1:153.
10. TCL, 1:154.
11. SFTP, 224.
12. AMTF, 445.
13. AMTF, 510.
14. POSR2, 165.
15. AMTF, 770.
16. Norm Cohen, "Robert W. Gordon and the Second Wreck of 'Old 97,'" *Journal of American Folklore* 87, no. 343 (Jan.–Mar. 1974): 12–38; Debora Kodish, *Good Friends and Bad Enemies: Robert Winslow Gordon and the Study of American Folksong* (Urbana: University of Illinois Press, 1986); Kodish, "Robert Winslow Gordon (1888–1961)," *Library of Congress*, accessed December 10, 2024, https://www.loc.gov/item/ihas.200196581/.
17. TCL, 1:40.
18. *Adventure,* August 23, 1926, 191–92.
19. TCL, 1:78.
20. *Adventure,* March 1, 1927, 204–5.
21. Kodish, "Robert."
22. TCL, 1:192.
23. POSR2, 153.
24. POSR2, 164.
25. AMTF, 198.
26. POSR2, 164.
27. POSR2, 166.
28. TCL, 1:74.
29. AMTF, 97.
30. TCP, 3:16.
31. AMTF, 97.
32. POSR2, 186.
33. TCP, 1:122.
34. TCL, 1:137.
35. TCP, 1:78.
36. WT, November 1928, 714.

37. TCL, 1:125.
38. TCL, 1:306.
39. Smith, *Weird Tales*, 33; Terence E. Hanley, "Who Wrote the Most Poems for Weird Tales?," *Teller of Weird Tales*, November 15, 2011, https://tellersofweirdtales.blogspot.com/2011/11/who-wrote-most-poems-for-weird-tales.html.
40. Glenn Lord, *Ultima Thule* (Omaha: Joe & Mona Marek, 2000), 9 (hereafter UT).
41. TCL, 3:126.
42. TCL, 1:254.
43. Louinet, "REH and *The Poet's Scroll*," *Robert E. Howard Foundation Newsletter* 9, no. 1 (Spring 2015): 3.
44. TCL, 1:348–49.
45. TCL, 1:349.
46. Lindsey W. Tyson letter, October 10, 1977, LSdC; Lord, *Howard Collector*, 234–35.
47. Benjamin Musser, *"As the Poet Says—": 250 Prose Comments on the Supreme Art* (New York: Parnassus Press, 1931).
48. AMTF, 544.
49. AMTF, 81.
50. Lord, *The Howard Collector* (hereafter HC) (Summer 1963): 2.
51. Lord, *Howard Collector*, 211–12.
52. AMTF, 32.
53. AMTF, 233, 463.
54. Lovecraft, "In Memoriam."
55. WT, April 1929, 564.
56. WT, July 1930, 8.
57. WT, September 1937, 635; May 1939, 151; September 1928, 856.
58. Carter, *Imaginary Worlds*, 187.
59. WT, February 1935, 269.
60. Raymond Chandler, "The Simple Art of Murder (1950)," University of Texas, April 8, 2021, http://www.en.utexas.edu/Classes/Bremen/e316k/316kprivate/scans/chandlerart.html, 9.
61. Mary Welsh Hemingway, *How It Was* (New York: Knopf, 1976), 352.
62. TCL, 1:123; Burke, "The Active Voice: Robert E. Howard's Personae," *Dark Man: The Journal of Robert E. Howard Studies*, no. 3 (April 1993): 24.
63. Herron, *Dark Barbarian*, 58.
64. SK, 400.
65. G. K. Chesterton, *The Ballad of the White Horse* (1911; repr., Mineola, NY: Dover Publications, 2010), v.
66. Burke, "Active Voice," 24.
67. BO2, 3.
68. Sam Moskowitz, *A. Merritt: Reflections in the Moon Pool* (Philadelphia: Oswald Train, 1985), 209.
69. HS, xvii–xviii.
70. Herron, *Dark Barbarian*, 25.
71. Howard, *Grim Land*, 4; see also Frank Coffman, "Robert E. Howard and Poetic Narrative: The Bardic Tradition and 'Popular Modernities,'" *Dark Man: The Journal of Robert E. Howard Studies* 2, nos. 1/2 (Spring 2006): 7.
72. Herron, *Dark Barbarian*, 52.
73. TCL, 2:208.
74. POSR2, 167.
75. AMTF, 494.
76. AMTF, 549.
77. Lindsey W. Tyson letter, n.d., LSdC.

78. AMTF, 494.
79. TCL, 2:61.
80. *Waxahachie Daily Light*, August 3, 1927.
81. Howard Payne College, *Catalogue 1927–1928*.

Notes for Chapter 13

1. TCP, 2:261.
2. Bill Bryson, *One Summer: America, 1927* (New York: Anchor, 2013).
3. TCL, 3:235.
4. AMTF, 52.
5. TCL, 1:122.
6. LSOL, 152.
7. Preece, "Robert's Lady Cousin," *Simba*, no. 2 (September 1978): 43.
8. Vinson to Preece postcard, August 20, 1927, TA&M; Roehm, "Pre-Junto Convention," *REH: Two-Gun Raconteur*, January 21, 2014, https://web.archive.org/web/20150907091654/http://www.rehtwogunraconteur.com/pre-junto-convention/.
9. HP, "Chapter I."
10. HP, "Chapter I."
11. HP, "Chapter I."
12. LC, 95.
13. HP, "Chapter I."
14. LC, 95.
15. HP, "Chapter I."
16. HP, "Chapter I."
17. Preece, "Robert's Lady Cousin," 43.
18. Ibid, 43–44.
19. Roehm, "Mary, Mary."
20. HP, "Chapter I."
21. Preece, "Robert's Lady Cousin," 43.
22. LC, 95.
23. HP, "Chapter II."
24. SFTP, xix.
25. TCL, 1:122.
26. TCL, 1:122, 130.
27. POSR2, 203.
28. TCL, 1:176.
29. DOTS, 24.
30. TCL, 1:136.
31. POSR2, 201.
32. TCL, 2:203.
33. TCL, 1:74.
34. Dowd, "Irish-American," 17.
35. LC, 100–101.
36. Preece, "Robert's Lady Cousin," 43.
37. LC, 97.
38. LC, 100–101.
39. TCL, 1:356.
40. LC, 93.
41. LC, 97.

42. TCL, 2:164; POSR2, 370.
43. TCL, 1:359.
44. Lovecraft, *H. P. Lovecraft: Letters to F. Lee Baldwin, Duane W. Rimel, and Nils Frome*, ed. David E. Schultz and S. T. Joshi (New York: Hippocampus Press, 2016), 128.
45. Christopher Dowd, *The Construction of Irish Identity in American Literature* (New York: Routledge, 2011), 19.
46. Lindsey W. Tyson letter, September 27, 1978, LSdC.
47. POSR1, 140–41; POSR2, 212.
48. Dowd, *Construction*, 19.
49. AMTF, 432–33.
50. AMTF, 433.
51. Leroy Butler interview, July 20, 1977, LSdC.
52. Leroy Butler interview, SFOHA.
53. Floyce Butler interview, July 20, 1977, LSdC.
54. TCL, 1:340.
55. TCL, 2:28.
56. Dowd, *Construction*, 20.
57. Dowd, *Construction*, 20, 23.
58. SK, 400.
59. Burke, "Active Voice," 22.
60. AMTF, 49.
61. Burke, "Active Voice," 24.
62. Dowd, "Irish-American," 15; Dowd, *Construction*; David O'Connell, *The Irish Roots of Margaret Mitchell's* Gone with the Wind, 2nd ed. (n.p.: O'Connell, 2019).
63. Dowd, *Construction*, 18.
64. SotN, xvi.
65. TCL, 2:23; FOI, 2:323.
66. Nora Hopper, *Under Quicken Boughs*. London: John Lane, 1896, 65; TCL, 2:3.
67. TCL, 2:23–24.
68. WT, February 1932, 150; December 1931, 580.
69. SotN; Burke, "Active Voice," 25.
70. UT, 12.
71. Holmes and Knight, "Conan the Argonaut," 5.
72. LC, 102.
73. LC, 341; Roehm, "A Pretty Good Paper': The Junto," *REH: Two-Gun Raconteur*, January 16, 2014, https://web.archive.org/web/20150907092703/http://www.rehtwo-gunraconteur.com/a-pretty-good-paper-the-junto-part-1/.
74. LC, 96.
75. HP, "Chapter V."
76. *Washington Post*, March 24, 1977.
77. Booth Mooney, *The Lyndon Johnson Story* (New York: Farrar, Strauss and Cudahy, 1956); *Sam Houston* (Chicago: Follett, 1966); and *General Billy Mitchell* (Chicago: Follett Publishing, 1968); Harold Preece, *The Dalton Gang: End of an Outlaw Era* (New York: Hastings House, 1963); *Lone Star Man: The Life of Ira Aten* (New York: Hastings House, 1960).
78. LC, 96.
79. TCL, 1:183; SFTP, 60.
80. Roehm, "Mary, Mary," 2.
81. Roehm, "Pretty Good."
82. TCL, 1:258.
83. SFTP, 60.

84. LC, 341; Roehm, "Pretty Good."
85. Lord, *Howard Collector*, 239–40.
86. SK, 398.
87. TCL, 1:162–63.
88. POSR2, 118.
89. POSR2, 121.
90. POSR2, 203.
91. POSR2, 204.
92. POSR2, 365–66.
93. POSR2, 212–13.
94. POSR2, xii.
95. POSR2, ix.
96. POSR2, 240–46.
97. POSR2, 212–13.
98. UT, 10.
99. POSR2, 213.
100. Chandler, "Simple Art," 1.
101. David A. Hardy, "The Great Game," *Cimmerian* 1, no. 2 (June 2004): 3.
102. Herron, *Dark Barbarian*, 117.

Notes for Chapter 14

1. TCP, 2:213.
2. OWWA, 78–79.
3. AMTF, 169
4. TCL, 1:163.
5. WT, October 1935, 524.
6. BMM, xvii.
7. TCL, 3:269.
8. TCL, 1:172.
9. TCL, 1:188.
10. TCL, 1:207.
11. WT, July 1928, 144.
12. TCL, 1:207.
13. Murphy, *Flame and Crimson.*
14. WT, August 1928, 152.
15. SK, 32.
16. Dierk Günther, "Faces of Kane: Exploring the Identity of Robert E. Howard's Puritan Swordsman," *Dark Man: The Journal of Robert E. Howard and Pulp Studies* 10, no. 1 (June 2019): 21.
17. SK, 48.
18. Günther, "Faces of Kane," 23.
19. Genesis 4:12; Günther, "Faces of Kane," 28.
20. WT, October 1928, 570.
21. UT, 11.
22. WT, September 1932, 430.
23. WT, October 1932, 571, 574.
24. Howard, *Pirate Adventures* (Plano, TX: Robert E. Howard Foundation Press, 2012), ix–x.
25. WT, May 1930, 584.
26. WT, January 1934, 134; July 1935, 144.
27. Lovecraft, "In Memoriam."

28. WTS, 46; Pelan and Walters, *Conversations*, 114.
29. Lovecraft, *Letters to C. L. Moore and Others*, ed. David E. Schultz and S. T. Joshi (New York: Hippocampus Press, 2017), 254 (hereafter LMO).
30. AMTF, 320.
31. SFTP, 226.
32. Roehm, "Missing Mexico Trip."
33. TCL, 1:198.
34. TCL, 1:199.
35. TCL, 3:236.
36. TCL, 1:199.
37. TCL, 1:199.
38. Derie, *Weird Talers*; regarding Howard and prostitution see also Zora May and Elliott Bryant interview, October 18, 1978; Harold Preece letter, January 3, 1979, LSdC.
39. Lindsey W. Tyson letter, n.d., LSdC.
40. TCP, 2:33.
41. Lindsey W. Tyson answers to questions, n.d., LSdC.
42. Lindsey W. Tyson letter, October 10, 1977, LSdC.
43. TCL, 1:212.
44. TCL, 1:213.
45. TCL, 1:214.
46. SFTP, 229.
47. POSR2, xi.
48. SFTP, 61.
49. Roehm, "A Day in the Life," *REH: Two-Gun Raconteur*, May 7, 2012, https://web.archive.org/web/20130121131744/http://rehtwogunraconteur.com/?p=18981.
50. TCL, 1:224.
51. TCL, 1:216.
52. TCL, 1:215.
53. TCL, 1:216.
54. Joe Urschel, *The Year of Fear: Machine Gun Kelly and the Manhunt That Changed the Nation* (New York: Minotaur Books, 2015); Todd B. Vick, "Bootleggers & Gangsters: A Day in the Life of Robert E. Howard," *On An Underwood No. 5*, November 16, 2017, http://onanunderwood5.blogspot.com/2017/11/bootleggers-gangsters-day-in-life-of.html.
55. TCL, 1:213.
56. Lindsey Tyson interview, March 7, 1978, LSdC; SFOHA.
57. Earl Baker interview, June 11, 1978, LSdC.
58. Lindsey Tyson interview, March 7, 1978, LSdC.
59. Earl Baker interview, January 21, 1979, LSdC.
60. Vera Baker Nichols interview, March 8, 1978, LSdC.
61. Earl Baker interview, January 21, 1979, and no date, LSdC.
62. TCL, 1:207.
63. TCL, 1:338.
64. TCL, 1:282.
65. Roehm, "Pretty Good."
66. TCL, 1:279.
67. Roehm, "The Diabolical Blond," *REH: Two-Gun Raconteur*, no. 17 (Summer 2014): 13–15.
68. Roehm, "Diabolical Blond," 13.
69. Roehm, "Pretty Good."
70. SFTP, 223.
71. TCL, 1:216.

72. TCL, 1:162.
73. TCL, 1:287.
74. Earl Baker interview, no date; Ruth Baum Browning interview, April 16, 1978, LSdC; De Camp, De Camp, and Griffin, *Dark Valley Destiny*.
75. Roehm. "Diabolical Blond."
76. Preece, "Women"; Roehm. "Diabolical Blond," 15.
77. TCL, 1:340.
78. OWWA, 144.
79. Floyce Butler interview, July 20, 1977, LSdC.
80. Herman, "Interview."
81. IMH, 206.
82. IMH, 206.
83. AMTF, 98.
84. IMH, 206.
85. IMH, 207.
86. IMH, 206.
87. SFTP, 223.
88. See chapters 8 and 10.
89. See POSR2, 371; AMTF, 604.
90. IMH, 206; Louinet, "A Man."
91. IMH, 206.
92. IMH, 206.
93. Photo of Howard family Bible courtesy of Rob Roehm.
94. IMH, 206.
95. Jack Scott interview, March 12, 1981, SWC.
96. WEST, vi.
97. CPR, November 23.
98. Roehm, "Comer Connection," 4.
99. LSOL; Roehm, "Pretty Good."
100. LC, 98.
101. LSOL, 183.
102. TCL, 1:226.
103. Glenn Lord, *The Book of Robert E. Howard* (New York: Berkley Books, 1980), ix.

Notes for Chapter 15

1. TCP, 2:28.
2. TCL, 1:305.
3. TCL, 1:306.
4. SFTP, 221.
5. Nat Fleischer, Sam Andre, and Nigel Collins, *An Illustrated History of Boxing*, 6th ed. (Toronto: Citadel Press, 2002).
6. Paul Beston, *The Boxing Kings: When American Heavyweights Ruled the Ring* (Lanham, MD: Rowman & Littlefield, 2017), 1.
7. FOI, 2:vii.
8. Lindsey W. Tyson letter, October 10, 1977, LSdC.
9. FOI, 2:vii.
10. Beston, *Boxing Kings*; Damon Runyon, *Jack Dempsey: A Tale of Two Fists*, ed. Paul Duncan (Reading, PA: Wordsmith, 2019).
11. Runyon, *Jack Dempsey.*
12. FOI, 2:vii.

13. Joyce Carol Oates, *On Boxing* (London: Bloomsbury, 1987), vii.
14. FOI, 4:viii.
15. Don Herron, *The Barbaric Triumph* (Cabin John, MD: Wildside Press, 2004), 12.
16. FOI, 1:x.
17. Austin Newton letter, n.d.; Earl J. Baker interview, October 16, 1978; Earl J. Baker interview, no date, LSdC; SFTP.
18. SFTP, xiii.
19. Herron, *Barbaric Triumph*, 12.
20. TCL, 2:203; FOI, 1:xvii–xviii.
21. AMTF, 239–40.
22. Harold Preece letter, July 26, 1928, TA&M; *Fort Worth Record-Telegram*, July 13, 1928.
23. *Fort Worth Record-Telegram*, July 13, 1928; Brian Leno, *Ringside with Robert E. Howard* (n.p.: Cimmerian Press, 2019).
24. Harold Preece letter, July 26, 1928, TA&M.
25. FOI.
26. Howard, *Waterfront Fists and Others: The Collected Fight Stories of Robert E. Howard*, ed. Paul Herman, introduction by Mark Finn (Rockville, MD: Wildside Press, 2003), 13.
27. TCL, 1:209.
28. Leno, "Out of the Shadows—Finally, 'Kid' Dula," *REH: Two-Gun Raconteur*, June 16, 2012, https://web.archive.org/web/20121015041419/rehtwogunraconteur.com/?p=19757.
29. FOI, 4:viii.
30. Burke, "Active Voice," 23.
31. AMTF, 539.
32. Labor, *Jack London*, xii.
33. FOI, 1:xvi.
34. Marshall B. Tymn and Mike Ashley, *Science Fiction, Fantasy, and Weird Fiction Magazines* (Westport, CT: Greenwood Press, 1985), 315–17.
35. Leno, "The Fouling of Robert E. Howard," *Cimmerian* 4, no. 2 (April 2007): 17; see also Jeffrey Shanks, "Ace Jessel and the Ghost of Tom Molineaux," *REH: Two-Gun Raconteur*, no. 16 (Winter 2012): 21–25.
36. Howard, "The Apparition in the Prize Ring," *Ghost Stories* 6, no. 4 (April 1929): 19–23.
37. HS, 69.
38. HS, 319.
39. HS, 344.
40. Goulart, *Cheap Thrills*, 180.
41. Goulart, *Cheap Thrills*, 187–88.
42. FOI, 1:409.
43. FOI, 1:410.
44. FOI, 1:413.
45. TCL, 3:269; London, *Martin Eden.*
46. AMTF, 816.
47. Mark Finn, "The Runyonesque Raconteur," *Cimmerian* 1, no. 2 (June 2004): 15.
48. Finn, "Runyonesque," 13.
49. FOI, 2:319.
50. TCL, 1:347.
51. FOI, 2:3.
52. TCL, 2:12.
53. FOI, 2:321.
54. FOI, 2:xvi.
55. TCL, 2:13.

56. TCL, 2:33.
57. TCL, 2:33.
58. Patrice Louinet, "One Gent Too Many on Bear Creek," *REH: Two-Gun Raconteur*, no. 16 (Winter 2012): 43–48.
59. FOI, 1:417.
60. TCL, 1:110.
61. TCL, 2:136.
62. AMTF, 168.
63. TCL, 2:266.
64. *New York Times*, December 28, 1932.
65. AMTF, 788.
66. FOI, 4:346.
67. FOI, 4:343.
68. TCL, 3:235; FOI, 1:414; FOI, 4:346.
69. Howard, *Boxing Stories* (Lincoln: University of Nebraska Press, 2005), ix.
70. FOI, 2:xii–viii; ABE, 1"vi.
71. Finn, "Bare Knuckles and Bulldogs: An Introduction to the Boxing Fiction of Robert E. Howard," in Howard, *Waterfront*, 9.
72. Finn, "Bare Knuckles," 355–56.
73. Finn, "Bare Knuckles," 358.
74. "History," *Battle of Flowers Association*, September 21, 2019, https://www.battleof-flowers.org/about-us/history/.
75. *Waco News*, April 27, 1929.
76. Norris R. Chambers letter, July 7, 1978, LSdC.
77. Roehm, "Letters to Glenn," *REHupa*, no. 235 (June 2012): 3.
78. Jack Scott interview notes, February 21, 1980, LSdC.
79. *Austin American*, March 6, 1929.
80. CPR, May 3, 1929; *Texas Spur*, May 3, 1929.
81. CPR, May 3, 1929.
82. CPR, May 10, 1929; *Texas Spur*, May 10, 17, 1929.
83. *Texas Spur*, May 10, 24, 1929.
84. *Texas Spur,* June 7, 1929.
85. CPR, June 7, 1929.
86. *Texas Spur,* June 14, 1929.
87. CPR, July 5, 1929.

Notes for Chapter 16

1. TCP, 1:164.
2. TCL, 1:229.
3. Patrice Louinet, "A Short History of the Kull Series," *Dark Man: The Journal of Robert E. Howard Studies*, no. 6 (Summer 2001): 31.
4. TCL, 1:229.
5. Plato, *Timaeus*, trans. Benjamin Jowett (New York: Scribner's Sons, 1871).
6. Ignatius Donnelly, *Atlantis : The Antediluvian World* (New York: Harper & Brothers, 1882).
7. TCL, 1:230.
8. KULL, 294.
9. TCL, 3:269.
10. KULL.
11. TCL, 3:269.
12. KULL, 294.

13. Louinet, "Short History," 30.
14. Pelan and Walters, *Conversations*, 115.
15. KULL, 292–93: See also Murphy, "Pulps to Paperbacks."
16. POSR2, 184.
17. POSR2, 200.
18. POSR2, 201.
19. TCL, 1:136.
20. Louinet, "Robert E. Howard," 163.
21. TCL, 1:230.
22. KULL, 13.
23. KULL, 14.
24. KULL, 293.
25. KULL, 24.
26. Louinet, "Robert E. Howard," 163.
27. Murphy, *Flame and Crimson*, 58; Fritz Leiber, "Letter," *Ancalagon*, no. 2 (April 1961): 6.
28. Murphy, *Flame and Crimson*, 31.
29. Farah Mendlesohn and Edward James, *A Short History of Fantasy* (Faringdon, UK: Libri, 2012).
30. Douglas A. Anderson, *Tales before Tolkien: The Roots of Modern Fantasy* (New York: Ballantine, 2003); Mendlesohn and James, *Short History.*
31. Murphy, *Flame and Crimson*, 9.
32. Jason Waltz, "The Color and the Dash," in *Swords & Heroes*, ed. Lyndon Perry (Vega Baja, PR: Tule Fog Press, 2023), 1.
33. Murphy, *Flame and Crimson*, 9.
34. Carter, *Imaginary Worlds*, 64; Pelan and Walters, *Conversations*, 114.
35. Murphy, *Flame and Crimson*, 63.
36. Charles A. Gramlich, "Robert E. Howard in the Gothic Tradition," *Dark Man: The Journal of Robert E. Howard Studies*, no. 8 (Winter 2004): 15.
37. Justin Everett and Jeffrey H. Shanks, *The Unique Legacy of* Weird Tales*: The Evolution of Modern Fantasy and Horror* (Lanham, MD: Rowman & Littlefield, 2015), 64.
38. Gramlich, "Robert E. Howard," 15.
39. Louinet, "Robert E. Howard," 170.
40. KULL, 288.
41. WT, October 1929, 436.
42. Sam Moskowitz, "The Most Popular Stories in Weird Tales, 1924 to 1940: With Statistics and Analytical Commentary," in *World Fantasy Convention 1983: Sixty Years of* Weird Tales, ed. Robert Weinberg, 27–37 (N.p.: Weird Tales, 1983).
43. WT, October 1929, 438.
44. WT, October 1929, 570.
45. Everett and Shanks, *Unique Legacy*, 65.
46. KULL, 287; BMM, 353; Louinet, "Short History."
47. KULL, 297–98.
48. KULL, 55.
49. SFTP, 221–22.
50. WT, January 1930, 6.
51. WT, November 1929, 716.
52. Herron, *Dark Barbarian*, 159; KULL; James Maliszewski, "The Mirrors of Tuzun Thune," *Grognardia*, January 18, 2021, http://grognardia.blogspot.com/2021/01/pulp-fantasy-library-mirrors-of-tuzun.html.

53. Louinet, “Short History,” 37.
54. KULL, 298.
55. KULL, 301.
56. POSR2, 382.
57. CC, 436.
58. LMO, 33.
59. AMTF, 766.
60. CC, 429.
61. WT, May 1932, 582.
62. WT, April 1934, 524.
63. WT, December 1935, 782; WT, April 1936, 506.
64. WT, May 1937, 636.
65. Louinet, “Short History,” 36.
66. Howard and Richard Lupoff, *The Return of Skull-Face* (West Linn, OR: FAX Collector’s Editions, 1977), 8.
67. Pelan and Walters, *Conversations,* 116.
68. WT, December 1929, 819.
69. Deuce Richardson, “The Call of Kathulos: Kull, Skull and ‘Call,’” *Cimmerian*, February 11, 2009, http://thecimmerian.com/2009/02/11/the-call-of-kathulos-kull-skull-and-call/.
70. AMTF, 510.
71. *Collier’s,* February 2, 1913, 29.
72. WT, October 1929, 451.
73. Pelan and Walters, *Conversations,* 118; Louinet, “Short History,” 36.
74. TCL, 1:344.
75. Howard and Lupoff, *Return*, 2–3.
76. WT, December 1929, 728.
77. WT, January 1930, 8.
78. WT, February 1930, 150.
79. WT, December 1931, 580; June 1933, 737.
80. WT, December 1929, 854.
81. WT, February 1930, 148.
82. CPR, July 12, 1929; Roehm, *Brownwood Connection*, 51.
83. Roehm, *Brownwood Connection*, 51; CPR, July 26, 1929.
84. Tevis Clyde Smith Jr., *Pecan Valley Days* (Brownwood, TX: T. C. Smith Jr., 1956), 44.
85. Roehm, *Brownwood Connection*, 51.
86. Louinet, *Howard Guide*, 51d.
87. CPR, July 5, 1929.
88. Roehm, “The Texas Spur,” *Howard History: The Life and Times of Robert E. Howard*, May 10, 2021, https://howardhistory.com/2021/05/10/the-texas-spur/.
89. Roehm, *Brownwood Connection*, 47.
90. Tevis Clyde Smith, *Don’t Blame the Python* (Brownwood, TX: Tevis Clyde Smith, 1975), 6.
91. Lord, *Howard Collector*, 238–39.
92. SFTP, xxii.
93. TCL, 1:355.
94. CPR, August 9, 1929, and November 1, 1929.
95. TCL, 1:356.
96. TCL, 1:358.
97. LC, 76.

Notes for Chapter 17

1. TCP, 3:320.
2. Lovecraft, "Letter: H. P. Lovecraft to E. Hoffmann Price, dated July 5, 1936," *Howard Collector* 3, no. 1 (Autumn 1970): 17.
3. John D. Haefele, *Lovecraft: The Great Tales* (n.p.: Cimmerian Press, 2021).
4. Lovecraft, "Letters to Farnsworth Wright," *Lovecraft Annual*, no. 8 (2014): 22.
5. TCL, 1:191.
6. WT, May 1928, 711.
7. TCL, 3:386.
8. OWWA, 151.
9. TTI, 120.
10. Joshi, *I Am Providence*.
11. Haefele, *Lovecraft.*
12. Pelan and Walters, *Conversations*, 13.
13. WT, October 1933, 517–18.
14. WT, March 1932, 292.
15. Haefele, *Lovecraft*, 137; See also Joshi, *I Am Providence,* 460; Derie, "Little People."
16. WT, August 1930, 152.
17. WTS, 33.
18. AMTF, 7; Derie, *Weird Talers*, 13.
19. WT, June 1930, 853. Note: The original *Weird Tales* printing mistakenly wrote "*aodaun*" for "*aodann*."
20. LMO, 47.
21. Fiona Macleod, *The Sin-Eater and Other Tales* (Chicago: Patrick Geddes, 1895), 45–46.
22. SLL, 1:258.
23. TCL, 2:36.
24. TCL, 2:36.
25. John Davis, *A History of Wales* (New York: Penguin Books, 2007).
26. TCL, 2:36.
27. Derie, *Weird Talers*; Down, "Irish-American"; Edward O'Reilly, *An Irish-English Dictionary* (Dublin: James Duffy, 1864).
28. Lovecraft and Derleth, *Essential Solitudes: The Letters of H. P. Lovecraft and August Derleth*, 2 vols., ed. David E. Schultz and S. T. Joshi (New York: Hippocampus Press, 2008), 1:268 (hereafter ES); DS 220.
29. DS, 220.
30. LPS, 242.
31. SLL, 5:277.
32. ES, 1:271.
33. Derie, *Weird Talers*, 53.
34. AMTF.
35. Derie, *Weird Talers*, 55.
36. AMTF, 17.
37. AMTF, 26, 37.
38. TCL, 2:52.
39. TCL, 2:52–53.
40. TCL, 2:53.
41. TCL, 2:32–33, 37.
42. TCL, 2:38.
43. TCL, 2:37.
44. TCL, 2:38.

45. TCL, 2:38.
46. Beston, *Boxing Kings.*
47. TCL, 2:23.
48. TCL, 2:15.
49. Jack Scott interview, March 12, 1981, SWC.
50. *Dallas Morning News*, January 6, 2003.
51. *Abilene Daily Reporter*, June 4, 1930.
52. SFOHA.
53. Jack Scott interview, March 12, 1981, SWC.
54. Jack Scott interview, March 12, 1981, SWC.
55. Louinet, "A Conversation with Jack Scott," *Unaussprechlichen Kulten*, no. 1 (October 1990): 26–29.
56. Jack Scott interview, March 12, 1981, SWC.
57. Louinet, "Conversation."
58. Jack Scott interview, July 19, 1977, LSdC.
59. Charles A. Rodenberger, *Transcript of the Oral History of Jack Scott* (Cross Plains, TX: Friends of the Cross Plains Public Library, 2001), 90 (hereafter JS).
60. TCL, 2:13.
61. Johnson, *Odd Type*.
62. Johnson, *Odd Type*, 3.
63. Johnson, *Odd Type*, 8.
64. Johnson, *Odd Type*, 7.
65. Johnson, *Odd Type*, 9.
66. Johnson, *Odd Type*, 23.
67. Johnson, *Odd Type*, 23.
68. J. H. Childs interview, October 18, 1978, LSdC.
69. Burke, *Robert E. Howard*, 7, 9.
70. Jack Scott interview, April/May 2001, SWC.
71. AMTF, 604.
72. Norris R. Chambers interview, July 22, 1977, LSdC.
73. Norris R. Chambers interview, July 22, 1977, LSdC.
74. IMH, 204; see also JS, 28.
75. Leroy Butler interview, July 20, 1977, LSdC.
76. IMH, 204.
77. TCL, 2:116.

Notes for Chapter 18

1. TCP, 2:72.
2. AMTF, 255.
3. BMM, xviii.
4. AMTF, 254.
5. AMTF, 272.
6. BMM, xviii, 343.
7. BMM, 323.
8. BMM, 343.
9. TCL, 2:91.
10. POSR2, 116–17.
11. BMM, xviii.
12. Everett and Shanks, *Unique Legacy*, 123.

13. AMTF, 38.
14. TCL, 2:36.
15. AMTF, 38.
16. Everett and Shanks, *Unique Legacy*, 122.
17. AMTF, 171, 45.
18. BMM, 208, 353; Everett and Shanks, *Unique Legacy*, 123.
19. TCL, 3:269.
20. AMTF, 255.
21. AMTF, 271–72.
22. Howard, *A Song of the Race* (Plano, TX: Robert E. Howard Foundation, 2009).
23. BMM, 346; see also BMM 237–42.
24. TCL, 1:21–22.
25. BMM, 289–20.
26. IMH, 5.
27. KULL, 303.
28. Louinet, *Howard Guide*, 52.
29. TCL, 2:14.
30. TCL, 2:61.
31. TCL, 2:18.
32. Louinet, *Howard Guide*, 54.
33. TCL, 2:18.
34. TCL, 2:61.
35. Moskowitz, "Most Popular."
36. WT, November 1931, 570–71.
37. WT, February/March 1931, 154; January 1931, 4.
38. WT, August 1932, 150.
39. WT, January 1931, 4.
40. AMTF, 27.
41. Everett and Shanks, *Unique Legacy*, 124.
42. Everett and Shanks, *Unique Legacy*, 124–25.
43. BMM, 220.
44. BMM, 358.
45. BMM, xxi.
46. FOI, 3–315.
47. AMTF, 271–72.
48. IMH, 10.
49. WT, May 1933, 665–66.
50. WT, January 1933, 142.
51. AMTF, 462; see also Clark Ashton Smith, *The Selected Letters of Clark Ashton Smith*, ed. Davide E. Schultz and Scott Connors (Sauk City, WI: Arkham House, 2003), 193 (hereafter CAS).
52. WTS, 55.
53. HS, xxii; WTS, 55; Clute, "Introduction," xvi.
54. BMM, 359.
55. BMM, xxii.
56. SotN.
57. TCL, 2:33.
58. TCL, 2:115; Louinet, *Howard Guide*, 54.
59. AMTF, 45–46.
60. AMTF, 41.
61. TCL, 2:112.

62. "Personal History," October 21, 1930, LSdC.
63. "Varicocele," *Johns Hopkins Medicine*, December 14, 2022, https://www.hopkinsmedicine.org/health/conditions-and-diseases/varicocele.
64. "Personal History," October 21, 1930, LSdC.
65. "Personal History," October 21, 1930, LSdC.
66. "Personal History," October 21, 1930, LSdC; F. G. Gosling, *Before Freud : Neurasthenia and the American Medical Community, 1870–1910* (Champaign: University of Illinois Press, 1987).
67. Gosling, *Before Freud*; Roy Proter and Marijke Gijswijt-Hofstra, *Cultures of Neurasthenia: From Beard to the First World War* (Amsterdam: Clio Medica, 2001).
68. Porter and Gijswijt-Hofstra, *Cultures of Neurasthenia,* 39.
69. George M. Beard, *Sexual Neurasthenia, [Nervous Exhaustion]: Its Hygiene, Causes, Symptoms, and Treatment*, ed. A. D. Rockwell (New York: E. B. Treat, 1886), 15.
70. DOTS; Beard, *Sexual Neurasthenia.*
71. Beard, *Sexual Neurasthenia*, 15.
72. Robert D. Richardson, *William James: In the Maelstrom of American Modernism* (Boston: Houghton Mifflin, 2006).
73. Kim Townsend, *Manhood at Harvard: William James and Others* (New York: W. W. Norton, 1996), 32.
74. Townsend, *Manhood at Harvard*, 50.
75. Porter and Gijswijt-Hofstra, *Cultures of Neurasthenia*, 1.
76. Porter and Gijswijt-Hofstra, *Cultures of Neurasthenia*, 1; Gosling, *Before Freud.*
77. "Personal History," October 21, 1930, LSdC.
78. TCL, 2:114.
79. LC, 76.

Notes for Chapter 19

1. TCP, 1:213.
2. AMTF, 126.
3. POSR2, 28.
4. SFTP, 242–43.
5. POSR2, 28.
6. IMH, 205–6.
7. SFTP, 242.
8. OWWA, 64.
9. OWWA, 65.
10. OWWA, 64.
11. OWWA, 65.
12. LPS, 243.
13. OWWA, 91–92.
14. Louinet, *Howard Guide*, 52.
15. TCL, 2:38.
16. TCL, 2:40.
17. Weinberg, *WT50*, 4.
18. WT, October 1925, 562.
19. AMTF, 160.
20. TCL, 2:113.
21. TCL, 2:40.
22. *Oriental Stories/The Magic Carpet Magazine*, hereafter OS, October 1930, 139.
23. TCL, 2:75.

24. TCL, 2:110.
25. OS, December 1930-January 1931, 150.
26. DS, 278–79.
27. AMTF, 101.
28. SK, 401.
29. SFTP, 3.
30. SW, 520.
31. TCL, 2:54; SFTP, 108.
32. OS, February–March 1931, 292.
33. OS, April–May–June 1931, 572; see also TCL, 2:153.
34. TCL, 2:75.
35. TCL, 2:113.
36. Howard, *Lord of Samarcand and Other Adventure Tales of the Old Orient*, ed. Rusty Burke, introduction by Patrice Louinet (Lincoln: University of Nebraska Press, 2005), viii.
37. TCL, 2:183.
38. SW, 523.
39. OS, Summer 1932, 426.
40. SW, 524.
41. SW, 525.
42. TCL, 2:226.
43. Dennis McHaney, *Robert E. Howard, Oriental Stories, The Magic Carpet Magazine, & The Souk* (Memphis, TN: Old Tiger Press, 2005), 17.
44. McHaney, *Robert E. Howard*, 19.
45. IMH, 12; UT, 28.
46. AMTF, 550.
47. AMTF, 651.
48. Herron, *Dark Barbarian*, 144; Willard Oliver, "The Personal and Literary Influences of Jack London's *The Star Rover* on Robert E. Howard," *Dark Man: The Journal of Robert E. Howard and Pulp Studies* (forthcoming).
49. AMTF, 83.
50. AMTF, 915.
51. AMTF, 126.
52. Howard, *The Bloody Crown of Conan* (New York: Del Rey, 2003), 349 (hereafter BCC).
53. Sylvia Cranston, *H. P. B.: The Extraordinary Life & Influence of Helena Blavatsky, Founder of the Modern Theosophical Movement* (New York: G. P. Putnam's Sons, 1993).
54. Norris R. Chambers letter, January 7, 1978, LSdC; Yogi Ramacharaka, *Fourteen Lessons in Yogi Philosophy and Oriental Occultism* (London: Yoga Publication Society, 1904), 222.
55. DOTS, 26; Barbara Barrett, "Robert E. Howard and Past Lives, Reincarnation, Dreams and Race Memories," *REH: Two-Gun Raconteur*, no. 17 (Summer 2014): 50.
56. SotN, 15.
57. SotN, 16.
58. WT, February 1936, 254, 252.
59. AMTF, 791.
60. TCL, 2:161.
61. Morgan Holmes, "Robert E. Howard and the Clayton Magazines," *Blood 'N' Thunder*, nos. 46/47 (Winter/Spring 2016): 58.
62. TCL, 2:167.
63. Farnsworth Wright, "The Grey God Passes." Unpublished letter, December 28, 1931, https://www.jwkbooks.com/pages/books/23179/robert-howard/the-grey-god-passes-typed-manuscript-tms-36-leaves-not-dated-circa-1930-31.
64. TCL, 2:259.

65. TCL, 2:153.
66. SLL, 3:173.
67. AMTF, 114.
68. DOTS, 45.
69. Waldrop, "Journey," 158.
70. Howard, "The Ghost of Camp Colorado," *Texaco Star* (April 1931): 13.
71. TCL, 2:160.
72. TCL, 2:113; see also AMTF, 118.
73. AMTF, 118.
74. Tymn and Ashley, *Science Fiction*, 729.
75. WT, February/March 1931, 148.
76. TCL, 2:156.
77. WT, April/May 1931, 292.
78. IMH, 189.
79. AMTF, 174–75.
80. WT, June/July 1931, 440.
81. AMTF, 174–75.
82. SFTP, xxii.
83. TCL, 2:155.
84. Roehm, "Vinson Papers."
85. TCL, 2:157; SFTP, 181.
86. TCL, 2:137.
87. Lindsey W. Tyson letter, October 10, 1977, LSdC.
88. TCL, 2:136, 158.
89. AMTF, 164.
90. TCL, 2:155.
91. TCLS, 157; SFTP, 181.
92. Harold Preece to Tevis Clyde Smith, March 27, 1931, TA&M.
93. TCL, 2:157; SFTP, 181–83.
94. AMTF, 166.
95. Frank Thurston Torbett letter, April 16, 1978, LSdC.
96. Frank Thurston Torbett interview, March 9, 1978, LSdC.

Notes for Chapter 20

1. TCP, 1:138.
2. WT, May 1928, 711–12.
3. AMTF, 37.
4. Joshi, *I am Providence*; Robert M. Price, *H. P. Lovecraft and the Cthulhu Mythos* (Mercer Island, WA: Starmont House, 1990).
5. Jeremy Agnew, *The Age of Dimes and Pulp: A History of Sensationalist Literature, 1830–1960* (Jefferson, NC: McFarland, 2018), 198.
6. AMTF, 40.
7. TCL, 2:63.
8. TCL, 3:95–96.
9. WT, August 1932, 271.
10. DS, 467.
11. WT, March 1930, 292.
12. AMTF, 40.
13. WT, August 1931, 41.
14. HC, Autumn 1973, 47.

15. AMTF, 32–33; BMM, 357; Everett and Shanks, *Unique Legacy*, 125–26.
16. WT, April/May 1931, 355.
17. BMM, 357.
18. AMTF, 95.
19. ES, 1:336, 353.
20. WT, August 1931, 4.
21. Blanche Colton Williams, ed., *O. Henry Memorial Award: Prize Stories of 1931* (Garden City, NY: Doubleday, 1931), 359.
22. TCL, 2:113–14.
23. AMTF, 229–30.
24. E.g., WT, August 1935, 270.
25. Morgan Holmes, "Enter the Barbarian," *Cimmerian* 4, no. 6 (December 2007): 10.
26. TCL, 2:116.
27. TCL, 2:114.
28. TCL, 2:182.
29. AMTF, 264.
30. Lovecraft, *Letters to Richard F. Searight*, ed. David E. Schultz and S. T. Joshi (West Warwick, RI: Necronomicon Press, 1992), 40.
31. AMTF, 279.
32. AMTF, 194.
33. BMM, 358.
34. UT, 13.
35. TCL, 2:226.
36. TCL, 2:247.
37. TCL, 2:245.
38. Louinet, "Grief & Greed? Isaac Mordecai Howard and the Robert E. Howard Estate, June 1936–March 1937." *Dwelling in Dark Valley*, June 2001, http://www.robert-e-howard.org/Dwelling2.html.
39. Glenn Lord, "REH, HPL and the Cthulhu Mythos," *REH: Two-Gun Raconteur*, no. 7 (Spring 2005): 9.
40. Finn, "Robert E. Howard," 172.
41. Fred Blosser, *Ar-I-E'ch and the Spell of Cthulhu* (n.p.: Pulp Hero Press, 2018); Haefele, *Lovecraft*; Everett and Shanks, *Unique Legacy*, 63–79.
42. Jack Scott interview, April/May 2001, SWC.
43. *Abilene Reporter-News*, November 6, 1932.
44. Jack Scott interview, April/May 2001, SWC.
45. CPR, October 3, 1931.
46. Jack Scott interview, April/May 2001, SWC.
47. UT; LC, 76.
48. AMTF, 190.
49. Lindsey W. Tyson answers to questions, n.d., LSdC; IMH, 133.
50. IMH, 133.
51. ABE, 1:xvi.
52. AMTF, 236.
53. TCL, 2:226.
54. SFTP, xxv–xxvi; Derie, *Weird Talers*.
55. TCL, 3:202.
56. AMTF, 228.
57. TCL, 2:226.
58. AMTF, 199.
59. AMTF, 224.

60. TCL, 2:222.
61. Derie, *Weird Talers*, 205.
62. Derie, *Weird Talers*, 206.
63. AMTF, 216.
64. Mrs. Virginia Sargent informant notes, LSdC.
65. Jack Scott interview notes, April 1, 1965, LSdC.
66. TCL, 2:203.
67. TCL, 2:165.

Notes for Chapter 21

1. TCP, 3:102.
2. AMTF, 152.
3. Goulart, *Cheap Thrills.*
4. AMTF, 152.
5. L'Amour, *Education.*
6. AMTF, 510.
7. Lee Clark Mitchell, *Westerns: Making the Man in Fiction and Film* (Chicago: University of Chicago Press, 1996), 3.
8. Finn, "Robert E. Howard," 173.
9. Howard, *The End of the Trail: Western Stories*, ed. with an introduction by Rusty Burke (Lincoln: University of Nebraska Press, 2005), xi.
10. WEST, vi.
11. Jeffrey Shanks and Mark Finn, "Vaqueros and Vampires in the Pulps: Robert E. Howard and the Dawn of the Undead West," in *Undead in the West II: They Just Keep Coming*, ed. Cynthia J. Miller and A. Bowdoin Van Riper, 3–25 (Lanham, MD: Scarecrow Press, 2013); WEST, xii. Note: There are those who believe Howard did not create this genre; cf., Todd B. Vick, "Wild, Wild Vampires," *Weird Fiction Review*, no. 9 (Winter 2018): 109–22.
12. Shanks and Finn, "Vaqueros and Vampires," 3.
13. Finn, "Texas as Character in Robert E. Howard's Fiction," *Dark Man: The Journal of Robert E. Howard Studies*, no. 8 (Winter 2004): 5.
14. HS, xxii; Finn, "Robert E. Howard," 174; HC (Spring 1968): 24–29.
15. DS, 364.
16. AMTF, 287.
17. AMTF, 292.
18. WT, July 1932, 6.
19. BO2, xxi.
20. WT, July 1932, 6.
21. Bobby Derie, "That Fool Olson," *Lovecraft Annual* (2018): 90–104.
22. TCL, 2:281.
23. AMTF, 307.
24. Shanks and Finn, "Vaqueros and Vampires," 10.
25. AMTF, 279.
26. TCL, 3:14.
27. AMTF, 386.
28. HS, xxiii.
29. TCL, 3:146.
30. WEST; James Reasoner, "Far and Away: The Wandering Heroes of Robert E. Howard," in Howard, *Treasures of Tartary* (Rockville, MD: Wildside Press, 2004), 9.
31. L. Sprague De Camp, *The Blade of Conan* (New York: Ace, 1979), 107.
32. TCL, 3:243.

33. Howard, *End of the Trail*, xv.
34. Morgan Holmes, "The Wild Wild West of Robert E. Howard: Defending the Westerns Written by Conan's Creator," *Blood 'N' Thunder* 48 (Summer 2016): 50.
35. IMH, 37.
36. Reasoner, "Far and Away," 9.
37. Clute, "Introduction," xvii.
38. UT, 16.
39. Holmes, "Wild," 50.
40. HC (Winter 1965): 13.
41. Roehm, "The Kline Connection," *Howard History: The Life and Times of Robert E. Howard*, November 2, 2018, https://howardhistory.com/2018/11/02/the-kline-connection/.
42. Howard, *End of the Trail*, xiii.
43. AMTF, 260.
44. TCL, 3:53.
45. WEST, xiii.
46. Holmes, "Wild," 49.
47. WEST, xiv; BO2, xx.
48. AMTF, 396.
49. AMTF, 273.
50. Fehrenbach, *Lone Star*, 653.
51. AMTF, 259.
52. AMTF, 259.
53. TCL, 2:279.
54. Ed Hulse, "The Glories of *Short Stories*," in *The Best of Blood 'N' Thunder*, vol. 2, ed. Ed Hulse (Morris Plains, NJ: Murania Press, 2013), 20.
55. TCL, 2:289.
56. TCL, 2:302.
57. AMTF, 307–8.
58. WT, February 1932, 148.
59. TCL, 2:302.
60. TCL, 2:303.
61. AMTF, 302.
62. TCL, 3:141.
63. AMTF, 302.
64. Gosling, *Before Freud*.
65. AMTF, 301.
66. TCL, 2:276.
67. TCL, 2:302.
68. TCL, 2:303.
69. TCL, 2:276.
70. TCL, 2:278.
71. Roehm, "Robert E. Howard's Automobiles: '*License and Registration, Please*,'" *Howard History: The Life and Times of Robert E. Howard*, October 2020, https://howardhistory.files.wordpress.com/2020/10/reh-cars3.pdf.
72. IMH, 205.
73. Lindsey W. Tyson letter, n.d., LSdC.
74. Catherine de Camp notes from Leroy Buter Interview, July 20, 1977, LSdC.
75. Fehrenbach, *Lone Star*, 649.
76. Jack Scott interview, July 19, 1977, LSdC.
77. Lindsey W. Tyson letter, February 18, 1977; Interview with Lindsey W. Tyson notes, August 1977; Lindsey W. Tyson letter, September 27, 1978, LSdC; Roehm, "Robert E. Howard's Automobiles."

78. Lindsey W. Tyson letter, February 18, 1977, LSdC.
79. Leroy Butler interview, SFOHA.
80. OWWA, 60.
81. Roehm, "Good Ol' Boys"; Herron, "Last," 25.
82. TCL, 2:246.
83. TCL, 3:269; Louinet, "Birth of Conan," 2.

Notes for Chapter 22

1. TCP, 1:145.
2. AMTF, 279.
3. TCL, 3:269; Louinet, "Birth of Conan," 2.
4. BO2, xix.
5. David Piske, "Barbarism and Civilization in the Letters of Robert E. Howard and H. P. Lovecraft: A Summary with Commentary," *On An Underwood No. 5*, August 19, 2015, http://onanunderwood5.blogspot.com/2015/08/barbarism-and-civilization-in-letters.html.
6. AMTF, 307, 338.
7. AMTF, 338.
8. AMTF, 594–95.
9. BCC, xiv.
10. CC, xxii.
11. CC, 430.
12. Herron, *Famous Someday*; See also Herron, "Robert'll Be Famous."
13. Herron, "COnun and TarZAN," *Cimmerian* 3, no. 6 (June 2006): 27.
14. Novalyne Price Ellis, "Novalyne Price Ellis's Q&A Session after Her Nolacon Speech (Transcribed by Adrian and Clark in Mailing #96)," *Nemedian Chroniclers*, no. 33 (December 2020): 41.
15. Ellis, "Letter to Mr. Thomas W. Collins," *Barbarian Scroll*, no. 6 (February 1989): 6.
16. TCL, 3:338.
17. LMO, 32–33.
18. TCL, 3:248.
19. TCL, 3:248; CC, 431.
20. Herron, *Dark Barbarian*, 42–43.
21. CC, 430; Homer, *The Odyssey of Homer*, trans. Alexander Pope (New York: John Wurtele Lovell, 1880), 152–53.
22. KULL; Louinet, "Birth of Conan."
23. CC, xxi.
24. TCL, 3 :143.
25. CC, 438.
26. TCL, 3 :428.
27. IMH, 10.
28. TCL, 3:135.
29. UT, 23.
30. CC, xix.
31. WT, February 1933, 262.
32. WT, February 1933, 264.
33. CC, 439.
34. TCL, 2:259.
35. CC, xxii, 440.
36. Louinet, "Birth of Conan," 11.
37. CC, 439.
38. CC, 381.

39. Rusty Burke, "A Statistical Analysis of REH's Vocabulary," *Cimmerian* 5, no. 1 (February 2008): 29.
40. Lovecraft, *Letters to Robert Bloch and Others*, ed. David E. Schultz and S. T. Joshi (New York: Hippocampus Press, 2015), 319.
41. Steven Tompkins, "The Shortest Distance between Two Towers," *Cimmerian* 3, no. 3 (March 2006): 10.
42. Louinet, "Birth of Conan," 11.
43. AMTF, 284.
44. UT, 24; WT May 1933, 668.
45. Louinet, "Birth of Conan," 11.
46. WT, March 1933, 394.
47. CC, 445.
48. DS, 557.
49. CC, 133.
50. UT, 24; WT, July 1934, 144.
51. UT, 23; WT, August 1933, 264.
52. WT, August 1933, 262.
53. TCL, 3:394.
54. Pelan and Walters, *Conversations,* 631.
55. WTS, 205.
56. Pelan and Walters, *Conversations*, 631.
57. Pelan and Walters, *Conversations*, 631.
58. WTS, 205.
59. WT, August 1933, 262.
60. WTS, 209.
61. WTS, 68.
62. Pelan and Walters, *Conversations*, 634.
63. Pelan and Walters, *Conversations*, 636.
64. Louinet, *Robert E. Howard Guide*, 23.
65. WT, June 1934, 784.
66. WT, November 1933, 650; December 1933, 776.
67. CC, 451.
68. WT, May 1933, 666.
69. WT, June 1933, 787.
70. WT, July 1935, 140.
71. TCL, 3:51; WT, December 1933, 775; Jamie Williamson, *The Evolution of Modern Fantasy: From Antiquarianism to the Ballantine Adult Fantasy Series* (New York: Palgrave MacMillan, 2015), 177.
72. BCC, xvi.
73. TCL, 2:420.
74. AMTF, 549–50.
75. WT, December 1933, 774.
76. WT, October 1933, 518.
77. AMTF, 353.
78. WT, April 1934, 520; November 1934, 651.
79. WT, November 1934, 651–52.
80. E.g., WT, March 1935, 396.
81. Bloch, *Once around the Bloch: An Unauthorized Autobiography* (New York: Tor Books, 1993), 72.
82. Goulart, *Cheap Thrills*, 157.
83. CPR, July 22, 1932; August 26, 1932.

84. TCL, 2:339.
85. AMTF, 346.
86. TCL, 2:343.
87. AMTF, 378.
88. AMTF, 436.
89. AMTF, 495–96.
90. AMTF, 436, 495–96.
91. AMTF, 495–96.
92. Joshi, *I am Providence*.
93. AMTF, 379, 340.
94. IMH, 205; see also Herron, *Famous Someday;* DOTS, 9.
95. AMTF, 338; Murphy, *Flame and Crimson*, 70; DOTS, 9.
96. Fehrenbach, *Lone Star*, 622.
97. Burke, "Robert E. Howard: New Deal Heroic Fantasist," *Dark Man: The Journal of Robert E. Howard Studies* 2, nos. 1/2 (Spring 2006): 20.
98. Richard Slotkin, *Gunfighter Nation: The Myth of the Frontier in Twentieth-Century America* (New York: Atheneum, 1992), 22.
99. AMTF, 501.
100. AMTF, 502.
101. AMTF, 432–33.
102. SFTP, 224.
103. AMTF, 432–33.
104. AMTF, 496–97.
105. TCL, 2:425–26.
106. LC, 77.
107. E. Hoffman Price, "Robert E. Howard & His Heroes," *Amra* 2, no. 15 (May 1961): 14.
108. Holmes and Knight, "Conan the Argonaut," 18.

Notes for Chapter 23

1. TCP, 1:89.
2. AMTF, 605.
3. Price, *Book of the Dead*, 31.
4. Price, *Book of the Dead*, 32.
5. OAK, 12.
6. OAK, 15, E. Hoffmann Price, "Otis Adelbert Kline: In Memoriam," *ERBzine*, December 17, 2020, https://www.erbzine.com/mag0/0037.html.
7. Derie, *Weird Talers*, 159–60.
8. Roehm, "Kline Connection."
9. Roehm, "Kline Connection."
10. Derie, *Weird Talers*, 179.
11. TCL, 3:340.
12. OWWA, 59.
13. OWWA, 106.
14. Cave, *Magazines*, 27.
15. De Camp, *Blade*, 123; Howard, *Two-Fisted Detective* (Bloomfield, NJ: Cryptic Publications, 1984), 2.
16. James Morton, *The First Detective: The Life and Revolutionary Times of Eugène-François Vidocq* (London: Ebury Press, 2004); Kenneth Silverman, *Edgar A. Poe: Mournful and Never-Ending Remembrance* (New York: Harper Perennial, 2008).

17. Vincent Starrett, *The Private Life of Sherlock Holmes* (New York: Macmillan, 1933).
18. "Black Mask History," *Black Mask Magazine*, February 22, 2023, https://blackmask-magazine.com/black-mask-history/.
19. Slotkin, *Gunfighter Nation*, 219.
20. Chandler, "Simple Art of Murder."
21. DeForest, *Storytelling*, 62.
22. TCL, 3:126.
23. De Camp, *Blade*, 124.
24. UT, 23.
25. AMTF, 634.
26. Howard, *Two-Fisted Detective*, 2.
27. De Camp, *Blade*, 125–26.
28. Derie, *Weird Talers*, 162.
29. UT, 24.
30. Fred Blosser, "Sleuths, Secrets, and Grisly Mysteries: The Detective Fiction of Robert E. Howard," in *Two-Gun Bob*, ed. Benjamin Szumskyj (New York: Hippocampus Press, 2006), 47.
31. AMTF, 634.
32. TCL, 3:235.
33. TCL, 3:302
34. Chandler, "Simple Art of Murder."
35. Julian Symons, *Bloody Murder: From the Detective Story to the Crime Novel*, 3rd ed. (New York: Mysterious Press, 1993), 107.
36. AMTF, 435.
37. Howard, *Steve Harrison's Casebook* (Plano, TX: Robert E. Howard Foundation Press, 2010), vii, xiii (hereafter SHC).
38. CC, 451.
39. BCC, 347.
40. CC, 452.
41. WT, October 1934, 528.
42. WT, October 1934, 523.
43. Herron, *Famous Someday;* see also Herron, "Robert'll Be Famous."
44. Herron, *Famous Someday;* see also Herron, "Robert'll Be Famous."
45. UT, 29.
46. TCL, 3:141.
47. UT, 3.
48. AMTF, 610.
49. AMTF, 521.
50. AMTF, 536.
51. AMTF, 537.
52. AMTF, 546.
53. AMTF, 604.
54. Howard, *Drafted: Unsent Letters to H. P. Lovecraft* (Plano, TX: Robert E. Howard Foundation, 2013), 8.
55. ES, 2:528.
56. Dorothy M. Grobe Litersky, *Derleth: Hawk . . . and Dove* (Aurora, CO: National Writers Press, 1997).
57. Derie, *Weird Talers*, 83.
58. Donald Sidney-Fryer, *The Golden State Phantasticks* (New York: Hippocampus Press, 2011), 10.

59. Sidney-Fryer, *Golden State*, 14.
60. TTI, 89–90.
61. Pelan and Walters, *Conversations*, 57.
62. Smith, *Weird Tales*, 12.
63. TCL, 3:96.
64. CAS, 219.
65. DOTS, 6.
66. OWWA, 15.
67. DOTS, 6.
68. OWWA, 15.
69. Lindsey W. Tyson letter, October 10, 1977, LSdC.
70. Jack Scott interview, July 19, 1977, LSdC.
71. Burke, "Novalyne Price Ellis."
72. DOTS, 44.
73. SD, 116; *Dallas Morning News,* May 1, 1924.
74. Burke, "Novalyne Price Ellis, 1908–1909," in *Robert E. Howard's Myth Maker*, ed. Roy Thomas (Cross Plains, TX: Cross Plains Comics, 1999).
75. SD, 177.
76. Roehm, "Novalyne and Daniel Baker," *REH: Two-Gun Raconteur*, March 5, 2010, https://web.archive.org/web/20111114110736/http://rehtwogunraconteur.com/?p=648.
77. OWWA, 16.
78. OWWA, 16.
79. OWWA, 17.
80. OWWA, 17–18.
81. OWWA, 18.
82. OWWA, 20.
83. OWWA, 15.
84. AMTF, 609.
85. TCL, 3:151.
86. TCL, 3:101–2.
87. AMTF, 610, 778; TCL, 3:52–53, 93, 101–2.
88. TCL, 3:13.
89. Herman, "Interview."
90. TCL, 3:13; AMTF, 769.
91. AMTF, 905.
92. BB, November 21, 1933; Comanche County, Tevis Clyde Smith Jr. Marriage Record.
93. SFTP, xxviii.
94. OWWA, 175.
95. CPR, December 22, 1933; TCL, 3:153.
96. Interview with Lindsey Tyson, undated letter, LSdC.
97. TCL, 3:151.
98. AMTF, 716–18.
99. Roehm, "In the Middle of the Street," *Cimmerian* 5, no. 3 (June 2008): 4–10.
100. Interview with Lindsey Tyson, undated letter, LSdC.
101. TCL, 3:183–84.
102. Roehm, *Robert E. Howard in* The Fantasy Fan (Los Angeles: Roehm's Room Press, 2006), 19.
103. LC, 78.
104. TCL, 3:151.
105. TCL, 3:141.

Notes for Chapter 24

1. TCP, 2:371.
2. UT, 4.
3. AMTF, 610.
4. UT, 4.
5. Cave, *Magazines*, 40–41.
6. TCL, 3:140.
7. Holmes, "Enter the Barbarian," 14.
8. Norris R. Chambers letter, October 28, 1978, LSdC.
9. Lindsey W. Tyson letter, October 10, 1977, LSdC.
10. TCL, 1:208.
11. Lord, *Howard Collector*, 194.
12. Finn, *Blood and Thunder*.
13. Boatright, "Art of Tall Lying," 357.
14. Boatright, "Art of Tall Lying," 358.
15. Boatright, "Art of Tall Lying," 360.
16. TCL, 2:424.
17. Goulart, *Cheap Thrills*, 141.
18. ABE, 2:vi.
19. ABE, 2:vi; Boatright, "Art of Tall Lying," 363.
20. Howard, *The Riot at Bucksnort and other Western Tales*, ed. and with an introduction by David Gentzel (Lincoln: University of Nebraska Press, 2005), 1.
21. Nick Carr, *The Western Pulp Hero: An Investigation into the Psyche of an American Legend* (Cabin John, MD: Wildside Press, 2009), 10.
22. Herron, *Dark Barbarian*, 143.
23. De Camp, *Blade of Conan*, 109.
24. Howard, *Riot at Bucksnort*, xii.
25. AMTF, 788.
26. Hoffmann, *Book of the Dead*, 76.
27. TCL, 3:151.
28. BCC, 349–50; Howard, *The Conquering Sword of Conan* (New York: Del Rey, 2005), 369 (hereafter CS).
29. WT, November 1934, 650–54.
30. WT, November 1934, 654; January 1935, 142.
31. WT, November 1934, 143.
32. BCC, 351.
33. UT, 29.
34. BCC, 351.
35. WT, August 1939, 159.
36. BCC, 357.
37. Herron, *Dark Barbarian,* 142; HC, Autumn 1970, 27.
38. BCC, 357.
39. TCL, 3:243; UT, 5.
40. AMTF, 837.
41. WT, February 1936, 256.
42. WT, February 1936, 255.
43. WT, June 1936, 768.
44. WT, June 1936, 765.
45. Louinet, "One Gent," 43.
46. ABE, 2:viii.
47. Herron, *Dark Barbarian*, 144.

48. Herron, "Ur *Gent*," *Cimmerian* 3, no. 8 (August 2006): 13–17.
49. IMH, 31.
50. Louinet, "One Gent," 47.
51. Herron, *Dark Barbarian*, 145.
52. "Letter from the Board," *Robert E. Howard Foundation Newsletter* 16, no. 4 (Winter 2022–2023): 2.
53. LC, 81; WT, November 1929.
54. AMTF, 331.
55. AMTF, 761.
56. TCL, 3:193–94; Lovecraft, *O Fortunate Floridian: H. P. Lovecraft's Letters to R. H. Barlow*, ed. S. T. Joshi and David E. Schultz. Tampa: University of Tampa Press, 2007), 130 (hereafter OFF).
57. LC, 82.
58. AMTF, 767.
59. TCL, 3:343.
60. LC, 83.
61. Price, *Book of the Dead*, 71.
62. E. Hoffmann Price letter, February 10, 1979, LSdC.
63. Price, *Book of the Dead*, 71.
64. E. Hoffmann Price letter, September 2, 1979, LSdC.
65. LC, 83.
66. Price, *Book of the Dead*, 72.
67. Lord, *Howard Collector*, 191.
68. LC, 85.
69. LC, 86.
70. LC, 82.
71. SFTP, 256; DOTS, 43.
72. TCL, 3:343.
73. LC, 86.
74. LC, 82–83.
75. LC, 87.
76. Lindsey W. Tyson letter, February 18, 1977, LSdC.
77. OWWA, 153.
78. DOTS, 25.
79. Bill Ingram interview, July 29, 1952, OIL.
80. LC, 84.
81. Pelan and Walters, *Conversations*, 183.
82. LC, 84.
83. Price, *Book of the Dead*, 82; Lord, *Howard Collector*, 192–93.
84. Price, *Book of the Dead*, 73.
85. LC, 85; see also Hoffmann, *Book of the Dead.*
86. AMTF, 767.
87. AMTF, 780.
88. AMTF, 212.
89. AMTF, 133.
90. AMTF, 780.
91. AMTF, 780.
92. AMTF, 781.
93. AMTF, 214.
94. AMTF, 785.
95. Lord, *Howard Collector*, 224.
96. AMTF, 851; Lindsey Tyson interview, March 7, 1978, LSdC.

97. AMTF, 765.
98. Lindsey W. Tyson interview notes, June 23, 1977, LSdC.
99. TCL, 3:200.
100. TCL, 3:189.
101. Cave, *Magazines*, 41.
102. Price, *Book of the Dead*, 72.

Notes for Chapter 25

1. TCP, 1:194.
2. AMTF, 851.
3. TCL, 3:269.
4. Howard, *The Best of Robert E. Howard*, vol. 1, *Crimson Shadows* (New York: Del Rey, 2007), xxi (hereafter BO1); Hardy, "Indomitable Wildness," 5; Howard, *The Early Adventures of El Borak* (Plano, TX: Robert E. Howard Foundation Press, 2010).
5. BO1, xxi; EB, 534.
6. Hardy, "Great Game," 4.
7. Hardy, "Indomitable Wildness," 5.
8. AMTF, 909.
9. Hardy, "Great Game,"4
10. Hardy, "Indomitable Wildness," 4–5.
11. BO1, xxi.
12. Burke, "Howard Bookshelf."
13. Morgan Holmes, "*Top-Notch*, Street & Smith and F. Orlin Tremaine," *REH: Two-Gun Raconteur*, no. 15 (Summer 2011): 33.
14. Holmes, "*Top-Notch*," 34.
15. Burke, "Robert E. Howard Fiction and Verse Timeline," *Howard Works*, accessed January 8, 2025, https://howardworks.com/timeline.htm.
16. EB, 542.
17. Hardy, "Indomitable Wildness," 7.
18. Hardy, "Indomitable Wildness," 13.
19. EB, 546.
20. EB, 118.
21. OWWA, 59.
22. CS, 369.
23. BCC, 359.
24. BCC, 268–70.
25. BCC, 359.
26. BCC, 359.
27. WT, December 1934, 659.
28. WT, February 1935, 268–69.
29. WT, February 1935, 270.
30. WT, February 1935, 271.
31. IMH, 24.
32. WT, February 1935, 272.
33. BCC, 359.
34. Roehm, "Robert E. Howard's Automobiles."
35. James Cross interview by Charlotte Laughlin, Charlotte Laughlin letter, February 1, 1979; Kate Merryman letter, no date, LSdC.
36. Roehm, "Robert E. Howard's Automobiles."
37. James Cross interview by Charlotte Laughlin, Charlotte Laughlin letter, February 1, 1979, LSdC.

38. Floyce Butler interview, July 20, 1977, LSdC.
39. DOTS, 14.
40. Floyce Butler interview, July 20, 1977, LSdC.
41. Annie Newton Davis interview, January 21, 1981, SWC.
42. Herman, "Interview."
43. Lindsey Tyson letter, January 20, 1977, LSdC.
44. AMTF, 836.
45. TCL, 3:246.
46. LC, 78.

Notes for Chapter 26

1. TCP, 3:267.
2. Burke, "Novalyne Price Ellis."
3. OWWA, 25.
4. OWWA, 11.
5. OWWA, 107.
6. OWWA, 177.
7. OWWA, 26.
8. OWWA, 27.
9. CPR, August 31, 1934.
10. CPR, September 7, 1934.
11. Beeler, *Footsteps*, 77.
12. OWWA, 39.
13. OWWA, 39.
14. OWWA, 40.
15. OWWA, 41.
16. OWWA, 45.
17. CS, 79.
18. OWWA, 69.
19. OWWA, 45.
20. OWWA, 46.
21. OWWA, 47.
22. OWWA, 48.
23. OWWA, 59.
24. OWWA, 48.
25. OWWA, 49.
26. OWWA, 49.
27. Johnson, *Odd Type*, 60.
28. OWWA, 50.
29. Roehm, "Letters to Glenn," 5.
30. OWWA, 54.
31. OWWA, 55.
32. OWWA, 57.
33. OWWA, 58.
34. OWWA, 59.
35. OWWA, 63; see also DOTS, 8.
36. OWWA, 80.
37. OWWA, 139.
38. DOTS, 12.
39. OWWA, 65.
40. OWWA, 70.

41. OWWA, 71.
42. OWWA, 71.
43. AMTF, 821.
44. OWWA, 121.
45. OWWA, 75.
46. OWWA, 119.
47. OWWA, 129.
48. OWWA, 131.
49. DOTS, 22.
50. Roehm, "Letters to Glenn," 4.
51. OWWA, 106, 110.
52. OWWA, 118.
53. OWWA, 102.
54. OWWA, 86.
55. OWWA, 86-87.
56. OWWA, 90; see also DOTS, 11.
57. OWWA, 134.
58. OWWA, 66.
59. Novalyne Price Ellis to Bill Cavalier, April 23, 1991, *REHupa*, no. 109.
60. OWWA, 83.
61. OWWA, 75.
62. OWWA, 85.
63. Herron, "Last," 23; Zora May Bryant interview, October 18, 1978; LSdC, Jack Scott interview notes, April 1, 1965, LSdC.
64. Johnson, *Odd Type*, 37.
65. Johnson, *Odd Type*, xviii.
66. OWWA, 85; see also DOTS, 27.
67. OWWA, 82.
68. OWWA, 149.
69. OWWA, 136–37.
70. OWWA, 64.
71. OWWA, 81.
72. OWWA, 114.
73. OWWA, 105.
74. OWWA, 105.
75. OWWA, 163–64.
76. OWWA, 166.
77. OWWA, 167.
78. OWWA, 170.
79. OWWA, 180.
80. OWWA, 181.

Notes for Chapter 27

1. TCP, 1:207.
2. OWWA,.181.
3. OWWA, 181–82.
4. AMTF, 838–39.
5. TCL, 3:285.
6. IMH, 64; AMTF, 838–39.
7. AMTF, 838–39.

8. AMTF, 838–39.
9. TCL, 3:285.
10. DOTS, 18.
11. IMH, 64.
12. Lindsey Tyson letter, January 20, 1977, LSdC.
13. AMTF, 501.
14. AMTF, 502.
15. DOTS, 44.
16. IMH, 64.
17. LC, 78.
18. Herman, "Interview."
19. Burke, *Robert E. Howard*, 6.
20. OWWA, 182.
21. OWWA, 187.
22. OWWA, 189.
23. OWWA, 190.
24. OWWA, 190.
25. OWWA, 191.
26. SFTP, 223; Lindsey W. Tyson interview notes, June 23, 1977, LSdC.
27. OWWA, 145–46.
28. OWWA, 112.
29. SK, 403.
30. DOTS, 42.
31. OWWA, 146.
32. OWWA, 192.
33. OWWA, 193.
34. OWWA, 194.
35. OWWA, 194–97.
36. OWWA, 200, 206.
37. Lindsey W. Tyson letter, n.d., LSdC.
38. OWWA, 208.
39. Leo Grin, "Heart's Blood," *Cimmerian* 1, no. 4 (October 2004): 22.
40. Johnson, *Odd Type*, 91–92.
41. Kay Redfield Jamison, "Manic-Depressive Illness and Creativity," *Scientific American* 272, no. 2 (February 1995): 62–67.
42. John Locke, *Pulp Fictioneers: Adventures in the Storytelling Business* (Silver Spring, MD: Adventure House, 2004), 34.
43. Anonymous, "A Penny a Word," *American Mercury* 37, no. 147 (March 1936): 286.
44. Anonymous, "Penny a Word," 287.
45. Anonymous, "Penny a Word," 287.
46. Anonymous, "Penny a Word," 289.
47. Anonymous, "Penny a Word," 287.
48. AMTF, 198.
49. TCL, 3:307.
50. SK, 403; Kate Merryman interview, July 18, 1977, LSdC.
51. Derie, *Weird Talers*, 256.
52. TCL, 3:285.
53. TCL, 3:285.
54. TCL, 3:285–86.
55. TCL, 3:286.
56. OWWA, 209.

57. OWWA, 212.
58. OWWA, 209.
59. OWWA, 212.
60. IMH, xv; Kate Merryman interview, July 18, 1977, LSdC.
61. Lindsey W. Tyson letter, October 10, 1977, LSdC,.
62. AMTF, 865.
63. TCL, 3:303; OWWA, 228.
64. AMTF, 867.
65. AMTF, 865–66.
66. OWWA, 229.
67. Roehm, "Letters to Glenn," 5.
68. AMTF, 873.
69. Roehm, "Vinson Papers."
70. OWWA, 230.
71. TCL, 3:314; OWWA, 230–31.
72. OWWA, 249.
73. OWWA, 249.
74. DOTS, 43.
75. Jack Scott interview notes, February 21, 1980; Elliott Bryant interview, October 18, 1978, LSdC.
76. CPR, July 19, 1935.
77. AMTF, 877–78.
78. AMTF, 863.
79. AMTF, 863.
80. AMTF, 885.
81. AMTF, 895.
82. WT, January 1936, 128; May 1935, 654.
83. WT, June 1935, 783.
84. UT, 25.
85. OWWA, 9; SFTP, xxviii.
86. AMTF, 905.
87. OWWA, 127.
88. Ellis, "Novalyne Price," 42; notes from interview with Katherine Merryman, March 7, 1978, LSdC.
89. Kate Merryman interview, July 18, 1977, LSdC.
90. *Empire-Tribune*, July 29, 1984.
91. AMTF, 901–4.
92. TCL, 3:385.
93. AMTF, 905–6.
94. AMTF, 908.
95. AMTF, 923.
96. TCL, 3:344.
97. LC, 79.
98. Derie, *Weird Talers*, 258.

Notes for Chapter 28

1. TCP, 2:182.
2. OWWA, 139.
3. Will Murray, "An Informal History of the Spicy Pulps," in *Windy City Pulp Stories #9*, ed. Tom Roberts (Normal, IL: Black Dog, 2009), 12.
4. Murray "Informal History," 7.

5. Murray "Informal History," 12; Damon Sasser, "REH Splashes the 'Spicys,'" *REH: Two-Gun Raconteur*, August 15, 2011, https://web.archive.org/web/20160327113931/http://www.rehtwogunraconteur.com/reh-splashes-the-spicys-part-i/
6. OWWA, 140.
7. OWWA, 141.
8. OWWA, 139.
9. Roehm, "Letters to Glenn," 4.
10. Morgan Holmes, "The Saga of Wild Bill Clanton and Two Gun Bob: The Spicy Robert E. Howard," in Roberts, *Windy City Pulp Stories #9*, 42; David C. Smith, *Robert E. Howard: A Literary Biography* (San Bernardino, CA: Pulp Hero Press, 2018), 158.
11. OWWA, 201.
12. IMH, 31–32.
13. OWWA, 140.
14. OWWA, 142.
15. IMH, 32.
16. TCL, 3:382; Sasser, "REH Splashes"; Louinet, "The Red-Bearded Viking of Skaggerack," *Dwelling in Dark Valley*, no. 3 (September 2001), http://www.robert-e-howard.org/Louinet/reh_frames.html.
17. O. Foerster Schully, "Markets in False Face," *Author & Journalist* 20 (November 1935): 16.
18. AMTF, 909.
19. Sasser, "REH Splashes"; TCL, 3:383.
20. IMH, 31.
21. Holmes, "Saga," 43; UT, 25.
22. Sasser, "REH Splashes."
23. Charles Hoffman, "Blood Lust," *Cimmerian* 2, no. 5 (October 2005): 6.
24. AMTF, 909.
25. TCL, 3:383.
26. DOTS, 18.
27. Robert Kenneth Jones, *The Shudder Pulps: A History of the Weird Menace Magazines of the 1930s* (West Linn, OR: FAX Collector's Editions, 1975), 75.
28. Louinet, "Red-Bearded Viking."
29. Roehm, "Letters to Glenn," 4.
30. Pelan and Walters, *Conversations*, 584.
31. IMH, 283.
32. Will Murray, "Spicy Adventurers," in Roberts, *Windy City Pulp Stories #9*, 38.
33. WT, April 1936, 509.
34. WT, May 1936, 638; WT June 1936, 761.
35. TCL, 3:391.
36. TCL, 3:368.
37. TCL, 3:385.
38. TCL, 3:385.
39. Holmes and Knight, "Conan the Argonaut," 4.
40. OWWA, 261.
41. TCL, 3:382.
42. TCL, 3:384.
43. OWWA, 264.
44. OWWA, 265.
45. OWWA, 266.
46. OWWA, 266.
47. Grin, "In Defense."
48. OWWA, 275.
49. DOTS, 13; Ellis, "Letter," 7.

50. OWWA, 267.
51. AMTF, 952.
52. Katherine Merryman and Alice Younglove interview, March 7, 1978, LSdC.
53. OWWA, 266.
54. OWWA, 266–67.
55. OWWA, 267.
56. OWWA, 267.
57. OWWA, 267.
58. OWWA, 267.
59. OWWA, 267.
60. OWWA, 269–70.
61. OWWA, 270.
62. TCL, 3:388.
63. TCL, 3:388–89.
64. OWWA, 274.
65. Roehm, "Letters to Glenn," 2.
66. Joseph W. McKnight, "McKnight, Joseph Banning," *Handbook of Texas Online*, updated April 7, 2020, https://www.tshaonline.org/handbook/entries/mcknight-joseph-banning.
67. TCL, 3:385.
68. AMTF, 922.
69. AMTF, 921.
70. Dormandy, *White Death*, 261.
71. IMH, 64.
72. IMH, 76.
73. AMTF, 921.
74. IMH, 76.
75. AMTF, 921.
76. AMTF, 951–52.
77. Barbara Bates, *Bargaining for Life: A Social History of Tuberculosis, 1876–1938* (Philadelphia: University of Pennsylvania Press, 1992); Daniel, *Captain of Death*; Dormandy, *White Death.*
78. Barrett, "Hester Jane Ervin.".
79. Grin, "In Defense."

Notes for Chapter 29

1. TCP, 3:90.
2. Frederick Jackson Turner, *The Frontier in American History* (New York: Henry Holt, 1921), 38.
3. Jay B. Hubbell, "The Frontier in American Literature," *Southwest Review* 10, no. 2 (January 1925): 85.
4. Dobie, *Coronado's Children* (New York: Grosset & Dunlap, 1930), i.
5. Walter Prescott Webb, *The Great Plains* (Lincoln: University of Nebraska Press, 1959), 321.
6. Larry McMurtry, *In a Narrow Grave: Essays on Texas* (New York: Liveright Publishing, 2018), 67.
7. AMTF, 89.
8. McMurtry, *In a Narrow Grave*, 73; POSR2, 378.
9. AMTF, 812–13.
10. AMTF, 91.
11. AMTF, 648.
12. AMTF, 502.

13. AMTF, 201.
14. AMTF, 223.
15. Fehrenbach, *Lone Star*, 612.
16. McMurtry, *In a Narrow Grave*, 67–68.
17. Finn, "Robert E. Howard," 173.
18. TCL, 3:235.
19. OWWA, 178.
20. OWWA, 180.
21. OWWA, 179–80.
22. AMTF, 817.
23. AMTF, 191.
24. John Bullard, "'Beyond the Black River': Is It Really 'Beyond the Brazos River'?" *Adventures Fantastic*, March 23, 2020, http://adventuresfantastic.com/beyond-the-black-river-is-it-really-beyond-the-brazos-river-part-1/.
25. Karl Edward Wagner, "Afterword," in *Red Nails*, ed. Karl Edward Wagner, 281–95 (New York: Berkeley Medallion Books, 1977), 285.
26. CS, 99.
27. DOTS, 45.
28. CS, 100.
29. AMTF, 857.
30. CS, 56.
31. Natalie Wooley, "The Adventure Story," *Californian*, no. 3 (Winter 1935): 9.
32. De Camp, *Spell of Conan*, 30; Louinet, "Robert E. Howard," 169; Wagner, "Afterword."
33. CS, 377–78.
34. AMTF, 908–9.
35. Wagner, "Afterword," 287–88.
36. CS, xix.
37. TCL, 3:338.
38. CS, 381.
39. CS, 383.
40. CS, xx.
41. DOTS, 44.
42. Novalyne Price Ellis to Rusty Burke, November 16, 1990, *REHupa*, no. 107.
43. WT, October 1936, 380
44. WT, October 1936, 382.
45. WT, October 1936, 384; November 1936, 512.
46. TCL, 2:166.
47. McMurtry, *In a Narrow Grave*, 65.
48. TCL, 2:166.
49. TCL, 2:61.
50. AMTF, 129; see also 111.
51. ES, 1:283.
52. OFF, 56; DS, 286–87; ES, 2:523–24; SLL, 4:180–81, 350.
53. SK, 401.
54. TCL, 3:52–53.
55. OWWA, 143, 227.
56. OWWA, 123.
57. TCL, 2:136.
58. TCL, 3:345.
59. OWWA, 180.
60. OWWA, 179–80.

61. DOTS, 46.
62. McMurtry, *In a Narrow Grave*, 75–76.
63. J. Frank Dobie, *Some Part of Myself* (Boston: Little, Brown, 1967), 271.
64. Lovecraft, "In Memoriam"; IMH, 249.
65. AMTF, 953.
66. *Houston Post*, March 20, 1966.
67. Grin, "In Defense Of."
68. AMTF, 952.
69. Herman, "Interview."
70. AMTF, 952.
71. Herbert W. Berger and Ervido Mejia, "Tuberculous Pleurisy," *Chest* 63, no. 1 (January 1973): 88–92; William Osler, *Tuberculosis Pleurisy* (Boston: David Clapp & Son, 1893).
72. AMTF, 952.
73. TCL, 3:390.
74. OWWA, 277.

Notes for Chapter 30

1. TCP, 2:311.
2. Lindsey Tyson interview, March 7, 1978, LSdC; Herron, "Last," 24.
3. AMTF, 952.
4. AMTF, 952; Bynum, *Spitting Blood*; Dormandy, *White Death*.
5. AMTF, 952.
6. Dormandy, *White Death*, 221.
7. Bynum, *Spitting Blood*, 66.
8. AMTF, 952.
9. CPR, April 17, 1936.
10. Caroline Henderson, *Letters from the Dust Bowl*, ed. Alvin O. Turner (Norman: University of Oklahoma Press, 2003), 141.
11. TCL, 3:400.
12. TCL, 3:395.
13. OWWA.
14. OWWA, 287.
15. OWWA, 291.
16. OWWA, 280.
17. OWWA, 295.
18. CPR, May 15, 1936.
19. TCL, 3:422; OWWA, 297.
20. LC, 79.
21. TCL, 3:395.
22. TCL, 3:402.
23. TCL, 3:403.
24. TCL, 3:398.
25. TCL, 3:423.
26. Bill Schelly, *Otto Binder: The Life and Work of a Comic Book and Science Fiction Visionary* (Berkeley: North Atlantic Books, 2016); IMH, xviii.
27. Roehm, "Kline Connection."
28. Schelly, *Otto Binder*, 43.
29. OWWA, 278.
30. TCL, 3:402.
31. SK, 405.
32. Howard, *Pictures*, 171.

33. Howard, *Pictures*, 173.
34. Anonymous, "Penny a Word," 287.
35. Anonymous, "Penny a Word," 287.
36. Anonymous, "Penny a Word," 289.
37. Anonymous, "Penny a Word," 291.
38. TCL, 2:165; POSR2, 371.
39. Jones, *Shudder Pulps*, 226.
40. AMTF, 952–53.
41. DOTS, 13.
42. IMH, 64.
43. IMH, 205.
44. IMH, 64.
45. Kate Merryman interview, July 18, 1977, LSdC.
46. IMH, 78.
47. TCL, 3:423.
48. IMH, 65.
49. IMH, 65; Misc. Notes on Texas Trip, October 1978, LSdC.
50. Lorene Bishop interview, October 19, 1978, LSdC.
51. Kate Merryman interview, July 18, 1977, LSdC.
52. Katherine Merryman and Alice Younglove interview notes, March 7, 1978, LSdC.
53. Kate Merryman interview, July 18, 1977, LSdC,.
54. IMH, 76; Kate Merryman interview, July 18, 1977, Lois Garrett interview, October 18, 1978, LSdC.
55. CPR, June 19, 1936; Lindsey W. Tyson letter, n.d., Kate Merryman letter, n.d., LSdC,; IMH, 49.
56. Kate Merryman interview, July 18, 1977, LSdC.
57. Alice Younglove interview, July 18, 1977, LSdC.
58. Herman, "Interview."
59. IMH, 59.
60. IMH, 64; Herron, "Last," 26.
61. IMH, 64; Herron, "Last," 26; Katherine Merryman and Alice Younglove interview notes, March 7, 1978, LSdC,.
62. IMH, 64.
63. Katherine Merryman and Alice Younglove interview notes, March 7, 1978, LSdC.
64. Kate Merryman interview, October 18, 1978, LSdC.
65. Louinet, *Howard Guide*, 62; Robert Baker interview, January 21, 1979, LSdC.
66. IMH, 59.
67. HC (Spring 1972): 2; Louinet, "Grief & Greed"; SK, 405.
68. SK, 405; Jack Scott interview, March 12, 1981, SWC; Louinet, *Howard Guide*, 62.
69. Lindsey W. Tyson letter, January 20, 1977; interviews about Robert E. Howard in Texas, various dates, LSdC.
70. Kate Merryman interview, October 18, 1978, LSdC.
71. BB, June 12, 1936.
72. IMH, 64.
73. IMH, 64, 77.
74. Roehm, "Letters to Glenn," 3.
75. IMH, 63.
76. CPR, June 12, 1936.
77. IMH, 63.
78. BB, June 11, 1936; Mr. Cross interview by Charlotte Laughlin, letter dated February 1, 1979, LSdC; Robert E. Howard Death Record.
79. TCP, 1:248–52.

80. Burke, "Toward Other Lands," 21.
81. SFTP, 246.
82. IMH, 51; Roehm, "Letters to Glenn," 3; LSdC, Kate Merryman interview, July 18, 1977.
83. Burke, "Toward Other Lands," 21.
84. De Camp, De Camp, and Griffin, *Dark Valley Destiny.*
85. Louinet, *Howard Guide*, 22.
86. Grin, "Heart's Blood," 22.
87. DOTS, 47.
88. Grin, "Heart's Blood," 21.
89. Novalyne Price Ellis to Rusty Burke, November 16, 1990, *REHupa*, no. 107
90. AMTF, 605.
91. DOTS, 47.
92. Grin, "Heart's Blood," 22.
93. TCL, 1:227.
94. AMTF, 595.
95. SK, 403.
96. SFTP, 223.
97. Louinet, *Howard Guide*, 22.
98. Burke, "Toward Other Lands," 21.
99. Burke, "Toward Other Lands," 22.
100. IMH, 63.
101. IMH, 58–59.
102. IMH, 63.
103. Kate Merryman letter, April 17, 1978, LSdC.
104. Kate Merryman letter, April 17, 1978, LSdC; Herron, *Famous Someday*.
105. Kate Merryman letter, n.d., LSdC.
106. Kate Merryman interview, July 18, 1977, LSdC.
107. Alice Younglove interview, October 18, 1978, LSdC.
108. CPR, June 19, 1936.
109. Louinet, "Conversation," 26.
110. Jack Scott interview, March 12, 1981; see also Jack Scott interview, April/May 2001, SWC.
111. BB, June 11, 1936.
112. CPR, November 6, 2003.
113. IMH, 58–59.
114. IMH, 211.
115. AMTF, 952–53.
116. TCL, 3:401.
117. IMH, 64.
118. Robert E. Howard Death Record.

Notes for Epilogue

1. IMH, 60.
2. IMH, 64.
3. Hester Jane Ervin Howard Death Record.
4. Kate Merryman interview, October 18, 1978, LSdC; visit to Robert E. Howard home in Cross Plains, October 18, 1978.
5. IMH, 106.
6. Questions for Kate Merryman, April 6, 1978, LSdC.
7. Kate Merryman interview, October 18, 1978, LSdC.
8. CPR, June 19, 1936.

9. Louinet, "Conversation," 28; see also Jack Scott interview, March 12, 1981, SWC; CPR, June 19, 1936.
10. Louinet, "Conversation," 28.
11. BB, June 15, 1936.
12. Norris R. Chambers interview, July 22, 1977, LSdC.
13. Waldrop, "Journey," 161.
14. BB, June 15, 1936.
15. Charlotte Laughlin letter, February 1, 1979; Norris R. Chambers interview, July 22, 1977, LSdC.
16. Kate Merryman letter, n.d., LSdC.
17. Robert Baker interview, January 21, 1979; Katherine Merryman and Alice Younglove interview, March 7, 1978, LSdC.
18. Katherine Merryman and Alice Younglove interview, March 7, 1978, LSdC.
19. Lindsey Tyson interview, March 7, 1978, LSdC.
20. Roehm, "The Legend of the Trunk," *REH: Two-Gun Raconteur*, January 14, 2014, https://web.archive.org/web/20150911053806/http://www.rehtwogunraconteur.com/the-legend-of-the-trunk-part-1; Louinet, "Grief & Greed?"
21. Callahan County Bond and Oath of Temporary Administration, June 15, 1936, LSdC.
22. I. M. Howard Bond and Oath of Temporary Administrator, June 16, 1936, LSdC.
23. Callahan County Bond and Oath of Temporary Administrator, June 16, 1936, LSdC.
24. I. M. Howard Bond and Oath of Temporary Administrator, June 16, 1936, LSdC.
25. "Postal Savings System," *US Postal Service*, September 15, 2020, https://about.usps.com/who-we-are/postal-history/postal-savings-system.pdf.
26. Jack Scott interview, March 12, 1981; see also Jack Scott interview, April/May 2001, SWC.
27. CPR, June 12, 1936.
28. Louinet, "Conversation," 26, 28.
29. IMH, 60.
30. Douglas A. Anderson, "'All Fled, All Done': Redux on Robert E. Howard's Famous Couplet," *A Shiver in the Archives*, January 18, 2019, http://ashiverinthearchives.blogspot.com/2019/01/all-fled-all-done-redux-on-robert-e.html; Burke, "All Fled, All Done," *Dark Man: The Journal of Robert E. Howard Studies*, no. 5 (Winter 2001): 15–17.
31. Burke, "The Note," *Cimmerian* 3, no. 1 (January 2006): 10.
32. Kate Merryman interview, July 18, 1977, LSdC.
33. Burke, "Note," 8–9.
34. CPR, July 3, 1936.
35. Jack Scott interview, SFOHA; interview with Jack Scott notes, February 21, 1980, LSdC; Jack Scott interview, March 12, 1981 & April/May 2001, SWC.
36. Herron, *Famous Someday*.
37. Herron, *Famous Someday*.
38. Roehm, "Robert E. Howard's Automobiles"; Charlotte Laughlin interview of James Cross notes; interview with Jack Scott notes, February 21, 1980, LSdC.
39. IMH, 58.
40. IMH, 107.
41. *Ranger Daily Times*, November 14, 1944; CPR, November 17, 1944; IMH, xvi.
42. OWWA, 302.
43. OWWA, 305.
44. OWWA, 316.
45. DOTS, 20.
46. Burke, "Novalyne Price Ellis."
47. DOTS, 30.
48. SFTP, 252.

49. Lindsey W. Tyson interview notes, June 23, 1977, LSdC; WT, May 1938, 633.
50. LC, 9.
51. LMO; Roehm, "June 1936," *REHupa*, no. 211 (June 2008): 1–23.
52. LPS, 238–39.
53. IMH, 53.
54. DS, 654.
55. LPS, 239.
56. IMH, 54.
57. Lovecraft, "In Memoriam."
58. IMH, 99; Lovecraft, "In Memoriam."
59. TTI, 227.
60. Murphy, "Pulps to Paperbacks," 47.
61. Pelan and Walters, *Conversations*, 636.
62. WT, August/September 1936, 250.
63. IMH, 67.
64. TTI, 219.
65. TTI, 218–19.
66. TTI, 219.
67. WTS, 4.
68. IMH, 52.
69. WT, January 1937, 122.
70. WT, November 1936, 510.
71. WT, November 1936, 509–10.
72. WT, January 1937, 122–23.
73. WT, September 1937, 379-380; WT, April 1937, 510.
74. WT, December 1936, 640; WT, February 1937, 249.
75. WT, November 1936, 508.
76. WT, July 1937, 128.
77. WT, July 1938, 124.
78. WT, January 1939, 123.
79. WT, November 1936, 506.
80. WT, January 1937, 124.
81. WT, March 1937, 380.
82. WT, December 1936, 637–38.
83. WT, November 1936, 510.
84. WT, April 1937, 507.
85. WT, July 1938, 124.
86. WT, October 1937, 508.
87. Stefan Dziemianowicz, "The Gnome Press Story," *Weird Fiction Review*, no. 9 (Winter 2018): 193–228.
88. Herron, *Dark Barbarian*, 129; BO2, xviii; Louinet, "Robert E. Howard," 165.
89. Norris R. Chambers interview, July 22, 1977, LSdC.
90. Herron, *Famous Someday*; see also Herron, "Robert'll Be Famous."
91. LPS, 275.
92. LPS, 243; *Hamlet*, Act 1, Scene 2.

Notes for Acknowledgments

1. LC, 31; POSR2, 25.
2. SFTP, 227.

Bibliography

Primary Sources

AMTF Lovecraft, H. P., and Robert E. Howard. *A Means to Freedom: The Letters of H. P. Lovecraft and Robert E. Howard.* Edited by S. T. Joshi, David E. Schultz, and Rusty Burke. New York: Hippocampus Press, 2017.

BB *Brownwood Bulletin.* Portal to Texas History. University of North Texas. https://texashistory.unt.edu/explore/collections/BROW/.

CAS Smith, Clark Ashton. *The Selected Letters of Clark Ashton Smith.* Edited by Davide E. Schultz and Scott Connors. Sauk City, WI: Arkham House, 2003.

CPR *Cross Plains Review.* Southwest Collection. Texas Tech University. https://newspapers.swco.ttu.edu/handle/20.500.12255/55668.

DOTS Ellis, Novalyne Price. *Day of the Stranger: Further Memories of Robert E. Howard.* West Warwick, RI: Necronomicon Press, 1989.

DS Lovecraft, H. P., and Clark Ashton Smith. *Dawnward Spire, Lonely Hills: The Letters of H. P. Lovecraft and Clark Ashton Smith.* Edited by David E. Schultz and S. T. Joshi. New York: Hippocampus Press, 2020.

ES Lovecraft, H. P., and August Derleth. *Essential Solitudes: The Letters of H. P. Lovecraft and August Derleth.* 2 vols. Edited by David E. Schultz and S. T. Joshi. New York: Hippocampus Press, 2008.

HC Lord, Glenn. *The Howard Collector.* 18 issues. 1961–1973.

HP Harold Preece Papers, 1922–2017. Dolph Briscoe Center for American History. University of Texas at Austin, Austin, TX.

IMH Howard, Isaac M. *The Collected Letters of Doctor Isaac M. Howard.* Edited by Rob Roehm. Plano, TX: Robert E. Howard Foundation Press, 2011.

JS Rodenberger, Charles A. *Transcript of the Oral History of Jack Scott.* Cross Plains, TX: Friends of the Cross Plains Public Library, 2001.

LC Lord, Glenn. *The Last Celt: A Bio-Bibliography of Robert E. Howard, the Creator of Conan.* New York: Berkley Windhover Books, 1976.

LMO Lovecraft, H. P. *Letters to C. L. Moore and Others.* Edited by David E. Schultz and S. T. Joshi. New York: Hippocampus Press, 2017.

LPS Lovecraft, H. P. *Letters to E. Hoffmann Price and Richard F. Searight.* Edited by David E. Schultz and S. T. Joshi. New York: Hippocampus Press, 2021.

LSdC L. Sprague de Camp and Catherine Crook de Camp Collection. Harry Ransom Center. University of Texas at Austin, Austin, TX.

LSOL Klatt, Herbert C. *Lone Scout of Letters.* Edited by Rob Roehm. Lancaster, CA: Roehm's Room Press, 2011.

OAK Kraft, David Anthony, ed. *OAK Leaves: The Official Journal of Otis Adelbert Kline and His Works.* Modern Limited Publications, 16 issues.

OFF Lovecraft, H. P. *O Fortunate Floridian: H. P. Lovecraft's Letters to R. H. Barlow.* Edited by S. T. Joshi and David E. Schultz. Tampa: University of Tampa Press, 2007.

OIL Oral History of the Texas Oil Industry Collection, 1952–1960. Dolph Briscoe Center for American History. University of Texas at Austin, Austin, TX.

OS *Oriental Stories/The Magic Carpet Magazine.* Popular Fiction, 1930–1934.

OWWA Ellis, Novalyne Price. *One Who Walked Alone: Robert E. Howard: The Final Years.* West Kingston, RI: Donald M. Grant Publishers, 1986.

RWM Smith, Tevis Clyde. *Report on a Writing Man & Other Reminiscences of Robert E. Howard.* Edited by Rusty Burke. West Warwick, RI: Necronomicon Press, 1991.

SD Howard, Robert E. *School Days in the Post Oaks: Cross Plains and Brownwood in the 1920s.* Edited by Rob Roehm. Plano, TX: Robert E. Howard Foundation Press, 2011.

SFOHA Lane, Daryl (interviewer). Science Fiction Radio Show Collection. Science Fiction Oral History Association Archives. http://sfoha.org/catalog/wb.html.

SFTP Smith, Tevis Clyde. *"So Far the Poet . . ." & Other Writings.* Edited by Rusty Burke and Rob Roehm. Plano, TX: Robert E. Howard Foundation Press, 2010.

SLL Lovecraft, H. P. *Selected Letters: H. P. Lovecraft.* 5 vols. Edited by August Derleth and Donald Wandrei. Sauk City, WI: Arkham House, 1965.

SWC Oral Histories. Southwest Collection. Texas Tech University, Lubbock, TX.

TA&M Robert E. Howard Collection. Cushing Library. Texas A&M University, College Station, TX.

TCL Howard, Robert E. *The Collected Letters of Robert E. Howard.* 2nd ed. 3 vols. Edited by Rob Roehm and John Bullard. Plano, TX: Robert E. Howard Foundation Press, 2021.

TCP Howard, Robert E. *The Collected Poetry of Robert E. Howard.* 2nd ed. 3 vols. Edited by Paul Herman. Plano, TX: Robert E. Howard Foundation Press, 2023.

TTI Locke, John. *The Thing's Incredible! The Secret Origins of Weird Tales, 1923–24.* Elkhorn, CA: Off-Trail Publications, 2018.

UT Lord, Glenn. *Ultima Thule.* Omaha: Joe & Mona Marek, 2000.

WT *Weird Tales.* Rural Publishing Company, 1923–1940.

WTS Weinberg, Robert. *The Weird Tales Story: Expanded and Enhanced.* N.p.: Pulp Hero Press, 2021.

Howard P. Lovecraft Collection. Brown University Library. Providence, RI. http://library.brown.edu/.

Lovecraft, H. P. *H. P. Lovecraft: Letters to F. Lee Baldwin, Duane W. Rimel, and Nils Frome.* Edited by David E. Schultz and S. T. Joshi. New York: Hippocampus Press, 2016.

Lovecraft, H. P. *Letters to Richard F. Searight.* Edited by David E. Schultz and S. T. Joshi. West Warwick, RI: Necronomicon Press, 1992.

Lovecraft, H. P. *Letters to Robert Bloch and Others.* Edited by David E. Schultz and S. T. Joshi. New York: Hippocampus Press, 2015.

Lovecraft, H. P. *Miscellaneous Writings.* Sauk City, WI: Arkham House, 1995.

Robert E. Howard Publications

ABE Howard, Robert E. *The Adventures of Breckinridge Elkins.* 2 vols. Plano, TX: Robert E. Howard Foundation Press, 2016.

BCC Howard, Robert E. *The Bloody Crown of Conan.* New York: Del Rey, 2003.

BMM Howard, Robert E. *Bran Mak Morn: The Last King.* New York: Del Rey, 2005.

BO1 Howard, Robert E. *The Best of Robert E. Howard.* Vol. 1, *Crimson Shadows.* New York: Del Rey, 2007.

BO2 Howard, Robert E. *The Best of Robert E. Howard.* Vol. 2, *Grim Lands.* New York: Del Rey, 2007.

CC Howard, Robert E. *The Coming of Conan the Cimmerian.* New York: Del Rey, 2002.

CS Howard, Robert E. *The Conquering Sword of Conan.* New York: Del Rey, 2005.

EB Howard, Robert E. *El Borak and other Desert Adventures.* New York: Del Rey, 2010.

FOI Howard, Robert E. *Fists of Iron: The Collected Boxing Fiction of Robert E. Howard.* 4 vols. Edited by Patrice Louinet, Christopher Gruber, and Mark Finn. Plano, TX: Robert E. Howard Foundation Press, 2019.

HS	Howard, Robert E. *The Horror Stories of Robert E. Howard.* New York: Del Rey, 2008.
KULL	Howard, Robert E. *Kull: Exile of Atlantis.* New York: Del Rey, 2006.
POSR1	Howard, Robert E. *Post Oaks and Sand Roughs.* Hampton Falls, NH: Donald M. Grant, Publishers, 1990.
POSR2	Howard, Robert E. *Post Oaks and Sand Roughs & Other Autobiographical Writings.* Edited by Rob Roehm. Plano, TX: Robert E. Howard Foundation Press, 2019.
Sentiment	Howard, Robert E. *Sentiment: An Olio of Rarer Works.* Edited by Rob Roehm. Plano, TX: Robert E. Howard Foundation Press, 2009.
SK	Howard, Robert E. *The Savage Tales of Solomon Kane.* New York: Del Rey, 1998.
SotN	Howard, Robert E. *Swords of the North.* Plano, TX: Robert E. Howard Foundation Press, 2014.
SW	Howard, Robert E. *Sword Woman and other Historical Adventures.* New York: Del Rey, 2011.
TLT	Howard, Robert E. *The Last of the Trunk.* Edited by Patrice Louinet. Plano, TX: Robert E. Howard Foundation Press, 2007.
WEST	Howard, Robert E. *Western Tales.* Plano, TX: Robert E. Howard Foundation Press, 2013.

Howard, Robert. E. *A Song of the Race.* Plano, TX: Robert E. Howard Foundation, 2009.

Howard, Robert E. "The Apparition in the Prize Ring." *Ghost Stories* 6, no. 4 (April 1929): 19–23.

Howard, Robert. E. *Boxing Stories.* Lincoln: University of Nebraska Press, 2005.

Howard, Robert. E. *Drafted: Unsent Letters to H. P. Lovecraft.* Plano, TX: Robert E. Howard Foundation, 2013.

Howard, Robert E. *The Early Adventures of El Borak.* Plano, TX: Robert E. Howard Foundation Press, 2010.

Howard, Robert E. *The End of the Trail: Western Stories.* Edited with an introduction by Rusty Burke. Lincoln: University of Nebraska Press, 2005.

Howard, Robert E. "The Ghost of Camp Colorado." *Texaco Star* (April 1931): 13–15.

Howard, Robert. E. *Lord of Samarcand and Other Adventure Tales of the Old Orient.* Edited by Rusty Burke. Introduction by Patrice Louinet. Lincoln: University of Nebraska Press, 2005.

Howard, Robert E. *Nameless Cults: The Cthulhu Mythos Fiction of Robert E. Howard.* Oakland, CA: Chaosium Book, 2001.

Howard, Robert E. *Pictures in the Fire: Remaining Weird Tales and Esoterica.* Plano, TX: Robert E. Howard Foundation Press, 2018.

Howard, Robert E. *Pirate Adventures.* Plano, TX: Robert E. Howard Foundation Press, 2012.

Howard, Robert E., and Richard Lupoff. *The Return of Skull-Face.* West Linn, OR: FAX Collector's Editions, 1977.

Howard, Robert E. *The Riot at Bucksnort and other Western Tales.* Edited and with an introduction by David Gentzel. Lincoln: University of Nebraska Press, 2005.

Howard, Robert E. *Steve Harrison's Casebook.* Plano, TX: Robert E. Howard Foundation Press, 2010.

Howard, Robert E. *Two-Fisted Detective.* Bloomfield, NJ: Cryptic Publications, 1984.

Howard, Robert. E. *Waterfront Fists and Others: The Collected Fight Stories of Robert E. Howard.* Edited by Paul Herman. Introduction by Mark Finn. Rockville, MD: Wildside Press, 2003.

Howard, Robert E. *West Is West & Others.* Edited by Rob Roehm and Alex Runions. N.p.: Roehm's Room Press, 2006.

Secondary Sources

Books

Abernethy, Francis Edward. *Texas Toys and Games.* Denton: University of North Texas Press, 1989.

Agnew, Jeremy. *The Age of Dimes and Pulp: A History of Sensationalist Literature, 1830–1960.* Jefferson, NC: McFarland, 2018.

Allen, Estill Franklin. *Cross Plains-Burkett, Texas, Methodists.* Cross Plains, TX: First United Methodist Church, 1985.

Anderson, Ann. *Snake Oil, Hustlers and Hambones: The American Medicine Show*. Jefferson, NC: McFarland, 2000.

Anderson, Douglas A. *Tales before Tolkien: The Roots of Modern Fantasy*. New York: Ballantine, 2003.

Asbury, Herbert. *The French Quarter: An Informal History of the New Orleans Underworld.* New York: Thunder's Mouth Press, 2003.

Ashley, Mike. *The Time Machines: The Story of the Science-Fiction Pulp Magazines from the Beginning to 1950.* Liverpool: Liverpool University Press, 2000.

Barry, John M. *The Great Influenza: The Epic Story of the Deadliest Plague in History.* New York: Penguin Books, 2004.

Barton, Jim Tom. *Eight from Decatur: Growing up in North Texas.* College Station: Texas A&M University Press, 1980.

Bates, Barbara. *Bargaining for Life: A Social History of Tuberculosis, 1876–1938.* Philadelphia: University of Pennsylvania Press, 1992.

Beard, George M. *Sexual Neurasthenia [Nervous Exhaustion]: Its Hygiene, Causes, Symptoms, and Treatment.* Edited by A. D. Rockwell. New York: E. B. Treat, 1886.

Beeler, Ann L. *Footsteps of Approaching Thousands.* Cross Plains, TX: Cross Plains Public Library, 2011.

Beston, Paul. *The Boxing Kings: When American Heavyweights Ruled the Ring.* Lanham, MD: Rowman & Littlefield, 2017.

Biographical and Historical Memoirs of Southern Arkansas. Chicago: Goodspeed Publishing, 1890.

Bloch, Robert. *Once around the Bloch: An Unauthorized Autobiography.* New York: Tor Books, 1993.

Blosser, Fred. *Ar-I-E'ch and the Spell of Cthulhu.* N.p.: Pulp Hero Press, 2018.

Boyle, Eric W. *Quack Medicine: A History of Combating Health Fraud in Twentieth-Century America.* Santa Barbara, CA: Praeger, 2013.

Bradley, Ora Lewis. *The Country Doctor's Wife.* New York: House of Field, 1940.

Brands, H. W. *The Age of Gold: The California Gold Rush and the New American Dream.* New York: Anchor Books, 2002.

Brown, Teri. *Cross Plains Remembered.* Cross Plains, TX: Barbarian Festival Committee, 2011.

Bryson, Bill. *One Summer: America, 1927.* New York: Anchor, 2013.

Bryson, J. Gordon. *One Hundred Dollars & A Horse: The Reminiscences of a Country Doctor.* New York: William Morrow, 1965.

Burke, Rusty. *REH: A Short Biography of Robert E. Howard.* New York: Cross Plains Comics, 1999.

Burke, Rusty. *Robert E. Howard in Cross Plains: A Guide for the Howard Fan.* Washington, DC: Rusty Burke, 2006.

Burns, T. A., and Merrill Burkett. *History of Coleman County and Its People.* San Angelo, TX: Coleman County Historical Commission, 1985.

Burroughs, Bryan. *The Big Rich: The Rise and Fall of the Greatest Texas Oil Fortunes.* New York: Penguin Press, 2009.

Bynum, Helen. *Spitting Blood: The History of Tuberculosis.* Oxford: Oxford University Press, 2012.

Caldwell, Mark. *The Last Crusade: The War on Consumption, 1862–1954.* New York: Atheneum, 1998.

Campbell, Randolph B. *Gone to Texas: A History of the Lone Star State.* New York: Oxford University Press, 2003.

Carr, Nick. *The Western Pulp Hero: An Investigation into the Psyche of an American Legend.* Cabin John, MD: Wildside Press, 2009.

Carter, Lin. *Imaginary Worlds.* New York: Ballantine Books, 1973.

Catalogue of Howard Payne College, 1927–1928. Brownwood: Howard Payne College, 1928.
Cave, Hugh B. *Magazines I Remember*. Chicago: Tattered Pages Press, 1994.
Chesterton, G. K. *The Ballad of the White Horse*. 1911. Reprint, Mineola, NY: Dover Publications, 2010.
Clark, John W. *Early English: A Study of Old and Middle English*. New York: Norton, 1964.
Clarke, Mary Whatley. *The Palo Pinto Story*. Fort Worth: Manney Company, 1956.
Cranston, Sylvia. *H. P. B.: The Extraordinary Life & Influence of Helena Blavatsky, Founder of the Modern Theosophical Movement*. New York: G. P. Putnam's Sons, 1993.
Daniel, Thomas M. *Captain of Death: The Story of Tuberculosis*. Rochester: University of Rochester Press, 1997.
Davis, John. *A History of Wales*. New York: Penguin Books, 2007.
Davis, Miriam C. *The Axeman of New Orleans*. Chicago: Chicago Review, 2018.
De Camp, L. Sprague. *The Blade of Conan*. New York: Ace, 1979.
De Camp, L. Sprague. *The Spell of Conan*. New York: Ace, 1980.
De Camp, L. Sprague, Catherine Crook de Camp, and Jane Whittington Griffin. *Dark Valley Destiny: The Life of Robert E. Howard*. New York: Bluejay Books, 1983.
Deffenbaugh, Walter S., and Ward W. Keesecker. *Compulsory School Attendance Laws and Their Administration*. Washington, DC: Government Printing Office, 1935.
DeForest, Tim. *Storytelling in the Pulps, Comics, and Radio: How Technology Changed Popular Fiction in America*. Jefferson, NC: McFarland, 2004.
Derie, Bobby. *Weird Talers: Essays on Robert E. Howard and Others*. New York: Hippocampus Press, 2019.
Dobie, Bertha McKee, Terrell Maverick Webb, Llerena Friend, Thomas Thompson, Joe Bertram Frantz, John Graves, A. C. Greene, et al. *Growing Up in Texas*. Austin: Encino Press, 1972.
Dobie, J. Frank. *Coronado's Children*. New York: Grosset & Dunlap, 1930.
Dobie, J. Frank. *The Flavor of Texas*. 1936. Reprint, Austin: Jenkins Publishing, 1975.
Dobie, J. Frank. *Some Part of Myself*. Boston: Little, Brown, 1967.
Donnelly, Ignatius. *Atlantis: The Antediluvian World*. New York: Harper & Brothers, 1882.
Dormandy, Thomas. *The White Death: A History of Tuberculosis*. Washington Square: New York University Press, 2000.
Dowd, Christopher. *The Construction of Irish Identity in American Literature*. New York: Routledge, 2011.
Duhigg, Charles. *The Power of Habit: Why We Do What We Do in Life and Business*. New York: Random House, 2014.
Elliot, G. F. Scott. *The Romance of Early British Life: From the Earliest Times to the Coming of the Danes*. London: Seeley, Service, 1909.
Everett, Justin, and Jeffrey H. Shanks. *The Unique Legacy of* Weird Tales*: The Evolution of Modern Fantasy and Horror*. Lanham, MD: Rowman & Littlefield, 2015.
Fehrenbach, T. R. *Lone Star: A History of Texas and the Texans*. 1968. Reprint, New York: Tess Press, 2000.
Finn, Mark. *Blood and Thunder: The Life and Art of Robert E. Howard*. Plano, TX: Robert E. Howard Foundation Press, 2014.
Fleischer, Nat, Sam Andre, and Nigel Collins. *An Illustrated History of Boxing*. 6th ed. Toronto: Citadel Press, 2002.
Flexner, Abraham. *Medical Education in the United States and Canada: A Report to the Carnegie Foundation for the Advancement of Teaching*. New York: Carnegie Foundation, 1910.
Funderburg, Anne Cooper. *Sundae Best: A History of Soda Fountains*. Bowling Green, OH: Bowling Green State University Popular Press, 2002.
Gijswijt-Hofstra, Marijke, and Roy Porter. *Cultures of Neurasthenia: From Beard to the First World War*. Amsterdam: Rodopi, 2001.

Goodstone, Tony. *The Pulps: Fifty Years of American Pop Culture*. New York: Bonanza Books, 1970.

Gosling, F. G. *Before Freud: Neurasthenia and the American Medical Community, 1870–1910.* Champaign: University of Illinois Press, 1987.

Goulart, Ron. *Cheap Thrills: The Amazing! Thrilling! Astonishing! History of Pulp Fiction.* New Rochelle, NY: Arlington House, 1972.

Haefele, John D. *Lovecraft: The Great Tales*. N.p.: Cimmerian Press, 2021.

Haycox, Ernest, Jr. *On a Silver Desert: The Life of Ernest Haycox*. Norman: University of Oklahoma Press, 2003.

Hemingway, Mary Welsh. *How It Was*. New York: Knopf, 1976.

Henderson, Caroline. *Letters from the Dust Bowl*. Edited by Alvin O. Turner. Norman: University of Oklahoma Press, 2003.

Herron, Don. *The Barbaric Triumph*. Cabin John, MD: Wildside Press, 2004.

Herron, Don, ed. *The Dark Barbarian: The Writings of Robert E. Howard: A Critical Anthology.* 1984. Reprint, Berkeley Heights, NJ: Wildside Press, 2000.

Herron, Don. *Famous Someday*. N.p.: Cimmerian Press, 2018.

Homer. *The Odyssey of Homer*. Translated by Alexander Pope. New York: John Wurtele Lovell, 1880.

Hopper, Nora. *Under Quicken Boughs*. London: John Lane, 1896.

Johnson, Celia Blue. *Odd Type Writers*. New York: Perigee, 2013.

Jones, Robert Kenneth. *The Shudder Pulps: A History of the Weird Menace Magazines of the 1930s*. West Linn, OR: FAX Collector's Editions, 1975.

Joshi, S. T. *I Am Providence: The Life and Times of H. P. Lovecraft*. New York: Hippocampus Press, 2013.

King, Stephen. *Danse Macabre*. New York: Gallery Books, 1981.

Kinglsey, Rev. C. *Hereward the Wake: Last of the English*. London: Macmillan, 1866.

Kodish, Debora. *Good Friends and Bad Enemies: Robert Winslow Gordon and the Study of American Folksong*. Urbana: University of Illinois Press, 1986.

Krist, Gary. *Empire of Sin: A Story of Sex, Jazz, Murder, and the Battle for Modern New Orleans.* New York: Broadway Books, 2015.

Labor, Earle. *Jack London: An American Life*. New York: Farrar, Straus and Giroux, 2013.

Leno, Brian. *Ringside with Robert E. Howard*. N.p.: Cimmerian Press, 2019.

Litersky, Dorothy M. Grobe. *Derleth: Hawk . . . and Dove*. Aurora, CO: National Writers Press, 1997.

Locke, John. *Pulp Fictioneers: Adventures in the Storytelling Business*. Silver Spring, MD: Adventure House, 2004.

Locke, John. *Pulpwood Days*. Vol. 1, *Editors You Want to Know*. Castroville, CA: Off-Trail Publications, 2007.

London, Jack. *Martin Eden*. New York: Penguin Books, 1984.

London, Jack. *The Star Rover*. Orinda, CA: Seawolf Press, 2018.

Long, Frank Belknap. *Howard Phillips Lovecraft: Dreamer on the Nightside*. Cabin John, MD: Wildside Press, 2016.

Lord, Glenn. *The Book of Robert E. Howard*. New York: Berkley Books, 1980.

Lord, Glenn, ed. *The Howard Collector: By and about Robert E. Howard*. New York: Ace Books, 1979.

Louinet, Patrice. *The Robert E. Howard Guide*. Tallahassee, FL: Skelos Press, 2018.

Macleod, Fiona. *The Sin-Eater and Other Tales*. Chicago: Patrick Geddes, 1895.

Manire, William. *Buggies to iPhones: A 96-Year-Old Man Remembers His Youth in Roanoke, Texas*. Roanoke: Manire, 2019.

McHaney, Dennis. *Robert E. Howard, Oriental Stories, The Magic Carpet Magazine, & The Souk.* Memphis, TN: Old Tiger Press, 2005.

McMurtry, Larry. *In a Narrow Grave: Essays on Texas*. New York: Liveright Publishing, 2018.

Mendlesohn, Farah, and Edward James. *A Short History of Fantasy*. Faringdon, UK: Libri, 2012.

Meyers, Jeffrey. *Hemingway: A Biography*. New York: Harper & Row, 1985.

Mitchell, Lee Clark. *Westerns: Making the Man in Fiction and Film*. Chicago: University of Chicago Press, 1996.

Mooney, Booth. *General Billy Mitchell*. Chicago: Follett Publishing, 1968.

Mooney, Booth. *The Lyndon Johnson Story*. New York: Farrar, Strauss and Cudahy, 1956.

Mooney, Booth. *Sam Houston*. Chicago: Follett, 1966.

Moore, Allen H. *Mustard Plasters and Printer's Ink: A Kaleidoscope of a Country Doctor's Observations about People, Places and Things*. New York: Exposition Press, 1959.

Morton, James. *The First Detective: The Life and Revolutionary Times of Eugène-François Vidocq*. London: Ebury Press, 2004.

Moskowitz, Sam. *A. Merritt: Reflections in the Moon Pool*. Philadelphia: Oswald Train, 1985.

Murphy, Brian. *Flame and Crimson: A History of Sword-and-Sorcery*. N.p.: Pulp Hero Press, 2019.

Musser, Benjamin. *"As the Poet Says—": 250 Prose Comments on the Supreme Art*. New York: Parnassus Press, 1931.

Myers, John Myers. *The Westerners: A Roundup of Pioneer Reminiscences*. Lincoln: University of Nebraska Press, 1969.

Nichols, James W. *On the Banks of Turkey Creek*. Cross Plains, TX: 1st Book Library, 2003.

Noel, Mary. *Villains Galore: The Heyday of the Popular Story Weekly*. Berkeley: University of California, 1954.

Oates, Joyce Carol. *On Boxing*. London: Bloomsbury, 1987.

O'Connell, David. *The Irish Roots of Margaret Mitchell's* Gone with the Wind. 2nd ed. N.p.: O'Connell, 2019.

Oliver, Neil. *A History of Scotland*. London: Weidenfeld & Nicolson, 2009.

O'Reilly, Edward. *An Irish-English Dictionary*. Dublin: James Duffy, 1864.

Osler, William. *Tuberculosis Pleurisy*. Boston: David Clapp & Son, 1893.

Palmer, Alex. *The Santa Claus Man: The Rise and Fall of a Jazz Age Con Man and the Invention of Christmas in New York*. Guilford, CT: Lyons Press, 2016.

Pelan, John, and Jerad Walters, eds. *Conversations with the* Weird Tales *Circle*. Lakewood, CO: Centipede Press, 2009.

Petterchak, Janice A. *Lone Scout: W. D. Boyce and American Boy Scouting*. Ann Arbor: Legacy Press, 2003.

Plato. *Timaeus*. Translated by Benjamin Jowett. New York: Scribner's Sons, 1871.

Porter, Roy, and Marijke Gijswijt-Hostra. *Cultures of Neurasthenia: From Beard to the First World War*. Amsterdam: Clio Medica, 2001.

Preece, Harold. *The Dalton Gang: End of an Outlaw Era*. New York: Hastings House, 1963.

Preece, Harold. *Lone Star Man: The Life of Ira Aten*. New York: Hastings House, 1960.

Price, E. Hoffmann. *Book of the Dead: Friends of Yesteryear: Fictioneers & Others (Memories of the Pulp Fiction Era)*. Sauk City, WI: Arkham House, 2001.

Price, Robert M. *H. P. Lovecraft and the Cthulhu Mythos*. Mercer Island, WA: Starmont House, 1990.

Ramacharaka, Yogi. *Fourteen Lessons in Yogi Philosophy and Oriental Occultism*. London: Yoga Publication Society, 1904.

Richardson, Robert D. *William James: In the Maelstrom of American Modernism*. Boston: Houghton Mifflin, 2006.

Roehm, Rob. *The Brownwood Connection: A Guide for Robert E. Howard Fans*. Plano, TX: Robert E. Howard Foundation Press, 2010.

Roehm, Rob. *Robert E. Howard in* The Fantasy Fan. Los Angeles: Roehm's Room Press, 2006.

Runyon, Damon. *Jack Dempsey: A Tale of Two Fists*. Edited by Paul Duncan. Reading, PA: Wordsmith, 2019.

Ryan, Frank. *The Forgotten Plague: How the Battle against Tuberculosis Was Won—and Lost*. Boston: Little, Brown, 1992.

Schelly, Bill. *Otto Binder: The Life and Work of a Comic Book and Science Fiction Visionary*. Berkeley: North Atlantic Books, 2016.

Sidney-Fryer, Donald. *The Golden State Phantasticks*. New York: Hippocampus Press, 2011.

Silverman, Kenneth. *Edgar A. Poe: Mournful and Never-Ending Remembrance*. New York: Harper Perennial, 2008.

Slawenski, Kenneth. *J. D. Salinger: A Life*. New York: Random House, 2010.

Slotkin, Richard. *Gunfighter Nation: The Myth of the Frontier in Twentieth-Century America*. New York: Atheneum, 1992.

Smith, David C. *Robert E. Howard: A Literary Biography*. San Bernardino, CA: Pulp Hero Press, 2018.

Smith, Reginald. Weird Tales *in the Thirties*. Santa Ana, CA: Reginald Smith, 1966.

Smith, Tevis Clyde. *Don't Blame the Python*. Brownwood: Tevis Clyde Smith, 1975.

Smith, Tevis Clyde, Jr. *Pecan Valley Days*. Brownwood, TX: T. C. Smith Jr., 1956.

Starrett, Vincent. *The Private Life of Sherlock Holmes*. New York: Macmillan, 1933.

Symons, Julian. *Bloody Murder: From the Detective Story to the Crime Novel*. 3rd ed. New York: Mysterious Press, 1993.

Texas Central Railroad Company. *Eighteenth Annual Report of the Texas Central Railroad Company for the Year Ending June 30, 1910*. Waco: Hill Printing and Stationery, 1910.

Torbett, J. W., Sr. *The Doctor's Scrapbook*. Marlin, TX: Torbett, 1947.

Townsend, Kim. *Manhood at Harvard: William James and Others*. New York: W. W. Norton, 1996.

Trudeau, Edward Livingston. *An Autobiography*. Garden City, NY: Doubleday Page, 1916.

Turner, Frederick Jackson. *The Frontier in American History*. New York: Henry Holt, 1921.

Tymn, Marshall B., and Mike Ashley. *Science Fiction, Fantasy, and Weird Fiction Magazines*. Westport, CT: Greenwood Press, 1985.

Urschel, Joe. *The Year of Fear: Machine Gun Kelly and the Manhunt That Changed the Nation*. New York: Minotaur Books, 2015.

Vandagriff, Jon R. *The Story of Parker County, Texas*. Virginia Beach: Donning Company, 2010.

Webb, Walter Prescott. *The Great Plains*. Lincoln: University of Nebraska Press, 1959.

Weinberg, Robert. *WT50: A Tribute to* Weird Tales. Oak Lawn, IL: Weinberg, 1974.

Williams, Blanche Colton, ed. *O. Henry Memorial Award: Prize Stories of 1931*. Garden City, NY: Doubleday, 1931.

Williams, Robert H. *Joyful Trek: A Texan's Times and Travels*. Lubbock: Texas Tech University Press, 1996.

Williamson, Jamie. *The Evolution of Modern Fantasy: From Antiquarianism to the Ballantine Adult Fantasy Series*. New York: Palgrave MacMillan, 2015.

Worley, John F. *Brownwood City Directory, 1923*. Dallas: John F. Worley Directory, 1923.

Zadra, Antonio, and Robert Stickgold. *When Brains Dream: Exploring the Science & Mystery of Sleep*. New York: W. W. Norton, 2021.

Articles and Chapters

Anderson, Douglas A. "'All Fled, All Done': Redux on Robert E. Howard's Famous Couplet." *A Shiver in the Archives*, January 18, 2019. http://ashiverinthearchives.blogspot.com/2019/01/all-fled-all-done-redux-on-robert-e.html.

Anonymous [Victor Rosseau]. "A Penny a Word." *American Mercury* 37, no. 147 (March 1936): 285–92.

Ashton, Dorothy C. "Cross Cut, TX." *Handbook of Texas Online*, updated December 1, 1994. https://www.tshaonline.org/handbook/entries/cross-cut-tx.

Barrett, Barbara. "Hester Jane Ervin Howard and Tuberculosis (Revised)." *REHupa*, no. 250 (December 2014): 1–68.

Barrett, Barbara. "Robert E. Howard and Past Lives, Reincarnation, Dreams and Race Memories." *REH: Two-Gun Raconteur*, no. 17 (Summer 2014): 35–51.

Beaumont, Charles. "The Bloody Pulps." *Playboy* 9, no. 9 (September 1962): 90–92.

Berger, Herbert W., and Ervido Mejia. "Tuberculous Pleurisy." *Chest* 63, no. 1 (January 1973): 88–92.

"Big Spring Troop 1." *West Texas Scouting History*, October 20, 2020. https://www.westtexasscoutinghistory.net/troop_bigspring_troop1.html.

Black, Sharon Stephens. "Mary Bohannon of Bagwell, Red River Co., Texas." *Red River County Texas Genealogical Society Quarterly* 19 (Spring 2002): 3–7.

"Black Mask History." *Black Mask Magazine*, February 22, 2023. https://blackmaskmagazine.com/black-mask-history/.

Bleiler, Richard. "A History of *Adventure* Magazine." *Galactic Central*, July 28, 2022. http://www.philsp.com/articles/magazines/adventure.html.

Blosser, Fred. "Sleuths, Secrets, and Grisly Mysteries: The Detective Fiction of Robert E. Howard." In *Two-Gun Bob*, edited by Benjamin Szumskyj, 39–58. New York: Hippocampus Press, 2006.

Boatright, Mody C. "The Art of Tall Lying." *Southwest Review* 34, no. 4 (Autumn 1949): 357–62.

Brackett, Leigh. "Introduction." In *The Sword Woman*, by Robert E. Howard, 5–11. New York: Zebra Books, 1977.

Bullard, John. "'Beyond the Black River': Is It Really 'Beyond the Brazos River'?" *Adventures Fantastic*, March 23, 2020. http://adventuresfantastic.com/beyond-the-black-river-is-it-really-beyond-the-brazos-river-part-1/.

Burke, Rusty. "The Active Voice: Robert E. Howard's Personae." *Dark Man: The Journal of Robert E. Howard Studies*, no. 3 (April 1993): 22–26.

Burke, Rusty. "All Fled, All Done." *Dark Man: The Journal of Robert E. Howard Studies*, no. 5 (Winter 2001): 15–17.

Burke, Rusty. "Bob Howard and the Bullies." *Iron Harp* 2, no. 1 (March 2002). http://www.robert-e-howard.org/IronHarp3.html.

Burke, Rusty. "A Deep Dark Current Flows Forever." *REHupa*, no. 200 (August 2006): 1–19.

Burke, Rusty. "The Note." *Cimmerian* 3, no. 1 (January 2006): 5–12.

Burke, Rusty. "Novalyne Price Ellis, 1908–1909." In *Robert E. Howard's Myth Maker*, edited by Roy Thomas. Cross Plains, TX: Cross Plains Comics, 1999.

Burke, Rusty. "The Old Deserted House: Images of the South in Howard's Fiction." *Dark Man: The Journal of Robert E. Howard Studies*, no. 2 (July 1991): 13–21.

Burke, Rusty. "The Reverend Joseph O. Ashbord." *REHupa*, no. 246 (April 2014): 1–5.

Burke, Rusty. "The Robert E. Howard Bookshelf." *Howard History*, December 28, 2020. https://howardhistory.com/the-robert-e-howard-bookshelf/#l007.

Burke, Rusty. "Robert E. Howard and Edgar Rice Burroughs." *Pavilion Blog*, September 1, 2020. https://www.thedarkmanjournal.org/the-pavilion-blog/robert-e-howard-and-edgar-rice-burroughs.

Burke, Rusty. "Robert E. Howard Fiction and Verse Timeline." *Howard Works*, accessed January 8, 2025, https://howardworks.com/timeline.htm.

Burke, Rusty. "Robert E. Howard: New Deal Heroic Fantasist." *Dark Man: The Journal of Robert E. Howard Studies* 2, nos. 1/2 (Spring 2006): 18–26.

Burke, Rusty. "Robert E. Howard in New Orleans." Parts 1 and 2. *REHupa*, no. 241 (June 2013): no page numbers; *REHupa*, no. 243 (October 2013): no page numbers.

Burke, Rusty. "A Statistical Analysis of REH's Vocabulary." *Cimmerian* 5, no. 1 (February 2008): 28–29.

Burke, Rusty. "Toward Other Lands: An Approach to Robert E. Howard." *Dark Man: The Journal of Robert E. Howard Studies*, no. 1 (August 1990): 17–22.

Burns, Chester R. "Health and Medicine." *Handbook of Texas Online*, updated November 5, 2020. https://www.tshaonline.org/handbook/entries/health-and-medicine.

Celis, Bill. "REH: College Fictioneer." *Weird Adventures* 1, no. 1 (May 1978): 14–16.

Chambers, Norris. "A Brief History of Cross Cut, Texas." *Cross Cut, Texas; Presented by Norris Chambers*, February 22, 2021. https://www.norrisc.com/crosscut/xcut.html.

Chambers, Norris. "How We Built a Steam Engine!" *Norris Chambers Old Timer's Tales*, February 22, 2021. http://www.norrisc.com/steamengine.html.

Chambers, Norris. "Old Time Fishing." *Norris Chambers Old Timer's Tales,* February 23, 2021. http://www.norrisc.com/fish.html.

Chambers, Norris. "Railroad Remembrances." *Norris Chambers Old Timer's Tales*, February 22, 2021. https://www.norrisc.com/train.html.

Chandler, Raymond. "The Simple Art of Murder (1950)." University of Texas, April 8, 2021. http://www.en.utexas.edu/Classes/Bremen/e316k/316kprivate/scans/chandlerart.html.

Chase, Ira Carleton, ed. "Copy of Report of Committee Appointed by the Medical Association of Arkansas." *Texas State Journal of Medicine*, no. 4 (June 1908): 37–38.

Clute, John. "Introduction." In Robert E. Howard, *Heroes in the Wind: From Kull to Conan.* New York: Penguin Books, 2009.

Coffman, Frank. "Robert E. Howard and Poetic Narrative: The Bardic Tradition and 'Popular Modernities.'" *Dark Man: The Journal of Robert E. Howard Studies* 2, nos. 1/2 (Spring 2006): 4–17.

Cohen, Norm. "Robert W. Gordon and the Second Wreck of 'Old 97.'" *Journal of American Folklore* 87, no. 343 (Jan.–Mar. 1974): 12–38.

Cravens, Chris. "Weatherford, Mineral Wells and Northwestern Railway." *Handbook of Texas Online*, updated March 5, 2019. https://www.tshaonline.org/handbook/entries/weatherford-mineral-wells-and-northwestern-railway.

Curtis, Eric W. "Two Victorian Botanists: Professor Roger Hennedy and Professor George Francis Scott Elliot." *Glasgow Naturalist* 25, part 2 (2009): 49–55.

"Dark Valley Creek." *Handbook of Texas Online*, updated December 1, 1994. https://www.tshaonline.org/handbook/entries/dark-valley-creek.

Derie, Bobby. "Conan and the Little People: Robert E. Howard and Lovecraft's Theory." *On An Underwood No. 5*, January 13, 2019. http://onanunderwood5.blogspot.com/2019/01/conan-and-little-people-robert-e-howard.html.

Derie, Bobby. "A Letter from Seabury Quinn." *On An Underwood No. 5*, March 22, 2020. http://onanunderwood5.blogspot.com/2020/03/a-letter-from-seabury-quinn-by-bobby.html.

Derie, Bobby. "That Fool Olson." *Lovecraft Annual* (2018): 90–104.

Derie, Bobby. "Wolf Prints (or, The legacy of 'In the Forest of Villefère')." *Weird Beginnings* (2019): 20–21.

Dowd, Christopher. "The Irish-American Identities of Robert E. Howard and Conan the Barbarian." *New Hibernia Review* 20, no. 2 (Summer 2016): 15–34.

"Dr. Isaac M. Howard." *Texas State Journal of Medicine* (February 1945): 560.

Dziemianowicz, Stefan. "The Gnome Press Story." *Weird Fiction Review*, no. 9 (Winter 2018): 193–228.

Ellis, Novalyne Price. "Letter to Mr. Thomas W. Collins." *Barbarian Scroll*, no. 6 (February 1989): 6–8.

Ellis, Novalyne Price. "Novalyne Price Ellis's Q&A Session after Her Nolacon Speech (Transcribed by Adrian and Clark in Mailing #96)." *Nemedian Chroniclers*, no. 33 (December 2020): 32–44.

Finn, Mark. "Bare Knuckles and Bulldogs: An Introduction to the Boxing Fiction of Robert E. Howard." In Howard, *Waterfront*, 9–10.

Finn, Mark. "Robert E. Howard." In *Conversations with Texas Writers*, edited by Frances Leonard and Ramona Cearley, 170–76. Austin: University of Texas Press, 2005.

Finn, Mark. "The Runyonesque Raconteur." *Cimmerian* 1, no. 2 (June 2004): 13–20.

Finn, Mark. "Texas as Character in Robert E. Howard's Fiction." *Dark Man: The Journal of Robert E. Howard Studies*, no. 8 (Winter 2004): 3–12.

Gramlich, Charles A. "Robert E. Howard in the Gothic Tradition." *Dark Man: The Journal of Robert E. Howard Studies*, no. 8 (Winter 2004): 13–24.

Grin, Leo. "Hail to the King." *Cimmerian* 3, no. 1 (January 2006): 3–4.

Grin, Leo. "Heart's Blood." *Cimmerian* 1, no. 4 (October 2004): 21–23.

Grin, Leo. "In Defense of Hester Jane Ervin Howard." *Cimmerian*, October 2, 2008. https://web.archive.org/web/20110708132217/www.thecimmerian.com/in-defense-of-hester-jane-ervin-howard/.

Günther, Dierk. "Faces of Kane: Exploring the Identity of Robert E. Howard's Puritan Swordsman." *Dark Man: The Journal of Robert E. Howard and Pulp Studies* 10, no. 1 (June 2019): 20–37.

Hanley, Terence E. "Who Wrote the Most Poems for Weird Tales?" *Teller of Weird Tales*, November 15, 2011. https://tellersofweirdtales.blogspot.com/2011/11/who-wrote-most-poems-for-weird-tales.html.

Hardy, David A. "The Great Game." *Cimmerian* 1, no. 2 (June 2004): 3–12.

Hardy, David A. "Indomitable Wildness, Unquenchable Vitality." *Cimmerian* 3, no. 4 (April 2006): 4–20.

Herman, Paul. "Interview of Larry McDonough by Paul Herman." *Another Thought*, no. 1 (June 2001). http://www.robert-e-howard.org/AnotherThought1.html.

Herman, Paul. "Introduction." In *A Rhyme of Salem Town and Other Poems*, by Robert E. Howard, 1–3. Plano, TX: Robert E. Howard Foundation Press, 2006.

Herron, Don. "COnun and TarZAN." *Cimmerian* 3, no. 6 (June 2006): 27.

Herron, Don. "The Last of the Baker Kids: A Talk with Marie Baker Andrews." *Cimmerian* 3, no. 3 (March 2006): 22–26.

Herron, Don. "'Robert'll Be Famous Someday': An Interview with Norris Chambers." *Cimmerian* 3, no. 10 (October 2006): 4–24.

Herron, Don. "Ur *Gent*." *Cimmerian* 3, no. 8 (August 2006): 13–17.

"History." *Battle of Flowers Association*, September 21, 2019. https://www.battleofflowers.org/about-us/history/.

"History." *Crazy Water*, October 22, 2020. http://drinkcrazywater.com/crazy-water-history/.

Hoffman, Charles. "Blood Lust." *Cimmerian* 2, no. 5 (October 2005): 4–14.

Hoffman, Charles. "Book Review: Robert E. Howard. Post Oaks and Sand Roughs." *Dark Man: The Journal of Robert E. Howard Studies*, no. 1 (August 1990): 35–36.

Hoffman, Charles. "'The Shadow Kingdom' and the Origins of Gothic Horror in Robert E. Howard's Heroic Fantasy." *Skelos*, no. 2 (Winter 2017): 84–97.

Holmes, Morgan. "Enter the Barbarian." *Cimmerian* 4, no. 6 (December 2007): 9–14.

Holmes, Morgan. "Robert E. Howard and the Clayton Magazines." *Blood 'n' Thunder*, nos. 46/47 (Winter/Spring 2016): 56–63.

Holmes, Morgan. "The Saga of Wild Bill Clanton and Two Gun Bob: The Spicy Robert E. Howard." In *Windy City Pulp Stories #9*, edited by Tom Roberts, 40–46. Normal, IL: Black Dog, 2009.

Holmes, Morgan. "*Top-Notch*, Street & Smith and F. Orlin Tremaine." *REH: Two-Gun Raconteur*, no. 15 (Summer 2011): 33–34.

Holmes, Morgan. "The Wild Wild West of Robert E. Howard: Defending the Westerns Written by Conan's Creator." *Blood 'n' Thunder*, no. 48 (Summer 2016): 44–54.

Holmes, Morgan, and George Knight. "Conan the Argonaut." *Cimmerian* 5, no. 4 (August 2008): 4–23.

Hubbell, Jay B. "The Frontier in American Literature." *Southwest Review* 10, no. 2 (January 1925): 84–92.

Hulse, Ed. "The Glories of *Short Stories*." In *The Best of Blood 'n' Thunder*, vol. 2, edited by Ed Hulse, 9–36. Morris Plains, NJ: Murania Press, 2013.

Jamison, Kay Redfield. "Manic-Depressive Illness and Creativity." *Scientific American* 272, no. 2 (February 1995): 62–67.

Kingman, James H. "Tuberculosis in Some of Its Aspects." *Atlantic Medical Weekly: A Journal of Reform and Progress in the Medical Sciences* 4, no. 19 (November 9, 1895): 289–96.

Kodish, Debora G. “Robert Winslow Gordon (1888–1961).” *Library of Congress*, accessed December 10, 2024. https://www.loc.gov/item/ihas.200196581/.

Kohoutek, Karen Joan. “By the Phoenix on This Sword I Rule!” *On An Underwood No. 5*, July 22, 2018. http://onanunderwood5.blogspot.com/2018/07/by-phoenix-on-this-sword-i-rule-by.html.

L’Amour, Louis. *Education of a Wandering Man*. New York: Bantam, 1989.

“Leading Causes of Death, 1900–1998.” *Centers for Disease Control*, February 13, 2020. https://www.cdc.gov/nchs/data/dvs/lead1900_98.pdf.

Leiber, Fritz. “Letter.” *Ancalagon*, no. 2 (April 1961): 6–7.

Leno, Brian. “The Fouling of Robert E. Howard.” *Cimmerian* 4, no. 2 (April 2007): 14–20.

Leno, Brian. “Out of the Shadows—Finally, ‘Kid’ Dula.” *REH: Two-Gun Raconteur*, June 16, 2012. https://web.archive.org/web/20121015041419/rehtwogunraconteur.com/?p=19757.

Leno, Brian. “When Yaller Rock County Came to Chawed Ear.” *Cimmerian* 5, no. 5 (October 1928): 4–13.

“Letter from the Board.” *Robert E. Howard Foundation Newsletter* 16, no. 4 (Winter 2022–2023): 2.

Limmer, John. “The Chambers.” *Norris Chambers Old Timer’s Tales*, May 20, 2021. http://www.norrisc.com/crosscut/xcutchamb1.html.

Limmer, John. “The 3 R’s.” *Norris Chambers Old Timer’s Tales*, May 20, 2021. http://www.norrisc.com/crosscut/xcutschoolsite.html.

Long, Christopher. “Callahan County.” *Handbook of Texas Online*, updated October 19, 2020. https://www.tshaonline.org/handbook/entries/callahan-county.

Lord, Glenn. “Herbert Klatt.” *Dark Man: The Journal of Robert E. Howard Studies*, no. 1 (August 1990): 24–27.

Lord, Glenn. “REH, HPL and the Cthulhu Mythos.” *REH: Two-Gun Raconteur*, no. 7 (Spring 2005): 8–9.

Louinet, Patrice. “The Birth of Conan.” *Dark Man: The Journal of Robert E. Howard Studies*, no. 4 (May 1997): 1–12.

Louinet, Patrice. “A Conversation with Jack Scott.” *Unaussprechlichen Kulten*, no. 1 (October 1990): 26–29.

Louinet, Patrice. “Grief & Greed? Isaac Mordecai Howard and the Robert E. Howard Estate, June 1936–March 1937.” *Dwelling in Dark Valley*, June 2001. http://www.robert-e-howard.org/Dwelling2.html.

Louinet, Patrice. “The Long Road to Dark Valley.” *REH: Two-Gun Raconteur*, January 18, 2013. https://web.archive.org/web/20150907100640/www.rehtwogunraconteur.com/the-long-road-to-dark-valley-introduction/.

Louinet, Patrice. “A Man and His Dog: Or, Not So Trivial Facts about Patch and His Death.” *Dwelling in Dark Valley*, no. 1 (March 2001): http://www.robert-e-howard.org/DwellingDarkValley.html.

Louinet, Patrice. “One Gent Too Many on Bear Creek.” *REH: Two-Gun Raconteur*, no. 16 (Winter 2012): 43–48.

Louinet, Patrice. “Pigeons from . . . Bagwell.” *Dwelling in Dark Valley*, no. 4 (Spring 2002). http://www.robert-e-howard.org/Louinet/dwelling4a.htm.

Louinet, Patrice. “The Red-Bearded Viking of Skaggerack.” *Dwelling in Dark Valley*, no. 3 (September 2001). http://www.robert-e-howard.org/Louinet/reh_frames.html.

Louinet, Patrice. “REH and *The Poet’s Scroll*.” *Robert E. Howard Foundation Newsletter* 9, no. 1 (Spring 2015): 3.

Louinet, Patrice. “Robert E. Howard, Founding Father of Modern Fantasy for the First Time Again.” *Contemporary French and Francophone Studies* 15, no. 2 (March 2011): 163–70.

Louinet, Patrice. “A Short History of the Kull Series.” *Dark Man: The Journal of Robert E. Howard Studies*, no. 6 (Summer 2001): 30–41.

Louinet, Patrice. "'The Wright Hook' (Or, The origin of 'Spear and Fang')." *REH: Two-Gun Raconteur*, October 25, 2016. https://web.archive.org/web/20170417100627/http://www.rehtwogunraconteur.com/the-wright-hook-or-the-origin-of-spear-and-fang/.

Lovecraft, H. P. "In Memoriam: Robert Ervin Howard." *Fantasy Magazine*, no. 38 (1936).

Lovecraft, H. P. "Letter: H. P. Lovecraft to E. Hoffmann Price, dated July 5, 1936." *Howard Collector* 3, no. 1 (Autumn 1970): 14–20.

Lovecraft, H. P. "Letters to Farnsworth Wright." *Lovecraft Annual*, no. 8 (2014): 5–59.

Maliszewski, James. "The Mirrors of Tuzun Thune." *Grognardia*, January 18, 2021. http://grognardia.blogspot.com/2021/01/pulp-fantasy-library-mirrors-of-tuzun.html.

McKnight, Joseph W. "McKnight, Joseph Banning." *Handbook of Texas Online*, updated April 7, 2020. https://www.tshaonline.org/handbook/entries/mcknight-joseph-banning.

Moskowitz, Sam. "The Forgotten Creator of Weird Tales: An Introduction." In *Worlds of Weird*, edited by Leo Margulies, 9–13. New York: Pyramid Books, 1965.

Moskowitz, Sam. "The Most Popular Stories in Weird Tales, 1924 to 1940: With Statistics and Analytical Commentary." In *World Fantasy Convention 1983: Sixty Years of* Weird Tales, edited by Robert Weinberg, 27–37. N.p.: Weird Tales, 1983.

Murphy, Brian. "From Pulps to Paperbacks: The Role of Medium in the Development of Sword-and-Sorcery Fiction." *Journal of American Culture* 43, no. 1 (March 2021): 43–53.

Murray, Will. "An Informal History of the Spicy Pulps." In *Windy City Pulp Stories #9*, edited by Tom Roberts, 7–17. Normal, IL: Black Dog, 2009.

Murray, Will. "Spicy Adventurers." In *Windy City Pulp Stories #9*, edited by Tom Roberts, 28–39. Normal: Black Dog, 2009.

National Oceanic & Atmospheric Administration. "Global Summary for March 1932." *National Centers for Environmental Information*, November 27, 2020. https://www.ncdc.noaa.gov/cdo-web/datasets#GSOM.

National Park Service. "3rd Regiment, Tennessee Cavalry (Forrest's)." *National Park Service: The Civil War*, November 9, 2021. https://www.nps.gov/civilwar/search-battle-units-detail.htm?battleUnitCode=CTN0003RC.

Odintz, Mark. "Brownwood, TX." *Handbook of Texas Online*, updated September 20, 2023. https://www.tshaonline.org/handbook/entries/brownwood-tx.

Oliver, Willard M. "Ghosties, Haunts, and Conjure-Men: Robert E. Howard and the Yarns of Mary Bohannon." *REHupa*, no. 191 (October 2021): 15–46.

Oliver, Willard M. "The Personal and Literary Influences of Jack London's *The Star Rover* on Robert E. Howard." *Dark Man: The Journal of Robert E. Howard and Pulp Studies* (forthcoming).

Oliver, Willard M. "Robert E. Howard and Jack London's *Martin Eden*: Analyzing the Influence of *Martin Eden* on Howard and His Semi-Autobiography." *Dark Man: The Journal of Robert E. Howard and Pulp Studies* 11, no. 1 (June 2020): 6–32.

Piske, David. "Barbarism and Civilization in the Letters of Robert E. Howard and H. P. Lovecraft: A Summary with Commentary." *On An Underwood No. 5*, August 19, 2015. http://onanunderwood5.blogspot.com/2015/08/barbarism-and-civilization-in-letters.html.

"Postal Savings System." *US Postal Service*, September 15, 2020. https://about.usps.com/who-we-are/postal-history/postal-savings-system.pdf.

Preece, Harold. "Quest for Books." *Fantasy Crossroads*, nos. 10–11 (March 1977): 46–47.

Preece, Harold. "Robert's Lady Cousin." *Simba*, no. 2 (September 1978): 43–44.

Preece, Harold. "Women and Robert Ervin Howard." *Fantasy Crossroads* 1, no. 3 (May 1975): 20–23.

Price, E. Hoffmann. "Otis Adelbert Kline: In Memoriam." *ERBzine*, December 17, 2020. https://www.erbzine.com/mag0/0037.html.

Price, E. Hoffmann. "Robert E. Howard & His Heroes." *Amra* 2, no. 15 (May 1961): 14.

Reasoner, James. "Far and Away: The Wandering Heroes of Robert E. Howard." In Robert E. Howard, *Treasures of Tartary*, 7–10. Rockville, MD: Wildside Press, 2004.

Richardson, Deuce. "The Call of Kathulos: Kull, Skull and 'Call.'" *Cimmerian*, February 11, 2009. http://thecimmerian.com/2009/02/11/the-call-of-kathulos-kull-skull-and-call/.

Roehm, Rob. "1915." *REHupa*, no. 256 (December 2015): 1–4.

Roehm, Rob. "1918." *REHupa*, no. 263 (February 2017): 1–4.

Roehm, Rob. "508 Coleman Street." *REH: Two-Gun Raconteur*, April 3, 2015. https://web.archive.org/web/20150907153854/http://www.rehtwogunraconteur.com/508-coleman-street/.

Roehm, Rob. "Austin, Who?" *REHupa*, no. 231 (October 2011): 1–12.

Roehm, Rob. "Back to School." *Howard History: The Life and Times of Robert E. Howard*, September 24, 2018. https://howardhistory.com/2018/09/24/back-to-school/.

Roehm, Rob. "The Birth of a Writer." *REHupa*, no. 280 (December 2019): 1–4.

Roehm, Rob. "Brownwood High School." *REH Two-Gun Raconteur*, April 21, 2010. https://web.archive.org/web/20100722021701/http://rehtwogunraconteur.com/?p=3842.

Roehm, Rob. "Class of '22." *REHupa*, no. 241 (June 2013): 1–6.

Roehm, Rob. "The Comer Connection." *REHupa*, no. 240 (April 2013): 1–4.

Roehm, Rob. "Dating the Right Hook." *Howard History: The Life and Times of Robert E. Howard*, February 1, 2018. https://howardhistory.com/2018/02/01/dating-the-right-hook/.

Roehm, Rob. "A Day in the Life." *REH: Two-Gun Raconteur*, May 7, 2012. https://web.archive.org/web/20130121131744/http://rehtwogunraconteur.com/?p=18981.

Roehm, Rob. "The Diabolical Blond." *REH: Two-Gun Raconteur*, no. 17 (Summer 2014): 13–15.

Roehm, Rob. "Down the Nueces." *Howard History: The Life and Times of Robert E. Howard*, December 9, 2018. https://howardhistory.com/2018/12/09/down-the-nueces/.

Roehm, Rob. "The Earliest Howards." *Howard History: The Life and Times of Robert E. Howard*, January 18, 2019. https://howardhistory.com/2019/01/18/the-earliest-howards-part-1/

Roehm, Rob. "Ervins in Oklahoma." *REH Two-Gun Raconteur*, June 21, 2012. https://web.archive.org/web/20130121131150/http://rehtwogunraconteur.com/?p=19789.

Roehm, Rob. "Family Legend." *Howard History: The Life and Times of Robert E. Howard*, August 30, 2019. https://howardhistory.com/2019/08/30/family-legend/.

Roehm, Rob. "The First Isaac M. Howard." *Howard History: The Life and Times of Robert E. Howard*, October 10, 2019. https://howardhistory.com/2019/10/10/the-first-isaac-m-howard/.

Roehm, Rob. "Footnotes #2." *Howard History: The Life and Times of Robert E. Howard*, November 1, 2018. https://howardhistory.com/2018/11/01/footnotes-2/.

Roehm, Rob. "Good Ol' Boys." *Howard History: The Life and Times of Robert E. Howard*, September 24, 2018. https://howardhistory.com/2018/09/24/good-ol-boys/.

Roehm, Rob. "Hawkshaw & Howard." *Howard History: The Life and Times of Robert E. Howard*, February 2, 2018. https://howardhistory.com/2018/02/02/hawkshaw-howard/.

Roehm, Rob. "Henry's Will." *REHupa*, no. 252 (April 2015): 1–4.

Roehm, Rob. "The Howards Are a Moving People." *Howard History: The Life and Times of Robert E. Howard*, December 13, 2019. https://howardhistory.com/2019/12/13/the-howards-are-a-moving-people/.

Roehm, Rob. "In the Middle of the Street." *Cimmerian* 5, no. 3 (June 2008): 4–10.

Roehm, Rob. "Isaac M. Howard in the 1880s." *REH: Two-Gun Raconteur*, October 18, 2012. https://web.archive.org/web/20130121130544/http://rehtwogunraconteur.com/?p=20488.

Roehm, Rob. "June 1936." *REHupa*, no. 211 (June 2008): 1–23.

Roehm, Rob. "The Kline Connection." *Howard History: The Life and Times of Robert E. Howard*, November 2, 2018. https://howardhistory.com/2018/11/02/the-kline-connection/.

Roehm, Rob. "The Legend of the Trunk." *REH: Two-Gun Raconteur*, January 14, 2014. https://web.archive.org/web/20150911053806/http://www.rehtwogunraconteur.com/the-legend-of-the-trunk-part-1.

Roehm, Rob. "Letters to Glenn." *REHupa*, no. 235 (June 2012): 3–6.

Roehm, Rob. "A Little History . . ." *REHupa*, no. 201 (October 2006): 1–4.

Roehm, Rob. "The Lost Ervin Mine." *Howard History: The Life and Times of Robert E. Howard*, October 18, 2019. https://howardhistory.com/2019/10/18/the-lost-ervin-mine/.

Roehm, Rob. "Mary, Mary, Quite Contrary." *REHupa*, no. 251 (February 2015): 1–4.

Roehm, Rob. "The Missing Mexico Trip." *Howard History: The Life and Times of Robert E. Howard*, October 19, 2018. https://howardhistory.com/2018/10/19/the-missing-mexico-trip/.

Roehm, Rob. "My Name Is Earl." *REHupa*, no. 229 (June 2011): 1–5.

Roehm, Rob. "The Mystery of the Wichita Falls Country." *Howard History: The Life and Times of Robert E. Howard*, May 1, 2019. https://howardhistory.com/2019/05/01/the-mystery-of-the-wichita-falls-country/.

Roehm, Rob. "Novalyne and Daniel Baker." *REH: Two-Gun Raconteur*, March 5, 2010. https://web.archive.org/web/20111114110736/http://rehtwogunraconteur.com/?p=648.

Roehm, Rob. "Oglethorpe County, GA." *Howard History: The Life and Times of Robert E. Howard*, February 13, 2019. https://howardhistory.com/2019/02/13/oglethorpe-county-ga/.

Roehm, Rob. "Peaster, Texas." *REHupa*, no. 245 (February 2014): 1–2.

Roehm, Rob. "Post Oaks and Football." *Howard History: The Life and Times of Robert E. Howard*, February 1, 2018. https://howardhistory.com/2018/02/01/post-oaks-and-football/.

Roehm, Rob. "Pre-Junto Convention." *REH: Two-Gun Raconteur*, January 21, 2014. https://web.archive.org/web/20150907091654/http://www.rehtwogunraconteur.com/pre-junto-convention/.

Roehm, Rob. "'A Pretty Good Paper': The Junto." *REH: Two-Gun Raconteur*, January 16, 2014. https://web.archive.org/web/20150907092703/http://www.rehtwogunraconteur.com/a-pretty-good-paper-the-junto-part-1/.

Roehm, Rob. "A Question of Birth." *REHupa*, no. 238 (December 2012): 1–2.

Roehm, Rob. "The Rise and Fall of Robert T. Ervin." *REHupa*, no. 286 (December 2020): 1–8.

Roehm, Rob. "The Road to Cross Plains." *REHupa*, no. 261 (October 2016): 8.

Roehm, Rob. "Robert E. Howard and the Lone Scouts." *Dark Man: The Journal of Robert E. Howard Studies* 7, no. 1 (December 2012): 45–57.

Roehm, Rob. "Robert E. Howard's Automobiles: '*License and Registration, Please*.'" *Howard History: The Life and Times of Robert E. Howard*, October 2020. https://howardhistory.files.wordpress.com/2020/10/reh-cars3.pdf.

Roehm, Rob. "Squire James Henry." *Howard History: The Life and Times of Robert E. Howard*, December 3, 2020. https://howardhistory.com/2020/12/.

Roehm, Rob. "The Summer of '24." *REHupa*, no. 246 (April 2014): 1–2.

Roehm, Rob. "Tell of Gloria's Life." *REHupa*, no. 273 (October 2018): 1–8.

Roehm, Rob. "The Texas Spur." *Howard History: The Life and Times of Robert E. Howard*, May 10, 2021. https://howardhistory.com/2021/05/10/the-texas-spur/.

Roehm, Rob. "Training Dr. Howard." *Howard History: The Life and Times of Robert E. Howard*, September 17, 2020. https://howardhistory.com/2020/09/17/training-dr-howard/.

Roehm, Rob. "Upson County, GA." *Howard History: The Life and Times of Robert E. Howard*, February 21, 2019. https://howardhistory.com/2019/02/21/upson-county-ga/.

Roehm, Rob. "The Vinson Papers." *Howard History: The Life and Times of Robert E. Howard*, October 19, 2021. https://howardhistory.com/2021/10/19/the-vinson-papers-part-1/.

Roehm, Rob. "The Virginia Howards." *Howard History: The Life and Times of Robert E. Howard*, January 22, 2019. https://howardhistory.com/2019/01/22/the-virginia-howards/.

Roehm, Rob. "We Spent the Winter in San Antonio." *Howard History: The Life and Times of Robert E. Howard*, December 10, 2018. https://howardhistory.com/2018/12/10/we-spent-the-winter-in-san-antonio/.

Roehm, Rob. "William Benjamin Howard." *Howard History: The Life and Times of Robert E. Howard*, August 23, 2020. https://howardhistory.com/2020/08/23/william-benjamin-howard/.

Roehm, Rob. "Willie and Oscar." *REHupa*, no. 293 (February 2022): 1–4.

Roehm, Rob. "Yellow Jacket." *REH: Two-Gun Raconteur*, September 17, 2010. https://web.archive.org/web/20150911051745/http://www.rehtwogunraconteur.com/yellow-jacket/.

Sasser, Damon. "I Knew Robert E. Howard." *R.E.H. Two-Gun Raconteur*, August 8, 2011. https://web.archive.org/web/20111114171638/http://rehtwogunraconteur.com/?p=6126.

Sasser, Damon. "REH Splashes the 'Spicys.'" *REH: Two-Gun Raconteur*, August 15, 2011. https://web.archive.org/web/20160327113931/http://www.rehtwogunraconteur.com/reh-splashes-the-spicys-part-i/.

Schlesinger, Arthur M. "Patriotism Names the Baby." *New England Quarterly* 14, no. 4 (December 1941): 611–18.

Schully, O. Foerster. "Markets in False Face." *Author & Journalist* 20 (November 1935): 15–16.

Schwartz, Julius. "Titans of Science Fiction: Farnsworth Wright." *Science Fiction Digest* 1, no. 7 (March 1933): 3–4.

Shanks, Jeffrey. "Ace Jessel and the Ghost of Tom Molineaux." *REH: Two-Gun Raconteur*, no. 16 (Winter 2012): 21–25.

Shanks, Jeffrey. "Gouged Eyes and Chawed Ears: The Rough-and-Tumble World of Breckenridge Elkins." *REH: Two-Gun Raconteur*, no. 15 (Summer 2011): 47–52.

Shanks, Jeffrey, and Mark Finn. "Vaqueros and Vampires in the Pulps: Robert E. Howard and the Dawn of the Undead West." In *Undead in the West II: They Just Keep Coming*, edited by Cynthia J. Miller and A. Bowdoin Van Riper, 3–25. Lanham, MD: Scarecrow Press, 2013.

"Sleep." *Reclamation Record* 12, no. 12 (December 1921): 566–67.

Taves, Brian. "An Author in Search of His Genre: Talbot Mundy's Earliest Stories." In *The Best of Blood 'n' Thunder*, edited by Ed Hulse, 201–28. Morris Plains, NJ: Murania Press, 2013.

Tompkins, Steven. "The Shortest Distance between Two Towers." *Cimmerian* 3, no. 3 (March 2006): 4–15.

"Treatment of Tuberculosis in General." *Southern California Practitioner* 16, no. 11 (November 1901): 413–16.

"Varicocele." *Johns Hopkins Medicine*, December 14, 2022. https://www.hopkinsmedicine.org/health/conditions-and-diseases/varicocele.

Vick, Todd B. "Bootleggers & Gangsters: A Day in the Life of Robert E. Howard." *On An Underwood No. 5*, November 16, 2017. http://onanunderwood5.blogspot.com/2017/11/bootleggers-gangsters-day-in-life-of.html.

Vick, Todd B. "The Carnival, The Girl, and The Smitten Teenager." *On An Underwood No. 5*, October 6, 2019. http://onanunderwood5.blogspot.com/2019/10/the-carnival-girl-and-smitten-teenager.html.

Vick, Todd B. "Wild, Wild Vampires." *Weird Fiction Review*, no. 9 (Winter 2018): 109–22.

Wagner, Karl Edward. "Afterword." In *Red Nails*, edited by Karl Edward Wagner, 281–95. New York: Berkeley Medallion Books, 1977.

Waldrop, Howard. "Journey to Cross Plains." In *The Robert E. Howard Reader*, edited by Darrell Schweitzer, 155–61. Berkeley Heights, NJ: Wildside Press, 2010.

Waltz, Jason. "The Color and the Dash." In *Swords & Heroes*, edited by Lyndon Perry. Vega Baja, PR: Tule Fog Press, 2023.

Weinberg, Robert. "Introduction: The Long Journey of the Morning Star." In Harold Lamb, *Swords from the West*, xiii–xv. Lincoln: University of Nebraska Press, 2009.

Wooley, Natalie H. "The Adventure Story." *Californian*, no. 3 (Winter 1935): 9.

Wright, Farnsworth. "The Grey God Passes." Unpublished letter, December 28, 1931. https://www.jwkbooks.com/pages/books/23179/robert-howard/the-grey-god-passes-typed-manuscript-tms-36-leaves-not-dated-circa-1930-31.

Dissertation

Drone, Craig Alan. "On to the Orient: The History, Restoration, and Preservation of the Kansas City, Mexico, and Orient Railway Depot in San Angelo, Texas." PhD diss., Texas Tech University, 1990.

Videos

Friberg, Ben. "Howard Family." *YouTube*, June 30, 2015. Video, 38:15. https://www.youtube.com/watch?v=H-RkpZsaPhc.

Friberg, Ben. "Margaret McNeel on Robert E. Howard." *YouTube*, January 14, 2012. Video, 5:09. https://www.youtube.com/watch?v=MxveGf1-cpI.

Friberg, Ben. "Memories of Robert E. Howard." *YouTube*, February 18, 2010. Video, 7:12. https://www.youtube.com/watch?v=8r6HASJNcpk.

Friberg, Ben. "Travels with Ol' Two-Gun: with Rob Roehm." *YouTube*, June 26, 2017. Video, 29:37. https://www.youtube.com/watch?v=-_jaJPxgovQ.

Friberg, Ben. "Travels with Ol' Two-Gun: with Todd Vick." *YouTube*, June 26, 2017. Video, 19:35. https://www.youtube.com/watch?v=cOCrBpTP4Ww.

Index

D

E

F

G

H

I

J

K

L

P

Q

R

S

T

About the Authors

Rob Roehm is the editor of *The Collected Letters of Robert E. Howard* and other collections put out by the REH Foundation Press. His essays have appeared in various publications, most recently in *The Weird Tales Story: Expanded and Enhanced* (Pulp Hero Press, 2021). Roehm has traveled to every location in the United States that Robert E. Howard mentions visiting—from New Orleans to Santa Fe and dozens of Texas towns in between—and his research has been recognized by numerous awards from the Robert E. Howard Foundation. He writes about his discoveries, infrequently, at howardhistory.com.

Willard M. Oliver is, in the words of Robert E. Howard, just "some lined-faced scrivener." He serves as a professor of criminal justice at Sam Houston State University in Huntsville, Texas; is a retired major in the Military Police Corps, United States Army; and is a former police officer. The author/editor of fifty books, this is his second biography. He is a member of the Robert E. Howard United Press Association, has published articles in the *Dark Man: The Journal of Robert E. Howard Studies* and others, and has been recognized for his work by the Robert E. Howard Foundation. He lives with his family in Huntsville, Texas.